BARRON'S

CLEP®

10TH EDITION

English Composition
William C. Doster
Elizabeth Schmid
Wendy Jo Ward, M.Ed.
Miami-Dade College

Humanities
Ruth S. Ward

Mathematics
Shirley O. Hockett, M.A.
Ithaca College (retired)
David Bock, M.S.
Cornell University

Natural Sciences
Adrian W. Poitras
Louis Gotlib, M.A.T.
Wissahickon Sr. High School

Social Sciences—History
Robert Bjork
Michael Colucci
    Social Studies Teaching Consultant

Introductions
John Bechtle, D.Min.
    Director, The Telos Institute International

BARRON'S

All inquiries should be addressed to:
Barron's Educational Series, Inc.
250 Wireless Boulevard
Hauppauge, New York 11788
http://www.barronseduc.com

Book ISBN-13:   978-0-7641-3639-9
Book ISBN-10:   0-7641-3639-9
CD ISBN-13:   978-0-7641-8452-9
CD ISBN-10:   0-7641-8452-0
Pkg. ISBN-13:   978-0-7641-9320-0
Pkg. ISBN-10:   0-7641-9320-1

Library of Congress Catalog Card No. 2007007101

Library of Congress Cataloging-in-Publication Data

CLEP / William Doster . . . [et al.].—10th ed.
    p. cm.
    Rev. ed. of: How to prepare for the CLEP, College-Level Examination
Program general examinations / William C. Doster . . . [et al.]. 9th ed.
c2003.
    Includes bibliographical references and index.
    ISBN-13: 978-0-7641-3639-9 (alk. paper)
    ISBN-10: 0-7641-3639-9 (alk. paper)
    ISBN-13: 978-0-7641-8452-9 (alk. paper)
    ISBN-10: 0-7641-8452-0 (alk. paper)
    1. College-level examinations—Study guides. 2. College Entrance
Examination Board. College-Level Examination Program.   I. Doster, William C.
II. How to prepare for the CLEP, College-Level Examination Program general
examinations.   III. Title: College-Level Examination Program general
examinations.

    LB2353.68.B37 2007
    378.1'662—dc22
                                                           2007007101

Printed in the United States of America

9 8 7 6 5 4

Contents

16 Background and Practice Questions   607

17 Sample Examinations   669

Introduction to the College-Level Examination Program

CHAPTER 1

WHAT IS THE CLEP EXAM PROGRAM?

The College-Level Examination Program (CLEP) is a nation-wide testing program developed by the College Board, in cooperation with Educational Testing Service (ETS). It began in 1965 and is now administered at 1300 colleges. Nearly 3000 colleges award credit to students who perform well on the exams.

WHO TAKES CLEP EXAMS?

Most students who take the CLEP Exams are people who have acquired significant amounts of knowledge outside the college classroom. By taking CLEP Exams, they can demonstrate that they have achieved college-level learning so that they are not required to enroll in certain courses when they pursue a college degree.

CLEP Exams have proven valuable for:

- Adult learners who have engaged in self-study and achieved significant learning on the job.

- Home-educated students who have undertaken advanced studies during their high school years.

- High school students who have taken advanced courses during their high school years.

- Students from nonaccredited institutions who need to have their records validated so they can pursue a degree at an accredited institution.

- Applicants for employment with government agencies who value a standardized evaluation of skills.

- Individuals who desire to evaluate their level of learning for the purpose of personal growth, rather than pursuit of a college degree.

CLEP SUBJECT EXAMS

This book will help you prepare for the five of the CLEP Exams that cover the material typically taught in introductory courses during the first two years of college: English Composition, Humanities, Mathematics, Natural Sciences, and Social Sciences and History.

Overview of Exams

Test	Content
English Composition (with Essay)	Part 1—Identifying sentence errors, improving sentences, revising work in progress
	Part 2—Essay
English Composition (without Essay)	Identifying sentence errors, improving sentences, revising work in progress, restructuring sentences, analyzing writing
Humanities	Literature (drama, poetry, fiction, non-fiction)
	Fine Arts (visual arts, music, performing arts, architecture)
Mathematics	Sets, logic, real number system, functions and graphs, probability and statistics
Natural Sciences	Biological science, physical science
Social Sciences and History	History, political science, sociology, economics, psychology, geology, anthropology

GENERAL INFORMATION ABOUT THE EXAMS COVERED IN THIS BOOK

Each of the CLEP Exams covered in this book emphasizes the general principles of the subject area being tested, not the mere facts anyone might remember from a specific course. More specific information about the areas covered is given in each of the sections of this book dealing with the five exams. In general, however, the entire battery of five tests covers what anyone might be expected to know from the first two years of college work or the equivalent.

Most colleges have a required series of courses that provide the type of general information and educational experience that every person should have as he or she goes into a specialized area; the CLEP General Examinations do not go beyond the content of these "general education" courses, as they are often called. Obviously, different schools provide varied content in each of these courses, and some schools have no such general education requirements. Students with different backgrounds may find that they are deficient in one area but very good in another. However, it is normally the overall, total score that matters.

You do not have to take all five General Examinations. You may choose any one or more of the exams, scheduling the test dates at your convenience.

HOW THE SYSTEM WORKS

The CLEP examination process requires you to interact with three different institutions.

1. The College Board
2. A local test center connected to the Educational Testing Service
3. A college (if you wish to receive college credit)

The **College Board** develops the CLEP Exams, keeps and reports the scores, and oversees the process. A network of 1300 **test centers**, located at colleges and universities, administer the exams. Over 2900 **colleges** grant credit for satisfactory scores.

Understanding how the process is organized will help you achieve your educational objectives most effectively. To earn college credit through CLEP Exams, you should take the following steps:

1. Become familiar with the exams and decide which one(s) you wish to take.
2. Make contact with the college where you intend to receive credit. Obtain information on their policies to learn how much credit is possible, what scores are required, and how your results will be handled.
3. Develop a plan to prepare for the exam, using materials like this handbook.
4. Contact a local test center and arrange for a testing date.
5. Take the exam at the test center.
6. Request that CLEP send your scores to the college of your choice.
7. Consult your college to request credit for your score.

HOW TO ARRANGE TO TAKE THE CLEP EXAMINATIONS

Educational Testing Service has established test centers at major colleges in all parts of the United States. To schedule a CLEP Exam, you must contact a local test center to make an appointment for the testing. Some test centers are open only to their own students; others are open to the public. You can locate the nearest test center by consulting the College Board web site at www.collegeboard.com/CLEP testcenters. You can also contact them by phone at (800) 257-9558.

Each test center will provide detailed information on their procedures, fees, and other information. In addition, the College Board maintains regional offices in each section of the country, which can provide additional information.

HOW SCORES ARE HANDLED

All CLEP Exams are now administered on computers. Most of them are scored immediately, so that you will know your score before you leave the exam session. An exception is the English Composition with Essay. Unlike exams in multiple-choice format, the English Composition essays are scored by college professors, rather than computers. Essays are scored twice a month, and scores are mailed to the student within two weeks of the scoring.

Because the exams are computer-based, you must be careful to follow instructions exactly. We suggest that you visit the College Board's web site at www.collegeboard.com. From there, click on "Taking the Tests," which will take you to a list of test links and information links for each test. Click on "CLEP" to reach the "About CLEP" page. From this page you can download the *CLEP Sampler* so that you can become familiar with the process of completing the exam on a computer.

The total number of questions you have answered correctly will be converted to a "scaled score" between 20 and 80. The scaled score will be reported to any college you designate. When you take the exam, you have the option to have the score sent to a college or employer at no charge. If you request a score report at a later date, there is a nominal fee.

FINAL CAUTION

Before you register for a CLEP Exam, consult the staff at the institution where you plan to have your scores sent. You should find out exactly how the scores will be interpreted, what uses will be made of the scores, and what specific scores are required by that college to receive credit.

Neither the College Board nor Educational Testing Service sets a passing or failing score. Evaluating your scores and granting credit is solely the responsibility of the college to which your scores are submitted. Since most institutions have different policies on these matters, you should have that information before you take the examinations.

NOTE

The format and content of the CLEP Examinations are changed periodically. You should check the CLEP web site or contact the nearest College Board regional office to obtain the latest information on each exam.

How to Use This Book in Preparing for the CLEP Examinations

HOW TO STUDY FOR THE CLEP EXAMINATIONS

The CLEP Examinations represent a survey of basic subjects. This book covers five basic subjects. When the test is constructed, each subject is outlined or divided up into a number of main topics. Questions are written that fall under the main headings. Because the test has only a limited number of questions, these questions will, for the most part, cover only the main points of any one category. Therefore, in studying for the examination the student should survey the entire subject, draw up an outline of the subject, review the main points in familiar areas, and study those topics with which he or she is less familiar.

This book helps you get used to the actual process of taking multiple-choice tests. At the same time each sample question reveals a topic or subject area that may be on the actual test. Because these questions and those presented on the actual test are not identical, it is best not to simply memorize answers to the questions in this book. Instead, when you run across questions you can't answer, check them off. When you find the answer, try to understand the concept or idea involved. You might keep track of the questions you miss and see if they fall in the same category. In this way you can direct your review toward those areas in which you are least proficient. You may have difficulty with a question because the question contains words you do not know. In this case, write the words down as you confront them and find out what they mean from a dictionary or other reference book.

Because the CLEP Examinations cover a wide area of general knowledge, it would be difficult to start from scratch, learning everything that might be included in the test. However, you should realize that you are not starting from scratch. If you are a recent high school graduate, you will discover that most of the material on the tests is material with which you are already familiar from high school and elementary school courses. If you have been out of school for some time, you will find that much of the material on the actual examination is familiar to you from newspapers, magazines, and your general experience.

In preparing for the test it is best to use books that outline the material to be covered in a brief but concise way. You need to know the main points of a subject. If you do not already have extensive knowledge in a field, it is unreasonable to expect to acquire it now and for the most part it will be unnecessary in terms of this particular examination. Main points you should know include the major persons in a field, the main events, principles involved, and the vocabulary of each field.

The Examination in College Mathematics covers material that is generally taught in a college course for nonmathematics majors. Some of the topics are sets, logic, the real number system, functions and graphs, and probability and statistics. The bibliography given in Chapter 10 will be helpful if you feel the need for a general review of mathematics.

It is important to remember that survey courses for freshmen and sophomores in college, for the most part, repeat a good deal of material that the student should have learned in high school. To be sure, college courses are more compact or concise and may go into the subject in greater depth. Nevertheless, many of the main topics covered are the same as those covered in high school. Do not be overwhelmed by the idea that these are "college" examinations for they are designed for the person who has acquired a basic education on his or her own. Working out the items offered in this book and answering the questions will be one way in which you can review what you have already learned, either in a classroom or on your own.

STRATEGIES FOR PREPARING FOR THE CLEP EXAMS

How the Book Is Laid Out

This book is arranged in five major parts, one part for each of the five CLEP Exams. Each part opens with a Trial Test, which gives you an idea of what the examination is like. It also lets you determine how you would score on the examination without any specific preparation or practice. Then there is a chapter that provides general information about the examination and a number of items illustrating the basic principles of the subject area as well as the different kinds of information you will need to have or the different responses you might be called upon to make. You will find these sample items arranged in small groups, and we have provided answers and explanations for these answers immediately following each group of questions. You may work through these groups of items at the pace you choose. The specific questions we give you will help you become familiar with the basic principles of the subject area. Each of these chapters includes a brief bibliography of reference works and textbooks that you may want to review if you find that you are weak in one of the subject areas. Most of these books are available in a good public library.

The rest of each section consists of a chapter containing two sample examinations. You may take these exams to track your progress as you prepare to take the CLEP Exam of your choice. An answer key is included at the end of each test so you can check yourself almost immediately. Answer explanations are also provided; these explanations will help you learn how to read each question carefully and answer exactly what is asked. They will also help you recognize your weak spots so you can plan your studies. We suggest that you follow the time limit that will be imposed during an actual CLEP Examination when you do the sample tests, just to get into the habit of having that limitation as part of the test procedure.

A Strategy for Studying for the CLEP Examinations

1. DECIDE WHICH EXAMS TO TAKE

You can't take all the exams on the same day, and most people will want to study for one or two exams at a time. If you do prepare for more than one test at a time, plan a schedule that allows you to skip back and forth between the two exam sections. This variety will give you a needed break.

Start with the subject you know best, so that you will have a quick initial success.

It is important to understand what kind of knowledge the CLEP Exams are designed to measure. The Exams represent a survey of five basic subjects. When the test is constructed, each subject is outlined or divided up into a number of main topics.

Questions are written to evaluate mastery of the main headings. Because the test has only a limited number of questions, these questions will, for the most part, cover only the main points of any one category. When you study, therefore, you should survey the entire subject, reviewing the main points in familiar areas and studying more intensively in the areas which are less familiar.

2. TAKE THE TRIAL TEST

You probably have a fairly accurate idea of which subjects are your strongest areas and which will require more intensive preparation.

By taking the Trial Test, you can confirm your self-evaluation and gain a more precise idea of how much preparation you should plan.

- If you have strong knowledge of the subject, you can simply use the material in this handbook to review. A score of 60 or above normally represents a fairly strong grasp of the material.

- If your knowledge of the subject is moderate, you should probably use one of the texts listed in the bibliography of each chapter to do a more extensive review of the subject. In preparing for the tests, it is best to use books that outline the material to be covered in a brief but systematic way. You may wish to obtain a textbook used by a local college. You need to know the main points of the subject, such as the major persons, the main events, the principles involved, and the vocabulary of each field.

- If you have a particularly weak background in one particular area, it may be more reasonable for you to take a college-level course in the subject. CLEP Examinations are designed to help you receive credit for what you have already learned, and if you do not already have adequate knowledge in a field, it is unreasonable to expect that you can master it without extensive study.

3. SET UP A PERSONAL STUDY PLAN

Determine your study goals and decide how much time you can devote to preparation. Set aside a time and place to work on the exam so that you can make steady progress.

4. WORK THROUGH THE CHAPTER ON BACKGROUND AND PRACTICE QUESTIONS

Do not attempt to take any of the complete Sample Examinations until you worked through all the sample items in this chapter. As you try the small groups of questions, you will see that each of these groups deals with just one part of the subject area. In the complete examinations, on the other hand, questions are arranged in a more random order to cover the whole subject area.

5. TAKE THE SAMPLE EXAMS

If you complete this entire book with the illustrative and sample test items we have prepared for you, you will have worked through almost 3000 different test items.

Why so many? We believe that this much practice is necessary for you to do well on the CLEP General Exam battery. We do not, of course, expect that anyone will attempt to finish the whole book in just a few days. Take your time, and you will be better off.

Observe the time limits when you take each Sample Examination, so that you will become accustomed to the discipline of working within time limits. Do not be disappointed if you do not finish each Sample Examination within the prescribed time limit. Test experts tell us that many people do not finish the tests for various reasons. Simply do the best you can. If you can get about 50% of each test correct, your score will be above the average score of all college sophomores in the United States.

The vocabulary level of the test items is about Grade 14, which means that the words used are those that any college sophomore should recognize and understand from his or her reading. Sentence structure and syntax are at the same level. It will be helpful to have a good dictionary available in case you find words that you do not understand.

You will take the actual CLEP Exams on a computer, but we have provided answer sheets for the Trial Tests and Sample Examinations.

This book helps you get used to the actual process of taking multiple-choice tests. In addition, each sample question reveals a topic or subject area that may be represented on the actual test. None of the questions in the book appear in an actual CLEP Exam, so it is best not to simply memorize answers to the questions in this book. Instead, you should use the following procedure:

a. Mark each question that you cannot answer.
b. Read the explanation of the question in the section following the test, and try to understand the concept you missed.
c. Look for patterns of weakness or blind spots. If several of the questions you missed fall into the same category, you can focus extra effort on study in that area.

6. BE SURE THAT YOU ARE COMFORTABLE WITH COMPUTER-BASED TESTING.

You will take your CLEP Exam on a computer, so it is important to become comfortable with that format so that you will not be distracted during the test. You can download the *CLEP Sampler* from the CLEP web site to recreate the experience of taking a CLEP Exam on your computer. www.collegeboard.com/student/testing/clep/prep.html

Strategies for Taking the CLEP Examinations

1. BEFORE THE TEST DAY

a. Get plenty of sleep. An important aid in taking an examination is to rest the night before. Fatigue can lower your self-confidence, your ability to concentrate, and your speed in taking the examination and can ultimately lower your score.

b. Eat normally. Do not take any tranquilizers or stimulants that might interfere with your performance. Do not drink too many liquids so that you can avoid the necessity of interrupting the exam for a visit to the restroom.

c. Plan to arrive early. Be sure that you know the location of the test center, including parking, so that you will not be delayed

d. Contact the test center to be sure that you know what ID to bring and what form of payment is acceptable.

2. ON THE TEST DAY

a. Arrive early so that you will not feel rushed and will have time to adjust to the surroundings. This will give you time to ask questions and arrange your personal belongings before the exam period starts.

b. Be sure you have remembered to bring the required personal identification and payment. Bring any registration forms required by the test center. Your personal identification should include a driver's license, passport, or other government-issued identification that includes your photograph and signature. You may also need secondary identification such as a social security card or student ID that includes your photo or signature.

A credit card is the most common method of payment, but you may also pay by check or money order.

c. Wear comfortable clothes. Since you do not know whether the examination room will be warm or cold, wear layers of clothing that can removed or added as needed.

d. Bring two pencils with good erasers, to write ideas for an essay or to do math calculations. You may not bring a mechanical pencil. Do not bring scratch paper; it will be provided by the test center. If you take the Mathematics Exam, you will not need a calculator; the test software includes a calculator.

3. DURING THE EXAM

Different strategies work for different people in taking exams. You should follow whatever procedure works best for you. Because each test is timed, however, it is crucial that you do not linger too long on any single question. As soon as it becomes obvious to you that you do not know the answer, you should move on to the next question. Many poor test takers get bogged down on one or two questions and don't have time to complete all the questions they could have answered.

Here is a strategy that seems to work for many people:

a. Read the question and try to *recall* the right answer.

b. If you do not recall the right answer, read the question again and see if you *recognize* the correct answer.

c. If you do not recognize the right answer, immediately go on to the next question. In this way you will spend your time on what you know. The secret of taking this type of test is to decide immediately whether or not you know the answer. If you cannot decide quickly, go on to the next item so that no time is wasted.

d. When you have completed all the answers that you were sure of, you will probably have time to go back and look more closely at the questions you skipped the first time around. When you come back to take a second look, you will find that you immediately recognize some of the answers.

e. For any items that still give you difficulty, you should use the process of elimination to weed out any obviously incorrect answers.

EXAMPLE

The scientist who invented the first usable electric light was

(A) Benjamin Franklin   (B) George Washington   (C) Thomas Edison   (D) Henry Ford   (E) Marie Curie

You may not know a thing about electricity but certainly you can eliminate the names of George Washington and Henry Ford. You have bettered your odds; your chances are now one-in-three instead of one-in-five. If you are still not sure which is correct, but have a hunch, then play that hunch.

f. Make your best guess. There is no penalty for wrong answers, so it is better to guess than to leave an item blank.

Often, you will have heard or read the correct answer, even though you do not consciously remember it. So you will often be correct if you follow your instincts. If you have chosen an answer and still aren't sure about it, it is usually best to stick with your first answer. Research studies have demonstrated that the first guess is more likely to be correct than a revised guess later on.

Other hints:

• Don't assume anything about the test instructions. You will be given time to read the test directions before the test begins. Even if you feel completely familiar with the directions from other experiences, take time to read them on this particular test, so that you know exactly what to expect.

• Relax. Don't let last minute nervousness get the better of you. Almost everyone is a little tense before an examination, and being a little keyed up can help you focus on the task at hand. But too much tension can interfere with your performance. If you freeze or clutch during the examination, then forget the questions for a few moments and concentrate on something else. Don't worry about the few minutes you lose. You'll waste more time and will be less efficient if you try to struggle through the test with that "locked up" feeling. Relax and be calm. Remind yourself that you're pretty smart and you have what it takes. Then, when you are calmer, go back to the exam.

- Pace yourself. Check the time fairly often to make sure you're not going too slowly. You should have finished one quarter of the questions when one quarter of the time is up, half of the questions when half the time is up. If you find you have been taking too long, try to speed up a bit for the rest of the test. And remember not to spend too long on any one question.

- Read all of the answer choices before choosing your answer. The first or second answer might seem correct, but the fourth or fifth one might be even better – and usually the directions instruct you to pick the *best* answer choice. [Note: You should use a slightly different approach when taking the College Mathematics Exam. See the section on the Math Exam for details.]

- Do not try to figure out a certain pattern of answers. Some students think that if the answer to one question is (A), the answer to the next question will probably be (D), and the correct response to the following question might be (B). The CLEP Exams are designed so that no such patterns exist.

- Do not look for "trick questions." CLEP Exams are written to ask straightforward questions to find out what you know. They do not build in traps or surprises.

When you finish this book, look back through the questions, and check to see just how much factual information you can recall from your experiences with the sample items. We think that you will be pleasantly surprised.

Good luck!

NOTE: No sample question in this book has ever appeared on an actual CLEP examination. The examinations are security tests, and all material on those tests is protected by copyright in the name of the Educational Testing Service. The test items in this book are meant to be similar in format to an actual CLEP examination, not actual items that you might find when you take one or more of the examinations.

Progress Chart

	Trial Test	Exam 1	Exam 2
English Composition 90 minutes			
Humanities 90 minutes			
Mathematics 90 minutes			
Natural Sciences 90 minutes			
Social Sciences- History 90 minutes			

THE ENGLISH COMPOSITION EXAMINATION

English Composition
ANSWER SHEET—TRIAL TEST

1 Ⓐ Ⓑ Ⓒ Ⓓ Ⓔ   26 Ⓐ Ⓑ Ⓒ Ⓓ Ⓔ   51 Ⓐ Ⓑ Ⓒ Ⓓ Ⓔ   76 Ⓐ Ⓑ Ⓒ Ⓓ Ⓔ
2 Ⓐ Ⓑ Ⓒ Ⓓ Ⓔ   27 Ⓐ Ⓑ Ⓒ Ⓓ Ⓔ   52 Ⓐ Ⓑ Ⓒ Ⓓ Ⓔ   77 Ⓐ Ⓑ Ⓒ Ⓓ Ⓔ
3 Ⓐ Ⓑ Ⓒ Ⓓ Ⓔ   28 Ⓐ Ⓑ Ⓒ Ⓓ Ⓔ   53 Ⓐ Ⓑ Ⓒ Ⓓ Ⓔ   78 Ⓐ Ⓑ Ⓒ Ⓓ Ⓔ
4 Ⓐ Ⓑ Ⓒ Ⓓ Ⓔ   29 Ⓐ Ⓑ Ⓒ Ⓓ Ⓔ   54 Ⓐ Ⓑ Ⓒ Ⓓ Ⓔ   79 Ⓐ Ⓑ Ⓒ Ⓓ Ⓔ
5 Ⓐ Ⓑ Ⓒ Ⓓ Ⓔ   30 Ⓐ Ⓑ Ⓒ Ⓓ Ⓔ   55 Ⓐ Ⓑ Ⓒ Ⓓ Ⓔ   80 Ⓐ Ⓑ Ⓒ Ⓓ Ⓔ
6 Ⓐ Ⓑ Ⓒ Ⓓ Ⓔ   31 Ⓐ Ⓑ Ⓒ Ⓓ Ⓔ   56 Ⓐ Ⓑ Ⓒ Ⓓ Ⓔ   81 Ⓐ Ⓑ Ⓒ Ⓓ Ⓔ
7 Ⓐ Ⓑ Ⓒ Ⓓ Ⓔ   32 Ⓐ Ⓑ Ⓒ Ⓓ Ⓔ   57 Ⓐ Ⓑ Ⓒ Ⓓ Ⓔ   82 Ⓐ Ⓑ Ⓒ Ⓓ Ⓔ
8 Ⓐ Ⓑ Ⓒ Ⓓ Ⓔ   33 Ⓐ Ⓑ Ⓒ Ⓓ Ⓔ   58 Ⓐ Ⓑ Ⓒ Ⓓ Ⓔ   83 Ⓐ Ⓑ Ⓒ Ⓓ Ⓔ
9 Ⓐ Ⓑ Ⓒ Ⓓ Ⓔ   34 Ⓐ Ⓑ Ⓒ Ⓓ Ⓔ   59 Ⓐ Ⓑ Ⓒ Ⓓ Ⓔ   84 Ⓐ Ⓑ Ⓒ Ⓓ Ⓔ
10 Ⓐ Ⓑ Ⓒ Ⓓ Ⓔ   35 Ⓐ Ⓑ Ⓒ Ⓓ Ⓔ   60 Ⓐ Ⓑ Ⓒ Ⓓ Ⓔ   85 Ⓐ Ⓑ Ⓒ Ⓓ Ⓔ
11 Ⓐ Ⓑ Ⓒ Ⓓ Ⓔ   36 Ⓐ Ⓑ Ⓒ Ⓓ Ⓔ   61 Ⓐ Ⓑ Ⓒ Ⓓ Ⓔ   86 Ⓐ Ⓑ Ⓒ Ⓓ Ⓔ
12 Ⓐ Ⓑ Ⓒ Ⓓ Ⓔ   37 Ⓐ Ⓑ Ⓒ Ⓓ Ⓔ   62 Ⓐ Ⓑ Ⓒ Ⓓ Ⓔ   87 Ⓐ Ⓑ Ⓒ Ⓓ Ⓔ
13 Ⓐ Ⓑ Ⓒ Ⓓ Ⓔ   38 Ⓐ Ⓑ Ⓒ Ⓓ Ⓔ   63 Ⓐ Ⓑ Ⓒ Ⓓ Ⓔ   88 Ⓐ Ⓑ Ⓒ Ⓓ Ⓔ
14 Ⓐ Ⓑ Ⓒ Ⓓ Ⓔ   39 Ⓐ Ⓑ Ⓒ Ⓓ Ⓔ   64 Ⓐ Ⓑ Ⓒ Ⓓ Ⓔ   89 Ⓐ Ⓑ Ⓒ Ⓓ Ⓔ
15 Ⓐ Ⓑ Ⓒ Ⓓ Ⓔ   40 Ⓐ Ⓑ Ⓒ Ⓓ Ⓔ   65 Ⓐ Ⓑ Ⓒ Ⓓ Ⓔ   90 Ⓐ Ⓑ Ⓒ Ⓓ Ⓔ
16 Ⓐ Ⓑ Ⓒ Ⓓ Ⓔ   41 Ⓐ Ⓑ Ⓒ Ⓓ Ⓔ   66 Ⓐ Ⓑ Ⓒ Ⓓ Ⓔ   91 Ⓐ Ⓑ Ⓒ Ⓓ Ⓔ
17 Ⓐ Ⓑ Ⓒ Ⓓ Ⓔ   42 Ⓐ Ⓑ Ⓒ Ⓓ Ⓔ   67 Ⓐ Ⓑ Ⓒ Ⓓ Ⓔ   92 Ⓐ Ⓑ Ⓒ Ⓓ Ⓔ
18 Ⓐ Ⓑ Ⓒ Ⓓ Ⓔ   43 Ⓐ Ⓑ Ⓒ Ⓓ Ⓔ   68 Ⓐ Ⓑ Ⓒ Ⓓ Ⓔ   93 Ⓐ Ⓑ Ⓒ Ⓓ Ⓔ
19 Ⓐ Ⓑ Ⓒ Ⓓ Ⓔ   44 Ⓐ Ⓑ Ⓒ Ⓓ Ⓔ   69 Ⓐ Ⓑ Ⓒ Ⓓ Ⓔ   94 Ⓐ Ⓑ Ⓒ Ⓓ Ⓔ
20 Ⓐ Ⓑ Ⓒ Ⓓ Ⓔ   45 Ⓐ Ⓑ Ⓒ Ⓓ Ⓔ   70 Ⓐ Ⓑ Ⓒ Ⓓ Ⓔ   95 Ⓐ Ⓑ Ⓒ Ⓓ Ⓔ
21 Ⓐ Ⓑ Ⓒ Ⓓ Ⓔ   46 Ⓐ Ⓑ Ⓒ Ⓓ Ⓔ   71 Ⓐ Ⓑ Ⓒ Ⓓ Ⓔ   96 Ⓐ Ⓑ Ⓒ Ⓓ Ⓔ
22 Ⓐ Ⓑ Ⓒ Ⓓ Ⓔ   47 Ⓐ Ⓑ Ⓒ Ⓓ Ⓔ   72 Ⓐ Ⓑ Ⓒ Ⓓ Ⓔ   97 Ⓐ Ⓑ Ⓒ Ⓓ Ⓔ
23 Ⓐ Ⓑ Ⓒ Ⓓ Ⓔ   48 Ⓐ Ⓑ Ⓒ Ⓓ Ⓔ   73 Ⓐ Ⓑ Ⓒ Ⓓ Ⓔ   98 Ⓐ Ⓑ Ⓒ Ⓓ Ⓔ
24 Ⓐ Ⓑ Ⓒ Ⓓ Ⓔ   49 Ⓐ Ⓑ Ⓒ Ⓓ Ⓔ   74 Ⓐ Ⓑ Ⓒ Ⓓ Ⓔ   99 Ⓐ Ⓑ Ⓒ Ⓓ Ⓔ
25 Ⓐ Ⓑ Ⓒ Ⓓ Ⓔ   50 Ⓐ Ⓑ Ⓒ Ⓓ Ⓔ   75 Ⓐ Ⓑ Ⓒ Ⓓ Ⓔ   100 Ⓐ Ⓑ Ⓒ Ⓓ Ⓔ

Trial Test

T his chapter contains a Trial Test in English Composition. Take this Trial Test to learn what the actual exam is like and to determine how you might score on the exam before any practice or review.

The CLEP General Exam in English Composition measures your knowledge of English, including usage, sentence correction, paragraph revising, analysis, and construction shift.

There are two forms of the General Exam in English Composition.

• The version *without essay* consists entirely of multiple-choice questions. It is arranged in two sections of 45 questions each.

• The version *with essay* consists of two parts: the first part involves 50 multiple-choice questions, and the second involves a single essay.

NUMBER OF QUESTIONS ON THE TRIAL TEST: 100

Time limit: 90 MINUTES

Directions. The following sentences test your knowledge of grammar, usage, diction (choice of words), and idiom.

Some sentences are correct.

No sentence contains more than one error.

You will find that the error, if there is one, is underlined and lettered, Assume that elements of the sentence that are not underlined are correct and cannot be changed. In choosing answers, follow the requirements of standard written English.

If there is an error, select the one underlined part that must be changed to make the sentence correct.

If there is no error, select answer (E).

1. The greatest <u>dramatists always imply</u> more in their plays than they seem to
                        A
say, <u>for they know how</u> to make use of <u>both denotation</u> and connotation
            B   C
<u>as well as</u> other technical devices of drama. <u>No error.</u>
      D   E

2. We <u>were told</u> by the director <u>that Marie was</u> the one
            A   B
<u>who the committee wanted</u> to hire <u>for the position.</u> <u>No error.</u>
            C   D   E

3. <u>Looking out</u> of the window was my pleasure for many
      A
hours, for I <u>could not</u> understand the countryside <u>until I had concentrated</u>
                  B   C
on the different <u>effects of it's beautiful</u> scenes. <u>No error.</u>
                        D   E

4. The new Ford having <u>slowed down a little</u>, the driver <u>greeted the riders</u>
                              A   B
in the short <u>distance between the buildings</u> and
                        C
the <u>display area</u> of the auto show. <u>No error.</u>
            D   E

5. Chinese art <u>with its subtle shadings</u> and almost suggestive
                        A
<u>curving lines</u> demonstrates those characteristics <u>that set them apart</u>
      B   C
from <u>all other people</u> of the world. <u>No error.</u>
            D   E

6. Brazil is larger <u>than any country</u> in the world; <u>if you argue with</u> this bold
      A   B   C
statement, look at the map of the world, <u>either an atlas</u> or any projection
                                                C
of the world on a flat surface. <u>No error.</u>
                                        E

7. A small <u>snack of candy are still</u> on the
                  A
<u>dish on the lower shelf of the cabinet</u> <u>if you want a taste</u>
                  B   C
before you <u>say good night.</u> <u>No error.</u>
                  D   E

8. In the court of Louis XVI, advisers belonged
           A   B

    to the Roman Catholic church who's honesty might have
                                                C

    been suspected by an impartial participant in the events of the
                                   D

    scene. No error.
           E

9. Most of the evidence the prosecutor so carefully presented in his
             A

    summation was ignored by the jury because the defense attorney made
                       B   C

    such an emotional speech explaining his client's actions. No error.
                          D   E

10. As Joel reflected on his experience at his last job, he has realized that he
           A   B

    learned some valuable life lessons that would help him at his current job.
                    C   D

    No error.
     E

11. In his speech, George Bush made many illusions, to the United States,
                            A

    its government and its citizens, its almost overwhelming diversity and
          B   C

    immensity, and its great past and future potential. No error.
                     D   E

12. All the new colognes, even for men, that are now on sale
            A

    at nearly every clothing store do not indicate that men prefer to smell like
                    B   C

    a spring garden nor a smelly saddle in a tack room. No error.
                  D   E

13. Reading a short novel from the beginning is worth more to one's
            A   B

    intelligence than plowing through *War and Peace* and
                       C

    skipping whole chapters of historical analysis. No error.
             D   E

14. Many current officeholders <u>must of been</u> aware that <u>their continuing effort</u>

                                     A   B

to waste money while <u>refusing to increase taxes</u> can only

                                                    C

<u>make budget deficits larger.</u> <u>No error.</u>

              D   E

15. Shakespeare's dramas and Austen's novels <u>seem to have</u> little in common

                                                                             A

<u>until a careful reader</u> enjoys both their <u>ability to keep a plot going</u> and

              B   C

their <u>most unique use</u> of language. <u>No error.</u>

              D   E

16. The <u>tragic love affair</u> of Romeo and Juliet <u>have inspired</u>

                A   B

<u>such different artists</u> as Shakespeare (dramatist) and Zeffirelli (filmmaker)

              C

to tell the story, <u>each using his</u> own special talents. <u>No error.</u>

                              D   E

17. Frank Sinatra and <u>Barbra Streisand have had.</u>

                                          A

<u>more influence upon contemporary music</u> <u>as any other singers</u>

                          B   C

<u>recording songs</u> by the thousands each week. <u>No error.</u>

              D   E

18. Some users of deadly <u>drugs have excused</u> <u>their fatal addiction</u> as their

                                    A   B

wanting to escape <u>the many problems</u> <u>that may afflict</u> those who have

                              C   D

been searching for happiness. <u>No error.</u>

                                                    E

19. <u>Whoever we select</u> <u>as our delegate</u> to the international

              A   B

<u>convention will have all</u> expenses paid <u>from the dues</u> of the local

              C   D

organization. <u>No error.</u>

                          E

20. Some experimenter <u>invented a better mousetrap</u> that was guaranteed to

                                          A

work <u>every</u> time, but the patent attorney arched his eyebrows

              B

<u>at the experimenter's</u> use of a nuclear warhead as <u>the agent of destruction.</u>

              C   D

<u>No error.</u>

      E

Directions: In each of the following sentences, part of the sentence or the entire sentence is underlined. Below each sentence you will find five ways of phrasing the underlined part. Select the answer that produces the most effective sentence, one that is clear and exact, without awkwardness or ambiguity. In choosing answers, follow the requirements of standard written English. Choose the answer that best expresses the meaning of the original sentence.

Answer (A) is always the same as the underlined part. Choose answer (A) if you think the original sentence needs no revision.

21. In these times of overwhelming social upheaval, we can understand that our past <u>was not as productive as we thought it was.</u>

    (A) was not as productive as we thought it was
    (B) was not so productive as we thought it was
    (C) was not as productive so that we thought about it
    (D) is not what we hoped it would be
    (E) was not as productive as we thought they were

22. The minister made the congregation a little upset <u>in the course of the initial</u> sermon by demanding money in the collection plates.

    (A) in the course of the initial
    (B) during his first
    (C) during the exciting
    (D) in the course of the foremost
    (E) in the coarse of the initial

23. It is an amazing observation <u>of today's modern world</u> that no one seems to have the ability of laughing at his or her mistakes.

    (A) of today's modern world
    (B) of the world of today
    (C) of today's world
    (D) with today's modern world
    (E) from all that I see around me today

24. <u>Americans has the responsibility of changing their government form if they</u> <u>believe it no longer responds to their needs.</u>

    (A) Americans has the responsibility of changing their government form if they believe it no longer responds to their needs.
    (B) When Americans find it no longer responds to their needs, they can change their form of government.
    (C) Americans can change their form of government if it no longer responds to their needs.
    (D) Americans who are unhappy with their government has the right to change its form.
    (E) Americans has the right to change their form of government; when they are unhappy with it.

25. The city council member introduced <u>an ordinance prohibiting rock concerts</u> within the city limits.

    (A) an ordinance prohibiting rock concerts
    (B) an ordinance that discouraged rock concerts
    (C) an ordinance that makes it possible for rock concerts
    (D) an ordinance for making illegal rock concerts
    (E) an ordinance permitting rock concerts

26. <u>The candidate for president worked hard for voters, dashing from precinct</u> <u>to precinct on a motor scooter.</u>

    (A) The candidate running for president worked hard for voters, dashing from precinct to precinct on a motor scooter.
    (B) On a motor scooter, the candidate rushed from place to place as they campaigned for election.
    (C) Rushing from place to place, the motor scooter was campaigning for voters.
    (D) The candidate campaigned hard for voters; rushing from place to place on a motor scooter.
    (E) The candidate having been campaigning hard for voters; rushing from place to place on a motor scooter.

27. <u>Suburbanites who are accustomed to riding trains on the daily round-trip do</u> <u>not get disturbed if exact schedules are not maintained.</u>

    (A) Suburbanites who are accustomed to riding trains on the daily round-trip do not get disturbed if exact schedules are not maintained.
    (B) Some of the suburbanites commuting into a city by train is not upset if a train is late once in a while.
    (C) A train being late once in a while does not upset those suburbanites whom expect such delays.
    (D) Schedules not being maintained as published do not disturb many suburbanites who commuted to a city for a job.
    (E) Those suburbanites who commute to the city by train doesn't and get bothered if trains are sometimes late.

28. When I think of astronauts undertaking strange experiments in outer space, my consciousness is filled with awe for the achievement of contemporary thinking.

    (A) is filled with awe
    (B) is filled up with awe
    (C) fills up with awe
    (D) was filled with admiration of awe
    (E) was filled up with awe for

29. Bill Smith showed his stupidity, for he refused to save money during his years of prosperous moneymaking.

    (A) showed his stupidity, for he refused
    (B) showed his stupidity; for he refused
    (C) showed his stupidity, he refused
    (D) showed his stupidity. For he
    (E) showed his stupidity, as a result

30. Jonathan's father, the male child of a native prince and a foreign sugarcane worker, was born in Grenada.

    (A) the male child of
    (B) being the male child of
    (C) having been sired by
    (D) the only male son of
    (E) the son of

31. Jessica wanted to succeed as a doctor or a lawyer, which is one of the highest ambitions anyone can have.

    (A) Jessica wanted to succeed as a doctor or a lawyer, which is one of the highest ambitions anyone can have.
    (B) Jessica wanted to succeed as a doctor or to be a lawyer, two of the highest ambitions anyone can have.
    (C) Jessica wanted to succeed in medicine or law, two professions in which people with high ambitions have been successful.
    (D) Among her other ambitions, Jessica wanted to study doctor and lawyer.
    (E) More than anything else, Jessica wanted to achieve eminence as a doctor or to be a lawyer.

32. Motorists who cross Death Valley is often told to take plenty of water for car radiators.

    (A) is often told to take
    (B) cannot but be warned
    (C) are advised to
    (D) is told to beware the dangers of dryness
    (E) could be constantly advised to

33. The judges of the writing contest had eliminated all but three of the original candidates, and now their only problem was choosing <u>the winner from among the remaining entrants</u>.

    (A) the winner from among the remaining entrants
    (B) the winner within the three finalists
    (C) the winner from between the finalists
    (D) the winner from the finalists
    (E) from among the three candidates

34. <u>Because George Washington knew how to submit an accurate expense account was the only reason he had so little trouble collecting money due him.</u>

    (A) Because George Washington knew how to submit an accurate expense account was the only reason he had so little trouble collecting money due him.
    (B) George Washington knew how to submit an accurate expense account; therefore, he had little trouble collecting money due him.
    (C) The reason that George Washington had so little trouble collecting money due him was because he knew how to submit an accurate expense account.
    (D) George Washington had little trouble collecting money due him, he knew how to submit an accurate expense account.
    (E) George Washington's expense account, having been so carefully submitted that the cost was paid almost immediately.

35. Since the package was actually addressed to both of us, you <u>should not of been so startled</u> when I opened it.

    (A) should not of been so startled
    (B) could not have been so startled
    (C) should of been so startled
    (D) would not have been so startled
    (E) should not have been so startled

36. Without being asked, <u>the woman took</u> a seat at one of the cocktail tables and ordered white wine.

    (A) the woman took
    (B) the woman should have taken
    (C) the woman has taken
    (D) the woman should of taken
    (E) the woman had took

37. In the South, dogwood and azaleas announce the arrival of spring <u>by bursting into bloom in many gardens</u>.

    (A) by bursting into bloom in many gardens
    (B) after they explode into bloom in every garden
    (C) even though they force their buds into bloom
    (D) since they have burst into bloom
    (E) while they bloom in every garden

38. A snowplow can clear streets and open spaces in a short while, <u>but they are troublesome to store</u> in the summertime.

    (A) but they are troublesome to store
    (B) but it can be troublesome to store
    (C) but some people have troubles when they store them
    (D) but problems when they store them
    (E) but they cannot be no trouble to store

39. Luggage inspectors at airports must confiscate food and exotic pets, not necessarily because they might contain weapons, <u>but diseases could be spread</u>.

    (A) but diseases could be spread
    (B) but the fact that they might cause diseases is terrifying
    (C) but what would we do if anyone got sick?
    (D) but because they might carry diseases
    (E) but they might could have diseases

40. Putin and <u>Bush have met publicly only once</u>, but they seem to agree on a number of things.

    (A) Bush have met publicly only once
    (B) Bush has met publicly only once
    (C) Bush has been meeting periodically
    (D) Bush will meet many times
    (E) Bush will be meeting several times

41. Ms. Cruz is <u>one of the commuters who takes</u> the train from Hunter's Point every evening.

    (A) one of the commuters who takes
    (B) one of the commuters that takes
    (C) one of the commuters and they take
    (D) one of the commuters who take
    (E) one of the commuters, they take

Directions: Each of the following selections is an early draft of a work in progress in which the sentences have been numbered for easy reference. Some parts of the selections need to be changed.

Read each selection and then answer the questions that follow. Some questions are about particular sentences or parts of sentences and ask you to improve the sentence structure and diction (word choice). In making these decisions, follow the conventions of standard written English. Other questions refer to the entire passage or parts of the passage and ask you to consider organization, development, and effectiveness of language in relation to purpose and audience.

Questions 42–48 are based on the following passage:

(1) Some people like to relax by engaging in sports like tennis or softball. (2) Others go in for yoga exercises or read spy stories or they like to work in the garden. (3) One woman I know works on her car whenever she feels tense and nervous. (4) Her car is always in tip-top shape, and she keeps up on the latest automotive technology, too. (5) Me, I play computer games.

(6) A lot of people claim computer games are a waste of time. (7) They say that teenagers are flipping shapes around on Tetris when they should be doing their homework while young children are zapping digitized monsters instead of getting some physical exercise. (8) But there is a place for computer games. (9) All you have to do is remember that they are games, and belong in relaxation time, so you shouldn't be doing them in work time.

(10) Sometimes computer games serve a very useful purpose. (11) A spy was discovered when his boss borrowed his computer to play a computer game and found a file with all the information the spy had collected to pass to the enemy.

(12) The great advantage of computer games is that they are always there. (13) If you need a break from the research paper you're working on or the calculus problem you're having trouble with, just hit a few keys and you're off on a game that may require some concentrated eye-hand coordination, but will give your brain a much-needed rest.

42. Which is the best version of the underlined portion of sentence 2 (reproduced below)?

    Others go in for yoga exercises or read spy stories or they like to work in the garden.

    (A) (as it is now)
    (B) and they like to work
    (C) and work
    (D) or work
    (E) or they work

43. What should be done with sentence 4?

    (A) Leave it as it is.
    (B) Delete it.
    (C) Combine it with sentence 3, using a colon.
    (D) Put it after sentence 5.
    (E) Combine it with sentence 3, using a comma.

44. What is the best version of the underlined portion of sentence 6 (reproduced below)?

    A lot of people claim computer games are a waste of time.

    (A) (as it is now)
    (B) Most people say
    (C) Many people claim that
    (D) They say
    (E) Although people claim that

45. What should be done with "while" in sentence 7?

    (A) It should be left as it is.
    (B) It should be deleted.
    (C) It should be replaced with a semicolon.
    (D) It should be replaced by "and that."
    (E) It should be replaced by "so that."

46. What should be done with paragraph 3?

    (A) It should be left as it is.
    (B) It should be deleted.
    (C) It should be placed before paragraph 1, so that it begins the essay.
    (D) It should be placed after paragraph 4, so that it ends the essay.
    (E) It should be combined with paragraph 2.

47. Which is the best version of the underlined portion of sentence 9 (reproduced below)?

    All you have to do is remember that they are games, and belong in relaxation time, so you shouldn't be doing them in work time.

    (A) (as it is now)
    (B) so you shouldn't do them in work time
    (C) so you shouldn't do them when you should be working instead
    (D) not in work time
    (E) not when you should be working

48. Which is the best version of sentence 12 (reproduced below)?

    The great advantage of computer games is that they are always there.

    (A) (as it is now)
    (B) The great advantage of computer games is their constant availability.
    (C) For those of us who use them, the great advantage of computer games is that they are always there on the computer.
    (D) Computer games are always there.
    (E) If you spend long hours working at a computer, the great advantage of computer games is that they are always there.

Questions 49–55 are based on the following passage:

(1) William Hazlitt and Percy Bysshe Shelley are the two most thoroughgoing radicals of the Romantic movement in English literature. (2) Shelley was a great poet and has had great influence. (3) His radicalism is less a matter of literary style than of attitude.

(4) Shelley came of a wealthy family and had all the advantages of education and social position that wealth could bring. (5) He was a vocal opponent of any form of oppression. (6) That oppression could come from politics or religion or from society.

(7) Many of his poems talk about and deal with the theme and topic of tyranny. (8) His tyrants are never admirable. (9) But you might say that they are never just people we can despise. (10) They are worthy opponents.

(11) Consider Ozymandias, whose statue lies shattered in the desert in Shelley's sonnet. (12) Ozymandias is gone, his empire is gone, but the "shattered visage" still bears the "sneer of cold command." (13) Shelley hated tyranny and even authority, but he never underestimated the power of the opposition.

49. The opening paragraph should be

    (A) left as it is
    (B) rewritten to omit Hazlitt
    (C) rewritten to include other English radicals
    (D) rewritten to include other European radicals of the Romantic period
    (E) rewritten to include some mention of Shelley's literary style

50. The best transitional word or phrase to introduce sentence 5 would be

    (A) Nonetheless
    (B) At the same time
    (C) Therefore
    (D) On the other hand
    (E) Besides

51. The best way to combine sentences 5 and 6 would be

    (A) He was a vocal opponent of any form of oppression, which includes oppression that could come from politics or religion or from society.
    (B) Any form of oppression, whether from politics or religion or from society, was something he was a vocal opponent of.
    (C) One thing he opposed was political, religious, or social oppression, often vocally.
    (D) He was a vocal opponent of any form of oppression—political, social, or religious.
    (E) Political, social, or religious oppression was opposed vocally by him.

52. Sentence 7 would best be rewritten

    (A) Many of his poems talk about and deal with the theme and topic of tyranny.
    (B) The theme and topic of many of Shelley's poems is tyranny.
    (C) Many of his poems are about tyranny.
    (D) The theme of many of his poems is about tyranny.
    (E) The topic of tyranny forms the theme that many of his poems talk about.

53. Which of the following is the best way to combine sentences 8 and 9?

    (A) His tyrants are never admirable, but you might say that they are never just people we can despise.
    (B) His tyrants are never admirable, even though you might say that they are never just people we can despise.
    (C) His tyrants are never admirable, but neither are they despicable.
    (D) Although his tyrants are never admirable, you might say that they are never just people we can despise.
    (E) Besides never being admirable, his tyrants are never people you could despise.

54. Which is the best version of sentence 11 (reproduced below)?

    Consider Ozymandias, whose statue lies shattered in the desert in Shelley's sonnet.

    (A) (as it is now)
    (B) Considering Ozymandias, his statue lies shattered in the desert in Shelley's sonnet.
    (C) Consider Ozymandias, about whose statue, lying shattered in the desert, Shelley wrote a sonnet.
    (D) Ozymandias's statue lies shattered in the desert.
    (E) Consider Shelley's sonnet on Ozymandias, whose statue lies shattered in the desert.

55. Which of the following is a valid criticism of the passage?

    (A) It fails to explain what the author means by "radical."
    (B) It does not give enough information about Shelley's life.
    (C) It fails to provide any specific information about any of Shelley's poems.
    (D) It does not discuss any of the other Romantic poets.
    (E) It does not discuss the Romantic movement in other European countries.

> **Directions:** Each of the following passages consists of a paragraph of numbered sentences. Since the paragraphs appear as they would within a larger piece of writing, they do not necessarily constitute a complete discussion of the issues presented.
>
> Read each paragraph carefully and answer the questions that follow it. The questions test your awareness of characteristics of prose that are important to good writing.

Questions 56–62 are based on the following passage:

(1) People often find excuses for not getting a flu vaccine each year. (2) Sometimes they get busy or do not understand the serious consequences of this respiratory infection. (3) In addition, people often confuse it with other milder infections. (4) The flu can cause prolonged stress on a body. (5) People with heart problems are especially vulnerable as are children and the elderly. (6) Even healthy people should get the shot each October or November. (7) For those squeamish of shots, there is even a nasal-spray vaccine. (8) On the other hand, people allergic to chicken egg should first consult their physicians before getting the shot. (9) Eggs are used in several vaccines. (10) If people got their annual flu vaccines, tens of thousands of people would not become hospitalized or possibly even die from this dangerous illness.

56. What should be done with sentence 9?

    (A) It should be placed before sentence 8.
    (B) It should be omitted.
    (C) It should end the paragraph.
    (D) It should begin with the word <u>however</u>.
    (E) It should be placed just after sentence 6.

57. From the tone of the passage, a reader might conclude

    (A) that it was written for a scientific journal
    (B) that this was an excerpt from a high school social studies assignment
    (C) that the author intended to persuade the readers to get a flu vaccine
    (D) that the author believes the formality of the passage will convey intellectual curiosity
    (E) that the author believes people overreact to insignificant illnesses

58. The paragraph is an example of

    (A) satire
    (B) argumentative writing
    (C) narration
    (D) a process paper
    (E) an informative paper

59. The function of sentence 5 is to

    (A) provide a contrast for sentence 4
    (B) exclude some people who don't need vaccines
    (C) imply that there is an alternative to vaccines
    (D) develop an argument against using eggs in vaccines
    (E) provide an example of whom the author feels most needs to take action

60. What is the best transition to begin sentence 6?

    (A) However,
    (B) Therefore,
    (C) In addition,
    (D) Furthermore,
    (E) Hence,

61. What tone does the author take in sentence 10?

    (A) Accusatory
    (B) Tense
    (C) Conciliatory
    (D) Advisory
    (E) Prophetic

62. Which of the following pairs of sentences could most logically be combined?

    (A) sentences 3 and 4
    (B) sentences 4 and 5
    (C) sentences 6 and 7
    (D) sentences 7 and 8
    (E) sentences 8 and 9

Questions 63–69 are based on the following passage:

(1) Language can convey pleasant or unpleasant thoughts; language can be used to speak tender thoughts of love and admiration or to declare unending hostility—the expressed ideas, themselves, are beside the point, however. (2) Can you imagine how thwarted a loving couple would be if they could not exchange outpourings of the affection they feel? (3) Suzanne Langer, a philosopher, in an essay called "The Language Line" says that it is not a collection of physical characteristics that separate people from the lower animals but very simply the ability to use language as a

vehicle of communication. (4) Since almost all language is used in a social context, we must include this characteristic as one of those essential to a definition of language.

63. What is the purpose of sentence 2?

    (A) To illustrate the point of sentence 1.
    (B) To intrude a new idea into the discussion.
    (C) To limit the uses of language to lovers' conversations.
    (D) To ask an unanswerable question.
    (E) To contradict the idea of sentence 1.

64. The author uses material from a Suzanne Langer essay in which of the following forms?

    (A) A direct quotation
    (B) A paraphrase
    (C) A summary
    (D) A qualified quotation
    (E) The reader cannot tell because the whole selection is not given.

65. In sentence 4, the phrase social context

    (A) should have been more clearly defined
    (B) may have several different meanings
    (C) is sociological jargon
    (D) indicates social aspects of communication implied in earlier sentences
    (E) refers to a radical political belief

66. The author identifies Ms. Langer as a philosopher

    (A) to explain the use of big words in the sentence
    (B) to lend intellectual support to his idea
    (C) to appeal to intellectual snobs among the readers
    (D) to limit the application of the remark to philosophy
    (E) to demonstrate his respect for Ms. Langer as a scholar

67. In sentence 1, the author uses

    (A) several positive and negative characteristics of language
    (B) an unnecessarily complex system of punctuation—a semicolon, dashes, commas
    (C) techniques of balancing complete opposite notions that language can express
    (D) the group of words after the dash to contradict the ideas expressed in the first part of the sentence
    (E) too much information for even a long sentence

68. That this passage was taken from a longer essay is shown most clearly in

    (A) sentence 1
    (B) sentence 4
    (C) sentence 2
    (D) sentence 3
    (E) sentences 1 and 3

69. Which of the following is the most accurate description of the apparent purpose of this passage?

    (A) to arouse the emotions
    (B) to justify the study of linguistics
    (C) to lead into a discussion of love
    (D) to lead into a definition of language
    (E) to show what human beings would be like without language

Directions: Each of the following selections is an early draft of a work in progress in which the sentences have been numbered for easy reference. Some parts of the selections need to be changed.

Read each selection and then answer the questions that follow. Some questions are about particular sentences or parts of sentences and ask you to improve the sentence structure and diction (word choice). In making these decisions, follow the conventions of standard written English. Other questions refer to the entire passage or parts of the passage and ask you to consider organization, development, and effectiveness of language in relation to purpose and audience.

Questions 70–76 are based on the following passage:

(1) There used to be an old ad that said, "They laughed when I sat down at the piano." (2) Well, all through my childhood, they just left when I sat down at the piano.

(3) Mother was determined that I should be a musician, and she started me on piano lessons when I was seven. (4) Little girls who take piano lessons also have to practice. (5) There's no point in taking piano lessons if you don't practice. (6) This is what she kept pointing out to my father and my two brothers. (7) "There's no point in having her take piano lessons if she doesn't practice," Mother told my father and my two brothers every evening at six o'clock, half an hour before dinner, when I did my practicing. (8) That's when my father went out to the garage. (9) That's when my brothers went up to their room. (10) That's when the dog started scratching the door to be let out. (11) Even my mother, who was the one who said I had to practice, headed for the kitchen and started banging pots and pans.

(12) It wasn't that my family didn't love me. (13) I was the baby of the family, and most of the time they were willing to spoil me rotten. (14) The problem was that they weren't deaf—not even tone-deaf. (15) They just couldn't bear to listen.

(16) Then I began to practice. (17) My fingers stumbled over even the easiest scales sitting at the piano. (18) I couldn't play anything without hitting the wrong notes. (19) And what is more, I therefore had no sense of rhythm.

70. What is the best position in the essay for paragraph 4?

    (A) (where it is now)
    (B) following paragraph 1
    (C) following paragraph 2
    (D) at the start of the essay
    (E) omitted from the essay

71. Which is the best word to replace "and" in sentence 3?

    (A) None. A semicolon should be used.
    (B) but
    (C) yet
    (D) because
    (E) so

72. What is the best way to treat sentences 5 and 6?

    (A) Combine them into a single sentence, joining them with "and."
    (B) Delete them.
    (C) Move them to the end of the paragraph.
    (D) Put them after sentence 7.
    (E) Put them at the beginning of the paragraph.

73. Keeping in mind the sense of the passage as a whole, which of the following would be the best transition word to introduce sentence 4?

    (A) However,
    (B) Therefore,
    (C) Consequently,
    (D) Thus,
    (E) Besides,

74. Which of the following would be the best way to combine sentences 8, 9, and 10?

    (A) with colons
    (B) with semicolons
    (C) with commas
    (D) with commas, adding "so" before each "that"
    (E) with commas and "and" between sentences 8 and 9 and "but" between sentences 9 and 10

75. Which of the following is the best version of the underlined portion of sentence 17 (reproduced below)?

    My fingers stumbled over even the easiest scales sitting at the piano.

    (A) It should be left as it is.
    (B) It should be deleted.
    (C) while sitting at the piano
    (D) seated at the piano
    (E) when on the piano bench

76. Which of the following is the best version of the underlined portion of sentence 19 (reproduced below)?

    And what is more, I therefore had no sense of rhythm.

    (A) (as it is now)
    (B) I had
    (C) Therefore, I had
    (D) And I thus had
    (E) What is more, I thus had

Questions 77–83 are based on the following passage:

(1) In 1869, Antonio Lopez de Santa Anna, the brave Mexican leader of the Alamo attack, moved to Staten Island, New York. (2) He had been exiled from Mexico because his forces slaughtered the Texas insurgents in their battle for independence. (3) Santa Anna had brought with him several objects from home, including a large lump of chicle, the elastic sap of the Sapodilla tree. (4) The Mayan Indians had been chewing this substance for hundreds of years. (5) Today, many people like breath mints as well as gum, although both products sell very well. (6) Santa Anna wasn't interested in chewing the chicle, he hoped that the inventor Thomas Adams could refine the substance into a substitute for rubber and Adams did his best, but he could not transform chicle into rubber.

(7) Adams was walking down the street one day he saw a small child buying a wax called "paraffin" at a pharmacy. (8) This gave Adams a great idea. (9) He asked the pharmacy manager if he would sell a brand new kind of gum. (10) The pharmacist agreed. (11) Dashing home, Adams immersed the chicle in water until it was soft. (12) Then he squeezed and was pressing the chicle into little round shapes. (13) They were a drab gray color, but every single ball of "gum" was sold the very next day. (14) With his profits, Adams went into business producing Adams New York Gum No. 1.

(15) The process of making chewing gum is surprisingly similar today. (16) Now, small pieces of latex—still obtained from the Sapodilla trees of Central and South America—are kneaded until soft. (17) Today, however, the chicle is added to a hot sugar-corn syrup mixture. (18) When the mixture is smooth, it is flavored, usually with mint (a great flavor), and rolled into thin strips or squares.

77. Which is the relationship between sentences 1 and 2?

    (A) cause-effect
    (B) chronological order
    (C) problem-solution
    (D) compare-contrast
    (E) no connection

78. A reasonable criticism of sentence 5 would be that it

    (A) does not serve as an example of the Alamo attack
    (B) endorses commercial products
    (C) is off the topic
    (D) lacks specific details to support the generalization
    (E) is not a complete sentence, since it lacks a verb

79. Which is the best version of sentence 6 (reproduced below)?

    Santa Anna wasn't interested in chewing the chicle, he hoped that the inventor Thomas Adams could refine the substance into a substitute for rubber and Adams did his best, but he could not transform chicle into rubber.

    (A) (as it is now)
    (B) Santa Anna wasn't interested in chewing the chicle but he hoped that the inventor Thomas Adams could refine the substance into a substitute for rubber and even though Adams did his best, but he could not transform chicle into rubber.
    (C) Santa Anna wasn't interested in chewing the chicle. He hoped that the inventor Thomas Adams could refine the substance into a substitute for rubber. Adams did his best, but he could not transform chicle into rubber.
    (D) Santa Anna wasn't interested in chewing the chicle; instead, he hoped that the inventor Thomas Adams could refine the substance into a substitute for rubber. Adams did his best, but he could not transform chicle into rubber.
    (E) Santa Anna hoped that the inventor Thomas Adams could refine the substance into a substitute for rubber because he wasn't interested in chewing the chicle and Adams could not transform chicle into rubber but he did his best.

80. Which is the best version of sentence 7 (reproduced below)?

    Adams was walking down the street one day he saw a small child buying a wax called "paraffin" at a pharmacy.

    (A) (as it is now)
    (B) Adams was walking down the street one day, he saw a small child buying a wax called "paraffin" at a pharmacy.
    (C) Adams was walking down the street one day when he saw a small child buying a wax called "paraffin" at a pharmacy.
    (D) At a pharmacy, a small child buying a wax called "paraffin" was seen by Adams as one day he was walking down the street.
    (E) A small child buying a wax called "paraffin" at a pharmacy was seen by Adams as he was walking down the street one day.

81. Sentence 12 is weak because

    (A) it is vague and unclear.
    (B) it is lacking a subject.
    (C) it has a misplaced modifier.
    (D) it has a dangling participle.
    (E) the verbs are not parallel.

82. Which is the best version of sentence 13 (reproduced below)?

    They were a drab gray color, but every single ball of "gum" was sold the very next day.

    (A) (as it is now)
    (B) They were a drab gray color, but every single ball of "gum" were sold the very next day.
    (C) Every single ball of "gum" was sold the very next day; they were a drab gray color.
    (D) Every single ball of a drab gray colored "gum" were sold the very next day.
    (E) A drab gray color, every single ball of "gum" was sold the very next day.

83. The apparent purpose of this passage is to

    (A) Persuade the reader that gum is an important product, in the past as well as the present
    (B) Explain the history of chewing gum
    (C) Compare and contrast marketing in the past and present
    (D) Describe how chewing gum is made
    (E) Highlight the contributions of people from other cultures

Directions: The following sentences test your knowledge of grammar, usage, diction (choice of words), and idiom.

Some sentences are correct.

No sentence contains more than one error.

You will find that the error, if there is one, is underlined and lettered. Assume that elements of the sentence that are not underlined are correct and cannot be changed. In choosing answers, follow the requirements of standard written English.

If there is an error, select the one underlined part that must be changed to make the sentence correct and fill in the corresponding oval on your answer sheet.

If there is no error, select answer (E).

84. The <u>schedule we face</u> is <u>much longer than</u> it <u>would of</u> been <u>had we begun</u>
          A   B   C   D

    the work on schedule in the spring. <u>No error.</u>
                                      E

85. <u>What Socrates represented</u> as ignorance and weakness in <u>himself</u> was
               A   B

    in fact <u>a noncommittal attitude</u> toward unproven assertions. <u>No error.</u>
      C   D   E

86. <u>Lack</u> of clarity <u>results</u> as often <u>from too few</u> words <u>as too many</u>. <u>No error.</u>
      A   B   C   D   E

87. <u>Had I known</u> then <u>what I know</u> now, I would not <u>then had done</u> what I
         A   B   C

    <u>did</u>. <u>No error.</u>
     D   E

88. It is difficult, if not <u>an impossibility</u>, to <u>engender</u> a sense of civic pride in
                           A   B

    a typical large city, where <u>more than half</u> the inhabitants were born
                                       C

    elsewhere and <u>do not plan</u> to remain. <u>No error.</u>
                 D   E

Directions: Effective revision requires choosing among the many options available to a writer. The following questions test your ability to use these options effectively.

Revise each of the following sentences according to the directions that follow it. Some directions require you to rephrase only part of the original sentence; others require you to recast the entire sentence. You may need to omit or add certain words in constructing an acceptable revision, but you should *keep the meaning of your revised sentence as close to the meaning of the original as the directions permit.* Your new sentence should follow the conventions of standard written English and should be clear and concise.

Look through the answer choices A–E under each question for the exact word or phrase that is included in your revised sentence. If you have thought of a revision that does not include any of the words or phrases listed, try to revise the sentence again so that it does include the wording in one of the answer choices.

When you take the test, you should feel free to make notes in your test book, but you will need to mark your answers on the separate answer sheet.

89. Comic books were the primers that taught me how to read and cereal boxes and ketchup labels also taught me to read.

    Begin with <u>Along</u>.

    (A) Along with comic books
    (B) Along with primers
    (C) Along with cereal boxes and ketchup labels
    (D) Along with learning how to read
    (E) Along with reading

90. Current college students are somewhat spoiled because they do not want to spend too much time in study.

    Eliminate <u>because</u>.

    (A) so do not want
    (B) but do not want
    (C) and do not want
    (D) when do not want
    (E) however do not want

91. Andrew Lloyd-Webber has many musicals filling theaters all over the world; also, he can buy whatever he wants after paying tremendous income taxes.

    Eliminate semicolon after <u>world</u>.

    (A) such
    (B) whenever
    (C) that
    (D) with
    (E) without

92. Many drug dealers are being caught, but many more roam the streets and create problems.

    Change the compound sentence to a complex one.

    (A) because of
    (B) even though
    (C) so as
    (D) inasmuch as
    (E) without

93. The generator, which provides power to the house, is used when the electricity goes out during a storm.

    Begin the sentence with <u>A generator provides</u>.

    (A) although the electricity
    (B) if the electricity
    (C) before the electricity
    (D) until the electricity
    (E) so that the electricity

94. The publisher was astounded by the sales of Maria Jones's first novel; there-fore, she was paid a much higher royalty arrangement for the second.

    Eliminate ; therefore.

    (A) novel, she
    (B) novel, so the publisher
    (C) novel, the publisher
    (D) novel; so she
    (E) novel; publisher

95. The new electronic ovens, which employ high-frequency sound waves rather than heat as a means of cooking food, use a clock instead of a thermostat as a control device.

    Begin with A thermometer is useless in.

    (A) because high-frequency sound waves employ
    (B) because heat employs
    (C) because the control device employs
    (D) because clocks employ
    (E) because they employ

96. Orphans are considered adoptable until they reach the age of seven; if no family has taken them by then, the welfare agency must be willing to keep the children until they finish high school.

    Begin with Orphans are not considered adoptable.

    (A) after they become seven years old
    (B) until they reach the age of seven
    (C) since they became seven years old
    (D) because they become seven years old
    (E) as they reach the age of seven

97. Any success in my efforts to write the great American novel will be com-pletely due to the lessons I learned from my tenth-grade English teacher.

    Substitute If I succeed for Any success.

    (A) is completely due
    (B) is completely attentive
    (C) is completely learned
    (D) is completely responsible
    (E) is completely effortless

98. Because Amanda Wingfield had a number of gentlemen callers in her youth, she assumed that the number of a girl's suitors was a measure of her popularity.

    Eliminate <u>because</u>.

    (A) youth, therefore
    (B) youth; therefore
    (C) youth. Therefore
    (D) youth, so therefore
    (E) youth; so thus

99. Some painkillers claim to be nonaddictive, no matter how many tablets a user takes, but others warn anyone's taking more than four every twenty-four hours.

    Begin with <u>Users may take an unlimited</u>.

    (A) to become addicted
    (B) for becoming addicted
    (C) from becoming addicted
    (D) with becoming addicted
    (E) without becoming addicted

100. When politicians prepare a speech for delivery to a conservation organization, they are sure to include some ringing phrases praising recycling and public responsibilty.

    Change <u>sure to include</u> to <u>surely include</u>.

    (A) When politicians prepared
    (B) Often when politicians prepare
    (C) Politicians who prepare
    (D) Politicians praising
    (E) Politicians cooking

STOP

If there is still time remaining, you may review your answers.

English Composition
ANSWER KEY—TRIAL TEST

1. E	26. A	51. D	76. B
2. C	27. A	52. C	77. A
3. D	28. A	53. C	78. C
4. A	29. A	54. E	79. D
5. C	30. E	55. A	80. C
6. B	31. C	56. B	81. E
7. A	32. C	57. C	82. A
8. C	33. D	58. E	83. B
9. E	34. B	59. E	84. C
10. B	35. E	60. A	85. E
11. A	36. A	61. D	86. D
12. D	37. A	62. B	87. C
13. E	38. B	63. A	88. A
14. A	39. D	64. E	89. C
15. D	40. A	65. D	90. C
16. B	41. D	66. B	91. D
17. C	42. D	67. C	92. B
18. E	43. B	68. B	93. B
19. A	44. C	69. D	94. C
20. E	45. D	70. C	95. E
21. A	46. B	71. E	96. A
22. B	47. D	72. B	97. D
23. C	48. E	73. A	98. B
24. C	49. B	74. B	99. E
25. A	50. A	75. B	100. C

SCORING CHART

After you have scored your Trial Test, enter the results in the chart below, then transfer your score to the Progress Chart on page 12. As you complete the Sample Examinations later in this part, you should be able to achieve increasingly higher scores.

Total Test	Number Right	Number Wrong	Number Omitted
100			

ANSWER EXPLANATIONS

1. **(E)** The sentence is correct.

2. **(C)** Who is a subject pronoun. An object pronoun, whom, is needed.

3. **(D)** It's is incorrect. Its (no apostrophe) is the correct form.

4. **(A)** This is a dangling modifier. The car isn't slowing itself down.

5. **(C)** Them is vague. It refers to Chinese people, and Chinese people are not mentioned.

6. **(B)** Any country should be any other country to make the comparison complete.

7. **(A)** Are is plural; snack is singular. Both words should use singular forms in the sentence.

8. **(C)** Who's is incorrect; use whose.

9. **(E)** The sentence is correct.

10. **(B)** Has realized is the present perfect tense. The simple past, realized, is needed.

11. **(A)** Illusions and allusions are very different words, therefore incorrect.

12. **(D)** Nor is the indirect comparison; use or.

13. **(E)** The sentence is correct.

14. **(A)** Must of should be must have, the correct verb form.

15. **(D)** Unique is an incomparable adjective; omit most.

16. **(B)** Have inspired is a plural form, not the required singular to agree with the singular affair (subject).

17. **(C)** As should be than. We say more than, not more as.

18. **(E)** The sentence is correct.

19. **(A)** Whoever, a nominative case form, should be whomever, the correct form for the direct object of select.

20. **(E)** The sentence is correct.

21. **(A)** Choice (B) contains a poor idiom (so-as). (C) is wordy. (D) It is is a vague usage. (E) they, a plural word, does not fit with the singular words.

22. **(B)** Choice (A) has too many words. (C) exciting changes the meaning of the sentence too much. (D) contains excess verbiage. (E) coarse is an incorrect word choice.

23. **(C)** Choice (A) Today's modern is redundant. (B) contains too many words. (D) with is an incorrect preposition. (E) is too wordy.

24. **(C)** <u>Has</u> in (A), (D), and (E) is a singular form when the sense of the idea is plural. (B) has <u>it</u>, <u>their</u>, and <u>they</u> as vague pronouns. The semicolon in (E) is also incorrect.

25. **(A)** Choice (B) and (E) change the meaning of the sentence too much. (C) is too wordy. (D) distorts the meaning of the sentence too much.

26. **(A)** Choice (B) <u>they</u> is a vague pronoun. (C) the sentence says <u>the motor scooter</u> was trying to get voters. (D) Use a semicolon to connect to independent clauses. "Rushing from place to place..." is a fragment. (E) is a vague sentence.

27. **(A)** Choice (B) has an error in agreement—<u>is</u> is singular, <u>some</u> is plural. (C) <u>Whom</u> is the wrong case for a subject. (D) <u>do not disturb</u> is present tense, <u>commuted</u> is past tense. (E) <u>doesn't</u> is singular, not plural.

28. **(A)** Choice (B) and (C) are wordy. (D) and (E) are also wordy and shift the tense of the verb.

29. **(A)** Choice (B) The semicolon produces an incomplete second clause. (C) This sentence contains a comma splice. (D) and (E), the second clause in each sentence is an incomplete sentence.

30. **(E)** Choice (A) <u>male child</u> is redundant. (B) <u>only male child</u> is not supported by the rest of the sentence. (C) <u>having been sired by</u> does not really make sense. (D) <u>male son</u> is repetitious.

31. **(C)** Choice (A) This sentence says that medicine or law are one job; note the singular <u>is</u>. (B) <u>A doctor or to be a lawyer</u> are distorted comparisons. (D) <u>Doctor</u> and <u>lawyer</u> are not parallel with <u>ambitions</u>. (E) has incorrect parallelism in the last part of the sentence.

32. **(C)** Choice (A) and (D) contain an error in agreement of subject and verb. (B) contains a vague phrase <u>cannot but be</u>. (E) <u>could</u> is not a strong enough word for the sentence.

33. **(D)** Choice (A) <u>Among</u> is redundant. (B) <u>within</u> is a poor word choice. (C) <u>between</u> implies there are two finalists. (E) <u>among</u> is redundant.

34. **(B)** Choice (A) <u>Because . . . the reason</u> is redundant. (C) <u>reason . . . was because</u> is repetitious. (D) the comma creates a comma splice. (E) the response to the sentence is a sentence fragment.

35. **(E)** Choice (A) and (C) <u>Of</u> is not a verb form. (B) <u>could</u> changes the tense relationship. (D) also changes the tense relationship.

36. **(A)** Choice (B) and (C) change the tense relationship. (D) <u>of</u> is not a verb form. (E) <u>had took</u> is an incorrect verb form.

37. **(A)** Choice (B) <u>After</u> is the wrong verb form because it involves a tense sequence that is not correct. (C) Even though makes no sense. (D) <u>since</u> also implies a past event. (E) <u>while</u> is an ambiguous word.

38. **(B)** (A) <u>They</u> is a pronoun-antecedent agreement error. *They* is plural. *Snowplows* is singular. (C) <u>some people</u> changes the meaning too much. (D) <u>they</u> is also a vague reference of a pronoun. (E) double negative.

39. **(D)** Choice (A) This is a shift from active to passive voice. (B) This is wordy and not parallel. (C) This is a shift in tone and not parallel. (E) This is not standard English.

40. **(A)** (B) and (C) <u>has</u> is singular, and the subject is plural. (D) and (E) change the meaning of the sentence.

41. **(D)** The <u>who</u> refers to the commuters, plural, so the verb must be the plural form, <u>take</u>.

42. **(D)** This is the only choice that maintains the parallel construction, <u>go</u> . . . or <u>read</u> . . . or <u>work</u>.

43. **(B)** This sentence has nothing to do with the topic of the passage, the value of computer games for relaxation, and so should be taken out.

44. **(C)** This choice corrects the original <u>a lot</u>, which is not acceptable in standard English. <u>Most</u> (B) is not justified by anything in the passage; <u>they say</u> (D) is vague and should be avoided whenever possible; and (E) begins a contrast the sentence does not complete.

45. **(D)** The two clauses are of comparable importance and are best joined with *and*.

46. **(B)** Again, the information contained here, though interesting, has nothing to do with the topic of the passage.

47. **(D)** This choice makes the contrasting phrase parallel to <u>in relaxation time</u>.

48. **(E)** This choice provides a logical justification for the claim made in sentence 12. Obviously, computer games are not "always there" for people who do not normally use a computer.

49. **(B)** Because Hazlitt is never mentioned again in the passage, there is no justification for mentioning him in the first sentence.

50. **(A)** <u>Nonetheless</u> is the only choice that makes clear that the information in sentence 5 is unexpected after the information in sentence 4.

51. **(D)** The other choices are wordy, awkward, or unnecessarily in the passive voice.

52. **(C)** The other choices all add words without adding any information.

53. **(C)** The parallel construction in this choice presents the information concisely and effectively.

54. **(E)** This is the most logical of the choices, because it is the sonnet, not the statue, that the author wants the reader to consider.

55. **(A)** The passage is about Shelley's radicalism, so an explanation of what the author means by "radical" would be useful. The other choices ask for irrelevant information.

56. **(B)** This sentence does not advance the paragraph. It hurts the unity of the paragraph.

57. **(C)** Choice (A) This paragraph does not contain scientific jargon or research. (B) This paper does not reflect social studies issues. (D) This paper is not formal. (E) The author does not mention overreacting. This paper contains a call to action.

58. **(E)** The paper does not have the characteristics of satire, argumentation, narration, or process work.

59. **(E)** Choice (A) There is no contrast to sentence 4. (B) The author advocates vaccines for these people. (C) There is no mention of an alternative to getting a vaccine. (D) This paragraph advises people to stay healthy by getting vaccinated.

60. **(A)** However shows a contrast between the most vulnerable and the healthy. Both groups are encouraged to get a vaccine.

61. **(D)** This paragraph advises people to stay healthy by getting a flu vaccine.

62. **(B)** There is a connection between the damage the flu can cause and who is most likely to suffer greater consequences from contracting the flu.

63. **(A)** Sentence 2 serves as a concrete example of the importance of language.

64. **(E)** Since the whole selection is not given, the reader cannot tell whether this is (B) a paraphrase, (C) a summary, or (D) a qualified quotation. The reader can tell, however, that it is not (A) a direct quotation.

65. **(D)** In sentences 1, 2, and 3, language as a means of communication is discussed. In each case, the examples used have to do with language in a social context.

66. **(B)** Writers often support their ideas with confirming statements from an authority in the field.

67. **(C)** The author makes effective use of the technique of balancing opposites in this sentence.

68. **(B)** Sentence 4, the last sentence of the passage, mentions that this is one characteristic of a definition of language. We can assume that other characteristics will be discussed in following paragraphs.

69. **(D)** The final sentence of the paragraph makes this clear.

70. **(C)** Paragraph 3 is a far better conclusion for the passage than paragraph 4 is. Putting paragraph 4 after paragraph 2 makes the sequence of events logical.

71. **(E)** So makes the cause-and-effect relationship clear.

72. **(B)** These sentences simply say what is said more effectively in sentence 7, so they should be removed.

73. **(A)** However, makes clear the problem created by sentence 3. The other choices make no sense in terms of the passage as a whole.

74. **(B)** These are independent sentences of equal and comparable importance, so a suitable way to join them is with semicolons.

75. **(B)** Because the scales were not sitting at the piano, the simplest way to deal with this dangling modifier is to remove it from the sentence.

76. **(B)** This choice keeps the sentence parallel with the other sentences in the paragraph and avoids unnecessary verbiage.

77. **(A)** There is a cause-and-effect relationship between these two sentences. The *cause* is *why* something happens; the *effect* is *what* happens, the result. Sentence 1 is the effect; sentence 2 is the cause. None of the other relationships is valid.

78. **(C)** The sentence is off the topic. (B) and (D) are incorrect. (A) and (E) are illogical.

79. **(D)** Eliminate (A) because it is a run-on sentence. (B) is stringy, with too many independent clauses strung together. (C) is choppy because it does not show the relationship between ideas. (E) does not make sense, largely because of the word "and" in the final clause. (D) correctly links ideas by using coordination.

80. **(C)** The original sentence is a run-on, where two independent clauses are incorrectly joined. (B) does not correct the error; rather, it creates a comma splice. Only a semicolon, colon, dash, or subordinating conjunction can join two independent clauses. (D) and (E) are in the passive voice, which should be used only when the doer of the action is unknown or the writer does not want to identify the doer to save embarrassment ("A mistake was made" rather than "You made a mistake"). (C) provides the best subordinating conjunction ("when") to show the relationship between clauses.

81. **(E)** The verbs are not parallel. The sentence should read: Then he *squeezed* and *pressed* the chicle into little round shapes.

82. **(A)** The sentence is correct as written. It is both grammatical and elegant.

83. **(B)** Choice (A) and (C) are not supported in the passage. (D) is incorrect because it is the subject of only the final paragraph. (E) is too limited for the same reason. (B) correctly states the author's purpose.

84. **(C)** Would of is nonstandard English; the verb should be would have been.

85. **(E)** There is no error in this sentence.

86. **(D)** Parallel constructions must follow. In this sentence, as from must be repeated.

87. **(C)** In this sentence, the correct form of the verb is would have done.

88. **(A)** An impossibility should be impossible to be parallel to difficult.

89. **(C)** Along with cereal boxes and ketchup labels, comic books were the primers that taught me how to read.

90. **(C)** Many current college students are somewhat spoiled and do not want to spend too much time studying.

91. **(D)** With his many musical hits filling theaters all <u>over the world</u>, Andrew Lloyd-Webber can buy whatever he wants, even after paying tremendous income taxes.

92. **(B)** <u>Even though</u> many drug dealers are being caught, many more roam the streets freely and create problems.

93. **(B)** A generator provides power to the house <u>if the electricity</u> goes out during a storm.

94. **(C)** Astounded by the sales of Maria Jones's first <u>novel, the publisher</u> offered a much higher royalty arrangement for the second.

95. **(E)** A thermometer is useless in electronic ovens <u>because they employ</u> sound waves rather than heat as a means of cooking food.

96. **(A)** Orphans are not considered adoptable <u>after they become seven years old;</u> . . .

97. **(D)** If I succeed in my efforts to write the great American novel, my tenth-grade English teacher <u>is completely responsible.</u>

98. **(B)** Amanda Wingfield had a number of gentlemen callers in her <u>youth; therefore,</u> she assumed that the number of a girl's suitors was a measure of her popularity.

99. **(E)** Users may take an unlimited number of tablets of some pain relievers <u>without becoming addicted</u>, but others warn against anyone's . . .

100. **(C)** <u>Politicians who prepare</u> a speech to a conservation organization surely include ringing praises . . .

CHAPTER 4

Background and Practice Questions

DESCRIPTION OF THE ENGLISH COMPOSITION EXAMINATION

Note: The College-Level Exam Program (CLEP) has four different examinations that cover the material a student is supposed to master in a college composition course:

1. The Examination in English Composition without Essay
2. The Examination in English Composition with Essay
3. A CLEP Subject Examination in College Composition.
4. Freshmen College Composition with Essay.

This chapter is designed to prepare you for the General Examinations, in English Composition with or without essay. It is *not* designed to prepare you for the Subject Examination in College Composition.

The Examination in English Composition evaluates your writing skills, including your grasp of acceptable grammar and usage and your ability to arrange ideas in clear, logical order. It covers material that is generally taught in freshmen composition courses. The exam is given in two parts, each requiring 45 minutes to complete. See the following chart for a summary of the content in the two forms of the exam.

> **TIP**
>
> Be sure you know which exam will be accepted by the institution to which you will send your score, so that you will take the appropriate examination.

English Composition With Essay

Content or Item Types	Time/Number of Questions
50% Multiple-Choice Questions	Part I
Identifying Sentence Errors	50 questions
Improving Sentences	45 minutes
Revising Works in Progress	Part II
50% Essay	1 essay
	45 minutes

English Composition Without Essay

Content or Item Types	Time/Number of Questions
Identifying Sentence Errors	90 questions
Improving Sentences	90 minutes
Revising Works in Progress	
Restructuring Sentences	
Analyzing Writing	

KINDS OF QUESTIONS THAT APPEAR ON THE EXAM

Both versions of the English Composition Exam (with or without essay) contain the following three types of questions:

1. **Identifying Sentence Errors:** You will be asked to identify wording that violates the standard conventions of written English.

2. **Improving Sentences:** You will choose the version of a phrase, clause, or sentence that best conveys the intended meaning.

   These two question types are used to measure your awareness of a variety of logical, structural, and grammatical relationships within sentences and acceptable usage, including the following:

   - Active and passive voice
   - Agreement between parts of sentences (subject and verb, pronoun and antecedent)
   - Sentence completeness and variety
   - Sentence joining (parallelism, coordination, subordination, modification)
   - Idiomatic use of language and diction
   - Economy and clarity of expression

3. **Revising Works in Progress:** You will identify ways to improve an early draft of an essay. This question type is used to measure your recognition of a variety of skills within a written context prose, including the following:

   - Thesis, or main idea
   - The organization of a paragraph or essay
   - The style, tone, language, or argument's purpose
   - Logic of argument (inductive/deductive reasoning)
   - Point of view and rhetorical emphasis
   - Sufficient details and relevant evidence
   - Sentence joining and variety
   - Coherence and sustaining appropriate tense

The version of the English Composition Exam without an essay contains two other types of questions that do not appear in the version with an essay:

4. **Analyzing Writing:** You are asked to read passages written in very different styles and answer questions about the content and organization of each passage, as well as the strategies used by each author.

5. **Restructuring Sentences:** You will choose the phrase that would appear in a sentence that has been rearranged to improve its clarity or change its emphasis.

STUDY SOURCES

For review, you might consult the following books.

Cazort, Douglas. *Under the Grammar Hammer: The 25 Most Important Grammar Mistakes and How to Avoid Them.* New York: Lowell House, 1997.

Choy, Penelope, Dorothy Goldbart Clark, and James R. McCormick. *Basic Grammar and Usage,* 5th ed. New York: Harcourt, 1997.

Feierman, Joanne. *Actiongrammar: Fast, No-Hassle Answers on Everyday Usage and Punctuation.* New York: Fireside, 1995.

Kipfer, Barbara Ann. *Twenty-First Century Manual of Style.* New York: Dell, 1995.

Partridge, Eric. *Usage and Abusage: A Guide to Good English.* New York: W. W. Norton & Company, 1995.

Princeton Language Institute. Holland, Joseph (ed.). *21st Century Grammar Handbook.* New York: Dell, 1993.

Rozakis, Laurie. *Random House Webster's Pocket Grammar, Usage and Punctuation.* New York: Random House Reference, 1998.

Shertzer, Margaret D. *The Elements of Grammar.* New York: MacMillan General Reference, 1996.

Strunk, W. and E. B. White. *The Elements of Style.* Prentice Hall, May 1999.

Sutcliffe, Andrea (ed.). *New York Public Library Writer's Guide to Style and Usage.* New York: HarperCollins, 1994.

Zahler, Diane, Ellen Lichtenstein, and Claudia H. C. Q. Sorsby. *21st Century Guide to Improving Your Writing.* New York: Dell, 1995.

Practice Questions for Identifying Sentence Errors

The directions and practice questions that follow will give you a good idea of what Sentence Error questions are like. The directions, reprinted here by permission of Educational Testing Service, are the actual directions you will find in the test booklet on the day of the exam.

Directions: The following sentences test your knowledge of grammar, usage, diction (choice of words), and idiom.

Some sentences are correct.

No sentence contains more than one error.

You will find that the error, if there is one, is underlined and lettered. Assume that elements of the sentence that are not underlined are correct and cannot be changed. In choosing answers, follow the requirements of standard written English.

If there is an error, select the one underlined part that must be changed to make the sentence correct.

If there is no error, select answer (E).

To help you review some of the basics of grammar and usage on which you will be tested, the practice questions for identifying sentence errors are grouped by type of grammatical error.

ERRORS IN CASE OF PRONOUNS

EXAMPLES

1. Between you and I, that whole celebration was really an elegant affair,
          A   B   C
   I thought. No error.
   D   E

   Explanation: The underlined error is choice (A); I should be me, objective case, object of preposition between.

2. The history teacher, whom I think was the best teacher I ever had,
                       A   B   C
   told us that he had served overseas during World War II. No error.
   D   E

   Explanation: The underlined error is choice (A); whom should be who, subjective case, subject of the verb was.

Now, try your hand with the following twelve sentences. You will find the answers and the explanations immediately following the group of sentences:

1. My aunt, <u>whom we admire</u>, has <u>given</u> we <u>boys ten</u> dollars each to spend
                A   B   C

    at <u>the fair</u> tomorrow. <u>No error.</u>
       D   E

2. When <u>I showed my</u> mother the suit <u>I had selected</u>, she <u>objected to me</u>
          A   B   C

    buying it; <u>she said it</u> was too expensive. <u>No error.</u>
            D   E

3. <u>Whomever</u> is going to the <u>meeting needs</u> to bring the
        A   B

    minutes from the <u>last meeting</u> <u>with him or her</u>. <u>No error.</u>
               C   D   E

4. <u>New York City</u> <u>with it's many</u> suburbs has been called America's fabulous
       A   B

    metropolis, <u>its dirtiest city</u>, and its <u>most exciting place for a</u> brief
               C   D

    vacation. <u>No error.</u>
           E

5. Abraham <u>Lincolns Gettysburg</u> Address has been called a <u>model of brevity</u>,
            A   B

    <u>the greatest short speech</u> that <u>anyone has ever</u> delivered, and a speech
            C   D

    worth more than a longer one would have been. <u>No error.</u>
                                       E

6. Please ask <u>whoever you</u> wish to serve as a fourth member of the
           A   B

    <u>board I am</u> appointing to study the pollution situation <u>in your county</u>.
       C   D

    <u>No error.</u>
      E

7. <u>The United Nations</u> has performed many useful tasks <u>through its various</u>
          A   B

    commissions although there <u>are representatives</u> on these commissions
                           C

    <u>whom everyone</u> knows are slow-moving. <u>No error.</u>
        D   E

8. The Nobel Prize for Literature <u>has been awarded</u> to
                                                     A

   <u>Toni Morrison, who's</u> novels are now <u>considered among the</u> greatest
                     B   C

   that <u>have</u> been written in the United States in the twentieth century.
          D

   <u>No error.</u>
       E

9. Even though we <u>know that</u> we are exercising our rights <u>under</u> the
                      A   B

   United States Constitution, <u>Ashley and myself</u> are arrested every
                                        C

   time we picket the animal shelter. <u>No error.</u>
        D   E

10. When the final <u>story has been</u> written for that final newspaper
                          A

    <u>sometime in</u> the future, you can be sure <u>that it's substance</u> will be some
         B   C

    violent act that <u>has</u> occurred. <u>No error.</u>
                        D   E

11. After the bell <u>rang and signaled</u> the end of classes for that day, the
                          A

    teacher <u>told Sandeep and I</u> that <u>we</u> would have to remain thirty
                    B   C

    minutes longer for <u>whispering in the back</u> of the room. <u>No error.</u>
                              D   E

12. A modern skyscraper <u>is usually constructed</u> with a steel frame, which is
                                  A

    <u>then covered</u> with concrete <u>slabs, stones</u> of some kind, brick, or any
           B   C

    other material that <u>will hide it's</u> metal skeleton. <u>No error.</u>
                             D   E

Answers and Explanations

1. **(B)** <u>We</u> should be <u>us</u>; it is the indirect object of the verb <u>has given</u>.

2. **(C)** <u>Me</u> should be <u>my</u>; the possessive case is used with the gerund; the object of the preposition is <u>buying</u> and not <u>me</u>.

3. **(A)** <u>Whomever</u> should be <u>whoever</u>; it is the subject of <u>is</u> and <u>needs</u>.

4. **(B)** <u>It's</u> should be <u>its</u>; the possessive case of it never has an apostrophe.

5. **(A)** <u>Lincolns</u> should be <u>Lincoln's</u>; this is a possessive, not a plural.

6. **(B)** <u>Whoever</u> should be <u>whomever</u>; objective case needed; object of <u>wish</u>.

7. **(D)** <u>Whom</u> should be <u>who</u>; subject of verb <u>are</u>.

8. **(B)** <u>Who's</u> should be <u>whose</u>; who's is a contraction of <u>who is</u>.

9. **(C)** <u>Myself</u> should be I; I, subject of <u>are arrested</u>; <u>myself</u> is a reflexive pronoun.

10. **(C)** <u>It's</u> should be <u>its</u>; possessive pronoun never has an apostrophe.

11. **(B)** <u>I</u> should be <u>me</u>; object of the verb <u>told</u>.

12. **(D)** <u>It's</u> should be <u>its</u>; it's is a contraction of <u>it is</u>.

ERRORS IN AGREEMENT OF SUBJECT AND VERB

EXAMPLES

1. The <u>top three winners</u> in the <u>state competition.</u> <u>goes</u> to the <u>national finals</u> to be
          A   B   C   D

   held this year in San Francisco, California. No error.
                                  E

   Explanation: The underlined error is choice (C); <u>goes</u> should be <u>go</u>, since the plural subject <u>winners</u> requires the plural verb <u>go</u>.

2. Either John or his two friends <u>is going</u> to find that <u>passing a test</u> on that material is
                         A   B   C

   not the easiest <u>thing they</u> have ever done in school. <u>No error</u>.
                 D   E

   Explanation: The underlined error is choice (A); <u>is going</u> should be <u>are going</u>, to agree with the plural word <u>friends</u>.

Now, try your hand at the next six items:

1. The committee <u>is deciding</u> now which <u>of the many</u> <u>applicants for the</u>
                A   B   C

   teaching position <u>are going</u> to be hired. <u>No error</u>.
              D   E

2. Despite what each <u>of the experts tell</u> us about <u>how to avoid</u> bankruptcy,
                      A   B

   some <u>people insist on</u> spending more money each year <u>than they</u> make.
              C   D

   <u>No error</u>.
    E

3. Each <u>of the critics were</u> assigned a <u>book to read</u>, to <u>discuss within</u> twenty
            A   B   C

   minutes, and <u>to offer</u> an opinion about. <u>No error</u>.
            D   E

4. Although <u>the influence</u> of television on <u>America's buying</u> proclivities
         A   B

   <u>have</u> been studied by many psychologists, no one has found exactly what
    C

   the <u>influence has been</u>. <u>No error</u>.
            D   E

5. No member of a <u>circus troop have</u> the right to <u>play strictly</u> to the
                    A   B

   audience so that other <u>members</u> of the team <u>do not get their</u> fair share
                             C   D

   of the applause. <u>No error</u>.
                   E

6. No matter <u>what statisticians report</u> to the American Automobile
                   A

   Association, accidents <u>just does not</u> happen on <u>today's superhighways</u>
                            B   C

   unless some <u>driver has been too</u> careless at the wheel of his or her car.
                     D

   <u>No error</u>.
    E

Answers and Explanations

1. **(D)** <u>Are</u> should be <u>is</u>; subject <u>which</u> is singular.

2. **(A)** <u>Tell</u> should be <u>tells</u>; subject <u>each</u> is singular.

3. **(A)** <u>Were</u> should be <u>was</u>; subject <u>each</u> is singular.

4. **(C)** <u>Have</u> should be <u>has</u>; subject <u>influence</u> is singular.

5. **(A)** <u>Have</u> should be <u>has</u>; subject <u>member</u> is singular.

6. **(B)** <u>Does</u> should be <u>do</u>; subject <u>accidents</u> is plural.

ERRORS IN AGREEMENT BETWEEN A PRONOUN AND ITS ANTECEDENT

EXAMPLES

1. The audience <u>was cheering</u> <u>Kevin Kline's</u> performance as Hamlet; <u>they refused</u>
            A   B   C

   to leave the theater <u>until he took</u> four curtain calls. <u>No error.</u>
                   D   E

   Explanation: The underlined error is choice (C); they should be it.

2. No one is able to find <u>their seats</u> in a <u>darkened theater</u> and must ask an usher to
                                   A   B

   bring <u>a flashlight.</u> No error.
           C   D

   Explanation: The underlined error is choice (A); their seats should be his seat.

Now, try your hand at the following seven items:

1. When anyone expresses <u>a desire</u> to <u>get married</u> <u>as quickly</u> as possible,
                               A   B   C

   <u>they always set</u> off gossiping tongues in the community. <u>No error.</u>
          D   E

2. When anyone <u>seeks employment</u> with a large corporation, <u>he or she should</u>
                          A   B

   always be sure <u>that his or her</u> qualifications fit <u>their needs.</u> <u>No error.</u>
                  C   D   E

3. Everyone always wants <u>their achievements</u> at work to be
                                A

   rewarded by <u>management</u> in the form of raises, promotions, and
                  B

   <u>other tangible signs of appreciation,</u> even though the ability to get
                  C

   along with <u>others is</u> often as important to success as accomplishment
                  D

   itself. <u>No error.</u>
       E

4. When anyone <u>looks up a word</u> in any of the desk dictionaries <u>to check its</u>
    A   B
    spelling, <u>you must make</u> sure that the word cannot be spelled
    C
    <u>in more than</u> one acceptable way. <u>No error.</u>
    D   E

5. The congregation was <u>sitting reverently</u> <u>in their pews</u> when the organ
    A   B
    <u>broke the silence</u> with the first <u>chords of a traditional</u> hymn. <u>No error.</u>
    C   D   E

6. The television industry <u>was</u> jolted when the Federal Communications
    A
    Commission announced that cigarette advertising would not <u>be permitted</u>
    B
    on television after <u>January 1, 1971</u>, a move that took away one <u>of their</u>
    C   D
    prime sources of revenues. <u>No error.</u>
    E

7. When you <u>finally decide upon</u> the career you will follow for the rest of
    A
    your life, <u>a person should</u> be sure that you have made <u>a choice that</u> will
    B   C
    bring you as much <u>personal gratification</u> as possible. <u>No error.</u>
    D   E

Answers and Explanations

1. **(D)** <u>They always set</u> should be <u>he or she always sets</u>; antecedent <u>anyone</u> is singular.

2. **(D)** <u>Their</u> should be its; antecedent <u>corporation</u> is singular.

3. **(A)** Their should be <u>his</u> or <u>her</u>; antecedent <u>everyone</u> is singular.

4. **(C)** <u>You</u> should be <u>he</u> or <u>she</u>; antecedent <u>anyone</u> is third person.

5. **(B)** <u>Their</u> should be <u>its</u>; antecedent <u>congregation</u> is singular here.

6. **(D)** <u>Their</u> should be <u>its</u>; antecedent <u>industry</u> is singular.

7. **(B)** <u>A person</u> should be <u>you</u>; antecedent <u>you</u> is second person.

ERRORS IN TENSE SEQUENCE

EXAMPLES

1. Almost every time Jack <u>drives</u> the family car, <u>he has left</u> it <u>completely</u>
       A   B   C
   <u>empty of gasoline.</u> <u>No error.</u>
       D   E

   Explanation: The underlined error is choice (B); <u>drives</u> should be <u>has driven</u>.

2. <u>If we could</u> <u>only enjoy</u> the pleasures of our youth <u>again</u>, we <u>may find</u> that we
             A   B   C
   <u>have not forgotten</u> them after all. <u>No error.</u>
       D   E

   Explanation: The underlined error is choice (C); <u>may</u> should be <u>might</u>.

Now, try your hand with these four sentences:

1. <u>This morning,</u> all banks in the New York <u>district announce</u> that interest
        A   B
   <u>rates</u> for all home loans would be raised to <u>8%.</u> <u>No error.</u>
      C   D   E

2. The chief strongly opposes the <u>idea of putting</u> a single police officer
                                       A
   <u>in cars</u> that <u>would be cruising</u> at night in <u>high crime districts.</u> <u>No error.</u>
     B   C   D   E

3. According to the schedule posted <u>on the skater's bulletin board,</u> <u>there are</u>
                                A   B
   three exhibitions before the season officially began but only

   <u>one after the playoffs</u> <u>had been completed</u> by the entire league. <u>No error.</u>
             C   D   E

4. If <u>John Paul Jones</u> had not been <u>victorious in his</u> naval battles, the
        A   B
   United <u>States will have</u> been a second-rate power <u>on the seas forever.</u>
                  C   D
   <u>No error.</u>
    E

Answers and Explanations

1. **(B)** <u>Announce</u> should be <u>announced</u>; correct tense sequence with <u>would be raised</u>.

2. **(C)** <u>Would</u> should be <u>will</u>; correct tense sequence with <u>opposes</u>.

3. **(B)** <u>Are</u> should be <u>were</u>; correct tense sequence with <u>had been completed</u>.

4. **(C)** <u>Will</u> should be <u>would have</u>; correct tense sequence after <u>had not been</u>.

ERRORS IN WORD CHOICES, DICTION, AND IDIOMS

An error in diction means that the writer has selected the incorrect word. An error in word choice means that the writer has selected a word that means almost what he or she wanted to say but not quite.

An error in idiom means that the writer has selected the wrong word to complete the idiom that he or she wanted to use.

EXAMPLES

1. She looked at both pictures <u>carefully</u>; she <u>could not</u> decide <u>which was the</u>
            A   B   C

   <u>most beautiful</u>. <u>No error</u>.
     D   E

   Explanation: The underlined error is choice (D); <u>most</u> should be <u>more</u>.

2. While Karen <u>was setting</u> out on the porch, <u>she saw</u> Wayne and
         A   B

   <u>Daryl walking</u>. <u>slowly</u> toward her from town. <u>No error</u>.
      C   D   E

   Explanation: The underlined error is choice (A); <u>setting</u> should be <u>sitting</u>.

3. When the baby woke up from <u>his nap</u>, he made <u>alot</u> of noise, <u>jumping up</u> and
        A   B   C   D

   down in his crib. <u>No error</u>.
         E

   Explanation: The underlined error is choice (C); <u>alot</u> should be <u>a lot</u>.

4. Without <u>no warning</u> <u>at all</u>, the kitten pounced on <u>the stuffed mouse</u> and shook it
       A   B   C

   vigorously, <u>tearing</u> it to shreds. <u>No error</u>.
       D   E

   Explanation: The underlined error is choice (A); <u>no</u> should be <u>any</u>.

5. The company is having some difficulty <u>of</u> <u>promoting</u> its new <u>cereal</u>; children
                 A   B C

   <u>must be sold the idea</u> of switching brands. <u>No error</u>.
     D   E

   Explanation: The underlined error is choice (A); <u>of</u> should be <u>in</u>.

EXAMPLES (Cont.)

6. Every day this summer, all the children in the neighborhood have gone to the
   $\quad\quad$ A $\quad\quad\quad\quad\quad\quad\quad\quad$ B $\quad\quad\quad\quad\quad\quad\quad\quad\quad$ C

   village pool, where they have swimmed for several hours. No error.
   $\quad\quad\quad\quad\quad\quad\quad\quad$ D $\quad\quad\quad\quad\quad\quad\quad\quad$ E

   Explanation: The underlined error is choice (D); swimmed should be swam or swum.

7. After all the votes have been counted and the winner declared, the new president
   $\quad\quad\quad\quad\quad\quad\quad$ A $\quad\quad\quad\quad\quad\quad\quad\quad\quad$ B $\quad\quad$ C

   will be formerly inducted into office. No error.
   $\quad\quad\quad\quad$ D $\quad\quad\quad\quad\quad\quad$ E

   Explanation: The underlined error is choice (D); formerly should be formally.

8. When gold was discovered in California in 1849, there was a mad stampede
   $\quad\quad\quad\quad$ A $\quad\quad\quad\quad\quad\quad\quad\quad\quad\quad$ B

   by people to both buy land in the area or lease claims near Sutter's Mill. No error.
   $\quad\quad\quad\quad$ C $\quad\quad\quad\quad\quad\quad\quad\quad\quad\quad$ D $\quad\quad\quad\quad\quad\quad\quad$ E

   Explanation: The underlined error is choice (D); or should be and.

9. No matter how hard the teacher tries to teach the class, her
   $\quad\quad\quad\quad\quad\quad\quad\quad\quad\quad\quad\quad$ A

   efforts have little affect upon the students who refuse to study the assigned
   $\quad\quad\quad\quad$ B $\quad\quad\quad$ C $\quad\quad\quad\quad\quad\quad\quad$ D

   materials. No error.
   $\quad\quad\quad\quad$ E

   Explanation: The underlined error is choice (C); affect should be effect.

10. With his great strength, Samson could of beaten any opponent in the wrestling
    $\quad\quad\quad$ A $\quad\quad\quad\quad\quad\quad\quad\quad\quad$ B

    arena, if he had not cut his hair. No error.
    $\quad\quad\quad\quad$ C $\quad$ D $\quad\quad$ E

    Explanation: The underlined error is choice (B); of should be have.

Now, try your hand at the following twenty-five sentences:

1. After Mother had tucked us into bed and kissed us good night, we continued
   $\quad\quad\quad\quad\quad\quad$ A $\quad\quad\quad\quad\quad\quad\quad\quad\quad$ B $\quad\quad\quad\quad$ C

   talking when we should of closed our eyes and gone to sleep. No error.
   $\quad\quad\quad\quad\quad\quad\quad\quad$ D $\quad\quad\quad\quad\quad\quad\quad\quad\quad\quad\quad\quad$ E

2. No matter <u>how hard</u> I try to finish an assignment, I <u>cannot do</u> it
              A   B

   if there is anything <u>laying around</u> that I can play with. <u>No error.</u>
     C   D   E

3. <u>My uncle Jack</u>, who <u>was setting</u> on the porch and enjoying <u>a cold drink,</u>
       A   B   C

   called out and told <u>me</u> to be careful about running into the street
                           D

   without looking. <u>No error.</u>
                     E

4. <u>I will</u> neither give you money to waste on that <u>junk or</u> offer any further
    A   B

   advice <u>if you</u> <u>proceed</u> against my wishes. <u>No error.</u>
           C   D   E

5. <u>Most all voters</u> who <u>support</u> conservative political candidates <u>also support</u>
         A   B   C

   many conservative <u>organizations that</u> have grown in membership within
                                D

   the past decade. <u>No error.</u>
                     E

6. <u>Because it was</u> the best offer that had been made, the owner decided to
           A

   <u>except</u> $100,500 for his home <u>although</u> it was worth more on <u>today's</u>
       B   C   D

   market. <u>No error.</u>
             E

7. He <u>is tired</u> of picking up all the dirty clothes <u>that</u> his roommate leaves
        A   B

   <u>laying</u> on the bathroom floor <u>every morning.</u> <u>No error.</u>
    C   D   E

8. George Gershwin, composer of many of the songs <u>by which</u> American
                                                     A

   popular music has gained a reputation <u>for greatness,</u> was <u>unhappy</u> and
                                           B   C

   dissatisfied <u>by his early works</u> and studied to improve his compositions.
                  D

   <u>No error.</u>
     E

9. Jealousy <u>has been called</u> the <u>more disastrous</u> of all the human emotions
      A   B
that can wrack the mind, <u>often susceptible</u> to all kinds of fears and
  C   D
anxieties. <u>No error.</u>
    E

10. Portia Jones, <u>one of the smartest lawyers</u> in the United States, <u>has</u> often
       A   B
remarked that <u>most all criminals</u> <u>really want</u> to be kept in jail. <u>No error.</u>
     C   D   E

11. <u>Between the several</u> choices on the menu, <u>I can hardly</u> decide <u>whether I will</u>
   A   B   C
order roast beef, fried chicken, broiled fish, <u>or baked ham.</u> <u>No error.</u>
              D   E

12. It is <u>really pitiful</u> to <u>see a small child</u> die <u>without never</u> having lived <u>long</u>
   A   B   C   D
enough to accomplish anything. <u>No error.</u>
          E

13. Ely Culbertson, <u>a famous professional</u> bridge player, said that thirteen
       A
<u>spades</u> dealt in one hand is the <u>most unique unusual bridge</u> hand he ever
 B   C
<u>saw.</u> <u>No error.</u>
 D E

14. No team <u>ever wants</u> to <u>loose a game</u>, even though <u>it seems that</u> some teams
    A   B   C
make many foolish mistakes and appear <u>to throw a game away.</u> <u>No error.</u>
           D   E

15. When the play <u>had less and less people</u> in its audience <u>as its run</u> grew
      A   B
longer, the producers <u>began to consider</u> the feasibility of trying to
       C
<u>extend its</u> run beyond six months. <u>No error.</u>
 D   E

16. <u>Most historians now</u> agree that the true story about John Smith and
   A
Pocahontas <u>has never been</u> told; maybe <u>some of them</u> are <u>even real sorry</u>
      B   C   D
that the facts are still hidden. <u>No error.</u>
        E

17. While <u>the driver was</u> <u>very carefully moving</u> ahead on the expressway
               A   B

    ramp, <u>she did not notice</u> that black Cadillac that was
                    C

    <u>speeding in back of</u> her. <u>No error.</u>
            D   E

18. Your letter <u>in regards to my</u> delinquent bill <u>has been sent</u> to my attorneys for
                     A   B

    possible <u>suit for slander</u> because it contains <u>several insinuations</u> that are
                  C   D

    untrue. <u>No error.</u>
            E

19. The opera diva always enjoyed <u>a few quit moments</u> alone
                                     A

    <u>in her dressing room</u> before <u>the performance started</u> so that she could
               B   C

    appear on stage <u>calm and relaxed.</u> <u>No error.</u>
                      D   E

20. There is <u>that bird again,</u> <u>diving at us</u> from her nest in the elm tree,
                 A   B

    trying to <u>peck</u> us on the head, and then flying <u>off somewheres else</u> to be
              C   D

    safe from our retaliation. <u>No error.</u>
                            E

21. The baby-sitter says <u>that we may have</u> no more cookies
                           A

    <u>without we come into</u> the house, do our homework <u>thoroughly,</u> and
             B   C

    ask politely <u>if there are</u> any more cookies in the jar. <u>No error.</u>
                  D   E

22. <u>In his statement</u> at the press conference, the president <u>inferred that</u>
     A   B

    opposition to his foreign policy could be found <u>only among those</u> who
                                              C

    had not voted for <u>him in the election.</u> <u>No error.</u>
                        D   E

23. Now that I have reached the <u>age of eighty-two,</u> I find that <u>I can't hardly do</u>
                                 A   B

    many of the things that were <u>very easy for me</u> when I was sixteen and
                                     C

    <u>still</u> vigorous. <u>No error.</u>
      D   E

24. Although I enjoyed the exotic dinner we were served <u>in San Francisco's</u>
                                                                                    A
<u>most famous Chinese</u> restaurant, <u>I felt badly</u> because I knew that I had
         B   C
eaten more <u>than I should have.</u> <u>No error.</u>
                    D   E

25. With a valid passport, an American citizen can go

<u>anywheres in the world,</u> <u>to any country</u> that will give him or her
         A   B
permission to enter <u>except a few</u> nations that the State Department has
                              C
ruled <u>"out of bounds"</u> for American tourists. <u>No error.</u>
              D   E

Answers and Explanations

1. **(D)** <u>Of</u> should be <u>have</u>.
2. **(D)** <u>Laying</u> should be <u>lying</u>.
3. **(B)** <u>Setting</u> should be <u>sitting</u>.
4. **(B)** <u>Or</u> should be <u>nor</u>.
5. **(A)** <u>Most</u> should be <u>Almost</u>.
6. **(B)** <u>Except</u> should be <u>accept</u>.
7. **(C)** <u>Laying</u> should be <u>lying</u>.
8. **(D)** Should be <u>with</u> not <u>by</u> his works.
9. **(B)** <u>More</u> should be <u>most</u>.
10. **(C)** <u>Most</u> should be <u>almost</u>.
11. **(A)** <u>Between</u> should be <u>Among</u>.
12. **(C)** <u>Never</u> should be <u>ever</u>.
13. **(C)** Eliminate <u>unique</u>.
14. **(B)** <u>Loose</u> should be <u>lose</u>.
15. **(A)** <u>Less and less</u> should be <u>fewer and fewer</u>.
16. **(D)** <u>Real</u> should be <u>really</u>.
17. **(D)** <u>In back of</u> should be <u>behind</u>.
18. **(A)** <u>Regards</u> should be <u>regard</u>.
19. **(A)** <u>Quit</u> should be <u>quiet</u>.
20. **(D)** <u>Somewheres</u> should be <u>somewhere</u>.

21. **(B)** <u>Without</u> should be <u>unless</u>.

22. **(B)** <u>Inferred</u> should be <u>implied</u>.

23. **(B)** Eliminate <u>hardly</u>.

24. **(C)** <u>Badly</u> should be <u>bad</u>.

25. **(A)** <u>Anywheres</u> should be <u>anywhere</u>.

ERRORS IN PARALLELISM

EXAMPLES

1. As the <u>locomotive</u> left the station, it jerked them <u>so that the passengers</u> were
           A   B
   <u>thrown from their seats</u> and <u>who fell</u> on the floor. <u>No error.</u>
          C   D   E

   Explanation: The underlined error is choice (D); the sentence parallels a verb phrase (thrown from their seats) with a dependent clause, beginning <u>who fell</u>. The correct phrasing should be <u>and fell</u>.

2. Almost everyone <u>enjoys watching</u> a baseball game on television, <u>having</u> a picnic in
                  A   B
   a peaceful park, <u>or to visit</u> some strange <u>place abroad</u>. <u>No error.</u>
                  D   C   E

   Explanation: The underlined error is choice (C); the sentence parallels two verbals (<u>watching</u> and <u>having</u>) with an infinitive <u>to visit</u>. The correct phrasing should be <u>or visiting</u>.

Now, try your hand with the following four sentences:

1. Dustin Hoffman, <u>one of Hollywood's great</u> stars, made his reputation
                          A
   playing a <u>confused young man</u>, a tubercular panhandler, <u>and he also has</u>
                  B   C
   enacted <u>other roles</u>. <u>No error.</u>
          D   E

2. No one can <u>decide between</u> two alternatives to raise <u>money</u>: either the
                A   B
   club <u>should sponsor</u> a cookie sale <u>or stage a festival</u> in the town's
            C   D
   auditorium. <u>No error.</u>
         E

3. In the 1970s, <u>many college</u> students protested social conditions by
A

sitting <u>in various</u> campus buildings, by burning campus structures,
B

<u>and they have also intimidated</u> <u>members of the administration.</u> <u>No error.</u>
C   D   E

4. <u>Rosie O'Donnell</u>, a stand-up comedienne <u>and who has</u> written a book
A   B

of jokes for children, has now <u>made a name for herself</u> as the host of two
C

<u>daytime talk shows.</u> <u>No error.</u>
D   E

Answers and Explanations

1. **(C)** The sentence parallels two nouns with an independent clause. The correct wording is <u>and other roles</u>.

2. **(D)** The same construction (a complete clause) should appear after both <u>either</u> and <u>or</u>.

3. **(C)** The sentence parallels two prepositional phrases with an independent clause. The correct wording is <u>by intimidating</u>.

4. **(B)** The sentence parallels a noun with a dependent clause. The correct wording is <u>who has</u> (omit <u>and</u>).

DANGLING ELEMENTS AND MISPLACED MODIFIERS

EXAMPLES

1. <u>Rising up above</u> the top of a <u>very high mountain,</u> we saw the sun make
A   B

its way <u>slowly</u> to the zenith at noon. <u>No error.</u>
C   D   E

Explanation: The underlined error is choice (A); the participial phrase cannot logically modify the first word after the comma.

2. The young man <u>who was</u> running <u>down the street.</u> <u>very rapidly</u> turned the corner
A   B   C

and <u>ran into</u> a friend who was looking for him. <u>No error.</u>
D   E

Explanation: The underlined error is choice (C); whether the adverb modifies <u>was running</u> or <u>turned</u> is not clear.

Now, here are four for practice:

1. Waddling up to the cold pool of water, I watched the penguin do
              A   B

   a belly flop onto the ice and dive into the water. No error.
        C   D   E

2. Looking ahead as far as the Detroit designers can predict, the automobile
             A

   will always have four wheels, a steering wheel, two headlights, and four
            B   C   D

   wheel brakes. No error.
           E

3. Chez Raddish is a superb and inexpensive restaurant where fine food
                   A   B

   is served by waiters and waitresses in appetizing forms. No error.
      C   D   E

4. The painter broke his hip when the ladder broke, climbing slowly rung
              A   B   C

   by rung until he reached the second floor of the building. No error.
                        D   E

Answers and Explanations

1. **(A)** The introductory phrase does not modify I.

2. **(A)** The introductory participial phrase does not modify automobile.

3. **(D)** The phrase in appetizing forms is misplaced. The phrase should appear after fine food.

4. **(C)** The participial phrase has no word in the sentence to modify. Who is climbing slowly? The ladder isn't.

INCORRECT VERB FORMS

Now, try the four sentences that follow:

1. "The Age of Aquarius" is <u>suppose</u> to be an age of youth, <u>an age of great</u>
   A   B
   accomplishments <u>by everyone</u>, an age in which all of our hopes and
   C
   aspirations <u>will be realized</u>. <u>No error</u>.
   D   E

2. Because of the <u>high yields</u> in the stock market, <u>many</u> investors
   A   B   C
   <u>have chose</u> to buy stocks in record numbers. <u>No error</u>.
   D   E

3. The driver of the car <u>should have went</u> right <u>to avoid</u> the <u>traffic snarl</u>,
   A   B   C
   but <u>he wasn't paying</u> attention. <u>No error</u>.
   D   E

4. After many repetitions <u>of the manual of arms</u>, a raw recruit <u>becomes use to</u>
   A   B
   <u>going through</u> the drill without thinking too hard about what
   C
   <u>he or she is doing</u>. <u>No error</u>.
   D   E

Answers and Explanations

1. **(A)** <u>Suppose</u> should be <u>supposed</u>.
2. **(D)** <u>Chose</u> should be <u>chosen</u>.
3. **(A)** <u>Went</u> should be <u>gone</u>.
4. **(B)** <u>Use</u> should be <u>used</u>.

SENTENCE PROBLEMS

Writing complete sentences helps you communicate your ideas clearly. There are three types of sentence errors: *sentence fragments, comma splices,* and *run-on sentences.* To help you identify these sentence construction errors, here are three definitions and some illustrations of the errors:

1. A *complete sentence* can be defined as a group of words that has a subject and a verb and conveys a complete idea. For example:

   The child hit the ball.

   That collection of words is a complete sentence; it has a subject (<u>child</u>) and a verb (<u>hit</u>). A complete sentence may be as short as this illustration or much longer, but the definition still holds: The word group conveys a complete idea.

2. A *sentence fragment* is a group of words that may look like a complete sentence but that lack a subject or a verb, or that include a word that makes the group incomplete. Look at the following examples:

   Looking up at the airplanes
   While the clouds turned darker and darker
   A terrible experience for all of us

   None of these is a complete sentence, because they don't convey a complete idea.

3. A *run-on sentence* is defined as two complete sentences that are written as if they were one complete sentence. Here is an example:

   The children worked hard they wanted to succeed.

   There are two complete sentences (The <u>children</u> <u>worked</u> <u>hard</u> and <u>they</u> <u>wanted</u> <u>to</u> <u>succeed</u>), and English convention says that we must have some logical separation of those complete sentences. If you use a comma—The <u>children</u> <u>worked</u> <u>hard</u>, <u>they</u> <u>wanted</u> <u>to</u> <u>succeed</u>—you will make another error called the *comma splice.*

   Here are some ways to correctly punctuate clauses.

   • Use a semicolon between two sentences to show that they are related. This combination is called coordination. Here are examples:

The baby cried; he was hungry.
The rain clouds worried the sponsors of the fair; they were afraid rain would keep people away.

- Use a comma with a coordinating conjunction for coordination. This creates a compound sentence. The coordinating conjuctions are as follows: *but, or, yet, for, and, nor, so.* Here are examples of compound sentences:

The job description mentioned a need for applicants to be knowledgeable of tax laws, so Humberto studied his old notes from college on the subject.
Min needed to stay home and study for her exam, but her boss asked her to come in to work.

- Use subordinating conjunctions for subordination, thereby creating complex sentences. Some common subordinating conjunctions include *because, when, if even though, although,* and *since.* Here are examples of complex sentences:

Even though his favorite football team was down by four touchdowns, Rick believed there could be a fourth quarter miracle.
Rick believed there could be a fourth quarter miracle even though his favorite football team was down by four touchdowns.

Look at some possible questions that might include errors in sentence construction.

EXAMPLE

1. The new Ford Focus model has captured the admiration of many automobile crit-ics, they have praised its sleek lines and daring styles.
   (A) critics, they have
   (B) critics; they have
   (C) critics they have
   (D) critics, whom have
   (E) critics, she has

   Explanation: The correct answer is (B). The semicolon corrects the comma splice. (C) is incorrect because omitting punctuation creates a run-on sentence. (D) is incorrect because whom is the objective form of the pronoun. (E) is also incorrect because she (a singular) cannot refer to critics (plural); also, the comma splice error has not been changed.

2. Tony Blair, prime minister of Great Britain, has changed the course of British history within his first years in office.
   (A) Britain, has changed
   (B) Britain, who has changed
   (C) Britain; has changed
   (D) Britain has changed
   (E) Britain, whom has changed

   Explanation: The correct answer is (A). (B) and (E) are incorrect because the relative pronouns would make the sentence incomplete; whom is also the incorrect case. (C) is incorrect because the semicolon signals that a comma splice has been corrected, and there is no comma splice in the sentence. (D) is incorrect because there needs to be a comma to set off the appositive phrase.

Now, try several of these types of sentences, illustrating the types of items you will find on an actual CLEP test:

1. A national magazine called Jimmy Carter "the best ex-president we have ever had" he has worked on many projects to help people.

   (A) have ever had" he has
   (B) have ever had" because he has
   (C) have ever had due to the fact that
   (D) have ever had" being that he has worked
   (E) have ever had," working

2. Dustin Hoffman won an Oscar for his performance as an autistic man, he lived in a sheltered home for many years before being rescued by his brother.

   (A) man, he lived in
   (B) man he lived in
   (C) man who lived
   (D) man whom he had lived in
   (E) man, he will live

Answers and Explanations

1. **(B)** <u>Because</u> makes the rest of the sentence a dependent clause. As written, there is a run-on sentence.

2. **(C)** The comma splice is eliminated. (B) is a run-on sentence. (D) uses an incorrect relative pronoun (<u>whom</u>). (E) is wrong because it is in the future tense, which is illogical in this sentence.

THE DANGLING MODIFIER

Another sentence structure problem is called the *dangling modifier*. This error arises when a modifier—a phrase or clause—does not have a specific word in the rest of the sentence to modify. For example:

At the age of five, my father died.

This sentence states that my father died when he was five years old, a biological impossibility.

<u>Correction</u>: When I was five years old, <u>my father</u> died.

Dangling modifiers do not occur only at the beginning of sentences. For example:

My brother fell and broke his leg in three places, which was too bad.

<u>Which was too bad</u> does not modify a specific word in the rest of the sentence but rather the idea that the rest of the sentence conveys.

Study a few more examples with corrections:

Looking up, four airplanes were overhead.

This sentence suggests four airplanes were looking up.

<u>Correction</u>: When I looked up, I saw four airplanes overhead.

The robber who was running down the street <u>rapidly</u> turned the corner.

(Does <u>rapidly</u> modify <u>was running</u> or <u>turned</u>? The modifier dangles between the two possibilities, creating an ambiguous sentence.)

<u>Correction</u>: The robber who was running rapidly down the street turned the corner.

or

The robber who was running down the street turned the corner rapidly.

While washing clothes, the clock struck three.

The clock wasn't washing clothes.

<u>Correction</u>: While I was washing clothes, the clock struck three.

My mother won a million dollars in the lottery, which was fortunate.

The lottery itself is not fortunate.

<u>Correction</u>: It was fortunate that my mother won a million dollars in the lottery.

CORRECT SENTENCES

Sentence Error questions include some sentences that are correct but that have portions underlined to distract the test taker. Here are some examples.

1. <u>Derek and José</u> started the race <u>this morning</u>; <u>we hope they</u> will reach the
    A   B   C
finish line <u>without having to quit</u>. <u>No error</u>.
          D   E

2. <u>The other night</u>, I was reading Sylvia Plath's poetry about her experiences
    A
when <u>I decided</u> that I wanted <u>to learn more</u> about this extraordinary
     B   C
<u>woman and her writing</u>. <u>No error</u>.
       D   E

3. George <u>Washington, the</u> father of our country, <u>had many problems</u> with
         A   B
the <u>Continental Congress</u>; many times he <u>had to beg</u> for funds to support
        C   D
his starving army. <u>No error</u>.
             E

4. <u>Walking up</u> four flights of stairs <u>is not easy</u> for anyone <u>who has</u> heart
     A   B   C
trouble or who gets <u>tired very easily</u>. <u>No error</u>.
                D   E

5. Many <u>builders of fine furniture</u> have used designs first created by <u>Adams</u>,
            A   B
Chippendale, Duncan-Phyffe, Morris, <u>as well as other</u> older furniture
                              C
<u>designers whose work</u> is preserved in museums all over the world.
        D
<u>No error</u>.
  E

6. Apple pie or <u>ice cream</u> — which has <u>more calories</u>? Even <u>the best</u> diet
            A   B   C
books <u>published cannot give anyone</u> a clear answer. <u>No error</u>.
           D   E

7. When the final score <u>flashed on the scoreboard</u>, cheers <u>rose from</u> the
                    A   B
crowd <u>that had been hoping</u> for that long-awaited victory over
           C
the traditional rival. <u>No error</u>.
      D   E

8. According to the code of ethics that <u>all lawyers accept</u>, no lawyer should
A
<u>take any</u> action, <u>within or outside</u> the courtroom, that might damage his
B   C
or her <u>client's right</u> to a fair trial. <u>No error.</u>
D   E

9. In any business, <u>the workers expect</u> to be paid <u>promptly when</u> pay day
A   B
comes; none of them can <u>finance his or her day-to-day</u> life without <u>such</u>
C   D
punctuality. <u>No error.</u>
E

10. Robin Williams <u>is famous</u> for <u>his expert comedy</u>, his ability to assume a
A   B
<u>number of different roles</u>, <u>and his knack of improvising</u> dialogue while the
C   D
television camera is on. <u>No error.</u>
E

TIP

Caution

On the actual CLEP examination, sentences will not be isolated by error as these practice pages and items have been organized; therefore, you will have to consider each underlined section carefully and consider the possibility that any one of the number of errors might be present. Also, do not forget that some sentences are correct and contain no error.

Practice Questions for Improving Sentences

These items test a student's ability to discern what is incorrect about the structure of a sentence, that is, what problems might exist in the sentence as written that would interfere with logical communication.

Directions: In each of the following sentences, part of the sentence or the entire sentence is underlined. Beneath each sentence you will find five versions of the underlined part. Answer (A) repeats the original; the other four are different.

Choose the answer that best expresses the meaning of the original sentence. If you think the original is better than any of the alternatives, choose (A); otherwise choose one of the others. Your choice should produce the most effective sentence—one that is clear and precise, without awkwardness or ambiguity.

EXAMPLES

1. The reason the company failed was because the president spent too much money.
   (A) The reason the company failed was because
   (B) The company failed because
   (C) Because the company failed
   (D) Because the reason was the company failed
   (E) The company failed was because

   Explanation: The correct answer is (B). The other choices are wordy or create illogical sentences.

2. When four years old, my father died.
   (A) When four years old
   (B) When four year's old
   (C) When he was four years old
   (D) When I was four years old
   (E) At the age of four

   Explanation: The correct answer is (D). The underlined section in the original sentence is a dangling modifier, and only answer (D) solves that problem.

3. Football teams pay athletes tremendous sums of money each year, the fans pay large sums for seats in the stadium.
   (A) year, the fans pay large sums
   (B) year, the fans paying large sums
   (C) year, for the fans pay large sums
   (D) year; the fans paying large sums
   (E) year, when the fans pay large sums

   Explanation: The correct answer is (C). The original sentence contains a comma splice, and only (C) corrects the problem logically.

EXAMPLES (Cont.)

4. The lazy old man was lying under his favorite tree, sipping his favorite soft drink, and reading his favorite novel for the fifth time.
   (A) man was lying under his favorite tree, sipping
   (B) man was laying under his favorite tree, sipping
   (C) man was lying under his favorite tree sipping
   (D) man laid under his favorite tree, sipping
   (E) man lied under his favorite tree, sipping

   Explanation: The correct answer is (A). (B) is incorrect; laying is the wrong word choice. (C) is incorrect; the comma after tree is omitted, distorting the parallelism of the original. (D) is incorrect; laid is the wrong word choice. (E) is also incorrect; lied is the wrong word choice.

5. People who attend baseball games often do not know enough about the fine points of offense and defense to enjoy them.
   (A) People who attend baseball games often do not know enough about the fine points of offense and defense to enjoy them.
   (B) People who attend baseball games do not know a sufficient amount about the fine points of offense and defense to appreciate them.
   (C) Some people who attend baseball games do not know enough about the fine points of offense and defense to enjoy the skill of the players.
   (D) People who attend baseball games often do not know enough about them to enjoy the fine points of offense and defense.
   (E) People who attend baseball games do not understand the fine points of offense and defense.

   Explanation: The correct answer is (C). (A) and (B) has them, which is a vague pronoun. (D) has the same problem even though them is moved within the sentence. (E) changes the meaning of the original too much.

Now that you have tried some items of this type, try six more.

1. The wooden house had once been a showpiece of antebellum architecture, but time and tide had reduced the structure to wrack and ruin.

   (A) but time and tide had reduced the structure to wrack and ruin
   (B) but time had reduced the structure to wrack and ruin
   (C) but time and tide had reduced the structure to ruin
   (D) but time reduced the structure to a ruin
   (E) but time had reduced the structure to a ruin

2. <u>Bill</u> had to be administered to by a doctor when his admittance to law school was refused.

    (A) Bill had to be administered to by a doctor when his admittance to law school was refused.
    (B) Bill had to be treated by a doctor when his admission to law school was refused.
    (C) Bill had to be treated by a doctor when his admittance to law school was refused.
    (D) Bill had to be administered to by a doctor when his admission to law school was refused.
    (E) Bill was administered to by a doctor when his admittance to law school was refused.

3. Our neighborhood ice cream vendor was refused a license <u>because he sold banana splits to customers that were rotten.</u>

    (A) because he sold banana splits to customers that were rotten
    (B) because he sold banana splits to customers who were rotten
    (C) because he sold banana splits that were rotten to customers
    (D) because he sold banana splits who were rotten to customers
    (E) because he sold rotten banana splits to customers

4. We could only wonder if he were going to attend college <u>this fall, or if he was planning to seek</u> immediate employment.

    (A) this fall, or if he was planning to seek
    (B) fall, or he was planning to seek
    (C) fall, or if he were planning to seek
    (D) fall or was planning to seek
    (E) fall; or he was planning to seek

5. Running the rapids <u>of the Colorado River in a small raft are considered</u> one of the greatest sporting thrills available to anyone.

    (A) the Colorado River in a small raft are considered
    (B) the Colorado River in a small raft is considered
    (C) the Colorado River with a small raft are considered
    (D) the Colorado River in small rafts are considered
    (E) the Colorado's River in a small raft is considered

6. <u>Each of you can do the problem if you will put your</u> mind to work and not give up too easily.

    (A) Each of you can do the problem if you will put your
    (B) Each of you can do the problem if they will put their
    (C) Each and everyone of you can finish the problem if they will put their
    (D) Each and everyone one of them can finish the problems if you will put their
    (E) Everyone of you can finish the problems if they will put their

Answers and Explanations

1. **(E)** Wrack and ruin and time and tide are clichés. Only choices (D) and (E) eliminate them; choice (D), however, introduces another error, an error in verb tense.

2. **(B)** Administered and admittance are errors in diction. (B) is correct.

3. **(E)** That was rotten (which modifies banana splits) is a misplaced modifier in any position except choice (E).

4. **(C)** Was must be changed to were to make the two parts of the sentence parallel in construction.

5. **(B)** Running … raft is the subject of the sentence; therefore, are must be is.

6. **(A)** The sentence is correct as it stands.

Practice Questions for Revising Work in Progress

This type of question appears in Section I of the test and also in Section II of the all-multiple-choice version. Candidates are given a passage that is a first draft in need of revision. They are then asked questions about ways to improve specific sentences or parts of sentences or about ways to improve the passage as a whole.

Directions: Each of the following selections is an early draft of a work in progress in which the sentences have been numbered for easy reference. Some parts of the selections need to be changed.

Read each selection and then answer the questions that follow. Some questions are about particular sentences or parts of sentences and ask you to improve the sentence structure and diction (word choice). In making these decisions, follow the conventions of standard written English. Other questions refer to the entire passage or parts of the passage and ask you to consider organization, development, and effectiveness of language in relation to purpose and audience.

Questions 1–4 are based on the following passage:

(1) Revision is an important part of writing. (2) Often the writer will discover that there are problems with the arrangement of the material. (3) This may call for transpositions. (4) When this happens, you can block and copy to rearrange your sentences in better order. (5) If the problem is that the writer has taken far too many words to say whatever it is that she wanted to say in the first place, it may be that a pencil will be the only tool needed to eliminate the excess verbiage. (6) This is true even if you write with a pen. (7) Do not think that you are a failure because your first draft needs major changes. (8) Few writers have ever been so expert that they can produce exactly what they want the first time.

1. Which of the following is a valid criticism of the passage as a whole?

    (A) It is inconsistent in its use of tenses.
    (B) It is inconsistent in its use of person (pronouns).
    (C) It does not discuss a real problem.
    (D) No one writes with a pen anymore.
    (E) It is not organized logically.

2. Which of the following is the best way to combine sentences 2 and 3 (reproduced below)?

Often the writer will discover that there are problems with the arrangement of the material. this may call for transpositions.

(A) Often the writer will call for transpositions to cope with problems with the arrangement of the material.
(B) Often the writer will discover that there are problems with the arrangement of the material and that transpositions are called for.
(C) Often the writer will discover that there are problems with the arrangement of the material, calling for transpositions.
(D) Often the writer will discover that the problems with the arrangement of the material mean that he should call for transpositions.
(E) Often the writer will discover that there are problems with the arrangement of the material, so he should call for transpositions.

3. Which of the following is a valid criticism of sentence 5?

(A) It is too long.
(B) It belongs at the end of the paragraph.
(C) It contains a mixed metaphor.
(D) It is too wordy.
(E) It contains a dangling modifier.

4. What should be done with sentence 6?

(A) It should be left as it is.
(B) It should be omitted.
(C) It should be moved to the end of the passage.
(D) It should follow sentence 3.
(E) It should follow sentence 2.

Answers and Explanations

1. **(B)** Sometimes the passage uses you (second person) and sometimes the passage uses *the writer/she* (third person). Either one would be acceptable, but not both.

2. **(C)** This combines the sentences with no grammatical problems and avoids having the writer, rather than the arrangement of the material, call for transposition.

3. **(D)** The sentence illustrates precisely the problem it describes.

4. **(B)** the sentence is irrelevant to the topic of the passage, so it should be removed.

Practice Questions for Restructuring Sentences (Without Essay)

Note: This type of item is found in Section II of the all-multiple-choice version of the exam.

Directions: Effective revision requires choosing among the many options available to a writer. The following questions test your ability to use these options effectively.

Revise each of the following sentences according to the directions that follow it. Some directions require you to change only part of the original sentence; others require you to change the entire sentence. You may need to omit or add certain words in constructing an acceptable revision, but you should keep the meaning of your revised sentences as close to the meaning of the original as the directions permit. Your new sentence should follow the conventions of standard written English and should be clear and concise.

Look through answer choices A–E under each question for the exact word or phrase that is included in your revised sentence. If you have thought of a revision that does not include any of the words or phrases listed, try to revise the sentence again so that it does include the wording in one of the answer choices.

You may make notes in your test book, but be sure to mark your answers on the separate answer sheet.

EXAMPLES

1. *Sentence:* Graduates of Harvard's law school are more likely to be hired by large Wall Street firms than graduates of a small midwestern law school.

   Directions: Substitute have fewer chances for are more likely.

   (A) of being hired
   (B) by being hired
   (C) with being hired
   (D) instead of being hired
   (E) as well as being hired

   Explanation: The correct answer is (A). Graduates of a small midwestern law school have fewer chances of being hired by large Wall Street firms than graduates of Harvard's law school.

EXAMPLES (Cont.)

2. *Sentence:* Since there were too many books on the weak table, Maria removed two of them and put them on the shelf.

   Directions: Begin with Maria removed.

   (A) on the weak table
   (B) by the weak table
   (C) from the weak table
   (D) upon the weak table
   (E) onto the weak table

   Explanation: The correct answer is (C). Maria removed two of the books from the weak table and placed them on the shelf.

3. *Sentence:* The waitress was discharged from her position at the restaurant because she refused to wear the uniform required for anyone serving food.

   Directions: Begin with The waitress refused.

   (A) food, therefore, she was discharged
   (B) food, and was discharged
   (C) food, but she was discharged
   (D) food and was discharged
   (E) food, as a result of which she was discharged

   Explanation: The correct answer is (D). The waitress refused to wear the uniform required of anyone serving food and was discharged from her position in the restaurant.

4. *Sentence:* The old man was tired of listening to his children's complaints; therefore, he disconnected his hearing aid.

   Directions: Begin with Tired.

   (A) complaints, and he
   (B) complaints, and the old man
   (C) complaints, the old man
   (D) complaints, he
   (E) complaints, so the old man

   Explanation: The correct answer is (C). Tired of listening to his children's complaints, the old man disconnected his hearing aid.

Now try several of this type of question and check the correct answers at the end of the group.

1. Certain specialized drugs have been used with remarkable success by doctors treating some mental disorders, particularly the manic-depressive syndrome, that thirty years ago would have required the patient to be hospitalized indefinitely.

   Begin with Thirty years ago, some mental.

   (A) patient, now these disorders
   (B) patient, and now these disorders
   (C) patients, for these disorders
   (D) patient, with these disorders
   (E) patient; now these disorders

2. He was trapped into a loveless marriage by an overly anxious woman; therefore, he was already weary of her before a month had passed.

   Begin with Trapped into.

   (A) woman, he
   (B) woman; he
   (C) woman, therefore, he
   (D) woman, so he
   (E) woman; therefore, he

3. Members of that loose coalition of groups calling themselves "The New Left" believe that the only solution for the nation's problems is the overthrow, through violence if necessary, of both corrupt capitalism and a corrupt governmental system.

   Substitute advocate for believe.

   (A) system for the only
   (B) system through the only
   (C) system as well as the only
   (D) system as the only
   (E) system by the only

4. Anyone's first flight is always a unique experience, no matter how many times he or she has seen pictures of planes flying or heard tales about the first flight of others.

   Begin with No matter and substitute anyone for he or she.

   (A) anyone's own
   (B) a person's own
   (C) his own
   (D) their own
   (E) theirs

5. The truck driver, tired after forty hours on the highway without rest, drank a cup of strong coffee; he knew that the coffee would keep him awake and alert for about three hours.

   Begin with The truck driver knew.

   (A) hours; so tired
   (B) hours; therefore, tired
   (C) hours, moreover, tired
   (D) hours; tired
   (E) hours, therefore, tired

6. The average laborer with no income except his or her monthly wages is frequently hard pressed for immediate cash to pay personal bills.

   Substitute whose only for with.

   (A) no income except his or her
   (B) income except his or her
   (C) income accepts his or her
   (D) income is his or her
   (E) no income but

7. The workers angrily charge that a corporation which hires minority group workers and then lays them off during a recession is actually intensifying the frustrations of black workers rather than helping them.

   Substitute a corporation's for a corporation.

   (A) actually intensifying
   (B) intensifies minority workers
   (C) actually intensifies
   (D) must actually intensify
   (E) actually brings on

8. According to an American Medical Association report, psychiatrists should be aware that certain types of patients are prone to severe depression.

   Begin with An American Medical Association.

   (A) bewares psychiatrists
   (B) arouses psychiatrists
   (C) defends psychiatrists
   (D) declares psychiatrists
   (E) warns psychiatrists

9. No depression in American history has ever lasted as long as the one which began in 1929; it is ironic that only the beginning of World War II in Europe brought prosperity to the United States.

   Begin with It is ironic, and substitute ended for brought.

   (A) the lasting depression
   (B) the longest depression
   (C) the 1929 beginning depression
   (D) no prosperity in the United States
   (E) no depression in American history

10. In their support of rising minority group aspirations, large corporations are not only evidencing true altruism in improving the lot of minorities but also producing social changes within the communities in which their plants are located.

    Substitute both for not only.

    (A) and
    (B) but
    (C) and so
    (D) as much as
    (E) for

Answers and Explanations

1. **(E)** Thirty years ago, some mental disorders would have required the indefinite hospitalization of the patient; now these disorders respond to treatment by certain specialized drugs.

2. **(A)** Trapped into a loveless marriage by an overly anxious woman, he was already weary of her before a month had passed.

3. **(D)** Members of that loose coalition of groups calling themselves "The new Left" advocate the overthrow, through violence if necessary, of both corrupt capitalism and a corrupt governmental system as the only solution for the nation's problems.

4. **(B)** No matter how many times anyone has seen pictures of planes flying or heard tales about the first flights of others, a person's own first flight is always a unique experience.

5. **(B)** The truck driver knew that a strong cup of coffee would keep him awake and alert for about three hours; therefore, tired after forty hours on the highway without rest, he drank a cup.

6. **(D)** The average laborer whose only income is his or her monthly wages is often hard pressed for immediate cash to pay personal bills.

7. **(C)** The workers angrily charge that a corporation's hiring minority group workers and then laying them off during a recession actually intensifies the frustration of black workers rather than helps them.

8. **(E)** An American Medical Association report <u>warns psychiatrists</u> that certain types of patients are prone to severe depression.

9. **(B)** It is ironic that only the outbreak of World War II ended <u>the longest depression</u> in American history and brought prosperity to the United States.

10. **(A)** In their support of rising minority group aspirations, large corporations are both evidencing true altruism in improving the lot of minorities <u>and</u> producing social changes within the communities in which their plants are located.

Practice Questions for Analyzing Writing (Without Essay)

Section II of the all-multiple-choice version uses several types of questions to measure the various skills needed to write an essay. One type of question is Analyzing Writing, based on a brief reading passage in which the sentences are numbered. Candidates are asked to read the passage and then answer questions about it that involve redrafting and revising the passage. The questions ask the candidate about such conceptual and rhetorical considerations as evaluation and organization of evidence, functions and relationships of sentences, and audience and purpose for writing. These questions constitute about 45 percent of Section II. The remainder of Section II contains Restructuring Sentences questions, and Identifying Sentence Errors and Revising Work in Progress questions described previously under Section I.

The following directions and sample questions will give you an idea of what the passage-based questions in this section are like.

> **Directions:** Each of the following passages consists of numbered sentences. Because the passages are part of longer writing samples, they do not necessarily constitute a complete discussion of the issues presented.
>
> Read each passage carefully and answer the questions that follow it. The questions test your awareness of a writer's purpose and of characteristics of prose that are important to good writing.

Questions 1–6 are based on the following passage:

(1) My basement is designed to be a family room, although we do not usually use it that way. (2) My desk is down here where it is cool, quiet, and away from the noise of the street outside the house. (3) My living room has three large windows which look out on my neighbors' driveway; thus, I can keep up with their comings and goings all hours of the day. (4) In my basement, I have my computer, all the files I need to do my writing, and a radio which I keep tuned to a good FM station. (5) I can get more work done if i have some "white noise" to block out the interference of other noises in the house. (6) When I withdraw to the basement to read papers or write, my family knows that they are not to disturb me except in case of an extreme emergency like the house catching on fire or something like that. (7) I also have my library stored down here so that I can reach for a book that I might need to refer to when I read or write. (8) There is also a bed; sometimes I get tired of typing and want to stretch out for a few minutes to rest my weary back and fingers.

1. What should be done with sentence 3?

   (A) It should begin the passage.
   (B) It should be omitted.
   (C) It should come after sentence 5.
   (D) It should come after sentence 8.
   (E) It should be combined with sentence 4.

2. Which of the following should be done with sentence 5?

   (A) It should be omitted.
   (B) It should be reduced to a clause, beginning *if*, and joined to sentence 7.
   (C) It should begin with *and* and be joined to sentence 8.
   (D) It should come at the beginning of the passage.
   (E) It should begin with *because* and be joined to sentence 4.

3. A logical concluding sentence for this passage would be which of the following?

   (A) My library is the most important thing in my life.
   (B) I spend many happy hours in my living room, watching my neighbors.
   (C) My basement is the center of my professional life; without it, I would be forced to write less than I do.
   (D) My basement is furnished with early American antiques.
   (E) My FM radio provides me with many hours of amusement.

4. The paragraph is an example of

   (A) descriptive writing
   (B) argumentative writing
   (C) comparison/contrast writing
   (D) writing that is too detailed to be interesting
   (E) fiction writing

5. The tone of the paragraph is

   (A) very formal
   (B) impressionistic
   (C) stentorian
   (D) relaxed and informal
   (E) satiric

6. From the paragraph, a reader might infer that the writer's profession is

   (A) nursing
   (B) teaching
   (C) radio announcing
   (D) preaching
   (E) automobile repairman

Answers and Explanations

1. **(B)** (B) shifts from the basement to the living room, and the whole paragraph is about the basement; thus, sentence 3 is irrelevant to the paragraph.

2. **(E)** (A) is incorrect, because sentence 5 adds important information. (B) and (C) would create illogical sentences. (D) is incorrect, because sentence 5 would not be a good topic sentence for the whole paragraph.

3. **(C)** All of the other choices focus on minor points in the paragraph; only (C) summarizes the paragraph effectively.

4. **(A)** The large number of descriptive details about the room lead to no other possible conclusion.

5. **(D)** The tone of a piece of writing is the author's attitude toward the material; the attitude here seems conversational.

6. **(B)** The number of specific references to writing and reading papers and consulting books makes this the most logical conclusion.

Practice Essays for Section II (Essay Version)

If you choose to take the English Composition with Essay CLEP Exam, you will be required to write an essay on an assigned topic. By choosing this version, you will not have to take two challenging sections in the "without essay" version: "Analyzing Writing" and "Restructuring Sentences." Although the time for planning and writing your essay is short, you can greatly improve your essay by following certain simple strategies of organizing your thoughts and developing them into a brief example of your writing ability.

First of all, carefully read the instructions:

> **Directions:** You will have 45 minutes to plan and write an essay on the topic specified. Read the topic carefully. You are expected to spend a few minutes considering the topic and organizing your thoughts before you begin writing. *Do not write on a topic other than the one specified. An essay on a topic of your own choice is not acceptable.*
>
> The essay is intended to give you an opportunity to demonstrate your ability to write effectively. You should, therefore, take care to express your thoughts on the topic clearly and exactly and to make them interesting to the reader. Be specific, using supporting examples whenever appropriate. Remember that how well you write is more important than how much you write.

From reading these directions you can conclude the following: organizing your thoughts is very important, supporting your thoughts with facts and examples is necessary, and demonstrating the ability to write effectively is your primary goal.

How is this to be done in such a short time? The following suggestions may be helpful to you.

1. The assigned topics will ask you to agree or disagree with a statement, often a controversial one. For example, you may be assigned a statement like this:

    Everything the government does for its citizens can be done better by private businesses. Agree or disagree.

    With time so limited, you *must* decide almost immediately whether you will support the statement or argue against it.

2. Since you have only a few minutes to think of reasons why you agree or disagree with the topic statement, you must go quickly to the core of the problem. Take a few minutes to think of several arguments to support your position. Pick three good points that will be easy to expand with good examples. Do not waste time nit-picking your brain. Quickly jot down three good reasons on the margin of your exam booklet, and then write a thesis sentence. An example of such a sentence might be: "I believe that many of the most important goals in a democracy can best be achieved by the government, not by private business; these goals include insuring the

purity of food and pharmaceutical drugs, controlling environmental pollution, and protecting the individual rights of all Americans."

3. Write your first paragraph. This should begin with a sentence or two that will catch the reader's attention and introduce your topic. Then present your thesis sentence.

4. In the second paragraph, present one of your supporting arguments. For the topic used in the sample, this might be the need to have the government monitor the purity of food and drugs. Make the point that private business, if left unregulated, might find it more profitable to cut corners and take chances with the public health. Add examples of the dangers such a policy might unleash.

5. Use your third and fourth paragraphs to present your other supporting arguments. You could discuss environmental pollution in the third paragraph and individual rights in the fourth, again pointing out the dangers of a world without environmental regulation and laws to protect the rights of all citizens.

6. In the fifth paragraph, sum up your argument briefly. Remember, it does not matter what your opinion is or whether the grader agrees with you. You will be judged only on the quality of your organizational and writing skills. Keep your organization simple and direct. Avoid repetition and wasted effort as much as possible, and stay precisely on the subject as outlined in your thesis sentence.

SAMPLE ESSAY 1

Anyone who listens to radio talk shows and reads letters to the editor these days knows that many people are angry with the "government." They seem to believe that private business can do anything the government does in a more efficient manner. I disagree. I believe that many of the most important goals in a democracy can best be achieved by the government, not by private business; these goals include insuring the purity of food and pharmaceutical drugs, controlling environmental pollution, and protecting the individual rights of all Americans.

Recent news stories about deaths from such bacteria as E. coli and salmonella show the importance of sanitary standards in the food business and the need for regulation by laws and inspections. Can we depend on a private business to regulate itself, without any monitoring? Most restaurants and delis try to prepare and serve products that will not harm their customers' health, but some might try to cut costs by taking chances that could prove fatal. Just as important is the federal government's examination of new prescription drugs to determine if they will be safe. Could we always trust the pharmaceutical companies, who are racing to be the first to market a new superdrug, to make such decisions? I prefer to trust the government.

Environmental pollution is a worldwide problem that must be solved if civilization as we know it is to survive for the next millennium. The purity of the air we breathe and the water we drink has a powerful adversary: industrial waste. Properly treating and disposing of such waste is expensive, and some businesses would prefer to ignore the problem. Only the government has the clout to force compliance with clean air and clean water standards. Only the government is willing to spend money on city transportation systems to reduce the number of cars and commuters that spoil the city air.

One of the most important parts of the Constitution of the United States is the Bill of Rights. Our democracy rests on the concept that every citizen has the basic right to "life, liberty, and the pursuit of happiness." Without the government, how long would it have taken for society to extend the right to vote to all its people? How long would it have taken for private business, without the laws enforced by the government, to give women equal rights in the workplace, including protection from sexual harassment?

There are some who argue that the government is too big, too wasteful of our taxes, and sometimes even repressive. Certainly there are worst-case scenarios that seem to offer evidence of these excesses. But in the matters of protecting the public health, the environment, and the basic human rights, I would prefer that the government take the major role. I think that to do otherwise would "put the foxes in charge of the henhouse," to use a wise rural axiom.

Probable Score: 7 or 8. *Essays in this high range show a high degree of competence and control, are well organized and clearly focused, and contain varied and appropriate detail. They also, of course, demonstrate the effective use of language and a mastery of grammar and mechanics.*

SAMPLE ESSAY 2

I am angry, and many people that I know are angry. Why are we so irate? It is because the government is taking so much of our money in taxes and wasting it on big-spending programs that could be handled more efficiently by private enterprise, which is the anchor of our democratic system of government. Anyone who reads the papers and is aware of what is going on knows that nowadays private companies are building and running prisons, setting up school systems, and delivering mail and packages far cheaper than the government can do these jobs. Besides that, these companies make a profit.

Every time I see a commercial on TV that has somebody running for office, I hear them say they are tough on crime. They should be. Crime is one of our country's greatest problems. To solve it we need to put more people in prison and lock the door on them for a long time. Do we want to trust the government to build prisons and staff them with guards? I don't think so. Let's put the job on the company with the lowest bid and save a big chunk of tax money.

What is the biggest cost in any county or city? It is education. The biggest share of taxes paid to local governments goes to building schools and paying schoolteachers. Let's turn the job over to private business. They know how to downsize and save money. They can begin with a whole new staff of teachers who are not in a union and who would love to have teaching jobs with summers off.

Have you tried to send a package or an overnight letter lately? If you used the post office you were in trouble. If you sent it by any of the companies that do the job efficiently and well, you were pleased with the result. Look at the way our postage is going up. Now it costs 37 cents to send a letter. How much will it be in the future? Who knows? If it were left to good old healthy competition and private enterprise, American business would find a way to keep the cost low.

Now you know why I am angry, along with many other people. When are we going to wake up and vote to cut down on the size of our government? When are income taxes going to be cut? This will only happen when we turn over more governmental jobs to private enterprise.

Probable score: 4–6. *Essays in the middle range show adequate competence, are organized, and are without serious grammatical errors. The topic is treated somewhat superficially, however, and the use of the language does not demonstrate a very high degree of skill.*

SAMPLE ESSAY 3

Everybody is talking about goverment. What is goverment? Do we have to have it? What would we do if we don't have it? I heard something once that say that goverment is by the people and for the people, something like that. Does that mean we get bossed by the people? What do the goverment do for the people?

I guess I am a person that don't like goverment. Don't like nobody telling me what to do. When to do it. What I can't do and can do.

Maybe we need the goverment for some things. A few things. Like the arm forces. If this country was like attacked by some other country or something, the arm forces could run them off. If we didn't have no goverment, we wouldn't have no arm forces.

Maybe we ought to let some smart people try to figure out how to do without goverment. I could live with that.

Probable score: 2. *The College Board Official Study Guide describes essays in the low range (2–3) as demonstrating "clear deficiencies." "They often fail to focus on the topic; they are thinly developed; diction is immature and awkward; and errors abound in grammar, mechanics, and syntax. The paper earning a score of 2 either fails to develop the topic or contains such an accumulation of errors that meaning is seriously obscured."*

EXERCISES IN PREPLANNING

The following exercises will help you become more efficient at quickly constructing a thesis sentence and planning your essay. Limiting yourself to no more than 5 minutes each, read the following essay topics and write three topic thesis sentences similar to the one used in Sample Essay 1.

a. *It's better to grow up in a small town than in a city. Agree or disagree.*

b. *Sports are overemphasized in high school budgets. Agree or disagree.*

c. *There is a very old proverb that reads: "He who hesitates is lost." Agree or disagree with this idea.*

d. *Articles in recent psychological journals theorize that the characters and personalities of teenagers are influenced more by peer groups and other forces outside the home than by parents. Agree or disagree.*

e. *Should women in the military be allowed to serve in combat?*

Here is one more sample essay. How would you grade it?

Directions: In 45 minutes write an essay on the following subject:

"The disadvantages of playing team sports in high school outweigh the advantages."
If you prefer, write on the advantages outweighing the disadvantages.

SAMPLE ESSAY 4

Many people believe that playing sports in high school will make you popular with the opposite sex, make you locally famous when you perform well and win the game for your team, and make you rich when you turn professional and sign a multimillion dollar contract. There is a possibility that all three of these results will come true, but the better chance is that team sports will take important time away from your education, lure you into an impossible dream of professional success, and even leave you with injuries that will affect your activities throughout life.

There are only 24 hours in a day, and if you spend three of these hours every weekday practicing a team sport, you have less time for the real purpose of high school: education. Much of the practice in team sports consists of running through repetitious drills. Physical tasks are repeated again and again until they become second nature. After practice and after games, most players are physically exhausted, unable to spend much quality time on their studies. Some ambitious people, who hope to one day enter a profession like law, may have to choose between high school sports or their lifelong dream.

Some players are so convinced they will become wealthy through professional sports that they focus only on athletics. They will later be unqualified to study for any high-level job because they are only proficient in one area: sports. The problem is that only a very few players go on to play in the pros. Putting all your eggs in the one basket called professional sports can lead to a life of frustration and disappointment.

I believe that a high school player has a greater chance of sustaining a nagging injury than of signing a professional contract. The knees are particularly vulnerable in contact sports like football. Also, young athletes beef up their torsos with exercise and even steroids in an effort to succeed in high school team sports. Many of these people become overweight after their athletic days are over and are vulnerable to all the health problems of carrying around too much fat.

I know that team sports can develop a sense of unselfish regard for the team instead of focusing on individual achievements. I know that one can learn discipline in this kind of athletic endeavor. But I also know that one can learn self-discipline by working hard on academic courses, which can open doors to college, graduate study, and to meaningful, life-fulfilling jobs. In my mind, the disadvantages of playing team sports in high school far outweigh the advantages.

ESSAY WRITING HINTS

1. Read the question very carefully. Notice the limitations of the topic (e.g., "Choose one side of this question") and any other instructions.
2. Allow a brief time (perhaps 5 minutes) to think about what you will say, and to decide how you will organize your ideas.
3. Jot down on the bottom of the instruction sheet important points that you want to include.
4. Bear in mind that there is no requirement as to length. A good essay of reasonable length will be rated higher than a poor one that is twice as long.

5. When you express a generalization, be sure to back it up with examples or other supporting evidence.

6. Allow time to read your essay critically. Look for misspellings, grammatical errors, ambiguities, and wordiness. Make necessary corrections and other changes as neatly as you can.

CONCLUSION

After you have worked through the sample questions in this chapter, you should be prepared for a whole CLEP Examination in English Composition. Three such examinations are given in the next chapter, models of those that you may encounter on an actual CLEP test. Again, we must caution you to ask the college to which your scores will be sent which version of the examination you are required to take—the version *with* the written composition or the version *without* the written composition. Good luck on this examination!

English Composition

ANSWER SHEET—SAMPLE EXAM 1

#						#						#						#					
1	Ⓐ	Ⓑ	Ⓒ	Ⓓ	Ⓔ	26	Ⓐ	Ⓑ	Ⓒ	Ⓓ	Ⓔ	51	Ⓐ	Ⓑ	Ⓒ	Ⓓ	Ⓔ	76	Ⓐ	Ⓑ	Ⓒ	Ⓓ	Ⓔ
2	Ⓐ	Ⓑ	Ⓒ	Ⓓ	Ⓔ	27	Ⓐ	Ⓑ	Ⓒ	Ⓓ	Ⓔ	52	Ⓐ	Ⓑ	Ⓒ	Ⓓ	Ⓔ	77	Ⓐ	Ⓑ	Ⓒ	Ⓓ	Ⓔ
3	Ⓐ	Ⓑ	Ⓒ	Ⓓ	Ⓔ	28	Ⓐ	Ⓑ	Ⓒ	Ⓓ	Ⓔ	53	Ⓐ	Ⓑ	Ⓒ	Ⓓ	Ⓔ	78	Ⓐ	Ⓑ	Ⓒ	Ⓓ	Ⓔ
4	Ⓐ	Ⓑ	Ⓒ	Ⓓ	Ⓔ	29	Ⓐ	Ⓑ	Ⓒ	Ⓓ	Ⓔ	54	Ⓐ	Ⓑ	Ⓒ	Ⓓ	Ⓔ	79	Ⓐ	Ⓑ	Ⓒ	Ⓓ	Ⓔ
5	Ⓐ	Ⓑ	Ⓒ	Ⓓ	Ⓔ	30	Ⓐ	Ⓑ	Ⓒ	Ⓓ	Ⓔ	55	Ⓐ	Ⓑ	Ⓒ	Ⓓ	Ⓔ	80	Ⓐ	Ⓑ	Ⓒ	Ⓓ	Ⓔ
6	Ⓐ	Ⓑ	Ⓒ	Ⓓ	Ⓔ	31	Ⓐ	Ⓑ	Ⓒ	Ⓓ	Ⓔ	56	Ⓐ	Ⓑ	Ⓒ	Ⓓ	Ⓔ	81	Ⓐ	Ⓑ	Ⓒ	Ⓓ	Ⓔ
7	Ⓐ	Ⓑ	Ⓒ	Ⓓ	Ⓔ	32	Ⓐ	Ⓑ	Ⓒ	Ⓓ	Ⓔ	57	Ⓐ	Ⓑ	Ⓒ	Ⓓ	Ⓔ	82	Ⓐ	Ⓑ	Ⓒ	Ⓓ	Ⓔ
8	Ⓐ	Ⓑ	Ⓒ	Ⓓ	Ⓔ	33	Ⓐ	Ⓑ	Ⓒ	Ⓓ	Ⓔ	58	Ⓐ	Ⓑ	Ⓒ	Ⓓ	Ⓔ	83	Ⓐ	Ⓑ	Ⓒ	Ⓓ	Ⓔ
9	Ⓐ	Ⓑ	Ⓒ	Ⓓ	Ⓔ	34	Ⓐ	Ⓑ	Ⓒ	Ⓓ	Ⓔ	59	Ⓐ	Ⓑ	Ⓒ	Ⓓ	Ⓔ	84	Ⓐ	Ⓑ	Ⓒ	Ⓓ	Ⓔ
10	Ⓐ	Ⓑ	Ⓒ	Ⓓ	Ⓔ	35	Ⓐ	Ⓑ	Ⓒ	Ⓓ	Ⓔ	60	Ⓐ	Ⓑ	Ⓒ	Ⓓ	Ⓔ	85	Ⓐ	Ⓑ	Ⓒ	Ⓓ	Ⓔ
11	Ⓐ	Ⓑ	Ⓒ	Ⓓ	Ⓔ	36	Ⓐ	Ⓑ	Ⓒ	Ⓓ	Ⓔ	61	Ⓐ	Ⓑ	Ⓒ	Ⓓ	Ⓔ	86	Ⓐ	Ⓑ	Ⓒ	Ⓓ	Ⓔ
12	Ⓐ	Ⓑ	Ⓒ	Ⓓ	Ⓔ	37	Ⓐ	Ⓑ	Ⓒ	Ⓓ	Ⓔ	62	Ⓐ	Ⓑ	Ⓒ	Ⓓ	Ⓔ	87	Ⓐ	Ⓑ	Ⓒ	Ⓓ	Ⓔ
13	Ⓐ	Ⓑ	Ⓒ	Ⓓ	Ⓔ	38	Ⓐ	Ⓑ	Ⓒ	Ⓓ	Ⓔ	63	Ⓐ	Ⓑ	Ⓒ	Ⓓ	Ⓔ	88	Ⓐ	Ⓑ	Ⓒ	Ⓓ	Ⓔ
14	Ⓐ	Ⓑ	Ⓒ	Ⓓ	Ⓔ	39	Ⓐ	Ⓑ	Ⓒ	Ⓓ	Ⓔ	64	Ⓐ	Ⓑ	Ⓒ	Ⓓ	Ⓔ	89	Ⓐ	Ⓑ	Ⓒ	Ⓓ	Ⓔ
15	Ⓐ	Ⓑ	Ⓒ	Ⓓ	Ⓔ	40	Ⓐ	Ⓑ	Ⓒ	Ⓓ	Ⓔ	65	Ⓐ	Ⓑ	Ⓒ	Ⓓ	Ⓔ	90	Ⓐ	Ⓑ	Ⓒ	Ⓓ	Ⓔ
16	Ⓐ	Ⓑ	Ⓒ	Ⓓ	Ⓔ	41	Ⓐ	Ⓑ	Ⓒ	Ⓓ	Ⓔ	66	Ⓐ	Ⓑ	Ⓒ	Ⓓ	Ⓔ	91	Ⓐ	Ⓑ	Ⓒ	Ⓓ	Ⓔ
17	Ⓐ	Ⓑ	Ⓒ	Ⓓ	Ⓔ	42	Ⓐ	Ⓑ	Ⓒ	Ⓓ	Ⓔ	67	Ⓐ	Ⓑ	Ⓒ	Ⓓ	Ⓔ	92	Ⓐ	Ⓑ	Ⓒ	Ⓓ	Ⓔ
18	Ⓐ	Ⓑ	Ⓒ	Ⓓ	Ⓔ	43	Ⓐ	Ⓑ	Ⓒ	Ⓓ	Ⓔ	68	Ⓐ	Ⓑ	Ⓒ	Ⓓ	Ⓔ	93	Ⓐ	Ⓑ	Ⓒ	Ⓓ	Ⓔ
19	Ⓐ	Ⓑ	Ⓒ	Ⓓ	Ⓔ	44	Ⓐ	Ⓑ	Ⓒ	Ⓓ	Ⓔ	69	Ⓐ	Ⓑ	Ⓒ	Ⓓ	Ⓔ	94	Ⓐ	Ⓑ	Ⓒ	Ⓓ	Ⓔ
20	Ⓐ	Ⓑ	Ⓒ	Ⓓ	Ⓔ	45	Ⓐ	Ⓑ	Ⓒ	Ⓓ	Ⓔ	70	Ⓐ	Ⓑ	Ⓒ	Ⓓ	Ⓔ	95	Ⓐ	Ⓑ	Ⓒ	Ⓓ	Ⓔ
21	Ⓐ	Ⓑ	Ⓒ	Ⓓ	Ⓔ	46	Ⓐ	Ⓑ	Ⓒ	Ⓓ	Ⓔ	71	Ⓐ	Ⓑ	Ⓒ	Ⓓ	Ⓔ	96	Ⓐ	Ⓑ	Ⓒ	Ⓓ	Ⓔ
22	Ⓐ	Ⓑ	Ⓒ	Ⓓ	Ⓔ	47	Ⓐ	Ⓑ	Ⓒ	Ⓓ	Ⓔ	72	Ⓐ	Ⓑ	Ⓒ	Ⓓ	Ⓔ	97	Ⓐ	Ⓑ	Ⓒ	Ⓓ	Ⓔ
23	Ⓐ	Ⓑ	Ⓒ	Ⓓ	Ⓔ	48	Ⓐ	Ⓑ	Ⓒ	Ⓓ	Ⓔ	73	Ⓐ	Ⓑ	Ⓒ	Ⓓ	Ⓔ	98	Ⓐ	Ⓑ	Ⓒ	Ⓓ	Ⓔ
24	Ⓐ	Ⓑ	Ⓒ	Ⓓ	Ⓔ	49	Ⓐ	Ⓑ	Ⓒ	Ⓓ	Ⓔ	74	Ⓐ	Ⓑ	Ⓒ	Ⓓ	Ⓔ	99	Ⓐ	Ⓑ	Ⓒ	Ⓓ	Ⓔ
25	Ⓐ	Ⓑ	Ⓒ	Ⓓ	Ⓔ	50	Ⓐ	Ⓑ	Ⓒ	Ⓓ	Ⓔ	75	Ⓐ	Ⓑ	Ⓒ	Ⓓ	Ⓔ	100	Ⓐ	Ⓑ	Ⓒ	Ⓓ	Ⓔ

Sample Examinations

This chapter includes three sample examinations, each with an answer key, scoring chart, and answer explanations. Take the first exam, check your answers, determine your raw score, and record it on the Progress Chart provided on page 12. Then, as you gain familiarity with the test, take the other two examinations and see your scores climb.

SAMPLE ENGLISH COMPOSITION EXAMINATION 1

NUMBER OF QUESTIONS: 100

Time limit: 90 MINUTES

Directions: The following sentences test your knowledge of grammar, usage, diction (choice of words), and idiom.

Some sentences are correct.

No sentence contains more than one error.

You will find that the error, if there is one, is underlined and lettered. Assume that elements of the sentence that are not underlined are correct and cannot be changed. In choosing answers, follow the requirements of standard written English.

If there is an error, select the <u>one underlined part</u> that must be changed to make the sentence correct.

If there is no error, select answer (E).

1. <u>Because of the cold, which seemed <u>to develop quite</u> suddenly, Luis woke
      A   B
<u>up feeling badly</u> and decided <u>not to go to work</u> yesterday. <u>No error.</u>
        C   D   E

2. The Red Cross first aid manual <u>provides the following</u> instructions for an
                                         A
emergency treatment of a heart attack victim: <u>loose his or her clothing,</u>
                                                    B
cover <u>him</u> or her with a blanket, and <u>give no medication</u> until a doctor
        C   D
arrives. <u>No error.</u>
              E

3. The <u>trees in the garden</u> <u>have developed</u> <u>their</u> <u>autumn leaf colors</u>: red,
          A   B   C   D
brown, orange, and yellow. <u>No error.</u>
                                 E

4. <u>After the professor</u> conferred with me about my paper, <u>pointing out to me</u>
          A   B
all the errors I made, <u>I could only</u> agree that my work <u>was not affective.</u>
                              C   D
<u>No error.</u>
    E

5. <u>Assuming that all</u> materials <u>will be delivered</u> by the deadlines the architect
          A   B
has established, we should occupy our new building by the end of October
but <u>certainly no later</u> than <u>November 15.</u> <u>No error.</u>
         C   D   E

6. A good umpire should <u>always be disinterested</u> in the game <u>whose rules</u> he
                              A   B
is there to interpret for the <u>players; he must</u> maintain complete <u>partiality</u>
                                    C   D
to avoid being charged with unfair decisions. <u>No error.</u>
                                                    E

7. <u>Just above the towering peaks,</u> we saw the glorious sun as <u>it was raising,</u>
                A   B
pouring streams of brilliant color over the <u>whole snow-capped mountain</u>
                                                  C
range and <u>the verdant valleys</u> below. <u>No error.</u>
                  D   E

8. Since 1945, <u>many former colonies</u> of the British Empire has achieved
   A
   independence <u>from the government</u> in London, and some historians <u>have</u>
   B C
   noted this development <u>with skepticism.</u> <u>No error.</u>
   D E

9. When Willie Mays <u>was a small boy</u>, he wanted very badly <u>to play baseball</u>
   A B
   in the major <u>leagues</u>, but <u>proving his competence</u> in sandlot and
   C D
   minor leagues was the only route he could take. <u>No error.</u>
   E

10. <u>Jack Benny</u>, one of the funniest comedians who worked in television,
    A
    <u>remained thirty-nine years old for more than thirty years;</u> <u>his portrayal</u> of a
    B C
    skinflint and a perpetual worrier have been and some of the
    <u>most successful acts</u> in show business history. <u>No error.</u>
    D E

11. <u>Few art critics</u> have been able to <u>except</u> the most recent exhibitions
    A B
    arranged by the curator of the Metropolitan Museum in New York;
    charges and countercharges of <u>lack of</u> artistic discrimination have filled the
    C
    <u>columns of the newspapers and magazines.</u> <u>No error.</u>
    D E

12. <u>Senate investigators</u> have charged that the major weapon systems
    A
    developed by the <u>Pentagon's research and development</u> sections have cost
    B
    many billions <u>more than the initial estimates</u> and contracts and that
    C
    <u>supplemental appropriations</u> must be passed immediately. <u>No error.</u>
    D E

13. Justification for his allegations <u>came from him and I,</u> as <u>the only two</u>
    A B
    witnesses to <u>the bizarre crime</u> the criminal committed against the
    C
    defendant <u>as she walked</u> by the packing house last night. <u>No error.</u>
    D E

14. Use <u>any</u> <u>set of criteria</u> you want, <u>but you will never convince</u> me that
      A   B   C

    Beethoven is <u>not equally as good</u> a composer as Johann Sebastian Bach.
                      D

    <u>No error.</u>
      E

15. In San Francisco's North Beach area, there <u>are many transient</u> young
                                    A

    people <u>whose weird costumes</u> seem to <u>flout conspicuously</u> every moral
                B   C

    code the <u>silent majority accepts</u> as holy. <u>No error.</u>
              D   E

16. <u>In a convoluted style</u>, the novel tells the tragic story <u>of a father's</u>
        A   B

    inhumanity to his daughter, a mother's rejection of her son, and

    <u>the strong trust</u> that developed <u>between the alienated</u> boy and girl.
          C   D

    <u>No error.</u>
      E

17. Until <u>transmissions were standardized</u> by the automobile industry in the
                      A

    late 1920s, drivers had <u>to learn several</u> different gear positions of the gear
         B   C

    shift lever, <u>which left</u> everyone confused. <u>No error.</u>
             D   E

18. We could <u>only ask ourselves</u> how any sane man could <u>have choosen such</u>
               A   B

    an ugly suit to wear <u>when</u>, rich as he is, he could have had the pick
                    C

    <u>of any of</u> the suits in the finest men's stores in the community. <u>No error.</u>
      D   E

19. That an artist <u>like Pablo Picasso</u> priced his paintings at more <u>than</u>
              A   B

    $100,000 each and actually sold as many <u>as he released</u> to the markets
                                      C

    <u>seem too</u> fantastic to be believed. <u>No error.</u>
      D   E

20. Whether students will <u>do well on</u> an examination <u>has depended</u> upon
                        A   B

    many factors: whether they know the material, whether they are feeling

    <u>good or bad</u>, or even whether the seat of the desk is properly adjusted
      C

    <u>to their height</u>. <u>No error.</u>
        D   E

Directions: In each of the following sentences, part of the sentence or the entire sentence is underlined. Beneath each sentence you will find five versions of the underlined part. Answer (A) repeats the original; the other four are different.

Choose the answer that best expresses the meaning of the original sentence. If you think the original is better than any of the alternatives, choose (A); otherwise choose one of the others. Your choice should produce the most effective sentence—one that is clear and precise, without awkwardness or ambiguity.

21. <u>There were fewer people in the auditorium than</u> we had expected; there were seats for everyone.

(A) There were fewer people in the auditorium than
(B) There were no more people in the auditorium than
(C) In the auditorium, there were a lot more people than
(D) There were more people in the auditorium than
(E) A great deal fewer people showed up in the auditorium as

22. During the Renaissance, <u>the Italian peasants could hardly find enough food</u> to keep their families alive and healthy.

(A) the Italian peasants could hardly find enough food
(B) the Italian peasants could hardly locate in the country more food than necessary
(C) the Italian peasants could scarcely find sufficient food
(D) the Italian peasants starved themselves with enough food
(E) the Italian peasants could not have found more than enough food

23. Attending college is a dream <u>which many of today's young people have had</u>.

(A) which many of today's young people have had
(B) which many of today's young people has had
(C) which many of today's young people is having
(D) which many of today's young people have been having
(E) which many of today's young people had been having

24. A good plumber can connect one pipe <u>with another so completely that</u> there will be no leak from the joint.

   (A) with another so completely that
   (B) into another with such a high degree of skill as
   (C) with another so that there will be completely
   (D) with another with such little skill that
   (E) with another with such accuracy that

25. My old dog <u>Skippy, who is out there lying in the sun,</u> has served me well for the past twelve years.

   (A) Skippy, who is out there lying in the sun,
   (B) Skippy that foolishly is not lying in the sun
   (C) Skippy, on the alert out there in the sun,
   (D) Skippy, working hard for his daily cookie treats,
   (E) Skippy whom we found out in the bright sun of noon

26. Many <u>others who are not so fortunate</u> will lose all the money they have invested in oil well speculation.

   (A) others who are not so fortunate
   (B) others who have had more fortunes
   (C) others who are not as fortunate
   (D) others whom we find to be among the more unfortunate
   (E) others who have had too many fortunes

27. <u>Marguerite spoke French with a charming accent for she had</u> studied the language with a former Russian countess in Paris.

   (A) Marguerite spoke French with a charming accent for she had
   (B) Marguerite spoke French with a very unique accent because she had
   (C) Marguerite, speaking French with a charming accent, had
   (D) Marguerite had often spoken French with a charming accent so that she had
   (E) Marguerite, speaking French with a charming accent, for she had

28. Frightened by the sound of footsteps, the puppy <u>ran upstairs and hide in the closet.</u>

   (A) ran upstairs and hide in the closet
   (B) ran upstairs, having hidden in the closet
   (C) ran upstairs; they went away
   (D) ran upstairs, which was hiding in the closet
   (E) ran upstairs and hid in the closet

29. The more money Mr. Getty accumulated, <u>the more he wanted.</u>

   (A) the more he wanted
   (B) he increased his desires
   (C) the more he accumulated
   (D) the greater quantity he desired
   (E) the larger in number became his disciples

30. No one doubts Lorraine Hansbury's skill as a <u>dramatist; but there is some critics who believe</u> her plays lack poetic dialogue and skillful exposition.

    (A) dramatist; but there is some critics who believe
    (B) dramatist; they say
    (C) dramatist, although some critics believe
    (D) dramatist, believing
    (E) dramatist, who some critics believe

31. The bus driver is always <u>pleasant to we riders even though</u> he must become impatient with some of us who never have the correct change.

    (A) pleasant to we riders even though
    (B) pleasant to us riders although
    (C) pleasant to us riders so that
    (D) pleasantly to us riders even though
    (E) impatient to those riders who

32. <u>The clever orator's presenting a specious argument caused her audience to become restless and inattentive.</u>

    (A) The clever orator's presenting a specious argument caused her audience to become restless and inattentive.
    (B) When the clever orator presented a specious argument, her audience became restless and inattentive.
    (C) The clever orator's presentation of a specious argument, causing her audience to become restless and inattentive.
    (D) The clever orator presenting a specious argument was when her audience became restless and inattentive.
    (E) The clever orator presented a specious argument because her audience became restless and inattentive.

33. <u>That type of person always</u> strongly resents any attempt by anyone to limit his actions.

    (A) That type of person always
    (B) That type of person who always
    (C) That type person that
    (D) He was that type of person who always
    (E) He is that type of persons

34. Because he was speeding, Jerry <u>was picked up</u> by the police.

    (A) was picked up
    (B) was arrested, and they were picked up
    (C) was arrested; then held
    (D) who was arrested
    (E) was arrested without charge

35. <u>While glancing through today's newspaper, I read that the cost of living has risen another four points.</u>

    (A) While glancing through today's newspaper, I read that the cost of living has risen another four points.
    (B) Glancing through today's newspaper, the cost of living has risen another four points.
    (C) Today's newspaper contained an item that the cost of living has risen another four points.
    (D) The cost of living having risen another four points, I read in today's newspaper.
    (E) I was glancing through today's newspaper when the cost of living rose another four points.

36. Each time <u>Billy Joel sitting down</u> at the piano, he plays at least one of his own songs.

    (A) Billy Joel sitting down
    (B) Billy Joel who sits down
    (C) Billy Joel while sitting down
    (D) Billy Joel, sitting down
    (E) Billy Joel sits down

37. While making a pathetic attempt to explain their behavior to the policeman, the young <u>thief and his accomplices was caught</u> in a web of contradictions.

    (A) thief and his accomplices was caught
    (B) thief and his accomplices who were caught
    (C) thief and his accomplices were caught
    (D) thief along with his accomplices were caught
    (E) thief who had a few accomplices were caught

38. Christine acts like a foolish child because <u>she trusts anyone that can tell</u> a story in a believable manner.

    (A) she trusts anyone that can tell
    (B) she is trusting to anyone who can tell
    (C) she can trust anyone that can tell
    (D) she trusts anyone who can tell
    (E) she is a person who trusts anyone that can tell

39. <u>Brianne remains convinced that she is as successful if not more successful than her friend Ariel.</u>

    (A) Brianne remains convinced that she is as successful if not more successful than her friend Ariel.
    (B) Brianne remains convinced that she is as successful as, if not more successful than, her friend Ariel.
    (C) Brianne is convinced that Ariel is much more successful than she is.
    (D) Ariel is really much more successful than Brianne.
    (E) Brianne may be more successful than her friend Ariel.

40. I cannot talk or write in class without the teacher's correcting or embarrassing me.

    (A) I cannot talk or write in class without the teacher's correcting or embarrassing me.
    (B) I cannot hardly talk or write in class without the teacher's correcting and embarrassing me.
    (C) I cannot talk or write in class without the teacher to correct or embarrass me.
    (D) To talk and write in class is a chore, because my teacher always correct and embarrass me.
    (E) Correcting and embarrassing me in class is the result whenever I talk or write.

41. In modern English, the most common form of inversion is done if you put the subject after the auxiliary verb.

    (A) is done if you put
    (B) is when you put
    (C) involves putting
    (D) is the way you put
    (E) is when they have put

Directions: Each of the following selections is an early draft of a work in progress in which the sentences have been numbered for easy reference. Some parts of the selections need to be changed.

Read each selection and then answer the questions that follow. Some questions are about particular sentences or parts of sentences and ask you to improve the sentence structure and diction (word choice). In making these decisions, follow the conventions of standard written English. Other questions refer to the entire passage or parts of the passage and ask you to consider organization, development, and effectiveness of language in relation to purpose and audience.

<u>Questions 42–48</u> are based on the following passage:

(1) Although the neighbors may complain, turning the empty lot on Maple Road into a soccer field would be a good deal for the entire community.

(2) Looking to the future, more and more children are playing soccer. (3) They need a safe place to play, a place where stray balls will not go flying into neighbors' yards or through neighbors' windows. (4) The Maple Road site is ideal for this, and all the neighbors are all on the other side of the road.

(5) The field at the high school where they are playing now is not a good place because it is needed for high school sports and the children who need the soccer field are in elementary school. (6) Besides, the field at the elementary school is too small.

(7) Turning the Maple Road lot into a soccer field would be an improvement. (8) At present, it is just a piece of wasteland, and people dump their garbage there. (9) If it is turned over to the soccer league, they will keep it cleaned up.

(10) As for the worries about noise and traffic, these can be dealt with easily. (11) The people on Maple Road who are opposing this project are just being obstructionist.

42. Which of the following is the best way to revise the underlined portion of sentence 2 (reproduced below)?

    Looking to the future, more and more children are playing soccer.

    (A) Looking to the future, more children, we see, are going to be
    (B) A look at the future shows us how many children are
    (C) If we look to the future, we see that more and more children are likely to be
    (D) In the future, more and more children are
    (E) If we look ahead, more children have been

43. The author of this letter could best improve the third paragraph by

    (A) first describing the children who need the soccer field and then describing the problems with the two school fields
    (B) giving more details about the kinds of children who play soccer
    (C) giving the exact locations of the school fields
    (D) omitting all mention of the elementary school field
    (E) explaining what sports the high school field is used for

44. The main problem with the introductory sentence is that

    (A) nobody knows where Maple Road is
    (B) the letter never explains why the soccer field would be good for the entire community
    (C) the term "community" is too vague
    (D) it fails to make clear the writer's position
    (E) the letter was not written by a resident of Maple Road

45. In context, the best phrase to replace "they" in sentence 9 would be

    (A) the neighbors
    (B) local residents
    (C) the members of the league
    (D) the garbage collectors
    (E) elementary school students

46. The final paragraph would be improved if it

    (A) restated the writer's position
    (B) said specifically how the problems of noise and traffic could be solved
    (C) showed how unpleasant the residents of Maple Road are
    (D) listed the organizations in favor of the soccer field
    (E) gave examples of soccer fields that have benefited their communities

47. Which would be the best word to replace "and" in sentence 4?

    (A) since
    (B) thus
    (C) or
    (D) while
    (E) whenever

48. Which is the best version of the underlined portion of sentence 7 (reproduced below)?

    Turning the Maple Road lot into a soccer field would be an improvement.

    (A) (as it is now)
    (B) would improve it
    (C) would bring about an improvement
    (D) would improve its appearance
    (E) would improve its locale

Questions 49–55 are based on the following passage:

(1) The side yard seems full of all kinds of oak trees, red, and white among them. (2) Some people find that oak trees are not evergreen, although there is one variety whose leaves turn brown, but those leaves do not leave the tree until almost spring. (3) If you look at an oak tree, you might think about some poet who has written a poem or who has talked about the wind as it moves through the oak trees in the fall. (4) Did you ever see a group of squirrels jumping around as they move nervously from limb to limb in the trees? (5) The whole side yard seems to come alive with this sudden leaping from place to place all over, for the branches seem almost unable to remain still.

(6) Once winter arrives, the scene has changed. (7) Everything is waiting for spring to come again. (8) The oaks are bare now and the leaves are not there anymore. (9) Therefore, the squirrels are gone. (10) The lively movement of summer is ended, which is because the bare branches stand stiff, barely moving in the wind.

49. Sentence 2

    (A) should be joined to sentence 1 with "and"
    (B) should be the topic sentence of the paragraph
    (C) should be placed after sentence 5
    (D) should be omitted
    (E) should be joined to sentence 1 with "however"

50. Which is the best version of the underlined portion of sentence 3?

    If you look at an oak tree, you might think about some poet who has written a poem or who has talked about the wind as it moves through the oak trees in the fall.

    (A) or who has talked about (no change)
    (B) or has talked on
    (C) or some poet who has published poems about
    (D) describing
    (E) while he describes

51. What should be done with sentence 5?

    (A) It should be left as it is.
    (B) It should be placed after sentence 2.
    (C) It should be placed after sentence 4.
    (D) It should be placed after sentence 1.
    (E) It should be used as the topic sentence of paragraph 2.

52. Which is the best version of sentence 8 (reproduced below)?

    The oaks are bare now and the leaves are not there anymore.

    (A) (as it is now)
    (B) The oaks are bare of leaves now.
    (C) The leaves are not there on the trees anymore.
    (D) The bare oak trees no longer have any leaves.
    (E) The leaves are not there anymore, leaving the oak trees bare.

53. Which is the best version of the underlined portion of sentence 10 (reproduced below)?

    The lively movement of summer is ended, which is because the bare branches stand stiff, barely moving in the wind.

    (A) (as it is now)
    (B) ended, caused by the bare branches that
    (C) stilled, which is caused by the branches that are now bare and
    (D) ended: the bare branches
    (E) ended, while the bare branches

54. What is the best thing to do with the word "Therefore" in sentence 9?

    (A) Leave it as it is (no change).
    (B) Omit it, and begin the sentence with "The."
    (C) Replace it with "As a result."
    (D) Replace it with "However."
    (E) Replace it with "Although."

55. Which is the best place for sentence 7?

    (A) where it is now (no change)
    (B) at the end of the second paragraph, after sentence 10
    (C) at the end of the first paragraph, after sentence 5
    (D) at the beginning of the second paragraph, before sentence 6
    (E) after sentence 8

Directions: Each of the following passages consists of numbered sentences. Because the passages are part of longer writing samples, they do not necessarily constitute a complete discussion of the issues presented.

Read each passage carefully and answer the questions that follow it. The questions test your awareness of a writer's purpose and of characteristics of prose that are important to good writing.

Questions 56–62 are based on the following passage:

(1) *Sesame Street* revolutionized the whole idea of television programming for children. (2) Until this program was produced and aired by the Public Broadcasting System, parents had no real options for children's television viewing except *Captain Kangaroo*, violent and crude cartoons on Saturday morning, and a few locally originated programs. (3) But *Sesame Street* is different. (4) Not only does it provide entertainment for viewers but it also provides educational opportunities for children under about ten. (5) The Sesame Street Generation, as some teachers are calling the group of children now in high school, know their numbers and the letters of the alphabet as well as many other facts about life. (6) Perhaps the most important lessons taught by this program derive from its interracial cast, for this program demonstrates that people of all races can live and play together without racially based friction. (7) Whatever this program has cost has been money well spent.

56. Sentences 2 and 3 might be combined. Which of the following is the correct form of the combination?

    (A) originated programs, *Sesame Street*
    (B) originated programs, however, *Sesame Street*
    (C) originated programs, but *Sesame Street*
    (D) originated programs, and *Sesame Street*
    (E) originated programs with the exception of *Sesame Street*

57. What should be done with sentence 5?

    (A) It should be left as it is.
    (B) It should be omitted.
    (C) It should be placed after sentence 7.
    (D) It should be combined with sentence 2.
    (E) It should be after sentence 1.

58. Which of the following might better replace sentence 7 as a conclusion to the passage?

    (A) *Sesame Street* has revolutionized children's television.
    (B) *Sesame Street* is an excellent television program.
    (C) The *Sesame Street* Generation will take over the world when it grows up.
    (D) The Public Broadcasting System should be congratulated for providing such an excellent television program as *Sesame Street.*
    (E) The money which the Public Broadcasting System has spent on *Sesame Street* may have some questionable returns.

59. Sentence 6 provides

    (A) irrelevant information for the reader
    (B) a second reason for public acclamation of *Sesame Street*
    (C) a plea for funds from the public to support the program
    (D) a justification for racial intolerance
    (E) praise for the cast's ability to react to children

60. The topic sentence of the paragraph is

    (A) 1
    (B) 2
    (C) 3
    (D) 4
    (E) 5

61. According to the paragraph, *Sesame Street* is a television program recommended for

    (A) adults only
    (B) for adolescent boys
    (C) for teenage girls
    (D) for mature teens
    (E) for children up to age ten

62. Which of the following is a valid criticism of the phrase "facts about life" in sentence 5?

   (A) It is ungrammatical.
   (B) It violates parallel construction.
   (C) It is vague and ambiguous.
   (D) It gives *Sesame Street* more credit than it deserves.
   (E) It is too formal to fit the tone of the passage.

Questions 63–69 are based on the following passage:

(1) For over a century, Helen Jackson's romantic story of Spanish and Indian life in California has been widely read and is now an American classic. (2) Originally published in 1884, *Ramona* has been issued in various editions, with a total of 135 printings. (3) *The Atlantic Monthly* has termed the story "one of the most artistic creations of American literature," while the late Charles Dudley Warner called it "one of the most charming creations of modern fiction." (4) Born in 1831, Mrs. Jackson was an ardent champion of the Native Americans to the end of her life, in 1885. (5) Three times, *Ramona* has been produced as a motion picture, been played on the stage, adapted for a pageant and may eventually be utilized for a grand opera.

Introduction to a 1935 reprint of *Ramona*

63. The function of sentence 1 is

   (A) to justify reprinting an 1884 novel in 1935
   (B) to define the phrase *American classic*
   (C) to identify Helen Jackson
   (D) to arouse the readers' interest in buying the book
   (E) to introduce the exotic (Spanish and Native American life in California) subject matter of the book.

64. Sentence 2

   (A) says that the book is one of the greatest novels ever written
   (B) congratulates the author for writing such a best-seller
   (C) reveals the plot of the book
   (D) documents the enormous popularity of the book
   (E) shows that the author of the introduction has not done much research

65. The quotations in sentence 3

    (A) are so brief as to be meaningless
    (B) provide concrete support for the figures in sentence 2
    (C) shift the introduction from the quantity of sales to the quality of the novel
    (D) play on the sympathy of the reader when Ms. Jackson's death in 1885 is mentioned
    (E) shift the central idea of the passage too quickly

66. The function of sentence 5 is to

    (A) add more figures to those of sentence 2
    (B) add information that does not mean much to the modern reader
    (C) say that popularity is a criterion for quality
    (D) imply that any book that has been made into a movie has to be good
    (E) provide more evidence of the book's popularity

67. Sentence 4

    (A) should be eliminated
    (B) gives a brief overview of Ms. Jackson's life
    (C) should have been used as the topic sentence of the passage
    (D) should be combined with sentence 1
    (E) explains Mrs. Jackson's interest in Indians

68. The passage concentrates

    (A) on Mrs. Jackson's life
    (B) on *Ramona's* popularity
    (C) on critics' opinions of *Ramona*
    (D) on Spanish and Native American life in California
    (E) on historical facts that are boring

69. From this passage you can conclude that its author

    (A) admires *Ramona*
    (B) has never read *Ramona*
    (C) is a novelist
    (D) is a poet
    (E) considers *Ramona* to be overly sentimental

Directions: Each of the following selections is an early draft of a work in progress in which the sentences have been numbered for easy reference. Some parts of the selections need to be changed.

Read each selection and then answer the questions that follow. Some questions are about particular sentences or parts of sentences and ask you to improve the sentence structure and diction (word choice). In making these decisions, follow the conventions of standard written English. Other questions refer to the entire passage or parts of the passage and ask you to consider organization, development, and effectiveness of language in relation to purpose and audience.

Questions 70–76 are based on the following passage:

(1) Lacy's wedding reception was very inexpensive. (2) As these things go. (3) We did not have a dinner at the reception. (4) Lacy, her mother, and her aunt did all the cooking ahead of time. (5) Flowers were few and simple—most of them came from our garden. (6) The bridal gown was on sale for half price. (7) The groom and ushers wore rented tuxedos that they had not purchased. (8) There was no champagne for the toast because the church does not permit alcoholic beverages in its parlor. (9) The wedding was beautiful, and the more than one hundred guests seemed to enjoy the festivities. (10) Lacy and Jared are now living in Decatur, where Jared sells insurance for a large company, which is one of the ones that specialize in life and health insurance programs.

70. What is the best way to combine sentences 1 and 2?

 (A) with a comma at the end of sentence 1
 (B) with a colon at the end of sentence 1
 (C) with a semicolon at the end of sentence 1
 (D) with "and" between them
 (E) with "but" between them

71. Which of the following is a valid criticism of sentence 3?

 (A) No one cares what was served at the reception.
 (B) Receptions rarely include dinner.
 (C) It should be the topic sentence of the paragraph.
 (D) It fails to explain who "we" are.
 (E) It is too short.

72. Once sentences 1 and 2 are combined (question 70), that sentence could be combined with sentences 3 through 8. What would be the best way to do this?

    (A) Change the period at the end of the new sentence 1 to a colon, and put semicolons at the end of sentences 3, 4, 5, 6, and 7.
    (B) Substitute semicolons for all the periods.
    (C) Substitute commas for all the periods.
    (D) Put a semicolon after the new sentence 1 and put commas after all the other sentences.
    (E) Put dashes after sentences 3, 4, 5, 6, and 7.

73. Which is the best version of the underlined portion of sentence 7 (reproduced below)?

    The groom and ushers wore rented tuxedos that they had not purchased.

    (A) (as it is now)
    (B) wore tuxedos that they rented so they did not have to buy them
    (C) rented their tuxedos
    (D) did not buy tuxedos so they rented them
    (E) rented tuxedos, which did not have to be bought

74. Which would be the best transition word or phrase to begin sentence 9?

    (A) Although,
    (B) Consequently,
    (C) As a result,
    (D) Even so,
    (E) At the same time,

75. Which is the best version of the underlined portion of sentence 10 (reproduced below)?

    Lacy and Jared are now living in Decatur, where Jared sells insurance for a large company, which is one of the ones that specialize in life and health insurance programs.

    (A) (as it is now)
    (B) company that specializes
    (C) company, which is specializing
    (D) company that is one of the ones that specialize
    (E) company that had specializations

76. What should be done with sentence 10?

    (A) It should be moved to the beginning of the passage.
    (B) It should begin a second paragraph.
    (C) It should be shorter and less detailed.
    (D) It should come immediately after sentence 2.
    (E) It should be combined with sentence 1.

Questions 77–83 are based on the following passage:

(1) In fact, this play piled up more continuous performances in the same theater than any play in American theatrical history. (2) *The Fantasticks*, a musical, ran at a small off-Broadway theater for about forty years. (3) An actress who made her debut in this simple musical comedy moved on to starring roles on television and in Hollywood. (4) Why this play, which was ignored by sophisticated critics when it opened, established such a record is a mystery to many people. (5) The story line is a kind of fairy tale, this is not very distinctive music, and the lyrics are full of clichés. (6) And the musical continued to attract audiences. (7) People who had gone to see it as children took their own children to it. (8) Couples who had attended in their youth celebrated their silver wedding anniversaries with a return visit. (9) It became a kind of good luck charm—as long as *The Fantasticks* was still running, all was right with the world.

77. What should be done with sentence 2?

   (A) It should be at the beginning of the passage
   (B) It should be at the end of the passage.
   (C) It should be placed immediately after sentence 4.
   (D) It should be omitted.
   (E) It should be left as it is.

78. What should be done with sentence 3?

   (A) It should be at the beginning of the passage.
   (B) It should be at the end of the passage.
   (C) It should be placed immediately after sentence 4.
   (D) It should be omitted.
   (E) It should be left as it is.

79. Where should sentence 5 be placed?

   (A) It should be at the beginning of the passage.
   (B) It should be at the end of the passage.
   (C) It should be placed immediately after sentence 3.
   (D) It should be omitted.
   (E) It should be left where it is.

80. What would be the best choice to replace "And" at the beginning of sentence 6?

   (A) Therefore
   (B) But
   (C) Thus
   (D) In this case
   (E) Finally

81. Which is the best version of the underlined portion of sentence 5 (reproduced below)?

    The story line is a kind of fairy tale, this is not very distinctive music, and the lyrics are full of clichés.

    (A) (as it is now)
    (B) this is not distinctive music
    (C) the music is not very distinctive
    (D) the music is distinguishable
    (E) this is terrible music

82. Which would be the best way to join sentences 7 and 8?

    (A) with a colon
    (B) with a comma followed by "but"
    (C) with a semicolon followed by "however,"
    (D) with a comma
    (E) with a semicolon

83. What punctuation mark could replace the dash in sentence 9 without changing the meaning of the sentence?

    (A) a period
    (B) a comma
    (C) a semicolon
    (D) a colon
    (E) a comma followed by "because"

Directions: Effective revision requires choosing among the many options available to a writer. The following questions test your ability to use these options effectively.

Revise each of the sentences below according to the directions that follow it. Some directions require you to change only part of the original sentence; others require you to change the entire sentence. You may need to omit or add certain words in constructing an acceptable revision, but you should keep the meaning of your revised sentence as close to the meaning of the original sentence as the directions permit. Your new sentence should follow the conventions of standard written English and should be clear and concise.

Look through answer choices A–E under each question for the exact word or phrase that is included in your revised sentence. If you have thought of a revision that does not include any of the words or phrases listed, try to revise the sentence again so that it does include the wording in one of the answer choices.

You may make notes in your test book, but be sure to mark your answers on the separate answer sheet.

84. In the tenth inning, Ozzie Smith knocked the ball into the left-field stands for a home run.

    Change <u>knocked</u> to <u>was knocked</u>.

    (A) from
    (B) at which
    (C) under
    (D) with
    (E) by

85. Looking up, we saw four Boeing 747s, flying in perfect formation.

    Begin with <u>While we were</u>.

    (A) looking
    (B) being looked
    (C) having looked
    (D) looked
    (E) having been looked

86. Unless a criminal charge can be proved in court, a defendant cannot be punished.

    Change <u>can</u> to <u>could</u>.

    (A) should
    (B) shall
    (C) will
    (D) would
    (E) must

87. The young man walked to the door; he wanted to see who had rung the bell.

    Begin with <u>Because he wanted</u>.

    (A) bell so
    (B) bell;
    (C) bell and
    (D) bell for
    (E) bell,

88. That humans are vertebrate animals has been affirmed by many scientific experiments.

    Begin with <u>Many scientific experiments</u>.

    (A) has
    (B) have
    (C) would
    (D) been
    (E) was

89. Some teachers declare vociferously that they are in the classroom to teach students, but their attitude contradicts what they say.

    Begin with <u>Some teachers who</u>.

    (A) contradicts what they say by
    (B) contradict what they say for
    (C) contradicts what they say from
    (D) contradict what they say by
    (E) contradicts what they say into

90. Insomnia, especially if long standing, is both one of the most troublesome of our afflictions and one of the most difficult to treat without special medication.

    Eliminate <u>both</u>.

    (A) so
    (B) so well as
    (C) as well as
    (D) as much as
    (E) thus

91. Dr. Martin Luther King, Jr., embraced nonviolence as a method of social reform when he was introduced to the philosophy of Mahatma Gandhi.

    Begin with <u>After being introduced</u>.

    (A) nonviolence as a method of social reform was embraced by Dr. Martin Luther King, Jr.
    (B) Dr. Martin Luther King, Jr., had been embracing nonviolence as a method of social reform.
    (C) to social reform
    (D) Dr. Martin Luther King, Jr., embraced nonviolence as a method of social reform.
    (E) Dr. Martin Luther King, Jr., was embracing nonviolence as a method of social reform.

92. No one can possibly comprehend that I can eat and relish fried squid or boiled seaweed, but I am not afraid to sample exotic dishes from strange places.

    Change <u>No one can possibly</u> to <u>Everyone finds it</u>.

    (A) possible that I can
    (B) comprehending that I can
    (C) comprehensible that I can
    (D) uncomprehending that I can
    (E) incomprehensible that I can

93. Some average children excel in math as they mature when they are taught music at an early age.

    Begin with <u>Some average children whose</u>.
    (A) whose skills in math
    (B) whose early education includes
    (C) they are excellent
    (D) who are average
    (E) as they mature

94. The doleful sound of the funeral bell reverberated through the village, and we could see the dismal cortege winding its way to the local cemetery.

    Begin with <u>With the doleful</u>.

    (A) reverberating through the village, so we
    (B) reverberating through the village; we
    (C) reverberating through the village, we
    (D) reverberating through the village, and we
    (E) reverberating through the village, thus we

95. A birth rate that continues to increase is no blessing to an island like Java, one of the most densely populated areas in the world with more than twelve hundred people per square mile.

    Begin with <u>Java, one of the most</u>.

    (A) needs an increasing birth rate
    (B) does not increase its birth rate each year
    (C) blesses an increasing birth rate
    (D) does not need an increasing birth rate
    (E) is not overpopulated

Directions: The following sentences test your knowledge of grammar, usage, diction (choice of words), and idiom.

Some sentences are correct.

No sentence contains more than one error.

You will find that the error, if there is one, is underlined and lettered. Assume that elements of the sentence that are not underlined are correct and cannot be changed. In choosing answers, follow the requirements of standard written English.

If there is an error, select the <u>one underlined part</u> that must be changed to make the sentence correct.

If there is no error, select answer (E).

96. After wandering in the woods for hours, we finally stumbled upon the
            A   B

    path that leads us back to the campground where we were staying.
           C   D

    No error.
     E

97. Although there have been many days of discouragement, when nothing
                    A   B

    seemed to go right, we now believe we are on the right track, we feel
              C   D

    confident again. No error.
            E

98. The medieval fortress outside the city,
                A

    which was built by Frederick Barbarossa, is the only example of Gothic
              B   C

    architecture still standing in the province. No error.
           D   E

99. Long after everyone else had switched over to expensive cassette and CD
       A   B

    players, Jerome was still playing his old LPs on a manually operated
      C   D

    turntable. No error.
          E

100. All things considered, there seems to be no reason why the present
         A   B

     members of the senior class should not enjoy the same privileges that their
                                                      C

     predecessors enjoy. No error.
           D   E

STOP

If there is still time remaining, you may review your answers.

English Composition
ANSWER KEY—SAMPLE EXAMINATION 1

1. C	21. A	41. C	61. E	81. C
2. B	22. A	42. C	62. C	82. E
3. E	23. A	43. A	63. D	83. D
4. D	24. E	44. B	64. D	84. E
5. A	25. A	45. C	65. C	85. A
6. D	26. C	46. B	66. E	86. A
7. B	27. A	47. A	67. B	87. E
8. A	28. E	48. D	68. B	88. B
9. E	29. A	49. D	69. A	89. D
10. C	30. C	50. D	70. A	90. C
11. B	31. B	51. A	71. D	91. D
12. E	32. B	52. B	72. A	92. E
13. A	33. A	53. D	73. C	93. B
14. E	34. A	54. B	74. D	94. C
15. E	35. A	55. B	75. B	95. D
16. E	36. E	56. C	76. B	96. C
17. D	37. C	57. A	77. A	97. D
18. B	38. D	58. D	78. D	98. B
19. D	39. B	59. B	79. E	99. E
20. B	40. A	60. A	80. B	100. D

SCORING CHART

After you have scored your Sample Examination 1, enter the results in the chart below; then transfer your score to the Progress Chart on page 12.

Total Test	Number Right	Number Wrong	Number Omitted
100			

ANSWER EXPLANATIONS

1. **(C)** <u>Badly</u> is an adverbial form; <u>bad</u> would be correct.

2. **(B)** <u>Loose</u> should be <u>loosen</u>, the correct form of the verb.

3. **(E)** The sentence is correct.

4. **(D)** <u>Affective</u> is an incorrect word—use <u>effective</u>.

5. **(A)** A dangling modifier—substitute <u>Because we assume</u>.

6. **(D)** <u>Partiality</u>—should be <u>impartiality</u>.

7. **(B)** <u>Raising</u> should be <u>rising</u>.

8. **(A)** <u>Colonies</u> is plural and the unmarked verb is singular; therefore, the correct version would be <u>many a colony</u>.

9. **(E)** The sentence is correct.

10. **(C)** <u>Portrayal</u> must be changed to plural to agree with <u>have</u>.

11. **(B)** <u>Except</u> should be <u>accept</u>.

12. **(E)** The sentence is correct.

13. **(A)** <u>I</u> should be <u>me</u>—the objective case form.

14. **(E)** The sentence is correct.

15. **(E)** The sentence is correct.

16. **(E)** The sentence is correct.

17. **(D)** The clause beginning <u>which</u> has no word in the sentence to modify.

18. **(B)** <u>Choosen</u> should be <u>chosen</u>.

19. **(D)** <u>Seem</u> should be <u>seems</u>—the subject is the whole clause, therefore singular.

20. **(B)** <u>Has depended</u> is an error in sequence of tenses; change to <u>depends</u>.

21. **(A)** Choices (B), (C), (D), and (E) are either wordy or change the meaning of the original.

22. **(A)** Choices (B) and (E) are wordy; (C) and (D) are illogical.

23. **(A)** The original sentence is correct; the other choices contain errors in verb forms.

24. **(E)** Choice (A) uses the word "completely," a poor word choice to describe the plumbing ability under discussion; (B) is wordy; (C) is illogical; (D) changes the meaning too much.

25. **(A)** Choice (B) contradicts meaning of original sentence; (C) and (D) change the meaning too much; (E) introduces an irrelevant idea.

26. **(C)** Choice (A) <u>so</u> is an incorrect idiom; (B) confuses <u>fortunate</u> and <u>fortune</u>; (D) is wordy; (E) also confuses <u>fortune</u> and <u>fortunate</u>.

27. **(A)** Choice (B) uses an incorrect phrase—very unique; (C) ignores cause-effect sense of the original; (D) confuses verb time sequences; (E) is a sentence fragment.

28. **(E)** Choice (A) hide should be hid; (B) having hidden is a dangling modifier; (C) and (D) have incorrect clauses.

29. **(A)** The other choices introduce grammatical errors of several kinds.

30. **(C)** Choice (A) has is, an error in subject-verb agreement; (B) they is a vague pronoun; (D) introduces a dangling modifier; (E) who has no verb to complete its meaning.

31. **(B)** Choice (A) we is incorrect case form; (C) is illogical; (D) incorrectly uses the adverb pleasantly instead of the adjective pleasant; (E) changes the meaning of the sentence.

32. **(B)** Choice (A) is illogical; (C) is a sentence fragment; (D) was when is an incorrect idiom; (E) because indicates a false cause-effect relationship.

33. **(A)** Choices (B) and (C) create sentence fragments; (D) creates a tense shift; (E) persons is an incorrect plural.

34. **(A)** Choice (B) presents information redundantly; (C) the semicolon is incorrect; (D) forms a sentence fragment; (E) is illogical

35. **(A)** Choice (B) the introductory phrase is a dangling modifier; (C) is incomplete, for the sense of the original sentence is incomplete; (D) the introductory phrase is a dangling modifier; (E) implies a false sequence of events.

36. **(E)** The other choices are illogical.

37. **(C)** Choice (A) was is an error in subject-verb agreement; (B) would be a sentence fragment; (D) and (E) were is incorrect subject-verb agreement.

38. **(D)** Choice (B) is wordy; the other choices use the incorrect word that.

39. **(B)** Choice (A) as successful if is an incorrect idiom; (C), (D) and (E) distort the original meaning.

40. **(A)** Choice (B) contains a double negative; (C) the infinitive seems awkward; (D) correct and embarrass are errors in subject-verb agreement; (E) is both awkward and an incomplete statement of the idea.

41. **(C)** This is the only choice that is neither illogical nor awkward.

42. **(C)** This choice avoids both the dangling modifier and an illogical sequence of tenses.

43. **(A)** In the original, sentence 6 seems to be tacked on as an afterthought, but it is clearly an important point. The rearrangement suggested in (A) would solve that problem.

44. **(B)** An introduction should be supported by what follows.

45. **(C)** In the original, the pronoun *they* in sentence 9 has no antecedent. In context, (C) provides the most logical choice.

46. **(B)** Simply saying that a problem can be easily solved is not likely to reassure those who are troubled by the problem. Because the purpose of the letter is to convince people that the writer's position is correct or desirable, the most effective addition to this paragraph would be a solution to the major problem raised by the opposition.

47. **(A)** The first part of this sentence is the result, and the second part is the cause. *Since* makes this connection clear.

48. **(D)** The problem with the original sentence is vagueness. (D) makes clear the kind of improvement the writer is suggesting.

49. **(D)** The information in this sentence has nothing to do with the rest of the passage, so the sentence should be left out.

50. **(D)** This is the most logical and least wordy choice.

51. **(A)** Because the *leaping* in sentence 5 refers to the squirrels in sentence 4, this sentence should not be moved.

52. **(B)** The problem with the original is wordiness. (B) solves this problem more gracefully than the other choices.

53. **(D)** The second part of the sentence is an illustration of the first, not a reason for it. A colon between the two makes this relationship clear.

54. **(B)** Because sentence 9 is simply another part of the description of the winter scene, no transition word is needed here.

55. **(B)** This sentence makes more sense as a conclusion for the paragraph.

56. **(C)** None of the other choices is grammatically correct.

57. **(A)** Sentence 5 should remain where it is. In sentence 4, the educational benefits of *Sesame Street* are mentioned, making it logical to move to a discussion of schools in sentence 5.

58. **(D)** Since cost was not mentioned elsewhere in the paragraph, it would be better to replace sentence 7 with a concluding sentence that did more to sum up the paragraph.

59. **(B)** The second reason provided in sentence 6 is the advocation of racial harmony.

60. **(A)** Sentence 1 makes the thesis statement the rest of the paragraph goes on to discuss and is, therefore, the topic sentence of the paragraph.

61. **(E)** Sentence 4 says that the program "provides educational opportunities for children under about ten."

62. **(C)** The phrase is not only vague but also suggests "facts of life," implying a discussion of sex that is not offered on *Sesame Street*.

63. **(D)** The writer has chosen two impressive facts about the book to arouse the reader's interest and has added a little color, as well, by mentioning that it is a romantic story of Spanish and Indian life.

64. **(D)** Sentence 2 offers further proof that the book has continuously been well-received.

65. **(C)** The writer is covering all ground in his or her praise of the book. In sentence 3, the writer uses the quotes to show that the book is not only popular, but that the critics find it to be of substance.

66. **(E)** The writer uses the information in sentence 5 as yet another means of showing the book's popularity.

67. **(B)** Sentence 4 gives a brief overview of Mrs. Jackson's life.

68. **(B)** Throughout the passage, fact after fact is given to show *Ramona's* popularity.

69. **(A)** Because the passage is full of praise for *Ramona*, it is reasonable to conclude that the author admires the book.

70. **(A)** Sentence 2 is a parenthetical comment that should be added to sentence 1 with no stronger punctuation than a comma.

71. **(D)** Pronouns always need clear antecedents to make clear to what or to whom they refer.

72. **(A)** Sentences 3 to 7 all illustrate the statement in sentence 1. The punctuation proposed in (A) makes this relationship clear.

73. **(C)** This choice avoids the unnecessary wordiness of the other choices.

74. **(D)** This is the only choice that makes clear the logical connection between sentence 9 and the earlier parts of the passage.

75. **(B)** This choice avoids the wordiness that characterizes the others.

76. **(B)** Because this sentence introduces a new topic, it belongs in a new paragraph.

77. **(A)** Sentence 2 is clearly the topic sentence, and also provides the reference for *this play* in sentence 1. The specific reference should always come first.

78. **(D)** This information has nothing to do with the topic of the passage, the continuing popularity of *The Fantasticks*.

79. **(E)** There is no problem with the location of this sentence.

80. **(B)** The relationship between sentence 5 and sentence 6 is one of contrast, so *but* would be the logical conjunction to join them.

81. **(C)** This puts the parallel thoughts in parallel construction.

82. **(E)** Two independent but comparable sentences can be joined by a semicolon.

83. **(D)** A dash and a colon are both acceptable ways to introduce an explanation.

84. **(E)** In the tenth inning, the ball was knocked into the left-field stands for a home run by Ozzie Smith.

85. **(A)** While we were *looking* up, we saw four Boeing 747s, flying in perfect formation.

86. **(A)** Unless a criminal charge could be proved, a defendant *should* not be punished.

87. **(E)** Because he wanted to see who had rung the *bell*, the young man walked to the door.

88. **(B)** Many scientific experiments *have* affirmed that humans are vertebrate animals.

89. **(D)** Some teachers who declare vociferously that they are in the classroom to teach students *contradict what they say* by their attitude.

90. **(C)** Insomnia, especially if long standing, is one of the most troublesome of our afflictions *as well as* one . . .

91. **(D)** After being introduced to the philosophy of Mahatma Gandhi, *Dr. Martin Luther King, Jr., embraced nonviolence as a method of social reform.*

92. **(E)** Everyone finds it *incomprehensible that I can* eat . . .

93. **(B)** Some average children *whose early education includes* music excel at math as they mature.

94. **(C)** With the doleful sound of the funeral bell *reverberating through the village, we* could see the dismal cortege winding . . .

95. **(D)** Java, one of the most densely populated areas in the world with more than twelve hundred people per square mile, *does not need an increasing birth rate.*

96. **(C)** The rest of the sentence is in the past tense, so *leads* should be *led*.

97. **(D)** A comma is not acceptable to join two independent clauses. One way to solve the problem would be to put a period after *track* and begin a new sentence with *we*.

98. **(B)** This clause is in the wrong place. It is unlikely that the entire city was built by Frederick Barbarossa.

99. **(E)** There is no error in this sentence.

100. **(D)** The verb *enjoy* should be in the past tense *enjoyed* because the seniors' predecessors are no longer present.

English Composition

ANSWER SHEET—SAMPLE EXAM 2

1 (A) (B) (C) (D) (E)	26 (A) (B) (C) (D) (E)	51 (A) (B) (C) (D) (E)	76 (A) (B) (C) (D) (E)
2 (A) (B) (C) (D) (E)	27 (A) (B) (C) (D) (E)	52 (A) (B) (C) (D) (E)	77 (A) (B) (C) (D) (E)
3 (A) (B) (C) (D) (E)	28 (A) (B) (C) (D) (E)	53 (A) (B) (C) (D) (E)	78 (A) (B) (C) (D) (E)
4 (A) (B) (C) (D) (E)	29 (A) (B) (C) (D) (E)	54 (A) (B) (C) (D) (E)	79 (A) (B) (C) (D) (E)
5 (A) (B) (C) (D) (E)	30 (A) (B) (C) (D) (E)	55 (A) (B) (C) (D) (E)	80 (A) (B) (C) (D) (E)
6 (A) (B) (C) (D) (E)	31 (A) (B) (C) (D) (E)	56 (A) (B) (C) (D) (E)	81 (A) (B) (C) (D) (E)
7 (A) (B) (C) (D) (E)	32 (A) (B) (C) (D) (E)	57 (A) (B) (C) (D) (E)	82 (A) (B) (C) (D) (E)
8 (A) (B) (C) (D) (E)	33 (A) (B) (C) (D) (E)	58 (A) (B) (C) (D) (E)	83 (A) (B) (C) (D) (E)
9 (A) (B) (C) (D) (E)	34 (A) (B) (C) (D) (E)	59 (A) (B) (C) (D) (E)	84 (A) (B) (C) (D) (E)
10 (A) (B) (C) (D) (E)	35 (A) (B) (C) (D) (E)	60 (A) (B) (C) (D) (E)	85 (A) (B) (C) (D) (E)
11 (A) (B) (C) (D) (E)	36 (A) (B) (C) (D) (E)	61 (A) (B) (C) (D) (E)	86 (A) (B) (C) (D) (E)
13 (A) (D) (D) (D) (E)	37 (A) (B) (C) (D) (E)	62 (A) (B) (C) (D) (E)	87 (A) (B) (C) (D) (E)
13 (A) (B) (C) (D) (E)	38 (A) (B) (C) (D) (E)	63 (A) (B) (C) (D) (E)	88 (A) (B) (C) (D) (E)
14 (A) (B) (C) (D) (E)	39 (A) (B) (C) (D) (E)	64 (A) (B) (C) (D) (E)	89 (A) (B) (C) (D) (E)
15 (A) (B) (C) (D) (E)	40 (A) (B) (C) (D) (E)	65 (A) (B) (C) (D) (E)	90 (A) (B) (C) (D) (E)
16 (A) (B) (C) (D) (E)	41 (A) (B) (C) (D) (E)	66 (A) (B) (C) (D) (E)	91 (A) (B) (C) (D) (E)
17 (A) (B) (C) (D) (E)	42 (A) (B) (C) (D) (E)	67 (A) (B) (C) (D) (E)	92 (A) (B) (C) (D) (E)
18 (A) (B) (C) (D) (E)	43 (A) (B) (C) (D) (E)	68 (A) (B) (C) (D) (E)	93 (A) (B) (C) (D) (E)
19 (A) (B) (C) (D) (E)	44 (A) (B) (C) (D) (E)	69 (A) (B) (C) (D) (E)	94 (A) (B) (C) (D) (E)
20 (A) (B) (C) (D) (E)	45 (A) (B) (C) (D) (E)	70 (A) (B) (C) (D) (E)	95 (A) (B) (C) (D) (E)
21 (A) (B) (C) (D) (E)	46 (A) (B) (C) (D) (E)	71 (A) (B) (C) (D) (E)	96 (A) (B) (C) (D) (E)
22 (A) (B) (C) (D) (E)	47 (A) (B) (C) (D) (E)	72 (A) (B) (C) (D) (E)	97 (A) (B) (C) (D) (E)
23 (A) (B) (C) (D) (E)	48 (A) (B) (C) (D) (E)	73 (A) (B) (C) (D) (E)	98 (A) (B) (C) (D) (E)
24 (A) (B) (C) (D) (E)	49 (A) (B) (C) (D) (E)	74 (A) (B) (C) (D) (E)	99 (A) (B) (C) (D) (E)
25 (A) (B) (C) (D) (E)	50 (A) (B) (C) (D) (E)	75 (A) (B) (C) (D) (E)	100 (A) (B) (C) (D) (E)

SAMPLE ENGLISH COMPOSITION EXAMINATION 2

NUMBER OF QUESTIONS: 100

Time limit: 90 MINUTES

Directions: The following sentences test your knowledge of grammar, usage, diction (choice of words), and idiom.

Some sentences are correct.

No sentence contains more than one error.

You will find that the error, if there is one, is underlined and lettered. Assume that elements of the sentence that are not underlined are correct and cannot be changed. In choosing answers, follow the requirements of standard written English.

If there is an error, select the one underlined part that must be changed to make the sentence correct.

If there is no error, select answer (E).

1. When <u>they fought</u> in the field, the <u>armies of</u> the two countries
          A   B
   <u>battled bravely</u> until <u>the war is over</u>. <u>No error</u>.
      C   D   E

2. The worker applied to <u>the union office</u> for retraining to <u>learn</u> a new trade,
                   A   B
   but <u>they refused</u> <u>his request</u>. <u>No error</u>.
        C   D   E

3. <u>Working both sides</u> of the street, the <u>con artist rushed</u> from house to house
         A   B
   <u>briskly making</u> his <u>pitch to home owners</u>. <u>No error</u>.
      C   D   E

4. The police officer <u>spoke harshly</u> to he and I about driving <u>too fast</u> on the
                 A   B   C
   residential <u>street and in</u> a school zone. <u>No error</u>.
           D   E

5. <u>Worrying about</u> what <u>was to happen</u> tomorrow, the <u>decision about</u> the
A   B   C
new job <u>was upsetting</u> Debbie's family routine. <u>No error.</u>
D   E

6. The president <u>of the board</u> of directors announced in Philadelphia today
A
that the company would <u>neither accede</u> to the monetary <u>demands of the</u>
B   C
strikers nor accept any further delays by union leaders <u>in accepting</u> a
D
settlement of the dispute. <u>No error.</u>
E

7. <u>Listening with rapt</u> attention while the orchestra was performing
A
<u>Beethoven's Fifth Symphony</u>, the concert hall was filled with <u>fashionably</u>
B   C
dressed music lovers who <u>followed the conductor's</u> every beat. <u>No error.</u>
D   E

8. The Pulitzer Prize Committee awarded <u>$25,000</u> to Scott Adams
A
<u>being as how the group voted</u> his <u>drawings in a national</u> newspaper the
B   C
best cartoons published in <u>America that year.</u> <u>No error.</u>
D   E

9. <u>Many expressions</u> that literate people <u>would not hesitate</u> to use in everyday
A   B
conversation they hesitate <u>to write because</u> an English teacher told them
C
such <u>phrases are colloquial.</u> <u>No error.</u>
D   E

10. The latest rock group has been playing on the stage for <u>more than an</u> hour
A
without repeating a song and <u>without</u> losing <u>their audience's</u> attention
B   C
<u>for even a few seconds.</u> <u>No error.</u>
D   E

11. Senator Snodgrass <u>must have</u> a very poor speech writer; <u>his inferences are</u>
A   B
always so subtle that the listener has to be <u>wary of drawing</u> hasty
C
conclusions <u>about what</u> he thinks he heard the senator say. <u>No error.</u>
D   E

12. Someone in the room dropped <u>their wallet</u> near the door,
    A

    <u>and the security guards</u> <u>brought it</u> to <u>their lost and found box</u> on the first
        B   C   D

    floor. <u>No error.</u>
      E

13. When David Brown called <u>the other afternoon</u>, Shari recognized the name
             A

    <u>immediately</u>, even after all these years, but she could not <u>locate the face</u>
     B   C

    from her memory of <u>the two hundred high school</u> graduates. <u>No error.</u>
             D   E

14. Investigators for <u>the Office of Education</u> spent many months reading
           A

    reports, collecting information, <u>and interviewing</u> witnesses; their
                B

    conclusion was that <u>about 70% of all</u> schools in the nation were above
           C

    standards either <u>in whole or in part.</u> <u>No error.</u>
          D   E

15. Our new computer has <u>more memory cells</u> than our old one; therefore,
            A

    the data <u>that can be recorded</u> and almost <u>instantaneously retrieved.</u>
         B   C

    <u>is unlimited.</u> <u>No error.</u>
     D   E

16. No <u>privately owned</u> telephone company in the United States <u>can deny</u> <u>its</u>
      A   B C

    employees <u>the right to join whatever</u> union they choose. <u>No error.</u>
        D   E

17. <u>True successful businesspersons</u> may belabor Congress for raising taxes on
        A

    their profits beyond <u>what they believe</u> they can afford to pay, but they can
           B

    <u>only admit</u> that <u>high taxes are necessary</u> during a period of increasing
     C   D

    deficits. <u>No error.</u>
       E

18. If a <u>local arrangements committee</u> can secure suitable hotel
                A
accommodations at <u>reasonable rates</u>, the board of <u>directors plan on having</u>
                   B   C
its annual <u>stockholders meeting</u> in Cleveland, Ohio. <u>No error.</u>
              D   E

19. Among the <u>luminaries whom</u> the successful <u>Washington diplomat</u> has
              A   B
invited to her <u>reception are</u> the secretary of state, the attorney general, the
              C
speaker of the House, and even <u>a presidential assistant</u> or two. <u>No error.</u>
                                D   E

20. All of the <u>new protein compounds</u> are <u>not to be found in unprocessed</u>
              A   B
foods; <u>they must be manufactured</u> in an expensive laboratory <u>that</u> few
                C   D
universities can afford to install. <u>No error.</u>
                                    E

Directions: In each of the following sentences, part of the sentence or the entire sentence is underlined. Beneath each sentence you will find five versions of the underlined part. Answer (A) repeats the original; the other four are different.

Choose the answer that best expresses the meaning of the original sentence. If you think the original is better than any of the alternatives, choose (A); otherwise choose one of the others. Your choice should produce the most effective sentence—one that is clear and precise, without awkwardness or ambiguity.

21. To make their children realize the significance of wise decision making, sometimes parents should let <u>them stew in the juice of their own concoction.</u>

  (A) let them stew in the juice of their own concoction
  (B) let them suffer the consequences of their actions
  (C) let them stew in their own consequences
  (D) reduce the penalties for deviant behavior
  (E) throw a lifeline to rescue them from the sea of despond

22. The government has passed a law regulating the sale of dangerous drugs <u>to teenagers, therefore, prescriptions</u> from licensed physicians are now required before a druggist can dispense them.

    (A) to teenagers, therefore, prescriptions
    (B) to teenagers, therefore; prescriptions
    (C) to teenagers; therefore, prescriptions
    (D) to teenagers, so therefore, prescriptions
    (E) to teenagers; and therefore prescriptions

23. If one considers the millions of years during which humanity has occupied this small space in the vastness of <u>space, they cannot help believing</u> that one person's life is truly insignificant.

    (A) space, they cannot help believing
    (B) space, but they cannot help but believe
    (C) space, he or she cannot help believing
    (D) space, he cannot help but believe
    (E) space, they cannot help but believing

24. Andy Warhol was a man of many talents; he painted many strange and unusual pictures, wrote a novel based on the experiences <u>of his coterie, and he produced</u> several experimental films for commercial distribution.

    (A) of his coterie, and he produced
    (B) of his coterie, and produced
    (C) of his coterie; and he has produced
    (D) of his coterie and have produced
    (E) of his coterie and he has produced

25. Many others <u>who are not so fortunate</u> will lose all the money they have invested in junk bonds.

    (A) others who are not so fortunate
    (B) others who is not so fortunate
    (C) others who is not as fortunate
    (D) others whom is not so fortunate
    (E) others whom are not so fortunate

26. The bus driver was always <u>pleasant to we riders even</u> though he must become impatient with some of us who never have the correct change.

    (A) pleasant to we riders even
    (B) pleasant to us riders even
    (C) pleasant to our riders even
    (D) pleasant to no riders
    (E) pleasant to their riders

27. Since Old Mother <u>Hubbard hadn't scarcely enough</u> food for herself, her friends wondered how she expected to feed a pet from her meager supply.

    (A) Hubbard hadn't scarcely enough
    (B) Hubbard had scarcely enough
    (C) Hubbard has scarcely enough
    (D) Hubbard had scarce enough
    (E) Hubbard scarcely have enough

28. While I was looking through the morning newspaper, <u>I read where the cost of living</u> had risen another four points, mainly because food prices had gone up again.

    (A) I read where the cost of living
    (B) I read when the cost of living
    (C) I read that the cost of living
    (D) I read because the cost of living
    (E) I read after the cost of living

29. <u>That type person always strongly resents</u> any attempt by anyone to inscribe limits around his actions.

    (A) That type person always strongly resents
    (B) That type person always strongly resent
    (C) That type of person always strongly resent
    (D) That type person always seldom resents
    (E) That type of person always strongly resents

30. Whenever a temptation to engage in an illegal activity arises while you are away from the protection of your <u>parents, remember that they have often informed</u> you that you should not do it.

    (A) parents, remember that they have often informed
    (B) parents; remember that they have often informed
    (C) parents, he should remember that they have often informed
    (D) parents, they should remember that they have often been informed
    (E) parents, they should remember that they have not informed

31. Reading a good novel can be as great a pleasure as seeing a professional football <u>game on television or catching a four-pound trout</u> in a clear stream in Michigan.

    (A) game on television or catching a four-pound trout
    (B) game on television or to catch a four-pound trout
    (C) game in television or catching a four-pound trout
    (D) game on television or caught a four-pound trout
    (E) game on television or to caught a four-pound trout

32. In her lecture, the novelist eluded to difficulties with her publisher who insisted that all controversial material be removed from her manuscript.

    (A) In her lecture, the novelist eluded to difficulties
    (B) In her lecture, the novelist alluded to difficulties
    (C) In her lecture, the novelist avoided her difficulties
    (D) In her lecture, the novelist inferred to difficulties
    (E) In her lecture, the novelist conferred to difficulties

33. The jury found the manager of the office so equally guilty as the clerk of the large establishment.

    (A) so equally guilty as the clerk
    (B) so much equally guilty as the clerk
    (C) as equally guilty just as the clerk
    (D) as guilty as the clerk
    (E) as if equally guilty as the clerk

34. Luckily, the arsonist was arrested before he set any more serious fires by the policeman who took him to jail.

    (A) was arrested before he set any more serious fires by the policeman who took him to jail
    (B) was arrested by the policeman who took him to jail after he set more serious fires
    (C) was arrested by the policeman who took him to jail before he could set any more serious fires
    (D) the policeman arrested him before he could set any more serious fires
    (E) was taken to jail by the policeman before he could set any more serious fires

35. I shopped in all the stores on Michigan Avenue before I found the exquisite old antique umbrella stand I wanted to give Masaki for a birthday present.

    (A) the exquisite old antique umbrella stand I wanted to give
    (B) the exquisite antique umbrella stand I wanted to give
    (C) the elaborate old antique umbrella stand I wanted to give
    (D) the exquisite antique old stand I wanted to give
    (E) the exquisite old stand for antique umbrellas I wanted to give

36. A good assistant can relieve an administrator of much of the paperwork that must be handled within any large organization to expedite its day to day operations.

    (A) that must be handled
    (B) that should have been handled
    (C) that must have been handled
    (D) that has got to be handled
    (E) that have to be handled

37. The majority political party could not <u>except the conditions of the minority</u>, and the coalition of parties collapsed.

    (A) except the conditions of the minority
    (B) reciprocate the conditions of the minority
    (C) calibrate the conditions of the minority
    (D) restrict the conditions of the minority
    (E) accept the conditions of the minority

38. That the United States is still suspicious of <u>terrorists is why Congress</u> is asked to increase defense spending.

    (A) terrorists is why Congress
    (B) terrorists is when Congress
    (C) terrorists is that Congress
    (D) terrorists explains why Congress
    (E) terrorists wants Congress

39. Working hard is not difficult for those <u>people whom are accustomed to</u> getting up early and coming home after dark.

    (A) people whom are accustomed to
    (B) people whom is accustomed to
    (C) people who are accustomed to
    (D) people that are accustomed to
    (E) people whose are accustomed to

40. In many countries, the ordinary people are neither permitted to decide <u>things for themselves or allowed</u> to say anything against the government.

    (A) things for themselves or allowed
    (B) things for themselves or could be allowed
    (C) things for themselves nor allowed
    (D) things for themselves and allowed
    (E) things for themselves therefore allowed

41. The inner chamber of the tomb had not been opened for nearly four thousand years, and there archaeologists discovered <u>the gilded chair, the alabaster jars of perfume, the golden crown, and other nice things.</u>

    (A) the gilded chair, the alabaster jars of perfume, the golden crown, and other nice things.
    (B) the gilded chair, the alabaster jars of perfume, the golden crown, and so on.
    (C) the gilded chair, the alabaster jars of perfume, the golden crown, and other things.
    (D) the gilded chair, the alabaster jars of perfume, the golden crown.
    (E) many wonderful things.

Directions: Each of the following selections is an early draft of a work in progress in which the sentences have been numbered for easy reference. Some parts of the selections need to be changed.

Read each selection and then answer the questions that follow. Some questions are about particular sentences or parts of sentences and ask you to improve the sentence structure and diction (word choice). In making these decisions, follow the conventions of standard written English. Other questions refer to the entire passage or parts of the passage and ask you to consider organization, development, and effectiveness of language in relation to purpose and audience.

Questions 42–48 are based on the following passage:

(1) For years now, presidents and others have been saying that we must win the war against drugs. (2) Drugs are destroying whole neighborhoods. (3) They are killing our young people. (4) Drugs also cause crime, and people can get rich easily selling drugs, and because there are enormous amounts of money involved they get into fights and that causes all kinds of violence. (5) Drug dealers kill not only each other but sometimes they also kill innocent bystanders, even small children.

(6) Our national leaders have urged us to wage war on this problem to cure the plague that is haunting us. (7) But urging users to say "no" hasn't worked. (8) Building new jails and hiring more police officers hasn't worked. (9) Telling users of the dangers of drugs hasn't worked. (10) What will?

(11) No one can be sure, but there have been plenty of suggestions ranging all the way from the recommendation that all casual users suffer the same legal penalties as pushers do to the legalization of drugs often with the caveat that there should of course be strict controls on the sale of these drugs so that they aren't sold to children and used to try to get additional people addicted.

(12) Everyone agrees that there is an emergency situation, but no one—not the administration, not Congress, not the American taxpayer—seems to be willing to spend the billions of dollars that are necessary to halt the widespread use of drugs.

42. What would be the best thing to do with sentence 1?

   (A) Leave it as it is.
   (B) Move it to the end of the first paragraph.
   (C) Move it to the beginning of the second paragraph.
   (D) Move it to the end of the passage.
   (E) Delete it.

43. Which is the best version of the underlined portion of sentence 4 (reproduced below)?

    Drugs also cause crime, and <u>people can get rich easily selling drugs, and because there are enormous amounts of money involved they get into fights and that causes</u> all kinds of violence.

    (A) (as it is now)
    (B) people sell drugs even though the enormous amounts of money cause
    (C) competition among drug dealers for the enormous sums of money involved leads to
    (D) seeking to get rich by selling drugs, the enormous amounts of money involved cause
    (E) seeking to get rich quick by selling drugs makes people get into fights over money that cause

44. A valid criticism of sentence 6 is that

    (A) it is too informal
    (B) it contains a mixed metaphor
    (C) it is irrelevant to the topic
    (D) it fails to say what should be done
    (E) the drug problem should not concern national leaders

45. Which of the following is a valid criticism of sentence 11?

    (A) It doesn't give any solutions.
    (B) It should make clear which side the author is on.
    (C) It tries to put too much information in a single sentence and should be broken up into two or more sentences.
    (D) Logically, it belongs after sentence 12.
    (E) It has a problem with subject-verb agreement.

46. A summary of recent research on the effectiveness of various drug treatment programs added to this passage would be most useful for which of the following audiences?

    (A) elementary school students
    (B) college students
    (C) professional drug rehabilitation counselors
    (D) high school teachers
    (E) former drug addicts

47. Which of the following words or phrases could be used to replace "caveat" in sentence 11 without changing the meaning of the sentence?

    (A) warning
    (B) intention
    (C) bearing in mind
    (D) possibility
    (E) purpose

48. Which of the following would be the best way to improve the final paragraph?

    (A) Add the author's personal experiences with drugs.
    (B) Delete the references to Congress and the president.
    (C) Explain how drugs affect the central nervous system.
    (D) Explain why it is necessary to spend billions of dollars.
    (E) Add a ringing denunciation of drug pushers.

Questions 49–55 are based on the following passage:

(1) Junipers are the most versatile plants we sell and are well suited to the New England climate. (2) They need to be planted in a sunny spot. (3) They tolerate relatively poor soil. (4) They tolerate salt air. (5) In addition, they will grow in windy sites. (6) All our plants are sold "B&B." (7) This means they are field-grown plants that are dug, balled, and wrapped in burlap. (8) There are three different types of junipers. (9) Ground cover types are good for steep slopes and around buildings, (10) They don't need a whole lot of maintenance. (11) Many of them will re-root wherever their stems touch the ground. (12) Spreading types work well in mass plantings where large areas need to be covered. (13) For example, you could plant them along a highway. (14) They also look attractive in mixed plantings with other evergreens. (15) They look attractive as foundation plants next to a house. (16) Upright types make attractive hedges or windbreaks when used in group plantings. (17) They are good for backgrounds or you can use them as individual specimens. (18) Ground cover types should be planted two to three feet apart. (19) Upright types should be planted four feet apart when used for hedges.

49. If this passage were to be divided into two paragraphs, which sentence should begin the second paragraph?

    (A) sentence 3
    (B) sentence 7
    (C) sentence 8
    (D) sentence 12
    (E) sentence 16

50. Which of the following would be the best way to combine sentences 1 and 2?

   (A) Junipers, which are the most versatile plants we sell and are well suited to the New England climate, but they need to be planted in a sunny spot.
   (B) Junipers are the most versatile plants we sell and are well suited to the New England climate because they need to be planted in a sunny spot.
   (C) Junipers are the most versatile plants we sell and are well suited to the New England climate if planted in a sunny spot.
   (D) Junipers are the most versatile plants we sell, well suited to the New England climate, and planted in a sunny spot.
   (E) Junipers, the most versatile plants we sell, are well suited to the New England climate if they need to be planted in a sunny spot.

51. Which of the following is the best way to combine sentences 3, 4, and 5?

   (A) They tolerate relatively poor soil; they tolerate salt air; in addition, they will grow in windy sites.
   (B) They tolerate relatively poor soil, salt air, and windy sites.
   (C) They tolerate relatively poor soil and salt air when grown in windy sites.
   (D) They tolerate relatively poor soil, and they tolerate salt air, and they will grow in windy sites.
   (E) They tolerate relatively poor soil and salt air; in addition, they will grow in windy sites.

52. Which is the best version of the underlined portion of sentence 10 (reproduced below)?

   They don't need a whole lot of maintenance.

   (A) (as it is now)
   (B) to be given a whole lot of
   (C) lots of
   (D) much
   (E) many

53. Which is the best version of the underlined portion of sentence 17 (reproduced below)?

   They are good for backgrounds or you can use them as individual specimens.

   (A) (as it is now)
   (B) or when used as
   (C) or are good as
   (D) or they are used as
   (E) or as

54. Which of the following pairs of sentences could most logically be combined?

    (A) sentences 7 and 8
    (B) sentences 11 and 12
    (C) sentences 12 and 13
    (D) sentences 15 and 16
    (E) sentences 17 and 18

55. Sentence 18 should

    (A) be omitted
    (B) follow sentence 11
    (C) follow sentence 19
    (D) follow sentence 13
    (E) follow sentence 8

Directions: Each of the following passages consists of numbered sentences. Because the passages are part of longer writing samples, they do not necessarily constitute a complete discussion of the issues presented.

Read each passage carefully and answer the questions that follow it. The questions test your awareness of a writer's purpose and of characteristics of prose that are important to good writing.

Questions 56–62 are based on the following passage:

(1) Combine the sugar and flour in a large bowl, and stir well. (2) In a saucepan, combine the butter, water, cocoa, and salt; bring to a boil. (3) Stir hot mixture into sugar-flour combination, and beat well. (4) Add eggs, one at a time, beating well after each egg has been added. (5) Dissolve baking soda in buttermilk, and stir well. (6) Stir in vanilla, and beat the batter for one minute. (7) Pour batter into baking pan, and place in oven. (8) Bake for twenty minutes or until a toothpick stuck into cake comes out clean. (9) Remove from oven and cool in baking pan for at least one hour. (10) Frost cake with a favorite icing. (11) Cut into squares and serve cold.

56. The paragraph is

    (A) a recipe for preparing a cake
    (B) a guide to making a fancy dessert
    (C) directions for making a cake
    (D) a section of a comparison/contrast composition
    (E) obviously from a gourmet's cookbook

57. All of the sentences

    (A) are actually sentence fragments because each has no subject
    (B) use the imperative mood of the verbs
    (C) are too short to be helpful to a cook
    (D) use the declarative mood of the verb
    (E) use the past tense of the verbs

58. One unique feature of paragraphs of this type is that

    (A) sentences can be used in any order
    (B) sentences provide several different bits of information
    (C) there is a definite sentence of conclusion
    (D) there is no expressed topic sentence or central idea
    (E) all of the sentences have a different construction

59. Sentences 1 through 6 assume that

    (A) the paragraph has been preceded by a list of ingredients with the amount of each one specified
    (B) the reader is an experienced cook
    (C) only children will use this recipe
    (D) the reader can interpret things for himself/herself
    (E) cakes are very easy to make

60. Sentence 7 is inadequate for this type of paragraph because

    (A) it is broken into two parts with the comma
    (B) the oven temperature is not given
    (C) the reader is told to do two things
    (D) the sentence is too short
    (E) the sentence conveys little information

61. One advantage of well-written paragraphs of this type is that the reader

    (A) does not have to read every word
    (B) does not need to do anything
    (C) is not expected to understand what is written
    (D) cannot make a serious mistake
    (E) is not required to interpret what is written

62. Which type of organization is most important for a paragraph of this type?

    (A) chronological
    (B) similarities followed by differences
    (C) differences followed by similarities
    (D) most to least important
    (E) least to most important

Questions 63–69 are based on the following passage:

(1) From my study window, I can see a grassy courtyard with some blooming flowers around the sides. (2) Across the courtyard is another apartment with a balcony which is larger than the one I have. (3) Usually, children are playing under the trees, and in the afternoons the noise of their activities is often distractive to my work. (4) From my balcony, I can see seven other balconies of varying sizes as well as seven patios that are attached to the apartments on the first floor. (5) Every Monday or Tuesday, depending upon the weather, several employees of the lawn upkeep service mow the grass, trim the shrubs, rake the clippings, and rake the area under the plants. (6) Just outside my study is a large oak tree that shades the windows from the afternoon sun; farther over in the courtyard are two more oak trees that are as tall as the two-story buildings. (7) Some tenants have planted petunias, marigolds, impatiens, and other annuals in flower boxes or at the edges of patios so that we have flowering plants to enjoy until frost comes. (8) One of the trees, a red maple, has already started the annual fall leaf color change so that in a couple of weeks we can hope for reds and browns in the branches to contrast with the green in the grass. (9) Then frost comes . . .

63. Sentence 1 lets the reader assume that

    (A) the paragraph will describe the courtyard
    (B) the writer will develop some abstract idea about the courtyard
    (C) the courtyard has some deep significance to the writer
    (D) the paragraph will go from a general statement to something more specific
    (E) the courtyard is not very attractive to the viewer

64. Sentence 5

    (A) seems a practical statement about the courtyard
    (B) demonstrates the apartment manager's concern for the unemployed
    (C) changes the subject too abruptly and should be omitted
    (D) produces the reason the author should remain in the apartment
    (E) praises the services of the lawn upkeep company

65. Sentence 3 implies that

    (A) the author does not like children
    (B) children enjoy the grassy courtyard
    (C) children cannot be trusted in the courtyard
    (D) the author has a job that requires peace and quiet
    (E) children should be encouraged in their activities

66. In sentence 7, the names of the plants that are in the courtyard illustrate what is said in

    (A) sentence 2
    (B) sentence 1
    (C) sentence 6
    (D) sentence 5
    (E) sentence 8

67. Sentence 8 relates most closely to what other sentence?

    (A) sentence 3
    (B) sentence 4
    (C) sentence 2
    (D) sentence 9
    (E) sentence 6

68. The effect of sentence 9, incomplete as it is, is

    (A) to summarize what the paragraph is all about
    (B) to signal the reader that the paragraph is exaggerated
    (C) to cast a coat of gloom on the mood of the paragraph
    (D) to lighten the whole mood of the paragraph
    (E) to show how the author can use an incomplete sentence ineffectively

69. In which sentences does the author give you information that tells you which season is being described?

    (A) sentences 1 and 5
    (B) sentences 1 and 9
    (C) sentences 3 and 6
    (D) sentences 7 and 8
    (E) sentences 2 and 4

Directions: Each of the following selections is an early draft of a work in progress in which the sentences have been numbered for easy reference. Some parts of the selections need to be changed.

Read each selection and then answer the questions that follow. Some questions are about particular sentences or parts of sentences and ask you to improve the sentence structure and diction (word choice). In making these decisions, follow the conventions of standard written English. Other questions refer to the entire passage or parts of the passage and ask you to consider organization, development, and effectiveness of language in relation to purpose and audience.

Questions 70–76 are based on the following passage:

(1) Many students now that they are entering college for the first time are confused by the attitude of the many faculty members who teach them. (2) Many college professors lecture about their many different subjects and assume, sometimes incorrectly, that new students understand the vocabulary that the professor uses, can define the terms from unfamiliar subjects, and that they know how to take notes adequately. (3) These skills are not those that most high school teachers teach or expect. (4) Both the professors and the students are frustrated because they do not understand each other in the classroom. (5) Many students hesitate to ask questions in class or during conferences, and they continue to be confused when they

listen to the lectures. (6) One thing colleges could do to fix up this problem is to offer a summer seminar in study skills for inexperienced students. (7) Those who take the class would gain valuable knowledge and develop skills that would be helpful to them throughout their college years. (8) Some colleges hesitate to offer such instruction because they say, "Here is the information you need, provided in the way we best provide it."

70. Which is the best version of the underlined portion of sentence 1 (reproduced below)?

    Many students now that they are entering college for the first time are confused by the attitude of the many faculty members who teach them.

    (A) (as it is now)
    (B) now they are entering
    (C) entering
    (D) that enter
    (E) now that they may be entering

71. Which is the best version of the underlined portion of sentence 2 (reproduced below)?

    Many college professors lecture about their many different subjects and assume, sometimes incorrectly, that new students understand the vocabulary that the professor uses, can define the terms from unfamiliar subjects, and that they know how to take notes adequately.

    (A) (as it is now)
    (B) and that know how
    (C) and that know
    (D) that know
    (E) and know how

72. A valid criticism of the first two sentences is that they

    (A) do not introduce the topic
    (B) are inconsistent in their verb tenses
    (C) repeat the word "many" too often
    (D) use pronouns with no logical antecedents
    (E) use an overly formal vocabulary

73. If this passage were to be divided into two paragraphs, which sentence should begin the second paragraph?

    (A) sentence 3
    (B) sentence 4
    (C) sentence 5
    (D) sentence 6
    (E) sentence 7

Exam 2

74. Which of the following would be the best choice to replace "and" in sentence 5?

    (A) but
    (B) or
    (C) while
    (D) yet
    (E) so

75. Which of the following would be the best replacement for "fix up" in sentence 6 to maintain the sense and the tone of the passage?

    (A) alleviate
    (B) get rid of
    (C) improve
    (D) maintain
    (E) disguise

76. Which of the following sentences would, if added to the end of the passage, make a suitable conclusion?

    (A) That's just not fair.
    (B) However, colleges need to remember that their goal should be to help students learn, not simply to provide students with information.
    (C) Well, a library card will do that job just as well.
    (D) Their best just isn't good enough.
    (E) So there!

Questions 77–83 are based on the following passage:

(1) If you drive from Florence to Arezzo through the Casentino, you will pass through a number of interesting places. (2) You take the main road to Pontassieve and then turn off onto the road for Vallombrosa. (3) The Casentino is the upper valley of the Arno. (4) The road to Vallombrosa goes through the villages of Pelago and Tosi. (5) After driving through a forest filled with pine, oak, and beech trees, you subsequently return to the main road just before Consuma. (6) Vallombrosa is now a popular summer resort. (7) Milton visited here when he was a young man, staying in the guest house of the famous and historic monastery of the Vallombrosan Order. (8) Just past Consuma, you will go across a mountain pass, and then one takes the road on the left to Pratovecchio and Stia. (9) The ruins of a twelfth-century castle that once belonged to the Guidi family lies near Pratovecchio. (10) Dante stayed with them when he was exiled from Florence. (11) Pratovecchio and Stia are two large villages in the Casentino. (12) Next the main road goes through Poppi and Bibbiena. (13) Poppi is a pretty little village and Bibbiena is the main town of the area. (14) You then go down across the plain and finally arrive at Arezzo.

77. Sentence 5 would be best placed

    (A) where it is now
    (B) after sentence 6
    (C) after sentence 7
    (D) after sentence 8
    (E) after sentence 9

78. One problem with sentence 8 is an inconsistency in

    (A) tenses
    (B) directions
    (C) pronouns
    (D) spelling
    (E) sentence structure

79. In the context of the passage as a whole, the best choice to replace "a number of interesting places" in sentence 1 would be

    (A) numerous interesting places
    (B) a variety of interesting places
    (C) a vast array of places of historic and literary interest
    (D) the whole of Italian history
    (E) a number of places of literary and historic interest

80. Sentence 3 could most logically be combined with

    (A) sentence 1
    (B) sentence 2
    (C) sentence 4
    (D) sentence 5
    (E) sentence 6

81. In sentence 5, "subsequently" should be

    (A) kept where it is
    (B) deleted
    (C) placed after "return"
    (D) replaced with "therefore"
    (E) replaced with "consequently"

Exam 2

82. Which of the following would be the best way to combine sentences 9 and 10 (reproduced below)?

    The ruins of a twelfth-century castle that once belonged to the Guidi family lies near Pratovecchio. Dante stayed with them when he was exiled from Florence.

    (A) Near Pratovecchio lie the ruins of a twelfth-century castle that once belonged to members of the Guidi family, who sheltered Dante when he was exiled from Florence.
    (B) The ruins of a twelfth-century castle that once belonged to the Guidi family lies near Pratovecchio; Dante stayed with them when he was exiled from Florence.
    (C) The ruins of a twelfth-century castle that once belonged to the Guidi family lies near Pratovecchio, with whom Dante stayed when he was exiled from Florence.
    (D) Dante took shelter with the Guidi family when he was exiled from Florence, and the ruins of a twelfth-century castle that once belonged to them lies near Pratovecchio.
    (E) The ruins of a twelfth-century castle lies near Pratovecchio that once belonged to the Guidi family, who sheltered Dante when he was exiled from Florence.

83. Sentence 11 could most logically be combined with

    (A) sentence 1
    (B) sentence 3
    (C) sentence 8
    (D) sentence 10
    (E) sentence 12

Directions: Effective revision requires choosing among the many options available to a writer. The following questions test your ability to use these options effectively.

Revise each of the sentences below according to the directions that follow it. Some directions require you to change only part of the original sentence; others require you to change the entire sentence. You may need to omit or add certain words in constructing an acceptable revision, but you should keep the meaning of your revised sentence as close to the meaning of the original sentence as the directions permit. Your new sentence should follow the conventions of standard written English and should be clear and concise.

Look through the answer choices A–E under each question for the exact word or phrase that is included in your revised sentence. If you have thought of a revision that does not include any of the words or phrases listed, try to revise the sentence again so that it does include the wording in one of the answer choices.

You may make notes in your test book, but be sure to mark your answers on the separate answer sheet.

84. Unfortunately, you have incorrectly inferred from my speech criticizing the college administration that I am unalterably opposed to the administration of President Banks.

    Begin with <u>My speech criticizing</u>.

    (A) no inference
    (B) no reference
    (C) no allegation
    (D) no implication
    (E) no desire

85. In any role Patti LuPone undertakes, she is always sheer magic and plays to the gallery as much as to front-row patrons.

    Begin with <u>Fans in the gallery as well as</u>.

    (A) enjoy the sheer magic of Patti LuPone
    (B) undertake the sheer magic of Patti LuPone
    (C) plays the sheer magic of Patti LuPone
    (D) always radiates sheer magic
    (E) act with sheer magic

Exam 2

86. Some historians insist that Columbus did not discover America but that he was preceded on these shores by both Eric the Red and a Mediterranean people, among others.

    Change was preceded to preceded.

    (A) Columbus on these shores
    (B) Eric the Red on these shores
    (C) him on these shores
    (D) a Mediterranean people on these shores
    (E) historians on these shores

87. If all species have some innate desire to reproduce, there is evidence that all living things have one thing in common at least.

    Change If all species have to All species having.

    (A) there was
    (B) was
    (C) is there
    (D) there is
    (E) is

88. A prudent individual should consider all the possibilities before investing money in any plan that seems to promise unlimited profits almost immediately.

    Begin with Before a prudent individual.

    (A) him
    (B) it
    (C) his
    (D) its
    (E) he

89. Neither the president of the class nor any of its members will be permitted to attend the rally in the park this afternoon.

    Substitute Either for Neither.

    (A) and any
    (B) for any
    (C) or any
    (D) with any
    (E) nor any

90. Won't Christine's parents object if you don't take her home by midnight?

    Change the question to a statement.

    (A) shall object
    (B) will object
    (C) will not object
    (D) shall not object
    (E) had not objected

91. Some people are so immature that they cannot accept any frustration without indulging in violent temper tantrums.

    Begin with <u>Some very immature people indulge</u>.

    (A) they are frustrated
    (B) any frustrations
    (C) he is frustrated
    (D) they frustrate
    (E) he frustrates

92. Without the slightest shred of evidence to support the allegation, the prosecutor charged the hostile witness with perjury and demanded his arrest.

    Change <u>the prosecutor charged</u> to <u>the prosecutor demanded</u>.

    (A) the hostile witness' allegation for perjury
    (B) the hostile witness' charged with perjury
    (C) the hostile witness' alleged perjury
    (D) the hostile witness' arrested for perjury
    (E) the hostile witness' arrest for perjury

93. The undertow was so strong that the lifeguard warned all swimmers to return to the beach and not risk being pulled out to sea.

    Begin with <u>All swimmers</u>.

    (A) although
    (B) how
    (C) as much as
    (D) because
    (E) where

94. Thoroughly spoiled children are so obnoxious that even their parents become disgusted with their atrocious behavior.

    Begin with <u>Thoroughly spoiled children behave so</u>.

    (A) atrociously
    (B) atrocious
    (C) disgustedly
    (D) behaviorally
    (E) behavioral

95. Conservative bankers do not agree that providing low interest rates for home loans is the best method of fighting inflation.

    Begin with <u>No conservative banker</u>.

    (A) does not agree
    (B) do agree
    (C) agrees
    (D) has been agreed
    (E) will have agreed

Exam 2

Directions: The following sentences test your knowledge of grammar, usage, diction (choice of words), and idiom.

Some sentences are correct.

No sentence contains more than one error.

You will find that the error, if there is one, is underlined and lettered. Assume that elements of the sentence that are not underlined are correct and cannot be changed. In choosing answers, follow the requirements of standard written English.

If there is an error, select the one underlined part that must be changed to make the sentence correct.

If there is no error, select answer (E).

96. Confirming our lengthy conversation, the shipment will be
    A   B   C
    ordered in a week. No error.
    D   E

97. We can all be grateful that the rain waited until the graduation ceremonies
                      A   B   C
    were over and finished. No error.
    D   E

98. "Nonsense," said the duchess as she puffed on a black cigar. No error.
         A   B   C   D   E

99. Nothing is easier than making a mistake; few things are harder than
            A   B
    to admit that you made one. No error.
    C   D   E

100. "I can see from your essay that you have read the book, unfortunately for
                                        A   B
    you, I can also see that you have not understood it," said the teacher.
         C   D
    No error.
    E

If there is still time remaining, you may review your answers.

English Composition

ANSWER KEY—SAMPLE EXAMINATION 2

1. D	21. B	41. D	61. E	81. B
2. C	22. C	42. E	62. A	82. A
3. C	23. C	43. C	63. A	83. C
4. B	24. B	44. B	64. C	84. D
5. A	25. A	45. C	65. D	85. A
6. E	26. B	46. C	66. B	86. A
7. A	27. B	47. A	67. E	87. E
8. B	28. C	48. D	68. C	88. E
9. E	29. E	49. C	69. D	89. C
10. C	30. A	50. C	70. C	90. B
11. B	31. A	51. B	71. E	91. A
12. A	32. B	52. D	72. C	92. E
13. C	33. D	53. E	73. D	93. D
14. D	34. C	54. C	74. D	94. A
15. D	35. B	55. B	75. A	95. C
16. E	36. A	56. C	76. B	96. C
17. A	37. E	57. B	77. C	97. D
18. C	38. D	58. D	78. C	98. E
19. E	39. C	59. A	79. E	99. C
20. B	40. C	60. B	80. A	100. B

SCORING CHART

After you have scored your Sample Examination 2, enter the results in the chart below; then transfer your score to the Progress Chart on page 12.

Total Test	Number Right	Number Wrong	Number Omitted
100			

ANSWER EXPLANATIONS

1. **(D)** <u>Is</u> is present tense and does not logically follow <u>fought</u> and <u>battled</u>, past tense.

2. **(C)** They, a vague reference of pronouns, seems to refer to the <u>union office</u>.

3. **(C)** <u>Briskly</u> is an ambiguous modifier.

4. **(B)** <u>He</u> and <u>I</u> are wrong pronoun forms; the objective case should be <u>him</u> and <u>me</u>.

5. **(A)** A dangling modifier.

6. **(E)** Sentence is correct.

7. **(A)** A dangling modifier.

8. **(B)** Incorrect idiom.

9. **(E)** Sentence is correct.

10. **(C)** Change <u>their</u> to <u>its</u> since the <u>latest rock group</u> is singular (see <u>has</u>).

11. **(B)** <u>Inferences</u> should be <u>implications</u>.

12. **(A)** <u>Their</u> (in <u>their wallet</u>) is plural and should be changed to either <u>a</u>, <u>his</u>, or <u>her</u>.

13. **(C)** <u>Locate the face</u> is a poor idiom; use <u>recognize</u>.

14. **(D)** <u>In whole</u> is poor word choice; use <u>wholly</u>.

15. **(D)** <u>Is</u> should be <u>are</u>; the word <u>data</u> is plural.

16. **(E)** Sentence is correct.

17. **(A)** <u>True</u> should be <u>truly</u>, the adverbial form.

18. **(C)** <u>Plan on having</u> is a poor idiom; uses <u>plans to have</u>.

19. **(E)** Sentence is correct.

20. **(B)** Eliminate <u>to be</u>—wordy.

21. **(B)** The original sentence contains a cliché; (B) corrects the problem.

22. **(C)** The comma in the original sentence is a comma splice.

23. **(C)** <u>They</u> is a plural; the antecedent is <u>one</u>, singular. (C) corrects the problem.

24. **(B)** Error in parallelism—the section beginning <u>and he</u> is a complete sentence, and the preceding section is a participle.

25. **(A)** The original sentence is correct.

26. **(B)** <u>We</u> should be <u>us</u>, the objective case.

27. **(B)** <u>Hadn't scarcely</u> is a double negative.

28. **(C)** <u>Where</u> is an incorrect word choice—<u>that</u> is correct.

29. **(E)** That type person is a poor idiom.

30. **(A)** The original sentence is correct.

31. **(A)** The original sentence is correct.

32. **(B)** Incorrect word choice, eluded should be alluded.

33. **(D)** The correct pair of conjunctions is as . . . as.

34. **(C)** A misplaced and ambiguous modifier—(C) corrects the problem.

35. **(B)** Old and antique are repetitious; (B) solves the problem.

36. **(A)** The original sentence is correct.

37. **(E)** Except has to be accept.

38. **(D)** The is why construction is ambiguous.

39. **(C)** Whom should be who, the correct case form.

40. **(C)** Neither—nor is the correct conjunction form.

41. **(D)** The sentence is stronger if you simply leave out a weak phrase like nice things.

42. **(E)** What is said in sentence 1 is repeated in sentence 6. The rest of the first paragraph has no direct connection with sentence 1.

43. **(C)** This is the clearest and most concise version.

44. **(B)** In this sentence, the drug problem is treated first as an enemy in a war, then as a plague, and finally as a ghost. It is best to stick to one metaphor at a time.

45. **(C)** Too many different points in a single sentence lead to confusion.

46. **(C)** Professionals in the field are the ones most likely to need this information.

47. **(A)** *Warning* is a synonym for *caveat*.

48. **(D)** Because the writer has already said that no one knows what to do about the drug problem, the paragraph needs to explain why it will not be a waste of money to spend billions of dollars.

49. **(C)** This sentence begins a new topic—types of junipers.

50. **(C)** This version avoids the awkward or illogical constructions in the other choices.

51. **(B)** This version puts the similar ideas concisely in parallel form.

52. **(D)** The original is too colloquial to fit the tone of the passage as a whole. (D) is the only acceptable alternative.

53. **(E)** This choice avoids excess words and maintains the parallel construction.

54. **(C)** The example in sentence 13 can easily be combined into sentence 12.

55. **(B)** Because sentence 18 is providing information about ground cover types of junipers, it should be with the rest of the information about this type of plant.

56. **(C)** Since the amounts for the ingredients are missing, this is not a complete recipe.

57. **(B)** All of the sentences use the imperative mood, the "you" being understood.

58. **(D)** Because this is a set of directions for baking a cake, there is no need for a topic sentence.

59. **(A)** Without a list specifying the amount of each ingredient, the directions would be meaningless.

60. **(B)** Without instructions about the proper oven temperature, the instructions in sentence 7 are not useful.

61. **(E)** The information is straightforward and, therefore, requires no interpretation on the reader's part.

62. **(A)** When you are giving instructions on how to do something, the only logical form of organization is step by step, or chronological.

63. **(A)** The narrative tone as well as the sense of the sentence makes the reader expect that a description of the courtyard will follow.

64. **(C)** The change from the mostly tranquil description of the courtyard to the activity of the gardeners disrupts the mood the author is creating.

65. **(D)** The author's statement about the children playing has neither negative nor positive implications. But the author's need for quiet is evident, since the noise of the children distracts the author from his work.

66. **(B)** In sentence 1, the author says he can see "blooming flowers." In sentence 7, he gives specific names of flowers to illustrate his point.

67. **(E)** Sentences 6 and 8 both describe the trees in the courtyard.

68. **(C)** Until this last sentence, the mood of the paragraph has been one of tranquillity and joy in the beauty of nature. The mood changes to one of gloom with the mention of frost and the visions that come with it.

69. **(D)** In sentence 7, *until frost comes* suggests that frost is not very far off. Sentence 8 says specifically that the *fall leaf color change* has already begun.

70. **(C)** There is no need for the extra words in any of the other choices.

71. **(E)** This is the only version that keeps the parallel construction.

72. **(C)** There is nothing grammatically wrong with repeating a word, and sometimes a writer will do it for rhetorical effect. In this case, however, the repetition calls unnecessary attention to an unimportant word.

73. **(D)** The first part of the passage describes the problem. Sentence 6 begins the discussion of a possible solution that could logically be a new paragraph.

74. **(D)** This is the only choice that makes clear the cause-effect relationship between the two parts of the sentence.

75. **(A)** *Alleviate* does not change the meaning, but is better suited to the formal tone of the passage than *fix up* is.

76. **(B)** This is a logical conclusion for the passage and maintains the tone.

77. **(C)** Because sentence 5 describes what you do after visiting Vallombrosa, it should come after all the discussion of Vallombrosa.

78. **(C)** Most of the passage is written in the second person (*you*), but the second part of sentence 8 switches to the third person (*one*). Either *one* or *you* would be perfectly acceptable, but the author must use the same case throughout.

79. **(E)** Specific is almost always better than vague. This makes choice (E) preferable to choices (A) or (B). Choices (C) and (D) claim more than the rest of the passage can justify.

80. **(A)** The Casentino may not be familiar to readers, so it should be identified when it is first mentioned.

81. **(B)** Because the first part of the sentence begins with *after*, the time sequence has already been established and *subsequently* is not needed.

82. **(A)** This is the only choice that is clear, grammatically correct, and free from misplaced or dangling modifiers.

83. **(C)** Identification of the villages should be provided when they are first mentioned.

84. **(D)** My speech criticizing the college administration contained *no implication* that I am unalterably opposed to the administration of President Banks.

85. **(A)** Fans in the gallery as well as front row patrons *enjoy the sheer magic of Patti LuPone*, playing any role she undertakes.

86. **(A)** Some historians insist that both Eric the Red and a Mediterranean people preceded *Columbus on these shores*; therefore, the claim that Columbus discovered America may be false.

87. **(E)** All species having some innate desire to reproduce is one piece of evidence that all living things have one thing in common at least.

88. **(E)** Before a prudent individual invests money in any plan that seems to promise unlimited profits at once, *he* should investigate all the possibilities.

89. **(C)** Either the president of the class *or any* of its members will not be permitted to attend the rally in the park this afternoon.

90. **(B)** Christine's parents *will object* if you don't take her home by midnight.

91. **(A)** Some very immature people indulge in violent temper tantrums whenever *they are frustrated.*

92. **(E)** Without the slightest shred of evidence to support the allegation, the prosecutor demanded *the hostile witness' arrest for perjury.*

93. **(D)** All swimmers were warned by the lifeguard to return to the beach *because* of the dangerous undertow that might pull them out to sea.

94. **(A)** Thoroughly spoiled children behave so *atrociously* that even their parents are disgusted by their obnoxious behavior.

95. **(C)** No conservative banker *agrees* that providing low interest rates for home loans is the best method of fighting inflation.

96. **(C)** This is a dangling modifier. According to the sentence, the shipment—not the speaker—confirmed the conversation. One possible revision: Confirming our lengthy conversation, I have arranged for the shipment to be ordered in a week.

97. **(D)** *Over* and *finished* are such close synonyms that only one of them is needed.

98. **(E)** There is no error in this sentence.

99. **(C)** To admit should be admitting to be parallel to *making*.

100. **(B)** There should be a period after book, and a new sentence should begin with unfortunately. In the original, it is not clear whether the phrase *unfortunately for you* belongs with the first part of the sentence or the second.

THE HUMANITIES EXAMINATION

Humanities

1 Ⓐ Ⓑ Ⓒ Ⓓ Ⓔ	39 Ⓐ Ⓑ Ⓒ Ⓓ Ⓔ	77 Ⓐ Ⓑ Ⓒ Ⓓ Ⓔ	115 Ⓐ Ⓑ Ⓒ Ⓓ Ⓔ
2 Ⓐ Ⓑ Ⓒ Ⓓ Ⓔ	40 Ⓐ Ⓑ Ⓒ Ⓓ Ⓔ	78 Ⓐ Ⓑ Ⓒ Ⓓ Ⓔ	116 Ⓐ Ⓑ Ⓒ Ⓓ Ⓔ
3 Ⓐ Ⓑ Ⓒ Ⓓ Ⓔ	41 Ⓐ Ⓑ Ⓒ Ⓓ Ⓔ	79 Ⓐ Ⓑ Ⓒ Ⓓ Ⓔ	117 Ⓐ Ⓑ Ⓒ Ⓓ Ⓔ
4 Ⓐ Ⓑ Ⓒ Ⓓ Ⓔ	42 Ⓐ Ⓑ Ⓒ Ⓓ Ⓔ	80 Ⓐ Ⓑ Ⓒ Ⓓ Ⓔ	118 Ⓐ Ⓑ Ⓒ Ⓓ Ⓔ
5 Ⓐ Ⓑ Ⓒ Ⓓ Ⓔ	43 Ⓐ Ⓑ Ⓒ Ⓓ Ⓔ	81 Ⓐ Ⓑ Ⓒ Ⓓ Ⓔ	119 Ⓐ Ⓑ Ⓒ Ⓓ Ⓔ
6 Ⓐ Ⓑ Ⓒ Ⓓ Ⓔ	44 Ⓐ Ⓑ Ⓒ Ⓓ Ⓔ	82 Ⓐ Ⓑ Ⓒ Ⓓ Ⓔ	120 Ⓐ Ⓑ Ⓒ Ⓓ Ⓔ
7 Ⓐ Ⓑ Ⓒ Ⓓ Ⓔ	45 Ⓐ Ⓑ Ⓒ Ⓓ Ⓔ	83 Ⓐ Ⓑ Ⓒ Ⓓ Ⓔ	121 Ⓐ Ⓑ Ⓒ Ⓓ Ⓔ
8 Ⓐ Ⓑ Ⓒ Ⓓ Ⓔ	46 Ⓐ Ⓑ Ⓒ Ⓓ Ⓔ	84 Ⓐ Ⓑ Ⓒ Ⓓ Ⓔ	122 Ⓐ Ⓑ Ⓒ Ⓓ Ⓔ
9 Ⓐ Ⓑ Ⓒ Ⓓ Ⓔ	47 Ⓐ Ⓑ Ⓒ Ⓓ Ⓔ	85 Ⓐ Ⓑ Ⓒ Ⓓ Ⓔ	123 Ⓐ Ⓑ Ⓒ Ⓓ Ⓔ
10 Ⓐ Ⓑ Ⓒ Ⓓ Ⓔ	48 Ⓐ Ⓑ Ⓒ Ⓓ Ⓔ	86 Ⓐ Ⓑ Ⓒ Ⓓ Ⓔ	124 Ⓐ Ⓑ Ⓒ Ⓓ Ⓔ
11 Ⓐ Ⓑ Ⓒ Ⓓ Ⓔ	49 Ⓐ Ⓑ Ⓒ Ⓓ Ⓔ	87 Ⓐ Ⓑ Ⓒ Ⓓ Ⓔ	125 Ⓐ Ⓑ Ⓒ Ⓓ Ⓔ
12 Ⓐ Ⓑ Ⓒ Ⓓ Ⓔ	50 Ⓐ Ⓑ Ⓒ Ⓓ Ⓔ	88 Ⓐ Ⓑ Ⓒ Ⓓ Ⓔ	126 Ⓐ Ⓑ Ⓒ Ⓓ Ⓔ
13 Ⓐ Ⓑ Ⓒ Ⓓ Ⓔ	51 Ⓐ Ⓑ Ⓒ Ⓓ Ⓔ	88 Ⓐ Ⓑ Ⓒ Ⓓ Ⓔ	127 Ⓐ Ⓑ Ⓒ Ⓓ Ⓔ
14 Ⓐ Ⓑ Ⓒ Ⓓ Ⓔ	52 Ⓐ Ⓑ Ⓒ Ⓓ Ⓔ	90 Ⓐ Ⓑ Ⓒ Ⓓ Ⓔ	128 Ⓐ Ⓑ Ⓒ Ⓓ Ⓔ
15 Ⓐ Ⓑ Ⓒ Ⓓ Ⓔ	53 Ⓐ Ⓑ Ⓒ Ⓓ Ⓔ	91 Ⓐ Ⓑ Ⓒ Ⓓ Ⓔ	129 Ⓐ Ⓑ Ⓒ Ⓓ Ⓔ
16 Ⓐ Ⓑ Ⓒ Ⓓ Ⓔ	54 Ⓐ Ⓑ Ⓒ Ⓓ Ⓔ	92 Ⓐ Ⓑ Ⓒ Ⓓ Ⓔ	130 Ⓐ Ⓑ Ⓒ Ⓓ Ⓔ
17 Ⓐ Ⓑ Ⓒ Ⓓ Ⓔ	55 Ⓐ Ⓑ Ⓒ Ⓓ Ⓔ	93 Ⓐ Ⓑ Ⓒ Ⓓ Ⓔ	131 Ⓐ Ⓑ Ⓒ Ⓓ Ⓔ
18 Ⓐ Ⓑ Ⓒ Ⓓ Ⓔ	56 Ⓐ Ⓑ Ⓒ Ⓓ Ⓔ	94 Ⓐ Ⓑ Ⓒ Ⓓ Ⓔ	132 Ⓐ Ⓑ Ⓒ Ⓓ Ⓔ
19 Ⓐ Ⓑ Ⓒ Ⓓ Ⓔ	57 Ⓐ Ⓑ Ⓒ Ⓓ Ⓔ	95 Ⓐ Ⓑ Ⓒ Ⓓ Ⓔ	133 Ⓐ Ⓑ Ⓒ Ⓓ Ⓔ
20 Ⓐ Ⓑ Ⓒ Ⓓ Ⓔ	58 Ⓐ Ⓑ Ⓒ Ⓓ Ⓔ	96 Ⓐ Ⓑ Ⓒ Ⓓ Ⓔ	134 Ⓐ Ⓑ Ⓒ Ⓓ Ⓔ
21 Ⓐ Ⓑ Ⓒ Ⓓ Ⓔ	59 Ⓐ Ⓑ Ⓒ Ⓓ Ⓔ	97 Ⓐ Ⓑ Ⓒ Ⓓ Ⓔ	135 Ⓐ Ⓑ Ⓒ Ⓓ Ⓔ
22 Ⓐ Ⓑ Ⓒ Ⓓ Ⓔ	60 Ⓐ Ⓑ Ⓒ Ⓓ Ⓔ	98 Ⓐ Ⓑ Ⓒ Ⓓ Ⓔ	136 Ⓐ Ⓑ Ⓒ Ⓓ Ⓔ
23 Ⓐ Ⓑ Ⓒ Ⓓ Ⓔ	61 Ⓐ Ⓑ Ⓒ Ⓓ Ⓔ	99 Ⓐ Ⓑ Ⓒ Ⓓ Ⓔ	137 Ⓐ Ⓑ Ⓒ Ⓓ Ⓔ
24 Ⓐ Ⓑ Ⓒ Ⓓ Ⓔ	62 Ⓐ Ⓑ Ⓒ Ⓓ Ⓔ	100 Ⓐ Ⓑ Ⓒ Ⓓ Ⓔ	138 Ⓐ Ⓑ Ⓒ Ⓓ Ⓔ
25 Ⓐ Ⓑ Ⓒ Ⓓ Ⓔ	63 Ⓐ Ⓑ Ⓒ Ⓓ Ⓔ	101 Ⓐ Ⓑ Ⓒ Ⓓ Ⓔ	139 Ⓐ Ⓑ Ⓒ Ⓓ Ⓔ
26 Ⓐ Ⓑ Ⓒ Ⓓ Ⓔ	64 Ⓐ Ⓑ Ⓒ Ⓓ Ⓔ	102 Ⓐ Ⓑ Ⓒ Ⓓ Ⓔ	140 Ⓐ Ⓑ Ⓒ Ⓓ Ⓔ
27 Ⓐ Ⓑ Ⓒ Ⓓ Ⓔ	65 Ⓐ Ⓑ Ⓒ Ⓓ Ⓔ	103 Ⓐ Ⓑ Ⓒ Ⓓ Ⓔ	141 Ⓐ Ⓑ Ⓒ Ⓓ Ⓔ
28 Ⓐ Ⓑ Ⓒ Ⓓ Ⓔ	66 Ⓐ Ⓑ Ⓒ Ⓓ Ⓔ	104 Ⓐ Ⓑ Ⓒ Ⓓ Ⓔ	142 Ⓐ Ⓑ Ⓒ Ⓓ Ⓔ
29 Ⓐ Ⓑ Ⓒ Ⓓ Ⓔ	67 Ⓐ Ⓑ Ⓒ Ⓓ Ⓔ	105 Ⓐ Ⓑ Ⓒ Ⓓ Ⓔ	143 Ⓐ Ⓑ Ⓒ Ⓓ Ⓔ
30 Ⓐ Ⓑ Ⓒ Ⓓ Ⓔ	68 Ⓐ Ⓑ Ⓒ Ⓓ Ⓔ	106 Ⓐ Ⓑ Ⓒ Ⓓ Ⓔ	144 Ⓐ Ⓑ Ⓒ Ⓓ Ⓔ
31 Ⓐ Ⓑ Ⓒ Ⓓ Ⓔ	69 Ⓐ Ⓑ Ⓒ Ⓓ Ⓔ	107 Ⓐ Ⓑ Ⓒ Ⓓ Ⓔ	145 Ⓐ Ⓑ Ⓒ Ⓓ Ⓔ
32 Ⓐ Ⓑ Ⓒ Ⓓ Ⓔ	70 Ⓐ Ⓑ Ⓒ Ⓓ Ⓔ	108 Ⓐ Ⓑ Ⓒ Ⓓ Ⓔ	146 Ⓐ Ⓑ Ⓒ Ⓓ Ⓔ
33 Ⓐ Ⓑ Ⓒ Ⓓ Ⓔ	71 Ⓐ Ⓑ Ⓒ Ⓓ Ⓔ	109 Ⓐ Ⓑ Ⓒ Ⓓ Ⓔ	147 Ⓐ Ⓑ Ⓒ Ⓓ Ⓔ
34 Ⓐ Ⓑ Ⓒ Ⓓ Ⓔ	72 Ⓐ Ⓑ Ⓒ Ⓓ Ⓔ	110 Ⓐ Ⓑ Ⓒ Ⓓ Ⓔ	148 Ⓐ Ⓑ Ⓒ Ⓓ Ⓔ
35 Ⓐ Ⓑ Ⓒ Ⓓ Ⓔ	73 Ⓐ Ⓑ Ⓒ Ⓓ Ⓔ	111 Ⓐ Ⓑ Ⓒ Ⓓ Ⓔ	149 Ⓐ Ⓑ Ⓒ Ⓓ Ⓔ
36 Ⓐ Ⓑ Ⓒ Ⓓ Ⓔ	74 Ⓐ Ⓑ Ⓒ Ⓓ Ⓔ	112 Ⓐ Ⓑ Ⓒ Ⓓ Ⓔ	150 Ⓐ Ⓑ Ⓒ Ⓓ Ⓔ
37 Ⓐ Ⓑ Ⓒ Ⓓ Ⓔ	75 Ⓐ Ⓑ Ⓒ Ⓓ Ⓔ	113 Ⓐ Ⓑ Ⓒ Ⓓ Ⓔ	
38 Ⓐ Ⓑ Ⓒ Ⓓ Ⓔ	76 Ⓐ Ⓑ Ⓒ Ⓓ Ⓔ	114 Ⓐ Ⓑ Ⓒ Ⓓ Ⓔ	

Trial Test

This chapter contains a Trial Test in Humanities. Take this Trial Test to learn what the actual exam is like and to determine how you might score on the exam before any practice or review.

The CLEP Exam in Humanities measures your knowledge of literature and the fine arts—the visual arts such as painting and sculpture, music, the performing arts such as drama, dance, and architecture.

NUMBER OF QUESTIONS ON THE TRIAL TEST: 150

Time limit: 90 MINUTES

Directions: Each of the questions or incomplete statements below is followed by five suggested answers or completions. Select the one that is best in each case.

1. Expressionism in art has most to do with

   (A) the intellect
   (B) the emotions
   (C) the dream world
   (D) geometric forms
   (E) decorative line

2. The Impressionists were least concerned with

   (A) the effects of light
   (B) informal treatment of subject matter
   (C) painting out of doors
   (D) interpenetration of forms
   (E) broken application of color

3. The length of a vibrating string or a column of air and the pitch either produces constituted the beginning of the science of

   (A) logarithms
   (B) rhythms
   (C) acoustics
   (D) theory
   (E) fuguery

4. The man who, practically single-handedly, unified the ballet and founded French opera was

    (A) Lully
    (B) Glinka
    (C) Gluck
    (D) Massenet
    (E) Offenbach

5. An important architect of the Romantic period was

    (A) Walter Gropius
    (B) Christopher Wren
    (C) James Wyatt
    (D) Joseph Paxton
    (E) Henri Labrouste

6. Ibsen did not write

    (A) plays about contemporary people
    (B) plays with realistic settings
    (C) plays employing well-made structure
    (D) comedies of manners
    (E) thesis plays

7. The release of emotions and the attaining of tranquillity therefrom in the theater is called

    (A) pyramidal plot structure
    (B) the author's use of hubris
    (C) the audience escaping dull lives by identifying with kings, aristocrats, and famous people
    (D) empathy
    (E) catharsis

8. One of the most characteristic types of 18th-century literature was the

    (A) novella
    (B) epic
    (C) nature poem
    (D) periodical essay
    (E) thesis play

9. Harriet Beecher Stowe unwittingly became a pioneer when she wrote the "propaganda novel"

    (A) *Erewhon*
    (B) *A Man's Woman*
    (C) *The Female Quixote*
    (D) *Uncle Tom's Cabin*
    (E) *The Mysterious Stranger*

10. "Brush my brow with burnished bronze" is an example of

    (A) alliteration
    (B) consonance
    (C) dissonance
    (D) onomatopoeia
    (E) free verse

11. Stravinsky's "Rite of Spring"

    (A) is a Baroque-style program piece
    (B) was called the destruction of music
    (C) is representative of the Classical styles
    (D) is in sonata-allegro form
    (E) is a symphony

12. An instrumental form usually associated with opera is

    (A) the overture
    (B) the symphony
    (C) the suite
    (D) the tone poem
    (E) the cadenza

13. The type of architecture shown is found in

    (A) India
    (B) Greece
    (C) The United States
    (D) Russia
    (E) Iran

14. Paintings that reflect an interest in the fantastic, dream associations, and the impossible are most likely to have been executed by

    (A) Cézanne, van Gogh, Toulouse-Lautrec
    (B) Gris, Braque, Picasso
    (C) Dali, Miró, de Chirico
    (D) Pollack, Motherwell, Mondrian
    (E) Renoir, Degas, Seurat

15. Confucius, Buddha, and Socrates, all born at the time when "the human mind seems first to have turned over in its sleep," lived in approximately

    (A) 1200–1100 B.C.
    (B) 2500–2400 B.C.
    (C) 5000 4000 B.C.
    (D) 800–700 B.C.
    (E) 600–400 B.C.

Questions 16 and 17 refer to the following quotation.

> *"O mother, mother, make my bed,*
> *O make it soft and narrow:*
> *Since my love died for me today,*
> *I'll die for him tomorrow."*

16. Which of the following describes these lines?

    (A) a couplet
    (B) a triolet
    (C) a quatrain
    (D) a tercet
    (E) a sestet

17. The lines are from the ballad

    (A) "Sir Patrick Spens"
    (B) "Barbara Allen"
    (C) "Lord Randall"
    (D) "The Three Ravens"
    (E) "Robin Hood and the Three Squires"

18. Pop art refers to

    (A) musical themes
    (B) abstract Expressionism
    (C) contemporary materialism and commercialism
    (D) the religious revival in contemporary art
    (E) a return to Classicism

19. The first to dedicate their art to the beauty of the human form were the

    (A) Egyptians
    (B) Renaissance artists
    (C) Romans
    (D) Greeks
    (E) French Impressionists

20. Frank Lloyd Wright's basic role in architecture was

    (A) to build a structure that was inexpensive
    (B) to use a minimum of materials
    (C) to build a structure in harmony with the past
    (D) to build a structure that looked as if it grew out of the ground
    (E) to build a structure that overpowers man and nature

21. Albert Camus said that capital punishment is

    (A) necessary and desirable
    (B) necessary but undesirable
    (C) murder
    (D) a 20th-century innovation
    (E) both (A) and (C)

22. One of the greatest of the Middle High German epics is

    (A) *The Nibelungenlied*
    (B) *The Story of Sigurd the Volsung*
    (C) *Beowulf*
    (D) *The Vikings at Helgeland*
    (E) *The Valkyrie*

23. A famous piece of music often associated with graduation exercises was written by

    (A) Elgar
    (B) Condon
    (C) Gluck
    (D) Palestrina
    (E) Haydn

24. A famous jazz guitarist of the 1940s was

    (A) F. Waller
    (B) B. Davidson
    (C) E. Condon
    (D) J. Teagarden
    (E) M. Feld

25. Shakespeare was noted for all but one of the following:

    (A) comedies
    (B) tragedies
    (C) bourgeois dramas
    (D) histories
    (E) tragicomedies

26. An outdoor amphitheater seating 20,000 people that has been the scene of ballets and popular concerts directed by world-famous orchestral conductors is the

    (A) Rose Bowl
    (B) Snow Bowl
    (C) Hollywood Bowl
    (D) Musitoreum
    (E) Sunshine Theater

27. The "father" of Greek tragedy was

    (A) Aristotle
    (B) Sophocles
    (C) Euripides
    (D) Aeschylus
    (E) Aristophanes

28. All but one of the following are parts of the Greek theater:

    (A) eccyclema
    (B) skene
    (C) deus ex machina
    (D) orchestra
    (E) movable panels

29. In music, the sign # is called a

    (A) flat
    (B) sharp
    (C) bass clef
    (D) treble clef
    (E) time signature

30. The term "Western man" or "Western civilization" refers to

    (A) the Western hemisphere
    (B) our present cultural tradition going back about 4,000 years
    (C) a force of history that always moves to the west
    (D) Europe
    (E) Canada and the United States

31. Richard Strauss is best known for his

    (A) fugues
    (B) motets
    (C) waltzes
    (D) madrigals
    (E) tone poems

32. Albert Camus, French existentialist writer, believed that the only real philosophical problem was that of suicide. What Shakespearean character expresses this same thought?

    (A) Iago
    (B) Cleopatra
    (C) Hamlet
    (D) Caliban
    (E) Julius Caesar

33. Cubism is indebted to the pioneering work of

    (A) Pollack
    (B) Cézanne
    (C) van Gogh
    (D) Munch
    (E) Hals

34. Which one of the following is not a stylistic (formal) element of Cubism?

    (A) compressed or "flat" space
    (B) multiple perspective
    (C) atmospheric perspective
    (D) interpenetration of line, color, and shape
    (E) an equal stress on negative and positive areas

35. The term *clerestory* would most likely be used by a(n)

    (A) poet
    (B) architect
    (C) sculptor
    (D) painter
    (E) musician

36. All of the following short stories were written by Edgar Allan Poe *except*

    (A) "The Fall of the House of Usher"
    (B) "The Murders in the Rue Morgue"
    (C) "Rappaccini's Daughter"
    (D) "The Purloined Letter"
    (E) "The Cask of Amontillado"

37. Sculpture is the art of

    (A) making lifelike figures
    (B) making statues of heroes
    (C) making memorials to heroes
    (D) cutting stone and marble
    (E) composing in mass and space

38. The philosopher famous for the doctrine that "to be is to be perceived" is

    (A) Berkeley
    (B) Leibniz
    (C) Hegel
    (D) Plato
    (E) Hume

39. The beginning of the Renaissance may be traced to the city of

    (A) Rome
    (B) San Miniate
    (C) Venice
    (D) Florence
    (E) Athens

40. The "School of Lyon" was

    (A) a 16th-century group of Neo-Platonist and Petrarchan poets
    (B) an 18th-century artistic movement
    (C) the college attended by Hugo and de Maupassant
    (D) a chamber music society founded by Massenet
    (E) an attempt to establish a classical spirit in French painting

41. The first American most naturalistic novel, *Maggie: A Girl of the Streets*, was written by

    (A) Anderson
    (B) Garland
    (C) Norris
    (D) Crane
    (E) Robinson

42. The painters Renoir, Monet, and Pissaro were

    (A) Expressionists
    (B) Cubists
    (C) Mannerists
    (D) Impressionists
    (E) Surrealists

43. The Romans made special use of

   (A) post and lintel construction
   (B) friezes carved over temple doorways
   (C) the rounded arch
   (D) the pointed arch
   (E) tempera painting

44. In music, a smooth transition from key to key is known as

   (A) modulation
   (B) constructioning
   (C) harmony
   (D) invention
   (E) translation

45. All of the following deal with the Trojan War or the men who fought in that war *except*

   (A) *The Odyssey*
   (B) *Agamemnon*
   (C) *The Iliad*
   (D) *Oedipus the King*
   (E) *The Aeneid*

46. This well-known landmark is found in

   (A) New York Harbor
   (B) Ceylon
   (C) India
   (D) Australia
   (E) Japan

47. The first major American author to be born west of the Mississippi was

   (A) William Dean Howells
   (B) Walt Whitman
   (C) Carl Sandburg
   (D) Mark Twain
   (E) Ellen Glasgow

48. "Twas brillig, and the slithy toves, Did gyre and gimble in the wabe," is an example of

   (A) *vers de société*
   (B) nonsense verse
   (C) a limerick
   (D) shaped verse
   (E) Goliardic verse

49. Farcical interludes in dramas

   (A) developed during the Middle Ages
   (B) dealt with sin
   (C) were essentially romantic comedies
   (D) developed during the Renaissance
   (E) adhered to the unities of time, place, and action

50. *The Decameron*, like *The Canterbury Tales*, has a specific dramatic framework. However, instead of pilgrims journeying to Canterbury, *The Decameron* has seven women and three men withdrawing from their native city for what purpose?

   (A) To seek the Holy Grail
   (B) To visit the Pope
   (C) To see Charles the Great
   (D) To make pilgrimage to the tomb of Abelard
   (E) To escape the Black Death

51. "All pigs are equal, but some pigs are more equal than others" is reminiscent of what novel?

   (A) *Lassie, Come Home*
   (B) *The Red Pony*
   (C) *Federico and his Falcon*
   (D) *Animal Farm*
   (E) *A Day at the Zoo*

52. An American tap dancer who appeared in musical comedies, revues, and motion pictures is

   (A) Mikhail Baryshnikov
   (B) Ray Jones
   (C) Adolph Bolm
   (D) David Klein
   (E) Ray Bolger

53. "The Grand Canyon Suite" was composed by

    (A) Anton Dvorák
    (B) George M. Cohan
    (C) Edward McDowell
    (D) Aaron Copland
    (E) Ferde Grofé

54. The medieval architect symbolized God's presence in the cathedral by

    (A) creating great areas of interior space
    (B) embellishing the surface with great columns and lacy decorations
    (C) creating the choir and high altar areas
    (D) combining the arts of painting and free-standing sculpture
    (E) placing gargoyles atop the roof to ward off evil spirits

55. "The lost generation" refers to those who lived during the period

    (A) 1900–1915
    (B) 1920–1940
    (C) 1940–1950
    (D) 1950–1960
    (E) 1960–1970

56. A leader of the "beat generation" was

    (A) Ernest Hemingway
    (B) John Steinbeck
    (C) Jack Kerouac
    (D) Ring Lardner
    (E) Flannery O'Connor

57. A short narrative from which a moral can be drawn is

    (A) a parable
    (B) an anecdote
    (C) an abstraction
    (D) an aphorism
    (E) a frame story

58. Lascaux and Altamira are

    (A) two French Gothic cathedrals
    (B) two painters working in a surrealistic style
    (C) caves in which prehistoric paintings have been found
    (D) mythological subjects used by Pierre Cot in "The Tempest"
    (E) leaders in the Fauve movement

59. A feeling of unrest and tension in a painting can be achieved by a powerful emphasis upon

    (A) horizontal line
    (B) vertical line
    (C) parallel line
    (D) diagonal line
    (E) linear grid pattern

60. The way in which we perceive abstractly is largely determined by

    (A) cultural conditioning
    (B) memory learning
    (C) individual genes
    (D) intellectual association
    (E) abstract behavior patterns

61. One of the first American "troubadors" and minstrels was

    (A) Vachel Lindsay
    (B) Edward McDowell
    (C) John Knowles Pain
    (D) Aaron Copland
    (E) Stephen Foster

62. An early American statesman, writer, inventor, and foreign correspondent, also known as the first American music critic, was

    (A) Paul Revere
    (B) Cotton Mather
    (C) Benjamin Franklin
    (D) Thomas Jefferson
    (E) Patrick Henry

63. "I have measured out my life with coffee spoons," said

    (A) Benjamin Compson
    (B) Lady Brett Ashley
    (C) Scarlet O'Hara
    (D) Phillip Jordan
    (E) J. Alfred Prufrock

64. A "mystery circle" may best be described as

    (A) based upon scriptures
    (B) basically religious
    (C) short biblical plays produced outside the church
    (D) performed by the guilds
    (E) all of the above

65. Which of the following has been hailed as a great novel of the women's movement?

    (A) *The Golden Notebook* by Doris Lessing
    (B) *Emma* by Jane Austen
    (C) *Wise Blood* by Flannery O'Connor
    (D) *Fluff* by Virginia Woolf
    (E) *Swain* by Carolyn Kimball

66. A satire on the medieval chivalric code is

    (A) *Don Quixote*
    (B) *Gulliver's Travels*
    (C) *Candide*
    (D) *Idylls of the King*
    (E) *Erewhon*

67. One of the most popular English painters of the 18th century, noted for his society portraits, was

    (A) John Singleton Copley
    (B) Sir Edward Burne-Jones
    (C) Thomas Gainsborough
    (D) John Constable
    (E) William Blake

68. Included among Johann Sebastian Bach's great works is

    (A) "The Well-Tempered Clavier"
    (B) "The Pathétique Sonata"
    (C) *The Student Prince*
    (D) "The Unfinished Symphony"
    (E) *Der Rosenkavalier*

69. Included among Beethoven's great works is

    (A) "The Symphonie Espagnole"
    (B) "The Moonlight Sonata"
    (C) "The Mass in B Minor"
    (D) *Messiah*
    (E) "The Minute Waltz"

70. Nicknamed "Red," the man who became famous for his novels about "main street" America was

    (A) Ernest Hemingway
    (B) John Steinbeck
    (C) Sinclair Lewis
    (D) Upton Sinclair
    (E) Booth Tarkington

71. The creative process is

    (A) limited to art
    (B) limited to art and music
    (C) limited to the humanities
    (D) limited to the arts and sciences
    (E) not limited

72. Of the Greek playwrights, Euripides is considered the most "modern" because he

    (A) usually disregards the unities
    (B) concentrates on message rather than moments
    (C) does not use women as protagonists
    (D) stresses his belief in reform
    (E) is most psychological in his treatment of conflict

73. Of which playwright is the following true: Nearly every character in his plays is at one time or another the hero of a tiny "microcosmic" drama that has a beginning, middle, and an end in itself, but does not become the basis for the total plot?

    (A) George Bernard Shaw
    (B) Henrik Ibsen
    (C) Arthur Miller
    (D) Anton Chekov
    (E) Oscar Wilde

74. The opera *I Pagliacci* was written by

    (A) Puccini
    (B) Leoncavallo
    (C) Mascagni
    (D) Verdi
    (E) Mozart

75. In music, this sign ♭ is called a

    (A) flat
    (B) sharp
    (C) bass clef
    (D) treble clef
    (E) time signature

76. The photograph at the right is

    (A) Nike of Samothrace
    (B) Venus de Milo
    (C) Mercury
    (D) Apollo Belvedere
    (E) Dionysius

©Bettmann/Corbis

77. The audiences who attended Shakespeare's plays were

    (A) aristocrats who enjoyed occasionally letting their hair down
    (B) commoners who had aristocratic taste in poetry
    (C) primarily drawn from the middle classes
    (D) a mixture of all classes
    (E) the most tightly knit "in group" in the history of the theater

78. All of the following represent serious barriers to critical perception of plays and films *except*

    (A) failing to remember that a drama is not reality
    (B) viewing the drama in terms of a particular occupation with which the viewer is familiar
    (C) reacting to the characterization of an ethnic type
    (D) accepting the drama on its own terms without any bias
    (E) entering the theater with the expectation of seeing one's moral values upheld

79. All of the following painters were called by critics "Fauve" or "wild beasts" *except*

    (A) Matisse
    (B) Dufy
    (C) Vlaminck
    (D) Rouault
    (E) Gauguin

80. The chief exponent of pointillism was

    (A) Cézanne
    (B) Monet
    (C) de Chirico
    (D) Courbet
    (E) Seurat

81. A leading rock group of the late 1960s took its name from the title of a novel by a German author who died in 1962 and whose works have recently won a new following. The book and the author are

    (A) *Steppenwolf* by Hermann Hesse
    (B) *Death in Venice* by Thomas Mann
    (C) *The Weavers* by Gerhart Hauptmann
    (D) *Siddhartha* by Hermann Hesse
    (E) *The Castle* by Franz Kafka

82. A chromatic scale is

    (A) all half steps played in order
    (B) every other half step played in order
    (C) no half steps played
    (D) only half steps played
    (E) all full steps played in order

Questions 83–85 refer to the following lines:

Come live with me, and be my love,
And we will all the pleasures prove,
That valleys, groves, hills, and fields,
Woods or steepy mountains yields.

83. These lines are from

    (A) "The Passionate Shepherd to His Love"
    (B) "The Shepherd's Wife's Song"
    (C) "A Strange Passion of a Lover"
    (D) one of Shakespeare's sonnets
    (E) "Troilus and Cressida"

84. The lines were written by

    (A) William Shakespeare
    (B) Christopher Marlowe
    (C) John Lyly
    (D) T.S. Eliot
    (E) Alexander Pope

85. The verse form is a

    (A) couplet
    (B) sestina
    (C) sonnet
    (D) quatrain
    (E) cinquaine

86. Most basic to a fundamental appreciation of art are

    (A) seeing and feeling
    (B) words and descriptions
    (C) knowing the life of the artist and understanding his or her ethnic background
    (D) understanding the theories of art and their corollaries
    (E) courses in art history

87. "Comfort ye, comfort ye, my people," saith your God. "Speak ye comfortably to Jerusalem, and cry unto her, that her warfare is accomplished, that her iniquity is pardoned."

    The source of this quotation, which is a portion of the libretto of Handel's Messiah and was taken directly from the Bible, was

    (A) Amos
    (B) Misab
    (C) Isaiah
    (D) Ezekiel
    (E) Hosea

Questions 88–90 refer to the following groups of people:

    (A) John Williams, Burt Bacharach, Henry Mancini

    (B) Sir George Solti, André Previn, Leonard Bernstein

    (C) John Steinbeck, William Faulkner, Sinclair Lewis

    (D) Andy Warhol, Joan Miró, Claes Oldenburg

    (E) Twyla Tharp, Michael Bennett, Gower Champion

88. Which is a group of contemporary symphony conductors?

89. Which is a group of novelists who won the Nobel Prize for Literature?

90. Which is a group of choreographers for Broadway musicals of the 1970s and 1980s?

91. *The Great Gatsby* was written by

    (A) Emerson
    (B) Lewis
    (C) Dreiser
    (D) Dos Passos
    (E) Fitzgerald

92. Nietzsche said that the noble man

    (A) never notices the unfortunate
    (B) always helps the unfortunate out of pity
    (C) always seeks to eradicate the unfortunate
    (D) helps the unfortunate, not from pity, but rather from an impulse generated out of a superabundance of power
    (E) always tries to trick the unfortunate into helping him

93. *Kiss Me Kate* is based upon William Shakespeare's play

    (A) *Romeo and Juliet*
    (B) *The Winter's Tale*
    (C) *A Midsummer Night's Dream*
    (D) *The Tempest*
    (E) *The Taming of the Shrew*

94. The artist van Gogh wrote that he

    (A) did his best not to put in detail
    (B) avoided using black altogether
    (C) could paint only when he was nervous
    (D) became an artist in order to travel and see the world
    (E) became an artist in order to prove he was sane

95. The musical notation indicates

    (A) the bass clef
    (B) crescendo
    (C) pianissimo
    (D) the treble clef
    (E) 1/2 time

96. A term used to describe choral music without instrumental accompaniment is

    (A) cantilena
    (B) a cappella
    (C) enharmonic
    (D) appoggiatura
    (E) oratorio

97. All of the following are part of Wagner's cycle of operas *Der Ring des Nibelungen* except

    (A) *Das Rheingold*
    (B) *Die Walküre*
    (C) *Die Meistersinger von Nürnberg*
    (D) *Siegfried*
    (E) *Die Götterdämmerung*

98. A Southern writer well known for her short stories, as well as her novels *Wise Blood* and *The Violent Bear It Away*, is

    (A) Gwendolyn Brooks
    (B) Jean Auel
    (C) Frances Cassidy
    (D) Flannery O'Connor
    (E) Elizabeth James

99. Baroque architecture is characterized by

    (A) severe simplicity
    (B) ornamentation and curved lines
    (C) post and lintel construction
    (D) steel and reinforced concrete
    (E) low, heavy domes

100. A good definition of art is

    (A) significant form
    (B) a production or procession of images expressing the personality of the artist
    (C) a reflection in visual form of the philosophy and culture of the period
    (D) nature seen through the emotion and intellect of man
    (E) all of the above

101. The first spoken line by Hamlet in the play is an aside: "A little more than kin, and less than kind." By this line, he indicates that

    (A) he already suspects Claudius of some sort of duplicity
    (B) he already knows that Claudius has killed his father
    (C) he already has designs on the throne
    (D) he is already plotting revenge
    (E) he intends to feign madness

102. The Connecticut Wits

    (A) were devoted to the modernization of the Yale curriculum and the declaration of independence of American letters from British influences
    (B) favored Unitarianism and Transcendentalism
    (C) included Timothy Dwight, john Trumbull, and Joel Barlow
    (D) all of the above
    (E) (A) and (C) above

103. A Latin-American writer, author of *One Hundred Years of Solitude*, is

    (A) Isabel Allende
    (B) Carlos Noriega
    (C) Gabriel García Márquez
    (D) Pablo Neruda
    (E) Guillermo González

104. The creator of Charlie Brown is

    (A) Bud Blake
    (B) Al Capp
    (C) Charles Schulz
    (D) Alex Kotsby
    (E) Fred Lasswell

105. "Each narrow cell in which we dwell" provides an example of

    (A) alliteration
    (B) internal rhyme
    (C) sprung rhythm
    (D) end rhyme
    (E) spondaic trimeter

106. A playwright who wrote a modern comic-psychological version of *Antigone* is

    (A) Arther Miller
    (B) Jean Anouilh
    (C) Edward Albee
    (D) Jean-Paul Sartre
    (E) Georges Clemenceau

107. This is an example of

(A) Mesopotamian sculpture
(B) Egyptian sculpture
(C) Indian sculpture
(D) prehistoric sculpture
(E) modern sculpture

Estate of David Smith,
courtesy of Marlborough Gallery, New York

108. Molière's audiences were predominantly

(A) peasants
(B) a great cross-section of the population
(C) people pretending to a higher station in life
(D) aristocrats
(E) middle class only

109. Edgar Allan Poe believed a short story should

(A) be sufficiently short to permit the reader to finish the work in a single sitting
(B) have a surprise ending
(C) delight and instruct the reader
(D) have complicated characters
(E) be realistic

110. The French word *genre* means

(A) plot
(B) category
(C) climax
(D) story
(E) introduction

111. What Renaissance writer do you associate with the Abbey of Theleme?

(A) Castiglione
(B) Shakespeare
(C) Ariosto
(D) Rabelais
(E) Cervantes

112. Ursula K. LeGuin is regarded primarily as a writer of

(A) poetry
(B) romantic fiction
(C) mysteries
(D) spy stories
(E) science fiction

113. A 19th-century novelist who anticipated many 20th-century discoveries and inventions was

(A) T.H. Huxley
(B) Mary Shelley
(C) Thomas Hardy
(D) Jules Verne
(E) Bram Stoker

114. According to tradition, who wrote *The Odyssey* and *The Iliad*?

(A) Achilles
(B) Tacitus
(C) Homer
(D) Vergil
(E) Thucydides

115. A form of music drama without stage action, of which Handel became a master, is the

(A) oratorio
(B) opera
(C) cantata
(D) castrati
(E) duet

116. The conductor's copy of the notes contains all the notes for each player in the orchestra. It is called the

    (A) score
    (B) libretto
    (C) manuscript
    (D) theme
    (E) thesis

117. The theme of John Steinbeck's *In Dubious Battle* is

    (A) the exodus of the Okies from Oklahoma
    (B) the growth of labor unions in America
    (C) the frustration of the war in Vietnam
    (D) the blacks' fight for freedom
    (E) World War II

118. An Aeschylean dramatic pattern made possible the first true plays because it introduced

    (A) villainy
    (B) humanism
    (C) plausibility
    (D) conflict between two characters
    (E) the family theme

119. The portrait below was painted by

    (A) da Vinci
    (B) Delacroix
    (C) van Gogh
    (D) Michelangelo
    (E) Dali

©Bettman/Corbis

120. In the play *Medea*, what was the name of Jason's ship?

    (A) *Tiki*
    (B) *Pelias*
    (C) *Dreadnaught*
    (D) *Medea*
    (E) *Argo*

121. Why did Jason set sail on his fateful voyage?

    (A) To search for the Golden Fleece
    (B) To make war on Sparta
    (C) To destroy the port of Colchis
    (D) To search for the Holy Grail
    (E) To put a stop to pirateering

122. The first permanent stringed orchestra in Europe, introduced during the reign of Louis XIV, was called the

    (A) Chapelle
    (B) Twenty-four viols
    (C) Grand Ecurie
    (D) Chambre
    (E) Academy

123. The architect associated with St. Paul's Cathedral is

    (A) Inigo Jones
    (B) Christopher Wren
    (C) Le Corbusier
    (D) Frank Lloyd Wright
    (E) Walter Gropius

124. The opening scene of Shakespeare's *Henry IV, Part I* establishes for the audience that

    (A) all is well in England
    (B) a pilgrimage to the Holy Land is in progress
    (C) it is raining
    (D) the king has two major problems confronting him
    (E) the king is dead

125. Byzantine art was a major contribution to the world because of its

    (A) sculpture
    (B) portraits
    (C) armor
    (D mosaics
    (E) glassware

126. The variety of styles in modern art is a reflection of

    (A) the complexity of modern life
    (B) a lack of purpose
    (C) a loss of values
    (D) foreign influence
    (E) our susceptibility to sensationalism and fads

127. In formal science, *all* statements are

    (A) intuitively true
    (B) given meaning by induction
    (C) hypothetically true
    (D) empirically truc
    (E) given meaning by experiment

128. The poem "Trees" was written by

    (A) E.E. Cummings
    (B) Edna St. Vincent Millay
    (C) Joyce Kilmer
    (D) Lawrence Ferlinghetti
    (E) John Frederick Nims

129. Voltaire's Candide journeyed from continent to continent to find his elusive Cunegonde, whose chief virtue was

    (A) beauty
    (B) physical indestructibility
    (C) piety
    (D) faithfulness
    (E) mental alertness

130. *The Tales of Hoffmann* was written by

    (A) De Maistre
    (B) Bierce
    (C) Poe
    (D) Hoffmann
    (E) Irving

131. The operatic score for *The Tales of Hoffmann* was written by

    (A) Offenbach
    (B) Adam
    (C) Rimsky-Korsakov
    (D) Schubert
    (E) Schumann

132. When the Christian Church came into power after the fall of the Roman Empire, it

    (A) used professional actors to perform plays
    (B) urged the wealthy to sponsor acting groups
    (C) emphasized the "here" rather than the "hereafter"
    (D) abolished all theatrical activities
    (E) began putting on plays in the church itself

133. The death of Seneca in A.D. 65 marks the

    (A) end of the Roman Empire
    (B) beginning of creative playwrighting
    (C) end of creative playwrighting until the Middle Ages
    (D) beginning of the Middle Ages
    (E) birth of comedy

134. Which of the following, written during the Revolutionary period, is often considered the first American novel?

    (A) *McTeague*
    (B) *Moby Dick*
    (C) *Huckleberry Finn*
    (D) *Golden Wedding*
    (E) *The Power of Sympathy*

135. The Artful Dodger is a character in the novel

    (A) *Oliver Twist*
    (B) *The Little Prince*
    (C) *Hard Times*
    (D) *David Copperfield*
    (E) *Vanity Fair*

136. One of the greatest jazz musicians of all time is

    (A) "Dizzy" Gillespie
    (B) Ray Charles
    (C) Pete Seeger
    (D) Arthel Watson
    (E) David Byrne

137. John Milton in *Paradise Lost* attempted to

    (A) justify the ways of men to God
    (B) justify the ways of God to men
    (C) explain evil
    (D) show that Satan and God have equal powers
    (E) explain why good and evil are necessary

138. The two great Italian writers of the 14th century were

    (A) Petrarch and Pirandello
    (D) Boccaccio and Silone
    (B) Petrarch and Boccaccio
    (E) Machiavelli and Borgia
    (C) Dante and Fellini

139. The ghost advises Hamlet, concerning his mother, to

    (A) make certain that she does not escape death
    (B) bring her to public trial and let the people of Denmark decide her fate
    (C) wash her incestuous sheets
    (D) allow heaven to decide her fate
    (E) deny her Christian burial so that her soul will wander forever, as his is doomed to do

140. A sonata is a musical composition for instruments. A cantata is

    (A) a slow symphony
    (B) an aria
    (C) a slow madrigal
    (D) a choral work
    (E) a round

141. "But I will start afresh and make dark things plain. In doing right by Laius, I protect myself . . . ," said

    (A) Phoebus
    (B) Oedipus
    (C) Ismene
    (D) Creon
    (E) Jocasta

Ruth S. Ward

142. The photograph above pictures

    (A) an Egyptian temple
    (B) an Etruscan temple
    (C) a Mayan temple
    (D) a Greek temple
    (E) a Roman temple

143. A chilling modern novel by Margaret Atwood is

    (A) *A Handmaid's Tale*
    (B) *Fear of Flying*
    (C) *The House of Sorrows*
    (D) *The Eiger Sanction*
    (E) *As I Lay Dying*

144. The rhyme scheme of Dante's *Divine Comedy* in its original Italian is

    (A) sestina
    (B) terza rima
    (C) sonnet
    (D) ballade
    (E) rondeau

145. The magnificent achievements of Gothic art are found especially in

    (A) the structures of the great cathedrals
    (B) the carving of statues on the porches of these cathedrals
    (C) the beauty of stained glass
    (D) the invention of the flying buttress
    (E) all of the above

146. All of the following Americans were awarded the Nobel Prize for Literature *except*

    (A) Pearl S. Buck
    (B) William Faulkner
    (C) Robert Frost
    (D) Ernest Hemingway
    (E) Eugene O'Neill

147. A soliloquy is

    (A) A short speech delivered to the audience while other characters are on stage
    (B) a few moments of pantomime by the main character in a play
    (C) a speech of some length spoken directly to the audience while the character speaking is alone on stage
    (D) a verbal exchange between two characters on stage
    (E) a short, comic speech by the protagonist

148. Which of the following painters produced a number of canvasses of jungle plants and animals?

    (A) Henri Rousseau
    (B) Paul Cézanne
    (C) Jackson Pollock
    (D) Mary Cassatt
    (E) Andy Warhol

149. Which of the following conductors began with opera and for many years headed the New York Philharmonic?

    (A) George Szell
    (B) Sir John Barbarolli
    (C) Herbert von Karajan
    (D) Arturo Toscanini
    (E) André Previn

150. A handkerchief plays a key role in which of the following tragedies?

    (A) *All for Love*
    (B) *Othello*
    (C) *King Lear*
    (D) *Antony and Cleopatra*
    (E) *Macbeth*

STOP

If there is still time remaining, you may review your answers.

Humanities

ANSWER KEY—TRIAL TEST

1. B	26. C	51. D	76. A	101. A	126. A
2. D	27. D	52. E	77. D	102. E	127. E
3. C	28. E	53. E	78. D	103. C	128. C
4. A	29. B	54. A	79. E	104. C	129. B
5. C	30. B	55. B	80. E	105. C	130. D
6. D	31. E	56. C	81. A	106. B	131. A
7. E	32. C	57. A	82. A	107. E	132. D
8. D	33. B	58. C	83. A	108. D	133. C
9. D	34. C	59. D	84. B	109. A	134. E
10. A	35. B	60. A	85. D	110. B	135. A
11. B	36. C	61. E	86. A	111. D	136. A
12. A	37. E	62. C	87. C	112. E	137. B
13. C	38. A	63. E	88. B	113. D	138. B
14. C	39. D	64. E	89. C	114. C	139. D
15. E	40. A	65. A	90. E	115. A	140. D
16. C	41. D	66. A	91. E	116. A	141. B
17. B	42. D	67. C	92. D	117. B	142. C
18. C	43. C	68. A	93. E	118. D	143. A
19. D	44. A	69. B	94. E	119. A	144. B
20. D	45. D	70. C	95. D	120. E	145. E
21. C	46. D	71. E	96. B	121. A	146. C
22. A	47. D	72. E	97. C	122. B	147. C
23. A	48. B	73. D	98. D	123. B	148. A
24. E	49. A	74. B	99. B	124. D	149. D
25. C	50. E	75. A	100. E	125. D	150. B

SCORING CHART

After you have scored your Trial Test, enter the results in the chart below, then transfer your score to the Progress Chart on page 12. As you complete the Sample Examinations later in this part of the book, you should be able to achieve increasingly higher scores.

Total Test	Number Right	Number Wrong	Number Omitted
100			

ANSWER EXPLANATIONS

1. **(B)** Expressionism in the arts was a movement during the latter part of the 19th and early part of the 20th centuries that emphasized the objective expression of inner experience through color, brushstrokes, symbols, and abstract shapes.

2. **(D)** The Impressionists were a group of late-19th-century painters who created a general impression of a scene or object by the use of color juxtapositions and small strokes to simulate actual reflected light.

3. **(C)** Acoustics is the study of sound.

4. **(A)** Jean Baptiste Lully (c. 1633–1687) was an Italian operatic composer who has been called "the father of French opera." In 1653 he was made court composer by Louis XIV, for whom he composed many ballets.

5. **(C)** James Wyatt (1746–1813) restored English Gothic cathedrals at Lincoln and Salisbury and built several buildings at Magdelen College, Oxford.

6. **(D)** A "comedy of manners" is a type of social farce. Ibsen wrote plays of a more serious nature.

7. **(E)** Aristotle said that the primary purpose of tragedy is to create a catharsis, or purgation, of the emotions.

8. **(D)** The best-known essayists of this period were Joseph Addison and Richard Steele, who contributed to both the *The Tattler* and *The Spectator*.

9. **(D)** *Uncle Tom's Cabin* ran as a serial in the *National Era*, an abolitionist paper, from June 1851 to April 1852, and was later published as a book.

10. **(A)** Alliteration is the occurrence in a phrase or line of speech or writing of two or more words having the same initial sound, as the "b" sound in "brush," "brow," "burnished," and "bronze."

11. **(B)** The ballet "The Rite of Spring" was first produced by Diaghileff's Ballets Russes in Paris in 1913. It raised a storm of protest and was performed only six times.

12. **(A)** An overture is an instrumental introduction to an opera.

13. **(C)** The photograph shows a pueblo in Taos, New Mexico.

14. **(C)** Dali, Miró, and de Chirico are three artists noted for their Surrealist paintings.

15. **(E)** This is a historical fact.

16. **(C)** A quatrain is a stanza or poem of four lines.

17. **(B)** "Barbara Allen" is an ancient British folk ballad.

18. **(C)** Pop art frequently depicts such things as Campbell's soup cans, flashy cars, and movie stars.

19. **(D)** The Greeks are noted for their graceful statues depicting the human body.

20. **(D)** Wright believed that a building should be built of the materials native to the area and should blend in with its particular surroundings.

21. **(C)** Camus says this in many essays, but no more strongly than in his "Reflections on the Guillotine."

22. **(A)** The *Nibelungenlied*, of unknown origin, was probably composed between the 12th and 14th centuries.

23. **(A)** This is the famous "Pomp and Circumstance" overture.

24. **(E)** None of the others were jazz guitarists.

25. **(C)** Shakespeare never wrote dramas about the middle class.

26. **(C)** The Hollywood Bowl opened in California in 1922.

27. **(D)** Aeschylus, the Athenian tragic poet, was the first of the three great tragedians, the others being Sophocles and Euripides.

28. **(E)** No scenery or props were employed by the Greeks in the open, outdoor theater.

29. **(B)** A sharp is a musical note raised one-half step in pitch.

30. **(B)** This is a standard definition of "Western man" or "Western civilization."

31. **(E)** A tone poem is an elaborate orchestral composition, usually in one movement, having no fixed form and based upon some nonmusical, poetic or descriptive theme. Strauss' best-known tone poem is "Thus Spake Zarathustra."

32. **(C)** Hamlet's famous "to be or not to be" soliloquy addresses this problem.

33. **(B)** Paul Cézanne (1839–1906) was a French post-Impressionist painter. He was noted for the use of very vivid colors, and for a striving for depth in place of flatness, which he achieved by very dark shadows and outlines.

34. **(C)** Cubism is a school of modern art characterized by the use of cubes and other abstract geometric forms rather than by a realistic representation of nature.

35. **(B)** A clerestory is an outside wall of a room or building that is carried above an adjoining roof and pierced with windows.

36. **(C)** "Rappaccini's Daughter" is a short story written by Nathaniel Hawthorne.

37. **(E)** Not all sculpture is a realistic portrayal of the human being; stone and marble can be cut for flooring and may be functional, but not necessarily artistic.

38. **(A)** George Berkeley (1685–1753) denied the independent existence of matter. His was the philosophy of subjective idealism, or immaterialism.

39. **(D)** Florence is a city in Tuscany, Italy. Among those who added luster to its name were the artist Michelangelo and the writers Dante and Boccaccio.

40. **(A)** The principal members of the School of Lyon, headed by Maurice Scève, were Antoine Heroet, Pernette de Guillet, and Louise Labè, all poets.

41. **(D)** Stephen Crane (1871–1900) was an American novelist, poet, and journalist. His *Red Badge of Courage* is a well-known tale of the American Civil War.

42. **(D)** Renoir, Monet, and Pissaro were 19th-century painters who attempted to create a general impression of a scene or object by the use of unmixed primary colors and small strokes to simulate actual reflected light.

43. **(C)** This is noticeable in Roman roads and aqueducts as well as in buildings.

44. **(A)** Modulation, in music, is defined as a shifting from one key to another by the transitional use of a chord common to both.

45. **(D)** *Oedipus the King*, a play written by Sophocles, concerns Oedipus, who killed his father and married his mother.

46. **(D)** The photograph is of the Opera House in Sydney, Australia.

47. **(D)** Mark Twain was the pseudonym of Samuel L. Clemens, who was born in Florida, Missouri, in 1835 and spent his childhood in Hannibal, Missouri.

48. **(B)** This example of nonsense verse is from the poem "Jabberwocky," by Lewis Carroll, and is to be found in *Through the Looking Glass*.

49. **(A)** With the fall of the Roman Empire, Christian forces had succeeded in driving the actors out of Rome. Modern drama, including farcical interludes, had its origins in the Middle Ages.

50. **(E)** The Black Death was an epidemic of plague in the 14th century.

51. **(D)** *Animal Farm* is a political satire by George Orwell.

52. **(E)** Bolger, the only tap dancer of the group, appeared in the musical *On Your Toes* and the motion picture *The Wizard of Oz*.

53. **(E)** Ferde Grofé was an American composer and arranger who became famous when he orchestrated Gershwin's *Rhapsody in Blue* in 1924. He also wrote other music describing the American scene, including "The Grand Canyon Suite."

54. **(A)** The great areas of interior space created the feeling of human insignificance and God's infinite and all-powerful presence.

55. **(B)** Some authors pictured the effects of the Great Depression and laborers brutalized by machines.

56. **(C)** Kerouac's novel *On the Road* ushered in a new movement in American literature.

57. **(A)** A parable is sometimes a religious lesson as well.

58. **(C)** Altamira is in northern Spain, and Lascaux is in south-central France.

59. **(D)** This is a basic principle of art.

60. **(A)** Modern psychologists and sociologists have demonstrated that cultural conditioning determines the way we perceive.

61. **(E)** Foster was the composer of "Old Folks at Home," "Oh Susannah," "My old Kentucky Home," and many other songs.

62. **(C)** Benjamin Franklin (1706–1790) was one of the most versatile of the early American fathers.

63. **(E)** The line comes from T. S. Eliot's poem "The Love Song of J. Alfred Prufrock."

64. **(E)** The mystery plays were the forerunner of modern drama.

65. **(A)** Lessing's *The Golden Notebook* appeared at the beginning of the Women's Liberation Movement in 1962.

66. **(A)** *Don Quixote*, the best-known work of Miguel de Cervantes, is a satire.

67. **(C)** Among Gainsborough's best-known works are "Mrs. Siddons" and "The Blue Boy."

68. **(A)** "The Well-Tempered Clavier," sometimes called "the Well-Tempered Clavichord," consists of forty-eight preludes and fugues.

69. **(B)** None of the other works was written by Beethoven.

70. **(C)** Among Lewis' best known novels are *Main Street* and *Babbitt*.

71. **(E)** All people have unlimited abilities.

72. **(E)** Aeschylus and Sophocles were more conservative and traditional in their approach.

73. **(D)** Chekhov is noted for presenting small "slices of life" in his plays.

74. **(B)** Leoncavallo wrote several operas, but only *I Pagliacci* was successful.

75. **(A)** A flat is a musical note one-half step lower than a specified note or tone.

76. **(A)** This famous Greek statue is presently to be seen in the Louvre in Paris.

77. **(D)** Shakespeare's plays contain elements such as song, dance, and ghostly apparitions because it was necessary for him to appeal to a diverse audience.

78. **(D)** In other words, the viewer must enter the theater with an open mind.

79. **(E)** Paul Gauguin was a French landscape and figure painter best known for his paintings of Tahitian subjects.

80. **(E)** Pointillism is characterized by the application of paint in small dots and brushstrokes so as to create an effect of blending and luminosity.

81. **(A)** Hermann Hesse was a Swiss author who wrote *Siddhartha*, *Demian* and *A Journey to the East*, as well as many other novels.

82. **(A)** This answer is true by definition.

83. **(A)** The poem was first published in *The Passionate Pilgrim* in 1599.

84. **(B)** The poem was published after Marlowe's death.

85. **(D)** A quatrain is a stanza of four lines.

86. **(A)** The appreciation of art is basically an emotional, sensory experience.

87. **(C)** Isaiah was one of the greatest of the Hebrew prophets.

88. **(B)** The other groups consist of those who are not symphony conductors.

89. **(C)** The others are not writers.

90. **(E)** The others are not choreographers.

91. **(E)** F. Scott Fitzgerald is probably the best-known writer of the "roaring 20s."

92. **(D)** Nietzsche wrote about the will to power, and the superman who, he believed, is to come.

93. **(E)** Kate is the name of the female lead in Shakespeare's play.

94. **(E)** Van Gogh became an artist, but he did not prove his point.

95. **(D)** This is a traditional musical notation.

96. **(B)** This is a definition of a cappella.

97. **(C)** *Die Meistersinger* is not part of the Germanic myth cycle.

98. **(D)** Mary Flannery O'Connor (1925–1964) lived most of her life in Milledgeville, Georgia.

99. **(B)** This ornate style in art and architecture developed in Europe about 1550 to 1700.

100. **(E)** "Art" is an abstract concept, and therefore may have many definitions.

101. **(A)** Hamlet's mother, Gertrude, is married to Claudius, but Hamlet mistrusts him.

102. **(E)** This group, also called the Hartford Wits, flourished in the late 18th and early 19th centuries.

103. **(C)** Márquez, author of *One Hundred Years of Solitude*, was awarded the Nobel Prize for literature in 1982.

104. **(C)** Schulz is the creator of *Peanuts*.

105. **(C)** Sprung rhythm is a forcefully accentual verse rhythm in which a stressed syllable is followed by an irregular number of unstressed or slack syllables to form a foot having a metrical value equal to that of the other feet in the line.

106. **(B)** Anouilh's play is also entitled *Antigone*.

107. **(E)** Metal is a popular medium for modern sculptors.

108. **(D)** Molière's attacks on bourgeois morality greatly appealed to his aristocratic audience.

109. **(A)** Poe, one of the first great American short story writers, coined this criterion.

110. **(B)** This is a translation from the French.

111. **(D)** François Rabelais (1494–1553) entered a monastery but later abandoned monasticism. His best-known work is *Gargantua and Pantagruel.*

112. **(E)** LeGuin's *The Left Hand of Darkness* is considered a classic in its field.

113. **(D)** Perhaps Verne's best-known work is *20,000 Leagues Under the Sea*, in which he anticipated the invention of the submarine.

114. **(C)** There is no proof, but tradition does hold that Homer was the author.

115. **(A)** Handel's most famous oratorios are on biblical subjects, such as *Esther*, *Deborah*, and *Samson*.

116. **(A)** The score is the written form of a musical composition. The conductor's copy is complete.

117. **(B)** This book shows how labor was oppressed by management in the early days of unionization.

118. **(D)** These characters are termed the protagonist and the antagonist. Without conflict, there can be no drama.

119. **(A)** The painting is of La Gioconda, popularly known as the Mona Lisa.

120. **(E)** Jason's men were called Argonauts, after the ship *Argo*.

121. **(A)** Jason stole the Golden Fleece from Aeetes, with the help of Aeetes' daughter, Medea.

122. **(B)** Louis XIV, the "Sun King," indulged his taste for luxury and elegance to the full. The arts flourished during his reign in France.

123. **(B)** Sir Christopher Wren (1632–1723) was one of the foremost architects of his day. All of his buildings exhibit elegance, vigor, and dignity.

124. **(D)** The king had learned of uprisings in both Scotland and Wales.

125. **(D)** A mosaic is a decorative design or picture made by setting small colored pieces, such as tile, in mortar.

126. **(A)** All the answers to the above are true, but only partial, explanations. "A," "the complexity of modern life," encompasses all of them and more.

127. **(E)** Formal science relies heavily upon experimentation for proof of a hypothesis.

128. **(C)** Kilmer's "Trees" is often recited on Arbor Day.

129. **(B)** Cunegonde's many experiences would have killed a weaker individual.

130. **(D)** Ernst Hoffmann (1776–1822) was a German musician, artist, and Romantic writer, who is one of the masters in the field of fantastic prose.

131. **(A)** Jacques Offenbach (1819–1880), a French composer of light operas, is best known for his adaptation of Hoffmann's stories.

132. **(D)** The Roman Church abolished all "immoral activities," theater among them.

133. **(C)** There was no theater under the Roman Church during the Dark Ages in Europe.

134. **(E)** This is the only work mentioned that was written during the Revolutionary period.

135. **(A)** *Oliver Twist* was written by Charles Dickens in 1838.

136. **(A)** John Brinks "Dizzy" Gillespie, along with Charlie Parker, created the style of jazz know as "bebop."

137. **(B)** Milton said this in *Paradise Lost.*

138. **(B)** The others are Italian, but not all 14th-century writers.

139. **(D)** Hamlet had been contemplating murder, but he listened to the ghost.

140. **(D)** A cantata is a vocal and instrumental composition comprising choruses, solos, and recitatives.

141. **(B)** Laius, king of Thebes, was the father of Oedipus, who killed him.

142. **(C)** Mayan architecture is to be found in sections of Mexico and Central America.

143. **(A)** Only *A Handmaid's Tale* was written by Atwood.

144. **(B)** Terza rima is composed of tercets that are not separate stanzas, because each is joined to the one preceding and the one following by a common rhyme: aba, bcb, cdc, ded, etc.

145. **(E)** All of the above are to be found in Gothic cathedrals.

146. **(C)** Robert Frost, one of America's most admired poets, never received the Nobel Prize.

147. **(C)** This is the answer by definition of "soliloquy."

148. **(A)** Henri Rousseau was a French primitive painter best known for his "Sleeping Gypsy" and "The Jungle."

149. **(D)** The others either did not begin with opera, did not head the New York Philharmonic, or did neither.

150. **(B)** It is Desdemona's handkerchief that spurs Othello to such jealousy that he kills her.

Background and Practice Questions

DESCRIPTION OF THE HUMANITIES EXAMINATION

The CLEP General Examination in Humanities measures your general knowledge of literature and the fine arts. It covers material that is generally taught in lower-division college courses designed to survey the humanities. The exam is given in two parts, each consisting of approximately 70 questions and each requiring 45 minutes to complete. See the following chart for approximate percentages of examination items:

Humanities Exam	
Content or Item Types	Time/Number of Questions
50% Literature	140 questions
10% Drama	90 minutes
10–15–20% Poetry	
15–20% Fiction	
10% Nonfiction	
10% Philosophy	
50% Fine Arts	
20% Visual arts (painting, sculpture)	
15% Performing arts (music)	
10% Performing arts (film, dance)	
5% Visual arts (architecture)	

The questions on this exam include aspects of the humanities that may not have been covered in courses you have taken in school. Your ability to answer these questions will depend on the extent to which you have maintained a general interest in the arts and kept current by reading widely; attending movies, theater, and concerts; visiting museums; and watching television.

A knowledge of foreign languages is not required to prepare for this exam. All literary works included are readily available in English translations.

The ability to read music is not necessary to answer the questions about music.

Though a few questions may appear rather technical, remember that no one is expected to have complete mastery of all fields of the humanities.

THE KINDS OF QUESTIONS THAT APPEAR ON THE EXAMINATION

There are two important aspects of the examination questions: (1) the knowledge and abilities they test for and (2) the formats in which they are presented.

Knowledge and Abilities Required

The questions require factual answers, not answers which depend upon your emotional responses or aesthetic tastes. Some questions cover material with which you should be familiar from course work. For other questions, the correct answer can be derived from your ability to analyze artistic creations, to recognize certain basic artistic techniques, and to make analogies between two works of art. You will be expected to identify literary passages and authors. In some cases, you will be presented with pictures of works of art that you will be expected to identify by artist, period, or in some other way.

The following questions illustrate the various types.

Knowledge of Factual Information

Questions 1–3 refer to the following groups of people.

    (A) John Williams, Burt Bacharach, Henry Mancini
    (B) Sir George Solti, Andre Previn, Leonard Bernstein
    (C) John Steinbeck, William Faulkner, Sinclair Lewis
    (D) Andy Warhol, Joan Miro, Claes Oldenburg
    (E) Twyla Tharp, Michael Bennett, Gower Champion

1. Which is a group of contemporary symphony conductors?

2. Which is a group of novelists who won the Nobel Prize for Literature?

3. Which is a group of choreographers for Broadway musicals of the 1970s and 1980s?

Recognition of Techniques and Identification with Artists and Periods

Questions 4–6 refer to the following lines.

> Come live with me, and be my love,
> And we will all the pleasures prove,
> That valleys, groves, hills, and fields,
> Woods or steepy mountains yields.

4. These lines are from

   (A) "The Passionate Shepherd to His Love"
   (B) "The Shepherd's Wife's Song"
   (C) "A Strange Passion of a Lover"
   (D) one of Shakespeare's sonnets
   (E) "Troilus and Cressida"

5. The lines were written by

   (A) William Shakespeare
   (B) Christopher Marlowe
   (C) John Lyly
   (D) T.S. Eliot
   (E) Alexander Pope

6. The verse form is a

   (A) couplet
   (B) sestina
   (C) sonnet
   (D) quatrain
   (E) cinquaine

Analysis of Artistic Creations

7.
   LADY BRACKNELL: "Do you smoke?"
   JACK: "Well, yes, I must admit I smoke."
   LADY BRACKNELL: "I am glad to hear it. A man should always have an occupation of some sort."

   This dialogue from Oscar Wilde's *The Importance of Being Earnest* illustrates

   (A) sympathy
   (B) empathy
   (C) scorn
   (D) comic pathos
   (E) linguistic wit

ANSWERS

1. **B**		2. **C**		3. **E**		4. **A**	
5. **B**		6. **D**		7. **E**			

STUDY SOURCES

If you would like to review some of the information that you may already have studied or fill in some gaps in your formal education, we recommend the following as excellent sources:

LITERATURE

Abrams, M.H. *The Norton Anthology of English Literature.* 4th ed. New York: W.W. Norton and Co., Inc., 1979.

Baker, Nancy L. *A Research Guide for Undergraduate Students: English and American Literature.* 2nd ed. New York: Modern Language Association of America, 1985.

Brooks, Cleanth, et al., eds. *American Literature: The Makers and the Making.* 4 volumes. New York: St. Martin's Press, Inc., 1974.

Grant, Michael. *Myths of the Greeks and Romans.* New York: New American Library, 1975.

Heiney, D.W. and L.H. Downs. *Contemporary Literature of the Western World.* 4 volumes. Hauppauge, NY: Barron's Educational Series, Inc., 1974.

Perrine, Laurence. *Sound and Sense: An Introduction to Poetry.* 5th ed. New York: Harcourt Brace Jovanovich, Inc., 1977.

FINE ARTS

Apel, Willi. *Harvard Dictionary of Music.* 2nd ed. Cambridge, MA: Harvard University Press, 1969.

Grout, Donald. *A History of Western Music.* 3rd ed. New York: W.W. Norton and Co., Inc., 1980.

Janson, H.W. *History of Art: A Survey of the Major Visual Arts from the Dawn of History to the Present Day.* 2nd ed. New York: Harry N. Abrams, Inc., 1977.

Whiting, Fran M. *An Introduction to the Theatre.* 4th ed. New York: Harper and Row Pubs., Inc., 1978.

In addition to these specific works, you might consult the excellent series of dictionaries for the various art forms published by Oxford University Press in New York. For very recent information, you might consult the music, art and book reviews and film criticisms which appear regularly in such publications as *Playboy, Esquire, Saturday Review, The National Review, The New Republic, The New York Times, The New York Review of Books, The New Yorker, The Film Quarterly,* and other periodicals.

For practice, we will now give you some sample questions in each of the areas that the CLEP Humanities Examination will cover; these questions should be considered typical.

Practice Questions on the Humanities

QUESTIONS ABOUT LITERATURE

Directions: Each of the questions or incomplete statements below is followed by five suggested answers or completions. Select the one that is best in each case.

1. What 17th-century poet attempted to "justify the ways of God to man"?

   (A) John Bunyan
   (B) Samuel Johnson
   (C) John Dryden
   (D) John Milton
   (E) John Donne

2. In poetry, the invention or use of a word whose sound echoes or suggests its meaning is called

   (A) amphibrach
   (B) sprung rhythm
   (C) onomatopoeia
   (D) zeugma
   (E) sententia

3. A Japanese poem of seventeen syllables is the

   (A) kyogen
   (B) haiku
   (C) sentyu
   (D) tanka
   (E) renka

4. The Greek theater contained all but one of the following:

   (A) masks
   (B) boots
   (C) proscenium
   (D) movable props
   (E) song and dance

5. A well-known 19th-century symbolist poem is "Afternoon of a Faun." This poem was written by

   (A) Baudelaire
   (B) Rimbaud
   (C) Valéry
   (D) Mallarmé
   (E) Claudel

6. A pastoral elegy, bewailing the death of Edward King, is

   (A) "In Memoriam"
   (B) "Lycidas"
   (C) "Thyrsis"
   (D) "Il Penseroso"
   (E) "Adonais"

7. An example of an Old English folk epic is

   (A) *The Canterbury Tales*
   (B) *The Iliad*
   (C) *Beowulf*
   (D) *A Midsummer Night's Dream*
   (E) *Paradise Lost*

8. The essence of comedy is

   (A) satire
   (B) surprise
   (C) mistaken identity
   (D) disguise
   (E) incongruity

9. The Greek word for "overweening pride" is

   (A) hamartia
   (B) catharsis
   (C) anagnorisis
   (D) peripety
   (E) hubris

10. The word *utopia* comes from a 16th-century book by

    (A) Sir Thomas More
    (B) Thomas à Becket
    (C) Samuel Beckett
    (D) William Shakespeare
    (E) Ben Jonson

11. A famous contemporary of John Dryden was

    (A) Alexander Pope
    (B) Ben Jonson
    (C) Thomas Macaulay
    (D) Leigh Hunt
    (E) John Milton

12. According to Aristotle, tragedy evokes pity and fear and produces a

    (A) catharsis
    (B) dénouement
    (C) climax
    (D) recognition
    (E) kothurnos

13. A Japanese play that exists as a harmony of all theatrical elements—poetry, music, dance, costume, mask, setting, and the interaction of performance—is the

    (A) kabuki
    (B) shinto
    (C) hari kiri
    (D) no
    (E) joruri

14. In the 16th century, people believed the main purpose of poetry was to

    (A) relieve the emotions
    (B) make science bearable
    (C) enliven life
    (D) delight and instruct
    (E) philosophize

15. Shakespeare's best-known comic character is

    (A) Titania
    (B) Falstaff
    (C) Henry VIII
    (D) Ariel
    (E) Friar Lawrence

16. A collection of medieval stories concerning a group of people on a pilgrimage is

    (A) *The Decameron*
    (B) *The Canterbury Tales*
    (C) *Sir Gawain and the Green Knight*
    (D) *Morte d'Arthur*
    (E) *Idylls of the King*

17. An American poet and novelist, awarded the Pulitzer Prize for her novel *The Color Purple*, is

    (A) Zora Neale Hurston
    (B) Ursula K. LeGuin
    (C) Barbara Bellows
    (D) Cynthia Blake
    (E) Alice Walker

18. "All are but parts of one stupendous whole, / Whose body Nature is, and God the soul" was written by

    (A) Matthew Arnold
    (B) Alexander Pope
    (C) Percy B. Shelley
    (D) John Milton
    (E) Robert Browning

19. A well-known British writer, born in Trinidad of Hindu parents, is

    (A) Derek Walcott
    (B) Malachi Smith
    (C) V.S. Naipaul
    (D) Abdur-Rahman Slade Hophinson
    (E) Erna Brodber

20. John Donne and his followers are known to literary historians as the

    (A) metaphysical poets
    (B) Molly Maguires
    (C) cavalier poets
    (D) graveyard school
    (E) Sons of Ben

21. The "hero" of Milton's *Paradise Lost* is

    (A) Satan
    (B) man
    (C) God
    (D) Adam
    (E) Jesus

22. A convention in drama wherein a character speaks his innermost thoughts aloud while alone on stage is the

    (A) aside
    (B) prologue
    (C) soliloquy
    (D) epilogue
    (E) proscenium

23. A fire-breathing monster, part lion, part goat, and part serpent, slain by Bellerophon, was the

    (A) medusa
    (B) chimera
    (C) phoenix
    (D) minotaur
    (E) hydra

24. The writer primarily responsible for the creation of the western as a literary genre is

    (A) Louis L'Amour
    (B) Jack London
    (C) Ernest Hemingway
    (D) Ambrose Bierce
    (E) Zane Grey

25. One of the great Sanskrit epics of Western India is

    (A) *The Mahabharata*
    (B) *Siddhartha*
    (C) *The Triptaka*
    (D) *The Analects*
    (E) *The Rubáiyát*

26. A well-known contemporary of William Shakespeare was

    (A) John Milton
    (B) Dante Alighieri
    (C) Geoffrey Chaucer
    (D) Christopher Marlowe
    (E) John Dryden

27. A 20th-century novel that made the public aware of the plight of migrant laborers is

    (A) *East of Eden*
    (B) *To a God Unknown*
    (C) *Cannery Row*
    (D) *The Grapes of Wrath*
    (E) *Tortilla Flat*

28. A poet who writes of ordinary people and of nature is considered a

    (A) naturalist
    (B) realist
    (C) romanticist
    (D) medievalist
    (E) Victorian

29. The "comedy of manners" was most popular during the

    (A) 16th century
    (B) 17th century
    (C) 18th century
    (D) 19th century
    (E) 20th century

30. The first book by a black author to be selected as a Book of the Month Club selection was

    (A) *The Invisible Man*
    (B) *Black Like Me*
    (C) *Giovanni's Room*
    (D) *Black Boy*
    (E) *Native Son*

31. A Greek divinity who punished crimes, particularly those of impicty and hubris, was

    (A) Artemis
    (B) Mercury
    (C) Clio
    (D) Clytaemnestra
    (E) Nemesis

32. Which Lawrence authored *Women in Love* and *Lady Chatterley's Lover*?

    (A) T.E. Lawrence
    (B) D.H. Lawrence
    (C) Ernest Lawrence
    (D) Gertrude Lawrence
    (E) Christian Lawrence

33. In Greek mythology, Demeter is the goddess of

    (A) the moon
    (B) the earth
    (C) rivers and lakes
    (D) agriculture
    (E) the hunt

34. The only two Americans to write poems for presidential inaugurations were

    (A) Sandberg and Ginsberg
    (B) Whitman and Lowell
    (C) Millay and Dickinson
    (D) Longfellow and Poe
    (E) Frost and Angelou

35. A 20th-century writer who refused the Nobel prize for literature was

    (A) Faulkner
    (B) Sartre
    (C) Camus
    (D) Lewis
    (E) Hemingway

Questions 36–38 refer to the following poem, "The Eagle" by Alfred, Lord Tennyson.

He clasps the crag with crooked hands;
Close to the sun in the lonely lands,
Ringed with the azure world, he stands.

The wrinkled sea beneath him crawls;
He watches from his mountain walls,
And like a thunderbolt he falls.

36. Which line contains a metaphor?

    (A) line 2
    (B) line 4
    (C) line 5
    (D) line 6
    (E) all of these lines

37. Which line contains a simile?

    (A) line 1
    (B) line 2
    (C) line 3
    (D) line 5
    (E) line 6

38. Which line contains an example of alliteration?

    (A) line 1
    (B) line 3
    (C) line 4
    (D) line 5
    (E) line 6

Answers

1. **D**	6. **B**	11. **E**	16. **B**	21. **B**	26. **D**	31. **E**	36. **B**
2. **C**	7. **C**	12. **A**	17. **E**	22. **C**	27. **D**	32. **B**	37. **E**
3. **B**	8. **E**	13. **D**	18. **B**	23. **B**	28. **C**	33. **D**	38. **A**
4. **D**	9. **E**	14. **D**	19. **C**	24. **E**	29. **C**	34. **E**	
5. **D**	10. **A**	15. **B**	20. **A**	25. **A**	30. **E**	35. **B**	

QUESTIONS ABOUT MUSIC

Directions: Each of the questions or incomplete statements below is followed by five suggested answers or completions. Select the one that is best in each case.

1. The assistant conductor or concertmaster of the orchestra is

   (A) the first chair violinist
   (B) the second chair violinist
   (C) a pianist
   (D) a harpist
   (E) standing in the wings ready to take over

2. The instrument with the stablest pitch and therefore the one asked to "sound your A" for all other players is the

   (A) piano
   (B) first violin
   (C) first oboe
   (D) clarinet
   (E) trumpet

3. The tone poem "Afternoon of a Faun" was composed by

   (A) Debussy
   (B) Liszt
   (C) Bizet
   (D) Rimsky-Korsakov
   (E) Poulenc

4. The first American music comes from the American Indian and, with its emphasis on single rhythms, American Indian music is primarily

   (A) emotional
   (B) formal
   (C) heterophonic
   (D) polyphonic
   (E) choral

5. Sir Andrew Lloyd Webber wrote the music for all of the following shows except

   (A) *Aspects of Love*
   (B) *Phantom of the Opera*
   (C) *Evita*
   (D) *Cats*
   (E) *Blood Brothers*

6. Composer of "4 minutes and 33 Seconds," in which the pianist sits at a piano for that length of time but does not play, is

   (A) Schoenberg
   (B) Bernstein
   (C) Ellington
   (D) Gershwin
   (E) Cage

7. The term "impressionism" was first applied to the music of

   (A) Ravel
   (B) Stravinsky
   (C) Debussy
   (D) Weill
   (E) Schoenberg

8. The music for the ballets "Rodeo," "Billy the Kid," and "Appalachian Spring" was written by

   (A) Howard Hanson
   (B) George Gershwin
   (C) Aaron Copland
   (D) Ferde Grofé
   (E) Elmer Bernstein

9. What American choreographer is best known for her "Fall River Legend" and "Rodeo"?

   (A) Agnes deMille
   (B) Isadora Duncan
   (C) Martha Graham
   (D) Loie Fuller
   (E) Doris Humphrey

10. The composer of the opera *Four Saints in Three Acts*, and the recipient of the Pulitzer Prize for his score to the documentary motion picture *Louisiana Story*, is

    (A) Aaron Copland
    (B) Kurt Weill
    (C) Erik Satie
    (D) Albert Roussel
    (E) Virgil Thomson

11. Running through music literature is a persistent thread that has affected, positively or negatively, the work of every composer from Bach to our 20th-century modernists. This thread is

    (A) melody
    (B) sonata
    (C) tone-poem
    (D) counterpart
    (E) atonality

12. The "Unfinished Symphony" was written by

    (A) Mendelssohn
    (B) Schubert
    (C) Brahms
    (D) Tchaikovsky
    (E) Chopin

13. The opera *The Barber of Seville* has music by

    (A) Puccini
    (B) Verdi
    (C) Mendelssohn
    (D) Rossini
    (E) Poulenc

14. The opera *The Marriage of Figaro* has music by

    (A) Mozart
    (B) Haydn
    (C) Verdi
    (D) Rossini
    (E) Puccini

15. A celebrated violinist who made his debut at Carnegie Hall at age eleven and toured the world before his twentieth birthday is

    (A) Georges Enesco
    (B) Aaron Copland
    (C) Elmer Bernstein
    (D) Yehudi Menuhin
    (D) André Previn

16. We get the word *octave* from a Latin word meaning

    (A) two
    (B) four
    (C) six
    (D) eight
    (E) nine

17. The direct ancestor of the symphony is the

    (A) concerto
    (B) sonata
    (C) motet
    (D) aria
    (E) overture

18. The method of four voices singing different tunes at the same time, yet linked by strict rules, is called a

    (A) motet
    (B) combo
    (C) chorus
    (D) fugue
    (E) baroque

19. Beethoven is best known for his

    (A) tone poems
    (B) operas
    (C) symphonies
    (D) waltzes
    (E) fugues

20. Many muscians agree that the greatest choral work ever written is

    (A) Beethoven's "Moonlight Sonata"
    (B) Bach's "Mass in B Minor"
    (C) Schubert's "Second Symphony"
    (D) Chopin's "Polonaise Militaire"
    (E) Bizet's *Carmen*

Answers

1. **A**	8. **C**	15. **D**
2. **C**	9. **A**	16. **D**
3. **A**	10. **E**	17. **E**
4. **D**	11. **E**	18. **A**
5. **E**	12. **B**	19. **C**
6. **E**	13. **D**	20. **B**
7. **C**	14. **A**	

QUESTIONS ABOUT FINE ARTS—PAINTING, ARCHITECTURE, SCULPTURE, DANCE

Directions: Each of the questions or incomplete statements below is followed by five suggested answers or completions. Select the one that is best in each case.

1. In painting, *chiaroscuro* refers to

    (A) a light-and-dark technique
    (B) brilliant colors
    (C) monochromes
    (D) perspective
    (E) a single-stroke technique

2. From 1692 to 1702 Giordano painted the ceiling of Charles II's palace, the Escorial, in

    (A) Versailles
    (B) Verona
    (C) Madrid
    (D) Rome
    (E) Milan

3. What is the main part of the interior of a church called?

   (A) The nave
   (B) The transept
   (C) The altar
   (D) The cruciform
   (E) The sacristy

4. One of the most famous modern ballet choreographers was

   (A) George Balanchine
   (B) Nicholas Sergeyev
   (C) Marius Petipa
   (D) Phillippe Taglioni
   (E) Rudolf von Laban

5. The artist famous for his painting on the ceiling of the Sistine Chapel is

   (A) Raphael
   (B) da Vinci
   (C) Michelangelo
   (D) Rembrandt
   (E) Delacroix

6. A painter noted for his madonnas is

   (A) Botticelli
   (B) van Gogh
   (C) Raphael
   (D) Picasso
   (E) Goya

7. The art of painting on freshly spread moist lime plaster with pigments suspended in a water vehicle is called

   (A) collage
   (B) pointillism
   (C) surrealism
   (D) primitivism
   (E) fresco

8. Perhaps the best known painting of Gustav Klimt is

   (A) *Ruth*
   (B) *The Last Temptation of Christ*
   (C) *Moses*
   (D) *The Kiss*
   (E) *The Thinker*

9. An artistic composition of fragments of printed matter and other materials pasted on a picture surface is called

   (A) dadaism
   (B) a fresco
   (C) art nouveau
   (D) a collage
   (E) pop art

10. Perhaps the outstanding master of the engraving and the woodcut was

    (A) Pieter Brueghel
    (B) Albrecht Dürer
    (C) William Blake
    (D) Leonardo da Vinci
    (E) Honoré Daumier

11. An Italian designer of the mid-20th-century known for his tiles painted to look like shelves of a bookcase was

    (A) Picasso
    (B) Miró
    (C) Ferrari
    (D) Fornasetti
    (E) Pucci

12. A "Spanish" painter noted for his thin-faced, elongated individuals was

    (A) Goya
    (B) Velásquez
    (C) El Greco
    (D) Picasso
    (E) Orozco

13. The first black choreographer to work at the Metropolitan Opera House was

    (A) Isadora Duncan
    (B) Alvin Ailey
    (C) Maya Angelou
    (D) Katherine Dunham
    (E) Katharine Graham

14. One of the 20th century's great British sculptors is

    (A) Ernst Barlach
    (B) Alberto Giacometti
    (C) Ossip Zadkine
    (D) Jacob Epstein
    (E) Alexander Calder

15. Inigo Jones was a

    (A) 17th-century architect and set designer
    (B) clarinetist with Bunk Johnson's orchestra
    (C) Restoration playwright
    (D) leading tenor with the La Scala Opera
    (E) 19th-century Impressionist painter

16. The American sculptor who designed two bridges for the Peace Park in Hiroshima and the Billy Rose Sculpture Garden for the National Museum in Jerusalem is

    (A) Cornell
    (B) Noguchi
    (C) Lipton
    (D) Calder
    (E) Duchamp

17. Perspective, as a unified system for representing space, was brought to perfection during the

    (A) Golden Age of Greece
    (B) Roman Republic
    (C) Byzantine period
    (D) Renaissance
    (E) nineteenth century

18. One of the many artists who designed sets and costumes for Sergei Diaghilev's Ballets Russes was

    (A) Claude Monet
    (B) Juan Gris
    (C) Jacques Lipchitz
    (D) Paul Gauguin
    (E) Paul Cezanne

19. An artist noted for her decorative sculpture and designs for metalwork is

    (A) Esther Moore
    (B) Edna St. Vincent Millay
    (C) Grandma Moses
    (D) Edith Sitwell
    (E) Francine Smythe

20. Edvard Munch's most famous painting is

    (A) *The Scream*
    (B) *Venus*
    (C) *The Persistence of Memory*
    (D) *Guernica*
    (E) *The Dream*

Answers

1. **A**	6. **C**	11. **D**	16. **B**
2. **C**	7. **E**	12. **C**	17. **D**
3. **A**	8. **D**	13. **D**	18. **B**
4. **A**	9. **D**	14. **D**	19. **A**
5. **C**	10. **B**	15. **A**	20. **A**

Humanities

ANSWER SHEET—SAMPLE EXAMINATION 1

1 Ⓐ Ⓑ Ⓒ Ⓓ Ⓔ	39 Ⓐ Ⓑ Ⓒ Ⓓ Ⓔ	77 Ⓐ Ⓑ Ⓒ Ⓓ Ⓔ	115 Ⓐ Ⓑ Ⓒ Ⓓ Ⓔ
2 Ⓐ Ⓑ Ⓒ Ⓓ Ⓔ	40 Ⓐ Ⓑ Ⓒ Ⓓ Ⓔ	78 Ⓐ Ⓑ Ⓒ Ⓓ Ⓔ	116 Ⓐ Ⓑ Ⓒ Ⓓ Ⓔ
3 Ⓐ Ⓑ Ⓒ Ⓓ Ⓔ	41 Ⓐ Ⓑ Ⓒ Ⓓ Ⓔ	79 Ⓐ Ⓑ Ⓒ Ⓓ Ⓔ	117 Ⓐ Ⓑ Ⓒ Ⓓ Ⓔ
4 Ⓐ Ⓑ Ⓒ Ⓓ Ⓔ	42 Ⓐ Ⓑ Ⓒ Ⓓ Ⓔ	80 Ⓐ Ⓑ Ⓒ Ⓓ Ⓔ	118 Ⓐ Ⓑ Ⓒ Ⓓ Ⓔ
5 Ⓐ Ⓑ Ⓒ Ⓓ Ⓔ	43 Ⓐ Ⓑ Ⓒ Ⓓ Ⓔ	81 Ⓐ Ⓑ Ⓒ Ⓓ Ⓔ	119 Ⓐ Ⓑ Ⓒ Ⓓ Ⓔ
6 Ⓐ Ⓑ Ⓒ Ⓓ Ⓔ	44 Ⓐ Ⓑ Ⓒ Ⓓ Ⓔ	82 Ⓐ Ⓑ Ⓒ Ⓓ Ⓔ	120 Ⓐ Ⓑ Ⓒ Ⓓ Ⓔ
7 Ⓐ Ⓑ Ⓒ Ⓓ Ⓔ	45 Ⓐ Ⓑ Ⓒ Ⓓ Ⓔ	83 Ⓐ Ⓑ Ⓒ Ⓓ Ⓔ	121 Ⓐ Ⓑ Ⓒ Ⓓ Ⓔ
8 Ⓐ Ⓑ Ⓒ Ⓓ Ⓔ	46 Ⓐ Ⓑ Ⓒ Ⓓ Ⓔ	84 Ⓐ Ⓑ Ⓒ Ⓓ Ⓔ	122 Ⓐ Ⓑ Ⓒ Ⓓ Ⓔ
9 Ⓐ Ⓑ Ⓒ Ⓓ Ⓔ	47 Ⓐ Ⓑ Ⓒ Ⓓ Ⓔ	85 Ⓐ Ⓑ Ⓒ Ⓓ Ⓔ	123 Ⓐ Ⓑ Ⓒ Ⓓ Ⓔ
10 Ⓐ Ⓑ Ⓒ Ⓓ Ⓔ	48 Ⓐ Ⓑ Ⓒ Ⓓ Ⓔ	86 Ⓐ Ⓑ Ⓒ Ⓓ Ⓔ	124 Ⓐ Ⓑ Ⓒ Ⓓ Ⓔ
11 Ⓐ Ⓑ Ⓒ Ⓓ Ⓔ	49 Ⓐ Ⓑ Ⓒ Ⓓ Ⓔ	87 Ⓐ Ⓑ Ⓒ Ⓓ Ⓔ	125 Ⓐ Ⓑ Ⓒ Ⓓ Ⓔ
12 Ⓐ Ⓑ Ⓒ Ⓓ Ⓔ	50 Ⓐ Ⓑ Ⓒ Ⓓ Ⓔ	88 Ⓐ Ⓑ Ⓒ Ⓓ Ⓔ	126 Ⓐ Ⓑ Ⓒ Ⓓ Ⓔ
13 Ⓐ Ⓑ Ⓒ Ⓓ Ⓔ	51 Ⓐ Ⓑ Ⓒ Ⓓ Ⓔ	89 Ⓐ Ⓑ Ⓒ Ⓓ Ⓔ	127 Ⓐ Ⓑ Ⓒ Ⓓ Ⓔ
14 Ⓐ Ⓑ Ⓒ Ⓓ Ⓔ	52 Ⓐ Ⓑ Ⓒ Ⓓ Ⓔ	90 Ⓐ Ⓑ Ⓒ Ⓓ Ⓔ	128 Ⓐ Ⓑ Ⓒ Ⓓ Ⓔ
15 Ⓐ Ⓑ Ⓒ Ⓓ Ⓔ	53 Ⓐ Ⓑ Ⓒ Ⓓ Ⓔ	91 Ⓐ Ⓑ Ⓒ Ⓓ Ⓔ	129 Ⓐ Ⓑ Ⓒ Ⓓ Ⓔ
16 Ⓐ Ⓑ Ⓒ Ⓓ Ⓔ	54 Ⓐ Ⓑ Ⓒ Ⓓ Ⓔ	92 Ⓐ Ⓑ Ⓒ Ⓓ Ⓔ	130 Ⓐ Ⓑ Ⓒ Ⓓ Ⓔ
17 Ⓐ Ⓑ Ⓒ Ⓓ Ⓔ	55 Ⓐ Ⓑ Ⓒ Ⓓ Ⓔ	93 Ⓐ Ⓑ Ⓒ Ⓓ Ⓔ	131 Ⓐ Ⓑ Ⓒ Ⓓ Ⓔ
18 Ⓐ Ⓑ Ⓒ Ⓓ Ⓔ	56 Ⓐ Ⓑ Ⓒ Ⓓ Ⓔ	94 Ⓐ Ⓑ Ⓒ Ⓓ Ⓔ	132 Ⓐ Ⓑ Ⓒ Ⓓ Ⓔ
19 Ⓐ Ⓑ Ⓒ Ⓓ Ⓔ	57 Ⓐ Ⓑ Ⓒ Ⓓ Ⓔ	95 Ⓐ Ⓑ Ⓒ Ⓓ Ⓔ	133 Ⓐ Ⓑ Ⓒ Ⓓ Ⓔ
20 Ⓐ Ⓑ Ⓒ Ⓓ Ⓔ	58 Ⓐ Ⓑ Ⓒ Ⓓ Ⓔ	96 Ⓐ Ⓑ Ⓒ Ⓓ Ⓔ	134 Ⓐ Ⓑ Ⓒ Ⓓ Ⓔ
21 Ⓐ Ⓑ Ⓒ Ⓓ Ⓔ	59 Ⓐ Ⓑ Ⓒ Ⓓ Ⓔ	97 Ⓐ Ⓑ Ⓒ Ⓓ Ⓔ	135 Ⓐ Ⓑ Ⓒ Ⓓ Ⓔ
22 Ⓐ Ⓑ Ⓒ Ⓓ Ⓔ	60 Ⓐ Ⓑ Ⓒ Ⓓ Ⓔ	98 Ⓐ Ⓑ Ⓒ Ⓓ Ⓔ	136 Ⓐ Ⓑ Ⓒ Ⓓ Ⓔ
23 Ⓐ Ⓑ Ⓒ Ⓓ Ⓔ	61 Ⓐ Ⓑ Ⓒ Ⓓ Ⓔ	99 Ⓐ Ⓑ Ⓒ Ⓓ Ⓔ	137 Ⓐ Ⓑ Ⓒ Ⓓ Ⓔ
24 Ⓐ Ⓑ Ⓒ Ⓓ Ⓔ	62 Ⓐ Ⓑ Ⓒ Ⓓ Ⓔ	100 Ⓐ Ⓑ Ⓒ Ⓓ Ⓔ	138 Ⓐ Ⓑ Ⓒ Ⓓ Ⓔ
25 Ⓐ Ⓑ Ⓒ Ⓓ Ⓔ	63 Ⓐ Ⓑ Ⓒ Ⓓ Ⓔ	101 Ⓐ Ⓑ Ⓒ Ⓓ Ⓔ	139 Ⓐ Ⓑ Ⓒ Ⓓ Ⓔ
26 Ⓐ Ⓑ Ⓒ Ⓓ Ⓔ	64 Ⓐ Ⓑ Ⓒ Ⓓ Ⓔ	102 Ⓐ Ⓑ Ⓒ Ⓓ Ⓔ	140 Ⓐ Ⓑ Ⓒ Ⓓ Ⓔ
27 Ⓐ Ⓑ Ⓒ Ⓓ Ⓔ	65 Ⓐ Ⓑ Ⓒ Ⓓ Ⓔ	103 Ⓐ Ⓑ Ⓒ Ⓓ Ⓔ	141 Ⓐ Ⓑ Ⓒ Ⓓ Ⓔ
28 Ⓐ Ⓑ Ⓒ Ⓓ Ⓔ	66 Ⓐ Ⓑ Ⓒ Ⓓ Ⓔ	104 Ⓐ Ⓑ Ⓒ Ⓓ Ⓔ	142 Ⓐ Ⓑ Ⓒ Ⓓ Ⓔ
29 Ⓐ Ⓑ Ⓒ Ⓓ Ⓔ	67 Ⓐ Ⓑ Ⓒ Ⓓ Ⓔ	105 Ⓐ Ⓑ Ⓒ Ⓓ Ⓔ	143 Ⓐ Ⓑ Ⓒ Ⓓ Ⓔ
30 Ⓐ Ⓑ Ⓒ Ⓓ Ⓔ	68 Ⓐ Ⓑ Ⓒ Ⓓ Ⓔ	106 Ⓐ Ⓑ Ⓒ Ⓓ Ⓔ	144 Ⓐ Ⓑ Ⓒ Ⓓ Ⓔ
31 Ⓐ Ⓑ Ⓒ Ⓓ Ⓔ	69 Ⓐ Ⓑ Ⓒ Ⓓ Ⓔ	107 Ⓐ Ⓑ Ⓒ Ⓓ Ⓔ	145 Ⓐ Ⓑ Ⓒ Ⓓ Ⓔ
32 Ⓐ Ⓑ Ⓒ Ⓓ Ⓔ	70 Ⓐ Ⓑ Ⓒ Ⓓ Ⓔ	108 Ⓐ Ⓑ Ⓒ Ⓓ Ⓔ	146 Ⓐ Ⓑ Ⓒ Ⓓ Ⓔ
33 Ⓐ Ⓑ Ⓒ Ⓓ Ⓔ	71 Ⓐ Ⓑ Ⓒ Ⓓ Ⓔ	109 Ⓐ Ⓑ Ⓒ Ⓓ Ⓔ	147 Ⓐ Ⓑ Ⓒ Ⓓ Ⓔ
34 Ⓐ Ⓑ Ⓒ Ⓓ Ⓔ	72 Ⓐ Ⓑ Ⓒ Ⓓ Ⓔ	110 Ⓐ Ⓑ Ⓒ Ⓓ Ⓔ	148 Ⓐ Ⓑ Ⓒ Ⓓ Ⓔ
35 Ⓐ Ⓑ Ⓒ Ⓓ Ⓔ	73 Ⓐ Ⓑ Ⓒ Ⓓ Ⓔ	111 Ⓐ Ⓑ Ⓒ Ⓓ Ⓔ	149 Ⓐ Ⓑ Ⓒ Ⓓ Ⓔ
36 Ⓐ Ⓑ Ⓒ Ⓓ Ⓔ	74 Ⓐ Ⓑ Ⓒ Ⓓ Ⓔ	112 Ⓐ Ⓑ Ⓒ Ⓓ Ⓔ	150 Ⓐ Ⓑ Ⓒ Ⓓ Ⓔ
37 Ⓐ Ⓑ Ⓒ Ⓓ Ⓔ	75 Ⓐ Ⓑ Ⓒ Ⓓ Ⓔ	113 Ⓐ Ⓑ Ⓒ Ⓓ Ⓔ	
38 Ⓐ Ⓑ Ⓒ Ⓓ Ⓔ	76 Ⓐ Ⓑ Ⓒ Ⓓ Ⓔ	114 Ⓐ Ⓑ Ⓒ Ⓓ Ⓔ	

Sample Examinations

This chapter contains three sample Humanities examinations, each with an answer key, scoring chart, and answer explanations. Calculate and record your scores and see your improvement on the Progress Chart on page 12.

SAMPLE HUMANITIES EXAMINATION 1

NUMBER OF QUESTIONS: 150

Time limit: 90 MINUTES

> **Directions:** Each of the questions or incomplete statements below is followed by five suggested answers or completions. Select the one that is best in each case.

1. The composer of *Carmina Burana* and *Die Kluge* is

   (A) Olivier Messiaen
   (B) Carl Orff
   (C) Leos Janácek
   (C) Peter Mennin
   (E) Nicolas Medtner

2. George Gershwin wrote all of the following except

   (A) *An American in Paris*
   (B) *Porgy and Bess*
   (C) *Cuban Overture*
   (D) *Rhapsody in Blue*
   (E) *The White Peacock*

3. Fernand Leger was a contemporary of

   (A) Michelangelo
   (B) da Vinci
   (C) Rubens
   (D) Braque
   (E) van Gogh

4. A major recurrent theme in the compositions of Willem de Kooning is

   (A) flowers
   (B) children
   (C) nightmares
   (D) birds
   (E) women

5. The first American writer to popularize the American Indian in literature was

   (A) Cooper
   (B) Hillerman
   (C) Twain
   (D) Irving
   (E) Longfellow

6. In a popular short story by F. Scott Fitzgerald, Bernice

   (A) runs away from school
   (B) steals a purse
   (C) elopes
   (D) bobs her hair
   (E) steals her sister's beau

7. Structural elements of architecture such as the pointed arch and the flying buttress were extensively used in the period known as

   (A) Byzantine
   (B) Gothic
   (C) Renaissance
   (D) Baroque
   (E) Victorian

8. The most intrinsically American and most durable of all motion picture genres is

   (A) romantic comedy
   (B) black comedy
   (C) musical comedy
   (D) the western
   (E) tragedy

9. "I have found that all the bronze my furnace contained had been exhausted in the head of this figure [of the statue of Perseus]. . . . It was a miracle. . . . I seemed to see in this head the head of god." This statement was made by

   (A) Grangousier
   (B) Cellini
   (C) Machiavelli
   (D) Michelangelo
   (E) Praxiteles

10. Which of the following plays was not written by Shakespeare?

   (A) *Titus Andronicus*
   (B) *Dr. Faustus*
   (C) *Love's Labour's Lost*
   (D) *The Tempest*
   (E) *Coriolanus*

11. The monarch known as the "Sun King" was

   (A) Charles II of England
   (B) Edward I of England
   (C) George VI of England
   (D) Henry IV of France
   (E) Louis XIV of France

12. The difference between sonata and sonata-allegro is

   (A) the sonata is more contrapuntal
   (B) the sonata is more homophonic
   (C) one is faster than the other
   (D) the sonata is a multi-movement work which might contain one or more movements in sonata-allegro form
   (E) the sonata-allegro form preceded the sonata

13. Impressionism in music originated in France under the leadership of

    (A) Debussy and Ravel
    (B) Poulenc and Hindemith
    (C) Stravinsky and Bartók
    (D) Debussy and Chopin
    (E) Sessions and Varese

14. Leonardo da Vinci was one of the greatest artists of the period known as

    (A) Baroque
    (B) the early Renaissance
    (C) the high Renaissance
    (D) Gothic
    (E) Byzantine

15. The word *philosophy* means literally

    (A) love of knowledge
    (B) knowledge of God
    (C) love of God
    (D) love of wisdom
    (E) science and progress

16. The play that shows the downfall of a man as a result of biological urges or his social environment is called

    (A) epic theater
    (B) neorealism
    (C) romantic tragedy
    (D) deterministic tragedy
    (E) Ibsenian irony

17. The unresolved or "open" ending is one of the trademarks of

    (A) Greek tragedy
    (B) Restoration comedy
    (C) Shakespearean comedy
    (D) Roman tragedy
    (E) modern plays and cinema

18. Dante's *Divine Comedy* contains how many cantos?

    (A) 3
    (B) 4
    (C) 33
    (D) 99
    (E) 100

19. The origins of Baroque architecture can be traced to Sansovino, Palladio, and

    (A) Bellini
    (B) Michelangelo
    (C) Giotto
    (D) da Vinci
    (E) Lorenzo

20. In the theater, a conventional character, a type that recurs in numerous works, is called

    (A) a tragic hero
    (B) a deus ex machina
    (C) a stock character
    (D) a redundant character
    (E) a supernumerary character

21. The greatest ballet dancer of the beginning of the 20th century and prima ballerina of the Maryinsky Theater was

    (A) Tamara Karsavina
    (B) Galina Ulanova
    (C) Anna Pavlova
    (D) Tamara Toumanova
    (E) Alexandra Danilova

22. The photo below is an example of

    (A) 17th-century art
    (B) 18th-century Spanish art
    (C) modern Mexican art
    (D) medieval art
    (E) American primitive art

23. Polyphonic texture is

    (A) chordal texture
    (B) unaccompanied melody
    (C) accompanied melody
    (D) a combination of melodies
    (E) common to all forms

24. *The Tempest* is a play of airy fancy and romantic charm, but it cannot be mistaken for a young man's work because

    (A) its comic situations are in reality serious
    (B) its conclusion offers no hope for mankind
    (C) it contains the kind of crowd-pleasing devices that can come only with experience
    (D) it abounds in wise reflections on human nature and human existence
    (E) we know that it was one of the best plays that Shakespeare ever wrote

25. A Danish writer, best known for the *Seven Gothic Tales* and *Winter's Tales*, was

    (A) Isak Dinesen
    (B) Karen Petersen
    (C) Inge Johanssen
    (D) Ingeborg Carlsen
    (E) Gerte Grimm

26. A well-known Spanish court painter of the 18th century was

    (A) Velásquez
    (B) Ribera
    (C) Pisarro
    (D) Goya
    (E) Pisano

27. The Greek playwright who introduced the third actor into tragedy was

    (A) Agamemnon
    (B) Euripides
    (C) Socrates
    (D) Thespis
    (E) Clytaemnestra

28. The Romantic period of literature gave birth to a special kind of horror story, the

    (A) pastoral romance
    (B) epic
    (C) vignette
    (D) Gothic novel
    (E) dramatic monologue

29. The story of the founding of Rome by the mythical Aeneas was written by

    (A) Augustus
    (B) Vergil
    (C) Homer
    (D) Sibyl
    (E) Romulus

30. Wagner's last opera concerning the search for the Holy Grail is

    (A) *Festspielhaus*
    (B) *Cosima*
    (C) *Siegfried*
    (D) *Parsifal*
    (E) *Wahnfried*

31. Rome contributed all of the following to architecture except

    (A) an emphasis on verticality
    (B) design of significant interiors
    (C) buildings for use
    (D) the arch and vault as a building principle
    (E) the flying buttress

32. A post-Impressionist painter best known for his South Seas subjects was

    (A) Paul Gauguin
    (B) Vincent van Gogh
    (C) Toulouse-Lautrec
    (D) Paul Cezanne
    (E) Georges Seurat

33. A modern playwright who believes in "aesthetic distancing" is

    (A) Arthur Miller
    (B) Eugene O'Neill
    (C) Jean Paul Sartre
    (D) Stanley Kubrick
    (E) Bertolt Brecht

34. The central figure in the Bayeux tapestry is

    (A) Alexander the Great
    (B) William the Conqueror
    (C) Edward the Confessor
    (D) Gregory the Great
    (E) Charlemagne

35. During the Hellenic period, the great center of Greek culture was located at

    (A) Alexandria
    (B) Antioch
    (C) Athens
    (D) Rhodes
    (E) Pergamon

Questions 36–38 refer to the following groups of people:

    (A) Paul Klee, Marc Chagall, Pablo Picasso
    (B) Samuel Barber, Alban Berg, George Gershwin
    (C) Paul Johnson, Mies van der Rohe, Louis Sullivan
    (D) Anne Jackson, Anne Tyler, Anne Bradstreet
    (E) Amy Lowell, May Senson, Nikki Giovanni

36. Which is a group of 20th-century painters?

37. Which is a group of 20th-century American poets?

38. Which is a group of 20th-century composers of opera?

39. All of the following are of the House of Atreus except

    (A) Agamemnon
    (B) Menelaus
    (C) Orestes
    (D) Iphigenia
    (E) Aphrodite

40. Willy Loman is one of the most famous characters in the modern American theater. He appears in

    (A) *Cat on a Hot Tin Roof*
    (B) *Murder in the Cathedral*
    (C) *The Sand Box*
    (D) *Oklahoma!*
    (E) *Death of a Salesman*

41. Which item does not belong in the following group?

    (A) a priori knowledge
    (B) deductive thinking
    (C) intuition
    (D) formal science
    (E) empirical knowledge

42. Which of the following Greek divinities is not properly identified?

    (A) Zeus, supreme god of the Greeks
    (B) Hephaestus, messenger of the gods
    (C) Aphrodite, goddess of love
    (D) Artemis, goddess of the moon
    (E) Apollo, god of the sun

43. A painter noted for his scenes of the American West was

    (A) Thomas Hart Benton
    (B) Frederick Remington
    (C) Grant Wood
    (D) Edward Hopper
    (E) John Marin

44. "Capriccio Espagnol" and "Scheherazade" were written by

    (A) Glinka
    (B) Moussorgsky
    (C) Tchaikovsky
    (D) Borodin
    (E) Rimsky-Korsakov

45. Which of the following composers served as a bridge between the Classical and Romantic periods?

    (A) Bruckner
    (B) Wagner
    (C) Tchaikovsky
    (D) Beethoven
    (E) Berlioz

46. John Steinbeck traveled America and reported on the people he met, the things he saw. His constant companion on one trip was his dog

    (A) Mitzi
    (B) Rocinante
    (C) Charlie
    (D) Joseph
    (E) Willie

47. "The Hand of God" and "The Kiss" are sculptures by

    (A) Rodin
    (B) Bertinelli
    (C) Michelangelo
    (D) Brancusi
    (E) Epstein

48. All of the following operas were written by Mozart except

    (A) *Don Giovanni*
    (B) *The Marriage of Figaro*
    (C) *Orpheus and Eurydice*
    (D) *The Magic Flute*
    (E) *Cosi fan tutte*

49. The American poet who wrote such works as "Abraham Lincoln Walks at Midnight" and "The Santa Fe Trail" was

    (A) Vachel Lindsay
    (B) William Carlos Williams
    (C) Walt Whitman
    (D) Carl Sandburg
    (E) Van Wyck Brooks

50. The medieval liturgical drama

    (A) was an outgrowth of the Roman theater
    (B) was an outgrowth of the Greek theater
    (C) sprang up independently of Roman and Greek theaters
    (D) was based upon pagan rites and rituals
    (E) owed much to such writers as Ben Jonson and William Shakespeare

51. The best known of the medieval morality plays is

    (A) *Quem Quaeritis Trope*
    (B) *The Castell of Perseverance*
    (C) *The Life of Christ*
    (D) *Hamlet*
    (E) *Everyman*

52. The first collected edition of Shakespeare's plays is known as

    (A) *The Collected Works of William Shakespeare*
    (B) *The First Quarto*
    (C) *The First Folio*
    (D) *"Othello" and Other Plays by William Shakespeare*
    (E) *Shakespeare's Plays: 1623*

53. An American author who vigorously attacked the "genteel tradition" and who took an active interest in American social problems was

    (A) Stephen Crane
    (B) Edward Arlington Robinson
    (C) Edgar Lee Masters
    (D) Theodore Dreiser
    (E) Thomas Wolfe

54. Two composers from the Baroque period are

    (A) Brahms and Berlioz
    (B) Stravinsky and Piston
    (C) Bach and Handel
    (D) Mozart and Haydn
    (E) Verdi and Puccini

55. Most jazz has a standard form of

    (A) sonata-allegro
    (B) rondo
    (C) theme and variation
    (D) fugue
    (E) canon

56. Surrealist art is associated with

    (A) frottage, the subconscious, paradox
    (B) anxiety, silence, the metaphysical
    (C) timelessness, literary origins, loneliness
    (D) fantasy, Freud, free association
    (E) all of these

57. Unlike most of the later troubadours, the *jongleurs* of the 11th century were

    (A) not of noble birth
    (B) accompanied by a small orchestra
    (C) able to sing the *chanson de geste*
    (D) more sophisticated
    (E) accompanied by two men

58. According to Plato, the principles of goodness and truth are

    (A) purely human conceptions
    (B) a result of class training
    (C) descriptions of the ways our minds work
    (D) objective realities that transcend human experience
    (E) rationalizations to conceal expediency and laziness

59. Two composers of the Italian Renaissance were

    (A) Ockeghem and Paderewski
    (D) Josquin and Cellini
    (B) Monteverdi and Bellini
    (E) Parmagianino and Cavalli
    (C) Palestrina and Josquin

60. *Metaphysics* is primarily the study of

    (A) morals
    (B) art
    (C) being as such
    (D) beauty and goodness
    (E) knowledge

61. The convention by which an actor, "unnoticed" by others on the stage, makes a brief comment to the audience, is the

    (A) soliloquy
    (B) perspective
    (C) aside
    (D) periphery
    (E) denouement

62. The Globe Theater

    (A) was closed on all sides but open on top
    (B) had a stage that extended into the audience area
    (C) depended upon natural lighting
    (D) was built in 1599
    (E) all of these

63. "One that lov'd not wisely but too well," describes

    (A) Hamlet
    (B) Romeo
    (C) Cleopatra
    (D) Othello
    (E) Desdemona

64. All except one of the following 20th-century authors have used materials from their Jewish backgrounds. The one exception is

    (A) Philip Roth
    (B) Saul Bellow
    (C) Bernard Malamud
    (D) Paul Goodman
    (E) John Updike

65. The art of painting on freshly spread moist lime plaster with pigments suspended in a water vehicle is called

    (A) collage
    (B) fresco
    (C) surrealism
    (D) primitivism
    (E) pointillism

©Bettman/Corbis

66. The building pictured above is an example of the architecture of

    (A) Christopher Wren
    (B) Inigo Jones
    (C) Frank Lloyd Wright
    (D) Joseph Paxton
    (E) Gustave Eiffel

67. Artists rediscovered man, glorified him as part of the world, and scientists discovered the world around man in the time of

    (A) the Roman Empire
    (B) the Middle Ages
    (C) the late 19th century
    (D) the Greek period
    (E) the Renaissance

68. All of the following were written by Ernest Hemingway except

    (A) *For Whom the Bell Tolls*
    (B) *The Old Lions*
    (C) *The Old Man and the Sea*
    (D) *Death in the Afternoon*
    (E) *The Sun Also Rises*

69. The Renaissance Italian author who, writing in the vernacular, opposed the extension of the pope's secular power was

    (A) Cellini
    (B) Machiavelli
    (C) Dante
    (D) Scotti
    (E) Manzoni

70. John Steinbeck once undertook a study of the tide pools with Dr. Ed Ricketts, a noted marine biologist. The trip is recorded in Steinbeck's

    (A) *Two Years Before the Mast*
    (B) *Tide Pools and Sea Urchins*
    (C) *Log of the Sea of Cortez*
    (D) *The Dory*
    (E) *Innocents Abroad*

71. In Shakespeare's plays,

    (A) All the female roles were played by boys when the plays were first produced
    (B) highly stylized language was a convention of the theater
    (C) the "tragic hero" was always of noble birth
    (D) the dialogue was written in poetic forms
    (E) all of the above

72. A Roman writer of comedy was

    (A) Menander
    (B) Hrosvitha
    (C) Plautus
    (D) Seneca
    (E) Sodomaeus

73. The American author who gave the English language the word *babbitry* was

    (A) Sinclair Lewis
    (B) Robinson Jeffers
    (C) Willa Cather
    (D) Edward Arlington Robinson
    (E) John Steinbeck

Questions 74 and 75 refer to the following line of poetry:

"How do I love thee? Let me count the ways."

74. This is the opening line of

    (A) *A Midsummer's Night Dream*
    (B) "Sonnets from the Portuguese"
    (C) "Burnt Norton"
    (D) "Sestina Altaforte"
    (E) "The Ballade of Dead Ladies"

75. The poem from which the line is taken was written by

    (A) William Shakespeare
    (B) T.S. Eliot
    (C) Ezra Pound
    (D) Robert Browning
    (E) Elizabeth Barrett Browning

The Granger Collection

76. The photograph above is an example of a style of painting popular during which century?

    (A) 15th
    (B) 17th
    (C) 18th
    (D) 19th
    (E) 20th

77. When the ghost in *Hamlet* appeared, most people in Shakespeare's audience would have

    (A) laughed, because the supernatural was considered ridiculous
    (B) recognized the figure as a dramatic symbol
    (C) been unimpressed, since the device had been over-used
    (D) reacted in a manner that we are unable to guess
    (E) believed in the actuality of ghosts appearing on stage

78. The architect who designed the Crystal Palace was

    (A) Charles Percier
    (B) P.F.L. Fontaine
    (C) Joseph Paxton
    (D) James Wyatt
    (E) Georges-Eugene Haussmann

79. Agamemnon's wife was

    (A) Jocasta
    (B) Clytaemnestra
    (C) Cassandra
    (D) Iphigenia
    (E) Antigone

80. When we speak of the study of *axiology*, we are talking about the interpretation of

    (A) existences
    (B) essences
    (C) substances
    (D) forms
    (E) values

81. The "green ey'd monster which doth mock the meat it feeds on" is

    (A) revenge
    (B) jealousy
    (C) pride
    (D) hatred
    (E) lust

82. Molière wrote during the reign of

    (A) Charles III
    (B) James II
    (C) Henry IV
    (D) Louis XIV
    (E) Elizabeth I

83. The Greek chorus did not

    (A) foretell the future
    (B) explain past actions
    (C) serve as the additional character in the play
    (D) philosophize
    (E) help to move scenery

84. Creon repents and goes to free Antigone, but she has already hanged herself. This is an example of

    (A) denouement
    (B) proscenium
    (C) deus ex machina
    (D) irony
    (E) *in medias res*

85. The modern meaning of deux ex machina in relation to drama is

    (A) a wheeled platform used as part of the scenery
    (B) a god from a machine
    (C) a mechanical device for staging elaborate effects
    (D) the catastrophic event at the climax of a play
    (E) an unsatisfactory resolution to problems of plot by means of an event for which the audience has not been prepared

86. Vincent van Gogh

    (A) faithfully followed the Impressionist techniques
    (B) felt that Impressionism did not allow the artist enough freedom to express his inner feelings
    (C) believed the artist must paint only what he could see, not what appeared in the mind
    (D) founded the movement in art called "abstract art"
    (E) led 17th-century art back to natural forms of realism

87. A single melody with subordinate harmony demonstrates

    (A) polyphonic texture
    (B) homophonic texture
    (C) monophonic texture
    (D) bitonality
    (E) rondo form

88. The musical terms *consonance* and *dissonance* are most properly used in a discussion of

    (A) texture
    (B) tone color
    (C) melody
    (D) rhythm
    (E) harmony

89. Gregorian chants are examples of which textures?

    (A) monophonic
    (B) contrapuntal
    (C) polyphonic
    (D) homophonic
    (E) modern

90. Which of the following is not characteristic of the Gregorian chant?

    (A) meter
    (B) use of Latin
    (C) use of eight church modes
    (D) male choir
    (E) a capella

91. A school of art known as *Surrealism* developed in the 1920s. A forerunner of the Surrealist school and the painter of *I and My Village* was

    (A) Picasso
    (B) Chagall
    (C) Klee
    (D) Kandinsky
    (E) Beckman

92. What author, sometimes called a western realist, wrote many tales of the American West and its mining towns?

    (A) A.P. Oakhurst
    (B) Ambrose Bierce
    (C) Stephen Crane
    (D) Bret Harte
    (E) M. Shipton

93. A singer, actress, poet, and playwright, perhaps best known for her autobiographical series, which includes *I Know Why the Caged Bird Sings* and *Gather Together in My Name,* is

    (A) Alice Walker
    (B) Linda Reed
    (C) Maya Angelou
    (D) Patricia Goldberg
    (E) Meryl Brooks

94. "The Rhapsody in Blue" was composed by

    (A) Paul Whiteman
    (B) Oscar Levant
    (C) Leonard Bernstein
    (D) Antheil Carpenter
    (E) George Gershwin

95. The first "King of Jazz" was a New Orleans barber named

    (A) Al Hirt
    (B) Bix Beiderbecke
    (C) Sidney Bechet
    (D) Charles Bolden
    (E) Papa Celestine

96. Almost every country in Europe has a national hero who has been enshrined in epic poems and myths. The national hero of Italy is

    (A) El Cid
    (B) Orlando Furioso
    (C) Beowulf
    (D) Roland
    (E) Giovanni Magnifioso

97. "The Canticle of the Sun" was written by

    (A) Dante
    (B) Chaucer
    (C) St. Francis of Assisi
    (D) Caedmon
    (E) The Venerable Bede

98. The 20th-century composer who first used the twelve-tone method was

    (A) Arnold Schoenberg
    (B) Leonard Bernstein
    (C) John Cage
    (D) George Gershwin
    (E) Richard Rodgers

99. Which of the following statements is *false?*

    (A) Satire is a means of showing dissatisfaction with an established institution or principle.
    (B) Satire is most easily accepted by an audience holding various beliefs or beliefs different from those of the playwright.
    (C) Satire was an early form of comedy.
    (D) *Lysistrata* is a classic example of satire.
    (E) Modern satire does not run the risk of being offensive.

100.

> LADY BRACKNELL: "Do you smoke?"
>
> JACK: "Well, yes, I must admit I smoke."
>
> LADY BRACKNELL: "I am glad to hear it. A man should always have an occupation of some sort."

The dialogue from Oscar Wilde's *The Importance of Being Earnest* illustrates

(A) sympathy
(B) empathy
(C) scorn
(D) comic pathos
(E) linguistic wit

101. Today's foremost American composer of musicals, noted for *Company, Sweeney Todd,* and *Sunday in the Park with George,* is

(A) Elmer Bernstein
(B) Stephen Sondheim
(C) Richard Rodgers
(D) Frederick Loewe
(E) Ernest Fleischman

102. Which American author, grandchild of a president, wrote a famous book about his own education?

(A) Henry Adams
(B) Robert Jackson
(C) Jonathan Tyler
(D) Elliot Roosevelt
(E) Howard Taft

103. In 1988 Toni Morrison won the Pulitzer Prize for her novel

(A) *Sula*
(B) *Song of Solomon*
(C) *I Know Why the Caged Bird Sings*
(D) *Beloved*
(E) *Tar Baby*

104. Best known for his book *I and Thou* is the philosopher

(A) Nietzsche
(B) Buber
(C) Russell
(D) Chardin
(E) Sartre

105. The Mexican painter whose murals can be seen in the Government Palace at Guadalajara is

(A) Rivera
(B) Orozco
(C) Siqueiros
(D) Hernández
(E) Cinfuentes

106. "I saw the sky descending black and white" is an example of

(A) iambic pentameter
(B) anapestic dimeter
(C) spondaic hexameter
(D) dactylic pentameter
(E) iambic tetrameter

107. Which of the following statements concerning courtly love is false?

(A) The idea was born in Provence in the 11th century.
(B) It was limited to the nobility.
(C) True love was considered impossible between husband and wife.
(D) Christian behavior was shunned.
(E) It glorified adultery.

108. The site of Apollo's great oracle was

    (A) Parnassus
    (B) Olympus
    (C) Athens
    (D) Crete
    (E) Delphi

109. The "Age of Faith" is a term that best applies to the

    (A) classical Greek period
    (B) Baroque period
    (C) Gothic period
    (D) Renaissance
    (E) 18th century

110. According to the Hedonist philosophers,

    (A) actions are right if they tend to promote pleasure
    (B) good acts depend primarily upon good intentions
    (C) good cannot be separated from work
    (D) duty makes an absolute demand upon us
    (E) right conduct involves obedience to some established authority

111. Giotto is noted for

    (A) writing a poem on a Grecian urn
    (B) discovering the principle of the flying buttress
    (C) the beginning of realistic painting in Western art, about 1300
    (D) impressionistic painting since 1900
    (E) inventing a secret process, now lost, for turning jewels into stained glass

Questions 112–114 refer to illustrations (A) through (E).

(A)

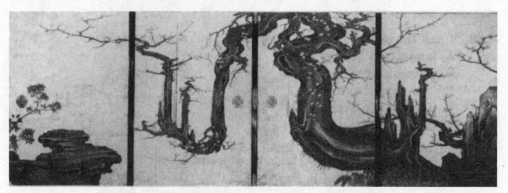

The Metropolitan Museum of Art, The Harry G.C. Packard Collection of Asian Art, Gift of Harry G.C. Packard and Purchase, Fletcher, Rogers, Harris Brisbane Dick and Louis V. Bell Funds, Joseph Pulitzer Bequest and The Annenberg Fund, Inc. Gift, 1975 (1975.268.48a-d) Image © The Metropolitan Museum of Art.

(B)

The Metropolitan Museum of Art, Purchased, special contributions and funds given or bequeathed by friends of the Museum, 1967 (67.241) Image © The Metropolitan Museum of Art.

(C)

The Metropolitan Museum of Art, Marquand Collection,
Gift of Henry G. Marquand, 1889 (89.15.21) Image ©
The Metropolitan Museum of Art.

(D)

The Metropolitan Museum of Art, Bequest of
Benjamin Altman, 1913 (14.40.618) Image
© The Metropolitan Museum of Art.

(E)

The Metropolitan Museum of Art,
Rogers Fund, 1947 (47.100.80)
Image © The Metropolitan
Musuem of Art.

112. Which is the Rembrandt?

113. Which is Japanese?

114. Which is an example of Impressionism?

115. The image below is a photograph of

    (A) the Parthenon
    (B) the Coliseum
    (C) Stonehenge
    (D) the Temple at Karnak
    (E) the Lighthouse at Knossos

Ruth S. Ward

116. In ancient and medieval mythology, the grif-fin is usually represented as a

    (A) winged horse
    (B) cross between a lion and agle
    (C) creature that is half man, half horse
    (D) winged lion with the head of a woman
    (E) devil with horns and cloven hooves

117. Deucalion is

    (A) the Greek Noah
    (B) the 10th book of the Bible
    (C) one of the daughters of Danaus
    (D) a whirlpool Odysseus encountered on his voyage
    (E) the hero of the Trojan War

118. "Ding, dong, bell;
    Pussy's in the well.
    Who put her in?
    Little Johnny Thin."

    The lines above are an example of

    (A) slant rhyme
    (B) a run-on line
    (C) sprung rhythm
    (D) hidden alliteration
    (E) ottava rima

119. A painter noted for his moving portraits, with bright light emerging from a dark can-vas, is

    (A) Pollock
    (B) Picasso
    (C) Rembrandt
    (D) Vermeer
    (E) van Gogh

120. The musical sign ♭

    (A) indicates false notes: falsetto
    (B) lowers the pitch of a note by a full step
    (C) precedes a note to be raised a full step
    (D) precedes a note to be raised by a half step
    (E) lowers the pitch of a note by a half step

121. Songs that are not as unreal as operatic arias but are much more sophisticated than folk songs are called

    (A) natural
    (B) erotic
    (C) lieder
    (D) appassionata
    (E) nova

122. As Candide journeyed from continent to continent, he searched for

    (A) Dr. Pangloss
    (B) the Oreillons
    (C) Providence
    (D) Cacambo
    (E) Cunegonde

123. The photograph below is a bust of

    (A) Queen Elizabeth I
    (B) Queen Nefertiti
    (C) the goddess Athena
    (D) Buddha
    (E) an unknown African warrior

©Bettman/Corbis

124. The photograph above is an example of

 (A) neolithic art
 (B) Corinthian art
 (C) Greek art
 (D) Egyptian art
 (E) Renaissance art

125. Winner of four 1996 Tony Awards, the musical Rent was based upon

 (A) Bellini's *Norma*
 (B) Verdi's *La Traviata*
 (C) Rossini's *William Tell*
 (D) Puccini's *La Boheme*
 (E) Mozart's *Don Giovanni*

126. Among *Rent's* other awards are

 (A) 1996 Pulitzer Price for Best American
 Drama
 (B) 1996 New York Drama Critics Circle
 Award for Best Musical
 (C) 1996 Outer Critics Circle Award for
 Best Off-Broadway Musical
 (D) 1996 Drama League Award for Best
 Musical
 (E) All of the above

127. Two principal forms of irony in tragedy are

 (A) Euripidean and Sophoclean
 (B) Aeschylean and Euripidean
 (C) Ibsenian and Shavian
 (D) Sophoclean and Aeschylean
 (E) comic and tragic

128. Leitmotif means

 (A) a note that is sung only once
 (B) a note or theme that is repeated
 (C) the leading motive
 (D) an aria
 (E) the first violinist is to take over leading
 the orchestra

129. Which of the following is not a convention
of the Elizabethan theater?

 (A) women's roles acted by young boys
 (B) setting established by dialogue
 (C) a chorus of elders
 (D) poetic language
 (E) the soliloquy

130. The basing of knowledge on scientific observation is best illustrated by

 (A) empiricists
 (B) rationalists
 (C) theologians
 (D) both rationalists and theologians
 (E) existentialists

131. In Greek mythology, the greatest of all musicians was

 (A) Dionysius
 (B) Musicus
 (C) Pan
 (D) Apollo
 (E) Orpheus

132. Odysseus' old nurse, who recognizes him
from a scar on his leg, was named

 (A) Argus
 (B) Euryclea
 (C) Menelaus
 (D) Calliope
 (E) Nausicaa

133. What Florentine autobiographer, goldsmith, and sculptor was a child of will rather than of reason and the quintessential Renaissance man?

    (A) Cellini
    (B) Lucagnolo
    (C) Urbrino
    (D) Francesco
    (E) Machiavelli

134. *Libretto* means the

    (A) rhythm of a musical composition
    (B) words of a musical composition, especially an opera
    (C) tempo of a musical composition
    (D) directions to the conductor
    (E) full orchestra is to play

135. A 20th-century poet who left America, went to England, and became one of England's most famous citizens was

    (A) Ezra Pound
    (B) Robinson Jeffers
    (C) Archibald MacLeish
    (D) Thomas Wolfe
    (E) T.S. Eliot

136. At the end of Saint-Exupéry's fairy tale, *The Little Prince*, the little prince

    (A) dies
    (B) goes home to his planet
    (C) falls into a deep sleep
    (D) decides to remain on earth
    (E) changes into a star

137. In 1900 the play *Madame Butterfly* was first produced in New York by

    (A) David Belasco
    (B) Bronson Howard
    (C) William Gillette
    (D) William Vaughan Moody
    (E) Eric Chang

138. A famous opera based on *Madame Butterfly* was written by

    (A) Puccini
    (B) Verdi
    (C) Strauss
    (D) Monteverdi
    (E) Offenbach

139. *M. Butterfly*, based on a true incident of a French diplomat who falls in love with a Chinese actress who turns out to be not only a spy but a man was written by

    (A) Lin Yutang
    (B) R.D. Liang
    (C) D.H. Hwang
    (D) Shi Ming
    (E) Dion Boucicault

140. Another version of *Madame Butterfly*, this one a musical set during the Vietnam War, is

    (A) *Indochine*
    (B) *Heaven and Earth*
    (C) *Apocalypse*
    (D) *Miss Saigon*
    (E) *Shogun*

141. The first black American writer to win the Nobel Prize for Literature was

    (A) Maya Angelou
    (B) Richard Wright
    (C) Toni Morrison
    (D) Langston Hughes
    (E) James Baldwin

142. A park dedicated to the sculptor Gustav Vigeland is to be found in

    (A) Oslo
    (B) Copenhagen
    (C) Paris
    (D) Helsinki
    (E) Stockholm

143. In music, a performer of unusual interpretive and technical skill is referred to as a(n)

    (A) savant
    (B) virtuoso
    (C) prima donna
    (D) maestro
    (E) maestoso

144. This art is an example of

    (A) Expressionism
    (B) Impressionism
    (C) Greek art
    (D) Byzantine art
    (E) primitive art

©Bettman/Corbis

145. The author of the one-act plays *The Toilet* and *Dutchman* is

    (A) Thomas Wolfe
    (B) James Baldwin
    (C) Lorraine Hansbury
    (D) LeRoi Jones (Imamu Amiri Baraka)
    (E) Countee Cullen

146. The modern musical *My Fair Lady* is based upon G.B. Shaw's play

    (A) *Man and Superman*
    (B) *Back to Methusaleh*
    (C) *Pygmalion*
    (D) *Candida*
    (E) *Arms and the Man*

Questions 147–149 refer to the following lines:

    (A) "I have measured out my life in coffee spoons."

    (B) "Do not go gentle into that good night,
        Old age should burn and rave at close day;
        Rage, rage, against the dying of the light."

    (C) "How did they fume, and stamp, and roar, and chafe!
        And swear, not Addison himself was safe."

    (D) "O Captain! my Captain! our fearful trip is done,
        The ship has weather'd every rack, the prize we sought is won,
        The port is near, the bells I hear, the people all exulting,
        While follow eyes the steady keel, the vessel grim and daring;
        But O heart! heart! heart!
          O the bleeding drops of red,
            Where on the deck my captain lies,
            Fallen cold and dead."

    (E) "Shall I compare thee to a summer's day?
        Thou art more lovely and more temperate."

147. Which alludes to the death of Abraham Lincoln?

148. Which is an example of a rhymed couplet?

149. Which is from a Shakespearean sonnet?

150. A cathedral noted for its famous rose windows is located at

    (A) Canterbury
    (B) Rome
    (C) London
    (D) Chartres
    (E) Istanbul

STOP

If there is still time remaining, you may review your answers.

Humanities
ANSWER KEY—SAMPLE EXAMINATION 1

1. B	26. D	51. E	76. D**	101. B	126. E
2. E	27. B	52. C	77. B	102. A	127. A
3. D	28. D	53. D	78. C	103. D	128. B
4. E	29. B	54. C	79. B	104. B	129. C
5. A	30. D	55. C	80. E	105. B	130. A
6. D	31. E	56. E	81. B	106. A	131. E
7. B	32. A	57. A	82. D	107. D	132. B
8. D	33. E	58. D	83. E	108. E	133. A
9. B	34. B	59. C	84. D	109. C	134. B
10. B	35. C	60. C	85. E	110. A	135. E
11. E	36. A	61. C	86. B	111. C	136. B
12. D	37. E	62. E	87. B	112. D	137. A
13. A	38. B	63. D	88. E	113. A	138. A
14. C	39. E	64. E	89. A	114. B	139. C
15. D	40. E	65. B	90. A	115. C	140. D
16. D	41. C	66. C*	91. B	116. B	141. C
17. E	42. B	67. E	92. D	117. A	142. A
18. E	43. B	68. B	93. C	118. C	143. B
19. B	44. E	69. C	94. E	119. C	144. D***
20. C	45. D	70. C	95. D	120. E	145. D
21. C	46. C	71. E	96. B	121. C	146. C
22. E	47. A	72. C	97. C	122. E	147. D
23. D	48. C	73. A	98. A	123. B	148. C
24. E	49. A	74. B	99. E	124. D	149. E
25. A	50. C	75. E	100. E	125. D	150. D

*The Solomon R. Guggenheim Museum.

**van Gogh, *The Starry Night*, 1889, Oil on Canvas, 29" x 36¼", Collection, the Museum of Modern Art, New York. Acquired through the Lillie B. Bliss Bequest.

***Enthroned Madonna and Child*, Byzantine School, National Gallery of Art, Washington, D.C., Andrew Mellon Collection.

SCORING CHART

After you have scored your Sample Examination 1, enter the results in the chart below; then transfer your score to the Progress Chart on page 12.

Total Test	Number Right	Number Wrong	Number Omitted
150			

ANSWER EXPLANATIONS

1. **(B)** Carl Orff believes that music in the long-accepted classical or romantic tradition has come to an end, and since 1935 has dedicated himself to the stage.

2. **(E)** *The White Peacock* was written by Charles T. Griffes.

3. **(D)** Fernand Leger (1881–1955), a Cubist, exhibited with both Braque and Picasso.

4. **(E)** De Kooning started his first series of women in 1938.

5. **(A)** James Fenimore Cooper (1789–1851) is best remembered for his *Leatherstocking Tales.*

6. **(D)** Fitzgerald, perhaps best known for his novel *The Great Gatsby,* also wrote short stories, one of the most popular being "Bernice Bobs Her Hair."

7. **(B)** "Gothic" pertains to an architectural style prevalent in western Europe from the 12th through the 15th centuries.

8. **(D)** Other countries have attempted to make westerns, but none has been successful.

9. **(B)** Benvenuto Cellini (1500–1571) was an Italian sculptor, metal-worker, and author.

10. **(B)** *Dr. Faustus* was written by Christopher Marlowe.

11. **(E)** Louis XIV (1638–1715) was king of France from 1643 to 1715.

12. **(D)** This is true by definition.

13. **(A)** Impressionism was the late-19th-century movement. The other composers listed are either not French, not Impressionist composers, or not both.

14. **(C)** The Renaissance originated in Italy in the 14th century, and later spread through Europe. Leonardo da Vinci (1452–1519) lived during the peak of the Italian Renaissance.

15. **(D)** This is true by definition.

16. **(D)** The point is that man is "determined" by heredity and/or environment.

17. **(E)** During other periods in time, all plays had a beginning, a middle, and an end.

18. **(E)** The poem is divided into three canticles, each made up of thirty-three cantos, plus the first canto in "Inferno," which serves as an introduction to the entire poem.

19. **(B)** Michelangelo was the famous painter of the Sistine Chapel.

20. **(C)** Stock characters, such as the braggart soldier, the jealous husband, and the stubborn father, appear as far back as the Greek and Roman comedies.

21. **(C)** Pavlova was promoted to prima ballerina in 1906, after a performance of *Swan Lake*.

22. **(E)** This American Primitive work was painted by an unknown artist, circa 1795.

23. **(D)** This is true by definition.

24. **(E)** It is believed *The Tempest* was written between 1611 and 1616. It was first published in the First Folio.

25. **(A)** Isak Dinesen was the pen name of Karen Dinesen von Blixen. She signed her stories "Isak," meaning "he who laughs."

26. **(D)** Goya was the leading painter, etcher, and designer of his day.

27. **(B)** None of the others were Greek playwrights.

28. **(D)** One of the most enduring popular examples of this genre is Mary Shelley's *Frankenstein*

29. **(B)** The work is *The Aeneid.*

30. **(D)** *Parsifal* was the first presented in 1882 in Bayreuth.

31. **(E)** The flying buttress was a development in Gothic architecture.

32. **(A)** Gauguin spent many years in Tahiti, painting native subjects.

33. **(E)** Brecht has even written plays within plays within plays so that the audience is always aware it is attending a play, and not experiencing reality.

34. **(B)** The Bayeux Tapestry depicts the Norman Conquest of England and the events leading up to it.

35. **(C)** Athens was the home of the arts, mathematics, philosophy, etc.

36. **(A)** The others are not 20th-century painters.

37. **(E)** The others are not 20th-century poets.

38. **(B)** The others are not 20th-century composers of opera.

39. **(E)** Aphrodite was the Greek goddess of love.

40. **(E)** The play was written by Arthur Miller, and it ushered in a new concept of tragedy.

41. **(C)** Intuition may be defined as the power or faculty of attaining to direct knowledge or cognition without rational thought. All the other terms imply rational thought.

42. **(B)** Hephaestus was the Greek god of fire and metalcraft.

43. **(B)** Remington is especially noted for his cowboys, Indians, and soldiers.

44. **(E)** Rimsky-Korsakov (1844–1908) was a Russian composer.

45. **(D)** Ludwig van Beethoven (1770–1827) studied with Mozart and Haydn and influenced the later Romantic composers.

46. **(C)** The book Steinbeck wrote was entitled *Travels with Charlie.*

47. **(A)** Auguste Rodin (1840–1917), the great French artist, was perhaps the greatest sculptor of his time.

48. **(C)** *Orpheus and Eurydice* was written by Gluck.

49. **(A)** Vachel Lindsay (1897–1931) was an American poet noted for his individualistic style, characterized by jazz-like rhythm.

50. **(C)** The medieval liturgical drama developed during the celebration of the mass.

51. **(E)** *Everyman* is a 15th-century allegorical play. Everyman, the hero, is summoned by Death to appear before God. Of all his friends and virtues, only Good Deeds may accompany him.

52. **(C)** The First Folio was printed in 1623.

53. **(D)** Two of Dreiser's best known novels are *An American Tragedy* and *Sister Carrie.*

54. **(C)** The other composers are not both from the Baroque period.

55. **(C)** Each time a musician plays a jazz work, he or she interprets the piece. Jazz is notoriously individualistic and variable.

56. **(E)** To select but one of the other answers would be to only partially explain Surrealism.

57. **(A)** These early medieval minstrels came from the lower classes. They usually accompanied themselves on a simple musical instrument, such as a lute.

58. **(D)** This is one of the basic tenets of Platonism.

59. **(C)** This is the only example of two composers, both Italian and of the Renaissance period.

60. **(C)** Metaphysics may be defined as relating to the transcendent or supersensible.

61. **(C)** This is true by definition. The aside differs from the soliloquy in that, in the latter, the character reveals his thoughts in the form of a monologue, without addressing a listener.

62. **(E)** To ignore any of the above would be to give an incomplete answer.

63. **(D)** This line is spoken after the death of Othello, and refers to his intense passion for Desdemona, which led to his murdering her in a fit of jealousy.

64. **(E)** Updike's best known works are *Rabbit, Run* and *Rabbit Redux.*

65. **(B)** This is true by definition.

66. **(C)** Wright was a modern architect who believed in functional buildings, made of materials native to the region.

67. **(E)** The clue is in the word *rediscovered.* Renaissance means rebirth or revival of interest in learning.

68. **(B)** Hemingway was a famous 20th-century American writer who won the Nobel Prize for literature.

69. **(C)** Dante's best-known work is *The Divine Comedy.*

70. **(C)** The Sea of Cortez, in Mexico, sometimes called the Gulf of California, separates Baja California from Sonora.

71. **(E)** The others are true, but only partial answers.

72. **(C)** Plautus and Terence were the great Roman writers of comedy.

73. **(A)** The word was coined from the title of Lewis' novel *Babbitt.*

74. **(B)** The sonnet sequence that opens with the line quoted is one of the most famous in English literature.

75. **(E)** Elizabeth Barrett wrote the sonnet sequence for her future husband, Robert Browning.

76. **(D)** The painting is *The Starry Night,* by van Gogh (1853–1890).

77. **(B)** Ghosts often appeared in Elizabethan plays as dramatic symbols. The audience was accustomed to the dramatic use of the ghost.

78. **(C)** Paxton first designed a similar but larger structure for the London Exhibition of 1851. In 1853 and 1854 he supervised the building of the Crystal Palace at Sydenham, England.

79. **(B)** Agamemnon was the leader of the Greeks in the Trojan War. Upon his return from the war Clytaemnestra and Aegisthus, her lover, murdered Agamemnon in his bath.

80. **(E)** This is true by definition.

81. **(B)** This line is from Shakespeare's *Othello.*

82. **(D)** Louis XIV ruled France from 1643 to 1715.

83. **(E)** The Greeks did not use scenery in their plays.

84. **(D)** Dramatic irony occurs when the audience understands the incongruity between a situation and the accompanying speeches while the characters in the play remain unaware of the incongruity.

85. **(E)** The modern meaning is that of a contrived or improbable conclusion.

86. **(B)** Van Gogh is generally considered a post-Impressionist.

87. **(B)** This is true by definition.

88. **(E)** Harmony, in music, refers to the structure of a musical composition from the point of view of its chordal characteristics and relationships.

89. **(A)** Gregorian chants contain a single melodic line.

90. **(A)** Gregorian chant is the monodic liturgical plainsong of the Roman Catholic Church.

91. **(B)** Chagall is also well known for his stained glass windows that adorn churches and synagogues throughout Europe and Israel.

92. **(D)** Two of Harte's best-known short stories are "The Outcasts of Poker Flat" and "The Luck of Roaring Camp."

93. **(C)** Angelou, born in Arkansas in 1928, also wrote *Singin' and Swingin' and Gettin' Merry Like Christmas* and *The Heart of a Woman.*

94. **(E)** Gershwin was also the composer of the folk opera *Porgy and Bess,* as well as many popular songs.

95. **(D)** The others are jazz figures, but none were barbers.

96. **(B)** Ariosto's "Orlando Furioso" is the best-known poem on the subject.

97. **(C)** Francis of Assisi was the founder of the Franciscan Order and one of the greatest of Christian saints.

98. **(A)** Schoenberg's twelve-tone system has become perhaps the most controversial musical development of the 20th century.

99. **(E)** Modern satire is often intentionally offensive.

100. **(E)** Wilde was noted for his linguistic wit.

101. **(B)** Sondheim's most recent works are *Into the Woods* and *Passion.* He also wrote the lyrics for *West Side Story.*

102. **(A)** The book is entitled *The Education of Henry Adams.*

103. **(D)** A novel in the "magical realism" mode, *Beloved* is based upon a true story of infanticide in Kentucky.

104. **(B)** Martin Buber's *I and Thou* posits a direct dialogue between the individual and God.

105. **(B)** Jose Clemente Orozco (1883–1949) was a painter of revolutionary murals. The imagination and emotional force of the murals in the Government Palace are impressively powerful.

106. **(A)** The iamb is a metrical foot consisting of a short syllable followed by a long or an unstressed syllable followed by a stressed. *Pentameter* means "five meters," or feet, and so iambic pentameter equals five iambs to the line.

107. **(D)** Under the rules of courtly love, the true knight was expected to be the epitome of the Christian man.

108. **(E)** Delphi is located near Mount Parnassus in ancient Greece. The legendary founder of the oracle was the goddess Gaea.

109. **(C)** The Gothic period approximates the Middle Ages. It was during this period that the Roman Catholic Church had its greatest hold on the populace.

110. **(A)** The Greek doctrine of hedonism states that pleasure is the highest good. In ancient times, hedonism was characteristic of the school of Aristippus.

111. **(C)** Giotto (c.1266–c.1337), Florentine painter and architect, was a perfector of form and movement. His faces and gestures are graceful and lifelike.

112. **(D)** The photograph is of a self-portrait by the 54-year-old Rembrandt, whose long series of self-portraits records every stage of his career.

113. **(A)** An ancient plum tree decorates these Japanese sliding screens from the study room of a Zen temple.

114. **(B)** Monet's *Terrace at Sainte-Adresse,* shown in this photograph, is an Impressionist painting.

115. **(C)** Stonehenge, a prehistoric structure, is on Salisbury Plain, in England.

116. **(B)** The origin of the griffin has been traced to the Hittites. It is also conspicuous in Assyrian and Persian sculpture.

117. **(A)** Deucalion and his wife, Pyrrha, are the principal figures in the Greek flood story.

118. **(C)** Sprung rhythm is a term for a mixed meter in which the foot consists of a stressed syllable which may stand alone, or be combined with from one to three more unstressed syllables.

119. **(C)** Rembrandt van Rijn (1606–1669), Dutch painter and etcher, was the greatest master of the Dutch school.

120. **(E)** This is a standard musical notation, a flat.

121. **(C)** The other words have nothing to do with songs.

122. **(E)** Cunegonde was the woman with whom Candide was in love.

123. **(B)** Nefertiti was an ancient Egyptian queen, wife of Akhenaton, a pharoah who ruled from 1367 to 1350 B.C.

124. **(D)** See above.

125. **(D)** *Rent*, Jonathan Larson's rock musical, relocates the story to the AIDS-era East Village in New York. Larson, its thirty-five-year-old composer, died of an aortic aneurysm on the eve of its first performance.

126. **(E)** *Rent* received Tony wards for Best Musical, Best Featured Actor (Wilson Jermaine Heredia), and Best Score and Best Book, both by Jonathan Larson.

127. **(A)** In Sophoclean irony the characters are symbols of tragic human fate. In Euripidean tragedy, the irony lies in the inner psyche of humans, who no longer struggle with fate, but fight with the demons of their own souls; each person is responsible for his or her actions.

128. **(B)** This is true by definition.

129. **(C)** The Elizabethan theater, unlike the Greek, did not make use of a chorus.

130. **(A)** Empiricism may be defined as the practice of relying upon observation and experiment, especially in the natural sciences.

131. **(E)** Orpheus was so skilled in singing and in playing the lyre that he could enchant not only men and animals, but even trees and stones.

132. **(B)** Euryclea appears in the *The Odyssey.*

133. **(A)** None of the others mentioned was as knowledgeable and talented in so many areas as Cellini.

134. **(B)** This is true by definition.

135. **(E)** T.S. Eliot is known as the author of "The Wasteland," "The Love Song of J. Alfred Prufrock," the play *Murder in the Cathedral,* and a large number of other works.

136. **(B)** Saint-Exupéry tells his reader to look up to the stars and listen for the laughter of the little prince.

137. **(A)** *Madame Butterfly* was based on a story by John Luther Long, who collaborated with Belasco on several other plays. Belasco, a pioneer in the movement toward natural methods in the theater, was also noted for his interesting effects of stage lighting.

138. **(A)** Puccini's opera was first performed in 1904, and is still one of the most popular of all operas.

139. **(C)** *M. Butterfly* opened at the National Theater in Washington, D.C., in 1988. The French diplomat, Bernard Bouriscot, claimed he had never seen his "girlfriend" naked, stating, "I thought she was very modest. I thought it was a Chinese custom."

140. **(D)** *Miss Saigon,* by Boubil and Schonberg, opened in 1989 in London and has been enjoying immense success throughout much of the world.

141. **(C)** Nobel Laureate Toni Morrison is the author of *Song of Solomon, The Bluest Eye, Beloved,* and *Jazz.*

142. **(A)** Vigeland studied in Oslo and Copenhagen, and in Paris with Rodin. Many of his sculpted figures represent the cycle of mankind from birth to death.

143. **(B)** This is true by definition.

144. **(D)** Byzantine refers to the style developed in Byzantium from the 5th century A.D. It is characterized by formality of design, frontal, stylized presentation of figures, rich use of color, especially gold, and generally religious subject matter.

145. **(D)** The contemporary American author LeRoi Jones changed his name to Imamu Amiri Baraka when he adopted the Muslim faith.

146. **(C)** Shaw's early-20th-century *Pygmalion* is one of his most frequently performed plays. *My Fair Lady* is the musical by Lerner and Loewe.

147. **(D)** The quote is from Walt Whitman's *O Captain! My Captain!*—a poem on Lincoln's death.

148. **(C)** These two lines are an example of a heroic couplet—two rhymed lines of verse of ten syllables each, having the same meter. The example here was written by Alexander Pope, a master of the heroic couplet. It is from Pope's "An Epistle to Dr. Arbuthnot."

149. **(E)** These are the first two lines of Shakespeare's Sonnet 18.

150. **(D)** The Gothic cathedral of Chartres is in northern France.

Humanities

ANSWER SHEET—SAMPLE EXAMINATION 2

1 (A) (B) (C) (D) (E)
2 (A) (B) (C) (D) (E)
3 (A) (B) (C) (D) (E)
4 (A) (B) (C) (D) (E)
5 (A) (B) (C) (D) (E)
6 (A) (B) (C) (D) (E)
7 (A) (B) (C) (D) (E)
8 (A) (B) (C) (D) (E)
9 (A) (B) (C) (D) (E)
10 (A) (B) (C) (D) (E)
11 (A) (B) (C) (D) (E)
12 (A) (B) (C) (D) (E)
13 (A) (B) (C) (D) (E)
14 (A) (B) (C) (D) (E)
15 (A) (B) (C) (D) (E)
16 (A) (B) (C) (D) (E)
17 (A) (B) (C) (D) (E)
18 (A) (B) (C) (D) (E)
19 (A) (B) (C) (D) (E)
20 (A) (B) (C) (D) (E)
21 (A) (B) (C) (D) (E)
22 (A) (B) (C) (D) (E)
23 (A) (B) (C) (D) (E)
24 (A) (B) (C) (D) (E)
25 (A) (B) (C) (D) (E)
26 (A) (B) (C) (D) (E)
27 (A) (B) (C) (D) (E)
28 (A) (B) (C) (D) (E)
29 (A) (B) (C) (D) (E)
30 (A) (B) (C) (D) (E)
31 (A) (B) (C) (D) (E)
32 (A) (B) (C) (D) (E)
33 (A) (B) (C) (D) (E)
34 (A) (B) (C) (D) (E)
35 (A) (B) (C) (D) (E)
36 (A) (B) (C) (D) (E)
37 (A) (B) (C) (D) (E)
38 (A) (B) (C) (D) (E)

39 (A) (B) (C) (D) (E)
40 (A) (B) (C) (D) (E)
41 (A) (B) (C) (D) (E)
42 (A) (B) (C) (D) (E)
43 (A) (B) (C) (D) (E)
44 (A) (B) (C) (D) (E)
45 (A) (B) (C) (D) (E)
46 (A) (B) (C) (D) (E)
47 (A) (B) (C) (D) (E)
48 (A) (B) (C) (D) (E)
49 (A) (B) (C) (D) (E)
50 (A) (B) (C) (D) (E)
51 (A) (B) (C) (D) (E)
52 (A) (B) (C) (D) (E)
53 (A) (B) (C) (D) (E)
54 (A) (B) (C) (D) (E)
55 (A) (B) (C) (D) (E)
56 (A) (B) (C) (D) (E)
57 (A) (B) (C) (D) (F)
58 (A) (B) (C) (D) (E)
59 (A) (B) (C) (D) (E)
60 (A) (B) (C) (D) (E)
61 (A) (B) (C) (D) (E)
62 (A) (B) (C) (D) (E)
63 (A) (B) (C) (D) (E)
64 (A) (B) (C) (D) (E)
65 (A) (B) (C) (D) (E)
66 (A) (B) (C) (D) (E)
67 (A) (B) (C) (D) (E)
68 (A) (B) (C) (D) (E)
69 (A) (B) (C) (D) (E)
70 (A) (B) (C) (D) (E)
71 (A) (B) (C) (D) (E)
72 (A) (B) (C) (D) (E)
73 (A) (B) (C) (D) (E)
74 (A) (B) (C) (D) (E)
75 (A) (B) (C) (D) (E)
76 (A) (B) (C) (D) (E)

77 (A) (B) (C) (D) (E)
78 (A) (B) (C) (D) (E)
79 (A) (B) (C) (D) (E)
80 (A) (B) (C) (D) (E)
81 (A) (B) (C) (D) (E)
82 (A) (B) (C) (D) (E)
83 (A) (B) (C) (D) (E)
84 (A) (B) (C) (D) (E)
85 (A) (B) (C) (D) (E)
86 (A) (B) (C) (D) (E)
87 (A) (B) (C) (D) (E)
88 (A) (B) (C) (D) (E)
89 (A) (B) (C) (D) (E)
90 (A) (B) (C) (D) (E)
91 (A) (B) (C) (D) (E)
92 (A) (B) (C) (D) (E)
93 (A) (B) (C) (D) (E)
94 (A) (B) (C) (D) (E)
95 (A) (B) (C) (D) (E)
96 (A) (B) (C) (D) (E)
97 (A) (B) (C) (D) (E)
98 (A) (B) (C) (D) (E)
99 (A) (B) (C) (D) (E)
100 (A) (B) (C) (D) (E)
101 (A) (B) (C) (D) (E)
102 (A) (B) (C) (D) (E)
103 (A) (B) (C) (D) (E)
104 (A) (B) (C) (D) (E)
105 (A) (B) (C) (D) (E)
106 (A) (B) (C) (D) (E)
107 (A) (B) (C) (D) (E)
108 (A) (B) (C) (D) (E)
109 (A) (B) (C) (D) (E)
110 (A) (B) (C) (D) (E)
111 (A) (B) (C) (D) (E)
112 (A) (B) (C) (D) (E)
113 (A) (B) (C) (D) (E)
114 (A) (B) (C) (D) (E)

115 (A) (B) (C) (D) (E)
116 (A) (B) (C) (D) (E)
117 (A) (B) (C) (D) (E)
118 (A) (B) (C) (D) (E)
119 (A) (B) (C) (D) (E)
120 (A) (B) (C) (D) (E)
121 (A) (B) (C) (D) (E)
122 (A) (B) (C) (D) (E)
123 (A) (B) (C) (D) (E)
124 (A) (B) (C) (D) (E)
125 (A) (B) (C) (D) (E)
126 (A) (B) (C) (D) (E)
127 (A) (B) (C) (D) (E)
128 (A) (B) (C) (D) (E)
129 (A) (B) (C) (D) (E)
130 (A) (B) (C) (D) (E)
131 (A) (B) (C) (D) (E)
132 (A) (B) (C) (D) (E)
133 (A) (B) (C) (U) (E)
134 (A) (B) (C) (D) (E)
135 (A) (B) (C) (D) (E)
136 (A) (B) (C) (D) (E)
137 (A) (B) (C) (D) (E)
138 (A) (B) (C) (D) (E)
139 (A) (B) (C) (D) (E)
140 (A) (B) (C) (D) (E)
141 (A) (B) (C) (D) (E)
142 (A) (B) (C) (D) (E)
143 (A) (B) (C) (D) (E)
144 (A) (B) (C) (D) (E)
145 (A) (B) (C) (D) (E)
146 (A) (B) (C) (D) (E)
147 (A) (B) (C) (D) (E)
148 (A) (B) (C) (D) (E)
149 (A) (B) (C) (D) (E)
150 (A) (B) (C) (D) (E)

SAMPLE HUMANITIES EXAMINATION 2

NUMBER OF QUESTIONS: 150

Time limit: 90 MINUTES

Directions: Each of the questions or incomplete statements below is followed by five suggested answers or completions. Select the one that is best in each case.

1. The first Caribbean writer to win the Nobel Prize for Literature was

   (A) Jamaica Kincaid
   (B) Derek Walcott
   (C) V.S. Naipaul
   (D) Geoffrey Philp
   (E) Ian McDonald

2. Lao Tzu, the Chinese philosopher, is regarded as the founder of

   (A) Zen
   (B) Mahayana Buddhism
   (C) Theravada Buddhism
   (D) Taoism
   (E) Shintoism

3. The seven daughters of Atlas who were changed into a cluster of stars to escape the hunter Orion were

   (A) Gorgons
   (B) Muses
   (C) Pleiades
   (D) Furies
   (E) Chimeras

4. The first black author to have a long-running Broadway hit was

   (A) Wright
   (B) Baldwin
   (C) Hughes
   (D) Hansbury
   (E) Morrison

5. Classicism is a style that embodies all of the following qualities except

   (A) balance
   (B) restraint
   (C) objectivity
   (D) form
   (E) abstraction

6. One of America's most renowned architects, designer of the JFK Library in Massachusetts, is

   (A) I.M. Pei
   (B) Jonathan Barnett
   (C) Charles Gwathmey
   (D) Frank Lloyd Wright
   (E) Richard Meier

7. One of the most popular operettas of all time, *La Grande-Duchess de Gerolstein*, was written by

   (A) Bizet
   (B) Gilbert and Sullivan
   (C) Offenbach
   (D) Lecocq
   (E) Halevy

8. The author of *Myra Breckinridge*, *Burr*, and *Empire* is

   (A) Gore Vidal
   (B) Kurt Vonnegut
   (C) Erich Segal
   (D) Philip Roth
   (E) Rod Steiger

9. Menotti wrote all of the following *except*

    (A) *The Medium*
    (B) *The Telephone*
    (C) *The Rake's Progress*
    (D) *The Consul*
    (E) *Amahl and the Night Visitor*

10. The architecture depicted in this photograph is typical of that found in

    (A) India
    (B) New Zealand
    (C) Russia
    (D) Hungary
    (E) China

Ruth S. Ward

11. A *priori* knowledge is

    (A) knowledge obtained from sensory experience
    (B) knowledge existing in the mind before sensory experience
    (C) a concept stressed particularly by the empiricist
    (D) a concept denied by the objective realist
    (E) knowledge verified by inductive evidence

12. The conclusion of *Candide* is that

    (A) "whatever is, is right"
    (B) "love conquers all"
    (C) "do unto others as you would have others do unto you"
    (D) "we must cultivate our garden"
    (E) "the end justifies the means"

13. The prefix "ur-" (as in *Ur-Faust*, *Ur-Hamlet*) means

    (A) early or primitive
    (B) alternate
    (C) pirated
    (D) last known
    (E) composite

14. All of the following are 19th-century Russian writers except

    (A) Chekhov
    (B) Nabokov
    (C) Tolstoy
    (D) Turgenev
    (E) Dostoevsky

15. The term *chamber music* can be applied to all of the following *except*

    (A) quartets
    (B) quintets
    (C) trios
    (D) symphonies
    (E) duo sonatas

16. An outside wall of a room or building carried above an adjoining roof and pierced with windows is called a

    (A) transept
    (B) clerestory
    (C) pilaster
    (D) transverse arch
    (E) atrium

17. A contemporary of E.A. Robinson, Edgar Lee Masters, Stephen Crane, and Theodore Dreiser, this poet holds a permanent place in American literature because his poetry is not only highly original, but also stresses the problems of his age. He is

    (A) Robert Morse Lovett
    (B) Walt Whitman
    (C) Vachel Lindsay
    (D) Robinson Jeffers
    (E) William Vaughn Moody

18. This female satirist, known especially for her novel *Ethan Frome* and *The Age of Innocence*, was influenced by Henry James, and her interests were centered mainly in the changing society of New York City. She is

    (A) Edith Wharton
    (B) Lily Bart
    (C) Zelda Fitzgerald
    (D) Dorothy Parker
    (E) Willa Cather

19. The blind seer who appears in several Greek tragedies is

    (A) Tiresias
    (B) Homer
    (C) Clytaemnestra
    (D) Oedipus
    (E) Agamemnon

20. A large composition for voices and orchestra, usually based on a religious text, is

    (A) an aria
    (B) an oratorio
    (C) a capella
    (D) a madrigal
    (E) a mass

21. France's two greatest writers of classical tragedy were

    (A) Molière and Rostand
    (B) Corneille and Racine
    (C) Jarry and Racine
    (D) Molière and Corneille
    (E) Balzac and Hugo

22. The author of *The Flies and The Clouds* was

    (A) Beckett
    (B) Sartre
    (C) Menander
    (D) Aristophanes
    (E) Molière

23. The painting below is

    (A) Whistler's *Arrangement in Gray and Black*
    (B) Klee's *Around the Fish*
    (C) Picasso's *Guernica*
    (D) Durer's *Four Horsemen of the Apocalypse*
    (E) Poussin's *Triumph of Neptune and Amphitrite*

©Bettman/Corbis

24. Of the following statements concerning a literary work read in translation, which is true?

   (A) It cannot escape the linguistic characteristics of the language into which it is turned.
   (B) Often one loses the *shade* of meaning when translating from an ancient language.
   (C) The translated work reflects the individuality of the age in which it is done.
   (D) Both A and B
   (E) All of the above

25. The author of "Waltzing Matilda" and "The Man from Snowy River" was the Australian poet

   (A) Hart Crane
   (B) "Banjo" Paterson
   (C) Lincoln Steffens
   (D) T.S. Eliott
   (E) Allen Ginsberg

26. The musical notation ♩: represents

   (A) the bass clef
   (B) the treble clef
   (C) sharp
   (D) flat
   (E) diminuendo

27. Which of the following is a multitalented writer of poetry, prose, and children's books, and a guide to Washington, D.C., restaurants?

   (A) Judith Viorst
   (B) Anita Kennedy
   (C) Nora Ephron
   (D) Frances Harmon
   (E) Rebecca Whitley

28. In the theater, the exploitation of "tender" emotions for their own sake—that is, whether motivated by the action or not—is called

   (A) virtue
   (B) temperamentality
   (C) melodrama
   (D) drama
   (E) sentimentality

29. If you raise a musical note from G to G sharp, or lower a note from E to E flat, you are practicing

   (A) staffing
   (B) writing musical shorthand
   (C) lengthening the composition
   (D) harmonizing
   (E) alteration

30. When the fingers of the hand that holds the bow are used to pluck the strings of an instrument, we call this

   (A) fortissimo
   (B) dissonance
   (C) pizzicato
   (D) diminuendo
   (E) espressivo

31. Perhaps the "perfect courtier" of the Renaissance was

   (A) Castiglione
   (B) Shakespeare
   (C) Maddox of Leicester
   (D) Henry VIII
   (E) Andrew the Chaplain

32. The beaker in the photograph below is

    (A) Egyptian
    (B) Peruvian
    (C) Byzantine
    (D) Roman
    (E) Greek

The Metropolitan Museum of Art, Rogers Fund, 1917
(17.230.14a,b) Gift of J. D. Beazley, 1927 (27.16)
Image © The Metropolitan Museum of Art.

Questions 33–35 refer to the following quotation:

"All nature is but Art, unknown to thee;
All Chance, Direction, which thou canst not
  see;
All Discord, Harmony not understood;
All partial Evil, universal Good:
And, spite of Pride, in erring Reason's spite,
One truth is clear, *Whatever is, is Right.*"

33. The preceding lines are from

    (A) Yeats' "Sailing to Byzantium"
    (B) Tennyson's "In Memoriam"
    (C) Whitman's "Song of Myself"
    (D) Wordsworth's "Ode on Intimations of
        Immortality"
    (E) Pope's "Essay on Man"

34. The verse form is the

    (A) sestina
    (B) ballad
    (C) heroic couplet
    (D) sonnet
    (E) haiku

35. The meter is

    (A) iambic pentameter
    (B) trochaic dimeter
    (C) anapestic tetrameter
    (D) iambic tetrameter
    (E) trochaic pentameter

36. The philosopher Nietzsche, from whom the
    Nazis derived some of their doctrines,
    taught that the basic human motivation is

    (A) intellectual curiosity
    (B) sensual pleasure
    (C) the desire for wealth
    (D) sex
    (E) the will to power

37. Two 20th-century composers of atonal
    music are

    (A) Bartók and Schoenberg
    (B) Stravinsky and Debussy
    (C) Ives and Wagner
    (D) Prokofiev and Poulenc
    (E) Rimsky-Korsakov and Rachmaninoff

38. The novels of Honoré de Balzac are known
    collectively as

    (A) *"Père Goriot" and Other Stories*
    (B) *The Collected Works of Honoré de Balzac*
    (C) *The Human Tragedy*
    (D) *The Human Comedy*
    (E) *Tales of the Tatras*

39. Which one of the following was a
    Renaissance painter?

    (A) Degas
    (B) Picasso
    (C) Michelangelo
    (D) Goya
    (E) Gainsborough

Exam 2

40. "To be, or not to be," is the beginning of a famous soliloquy from

    (A) *Dr. Faustus*
    (B) *Romeo and Juliet*
    (C) *Tamburlaine*
    (D) *Othello*
    (E) *Hamlet*

41. Just as Aristophanes used satire and humor to attack the existing society in early Athens, so did an American author use these media to express the discrepancy between American expectations and the very disturbing reality of his times. He is

    (A) Charles Brockden Brown
    (B) Augustus Longstreet
    (C) Robert Frost
    (D) Edwin Arlington Robinson
    (E) Mark Twain

42. A period of enthusiasm for the classics in art, architecture, literature, drama, etc., is known as

    (A) the Age of Enlightenment
    (B) the Neo-Classic Age
    (C) Romantic Age
    (D) the Classical Age
    (E) the Renaissance

43. The painter who became interested in politics and who, under Napoleon, became First Painter of the Empire was

    (A) Goya
    (B) Gros
    (C) Géricault
    (D) Ingres
    (E) David

44. Which word comes from the Greek term meaning "unknown" or "without knowledge"?

    (A) metaphysics
    (B) axiology
    (C) agnosticism
    (D) pragmatism
    (E) skepticism

45. After the Dark Ages, the first professional people to make songs popular were called

    (A) troubadours
    (B) barbershop quartets
    (C) castrati
    (D) church choirs
    (E) motets

46. In Greek drama, the protagonist's tragic flaw is frequently pride; in a Greek comedy, it is often

    (A) anguish
    (B) single-mindedness
    (C) open-mindedness
    (D) lust
    (E) super-intellectualism

47. Stimulated by the Cubist style, the Italian artists who introduced the additional concept of movement in "space-time" were the

    (A) Expressionists
    (B) Impressionists
    (C) Non-objectivists
    (D) Futurists
    (E) Romanticists

48. Henri Matisse is to Fauvism what Edvard Munch is to

    (A) Impressionism
    (B) Surrealism
    (C) Cubism
    (D) German Expressionism
    (E) *Die Brücke*

49. Franz Liszt

    (A) used classical forms in his music
    (B) experimented with atonal music
    (C) used romantic forms such as the tone poem
    (D) was a virtuoso performer on the violin
    (E) rejected the ideals of romanticism

50. In Greek legend, who killed his father, married his mother, and became King of Thebes?

    (A) Polynices
    (B) Agamemnon
    (C) Laius
    (D) Oedipus
    (E) Jason

51. Johann Strauss is best known for his

    (A) waltzes
    (B) tone poems
    (C) fugues
    (D) sonatas
    (E) symphonies

52. Often considered the "showpiece of French realism" is

    (A) Flaubert's *Madame Bovary*
    (B) Balzac's *Eugénie Grandet*
    (C) Hugo's *Les Misérables*
    (D) Zola's *Nana*
    (E) Voltaire's *The Huron*

53. In an orthodox sense, Arabic literature begins with

    (A) *The Rubáiyát*
    (B) *The Koran*
    (C) *The Book of the Dead*
    (D) *The Ramayana*
    (E) *The Mahabharata*

Questions 54 and 55 refer to the photograph below.

54. The work pictured is

    (A) Michelangelo's "David"
    (B) Michelangelo's "Pietá"
    (C) "The Nike of Samothrace"
    (D) Brancusi's "Father and Son"
    (E) Praxiteles' "Hermes"

©Bettman/Corbis

55. If you wanted to see sculpture of this type in the city where it was created, you would visit

    (A) Paris
    (B) Washington, D.C.
    (C) Rome
    (D) Athens
    (E) Munich

56. The view that the mind is passive, or a *tabula rasa* upon which experience writes, and that the senses are more reliable than reason, was held by

    (A) Hegel
    (B) Socrates
    (C) Locke
    (D) Kant
    (E) Plato

Exam 2

57. According to legend, what was the cause of the Trojan War?

   (A) Argos's need for more land
   (B) the sacrifice of Iphigenia
   (C) the adultery of Clytaemnestra
   (D) the murder of Aegisthus
   (E) the kidnapping of Helen by Paris

58. *The Executions of May Third, 1808* was painted by

   (A) Goya
   (B) Canova
   (C) Vignon
   (D) Ingres
   (E) David

59. A writer who exerted a profound influence on the development of the American short story was William Sidney Porter, better known as

   (A) Artemus Ward
   (B) Josh Billings
   (C) Edgar Allan Poe
   (D) Mark Twain
   (E) O. Henry

60. An American author best known for his depictions of the old French Quarter of New Orleans, ante-bellum plantations, and the survival of the chivalric code in the South is

   (A) Rhett Butler
   (B) George Washington Cable
   (C) Joel Chandler Harris
   (D) William Faulkner
   (E) Joseph Lee

61. The most sensitively expressive of all musical instruments made by the family of Stradivari is the

   (A) drum
   (B) violin
   (C) cymbal
   (D) oboe
   (E) piano

62. A contemporary of Johann Sebastian Bach, though not as great an innovator, nevertheless one of the most successful of the world's serious composers, was

   (A) Beethoven
   (B) Mendelssohn
   (C) Handel
   (D) Silbermann
   (E) Schmidt

63. The one-eyed giant whom Odysseus met on his voyage was named

   (A) Dryope
   (B) Polyphemus
   (C) Aeolus
   (D) Circe
   (E) Medea

64. The proximity of the audience to the players influenced some of the theatrical devices used by Shakespeare and made feasible

   (A) the soliloquy
   (B) the appearance of boys in feminine roles
   (C) the use of special effects
   (D) music with dance sequences
   (E) the use of pantomime

65. The three hideous sisters of Greek mythology, one of whom (Medusa) was killed by Perseus, were called

   (A) Gorgons
   (B) Sphinxes
   (C) Furies
   (D) Sirens
   (E) Charities

66. The music Beethoven wrote for the theater was all of the following except

   (A) based on a theme of the quest for individual liberty
   (B) based on the cause of popular freedom
   (C) reflective of high moral purpose
   (D) religious in nature
   (E) based on an ideal of human creativity

67. In poetry, the omission of one or more final unstressed syllables is called

    (A) anacrusis
    (B) catalexis
    (C) feminine rhyme
    (D) masculine rhyme
    (E) caesura

68. Penelope's chief suitor was named

    (A) Telemachus
    (B) Oedipus
    (C) Creon
    (D) Telegonus
    (E) Antinous

69. Because of his innovations of style, his free hand with form, and his use of extra-musical devices, the man often called the first Romantic composer is

    (A) Liszt
    (B) Beethoven
    (C) Haydn
    (D) Mozart
    (E) von Weber

70. The great French tragic dramatist of the Neo-Classic period was

    (A) Racine
    (B) Pascal
    (C) Molière
    (D) La Fontaine
    (E) Sainte-Beuve

71. A stale phrase used where a fresh one is needed is

    (A) parallelism
    (B) a cliché
    (C) denouement
    (D) poetic license
    (E) a pun

72. Poetry that is not so much read as looked at is called

    (A) structured poetry
    (B) nonsense verse
    (C) gnomic poetry
    (D) euphuistic verse
    (E) concrete verse

73. Shelley's elegy on the death of John Keats is

    (A) "In Memoriam"
    (B) "Adonais"
    (C) "Thyrsis"
    (D) "Lycidas"
    (E) "Stanzas Written in Dejection near Naples"

74. Thomas Henry Huxley was

    (A) primarily a man of letters
    (B) author of *Brave New World*
    (C) devoted to the popularization of science
    (D) noted for his florid, romantic style
    (E) the founder of *The Spectator*

75. A florid, ornate portion of prose or poetry, which stands out by its rhythm, diction, or figurative language, is called

    (A) pure poetry
    (B) a purple passage
    (C) quantitative verse
    (D) prosody
    (E) hyperbole

©Bettman/Corbis

76. The above painting is

(A) Donatello's *Annunciation*
(B) Correggio's *Holy Night*
(C) Raphael's *Sistine Madonna*
(D) Botticelli's *Birth of Venus*
(E) Rogier van der Weyden's *Nativity*

77. A well-known sonneteer of the 14th century was

(A) Petrarch
(B) Dante
(C) Shakespeare
(D) Shelley
(E) Boccaccio

78. Today's audiences would find strange the theater for which Shakespeare wrote because they

(A) prefer to attend matinees
(B) are not accustomed to intermissions
(C) prefer simple sets and costumes
(D) are not used to listening to such complex language
(E) are less well educated

79. The literal meaning of the word "Renaissance" is

(A) rebirth
(B) clarification
(C) analysis
(D) enlightenment
(E) question

80. Canio is the famous clown from the opera

(A) *I Pagliacci*
(B) *Rigoletto*
(C) *Cavalleria Rusticana*
(D) *Gianni Schicchi*
(E) *Così fan tutte*

81. The English language is most closely related to which of the following in the structure of its sentences?

(A) Latin
(B) German
(C) French
(D) Bulgarian
(E) Italian

82. The period in English literature called the "Restoration" is commonly regarded as running from

(A) 1300 to 1450
(B) 1500 to 1550
(C) 1660 to 1700
(D) 1798 to 1848
(E) 1848 to 1900

83. Below is a photograph of

    (A) a Greek temple
    (B) a Roman temple
    (C) an Egyptian temple
    (D) the University of South Florida
    (E) the University of Mexico

Ruth S. Ward

84. Walter Pater believed that one should

    (A) "cultivate one's own garden"
    (B) "justify the ways of God to man"
    (C) "follow the sun"
    (D) "burn with a hard, gem-like flame"
    (E) "contemplate the Absolute"

85. The expressive combination of reinforced concrete material, cantilevered construction, and a dramatic site are characteristic of the modern architect

    (A) J.J.P. Oud
    (B) Walter Gropius
    (C) Louis Sullivan
    (D) Frank Lloyd Wright
    (E) Le Corbusier

86. The "Theater of the Absurd" is basically

    (A) ridiculous
    (B) emotional
    (C) comic
    (D) tragic
    (E) intellectual

87. What daughter of an American president has successfully established herself as a mystery writer?

    (A) Amy Carter
    (B) Margaret Truman
    (C) Tricia Nixon Cox
    (D) Julie Nixon Eisenhower
    (E) Lynda Johnson Robb

88. Don Quixote's horse was named

    (A) Escudero
    (B) Rocinante
    (C) Sancho Panza
    (D) Dulcinea
    (E) Gringolet

89. A modern folklorist, author of *The Hero with a Thousand Faces*, is

    (A) Jacob Grimm
    (B) Margaret Hunt
    (C) Padriac Colum
    (D) Joseph Stern
    (E) Joseph Campbell

90. Sir Arthur Conan Doyle's famous character Sherlock Holmes, the Victorian sleuth, was

    (A) based on a character from Edgar Allan Poe
    (B) known to be addicted to cocaine
    (C) believed to be Jack the Ripper
    (D) based on a well-known detective of the time, James Edmunds
    (E) killed in an airplane accident

91. The institution of the villain in drama goes back to

    (A) the Greek epics
    (B) the medieval romance
    (C) Christianity and the writings of Machiavelli
    (D) the Protestant attack on corrupt clergy
    (E) an ancient source, probably a ritual

92. The slogan of the 19th-century Aesthetic Movement was

    (A) "Art is the opiate of the masses"
    (B) "Art is life"
    (C) "Art for art's sake"
    (D) "What is art, that it should have a sake?"
    (E) "Burn with a hard, gem-like flame"

93. The most famous medieval tapestry is the

    (A) Bayeux
    (B) Byzantine
    (C) Canterbury
    (D) Hastings
    (E) Norman

94. The main difference between the Pantheon (in Italy) and the Parthenon (in Greece) is that

    (A) the Parthenon was constructed of raw concrete
    (B) the Pantheon used red bricks and mortar
    (C) the Pantheon is topped with a dome, while the roof of the Parthenon is triangular
    (D) the Parthenon used plain pillars without any ornamentation, while those in the Pantheon are elaborately decorated
    (E) the floor space in the Parthenon is about four times larger

95. The Greek tragedy *Antigone* was written by

    (A) Socrates
    (B) Plato
    (C) Aristotle
    (D) Sophocles
    (E) Agamemnon

96. The poignant line "But where are the snows of yesteryear?" is from "The Ballade of Dead Ladies" by

    (A) François Villon
    (B) Percy Bysshe Shelley
    (C) John Keats
    (D) William Shakespeare
    (E) Lord Byron

97. Which of the following Hindu holy books especially influenced the so-called "beat generation" of poets and novelists?

    (A) *The Bhagavad-Gita*
    (B) *Upanishads*
    (C) *Carmina Burana*
    (D) *Jaina Sutras*
    (E) *Mahabharata*

98. When people started to sing different tunes together, which of the following had its beginnings?

    (A) monophony
    (B) jazz
    (C) polyphony
    (D) a capella
    (E) homophony

99. A stale phrase used where a fresh one is needed is

    (A) a cliché
    (B) parallelism
    (C) denouement
    (D) poetic license
    (E) a pun

100. The life of decadent Europe is contrasted unfavorably with life on an unspoiled, Eden-like island. This is indicative of an Age called

    (A) Elizabethan
    (B) Neo-Classic
    (C) Classic
    (D) Romantic
    (E) Victorian

101. *Waverly, Ivanhoe,* and *Quentin Durward* were written by

    (A) Sir Thomas Hardy
    (B) Sir Walter Scott
    (C) Henry Makepeace Thackeray
    (D) Charlotte Brontë
    (E) Emily Brontë

102. The medieval poem "Piers Plowman" belongs to the literature of

    (A) chivalry
    (B) social protest
    (C) mythology
    (D) social satire
    (E) pastoral philosophy

103. The greatest Spanish painter of the 17th century, who worked almost exclusively on portraits of the nobility and court figures, was

    (A) Velázquez
    (B) Murillo
    (C) Goya
    (D) Utrillo
    (E) El Greco

104. The French novelist George Sand was the mistress of which famous composer?

    (A) Verdi
    (B) Rachmaninoff
    (C) Prokofiev
    (D) Chopin
    (E) Mahler

105. In music, gradual decrease of tempo is called

    (A) retardando
    (B) accelerando
    (C) moderato
    (D) presto
    (E) allegro

106. The philosophy best represented by the statement "true ideas are those that work" is

    (A) rationalism
    (B) positivism
    (C) empiricism
    (D) pragmatism
    (E) Thomism

107. This is an example of

    (A) Hindu art
    (B) Chinese art
    (C) Egyptian art
    (D) primitive art
    (E) Etruscan art

108. The Russian writer thought to have coined the word "nihilist" was

    (A) Chekhov
    (B) Dostoevsky
    (C) Pushkin
    (D) Tolstoy
    (E) Turgenev

109. Which one of the following do most critics consider the greatest novel ever written?

    (A) *War and Peace*
    (B) *The Brothers Karamazov*
    (C) *The Forsyte Saga*
    (D) *The Sound and the Fury*
    (E) *Pride and Prejudice*

Exam 2

110. How many muses were there in Greek mythology?

    (A) 3
    (B) 4
    (C) 7
    (D) 9
    (E) 11

111. In three novels, called collectively U.S.A., this author employed interludes he dubbed "The Camera Eye" and "Newsreels." The author is

    (A) John Dos Passos
    (B) James Jones
    (C) John Steinbeck
    (D) Truman Capote
    (E) John P. Marquand

112. The "Father of the Irish Renaissance" was

    (A) George Moore
    (B) George Russell
    (C) J.M. Synge
    (D) W.B. Yeats
    (E) G.B. Shaw

113. Josiah Wedgwood began making pottery in England during which period?

    (A) Medieval
    (B) Renaissance
    (C) Neo-Classic
    (D) Romantic
    (E) Victorian

114. A contemporary choreographer whose ballets included "Fancy Free" and the dances in *West Side Story* is

    (A) Michael Kidd
    (B) Agnes de Mille
    (C) Jerome Robbins
    (D) John Cranko
    (E) Gene Kelly

115. All of the following are Italian film directors who have achieved worldwide fame since 1945 *except*

    (A) Roberto Rossellini
    (B) Michaelangelo Antonioni
    (C) Michelangelo Buonarroti
    (D) Federico Fellini
    (E) Vittorio de Sica

116. Which one of the following was *not* considered a medieval knightly virtue?

    (A) chastity
    (B) honesty
    (C) fortitude
    (D) faithfulness
    (E) duplicity

117. Chaucer wrote in the dialect of

    (A) Mercia
    (B) Wessex
    (C) Kent
    (D) Northumbria
    (E) London

Questions 118–120 refer to the following quotation:

> "Ring out the old, ring in the new;
> Ring, happy bells, across the snow:
> The year is going, let him go;
> Ring out the false, ring in the true."

118. The lines are quoted from

    (A) Tennyson's "In Memoriam"
    (B) Milton's "Lycidas"
    (C) Browning's "Pippa Passes"
    (D) Anonymous: "Christmas Bells"
    (E) Poe's "The Bells"

119. The verse form is a

    (A) sonnet
    (B) quatrain
    (C) couplet
    (D) tercet
    (E) cinquaine

120. The rhyme scheme is

   (A) a b a b
   (B) a b c d
   (C) a b b c
   (D) a b b a
   (E) a b c b

121. Impressionism found its most frequent expression in painting and music, but there was at least one sculptor who utilized the principles of Impressionism in his work:

   (A) Gustave Moreau
   (B) Odilon Redon
   (C) Giovanni Segantini
   (D) P.W. Steer
   (E) Auguste Rodin

122. A contemporary Russian novelist who experienced political difficulties with Soviet authorities because of his criticisms of Stalin and communism is

   (A) Ivan Denisovich
   (B) Konstantin Fedin
   (C) Pavel Antokolsky
   (D) Aleksandr Solzhenitsyn
   (E) Alexander Bek

123. The meter of a musical composition

   (A) has to do with regularly recurring accents
   (B) determines tempo
   (C) indicates texture
   (D) determines dynamics
   (E) is the same as rhythm

124. The most famous saint of Tibet is

   (A) Milarepa
   (B) Siddhartha
   (C) Tukela
   (D) the Dalai Lama
   (E) Naropa

125. When an author selects a title for a novel, he may quote another author. When Ernest Hemingway chose *For Whom the Bell Tolls* as the title for his novel about the Spanish Civil War, he was referring to

   (A) a poem by Andrew Marvell
   (B) a satire by Juvenal
   (C) a meditation by John Donne
   (D) a tragedy by John Ford
   (E) an essay by William Hazlitt

126. A Gilbert and Sullivan operetta that had a successful revival in London and on Broadway, and even made its way to the movie screen, is

   (A) *Iolanthe*
   (B) *The Mikado*
   (C) *The Pirates of Penzance*
   (D) *H.M.S. Pinafore*
   (E) *Ruddigore*

127. Samuel Johnson attached the label "Metaphysical Poets" to which of the following groups?

   (A) Donne, Marvel, Crashaw, and Herbert
   (B) Dryden, Pope, and Young
   (C) Greene, Jonson, and Herrick
   (D) Shakespeare, Milton, and Pope
   (E) Wordsworth, Keats, Shelley, and Byron

128. One of America's best-loved humorists, known for his satiric essays and hilarious cartoons, is

   (A) Berke Breathed
   (B) Walt Kelly
   (C) Mark Twain
   (D) William Zinsser
   (E) James Thurber

129. Which of the following lists of musical periods is arranged in the correct chronological sequence?

    (A) Renaissance, Classical, Baroque
    (B) Classical, Medieval, Romantic
    (C) Renaissance, Baroque, Romantic
    (D) Romantic, Renaissance, Baroque
    (E) Medieval, Baroque, Renaissance

130. The artist usually considered the father of modern abstract sculpture is

    (A) Brancusi
    (B) Maillol
    (C) Rodin
    (D) Lehmbruck
    (E) Archipenko

131. Most readers consider *Frankenstein* only a horror story about a fabricated monster. Few realize it has a social theme of

    (A) racial prejudice
    (B) class bigotry
    (C) the rejection by society of an individual who differs from the norm
    (D) sexual immorality
    (E) an individual's dependence upon drugs

132. *Frankenstein* was written in 1817 by

    (A) Sir Walter Scott
    (B) Horace Walpole
    (C) William Godwin
    (D) Mary Godwin
    (E) Mary Wollstonecraft Shelley

Questions 133–135 refer to the following quotation:

"It is an ancient Mariner
And he stoppeth one of three.
'By thy long gray beard and glittering eye,
Now wherefore stopp'st thou me?' "

133. The lines were written by

    (A) Keats
    (B) Eliot
    (C) Coleridge
    (D) Tennyson
    (E) Shelley

134. The form is a

    (A) tercet
    (B) quatrain
    (C) rondelay
    (D) haiku
    (E) sestina

135. The form of the whole poem is

    (A) a ballade
    (B) a dramatic monologue
    (C) a traditional ballad
    (D) a literary ballad
    (E) an unconventional form which the author invented for this poem and never used again

136. The contemporary American author of *The Fire Next Time* and *Tell Me How Long the Train's Been Gone* is

    (A) James Baldwin
    (B) Margaret Walker
    (C) LeRoi Jones (Imamu Amiri Baraka)
    (D) Frederick Douglass
    (E) John Williams

137. The immediate intention of the comic theater is to

    (A) show the absurdity of life
    (B) make us feel better
    (C) drive a group of people into hysterical laughter
    (D) act as an emotional tranquilizer
    (E) convert the audience into giggling optimists

138. In the beginning, conductors performed their task from

    (A) a podium
    (B) the right side of the stage
    (C) the left side of the stage
    (D) an instrument, usually a clavier
    (E) a pit hidden from the audience

139. "What animal goes in the morning on four feet, at noon on two, and in the evening on three?" is the riddle posed by the

    (A) Griffin
    (B) Jabberwock
    (C) Sphinx
    (D) Muses
    (E) Furies

140. While David extolled the virtues and nobility of the conqueror Napoleon in his paintings, another artist depicted the sufferings of a subjugated people. He was

    (A) Rodin
    (B) Gros
    (C) Géricault
    (D) Goya
    (E) Ingres

141. All of the following were essayists of the English Romantic Movement *except*

    (A) De Quincey
    (B) Lamb
    (C) Addison
    (D) Hazlitt
    (E) Hunt

142. The "vast chain of being" is an important concept of the

    (A) 16th century
    (B) 17th century
    (C) 18th century
    (D) 19th century
    (E) 20th century

143. The first composer to use hammering repetition as a dramatic device was

    (A) Schmoll
    (B) Beethoven
    (C) Oberon
    (D) Offenbach
    (E) Stravinsky

144. A 19th-century writer noted for his short stories about life in India and his novels, poems, and children's stories was

    (A) George Orwell
    (B) Thomas Hardy
    (C) John Masefield
    (D) Joseph Conrad
    (E) Rudyard Kipling

145. In the lines, "Hail to thee, blithe spirit!/Bird thou never wert," the bird referred to is a

    (A) sparrow
    (B) nightingale
    (C) robin
    (D) skylark
    (E) mockingbird

146. A defector from the Soviet Union and a British dame formed one of the greatest ballet teams of all time. They were

    (A) Mikhail Baryshnikov and Cyd Charisse
    (B) Vaslav Nijinsky and Isadora Duncan
    (C) Boris Chaliapin and Martha Graham
    (D) Rudolf Nureyev and Margot Fonteyn
    (E) Jacques d'Amboise and Maria Tallchief

147. Jane Austen's novels *Pride and Prejudice* and *Emma* deal with

    (A) the English lower middle-class
    (B) the English working class
    (C) the problem of getting married
    (D) child labor laws
    (E) the plight of coal miners in Wales

148. Robert Browning is especially noted for his

    (A) short stories
    (B) dramatic monologues
    (C) sonnets
    (D) ballads
    (E) dirges

149. The painting of Leda and the swan is associated with which Renaissance artist?

    (A) Michelangelo
    (B) Botticelli
    (C) da Vinci
    (D) Correggio
    (E) Masaccio

150. In scansion of poetry, the symbol / indicates

    (A) a slight pause within a line
    (B) a foot
    (C) read more slowly
    (D) read faster
    (E) stress the syllable

STOP

If there is still time remaining, you may review your answers.

Humanities
ANSWER KEY–SAMPLE EXAMINATION 2

1. B	31. A	61. B	91. C	121. E
2. D	32. E	62. C	92. C	122. D
3. C	33. E	63. B	93. A	123. A
4. C	34. C	64. A	94. C	124. A
5. E	35. A	65. A	95. D	125. C
6. A	36. E	66. D	96. A	126. C
7. C	37. A	67. B	97. A	127. A
8. A	38. D	68. E	98. C	128. E
9. C	39. C	69. E	99. A	129. B
10. E	40. E	70. A	100. D	130. A
11. B	41. E	71. B	101. B	131. C
12. D	42. B	72. E	102. B	132. E
13. A	43. E	73. B	103. A	133. C
14. B	44. C	74. C	104. D	134. B
15. D	45. A	75. B	105. A	135. D
16. B	46. B	76. D	106. D	136. A
17. E	47. D	77. A	107. D	137. B
18. A	48. D	78. D	108. E	138. D
19. A	49. C	79. A	109. A	139. C
20. B	50. D	80. A	110. D	140. D
21. B	51. A	81. B	111. A	141. C
22. C	52. A	82. C	112. D	142. C
23. D	53. B	83. E	113. C	143. B
24. E	54. E	84. D	114. C	144. E
25. B	55. D	85. D	115. C	145. D
26. A	56. C	86. E	116. E	146. D
27. A	57. E	87. B	117. E	147. C
28. E	58. A	88. B	118. A	148. B
29. E	59. E	89. E	119. B	149. C
30. C	60. B	90. B	120. D	150. E

Answer Key—Exam 2

SCORING CHART

After you have scored your Sample Examination 2, enter the results in the chart below; then transfer your score to the Progress Chart on page 12.

Total Test	Number Right	Number Wrong	Number Omitted
150			

ANSWER EXPLANATIONS

1. **(B)** Walcott's works include the long poem *Omeros,* his stage adaptation of Homer's *The Odyssey,* and his *Collected Poems,* published in 1986. He won the Nobel Prize in 1992.

2. **(D)** Lao Tzu emphasized the tao, the harmonious and inevitable way of the universe.

3. **(C)** In astronomy, the Pleiades is a star cluster in the constellation Taurus, which represents the seven sisters of Greek mythology.

4. **(C)** Langston Hughes' play *Mulatto* opened on Broadway in 1935, and played continuously for more than two years.

5. **(E)** This is true by definition.

6. **(A)** Pei also designed the East Building of the National Gallery of Art in Washington, D.C.

7. **(C)** Offenbach is also well known for his *La Vie Parisienne* and *Tales of Hoffman.*

8. **(A)** Writer and critic, much of Vidal's fiction deals satirically with history and politics.

9. **(C)** *Tile Rake's Progress* is a ballet by Gavin-Gordon.

10. **(E)** The photograph is of a pagoda. The architecture is typical of that found in the Orient.

11. **(B)** This is true by definition.

12. **(D)** These lines appear in the final chapter of Voltaire's novel.

13. **(A)** This is true by definition.

14. **(B)** Nabokov is a 20th-century writer.

15. **(D)** A large symphony orchestra is composed of string, wind, and percussion sections. The other answers refer to two to four instruments.

16. **(B)** This is true by definition.

17. **(E)** None of the other poets has all of the qualifications listed.

18. **(A)** Edith Wharton (1862–1937) was an American poet, short story writer, and novelist.

19. **(A)** Tiresias is important in many of the stories of Thebes. He is consulted also, in the underworld, by Odysseus.

20. **(B)** This is true by definition.

21. **(B)** Pierre Corneille (1606–1684) was the first of the great tragic writers of the era. Jean Racine (1639–1699) is generally described as France's greatest writer of tragedy.

22. **(D)** Aristophanes was the great Greek writer of comedy.

23. **(C)** *Guernica* depicts the ravaging of a small town by that name in Spain during the Revolution.

24. **(E)** To limit the answer to only one of the other statements would be to make an inadequate statement.

25. **(B)** Paterson, whose full name is Andrew Barton "Banjo" Paterson, is the only Australian in the group.

26. **(A)** This is a standard musical notation.

27. **(A)** Viorst, a contributing editor to *Redbook* magazine, has also written for television.

28. **(E)** This is true by definition.

29. **(E)** This is true by definition.

30. **(C)** This is true by definition.

31. **(A)** Baldassare Castiglione (1478–1529) wrote a handbook of manners, *The Courtier,* which was a guidebook for elegant deportment.

32. **(E)** The artistic style and decorations of the Greeks are far different from any of the others mentioned.

33. **(E)** The philosophy expressed is typical of the Neo-Classic period.

34. **(C)** Couplets are lines of poetry rhyming in pairs. The most widely used couplet form is the iambic pentameter, known as the heroic couplet.

35. **(A)** Iambic pentameter is five feet of unstressed/stressed syllables to the line.

36. **(E)** Nietzsche's *The Will to Power* was published in Germany in 1888. The first English translation appeared in 1909–10.

37. **(A)** The others are either not 20th-century composers, not composers of atonal music, or both.

38. **(D)** Honoré de Balzac (1799–1850) wrote *The Human Comedy.* The chief novels in this group are *Père Goriot* and *Eugénie Grandet.*

39. **(C)** Michelangelo (1475–1564) was the most famous artist of the Renaissance period.

40. **(E)** In his famous soliloquy, Hamlet is pondering whether or not to commit suicide.

41. **(E)** Perhaps Twain's most famous satire on contemporary society is *Huckleberry Finn.*

42. **(B)** The late 18th century and early 19th century are known as the Neo-Classic Age.

43. **(E)** Jacques Louis David (1748–1825) was one of the most famous painters of his day.

44. **(C)** This is true by definition.

45. **(A)** The troubadours were lyric poets of the 12th and 13th centuries attached to the courts of Provence and northern Italy.

46. **(B)** A character with one overriding purpose or opinion is often hilarious.

47. **(D)** Futurism, an artistic movement that originated in Italy about 1910, attempted to depict the dynamic quality of contemporary life influenced by the force and motion of modern machinery.

48. **(D)** Edvard Munch (1863–1944) was a Norwegian painter and printmaker who used intense colors and body attitudes to show love, sickness, anxiety, and death. He greatly influenced the German Expressionist movement of the early 1900s.

49. **(C)** Liszt wrote twelve tone poems, the form of which he invented.

50. **(D)** According to legend, Oedipus killed his father, married his mother, Jocasta, and had four children by her: Polynices, Eteocles, Antigone, and Ismene.

51. **(A)** Johann Strauss was a composer of comic operas, but his reputation rests on some 400 waltzes.

52. **(A)** Flaubert's *Madame Bovary,* published in 1859, was the first of the works that made him a model for later writers of the realistic school.

53. **(B)** *The Koran* is the sacred book of Islam, purportedly revealed by God to the Prophet Mohammed.

54. **(E)** Praxiteles was the most famous of the Attic sculptors.

55. **(D)** Praxiteles was from Athens, Greece.

56. **(C)** John Locke (1632–1704), an English philosopher, is best known for his *Essay Concerning the Human Understanding,* which poses the view of the tabula rasa.

57. **(E)** Paris kidnapped Helen, wife of Menelaus, king of Sparta, and brought her back to Troy. The Greek leaders rallied to aid Menelaus, and thus began the Trojan War.

58. **(A)** Goya (1746–1828) was a Spanish painter, etcher, and designer.

59. **(E)** O. Henry is noted for his surprise endings. One of his best known short stories is "The Gift of the Magi." The other writers did not use the pseudonym "O. Henry."

60. **(B)** The others were not writers of ante-bellum New Orleans chivalric literature.

61. **(B)** The Stradivarius is also perhaps the most famous and most expensive violin in the world.

62. **(C)** George Friedrich Handel (1685–1759) is perhaps best known as the composer of *The Messiah.*

63. **(B)** Polyphemus is the only cyclops Odysseus met.

64. **(A)** In the soliloquy, the actor could speak his innermost thoughts aloud.

65. **(A)** The others are mythological creatures, but no other fits the description.

66. **(D)** Beethoven was a prolific composer of symphonies, sonatas, and opera, but he did not write religious music.

67. **(B)** This is true by definition.

68. **(E)** The other characters were not suitors of Penelope.

69. **(E)** Von Weber (1786–1826) was a German who composed his first opera at age thirteen.

70. **(A)** The others were not tragic dramatists of the Neo-Classic period.

71. **(B)** This is true by definition.

72. **(E)** This is true by definition.

73. **(B)** John Keats, English Romantic poet, was a friend of Shelley

74. **(C)** Huxley was a 19th-century evolutionist and social reformer who was instrumental in popularizing science. He was the grandfather of Aldous Huxley, author of *Brave New World.*

75. **(B)** This is true by literary definition.

76. **(D)** Sandro Botticelli (1444–1510), a Florentine, was one of the great painters of the Renaissance; *The Birth of Venus* is one of his most famous paintings.

77. **(A)** Petrarch's sonnets, mostly inspired by Laura, form one of the most splendid bodies of verse in literature. Petrarch's sonnets were first imitated in England by Sir Thomas Wyatt; the form was later used by Milton, Wordsworth, and other sonneteers.

78. **(D)** The Elizabethan audience insisted upon inflated, poetic language.

79. **(A)** This answer is true by definition.

80. **(A)** *I Pagliacci* is an opera in two acts by Leoncavallo.

81. **(B)** English is considered a Germanic language. Old English and German are similar in many respects.

82. **(C)** In English literature, the Restoration generally refers to the period from the accession of Charles II to the throne in 1660 to the death of Dryden in 1770. This period is sometimes called "The Age of Dryden."

83. **(E)** Brilliantly colored mosaics are typical of the art and architecture of the University of Mexico.

84. **(D)** Pater was an important Victorian essayist and literary critic.

85. **(D)** Wright's immensely functional, yet artistic, buildings always blend in with the environment.

86. **(E)** One must be able to intellectualize the absurdity of life in order to enjoy this type of theater.

87. **(B)** Among Ms. Truman's novels are *Murder on Embassy Row, Murder in Georgetown,* and *Murder in the Smithsonian.*

88. **(B)** Rocinante was a run-down nag Don Quixote rode into his famous, or infamous, battles.

89. **(E)** Campbell also authored *The Masks of God* and *Myths to Live By.*

90. **(B)** The novel and movie *The Seven-Per-Cent Solution,* concerns Holmes' addiction, and his treatment by Dr. Sigmund Freud.

91. **(C)** In Christianity, the Devil is evil incarnate. In Machiavelli's *The Prince,* his greatest work, evil is permissible, if necessary.

92. **(C)** The "art for art's sake" movement was an attempt to break away from all theories and traditions of the past.

93. **(A)** This tapestry depicts scenes of the Norman Conquest of England and the events leading up to it.

94. **(C)** Other than this distinction, the two buildings are architecturally similar in many respects.

95. **(D)** Sophocles is the only playwright in this group.

96. **(A)** François Villon (1431–1463?) was a vagabond, a rogue, and the greatest lyric poet of his time.

97. **(A)** Allen Ginsberg, one of the most popular "beat" poets, was greatly influenced by Hindu philosophy and incorporated Hindu chants into some of his poetry.

98. **(C)** *Polyphony* means the simultaneous combination of two or more independent melodic parts, especially when in close harmonic relationship.

99. **(A)** This is true by definition.

100. **(D)** The Romantic Age originated in Europe toward the end of the 18th century. It asserted the validity of subjective experience.

101. **(B)** Sir Walter Scott (1771–1832) was a British novelist and poet.

102. **(B)** "Piers Plowman" is a 14th-century English allegorical poem satirizing and attacking the clergy and exalting the simple and truthful life.

103. **(A)** Diego Velázquez (1599–1660) was perhaps the most naturalistic and objective of all the court painters.

104. **(D)** George Sand's liaison with Chopin lasted from 1837 until 1847.

105. **(A)** This is true by definition.

106. **(D)** Another word for pragmatism is *practicality.*

107. **(D)** One should notice the lack of sophistication in the sculpture.

108. **(E)** *Fathers and Sons* is the most famous nihilist novel by Turgenev.

109. **(A)** This monumental work was written by the Russian writer Tolstoy.

110. **(D)** The Muses, the nine daughters of Zeus and Mnemosyne, were originally the patronesses of literature.

111. **(A)** This trilogy is Dos Passos' most famous work.

112. **(D)** W. B. Yeats (1865–1939) was influenced by Irish folklore and mythology and the French Symbolists. He brought to the Irish literary movement a sophistication of technique it had previously lacked.

113. **(C)** "Neo-Classic" refers to the 17th and 18th centuries in Europe.

114. **(C)** The others are well known figures in the field, but Robbins' dances in *West Side Story* have become classics.

115. **(C)** Michelangelo Buonarroti is another name for Michelangelo, the famous Italian Renaissance artist.

116. **(E)** Duplicity is not a virtue.

117. **(E)** Most of the educated people in England lived in London, and Chaucer spent most of his life there.

118. **(A)** Tennyson wrote this poem to commemorate the death of his very dear friend, Arthur Hallam.

119. **(B)** Quatrain means four lines of verse.

120. **(D)** The rhyme scheme is determined by listening to the vowel sounds of the last word of each line, and lettering alphabetically; therefore, new = a; snow = b; go (which has the same vowel sound as "snow") = b, and true (which has the same vowel sound as "new") = a.

121. **(E)** Auguste Rodin (1840–1917) was a French sculptor and perhaps the strongest influence on 20th-century art.

122. **(D)** Nobel Prize–winner Solzhenitsyn has written *Gulag Archipelago, Cancer Ward,* and *One Day in the Life of Ivan Denisovich.*

123. **(A)** The meter means a division of music into measures of bars.

124. **(A)** The name Milarepa, which means "Mila who wears the cotton cloth of an ascetic," lived from 1025 to 1135. His biography, written in the 15th century, containing many spiritual songs, is one of the greatest sources of inspiration in Tibetan Buddhism.

125. **(C)** John Donne was an English poet and preacher. The meditation referred to is his 17th.

126. **(C)** W.S. Gilbert and Sir Arthur Sullivan collaborated on fourteen operettas.

127. **(A)** The most conspicuous characteristics of this group of 17th-century poets are the use of conceits, harshness of versification, and a combination of different types of emotions.

128. **(E)** James Thurber (1894–1961) was well known for his stories and cartoons depicting the battles of the sexes.

129. **(B)** Classic: pertaining to the ancient Greek or Roman period; Medieval: pertaining to the Middle Ages; Romantic: pertaining to the late 18th and early 19th century.

130. **(A)** Constantin Brancusi (1876–1957) was a Rumanian abstract sculptor.

131. **(C)** Mary Shelley intended the monster to arouse the sympathy of her readers.

132. **(E)** Mary Shelley published her novel *Frankenstein* in 1818.

133. **(C)** The poem is "The Ancient Mariner."

134. **(B)** Quatrain means four lines of verse.

135. **(D)** A literary ballad is written in deliberate imitation of the form and spirit of a folk ballad. The ballad stanza is usually a quatrain in alternate 4- and 3-stress lines, rhyming abcb.

136. **(A)** Baldwin is one of America's best known contemporary black writers.

137. **(B)** A good laugh is the best cure for many ills.

138. **(D)** A clavier is a stringed keyboard instrument, such as a harpsichord.

139. **(C)** Oedipus solved the riddle by replying, "It is man."

140. **(D)** Goya (1746–1828) was a Spanish painter, etcher, and designer, and a leading representative of the Spanish school of his day.

141. **(C)** Addison was the leading prose stylist of the early 18th century.

142. **(C)** This is a concept first stated by Aristotle.

143. **(B)** Beethoven's Fifth Symphony is the most obvious example of the use of this technique.

144. **(E)** Kipling is well known for such works as *Gunga Din, Kim,* and *The Jungle Book.*

145. **(D)** The lines are from the poem "To a Skylark," by Shelley.

146. **(D)** Nureyev was the only one of the group to defect from the Soviet Union; Fonteyn is the only British dame listed.

147. **(C)** Getting married was of prime consideration to a woman in Victorian England.

148. **(B)** Browning's "My Last Duchess" is perhaps his best known dramatic monologue.

149. **(C)** This painting, to date, has not been found.

150. **(E)** This is a standard accent mark used when scanning poetry.

THE COLLEGE
MATHEMATICS EXAMINATION

College Mathematics

ANSWER SHEET—TRIAL TEST

1 Ⓐ Ⓑ Ⓒ Ⓓ
2 Ⓐ Ⓑ Ⓒ Ⓓ
3 [ ]
4 Ⓐ Ⓑ Ⓒ Ⓓ
5 Ⓐ Ⓑ Ⓒ Ⓓ
6 [ ]
7 Ⓐ Ⓑ Ⓒ Ⓓ
8 Ⓐ Ⓑ Ⓒ Ⓓ
9 Ⓐ Ⓑ Ⓒ Ⓓ
10 [ ]
11 Ⓐ Ⓑ Ⓒ Ⓓ
12 [ ]

13 Ⓐ Ⓑ Ⓒ Ⓓ
14 Ⓐ Ⓑ Ⓒ Ⓓ
15 Ⓐ Ⓑ Ⓒ Ⓓ
16 Ⓐ Ⓑ Ⓒ Ⓓ
17 Ⓐ Ⓑ Ⓒ Ⓓ
18 Ⓐ Ⓑ Ⓒ Ⓓ
19 Ⓐ Ⓑ Ⓒ Ⓓ
20 Ⓐ Ⓑ Ⓒ Ⓓ
21 Ⓐ Ⓑ Ⓒ Ⓓ
22 [ ]
23 Ⓐ Ⓑ Ⓒ Ⓓ
24 Ⓐ Ⓑ Ⓒ Ⓓ
25 Ⓐ Ⓑ Ⓒ Ⓓ
26 [ ]
27 Ⓐ Ⓑ Ⓒ Ⓓ

28 Ⓐ Ⓑ Ⓒ Ⓓ
29 Ⓐ Ⓑ Ⓒ Ⓓ
30 Ⓐ Ⓑ Ⓒ Ⓓ
31 Ⓐ Ⓑ Ⓒ Ⓓ
32 Ⓐ Ⓑ Ⓒ Ⓓ
33 Ⓐ Ⓑ Ⓒ Ⓓ
34 Ⓐ Ⓑ Ⓒ Ⓓ
35 Ⓐ Ⓑ Ⓒ Ⓓ
36 Ⓐ Ⓑ Ⓒ Ⓓ
37 Ⓐ Ⓑ Ⓒ Ⓓ
38 Ⓐ Ⓑ Ⓒ Ⓓ
39 Ⓐ Ⓑ Ⓒ Ⓓ
40 Ⓐ Ⓑ Ⓒ Ⓓ
41 Ⓐ Ⓑ Ⓒ Ⓓ
42 Ⓐ Ⓑ Ⓒ Ⓓ
43 Ⓐ Ⓑ Ⓒ Ⓓ
44 Ⓐ Ⓑ Ⓒ Ⓓ
45 Ⓐ Ⓑ Ⓒ Ⓓ

46 Ⓐ Ⓑ Ⓒ Ⓓ
47 Ⓐ Ⓑ Ⓒ Ⓓ
48 Ⓐ Ⓑ Ⓒ Ⓓ
49 Ⓐ Ⓑ Ⓒ Ⓓ
50 Ⓐ Ⓑ Ⓒ Ⓓ
51 Ⓐ Ⓑ Ⓒ Ⓓ
52 Ⓐ Ⓑ Ⓒ Ⓓ
53 Ⓐ Ⓑ Ⓒ Ⓓ
54 Ⓐ Ⓑ Ⓒ Ⓓ
55 Ⓐ Ⓑ Ⓒ Ⓓ
56 Ⓐ Ⓑ Ⓒ Ⓓ
57 Ⓐ Ⓑ Ⓒ Ⓓ
58 [ ]
59 Ⓐ Ⓑ Ⓒ Ⓓ
60 Ⓐ Ⓑ Ⓒ Ⓓ

Trial Test

This chapter contains a Trial Test in College Mathematics. Take this Trial Test to learn what the actual exam is like, and to determine how you might score on the exam before any practice or review.

The CLEP General Exam in College Mathematics measures your knowledge of the mathematical skills generally covered in college-level courses for nonmath majors, including sets, logic, the real number system, functions and their graphs, probability and statistics, and miscellaneous topics.

NUMBER OF QUESTIONS ON THE TRIAL TEST: 60

Time Limit: 90 MINUTES

Directions: You will have access to an online scientific calculator during this test.

For multiple-choice questions, select the *best* of the four choices, then type A, B, C, or D. For the other questions, type your numerical answer in the box on the computer screen. (Note: on this practice exam you may circle your choice or write your numerical answer in the box provided.)

Notes:

1. i represents $\sqrt{-1}$.

2. If the domain of a function f is not specified in a question, assume that it is the set of all real numbers for which $f(x)$ is defined.

3. Figures are drawn to scale and lie in a plane, *unless* otherwise specified.

1. Shade the set $R \cup (S \cap T)$ by clicking on the appropriate region(s)

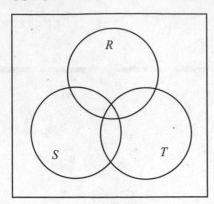

2. Which of the following graphs is for the line $2x + y = 2$?

(A)

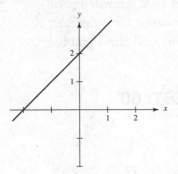

(B)

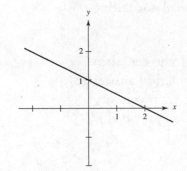

(C)

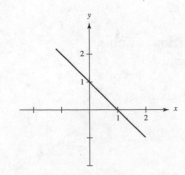

(D)

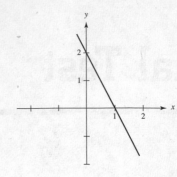

3. If $f(x) = 4 - x^3$, then $f(-2)$ equals

4. If $f(x) = x^3 + k$ and $f(x)$ is divisible by the factor $(x + 2)$, then $k =$

(A) –8
(B) –2
(C) 0
(D) 8

5. One card is selected from a set of 52. Represent the probability of choosing an ace or a black card as a fraction in lowest terms.

6. If an average grade of 60 on four tests is required to pass a course and Chris has grades of 52, 57, and 61 on the first three tests, what is the least grade she can get on the fourth test and pass the course?

7. If $R = \{x : x < 3\}$ and $S = \{x : x \geq 0\}$, then the number of integers in $R \cup S$ is

(A) none
(B) two
(C) three
(D) infinite

8. The statement "If she has passed this test, then she'll get college credit" is true. Which of the following is also true?

   (A) If she fails this test, then she'll not get college credit.
   (B) If she does not get college credit, then she has not passed this test.
   (C) She passes this test but does not get college credit.
   (D) If she gets college credit then she has passed this test.

9. If you roll two fair dice, what is the probability that the top faces will add up to 9?

   (A) $\dfrac{1}{18}$

   (B) $\dfrac{1}{9}$

   (C) $\dfrac{1}{6}$

   (D) $\dfrac{2}{9}$

10. If $g(x)$ is a linear function such that $g(-2) = -7$ and $g(3) = 8$, then $g(1)$ equals

11. The equation for the graph at the right is

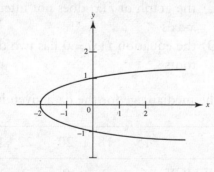

   (A) $x - 2y^2 + 2 = 0$
   (B) $x + y^2 + 2 = 0$
   (C) $x + 2y^2 - 2 = 0$
   (D) $x - y^2 + 2 = 0$

12. Two members of a group of 12 people are teachers. How many committees of 3 can be chosen so as to include at least one teacher?

13. If x is different from 0 and 1, then
$$\frac{x^2 - x}{x(x^2 - 1)} =$$

   (A) $\dfrac{1}{x+1}$

   (B) $\dfrac{1}{x-1}$

   (C) $\dfrac{1}{x(x+1)}$

   (D) $x + 1$

14. If $x^2 - x > 0$, then which of the following statements is false?

   (A) $x < 0$
   (B) $x > 1$
   (C) $0 < x < 1$
   (D) $x < 0$ or $x > 1$

15. A friend tells you that he has a special deck of cards in which all the cards with prime numbers are red. You would know that his assertion is false if you find a

   (A) red 6
   (B) red 7
   (C) black 6
   (D) black 7

16. Check (√) the appropriate boxes to indicate whether these numbers are rational or irrational.

Number(s)	Rational	Irrational
0		
x such that $x^2 = 8$		
$\dfrac{1}{6}$		
$\sqrt{121}$		

17. The difference between the mean and the median (mean minus median) for the set {35, 41, 52, 33, 49} is

(A) 0
(B) 1
(C) 2
(D) 3

18. Given the number line shown below, which of the statements is false?

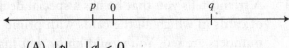

(A) $|p| - |q| < 0$
(B) $|p| + |q| > q$
(C) $|p| - |q| > p$
(D) $|p - q| > q$

19. The odds that the Panthers will beat the Lynxes in a game are 3 to 2. The probability that the Lynxes will win is

(A) $\dfrac{2}{3}$
(B) 0.65
(C) $\dfrac{3}{5}$
(D) 0.4

20. Two balls are drawn at the same time from a box of 5 of which 1 is red, 1 is blue, and 3 are black. The probability that both are black is

(A) $\dfrac{6}{25}$
(B) $\dfrac{3}{10}$
(C) $\dfrac{2}{5}$
(D) $\dfrac{3}{5}$

21. If the domain of the function $f(x) = 4x^2 + 12x + 9$ is the set of reals, then

(A) $f(x)$ is always positive
(B) $f(x)$ is nonnegative
(C) the graph of $f(x)$ does not intersect the x-axis
(D) the equation $f(x) = 0$ has two distinct roots

22. The median age for the data given is

AGE	15	18	20	22	30	31
FREQUENCY	6	2	9	2	8	1

23. If you choose an integer from 1 to 5 inclusive, then choose one from 6 to 9 inclusive, what is the probability that both integers will be divisible by 3?

    (A) $\dfrac{1}{3}$

    (B) $\dfrac{1}{10}$

    (C) $\dfrac{1}{12}$

    (D) $\dfrac{1}{15}$

24. For which of the following functions is the domain *not* the set of real numbers?

    (A) $f(x) = x^2$
    (B) $f(x) = 3x + 1$
    (C) $f(x) = \sqrt{x}$
    (D) $f(x) = 1$

25. For which real numbers is the function $f(x)$

    $= \dfrac{x}{x^2 - 9}$ *not* defined?

    (A) only $x = 0$
    (B) only $x = 3$
    (C) $x = 0$ or 3
    (D) $x = 3$ or -3

26. If n is divisible both by 6 and by 10, then it must also be divisible by

27. If $f(x) = ax + b$, $f(0) = 2$, and $f(1) = -1$, then

    (A) $a = 3, b = 2$
    (B) $a = 3, b = -2$
    (C) $a = -3, b = 2$
    (D) $a = -3, b = -2$

28. If m and n are real numbers, which of the following statements is false?

    (A) $2^m \cdot 2^n = 2^{mn}$
    (B) $(2^m)^n = 2^{mn}$
    (C) $2^m \div 2^n = 2^{m-n}$
    (D) $2^m \cdot 2^n = 2^{m+n}$

29. $\log_4 8 =$

    (A) $\dfrac{1}{2}$

    (B) $\dfrac{2}{3}$

    (C) $\dfrac{3}{2}$

    (D) 2

30. If $i = \sqrt{-1}$, then $i^{19} =$

    (A) 1
    (B) -1
    (C) i
    (D) $-i$

31. Which graph below represents the inequality $|x| < 2$?

    (A) ![number line with open interval between -2 and 2]

    (B) ![number line with closed interval between -2 and 2]

    (C) ![number line]

    (D) ![number line]

32. For what value of k do the equations

$$\begin{cases} 2x - y = 4 \\ 4x + ky = 3 \end{cases} \text{ have no solution?}$$

    (A) -8
    (B) -2
    (C) 2
    (D) 8

33. Which function has a graph symmetric to the origin?

    (A) $y = x^2$

    (B) $y = \dfrac{1}{x^2}$

    (C) $y = x + 3$

    (D) $y = \dfrac{1}{x}$

34. If S has 3 elements, then the number of ordered triples in $S \times S \times S$ is

    (A) 3
    (B) 9
    (C) 27
    (D) 81

35. Note: $R \cap \overline{S} = \{x \mid x \in R,\ x \notin S\}$. If $R \{x \mid x$ is a real number$\}$ and S is the set of all non-negative real numbers, then $R \cap \overline{S} =$

    (A) Ø, the empty set
    (B) the set of negative real numbers
    (C) $\{x \mid x \leq 0\}$
    (D) $\{0\}$

36. Suppose $f(x) = \begin{cases} x & \text{if } x \leq 1 \\ 2 - x^2 & \text{if } x > 1 \end{cases}$.

    Then the graph of f is

    (A)

    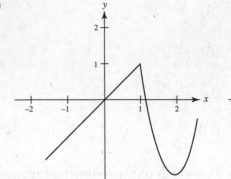

    (B)

    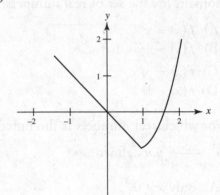

    (C)

    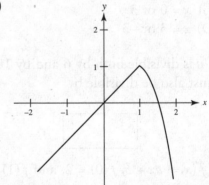

    (D)

    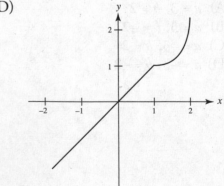

37. Which of the following is *not* the graph of a function?

    (A)

    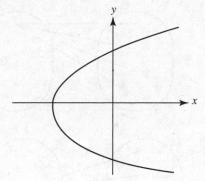

    (B)

    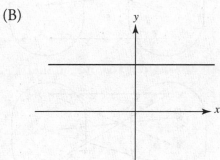

    (C)

    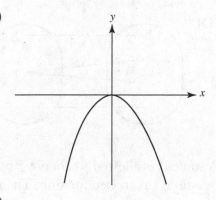

    (D)

    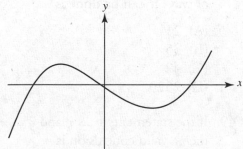

38. $\sim(p \vee \sim q)$ is true whenever

    (A) p is false and q is true
    (B) p is true
    (C) p is true
    (D) p and q are both false

39. Suppose $a < b$ (a, b real). Then it always follows that

    (A) $-a > -b$
    (B) $-a < -b$
    (C) $-a < b$
    (D) none of the preceding

40. The function whose graph is shown is

    (A) $y = x(x^2 + 4)$
    (B) $y = x(4 - x^2)$
    (C) $y = x(x^2 - 4)$
    (D) $y = x(x^2 + 2)$

    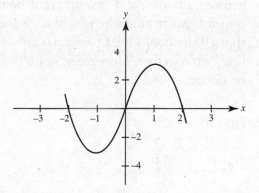

41. If $f(x) = \dfrac{1}{x+2}$ and $g(x) = \dfrac{1}{x} - 2$ for $x \neq 0$, -2, then $f(g(x)) =$

    (A) $\dfrac{1}{x+2} - 2$

    (B) $x + 2$

    (C) $\dfrac{1}{x}$

    (D) x

42. Which pair of integers (m,n) does *not* satisfy the inequality $3m - 2n \leq 4$?

    (A) $(-4,-9)$
    (B) $(-1,2)$
    (C) $(2,1)$
    (D) $(0,-2)$

43. The negation of "if p, then q" is

    (A) If not p, then not q.
    (B) If not q, then not p.
    (C) p is true, but q is false.
    (D) If q, then p.

44. If two fair dice are rolled, the probability that neither die shows a 3 or 4 is

    (A) $\dfrac{2}{9}$

    (B) $\dfrac{4}{9}$

    (C) $\dfrac{5}{9}$

    (D) $\dfrac{2}{3}$

45. Five different algebra books, four different geometry books, and two different books on probability are to be placed on a shelf so that all the books on a particular subject are lined up together. How many ways can this be done?

    (A) 40
    (B) 40 · 3!
    (C) 5! 4! 2!
    (D) (5! 4! 2!)3!

46. The notation $A \subset B$ says that "A is a subset of B." Which of the following statements is false?

    (A) Every nonempty set has at least 2 subsets.
    (B) If $P \subset Q$ then $P = Q$.
    (C) If $P = Q$ then $P \subset Q$.
    (D) The empty set is a subset of every set.

47. Which diagram does *not* define a function from $X(x_1, x_2, x_3, x_4)$ into $Y(y_1, y_2, y_3)$?

    (A)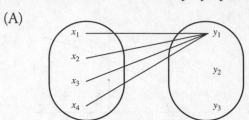

    (B)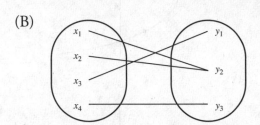

    (C)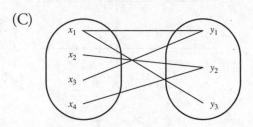

    (D)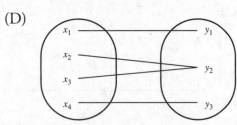

48. A student is allowed to choose 5 out of 7 questions on an examination. The number of ways it can be done is

    (A) 21
    (B) 35
    (C) 42
    (D) 2520

49. If the statements $p \rightarrow q$ and $q \rightarrow {\sim}r$ are true, then a valid conclusion is

    (A) $p \rightarrow r$
    (B) ${\sim}p \rightarrow r$
    (C) $r \rightarrow p$
    (D) $p \rightarrow {\sim}r$

50. Box I contains 2 red and 5 black marbles; box II contains 4 green and 2 black marbles. If 1 marble is drawn from each box the probability that they will be of different colors is

   (A) $\dfrac{20}{147}$

   (B) $\dfrac{5}{21}$

   (C) $\dfrac{4}{7}$

   (D) $\dfrac{16}{21}$

51. In base two, the next whole number after 101111 is

   (A) 110010
   (B) 110110
   (C) 111100
   (D) 110000

52. Which set is *not* closed under multiplication?

   (A) the set of squares of positive integers
   (B) the set of multiples of 7
   (C) the set of integers greater than 1
   (D) the set of negative integers

53. The set $\{x : x$ is an integer and $|x - 1| < 2\}$ equals

   (A) $\{1, 2\}$
   (B) $\{-2, -1, 1, 2\}$
   (C) $\{-2, -1, 0, 1, 2\}$
   (D) $\{0, 1, 2\}$

54. If $f(x) = x^2 + bx + c$, if $f(0) = 1$ and $f(1) = 2$, then $f(x) =$

   (A) $x^2 + 1$
   (B) $x^2 + x + 1$
   (C) $x^2 - x + 1$
   (D) $x^2 + 2x + 1$

55. The probability of Jane's winning a game of darts against Val is $\dfrac{1}{4}$. If they play three games, what is the probability that Jane will win at least one game?

   (A) $\dfrac{1}{2}$

   (B) $\dfrac{9}{16}$

   (C) $\dfrac{37}{64}$

   (D) $\dfrac{3}{4}$

56. It is known that m and n are positive integers, m is even, and n is odd. Check ($\surd$) the appropriate boxes to indicate whether each of these numbers is even or odd.

Number	Even	Odd
$mn + 2$		
m^n		
$5n + 1$		
n^m		

57. If $\log_{10} m = 0.1$, then $\log_{10} m^3 =$

   (A) 0.001
   (B) 0.3
   (C) 3.1
   (D) 3.3

58. If $m * n = m^2 - 2n$, then $3 * (2 * 1) =$

   (A) 23
   (B) 9
   (C) 7
   (D) 5

59. At a certain high school 20% of the students failed math, 25% failed physics, and 10% failed both. The probability that a student selected at random failed math if he failed physics is

    (A) $\dfrac{2}{7}$

    (B) $\dfrac{2}{5}$

    (C) $\dfrac{1}{2}$

    (D) $\dfrac{4}{5}$

60. The inverse of the function $y = 2^x$ is

    (A) $y = \log_2 x$
    (B) $y = -2^x$
    (C) $y = 2^{-x}$
    (D) $y = x^2$

STOP

If there is still time remaining, you may review your answers.

College Mathematics
ANSWER KEY—TRIAL TEST

1.

2. D
3. 12
4. D
5. $\dfrac{7}{13}$
6. 70
7. D
8. B
9. B
10. 2
11. A
12. 100
13. A

14. C
15. D
16.

17. B
18. C
19. D
20. D
21. B
22. 20
23. B
24. C
25. D
26. 30
27. C

28. A
29. C
30. D
31. A
32. B
33. D
34. C
35. B
36. C
37. A
38. A
39. A
40. B
41. D
42. A
43. C
44. B
45. D
46. B

47. C
48. A
49. D
50. D
51. D
52. D
53. D
54. A
55. C
56.

57. B
58. 5
59. B
60. A

SCORING CHART

After you have scored your Trial Test, enter the results in the chart below, then transfer your score to the Progress Chart on page 12. As you complete the Sample Examinations later in this part of the book, you should be able to achieve increasingly higher scores.

Total Test	Number Right	Number Wrong	Number Omitted
Total: 60			

ANSWER EXPLANATIONS*

1. **(B)** The set $R \cup (S \cap T)$ consists of elements in R or in both S and T.

Number(s)	Rational	Irrational
0	√	
x such that $x^2 = 8$		√
$\dfrac{1}{6}$	√	
$\sqrt{121}$	√	

2. **(D)** The line $2x + y = 2$ has x-intercept $+1$ and y-intercept $+2$.

3. **(12)** $f(-2) = 4 - (-2)^3 = 4 + 8 = 12$.

4. **(D)** $f(-2) = 0 = (-2)^3 + k \rightarrow k = 8$.

5. $\left(\dfrac{7}{13}\right)$ There are 26 black cards (including 2 aces) and 2 more (red) aces for a total of 28 cards out of 52.

6. **(70)** If x is the grade required on the fourth test to pass the course, then x must satisfy $\dfrac{52 + 57 + 61 + x}{4} \geq 60$. So $170 + x \geq 240$, or $x \geq 70$.

7. **(D)** The integers in R are ..., $-2, -1, 0, 1, 2$. The integers in S are $0, 1, 2, 3, \ldots$. Those in $R \cup S$ are $\ldots, -2, -1, 0, 1, 2, \ldots$, namely, the entire set of integers.

8. **(B)** The contrapositive of statement is $p \rightarrow q$ is $\sim q \rightarrow \sim p$.

9. **(B)** There are 36 possible sums, of which the pairs $(3,6)$, $(6,3)$, $(4,5)$, and $(5,4)$ sum to 9.

10. **(2)** $g(x) = ax + b$. Then $g(-2) = -2a + b = -7$, and $g(3) = 3a + b = 8$. Subtracting, we get $-5a = -15$ and $a = 3$. Then $b = -1$ and $g(x) = 3x - 1$. So $g(1) = 2$.

11. **(A)** Note that the graph has x-intercept -2 and two y-intercepts, -1 and $+1$.

12. **(100)** A committee must have one or two teachers. There are ${}_2C_1 \cdot {}_{10}C_2$ one-teacher committees and ${}_2C_2 \cdot {}_{10}C_1$ two-teacher committees. The sum is

$$2 \cdot \frac{10 \cdot 9}{1 \cdot 2} + 1 \cdot 10, \text{ or } 90 + 10. \text{ Why is } {}_{12}C_3 - {}_{10}C_3 \text{ also correct?}$$

*In some explanations of the Practice Sets we verify that incorrect answers are indeed incorrect—even though we have recommended that you not do this when taking the examination. Our intention here is to review and reinforce the mathematics, when time restrictions are not a factor. When working on one of the practice examinations, or on the CLEP Examination itself, time is a factor, and you should follow the instructions given on page 271 to the best of your ability. See also pages 298–299.

13. **(A)** $\dfrac{x^2 - x}{x(x^2 - 1)} = \dfrac{x(x-1)}{x(x-1)(x+1)} = \dfrac{1}{x+1}$ if $x \neq 0, 1$.

14. **(C)** $x^2 - x = x(x-1)$; the product is positive if $x > 1$ or if $x < 0$.

15. **(D)** A black 7 is a counterexample.

16.

Number(s)	Rational	Irrational
0	√	
x such that $x^2 = 8$		√
$\dfrac{1}{6}$	√	
$\sqrt{121}$	√	

Note that $\sqrt{121} = 11$, a rational number.

17. **(B)** The mean is the average, or 42; the median is the middle grade, or 41.

18. **(C)** Choose suitable values for p and q, for example $p = -1$ and $q = 3$. You may then verify that (A), (B), and (D) are true. But (C) is false since $|-1| - |3| = -2$, which is *not* greater than -1.

19. **(D)** The probability that the Lynxes will win is $2 \div (3 + 2)$, which equals $\dfrac{2}{5}$ or 0.4 .

20. **(B)** The probability is $\dfrac{_3C_2}{_5C_2}$, or $\dfrac{(3 \cdot 2)}{(5 \cdot 4)}$

21. **(B)** $f(x) = (2x + 3)^2$, which is zero if $x = -\dfrac{3}{2}$ otherwise $f(x) > 0$.

22. **(20)** The total number reported on (that is, the sum of the frequencies) is 28; the middle one (14th or 15th) is age 20.

23. **(B)** Only one of the first set of five integers is divisible by 3 (namely 3); both 6 and 9 in the second set of four integers are divisible by 3. The answer is $\dfrac{1}{5} \cdot \dfrac{2}{4}$ or $\dfrac{1}{10}$.

24. **(C)** $f(x) = \sqrt{x}$ is a function but its domain is the set of nonnegative numbers.

25. **(D)** Division by zero is excluded.

26. **(30)** Since $6 = 2 \cdot 3$ and $10 = 2 \cdot 5$, n must be divisible by 2, 3, and 5.

27. **(C)** $f(0) = b = 2$; $f(1) = a + b = -1$; so $a + 2 = -1$ and $a = -3$.

28. **(A)** $2^m \cdot 2^n = 2^{m+n}$ as in (D).

29. **(C)** If $\log_4 8 = x$, then $4^x = 8$ or $2^{2x} = 2^3$.

30. **(D)** $i^{19} = i^{16} \cdot i^3 = 1 \cdot (-i)$. Note that $i^2 = -1$; $i^3 = i(i^2) = i(-1) = -i$; $i^4 = (i^2)^2 = (-1)^2 = 1$; and so on.

31. **(A)** $|x| < a$ is equivalent to $-a < x < a$.

32. **(B)** The coefficients of y must be in the same ratio as those of x. Thus k must satisfy the proportion $k : -1 = 4 : 2$. It follows that $2k = -4$ or that $k = -2$.

33. **(D)** A graph of $y = f(x)$ is symmetric to the origin if $(-x, -y)$ lies on the graph, that is, if it satisfies the equation. Note that $(-y) = \dfrac{1}{(-x)}$ is equivalent to $y = \dfrac{1}{x}$.

34. **(C)** $S \times S$ has (3×3) or 9 elements, and $S \times S \times S$ has (9×3) elements.

35. **(B)** The set $R \cap \overline{S}$ contains all the elements of R that are not in S. Here S is the set of positive real numbers and 0.

36. **(C)** The graph consists of the line through the origin with slope 1 for $x \le 1$ and that part of the parabola (whose vertex is $(0,2)$ and which opens down) for $x > 1$.

37. **(A)** The graph of a function must pass the vertical-line test (a vertical line can intersect the graph at most at one point). Analytically, for each x in the domain, there is a *unique y*.

38. **(A)** Here is the truth table; note that $\sim(p \vee \sim q)$ is true only when p is false and q is true.

$\sim$	$(p$	$\vee$	$\sim$	$q)$
F	T	T	F	T
F	T	T	T	F
T	F	F	F	T
F	F	T	T	F
(5)	(1)	(4)	(3)	(2)

39. **(A)** $a < b$ implies that $(b - a) > 0$, so $-a > -b$.

40. **(B)** The intercepts can be read from the graph: they are 0, 2, −2. So only (B) and (C) are possible. But from the graph $f(1) > 0$ and for (C) $f(1) < 0$; so (C) is eliminated.

41. **(D)** $f(g(x)) = \dfrac{1}{\dfrac{1}{2} - 2 + 2} = x.$

42. **(A)** Substitute the first number in the ordered pair for m, the second for n. Only for (A) is $3m - 2n$ *greater* than 4.

43. **(C)** Here is the truth table.

p	q	$p \rightarrow q$	$\sim(p \rightarrow q)$
T	T	T	F
T	F	F	T
F	T	T	F
F	F	T	F

$\sim(p \rightarrow q)$ is true only when p is true and q is false.

44. **(B)** There are four ways out of six for each die to show a number other than 3 or 4. The answer is therefore $\frac{4}{6} \cdot \frac{4}{6}$ or $\frac{4}{9}$.

45. **(D)** There are 5! ways to arrange the algebra books, 4! ways to arrange the geometry books, and 2! ways to arrange the probability books. The three subjects can be arranged in 3! ways.

46. **(B)** As a counterexample to statement (B), let $P = \{1,2\}$ and $Q = \{1,2,3\}$. Then $P \subset Q$ but $P \neq Q$.

47. **(C)** Note, in (C), that x_1 maps into both y_1 and y_3. Since X is a function, $X(x_1)$ must be unique.

48. **(A)** The answer is the number of combinations of 7 elements taken 5 at a time, or $_7C_5$. Since $_7C_5 = {_7C_2}$, we get $\frac{(7 \cdot 6)}{(1 \cdot 2)}$ or 21.

49. **(D)** If p implies q and q implies $\sim r$ then p implies $\sim r$.

50. **(D)** Compute the probability of obtaining two marbles of the same color and subtract from 1. The probability of getting 2 blacks is $\left(\frac{5}{7}\right) \cdot \left(\frac{2}{6}\right)$ or $\frac{5}{21}$. The required probability is $1 - \frac{5}{21} = \frac{16}{21}$.

51. **(D)** Here is the addition:

$$\begin{array}{r} 1111 \quad \text{(carry)} \\ 101111 \\ +\underline{\qquad 1} \\ 110000 \end{array}$$

52. **(D)** The product of two negative integers is positive.

53. **(D)** If $|x - 1| < 2$, then x is within two units of 1; that is, $-1 < x < 3$.

54. **(A)** $f(0) = c = 1$ and $f(1) = 1 + b + c = 1 + b + 1 = 2$, so $b = 0$.

55. **(C)** The probability that Jane will lose a game against Val is $\frac{3}{4}$, and that she will lose all three games is $\left(\frac{3}{4}\right) \cdot \left(\frac{3}{4}\right) \cdot \left(\frac{3}{4}\right)$. The probability that she will win at least one game is $1 - \left(\frac{3}{4}\right)^3$, or $\frac{37}{64}$.

56.

Number	Even	Odd
$mn + 2$	√	
m^n	√	
$5n + 1$	√	
n^m		√

Let $m = 2$, $n = 3$. Note that (A), (B), (C) are all even, but $3^2 = 9$.

57. **(B)** $\log_{10} m^3 = 3 \log_{10} m = 3(0.1)$.

58. **(5)** $3 * (2 * 1) = 3 * (2^2 - 2 \cdot 1) = 3 * 2 = 3^2 - 2 \cdot 2 = 5$.

59. **(B)** The probability that a student failed math if he failed physics is the percentage of students who failed both out of the percentage of students who failed physics:

$$\frac{\text{probability the student failed both math and physics}}{\text{probability the student failed physics}} = \frac{0.10}{0.25} = \frac{2}{5}$$

60. **(A)** To find the inverse of a function, interchange x and y, then solve for y. For $y = 2^x$, we write $x = 2^y$, which yields, after taking the log of each side to base 2, $\log_2 x = y$.

CHAPTER 10

Background and Practice Questions

DESCRIPTION OF THE COLLEGE MATHEMATICS EXAMINATION

The CLEP General Examination in College Mathematics measures your knowledge of fundamental principles and concepts of mathematics. It covers material that is generally taught in a college course for nonmathematics majors. The exam is given in two parts, each consisting of approximately 30 questions and each requiring 45 minutes to complete. See the following chart for approximate percentages of examination items:

College Mathematics Exam	
Content or Item Types	**Time/Number of Questions**
10% Sets—union and intersection, subsets, Venn diagrams, Cartesian product	60 questions 90 minutes
10% Logic—truth tables, conjunctions, disjunctions, implications and negations, conditional statements, necessary and sufficient conditions, converse, inverse and contrapositive couterexamples	
20% Real Number System—prime and composite numbers, odd and even numbers, factors and divisibility, rational and irrational numbers, absolute value and order, open and closed intervals	
20% Functions and Their Graphs—properties and graphs of functions, domain and range, composition of functions and inverse functions	

College Mathematics Exam

Content or Item Types	Time/Number of Questions
25% Probability and Statistics—counting problems, including permutations and combinations, computation of probabilities of simple and compound events, simple conditional probability, mean, median, mode, and range, concept of standard deviation	
15% Additional Topics in Algebra and Geometry—complex numbers; logarithms and exponents; applications; perimeter and area of plane figures; properties of triangles, circles, and rectangles; Pythagorean theorem; parallel and perpendicular lines; algebraic equations and inequalities	

About half of the exam asks you to solve routine, straightforward problems, while the other half requires you to do nonroutine problems that involve understanding and application of basic concepts of mathematics.

The College Mathematics Exam does not emphasize arithmetical calculations, so a calculator is not required for the examination. However, the testing software includes a scientific (nongraphing, nonprogrammable) calculator for your use during the exam.

COMMON MATHEMATICAL SYMBOLS AND FORMULAS

Symbols used in arithmetic, algebra, geometry, and so forth:

$a = b$	a equals b
$a \neq b$	a does not equal b
$a \approx b$	a is approximately equal to b
$a > b$	a is greater than b
$a \geq b$	a is greater than or equal to b
$a < b$	a is less than b
$a \leq b$	a is less than or equal to b
$a < x < b$	x is greater than a and less than b
$|x|$	the absolute value, or magnitude, of x
$\sqrt{q}$	the square root of q
$\sqrt[3]{q}, \sqrt[4]{q}, \sqrt[n]{q},$	the cube root of q, the fourth root of q, the nth root of q
$a : b$	the ratio of a to b, "a is to b"
π	the constant pi (the ratio of the circumference of a circle to its diameter; approximately 22/7 or 3.14)
$0.\overline{18}$	the repeated decimal 0.1818. . .

Symbols used in set theory:[†]

$a \in S$	a is an element of set S
$a \notin S$	a is not an element of set S
$\{a, b, c\}$	the set containing the elements a, b, and c
$\emptyset$	the null or empty set
U	the universal set
$\overline{R}$ (or R' or $\widetilde{R}$)	the complement of set R: the set of all elements that are not in set R
$A \cup B$	the union of sets A and B
$A \cap B$	the intersection of sets A and B
$A \times B$	the Cartesian product of A and B: the set of all ordered pairs whose first element is in A and whose second element is in B
$A \cap \overline{B}$	the set of all elements in A that are not also in B
$A \subset B$	A is a subset of B. (Some authors use "$A \subset B$" to mean A is a proper subset of B and "$A \subseteq B$" to mean A is a subset, proper or improper, of B.)
$A \not\subset B$	set A is not a subset of set B

[†]*Most of these symbols are defined or illustrated when they first occur in the chapter.*

Symbols used in logic:[†]

$\sim p$	not p (the negation of p)
$p \wedge q$	p and q (conjunction)
$p \vee q$	p or q (disjunction: p or q or both)
$p \rightarrow q$	if p then q; or p implies q
$p \leftrightarrow q$	p if and only if q, or p is equivalent to q
$\exists_x$	there exists an x; for some x
$\forall_x$	for all x; for each x

Symbols used for functions:[†]

$f(x)$	A function f of a variable x (see definition of function on page 292).
$f(a)$	The value of the function $f(x)$ when x is equal to a; $f(a)$ is obtained by replacing x wherever it appears in $f(x)$ by a. For example, if $f(x) = x^2 - x + 1$, then $f(-2) = (-2)^2 - (-2) + 1 = 7$.
$f(g(x))$ or $(f \circ g)(x)$	The composite of functions f and g; $f(g(x))$ is obtained by replacing x wherever it appears in $f(x)$ by $g(x)$. For example, if $f(x) = 2x^2 - x + 3$ and $g(x) = 4 - x$, then $f(g(x)) = 2(4-x)^2 - (4-x) + 3$ $= 2x^2 - 15x + 31$ Note that $g(f(x)) = 4 - (2x^2 - x + 3)$ $= -2x^2 + x + 1$.

Symbols used in probability and statistics:[†]

$n!$	n factorial, the product of the first n positive integers: $n! = n(n-1)(n-2) \cdots 3 \cdot 2 \cdot 1$ For example, $6! = 6 \cdot 5 \cdot 4 \cdot 3 \cdot 2 \cdot 1 = 720$.
$_nP_r$ or $P(n,r)$	The number of *permutations* (or-dered arrangements) of a set of n objects taken r at a time: $$_nP_r = \frac{n!}{(n-r)!}$$

[†]*Most of these symbols are defined or illustrated when they first occur in the chapter.*

$_nC_r$ or $C(n,r)$ or $\binom{n}{r}$ — The number of *combinations* (selections in which order does not matter) of a set of n objects taken r at a time:

$$_nC_r = \frac{_nP_r}{r!} = \frac{n!}{r!(n-r)!}$$

$\displaystyle\sum_{k=1}^{n} f(k)$ — The sum obtained by letting k vary from 1 through n and adding up the resulting terms:

$$\sum_{k=1}^{n} f(k) = f(1) + f(2) + \cdots + f(n)$$

For example,

$$\sum_{k=1}^{n} 3(k) - 1 = 3(1) - 1 + 3(2) - 1$$
$$+3(3) - 1 + 3(4) - 1$$
$$= 2 + 5 + 8 + 11$$
$$= 26$$

$\overline{x}$ — The arithmetic mean (average) of a set of numbers (see definition of mean on page 292). If the set of numbers is $\{x_1, x_2, ..., x_n\}$, then

$$\overline{x} = \frac{\displaystyle\sum_{k=1}^{n} x_k}{n}$$

Other symbols:[†]

i — The imaginary unit in complex numbers; $i = \sqrt{-1}$.

(a,b) — The point in the plane whose abscissa (x-coordinate) is a and whose ordinate (y-coordinate) is b. Also, the ordered pair of elements a and b, where the set containing a and b is specified.

$a * b$ — Here "$*$" stands for some algebraic operation; thus $a * b$ is the element obtained by applying this operation to the ordered pair of elements (a,b). For example, if $*$ is ordinary subtraction on the set of integers, then

$$3 * 7 = 3 - 7 = -4.$$

1101_2 or 1101_{TWO} — This is a base-two numeral; its value in our (base-ten) system is

$(1 \times 2^3) + (1 \times 2^2) + (0 \times 2^1) + (1 \times 2^0)$

or $8 + 4 + 0 + 1 = 13$

[†]*Most of these symbols are defined or illustrated when they first occur in the chapter.*

DEFINITIONS OF SOME COMMON MATHEMATICAL TERMS

prime number   A positive integer other than 1 whose only factors are 1 and itself; for example, 2, 3, 5, . . ., 23, 29, . . ., 41, 43, ... There are infinitely many primes.

composite number   A positive integer that has a factor other than 1 and itself; for example, 4, 6, 8, 9, 10, 12, ...

function   A correspondence between two sets such that each element of one set, called the *domain*, is associated with one and only one element of the other set, called the *range*.

mean   The arithmetic average of a set of values; the mean of a set is equal to the sum of all the values in the set divided by the number of values in the set.

median   The middle value of a set (or the value halfway between the two middle values) when the values are arranged in order of size. The median of the set [1, 1, 4, 6, 7, 7, 10] is 6; the median of [l, 2, 4, 6, 6, 8] is 5.

COMMON GEOMETRIC FORMULAS

Sum of the angles of a triangle.
The sum is 180°.

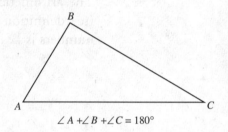

$\angle A + \angle B + \angle C = 180°$

Pythagorean Theorem.
In a right triangle, the square of the length of the hypotenuse equals the sum of the squares of the lengths of the other two sides:

$$c^2 = a^2 + b^2$$

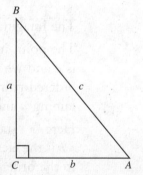

		Areas	**Perimeters**
RECTANGLE		$A = lw$	$P = 2l + 2w$
SQUARE		$A = s^2$	$P = 4s$
PARALLELOGRAM	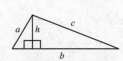	$A = bh$	
TRIANGLE	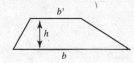	$A = \frac{1}{2}bh$	$P = a + b + c$
TRAPEZOID	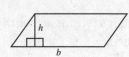	$A = \frac{1}{2}(b + b')\,h$	
CIRCLE		$A = \pi r^2$	

TYPES OF QUESTIONS

Most of the questions on the exam are of the multiple-choice type, where you select the best answer from among four choices. For other questions you may be asked to enter numbers or check marks in boxes provided, shade regions in a diagram, identify points on a number line, or put a list in order.

Here are the directions followed by six examples, with correct answers and explanations.

Directions: For each of the following questions select the best answer or write the correct answer in the box provided.

1. If $2x - y = 7$ and $3x + y = 8$, then $x + y$ equals

$$\boxed{2}$$

ANSWER

Solve the pair of equations simultaneously:

$$
\begin{aligned}
(1) \quad 2x - y &= 7 \\
(2) \quad 3x + y &= 8 \\
5x &= 15 \text{ (by adding (1) and (2))} \\
x &= 3
\end{aligned}
$$

Then, substituting for x in equation (1), we have

$$
\begin{aligned}
2(3) - y &= 7 \\
6 - y &= 7 \\
y &= -1
\end{aligned}
$$

So $x = 3$ and $y = -1$. Then $x + y = 3 + (-1) = 2$.

Note that we have inserted the answer "2" in the box provided.

2. Suppose $f(x) = \dfrac{x+1}{x-1}$. Then $f(1)$ equals

(A) -1
(B) 0
(C) 2
(D) none of these

ANSWER

Replacing x by 1, we get

$$f(1) = \frac{1+1}{1-1} = \frac{2}{0}.$$

Since division by zero is excluded, the function is not defined as $x = 1$.]

The correct answer is D.

3. If a is negative, indicate whether each of the following numbers is positive or negative by checking (√) the appropriate box.

Number	Positive	Negative
a^3		
a^4		
$10 - 2a$		
$\lvert a - 100 \rvert$		

ANSWER

Note that the product of three negative numbers is negative, so a^3 is negative. Check the appropriate box by clicking in it. Similarly, the product of four negative numbers is positive, so a^4 is positive.

The product of two negative numbers is positive, so $-2a$ is positive, and thus $10 - 2a$ is positive.

The absolute value is defined as follows:

$$\lvert x \rvert = \begin{cases} x, & \text{if } x \geq 0 \\ -x, & \text{if } x < 0 \end{cases}$$

Since a is given as negative, the quantity $a - 100$ is negative. The absolute value $\lvert a - 100 \rvert$ is therefore the opposite (or negative) of the negative quantity $a - 100$, a positive number.

The correct answer is

Number	Positive	Negative
a^3		√
a^4	√	
$10 - 2a$	√	
$\lvert a - 100 \rvert$	√	

4. In the Venn diagram shown, circle *R* represents days when it rained in New York City and circle *Y* represents days when the Yankees played baseball there. Shade the region that represents the days when it was raining and the Yankees did not play baseball.

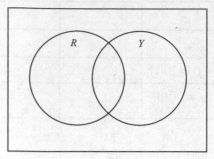

ANSWER

Click in the region inside circle *R* but outside circle *Y*.

The answer is

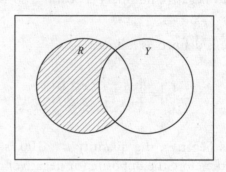

5. Mark the number line to identify the value of *x* for which the function $f(x) = \dfrac{6}{2+x}$ is undefined.

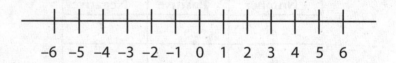

ANSWER

The function is undefined when the denominator equals 0. If $2 + x = 0$, then $x = -2$. Click on -2 to mark that point.

The answer is

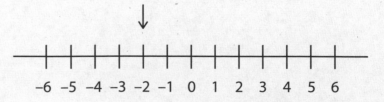

6. Arrange these numbers in increasing order, starting with the smallest number in the top box:

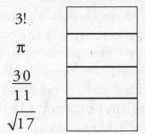

ANSWER

You don't need to know exact values to answer this question. Observe that $3! = 6$, π is a little more than 3, $\dfrac{30}{11}$ is a little less than 3, and $\sqrt{17} > 4$.

Create the correct order by clicking on the smallest number, $\dfrac{30}{11}$, and then clicking in the top box. Continue until you have placed all four numbers in the proper order.

The answer is

$3!$	$\dfrac{30}{11}$
π	π
$\dfrac{30}{11}$	$\sqrt{17}$
$\sqrt{17}$	$3!$

TIPS ON ANSWERING QUESTIONS

1. As soon as you recognize the correct answer to a multiple-choice question, indicate that choice in the answer column immediately and move on to the next question. Do not try to verify that the other choices are incorrect. You may notice that this point differs from the strategy explained in Chapter 2. In that chapter, we advised you to read *all* the answers carefully before selecting your answer. This advice works well on the other exams because more than one answer might be correct. On those exams, you are asked to pick the *best* answer, even if another answer might be possible. On the math exam, however, only one answer is correct. The others are definitely wrong. Therefore, you only need to find the one correct answer; there is no need to look further. For example:

   Which of the following Venn diagrams is for the set R ∩ S?

   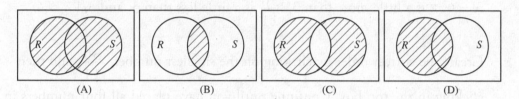

(A)	(B)	(C)	(D)

   Choice (A) is incorrect. Since choice (B) is correct, blacken space (B) on the answer sheet immediately without considering the remaining choices. Many multiple-choice questions can be answered using this strategy. Here are four examples: Which of the following statements is true *(or* false *or* impossible)? Which set is *not* empty? Which number is irrational? Which of the following graphs represents a function?

2. Be careful when solving an equation like $x^2 = 3x$. If you divide through by x, you will throw away a root. Instead, rewrite and factor as follows:
$$x^2 - 3x = 0$$
$$x(x - 3) = 0$$
$$x = 0 \text{ or } x = 3$$

3. Draw a sketch, if appropriate, and label the parts with given data or variables. To find a function or express a relation among variables, it may help to replace the variables by simple numbers.

4. Avoid excessive computation. Don't use pencil and paper unless you must. You will be allowed to use an online, scientific nongraphing, nonprogrammable calculator during the examination if you need to.

5. Do not spend too much time on any one question. If you're not sure of the answer, or if your equations or your computations seem unduly complicated, mark the question and return to it later if time permits.

6. Keep track of the time. Try to answer about 20 questions during the first 30 minutes. If you answer fewer, try to work a bit faster on the remaining questions.

7. You should not be concerned if you do not answer all the questions on the mathematics examination, because no one is expected to do all of them within the time limit. If you answer about half the questions correctly, your score will be approximately equal to the average score obtained by a test group of college sophomores with liberal arts backgrounds.

8. You are encouraged to guess whenever you do not know or are not sure of the answer since your score will be based only on the number of questions you answer correctly.

Try to keep in mind the tips given above and to use them when appropriate in answering the practice questions that follow.

STUDY SOURCES

Throughout this chapter, we will encourage you to develop a systematic approach to problem-solving, suggesting specific techniques and offering further hints on taking the test. You may find it helpful for your review to refer to one or more of the books listed below. These books, or others covering similar material, are available in public and school libraries.

The College Board Official Study Guide (2006) and its web site at *www.collegeboard.comlclep.*

Leff, Lawrence S. *Let's Review: Math A (2002); Math B (2002).* Hauppauge, NY: Barron's Educational Series.

Leff, Lawrence S. *EZ-101 College Algebra.* Hauppauge, NY: Barron's Educational Series, 2005.

Practice Questions on Mathematics

In this section we will use practice questions to review the skills and content tested on the CLEP College Mathematics Examination. The topics covered are those frequently taught in college courses designed for non-mathematics majors: survey courses, courses offered to meet general education requirements, or courses designed for majors in elementary education. You will be expected to understand conventional symbols and notation, especially as used for the topics of sets, logic, and functions. Contemporary mathematical terminology and symbolism will generally be used here to provide review.

In the material that follows, practice questions are given separately for each topic covered: sets, logic, the real number system, functions and graphs, and probability and statistics. The last group of questions is on additional algebra topics, including complex numbers, logarithms and exponents, and applications.

As noted earlier, most of the questions on the CLEP Examination are of the regular multiple-choice type. The others require that you enter type a numerical answer or checkmark in the boxes provided, shade regions in a diagram, identify points on a number line, or put a list in order.

Directions: Answer each of the following questions. Keep track of your answers so you can compare them with the correct ones beginning on page 303.

SETS

The subtopics are union and intersection; subsets; Venn diagrams; and Cartesian products.

EXAMPLES

1. If $R = \{0,1\}$ and $S = \{2,3,4\}$, then $R \cup S$ equals

   (A) $\{0\}$
   (B) $\{2,3,4\}$
   (C) $\{1,2,3,4\}$
   (D) $\{0,1,2,3,4\}$

   Explanation: $R \cup S$ denotes the *union* of sets R and S; it consists of *all* the elements in set R or in set S or in both. The correct answer is D.

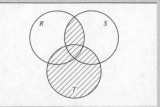

EXAMPLES (cont.)

2. The Venn diagram above is for the set

(A) $R \cap (S \cup T)$
(B) $(R \cap S) \cup T$
(C) $(R \cup S) \cap T$
(D) $R \cap S \cup T$

Explanation: The shaded area consists of elements that are either in both R and S, i.e., in $R \cap S$, or in T. The correct answer is B.

Follow the directions given above for this group of practice questions on sets. If you can eliminate one or more choices, then guess among the remaining ones. The correct answers and explanations will be found following the group of questions.

1. If $R = \{0,2,4\}$ and $S = \{0\}$, then $R \cap S =$

   (A) $\{0,2,4\}$
   (B) $\{2,4\}$
   (C) $\{0\}$
   (D) $\emptyset$

2. If $R = \{a,b\}$, $S = \{b,c\}$, and $T = \{a,c\}$, the $R \cap (S \cap T)$ equals

   (A) $\emptyset$
   (B) $\{a,b,c\}$
   (C) $\{a,b\}$
   (D) $\{c\}$

3. Which of the following is not a subset of $\{p,q,s,v,w\}$?

   (A) $\{p,q,s,v,w\}$
   (B) $\emptyset$
   (C) $\{p\}$
   (D) $\{p,q,t\}$

4. If $\overline{P}$ denotes the complement of set P, then shade the region(s) in the diagram corresponding to $\overline{R \cup S}$.

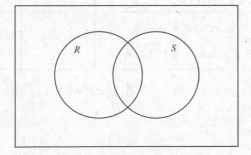

5. If $U = \{a,b,c\}$ and $V = \{d\}$, then $U \times V =$
   (A) $\{a,b,c,d\}$
   (B) $\emptyset$
   (C) $\{(a,d)(b,d)(c,d)\}$
   (D) $\{(d,a)(d,b)(d,c)\}$

6. If $R = \{x : 1 < x < 5\}$, then the number of integers in R is

7. $R = \{x : x \geq 0\}$ and $S = \{x : x \leq 3\}$. The number of integers in $R \cup S$ is

   (A) none
   (B) 2
   (C) 4
   (D) infinite

8. Which of the following is a Venn diagram for $(R \cup S) \cap T$?

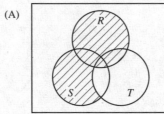

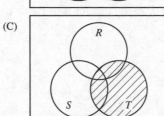

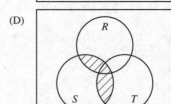

9. $V = \{a,b,c,d\}$ and $W = \{b,d,f\}$. Check the appropriate box to indicate whether each statement is true or false.

Statement	True	False
$W \subset V$		
$\{b,f\}$ is a subset of $V \cap W$		
$\{a,c\}$ belongs to $V \times W$		
$\{a,c,f\}$ is a subset of $V \cup W$		

10. If $R = \{x : x > 1\}$ and $S = \{x : x \leq 2\}$, then which of the following is false?

    (A) $R \cap S$ contains two integers
    (B) $1 \notin R$
    (C) $R \cap S = \{x : 1 < x \leq 2\}$
    (D) $1 \in S$

11. If $R = \{a,b\}$ and $S = \{a,c\}$, then the number of ordered pairs in $R \times S$ is

12. The number of subsets of $\{a,b,c\}$ is

   (A) 8
   (B) 6
   (C) 5
   (D) 3

13. $R \cap (S \cup T)$ equals

   (A) $(R \cap S) \cup T$
   (B) $(R \cap S) \cup (R \cap T)$
   (C) $(R \cup S) \cap (R \cup T)$
   (D) $(R \cup S) \cap T$

14. Which of the following is a false statement about the Venn diagram?

   (A) $S \subset R$
   (B) $R \cap S = S$
   (C) $(R \cap S) \subset R$
   (D) $R \cap S = \emptyset$

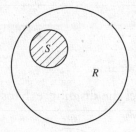

15. If $P = \{x | x \geq 1\}$ and $Q = \{x | x < 7\}$ then the number of integers in $P \cup Q$ is

   (A) none
   (B) 6
   (C) 7
   (D) infinite

ANSWERS AND EXPLANATIONS*

1. **(C)** $R \cap S$ is the *intersection* of sets R and S; it consists of the elements that are in both R and S.

2. **(A)** $S \cap T = \{c\}$; $R \cap (S \cap T) = \emptyset$ When the intersection of two sets is the empty (or null) set $\emptyset$, then the sets are said to be *disjoint*. Disjoint sets have *no* elements in common.

3. **(D)** Any element in a subset of a set must be an element of the set. Remember that the null set ∅ is a subset of every set.

4. **(A)** $\overline{T}$ denotes the complement of T; i.e., the elements not in T. $\overline{R \cup S}$ consists of elements in the universal set which are not in $R \cup S$.

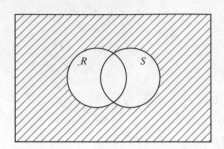

5. **(C)** $U \times V$ is the set of ordered pairs whose first element is an element of U and whose second is an element of V. $U \times V$ is called the *Cartesian product* of U and V.

6. **(3)** The integers are 2, 3, 4.

7. **(D)** Think of a number line:

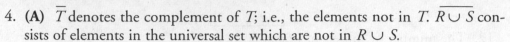

$R \cup S$ is the whole number line.

8. **(B)** Often it helps to label the disjoint, exhaustive sets as shown:

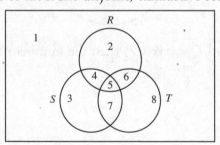

R consists of regions 2, 4, 5, 6
S consists of regions 3, 4, 5, 7
T consists of regions 5, 6, 7, 8
$(R \cup S) \cap T$ consists of (2, 3, 4, 5, 6, 7) ∩ (5, 6, 7, 8) = 5, 6, 7.

9.

Statement	True	False
$W \subset V$		√
$\{b,f\}$ is a subset of $V \cap W$		√
$\{a,c\}$ belongs to $V \times W$		√
$\{a,c,f\}$ is a subset of $V \cup W$	√	

Note that $V \cap W = \{b,d\}$, that $\{a,c\} \notin V \times W$, that $V \cup W = \{a,b,c,d,f\}$.

10. **(A)**

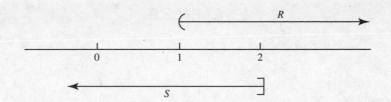

(Note that "∈ " denotes "is an element of," "∉ " denotes "is not an element of," some specified set.)

11. **(4)** $R \times S = \{(a,a), (a,c), (b,a), (b,c)\}$.

12. **(A)** The subsets of $\{a,b,c\}$ are $\emptyset$, $\{a\}$, $\{b\}$, $\{c\}$, $\{a,b\}$, $\{a,c\}$, $\{b,c\}$, and $\{a,b,c\}$.

13. **(B)** A Venn diagram helps.

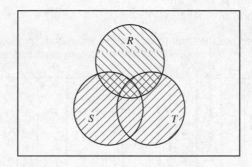

The crosshatched region is $R \cap (S \cup T)$ or $(R \cap S) \cup (R \cap T)$. See also the explanation to question 8 above. Note that $R \cap (S \cup T)$ includes regions 4, 5, 6.

14. **(D)** Note that $R \cap S = S$, and that $S \neq \emptyset$.

15. **(D)** Here are number line graphs representing sets P and Q.

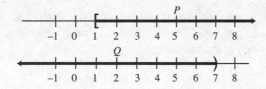

Note that the *union* of P and Q contains the entire set of integers.

LOGIC

The subtopics are truth tables; conjunctions and disjunctions; implications and negations; conditional statements; necessary and sufficient conditions; converse, inverse, and contrapositive; hypotheses and conclusions; and counterexamples.

EXAMPLES

1. The converse of the statement $p \to q$ is

   (A) $p \to \sim q$
   (B) $q \to p$
   (C) $\sim q \to \sim p$
   (D) $\sim p \to \sim q$

   Explanation: $p \to q$ denotes "if p then q"; its converse is "if q then p," i.e., $q \to p$.

   The correct answer is B.

2. Which of the following is false?

   (A) If p is false, then $p \to q$ is true.
   (B) If p and q are both false, then $p \leftrightarrow q$ is true.
   (C) If q is true, then $p \wedge q$ is true.
   (D) If p is true, then $p \vee q$ is true.

   Explanation: Here are the truth tables for the most common logical connectives:

p	$\wedge$	q
T	T	T
T	F	F
F	F	T
F	F	F

p	$\vee$	q
T	T	T
T	T	F
F	T	T
F	F	F

p	$\to$	q
T	T	T
T	F	F
F	T	T
F	T	F

p	$\leftrightarrow$	q
T	T	T
T	F	F
F	F	T
F	T	F

   Use the tables to verify (A), (B), and (D). Note that for $p \wedge q$ to be true, both p and q must be true. The correct answer is C.

3. The statement $p \to q$ may be translated as

   (A) q only if p
   (B) p is necessary for q
   (C) p is sufficient for q
   (D) p is necessary and sufficient for q

   Explanation: See the third truth table in Example 2. Note that $p \to q$ is true *except* when p is true and q is false. The statement $p \to q$ is called the *conditional* and may be translated by any of the following:

   if p then q
   p only if q
   p is sufficient for q
   q is necessary for p
   p implies q

   The correct answer is C.

   The fourth table in Example 2 is for the *biconditional* $p \leftrightarrow q$ and can be translated

   p if and only if q (p iff q)
   p is necessary and sufficient for q

   The biconditional is true when p and q have the same values and false when they have opposite values.

Follow the directions for multiple-choice questions. The correct answers and explanations follow the set of questions.

1. If p denotes "He is a professor" and q denotes "He is absent-minded," then the statement "It is not true that he is an absent-minded professor" can be written symbolically as

   (A) $p \wedge q$
   (B) $\sim(p \vee q)$
   (C) $\sim p \wedge q$
   (D) $\sim(p \wedge q)$

2. Let p be "Mary is smart" and q be "Mary is conscientious." Then $p \rightarrow q$ may be translated as

   (A) If Mary is conscientious, then she is smart.
   (B) If Mary is smart, then she is conscientious.
   (C) Mary is smart but not conscientious.
   (D) Mary is both smart and conscientious.

3. Which of the following is the negation of "If p, then not q"?

   (A) p and q
   (B) If not p then q
   (C) If q then not p.
   (D) q and not p

4. The statement $\sim p \vee q$ is false only when

   (A) p is true, q is false
   (B) p and q are both true
   (C) p is false, q is true
   (D) p and q are both false

5. Which of the following statements is *not* equivalent to "All mathematicians are clever"?

   (A) If a man is a mathematician, then he's clever.
   (B) If a man is not clever, then he's not a mathematician.
   (C) If a man is clever, then he's a mathematician.
   (D) A man is a mathematician only if he is clever.

6. The negation of the statement "If stock prices are rising, then food prices are high" is

   (A) If stocks are not rising, then food prices are not high.
   (B) If food prices are not high, then stocks are not rising.
   (C) If stocks are falling, then food prices are low.
   (D) Stocks are rising but prices are not high.

7. Let p be "A triangle is isosceles" and q be "A triangle is equilateral." Symbolically, the statement "In order for a triangle to be equilateral it must be isosceles" is

 (A) $p \leftrightarrow q$
 (B) $p \rightarrow q$
 (C) $q \leftrightarrow p$
 (D) $q \rightarrow p$

8. Which of the following is false?

 (A) $2 + 1 = 4$ if and only if $(-1)^2 = -1$.
 (B) $3 + 2 = 5$ if and only if $(-x)^2 = x^2$.
 (C) $1 + 1 = 3$ if $4 - 4 = 0$.
 (D) $x^2 = 4$ if and only if $x = 2$ or $x = -2$.

9. If a statement is true so is its

 (A) converse
 (B) contrapositive
 (C) inverse
 (D) negation

10. Consider the set of true implications: "If Carl enjoys a subject, then he studies it. If he studies a subject, then he does not fail it." Which of the following is a valid conclusion?

 (A) Since Carl failed history he did not enjoy it.
 (B) If Carl does not enjoy history, then he fails it.
 (C) If Carl does not study a subject, then he does not pass it.
 (D) Carl did not fail mathematics; therefore he enjoyed it.

11. The converse of the statement "If dentists have no cavities, then they use Screen toothpaste" is

 (A) If dentists have cavities, then they do not use Screen.
 (B) If dentists do not use Screen, then they have cavities.
 (C) If dentists use Screen, then they have no cavities.
 (D) Dentists must use Screen if they are to have no cavities.

12. To disprove the statement "$x^2 > 0$ for all real x," which value of x may be offered as a counterexample?

 (A) $x = -2$
 (B) $x = -1$
 (C) $x = 0$
 (D) $x = 1$

13. The negation of the statement "Some students have part-time jobs" is

 (A) All students have part-time jobs.
 (B) Some students do not have part-time jobs.
 (C) Only one student has a part-time job.
 (D) No student has a part-time job.

Answers and Explanations*

1. **(D)** $p \wedge q$ denotes "He is an absent-minded professor."

2. **(B)** A translation of $p \rightarrow q$ is "if p then q."

3. **(A)** "If p then not q" can be written $p \rightarrow \sim q$. This is equivalent to $\sim p \vee \sim q$. The negation is $\sim(\sim p \vee \sim q) = p \wedge q$.

4. **(A)** Look at the truth table:

p	$\sim p$	$\vee$	q
T	F	T	T
T	F	F	F
F	T	T	T
F	T	T	F

5. **(C)** A Venn diagram for the given statement shows mathematicians as a subset of clever men. Note that some clever men may not be mathematicians.

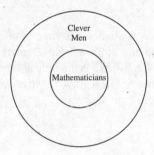

6. **(D)** The negation of "if p then q" is "p and not q."

7. **(D)** A restatement is "If a triangle is equilateral, then it is isosceles."

8. **(C)** "p if and only if q" or simply "p iff q" is called the biconditional and denoted by $p \leftrightarrow q$. It is true when p and q have the same truth values (both true or both false) and is false otherwise.

9. **(B)** A statement and its contrapositive are equivalent.

10. **(A)** Use contrapositives to work "backward." Since Carl failed history, he did not study it. Since he did not study history, he therefore did not enjoy it.

11. **(C)** The converse of "if r then s" is "if s then r."

12. **(C)** If $x \neq 0$, then $x^2 > 0$. But if $x = 0$, then $x^2 = 0$.

13. **(D)** Since "some" means "at least one," the negation of "some" is "none."

See footnote, page 303.

REAL NUMBER SYSTEM

The subtopics are prime and composite numbers; odd and even numbers; factors and divisibility; rational and irrational numbers; absolute value and order; and binary number system.

Here are introductory examples, with answers and explanations.

EXAMPLES

1. If a and b are real numbers, then $(a)[b + c] = (ab) + (a)(c)$ because

   (A) addition is commutative
   (B) multiplication is commutative
   (C) the real numbers are closed under multiplication
   (D) multiplication is distributive over addition

   Explanation: This is referred to briefly as the *distributive property*.

2. If $x^2 - x \geq 0$, then which of the following statements is true?

   (A) x must be positive.
   (B) x must be negative.
   (C) x must be greater than 1.
   (D) $x \leq 0$ or $x \geq 1$.

   Explanation: Since $x^2 - x = 0$ when $x = 0$, we can eliminate (A) and (B) immediately. Since $x^2 - x \geq 0$ for any negative x, (C) is false. Darken oval (D) immediately. Note that you need not justify choice (D), since it is the only alternative left. For completeness, we add here that (D) is true since $x^2 - x = x(x - 1)$, which equals 0 if $x = 0$ or 1, and is positive if x is negative or greater than 1.

Follow the directions for multiple-choice questions. If you can eliminate one or more choices, then guess among the remaining ones. The correct answers and explanations follow the set of questions.

Notes:

1. i represents $\sqrt{-1}$.

2. If the domain of a function f is not specified in a question, assume that it is the set of all real numbers for which $f(x)$ is defined.

3. Figures are drawn to scale and lie in a plane, *unless* otherwise specified.

1. Which of the following is *not* a prime number?

   (A) 2
   (B) 17
   (C) 27
   (D) 37

2. Which of the following statements is false?

   (A) If $ab > 0$, then a and b are both positive.
   (B) $a < 0 \rightarrow -a > 0$.
   (C) If $a > b$, then $-a < -b$.
   (D) If $0 < a < 1$, then $a^2 < a$.

3. Which of the following provide a counterexample to the false statement "If $a > b$, then $a^2 > b^2$"?

   (A) $a = 2, b = 1$
   (B) $a = 1, b = 0$
   (C) $a = -2, b = -1$
   (D) $a = 1, b = -1$

4. Which number is irrational?

   (A) $\sqrt[3]{-27}$

   (B) $\sqrt[3]{9}$

   (C) $\sqrt[4]{81}$

   (D) $\sqrt{16}$

5. The binary numeral 10110_2 corresponds to the base-ten numeral

6. Which of the following statements about the real number system is false?

   (A) The real numbers are closed under addition and multiplication.
   (B) Subtraction of reals is commutative.
   (C) Every number except 0 has a multiplicative inverse.
   (D) The square of every nonzero number is positive.

7. If none of the denominators below is zero, which of the following is true?

   (A) $\dfrac{2p + 4q}{p + 2q} = 2$

   (B) $\dfrac{2m + p}{2q} = \dfrac{m + p}{q}$

   (C) $\dfrac{q}{q + p} = \dfrac{1}{p}$

   (D) $\dfrac{3m}{3q + p} = \dfrac{m}{q + p}$

8. If $|a - 2| = a - 2$, then it is false that

   (A) $a > 0$
   (B) $a = 2$
   (C) $a > 2$
   (D) $a < 2$

9. Which of the following numbers is rational?

(A) $\sqrt{2}$

(B) $\sqrt{3}$

(C) $\sqrt{4}$

(D) $\sqrt{5}$

10. The prime factorization of 300 is

(A) $3^2 \cdot 10^2$
(B) $2 \cdot 3^2 \cdot 5^2$
(C) $2 \cdot 3 \cdot 5^2$
(D) $2^2 \cdot 3 \cdot 5^2$

11. Which of the following is meaningless?

(A) $0 \cdot 1$
(B) $\dfrac{0}{1}$
(C) 1^0
(D) $\dfrac{1}{0}$

12. Which statement is false?

(A) There is a rational number between every pair of rationals.
(B) There is an irrational between every pair of rationals.
(C) There is a rational number between every pair of irrationals.
(D) The sum of two irrational numbers is always irrational.

13. The repeating decimal 0.444 . . . equals the fraction

$$\frac{\boxed{}}{\boxed{}}$$

14. If $R = \{x : x$ is an integer$\}$ and $S = \{x : x$ is a positive real number$\}$, then $R \cap S$ equals

(A) $\{x : x$ is a positive integer$\}$ (B) the empty set   (C) R (D) S

15. $1001_2 + 11_2$ equals what number base 2?

$$\boxed{}$$

16. Given that a and b are positive integers with a odd and b even, check ($\sqrt{}$) the appropriate boxes to indicate whether each of the following numbers is even or odd.

Number	Even	Odd
$3a + b$		
$a^2 + 3b$		
$ab + 2a$		
b^a		

This number line with points q and t as shown is for questions 17 and 18.

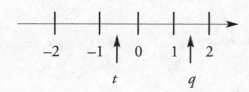

17. Which statement is false?

    (A) $q + t > 0$
    (B) $q - t > 0$
    (C) $q^2 > 1$
    (D) $t > -t$

18. Arrange these numbers in increasing order, starting with the smallest number in the top box:

$q + t$

$q - t$

$t - q$

qt

19. Which set is not empty?

    (A) $\{x : x + 2 = 2\}$
    (B) $\{x : |x| = -1\}$
    (C) $\{x : x$ is real and $x^2 + 1 = 0\}$
    (D) $\{x : x \neq x\}$

20. The set of different factors of 135 is

    (A) {3, 5}
    (B) {3, 7}
    (C) {5, 7}
    (D) {7, 9}

21. If p denotes "$x \le 1$" and q denotes "$x > -2$," then the set that satisfies $p \wedge q$ is

    (A) $-2 < x \le 1$
    (B) $1 \le x$ or $x > -2$
    (C) $x < -2$ and $x \ge 1$
    (D) $-2 \le x < 1$

22. To disprove the statement "If x is irrational, then x^2 is rational," choose x to be

    (A) $\sqrt{2}$
    (B) $\sqrt{9}$
    (C) π
    (D) 7

23. If p is divisible by 2 and q is divisible by 5, which of the following must be divisible by 10?

    (A) $pq + 15$
    (B) $5p + 2q$
    (C) $5(p + q)$
    (D) $p + q + 10$

Answers and Explanations*

1. **(27)** A prime number is an integer greater than 1 that has only itself and 1 as factors; $27 = 3 \cdot 9$.

2. **(A)** If a and b are both negative, then ab is positive. Verify the truth of (B), (C), and (D).

3. **(D)** $1 > -1$, but $(1)^2 \cdot (-1)^2$. (C) is not a counterexample because $-2 \ge -1$.

4. **(B)** Note that $\sqrt[3]{27} = -3\sqrt[4]{81} = 3$, and $\sqrt{16} = 4$.

5. **(22)** $10110_2 = 1 \cdot 2^4 + 0 \cdot 2^3 + 1 \cdot 2^2 + 1 \cdot 2^1 + 0 \cdot 2^0 = 22$.

6. **(B)** A counterexample to statement (B): $5 - 3 \ne 3 - 5$.

7. **(A)** $\dfrac{2p + 4q}{p + 2q} = \dfrac{2(p + 2q)}{p + 2q} = 2$ if $(p + 2q) \ne 0$.

8. **(D)** $|a - 2| = a - 2$ if $a - 2 \ge 0$, i.e., if $a > 2$ or $a = 2$. If $a \ge 2$, certainly $a > 0$.

9. **(C)** $\sqrt{4} = 2$.

10. **(D)** No other product given equals 300!

* See footnote, page 303.

11. **(D)** Division by 0 is impossible.

12. **(D)** $\sqrt{2} + (3 - \sqrt{2}) = 3$ is a counterexample to statement (D). (A), (B), and (C) are true.

13. $\left(\dfrac{4}{9}\right)$ Let $r = 0.444\ldots$ (where the three dots indicate an infinite number of 4's).

   Then $\qquad 10r = 4.44\ldots$

   $\qquad\qquad 9r = 4$

   and $r = \dfrac{4}{9}$. The technique shown here will work for all repeating decimals.

14. **(A)** The intersection of two sets contains those elements that are in both sets.

15. **(1100)** The addition in base 2 is as follows:

   $$\begin{array}{r} {\scriptstyle 1\ 1\ \text{(carry)}} \\ 1\ 0\ 0\ 1 \\ +\quad 1\ 1 \\ \hline 1\ 1\ 0\ 0 \end{array}$$

   where we replaced $1 + 1$ (or 2) in the units column by 10 and $1 + 1$ in the tens column by 100.

16.

Number	Even	Odd
$3a + b$		√
$a^2 + 3b$		√
$ab + 2a$	√	
b^a	√	

   Try $a = 3$ and $b = 2$

17. **(D)** Since $t < 0$, $-t > 0$.

18.

$q + t$	$t - q$
$q - t$	qt
$t - q$	$q + t$
qt	$q - t$

Note that $q + t$ is positive and less than q; $q - t$ is positive and greater than q; qt is negative but closer to 0 than $t - q$, the opposite of $q - t$.

19. **(A)** $\{x : x + 2 = 2\} = \{0\}$. None of the other sets contain any elements.

20. **(A)** Note that $135 = 3 \cdot 45 = 3 \cdot 3 \cdot 15 = 3 \cdot 3 \cdot 3 \cdot 5$ or $3^3 \cdot 5$.

21. **(A)** $(x \le 1) \wedge (x > -2)$ is true when both inequalities are satisfied. Thus, x must both exceed -2 and be less than or equal to 1.

22. **(C)** π is irrational, but so is π^2.

23. **(B)** Find p and q that satisfy the given conditions but for which the expressions in (A), (C), and (D) are not divisible by 10, for example, $p = 2$ and $q = 5$.

FUNCTIONS AND THEIR GRAPHS

The subtopics are domain and range; and linear, polynomial, and composite functions.

EXAMPLES

1. If $f(x) = x^3 - x - 1$, then $f(-1) =$

    [ ]

    Explanation: $f(-1) = (-1)^3 - (-1) - 1 = -1 + 1 - 1 = -1$.

2. If $R = \{1,2,3\}$, which of the following is a function from R into R?

    (A) $\{(1,3), (2,1)\}$
    (B) $\{(3,1), (2,3), (1,5)\}$
    (C) $\{(1,2), (2,2), (3,2)\}$
    (D) $\{(1,2), (2,3), (3,1), (3,3)\}$

    Explanation: A function from R into R may be defined as a set of ordered pairs in which each element of R must be a first element of exactly one pair, and the second element of that pair, its image, must belong to R. (A) is not a function because although $3 \varepsilon R$, it has no image; in (B), the image of 1 is 5, which is not in R; and in (D) the element 3 has *two* images. The correct answer is C.

3. Which of the following is the graph of a function $y = f(x)$?

    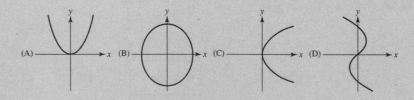

    Explanation: If $y = f(x)$ is a function, then for each x in the domain there is a *unique* y. A vertical line can cut the graph of a function at most once. The correct answer is A.

Follow the directions for multiple-choice questions. If you can eliminate one or more choices, then guess among the remaining ones. The correct answers and explanations follow the set of questions.

1. If $g(x) = x^2 - 2x + 1$, then $g(-x) =$

   (A) $x^2 - 2x + 1$
   (B) $-x^2 + 2x + 1$
   (C) $x^2 + 2x + 1$
   (D) $x^2 + 2x - 1$

2. Which of the following is the graph of $x + 2y = 2$?

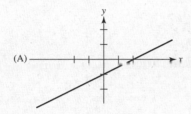
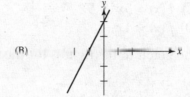
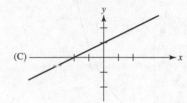
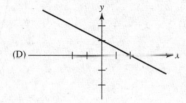

3. If $f(x) = x^2 - x + 3$, then $f(2) =$

4. If $f(x) = \dfrac{x+1}{(x-1)^3}$, then $f(0)$ equals

   (A) -1
   (B) 0
   (C) 1
   (D) none of these

5. If $f(x) = x^2 + 1$ then the domain of f is

   (A) $\{x : x > 0\}$
   (B) $\{x : -\infty < x < \infty\}$
   (C) $\{x : x \geq 0\}$
   (D) $\{x : x \geq 1\}$

6. The range of the function of question 5 is

   (A) all real numbers
   (B) all positive numbers
   (C) all numbers greater than one
   (D) all numbers y such that $y \geq 1$

7. Let $g(x) = \dfrac{x+1}{x^2 - x}$. Then the set of real numbers excluded from the domain of g is

   (A) $\{-1, 0, 1\}$
   (B) $\{0, 1\}$
   (C) $\{1\}$
   (D) $\{-1, 1\}$

8. A function $y = f(x)$ is even if $f(-x) = f(x)$. Which of the following functions is even?

   (A) $f(x) = 2x + 4$
   (B) $f(x) = x^2 + 2x$
   (C) $f(x) = 3x^2 + 5$
   (D) $f(x) = 4x$

9. The graph to the right is for the function

   (A) $2y = x^2 - 4$
   (B) $y = x^2 - 2$
   (C) $2y = x^2$
   (D) $y = x^2 - 4$

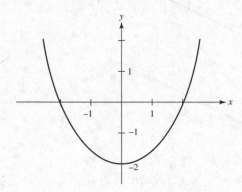

10. Which of the following points lies on the line $2x - 3y = 6$?

    (A) $(3, 2)$
    (B) $(0, 2)$
    (C) $(-3, 0)$
    (D) $(-3, -4)$

11. $f(x) = x(x - 2)$ and $g(x) = x + 1$. Then $f(g(0)) =$

12. With f and g defined as in question 11, $g(f(0)) =$

13. If $f(x) = x^2 - 2x + c$ and $f(0) = 1$, then $c =$

14. The graph of $y = x^2 - 3$ is obtained from that of $y = x^2$ by translating the latter

    (A) to the right 3 units
    (B) to the left 3 units
    (C) up three units
    (D) down 3 units

15. Which of the following is a polynomial function?

    (A) $y = 2^x$

    (B) $y = \dfrac{1}{x}$

    (C) $y = \log_2 x$

    (D) $y = \dfrac{1}{3}x^2$

16. Which of the following diagrams does *not* define a function from $\{a,b,c\}$ into $\{d,e,f\}$?

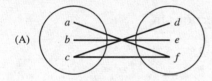

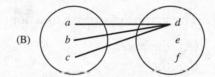

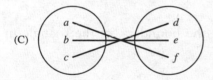

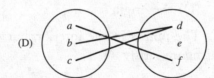

17. Let $f(x) = \begin{cases} x - 1 & \text{if } x < 2 \\ x^2 - 3 & \text{if } x \geq 2 \end{cases}$. The graph of f is

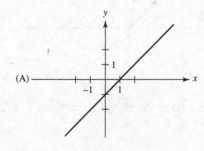

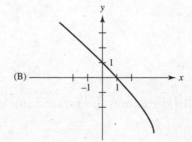

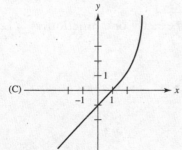

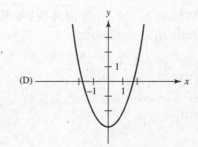

18. If $f(x) = 3x + 2$ and $g(x) = x^2 - 3$, then $f(g(x))$ equals

    (A) $9x^2 + 12x + 1$
    (B) $3x^2 - 7$
    (C) $3x^2 - 1$
    (D) $9x^2 + 6x + 1$

19. If $g(x) = 3x + k$ and $g(1) = -2$, then $g(2) =$

20. The graph below is for the set

    (A) $\{x : -2 < x < 1\}$
    (B) $\{x : x < -2, x = 1\}$
    (C) $\{x : x > 1, x \neq -2\}$
    (D) $\{x : x < -2 \text{ or } x > 1\}$

    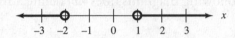

21. The graphs of inverse functions are reflections in

    (A) the x-axis
    (B) the y-axis
    (C) the line $y = x$
    (D) the origin

22. The points in the interior, but not on the boundary, of the triangle in the figure satisfy

    (A) $y < 2 - x, y > 0, x > 0$
    (B) $y > 2 - x, y > 0, x > 0$
    (C) $y \leq 2 - x, y \geq 0, x \geq 0$
    (D) $y < x - 2, y > 0, x > 0$

    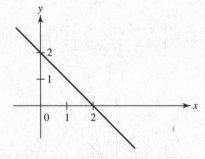

23. If $[x]$ denotes the greatest integer less than or equal to x, then $[-1.2]$ equals

24. Which of the equations below defines exactly one function $y = f(x)$ from the reals into the reals?

    (A) $y^2 = x^2 + 1$
    (B) $x^3 - y = 4$
    (C) $x - 4y^2 = 2$
    (D) $4x^2 + 9y^2 = 36$

25. Which of the following is the graph of a function $y = f(x)$?

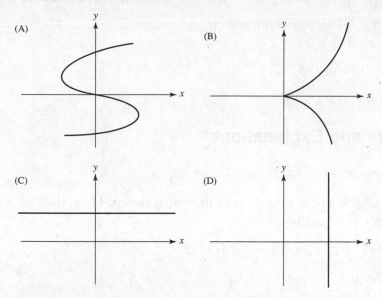

(A)

(B)

(C)

(D)

26. Which of the following descriptions of Chuck's activities may be illustrated by this graph of his distance from his office as a function of time, if he leaves his office at noon?

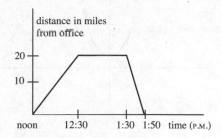

(A) Chuck drives 20 miles at 40 mph to visit his dentist, spends an hour there, then returns to his office in twenty minutes.

(B) Chuck drives at 60 mph to visit his dentist 20 miles away, spends an hour and 20 minutes there, then returns to his office in half an hour.

(C) Chuck drives 20 miles to his dentist in half an hour, spends an hour and 20 minutes there, then returns to his office in twenty minutes.

(D) At 40 mph, it takes Chuck a half hour to reach his dentist, with whom he spends an hour. Then he returns to his office in half an hour.

27. Which line is perpendicular to the line $4x + 3y = 7$?

(A) $4x + 3y = -\dfrac{1}{7}$

(B) $3x + 4y = 7$

(C) $4x - 3y = 7$

(D) $y = \dfrac{3}{4}x + 1$

28. If $f(x) = x^2 - 4$ and $g(x) = \sqrt{x}$, then the composite function $(f \circ g)(x)$ is

   (A) $x - 4$ (x is any real number)
   (B) $x - 4$ ($x \geq 0$)
   (C) $\sqrt{x^2} - 4$ ($|x| \geq 2$)
   (D) $\sqrt{x^2} - 4$ ($x \geq 2$)

Answers and Explanations*

1. **(C)** $g(-x) = (-x)^2 - 2(-x) + 1 = x^2 + 2x + 1$.

2. **(D)** Checking the intercepts of the line is fastest. Here, they are $x = 2$ and $y = 1$. Only (D) qualifies.

3. **(5)** $f(2) = 2^2 - 2 + 3 = 4 - 2 + 3 = 5$.

4. **(A)** $f(0) = \dfrac{0 + 1}{(0 - 1)^3} = \dfrac{1}{-1} = -1$.

5. **(B)** A sketch of the graph may help for questions 5 and 6.

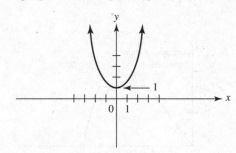

6. **(D)** See graph for Question 5.

7. **(B)** Set the denominator of g equal to zero. Note that $x^2 - x = x(x - 1) = 0$ when $x = 0$ or $x = 1$.

8. **(C)** Note that (A), (B), and (D) are not even.

9. **(A)** Check intercepts first. From the graph we see that $x = \pm 2$ and $y = -2$. Only $2y = x^2 - 4$ has these intercepts.

10. **(D)** The left side of the given equation must equal 6 when x and y are replaced by their coordinates.

11. **(−1)** $g(0) = 0 + 1 = 1$, $f(g(0)) = f(1) = 1(1 - 2) = 1 \cdot -1 = -1$.

12. **(1)** $f(0) = 0(0 - 2) = 0 \cdot -2 = 0$, and $g(f(0)) = 0 + 1 = 1$.

13. **(1)** $f(0) = 0^2 - 2(0) + c = 1 \rightarrow c = 1$.

14. **(D)** For a given x, each y-value of $y = x^2 - 3$ is 3 *less* than that of $y = x^2$.

15. **(D)** A polynomial in x is an expression of the form

$$a_0 x^n + a_1 x^{n-1} + a_2 x^{n-2} + \cdots + a_{n-1} x + a_n$$

where the a's are real numbers and n is a positive integer. The variable x never appears in the denominator and the exponents of x are always positive integers.

16. **(A)** Note in (A) that the element c has two images, d and f. Why do diagrams (B), (C), and (D) define functions?

17. **(C)** The graph consists of part of a straight line ($y = x - 1$ if $x < 2$) and part of a parabola ($y = x^2 - 3$ if $x \geq 2$). Checking intercepts helps.

18. **(B)** $f(g(x)) = 3(x^2 - 3) + 2 = 3x^2 - 9 + 2 = 3x^2 - 7$.

19. **(1)** Since $g(1) = 3(1) + k = -2$, $k = -5$. So $g(2) = 3(2) + (-5) = 1$.

20. **(D)** The x-axis has been darkened to the left of $x = -2$ and to the right of $x = 1$. The hollow circles tell us to exclude these two points.

21. **(C)** If point (a,b) is on the graph of $y = f(x)$, then (b,a) lies on the graph of its inverse.

22. **(A)** Since the line goes through the points $(0,2)$ and $(2,0)$, it has slope -1. Its equation is $y = 2 - x$. The coordinates (x,y) of each point in the interior of the triangle satisfy the inequalities $x > 0$, $y > 0$, and $y < 2 - x$.

23. **(−2)** The greatest integer less than or equal to -1.2 is -2. Verify this with a number line if necessary.

24. **(B)** When the exponent of y is 2, there may be 2 values of y for an x in the domain.

25. **(C)** The graphs in (A), (B), and (D) do not pass the vertical-line test.

26. **(A)** At 40 mph it takes Chuck half an hour to drive the 20 miles to the dentist; he arrives at 12:30. His distance from his office remains constant until 1:30, hence he is at the dentist's for one hour. At 60 mph he drives the 20 miles back to his office in 20 minutes, arriving at 1:50.

27. **(D)** Slopes of perpendicular lines are negative reciprocals of each other. The given line has slope $-\frac{4}{3}$; the line in (D) has slope $\frac{3}{4}$.

28. **(B)** $(f \circ g)(x) = f(g(x)) = f(\sqrt{x}) = (\sqrt{x})^2 - 4 = x - 4$. The domain of $(f \circ g)(x)$ is the set of all x in the domain of g for which $g(x)$ is in the domain of f. Here the domain of g is $\{x \mid x \geq 0\}$, eliminating choice (A).

PROBABILITY AND STATISTICS

The subtopics are counting problems, including permutations and combinations; computation of probabilities of simple and compound events; simple conditional probability; and the mean and median.

In any question on probability in this book, you may assume that a die or coin is fair; that is, that the outcomes (a particular face showing on the die, or head versus tail on the coin) are equally probable.

EXAMPLES

1. How many ways can an 8-member council elect a chairman, a vice chairman, and a secretary if no member may hold more than one office?

   (A) $\dfrac{8!}{3!}$

   (B) $\dfrac{8!}{5!}$

   (C) $\dfrac{8!}{3!\,5!}$

   (D) 8^3

   Explanation: The chairman can be elected in 8 ways, after which the vice chairman can be elected in 7 different ways; following this, the secretary can be chosen from among 6 different people. There are then $8 \cdot 7 \cdot 6$ different ways the officers can be elected. For this question the *order* matters. An ordered arrangement of n objects taken r at a time is called a *permutation,* and is denoted by $_nP_r$ or by $P(n,r)$. Note that

   $$_nP_r = \frac{n!}{(n-r)!}$$

   If common factors are eliminated from numerator and denominator, a product of exactly r factors remains. Thus

   $$\frac{8!}{5!} = \frac{8 \cdot 7 \cdot 6 \cdot 5 \cdot 4 \cdot 3 \cdot 2 \cdot 1}{5 \cdot 4 \cdot 3 \cdot 2 \cdot 1} = 8 \cdot 7 \cdot 6$$

2. How many different 3-member committees can be selected from a group of 5 people?

   (A) 60
   (B) 20
   (C) 10
   (D) 5

   Explanation: This question calls for a *combination* of 5 objects taken 3 at a time; i.e., a selection where order does *not* count. A combination of n objects taken r at a time is just the number of different r-element subsets that an n-element set has. We'll use the notation $_nC_r$; others used are $C(n,r)$, $C_{n,r}$, and $\binom{n}{r}$. Since there are $r!$ permutations of each r-element set, we find $_nC_r$ by dividing $_nP_r$ by $r!$. Here the answer is $_5C_3$ or

   $$\frac{5!}{2!\,3!} = \frac{5 \cdot 4 \cdot 3 \cdot 2 \cdot 1}{2 \cdot 1 \cdot 3 \cdot 2 \cdot 1} = 10$$

   For computation, it's easiest to remember $_5C_3$ as

   $$\frac{5 \cdot 4 \cdot 3}{1 \cdot 2 \cdot 3}$$

   where you have the same number of factors in the numerator as in the denominator. Also, $_nC_r = {}_nC_{n-r}$. In terms of committees, for example, each committee of r members determines a "left-over" committee of $(n-r)$ members. So there are the same number of each. So for example, to compute $_9C_7$ we use instead $_9C_2$. Recalling that $_9P_2 = 9 \cdot 8$, we have

   $$_9C_2 \frac{9 \cdot 8}{1 \cdot 2}$$

EXAMPLES (cont.)

3. A box contains 4 black and 3 white chips. Two chips are selected at random. The probability that one is black and one is white is

(A) $\frac{2}{7}$

(B) $\frac{3}{7}$

(C) $\frac{4}{7}$

(D) $\frac{7}{12}$

Explanation: The probability of an event is the ratio

$$\frac{\text{number of ways the event can occur}}{\text{total number of possible outcomes}}$$

There are $4 \cdot 3$ or 12 ways of selecting 1 black chip and 1 white chip. There are $_7C_2$ or $(7 \cdot 6) / (1 \cdot 2)$ ways of choosing 2 chips from 7. The answer is $\frac{12}{21}$ or $\frac{4}{7}$. The correct answer is C.

Follow the directions for multiple-choice questions. If you can, eliminate one or more choices, then guess among the remaining ones. The correct answers and explanations follow the set of questions.

1. The number of different license plates that start with one letter followed by three different digits selected from the set {0,1,2,3,4,6,6,7,8,9} is

(A) $26 \cdot 10 \cdot 10 \cdot 10$
(B) $26 \cdot 9 \cdot 9 \cdot 9$
(C) $26 \cdot 10 \cdot 9 \cdot 8$
(D) $16 \cdot 9 \cdot 8 \cdot 7$

2. The number of different license plates beginning with two different letters followed by two digits either of which may be any digit other than zero is

(A) $26^2 \cdot 8^2$
(B) $26 \cdot 25 \cdot 9 \cdot 9$
(C) $26^2 \cdot 9 \cdot 8$
(D) $26^2 \cdot 9^2$

3. A box contains 6 green pens and 5 red pens. The number of ways of drawing 4 pens if they must all be green is

4. How many committees consisting of 3 girls and 2 boys may be selected from a club of 5 girls and 4 boys?

   (A) 6
   (B) 20
   (C) 60
   (D) 72

5. In how many ways can 2 or more bonus books be selected from a set of 5 offered by a book club?

   ☐

6. The number of different ways a student can answer a 10-question true-false test is

   (A) 2
   (B) 20
   (C) 10^2
   (D) 2^{10}

7. The probability of obtaining a 5 when an ordinary die is rolled is the fraction

   $$\frac{}{}$$

8. If a penny is tossed 3 times, then the number of different possible outcomes is

   ☐

9. If a penny and a die are tossed, then the probability that the penny shows heads and the die an even number is the fraction

   $$\frac{}{}$$

10. The probability that at least 1 head shows in a toss of 3 coins is

    (A) $\dfrac{1}{8}$

    (B) $\dfrac{3}{8}$

    (C) $\dfrac{1}{2}$

    (D) $\dfrac{7}{8}$

11. A college that administered two tests to 100 freshmen got the following results: 14 failed both exams; 28 failed the mathematics exam; 33 failed the English exam. The number of students who passed both exams is

    (A) 53
    (B) 67
    (C) 72
    (D) 86

12. Given the data in question 11, what is the probability that a freshman failed both exams if he failed the math exam?

    (A) $\dfrac{19}{47}$

    (B) $\dfrac{14}{33}$

    (C) $\dfrac{1}{2}$

    (D) $\dfrac{28}{33}$

13. According to polls, candidates X, Y, and Z have a 0.5, 0.3, and 0.2 chance respectively of winning an election. If candidate Z withdraws, then Y's chance of winning is

    (A) 0.375
    (B) 0.4
    (C) 0.475
    (D) 0.5

14. Slips numbered 1 to 6 are placed in a bag. If two slips are drawn from the bag without replacement, then the probability that the sum will equal 7 is

    (A) $\dfrac{2}{5}$

    (B) $\dfrac{1}{3}$

    (C) $\dfrac{1}{5}$

    (D) $\dfrac{1}{15}$

15. A bag contains 2 red, 3 white, and 4 green balls. If 2 balls are drawn at random, what is the probability that at least 1 is green?

(A) $\dfrac{5}{18}$

(B) $\dfrac{13}{18}$

(C) $\dfrac{4}{9}$

(D) $\dfrac{59}{72}$

16. Based on a sample of 500,000 people, the American Cancer Society estimated that 750 people would die of cancer in 1973. The probability of death from cancer in 1973 for this sample was

(A) 0.17
(B) 0.015
(C) 0.0017
(D) 0.0015

17. If 2 cards are drawn from an ordinary deck of cards, the probability that they will both be clubs is

(A) $\dfrac{1}{8}$

(B) $\dfrac{1}{17}$

(C) $\dfrac{1}{16}$

(D) $\dfrac{1}{15}$

18. The number of distinguishable permutations of letters in the word CANAL is

(A) 31
(B) 4!
(C) 60
(D) 5!

19. The eye color of students in a class is given by the chart. The probability that a person selected at random is a male or has blue eyes is

	MALES	FEMALES
BROWN EYES	6	4
BLUE EYES	3	7

(A) $\dfrac{3}{20}$

(B) $\dfrac{3}{10}$

(C) $\dfrac{1}{3}$

(D) $\dfrac{4}{5}$

20. One bag contains 5 black and 3 green marbles. A second bag has 4 black and 2 green marbles. If one marble is chosen from each bag at random, the probability that they are both green is

(A) $\dfrac{1}{8}$

(B) $\dfrac{1}{4}$

(C) $\dfrac{1}{3}$

(D) $\dfrac{5}{14}$

21. If a pair of dice is cast, then the probability that the sum is greater than 9 is

(A) $\dfrac{1}{18}$

(B) $\dfrac{1}{12}$

(C) $\dfrac{1}{9}$

(D) $\dfrac{1}{6}$

22. Assume that the probability that it will rain on a day to be selected at random for a picnic is 10%. The probability that a Tuesday will be chosen and that that Tuesday will be dry is

(A) $\dfrac{10}{9}$

(B) $\dfrac{9}{10}$

(C) $\dfrac{9}{70}$

(D) $\dfrac{1}{70}$

Questions 23 and 24 are based on the following information:

A college registrar reports the following statistics on 360 students:

200 take politics   70 take politics and biology

150 take biology   50 take biology and mathematics

75 take mathematics   10 take politics and mathematics

5 take all 3 subjects

23. How many students in the report do not take politics, biology, or mathematics?

(A) 0

(B) 30

(C) 60

(D) 100

24. If a student in the report is chosen at random, what is the probability that he studies mathematics but neither politics nor biology?

(A) $\dfrac{1}{24}$

(B) $\dfrac{1}{18}$

(C) $\dfrac{1}{6}$

(D) $\dfrac{5}{24}$

25. If the average of the set of numbers {3, 5, 6, 11, x} is 7, then the median is

(A) 5

(B) $5\dfrac{1}{2}$

(C) 6

(D) 7

Answers and Explanations*

1. **(C)** We can show how to fill the 4 "slots" in the license plate schematically by

$$26 \ \times \ 10 \ \times \ 9 \ \times \ 8$$

□   □   □   □

where the number above a position indicates how many ways it may be filled. Note that a digit may *not* be repeated.

* See footnote, page 303.

2. **(B)** Here we have

$$26 \ \times \ 25 \ \times \ 9 \ \times \ 9$$
$$\square \qquad \square \qquad \square \qquad \square$$

The letter may not be repeated, but any of the 9 nonzero digits may be.

3. **(15)** $_6C_4$ or its equal, $_6C_2$, which is $(6 \cdot 5) / (1 \cdot 2)$.

4. **(C)** $_5C_3 \times {}_4C_2$, or $\dfrac{5 \cdot 4}{1 \cdot 2} \times \dfrac{4 \cdot 3}{1 \cdot 2}$, since $_5C_3 = {}_5C_2$.

5. **(26)** $_5C_2 + {}_5C_3 + {}_5C_4 + {}_5C_5 = 26$.

6. **(D)** The first may be answered in 2 ways, after which the second may be answered in 2 ways, after which the third and so on. This yields $2 \times 2 \times 2 \times \cdots \times 2$, where there are 10 twos, or 2^{10}. Note for just 3 T-F questions that there are 8 different ways of answering them. List them.

7. $\left(\dfrac{1}{6}\right)$ There are 6 possible outcomes, of which obtaining 5 is 1 outcome.

8. **(8)** A tree diagram may be useful:

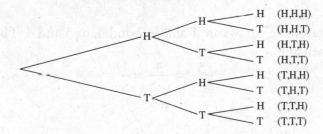

There are 8 possible outcomes. Note that the answer is obtainable immediately from

$$2 \ \times \ 2 \ \times \ 2$$
$$\square \qquad \square \qquad \square$$

where there are 2 outcomes on the first toss; for each of these there are 2 on the second; and for each of the first four there are 2 outcomes on the third.

9. $\left(\dfrac{1}{4}\right)$ The probability that the penny shows heads is $\dfrac{1}{2}$ and that the die shows an even number $\dfrac{1}{2}$. The answer is the product since the events are independent.

10. **(D)** The tree in the answer to question 8 shows that at least one H occurs in 7 of 8 possible outcomes. Or note that the probability of getting all (3) tails is $\dfrac{1}{2} \times \dfrac{1}{2} \times \dfrac{1}{2}$, or $\dfrac{1}{8}$; so the answer is $1 - \dfrac{1}{8}$.

11. **(A)** Draw a Venn diagram. Since 14 + 14 + 19, or 47, students failed one or both exams, it follows that 100 – 47 passed both.

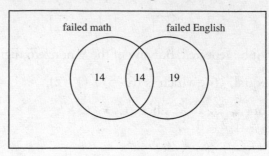

12. **(C)** $P(\text{failed both if failed math}) = \dfrac{P(\text{failed both})}{P(\text{failed math})} = \dfrac{^{14}\!/_{100}}{^{28}\!/_{100}} = \dfrac{1}{2}$

13. **(A)** Assuming that the chances for X and Y are increased proportionately when Z withdraws, Y's chance becomes

$$\frac{0.3}{05.+0.3}$$

14. **(C)** The "favorable" draws are 1 and 6, 2 and 5, or 3 and 4. The desired probability is therefore

$$\frac{3}{_6C_2} = \frac{3}{\dfrac{6\cdot5}{1\cdot2}} = \frac{1}{5}$$

15. **(B)** The probability that no ball drawn is green is

$$\frac{_6C_2}{_9C_2} = \frac{5\cdot4}{9\cdot8} = \frac{5}{19}$$

Therefore, the probability that at least 1 green ball is drawn equals $1-\dfrac{5}{18}$, or $\dfrac{13}{18}$.

16. **(D)** $\dfrac{750}{500,000} = 0.0015.$

17. **(B)** $\dfrac{_{13}C_2}{_{52}C_2} = \dfrac{13\cdot12}{1\cdot2} \div \dfrac{52\cdot51}{1\cdot2} = \dfrac{13\cdot12}{52\cdot51} = \dfrac{1}{17}.$

18. **(C)** If the two A's were distinguishable (perhaps subscripted), there would be 5! permutations. We divide by 2 to eliminate identical pairs of permutations.

19. **(D)** If M is the set of males and B is the set of blue-eyed people, then we want

$$\frac{P(M \cup B)}{\text{number in the class}} = \frac{6+3+7}{20} = \frac{4}{5}.$$

20. **(A)** $\dfrac{_3C_1}{8} \times \dfrac{_2C_1}{6} \times \dfrac{3}{8} \times \dfrac{1}{3} = \dfrac{1}{8}.$

21. **(D)** There are 6×6 or 36 possible outcomes when the pair of dice is cast. A sum that exceeds 9 can be obtained in the following 6 ways:

DIE I	DIE II
4	6
5	6
5	5
6	6
6	5
6	4

Therefore the probability of the event is $\dfrac{6}{36}$.

22. **(C)** The 2 events, day of the week selected and whether it rains, are independent. The desired product is $\dfrac{1}{7} \times \dfrac{9}{10}$.

23. **(C)** A Venn diagram helps.

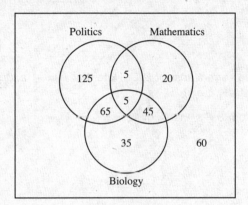

24. **(B)** Since 20 students out of 360 take mathematics but neither politics nor biology, the answer is $\dfrac{20}{360}$ or $\dfrac{1}{18}$.

25. **(C)** $(3 + 5 + 6 + 11 + x) \div 5 = 7 \rightarrow (25 + x) \div 5 = 7 \rightarrow x = 10$. The median of the set $\{3, 5, 6, 10, 11\}$ is the middle number, 6.

ADDITIONAL ALGEBRA TOPICS

The subtopics are complex numbers; logarithms and exponentials; algebra; and applications.

Here are some introductory examples.

EXAMPLES

1. If for all elements p, q, r in a mathematical system

   $p + (q + r) = (p + q) + r$, then the system satisfies

   (A) the commutative law for addition
   (B) the commutative law for multiplication
   (C) a distributive law
   (D) an associative law

   Explanation: The correct answer is D.

2. If $i = \sqrt{-1}$, then $i^7 =$

   (A) 1
   (B) −1
   (C) i
   (D) $-i$

   Explanation: The correct answer is D. Note that $i^2 = -1$ and $i^4 = (-1)(-1) = 1$; thus $i^7 = i^4 \cdot i^2 \cdot i = (1)(-1)(i) = -i$.

3. If $\log_b 2 = r$ and $\log_b 3 = s$, then $\log_b 18 =$

   (A) $r + 2s$
   (B) $2r + s$
   (C) $2rs$
   (D) $r^2 s$

   Explanation: Since $18 = 2 \cdot 3^2$, $\log_b 18 = \log_b 2 + \log_b 3^2 = \log_b 2 + 2 \log_b 3 = r + 2s$.

   The correct answer is A.

Follow the directions for multiple-choice questions. If you can eliminate one or more choices, then guess among the remaining ones. The correct answers and explanations follow the set of questions.

1. The roots of the equation $x^2 + 2 = 0$ are

   (A) $\pm\sqrt{2}$

   (B) $+2i$ (where $i = \sqrt{-1}$)

   (C) $\pm i\sqrt{2}$

   (D) $\pm\sqrt{2}i$

2. If $\log_a 2 = p$ and $\log_a 3 = s$, then $\log_a \dfrac{9}{2} =$

   (A) $\dfrac{2s}{p}$

   (B) $2s - p$

   (C) $\dfrac{s^2}{p}$

   (D) $2s + \dfrac{1}{p}$

3. $(a^x)^y$ (where x and y are integers) equals

   (A) a^{x+y}
   (B) $a^x \cdot a^y$
   (C) a^{xy}
   (D) ya^x

4. $(2 + i)(3 - i)$, where $i = \sqrt{-1}$ equals

   (A) 7
   (B) 5
   (C) $5 + i$
   (D) $7 + i$

5. If the roots of $x^2 + 2x + d = 0$ are real, then d *cannot* equal

   (A) 2
   (B) 1
   (C) 0
   (D) -1

6. If $p * q = p + pq - 1$ then $a * -1$ equals

   (A) $a + 1$
   (B) $-a + 1$
   (C) $-a - 1$
   (D) -1

7. If $f(x) = ax^3 + bx^2 + cx + d$ and $f(-1) = 0$, then f must be divisible by

   (A) x
   (B) $x - 1$
   (C) $x + 1$
   (D) $x^2 - 1$

8. $\dfrac{2^p}{2^{p+q}} =$

   (A) 2^q
   (B) 2^{2p-q}
   (C) 2^{-q}
   (D) $\dfrac{1}{q}$

9. If $\log_3 p = m$ and $\log_3 q = 2m$, then $\log_3 pq =$

   (A) $2m$
   (B) $3m$
   (C) $6m$
   (D) $3m^2$

10. Which set is not closed under ordinary multiplication?

    (A) $\{0, 1\}$
    (B) $\{-1, 1\}$
    (C) $\{1, 2\}$
    (D) $\{-1, 0, 1\}$

11. If $3^{x+1} = 3$, then $x =$

12. Which of the following is the graph of $y = \log_2 x$?

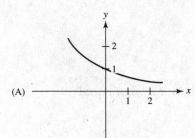

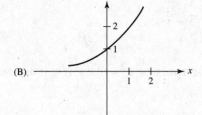

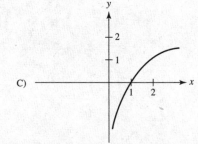

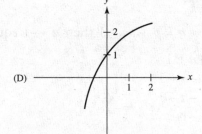

13. Let $f(x) = x^3 - 2x^2 - x + d$. If $f(1) = 0$, then the roots of $f(x) = 0$ are

    (A) 1, 2, and –2
    (B) 1, –1, and –2
    (C) –1, 2, and –2
    (D) 1, –1, and 2

14. $\sqrt{3} \cdot \sqrt{-27} =$

    (A) –9
    (B) $-9i$ (where $i = \sqrt{-1}$)
    (C) $9i$
    (D) 9

15. Which equation does *not* have real roots?

    (A) $x^2 + 1 = 0$
    (B) $x^2 - 2 = 0$
    (C) $x^2 + x - 1 = 0$
    (D) $x^2 + 4x = 0$

16. The set of prime factors of 1260 is

    (A) $\{3,4,5\}$
    (B) $\{2,5,7,9\}$
    (C) $\{2,3,5,7\}$
    (D) $\{4,5,7,9\}$

17. The roots of the equations $x^2 + 4x + 1 = 0$ are

    (A) real and equal
    (B) real and unequal
    (C) imaginary
    (D) complex

18. The complete factorization of $x^4 - 3x^2 - 4$ is

    (A) $(x^2 + 1)(x^2 - 4)$
    (B) $(x^2 + 1)(x^2 + 4)$
    (C) $(x + 1)(x - 1)(x + 2)(x - 2)$
    (D) $(x + 2)(x - 2)(x^2 + 1)$

19. If $f(x) = \log_2 x$ and $g(x) = 2^x$, then it is false that

    (A) $f(g(x)) = x$
    (B) $g(f(x)) = x$
    (C) $f(g(x)) = 1$
    (D) the graphs of f and g are symmetric to the line $y = x$

20. The slope of the line is $\dfrac{x}{2} - \dfrac{y}{5} - 2 =$ is

    (A) $\dfrac{5}{2}$

    (B) $\dfrac{2}{5}$

    (C) $-\dfrac{2}{5}$

    (D) $-\dfrac{5}{2}$

21. The *y*-intercept of the line in question 20 is

22. The roots of $x^2 + 2x + q = 0$ are not real if q exceeds

23. Suppose $2^a = 5$ and $4^b = 3$. Then 2^{a-2b} equals

(A) $\dfrac{5}{9}$

(B) $\dfrac{5}{3}$

(C) 2

(D) 15

24. When $x^3 - 3x^2 - 4x + 1$ is divided by $x + 2$, the remainder is

25. $2 \log m - 3 \log n$ is equal to

(A) $\dfrac{\log m^2}{\log n^3}$

(B) $\dfrac{2}{3} \log \dfrac{m}{n}$

(C) $\log \dfrac{m^2}{n^3}$

(D) $\log \left(\dfrac{m}{n} \right)^{\frac{2}{3}}$

26. If the lengths of all the sides of a cube are doubled, then the volume of the cube is multiplied by

(A) 2
(B) 3
(C) 6
(D) 8

27. A college graduate is offered a part-time job at a salary of \$20,000. He is promised a 5% raise every year. His salary in his third year can be expressed as

(A) \$20,000(.05)
(B) \$20,000(1.05)
(C) \$20,000(1.05)^2
(D) \$20,000(1.05)^3

28. $2^{\log_2 1} + 2^{\log_2 2} + 2^{\log_2 4} =$

    (A) 3
    (B) 5
    (C) 7
    (D) 14

29. If $\ln u = 4$ and $\ln v = 2$, then $\ln\left(\dfrac{u}{v^2}\right) =$

    (A) 0

    (B) 1

    (C) 2

    (D) 3

30. A rectangular garden has an area of 168 square feet. If its length exceeds its width by 2 feet, what is the perimeter of the garden?

    (A) 54 ft

    (B) 52 ft

    (C) 50 ft

    (D) 48 ft

Answers and Explanations*

1. **(C)** $x^2 = -2 \rightarrow x = \pm\sqrt{-2} = \pm\sqrt{2i}$ or $\pm i\sqrt{2}$.

2. **(B)** $\log_a \dfrac{9}{2} = \log_a 9 - \log_a 2 = \log_a 3^2 - \log_a 2 = 2\log_a 3 - \log_a 2 = 2s - p$.

3. **(C)** Note that, if x and y are integers, $(a^x)^y$ indicates a product of y factors, each equal to a^x:

$$(a^x)^y = a^x \cdot a^x \cdots a^x = a^{(x + x + \cdots + x)} = a^{xy}$$

4. **(D)** $(2 + i)(3 - i) = (2)(3) + (2)(-i) + (i)(3) + (i)(-i)$

$$= 6 + i - i^2 = 6 + i - (-1) = 7 + i.$$

5. **(A)** If the roots of $ax^2 + bx + c = 0$ are real, then $b^2 - 4ac \geq 0$. Here $a = 1$, $b = 2$, $c = d$, so $b^2 - 4ac = 4 - 4d$, which is greater than or equal to zero if $d \leq 1$.

6. **(D)** With $p = a$, $q = -1$, we get $a * -1 = a + a(-1) - 1 = -1$.

7. **(C)** If $f(x)$ is polynomial and $f(r) = 0$, then $f(x)$ is divisible by $(x - r)$. The converse is also true. These follow from the so-called *factor* and *remainder theorems* of algebra.

8. **(C)** $\dfrac{2^p}{2^{p+q}} = 2^{p-(p+q)} = 2^{p-p-q} = 2^{-q}$.

9. **(B)** $\log_3 pq = \log_3 p + \log_3 q = m + 2m = 3m$.

* See footnote, page 303.

10. **(C)** Note for the set $\{1, 2\}$ that $2 \cdot 2 = 4$, which is not in the set. Verify that the other sets are all closed under ordinary multiplication.

11. **(0)** $(3^{x+1} = 3 = 3^1) \rightarrow (x + 1 = 1) \rightarrow x = 0$.

12. **(C)** Some of the properties of the graph of $y = \log_2 x$ are $\log_2 1 = 0$, the domain is $\{x : x > 0\}$. Only the graph in (C) satisfies these.

13. **(D)** $f(1) = 1^3 - 2(1)^2 - 1 + d = d - 2$.
    Since $f(1) = 0$, $d = 2$ and $f(x) = x^3 - 2x^2 - x + 2$.
    Since $f(1) = 0$, $x - 1$ is a factor of $f(x)$.
    Indeed: $x^3 - 2x^2 - x + 2 = (x - 1)(x + 1)(x - 2)$.

14. **(C)** $\sqrt{3} \cdot \sqrt{-27} = \sqrt{3} \cdot \sqrt{27} \cdot \sqrt{-1} = \sqrt{81} \cdot i = 9i$.

15. **(A)** The roots in (A) are $\pm i$; verify that the roots of the others are all real. Remember, the roots of $ax^2 + bx + c = 0$ are

$$x = \frac{-b \pm \sqrt{b^2 - 4ac}}{2a};$$

the roots are real only if $b^2 - 4ac \geq 0$.

16. **(C)** $1260 = 4 \cdot 5 \cdot 7 \cdot 9 = 2^2 \cdot 3^2 \cdot 5 \cdot 7$.

17. **(B)** Since the discriminant equals $4^2 - 4(1)(1)$, which is positive, the roots are real and unequal. You do not need to find the roots.

18. **(D)** $x^4 - 3x^2 - 4 = (x^2 - 4)(x^2 + 1) = (x + 2)(x - 2)(x^2 + 1)$.

19. **(C)** Note that $f(g(x)) = \log_2 2^x = x \log_2 2 = x = g(f(x)) = 2^{\log_2 x}$. In the answer choices for question 12 on page 336, (B) shows the graph of $y = 2^x$ and (C) shows the graph of $y = \log_2 x$. They are symmetric to the line $y = x$.

20. **(A)** Rewriting the equation yields $5x - 2y - 20 = 0$ or $-2y = -5x + 20$. So $y = \frac{5}{2}x - 10$, which is in the form $y = mx + b$ with m the slope.

21. **(–10)** From answer 20 above, we see immediately that when $x = 0$, $y = -10$.

22. **(1)** The discriminant, which is $4 - 4q$, must be nonnegative for the roots to be real. So $4 - 4q \geq 0$ implies $1 \geq q$ or $q \leq 1$. Therefore, q cannot exceed 1.

23. **(B)** $2^{a-2b} = 2^a \cdot 2^{-2b} = 2^a \div 2^{2b} = 2^a \div 4^b = \frac{5}{3}$.

24. **(–11)** The fastest and simplest way to do this question is to know that if $f(x)$ is divided by $x - a$ then the remainder is $f(a)$. Here, therefore, the remainder is $f(-2)$, which equals $(-2)^3 - 3(-2)^2 - 4(-2) + 1$ or -11.

25. **(C)** We use two laws of logarithms here: $p \log q = \log q^p$ and $\log \frac{p}{q} = \log p - \log q$. So $2 \log m - 3 \log n = \log m^2 - \log n^3 = \log \frac{m^2}{n^3}$.

26. **(D)** Let the length originally be x; then the volume is x^3. After doubling the side the new volume is $(2x)^3 = 8x^3$, 8 times the original volume.

27. **(B)** The grad's salary (in dollars) each year is as follows:

    1st year: $20,000

    2nd year: $20,000 + (.05)(20000) = $20,000(1.05)

    3rd year: (2nd year amount)(1.05) = $20,000(1.05)(1.05) = $20,000(1.05)^2$

28. **(C)** Logarithms are exponents. $\text{Log}_a p$ is the number you must raise a to in order to get p. Hence $a^{\log_a p} = p$. Thus $2^{\log_2 1} + 2^{\log_2 2} + 2^{\log_2 4} = 1 + 2 + 4 = 7$

29. **(A)** $\ln\left(\dfrac{u}{v^2}\right) = \ln u - \ln v^2 = \ln u - 2\ln v = 4 - 2(2) = 0.$

30. **(B)** If l represents the length, then the width is $(l - 2)$, and the area is $l(l - 2)$. Solve the equation $l^2 - 2l = 168$; note that $l^2 - 2l - 168 = (l - 14)(l + 12)$, which equals 0 if $l = 14$. Hence the perimeter is $2(14) + 2(14 - 2) = 52$ feet.

Sample Examinations

This chapter has two sample CLEP College Mathematics Examinations. Each is followed by an answer key, a scoring chart, and answer explanations. The examination consists of 60 questions for which 90 minutes are allowed. Most questions are of the multiple-choice type; for others you may be asked to enter a checkmark ($\sqrt{}$) or a numerical answer in a box, click on a diagram, or arrange a list in order.

It is very important that you not spend too much time on any one question. It is probably best to answer first those questions that you are pretty sure about, returning after you've gone through the entire section to those questions that need more thought or work. Keep track of the time so you can pace yourself, remembering that it is not expected that anyone taking the test will answer every question.

For a reminder about the major topics that are covered in each part and the approximate number of questions for each topic, see page 287.

It will be helpful at this point to reread the tips on pages 298–299. Here, again, are some reminders and additional tips:

1. Read the test directions carefully and study any illustrative examples.
2. Pay attention to any notes about figures, which are intended to provide information useful in answering the questions and are drawn as accurately as possible except when specifically noted otherwise.
3. Answer the easy questions first; you will have a chance to go back to the others.
4. Remember the College Board's "rights-only" policy on grading. Your score will be based *only* on the number of questions you answer correctly.
5. There is no penalty for incorrect or omitted answers.
6. When practicing, it is sometimes worthwhile to verify that choices not selected are truly incorrect. However, when taking the actual examination it would be needlessly time-consuming (and therefore foolish) to do that. When you decide on the answer to a particular question, type it in and move on immediately to the next question.
7. Work steadily, trying not to be careless.
8. Pace yourself but try to take a breather from time to time.
9. Keep cool. Remember that practically no one answers every question.

College Mathematics

ANSWER SHEET—SAMPLE EXAMINATION 1

1 ☐

2 Ⓐ Ⓑ Ⓒ Ⓓ

3 ☐

4 Ⓐ Ⓑ Ⓒ Ⓓ E

5

6 ☐

7 ☐

8 Ⓐ Ⓑ Ⓒ Ⓓ

9 Ⓐ Ⓑ Ⓒ Ⓓ

10

Number(s)	Rational	Irrational	Imaginary
$\sqrt[3]{-125}$			
$\dfrac{5}{\sqrt{9}}$			
$\sqrt{18}$			
$\sqrt{3^2 - 4^2}$			

11 Ⓐ Ⓑ Ⓒ Ⓓ

12 Ⓐ Ⓑ Ⓒ Ⓓ

13 Ⓐ Ⓑ Ⓒ Ⓓ

14 Ⓐ Ⓑ Ⓒ Ⓓ

15 Ⓐ Ⓑ Ⓒ Ⓓ

16 Ⓐ Ⓑ Ⓒ Ⓓ

17 Ⓐ Ⓑ Ⓒ Ⓓ

18 Ⓐ Ⓑ Ⓒ Ⓓ

19 Ⓐ Ⓑ Ⓒ Ⓓ

20 Ⓐ Ⓑ Ⓒ Ⓓ

21 Ⓐ Ⓑ Ⓒ Ⓓ

22 Ⓐ Ⓑ Ⓒ Ⓓ

23 Ⓐ Ⓑ Ⓒ Ⓓ

24 Ⓐ Ⓑ Ⓒ Ⓓ

25 Ⓐ Ⓑ Ⓒ Ⓓ

26 Ⓐ Ⓑ Ⓒ Ⓓ

27 Ⓐ Ⓑ Ⓒ Ⓓ

28 Ⓐ Ⓑ Ⓒ Ⓓ

29 Ⓐ Ⓑ Ⓒ Ⓓ

30

Number	Prime	Composite
4		
5		
25		
39		

31 Ⓐ Ⓑ Ⓒ Ⓓ

32 Ⓐ Ⓑ Ⓒ Ⓓ

33 Ⓐ Ⓑ Ⓒ Ⓓ

34 Ⓐ Ⓑ Ⓒ Ⓓ

35 Ⓐ Ⓑ Ⓒ Ⓓ

36 Ⓐ Ⓑ Ⓒ Ⓓ

37 ☐

38 Ⓐ Ⓑ Ⓒ Ⓓ

39 Ⓐ Ⓑ Ⓒ Ⓓ

40 Ⓐ Ⓑ Ⓒ Ⓓ

41 Ⓐ Ⓑ Ⓒ Ⓓ

42 Ⓐ Ⓑ Ⓒ Ⓓ

43 Ⓐ Ⓑ Ⓒ Ⓓ

44 Ⓐ Ⓑ Ⓒ Ⓓ

45 Ⓐ Ⓑ Ⓒ Ⓓ

46 Ⓐ Ⓑ Ⓒ Ⓓ

47 ☐

48 ☐ ☐

49 Ⓐ Ⓑ Ⓒ Ⓓ

50 Ⓐ Ⓑ Ⓒ Ⓓ

51 Ⓐ Ⓑ Ⓒ Ⓓ

52 Ⓐ Ⓑ Ⓒ Ⓓ

53 Ⓐ Ⓑ Ⓒ Ⓓ

54 Ⓐ Ⓑ Ⓒ Ⓓ

55 Ⓐ Ⓑ Ⓒ Ⓓ

56 Ⓐ Ⓑ Ⓒ Ⓓ

57 Ⓐ Ⓑ Ⓒ Ⓓ

58 ☐

59 Ⓐ Ⓑ Ⓒ Ⓓ

60 Ⓐ Ⓑ Ⓒ Ⓓ

SAMPLE MATHEMATICS EXAMINATION 1

NUMBER OF QUESTIONS: 60

Time: 90 MINUTES

Directions: You will have access to an online scientific calculator during this test.

For multiple-choice questions, select the *best* of the four choices, then type A, B, C, or D. For the other questions, type your numerical answer in the box or click in the appropriate place on the computer screen. (Note: on this practice exam you may circle your choices or write your answers in the boxes provided.)

Notes:

1. represents $\sqrt{-1}$.

2. If the domain of a function f is not specified in a question, assume that it is the set of all real numbers for which $f(x)$ is defined.

3. Figures are drawn to scale and lie in a plane, *unless* otherwise specified.

1. If $g(x) = 2 - x^3$, then $g(-1) =$

2. The negation of the statement "He is tall, or he is handsome" is

   (A) He is tall and handsome
   (B) He is not tall or he is not handsome
   (C) He is neither tall nor handsome
   (D) He is tall but he is not handsome

3. The Early Bird dinner menu lists 2 salads, 6 entrees, and 3 desserts. If a guest may choose 1 of each course, how many different dinners are available?

4. If m and n are positive integers, then which of the following *cannot* be an integer?

   (A) $\dfrac{1}{m+n}$

   (B) $\sqrt{m+n}$

   (C) $\dfrac{m+n}{m-n}$

   (D) $\dfrac{m}{n}$

5. In the Venn diagram below shade the region(s) that represents the set $R \cap (S \cap T)$.

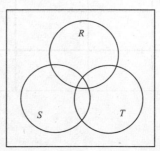

6. If students must answer 3 of 6 questions on a test, how many different choices do they have?

7. If $\log_4 x = \dfrac{3}{2}$, then x is equal to

8. The temperature of a fluid in a lab (in degrees Celsius) is a linear function of the time. Initially, at noon, the temperature was −4°C and at 2 P.M. it was −1°C. What was the temperature at 3 P.M.?

   (A) −2°C
   (B) 0°C
   (C) 0.5°C
   (D) 1.5°C

9. How many different 3-digit numbers less than 500 can be formed from the set of digits {2,3,4,5,6,7} if repetitions are not allowed?

   (A) 24
   (B) 30
   (C) 60
   (D) 80

10. Indicate whether each number is rational, irrational, or imaginary by checking the appropriate box.

Number(s)	Rational	Irrational	Imaginary
$\sqrt[3]{-125}$			
$\dfrac{5}{\sqrt{9}}$			
$\sqrt{18}$			
$\sqrt{3^2 - 4^2}$			

11. According to the local weather stations in cities X and Y, the probability that it will snow today in X is 0.2 and in Y is 0.4. Based on these predictions and assuming these events are independent, the probability that it will snow today in both cities is

    (A) 0.08
    (B) 0.48
    (C) 0.8
    (D) 0.92

12. Given the predictions in question 11, the probability that it will not snow today in either city X or city Y is

    (A) 0.08
    (B) 0.48
    (C) 0.52
    (D) 0.92

13. A car travels a scenic route at an average rate of 30 mph and returns along the same route at an average rate of 60 mph. Its average speed for the trip is

    (A) 40 mph
    (B) 45 mph
    (C) 50 mph
    (D) 55 mph

14. If $R = \{a,b,c,w\}$ and $S = \{a,c,d,w\}$, then $R \cap S$ equals

    (A) $\{a,b,c,d,w\}$
    (B) $\{a\}$
    (C) $\{a,c\}$
    (D) $\{a,c,w\}$

15. Which of the following sets is not infinite?

    (A) the set of multiples of 3
    (B) the set of prime numbers
    (C) the set of subsets of the set {1, 2, 3, . . . , 100}
    (D) the set of integers less than −100

16. Let *p* denote "Warren wears braces" and let *q* denote "Warren wears glasses." Then the statement "Warren wears neither braces nor glasses" is written symbolically as

    (A) $\sim p \vee \sim q$
    (B) $\sim p \vee q$
    (C) $\sim p \wedge \sim q$
    (D) $\sim p \wedge q$

17. The negation of "Every college graduate has studied geometry" is

    (A) Some college graduates have not studied geometry
    (B) No college graduate has studied geometry
    (C) Geometry is not necessary for graduation from college
    (D) If a person has studied geometry, then he is not a college graduate

18. Which of the following fractions *cannot* be written as a terminating decimal?

    (A) $\dfrac{2}{7}$

    (B) $\dfrac{5}{16}$

    (C) $\dfrac{17}{40}$

    (D) $\dfrac{19}{25}$

19. Which of the laws below holds for real numbers?

    (A) division is commutative
    (B) subtraction is associative
    (C) $(a + b) \div c = (a \div c) + (b \div c)$
    (D) $a - b = b - a$

20. Which of the following *cannot* be a rational number?

    (A) the sum of two irrational numbers
    (B) the product of two irrational numbers
    (C) the sum of a rational number and an irrational number
    (D) the quotient of two irrational numbers

21. If $f(x) = 2x^2 - 3x + 2$, then $f(-x) =$

    (A) $2x^2 + 3x + 2$
    (B) $-2x^2 + 3x - 2$
    (C) $-2x^2 + 3x + 2$
    (D) $-f(x)$

22. Which of the following equations has a graph that is symmetric to the *x*-axis?

    (A) $y = x$
    (B) $y = x^2 + 3$
    (C) $y^2 = x$
    (D) $y = x^3 - x$

23. Which graph of points, shown below, is not that of a function of *x*?

    (A)

    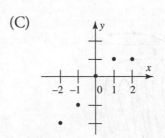

    (B)

    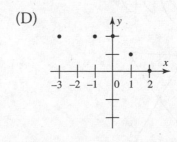

    (C)

    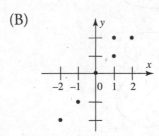

    (D)

    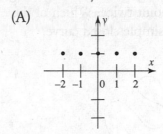

24. If a die is tossed twice in succession, the probability of getting 4 on the first roll or 5 on the second is

    (A) $\dfrac{1}{36}$

    (B) $\dfrac{7}{36}$

    (C) $\dfrac{11}{36}$

    (D) $\dfrac{1}{3}$

25. A simple closed curve is one that starts and stops at the same point without passing through any point twice. Which of the following is a simple closed curve?

    (A)

    (B)

    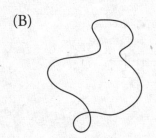

    (C)

    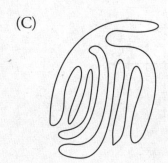

    (D)

    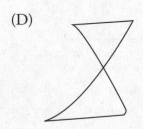

26. If $y > 0 > x$, then which of the following is necessarily positive?

    (A) $y + x$
    (B) $y - x$
    (C) $y^2 + x$
    (D) $x^2 - 1$

27. The graph shown is for the function $y =$

    (A) 2^x
    (B) 2^{-x}
    (C) $\log_2 x$
    (D) 3^x

    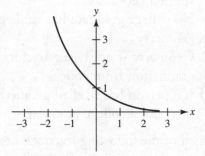

28. If $23_{\text{TEN}} = n_{\text{TWO}}$, then n equals

    (A) 10101
    (B) 10111
    (C) 11001
    (D) 11011

29. Which one of the following tables defines a function $y = f(x)$?

    (A)

x	1	1	2
y	3	4	5

    (B)

x	0	0	1
y	−1	1	2

    (C)

x	−1	0	1	1
y	0	1	2	3

    (D)

x	1	2	3	4
y	2	2	2	2

30. Indicate whether each number is prime or composite by checking the appropriate box.

Number	Prime	Composite
4		
5		
25		
39		

31. Let $f(x) = x + 2$ and $g(x) = x^2$; let p and q be the statements that the point (x,y) lies on the graph of f and on that of g, respectively. If $(x,y) = (1,3)$, which of the following is false?

    (A) $\sim q$
    (B) $p \vee q$
    (C) $p \wedge q$
    (D) $p \wedge \sim q$

32. For what value of k is the line $3y - kx = 6$ parallel to the line $y + 3x = 9$?

    (A) 9
    (B) 3
    (C) −3
    (D) −9

33. $(4 + i)(4 - i)$, where $i = \sqrt{-1}$, equals

    (A) 17
    (B) 15
    (C) $16 + 8i$
    (D) $8i$

34. If $(x + 1)$ is a factor of $f(x) = x^3 - 2x^2 + 3x + d$, then $d =$

    (A) −2
    (B) −1
    (C) 2
    (D) 6

35. If $4^m = 6$ and $4^n = 9$, then 4^{2m-n} equals

    (A) 3
    (B) 4
    (C) 27
    (D) 324

36. If $f(x) = \dfrac{x}{x^2 - 1}$, then the domain of f is

    (A) the real numbers
    (B) $x \neq 1$
    (C) $x \neq 1, -1$
    (D) $x \neq 0, 1, -1$

37. If 2 positive numbers are in the ratio of 6 to 11 and differ by 15, then the smaller number is

38. A registrar's records show that of 300 transfer students, 150 students signed up for a psychology course, 190 signed up for a computer course, and 70 signed up for both. The probability that a transfer student did not sign up for either psychology or computers is

    (A) $\dfrac{1}{10}$

    (B) $\dfrac{1}{2}$

    (C) $\dfrac{19}{30}$

    (D) $\dfrac{9}{10}$

39. How many subsets does the set $\{a,b,c\}$ have?

    (A) 3
    (B) 4
    (C) 7
    (D) 8

40. Which statement is equivalent to the statement "If she has invested wisely, then she is rich"?

    (A) If she is not rich, then she has not invested wisely
    (B) If she is rich, then she has invested wisely
    (C) To be rich, you must invest wisely
    (D) If she has not invested wisely, then she is not rich

41. If $\overline{P}$ denotes the complement of Set P, then the shaded set in the Venn diagram is

   (A) $\overline{V \cup W}$
   (B) $\overline{V \cap W}$
   (C) $\overline{V} \cap \overline{W}$
   (D) $\overline{V} \cup \overline{W}$

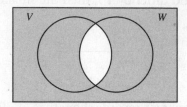

42. 30% of the boys in a school have brown hair, 20% have blue eyes, and 15% have both brown hair and blue eyes. If a boy chosen at random has brown hair, what is the probability that he also has blue eyes?

   (A) $\dfrac{3}{20}$

   (B) $\dfrac{3}{8}$

   (C) $\dfrac{1}{2}$

   (D) $\dfrac{3}{4}$

43. The graph of $\begin{cases} y \geq 1-x \\ x^2 + y^2 \leq 4 \\ x \geq 0, y \geq 0 \end{cases}$ is

(A)

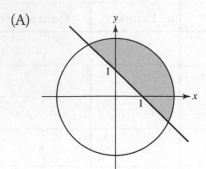

(B)

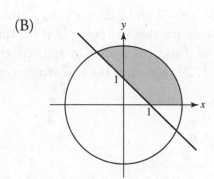

(C)

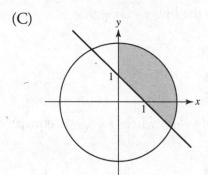

(D)

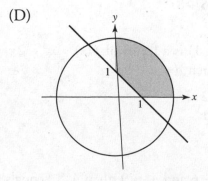

44. Which Venn diagram is *incorrect* if the following statements are true: $P \subset Q$; $P \cap R = \emptyset$?

(A)

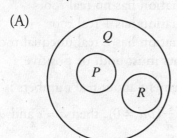

(B)

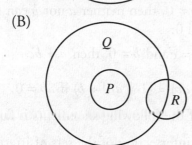

(C)

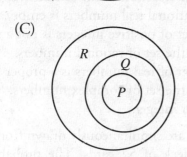

(D)

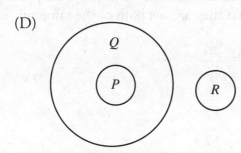

45. The solution set of $\{x : x$ is a real number and $x^3 - x^2 - 2x = 0\}$ is

(A) $\{0,1,2\}$
(B) $\{0,-1,2\}$
(C) $\{-1,2\}$
(D) $\{0,1,-2\}$

46. Let Z, Q, R denote respectively the sets of integers, of rationals, and of reals. Then it is false that

(A) $(3, 5) \in Z \times Z$
(B) $Z \times Z \subset Q \times Q$
(C) $(1, 1) \in Q \times Q$
(D) $Q \subset R \times R$

47. If $\log_2 2^x = 3$, then $x =$

48. There are 5 identical black socks and 5 identical brown ones in a drawer. If you reach in and choose 2 socks without looking, what fraction is the probability that you will get a matching pair?

$$\frac{\rule{2cm}{0.4pt}}{\rule{2cm}{0.4pt}}$$

49. The truth table of $p \rightarrow q$ is

p	q	(A)	(B)	(C)	(D)
T	T	T	T	T	T
T	F	F	F	F	F
F	T	T	F	F	T
F	F	F	F	T	T

50. A counterexample to the claim that if $(a^2 > b^2)$, then $(a > b)$ is

(A) $a = 3, b = 2$
(B) $a = -2, b = -1$
(C) $a = 1, b = 0$
(D) $a = \frac{1}{2}, b = \frac{1}{3}$

51. If $f(x) = x + \dfrac{4}{x}$ and $g(x) = \sqrt{x + 4},$ then $f(g(0))$ is

(A) 2
(B) 3
(C) 4
(D) undefined

52. Which of the following statements is true about the data represented by this histogram?

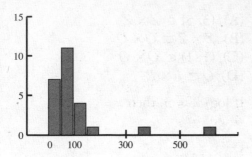

(A) The mean and the median are approximately equal.
(B) The mean is greater than the median.
(C) The median is greater than the mean.
(D) The relative sizes of the mean and median cannot be determined from the graph.

53. $(x - 1)(3 - x)^2 > 0$ if and only if

(A) $x > 1$
(B) $1 < x < 3$
(C) $x < 1$
(D) $x > 1, x \neq 3$

54. If the probability that an egg will hatch is 0.20, then the odds in favor of its hatching are

(A) $\dfrac{1}{5}$
(B) 1 to 5
(C) $\dfrac{1}{4}$
(D) 1 to 4

55. A student received quiz grades of 10, 7, 7, 10, 6, 9, 8, 7 in a language class. Her median score was

(A) 7
(B) $7\dfrac{1}{2}$
(C) 8
(D) $8\dfrac{1}{2}$

56. Suppose $q < 0$ in the equation $x^2 + px + q = 0$. Then

(A) the equation has no real roots
(B) the equation has 1 real root
(C) the equation has 2 real unequal roots
(D) the roots must both be positive

57. Which statement about real numbers is false?

(A) If $\dfrac{a}{b} = \dfrac{c}{d} (bd \neq 0)$, then $a = c$ and $b = d$.
(B) If $ab \neq 0$, then neither a nor b can equal 0.
(C) If $\dfrac{a}{b} = c$ and $b \neq 0$, then $a = bc$
(D) $1 \div (ab) = (1 \div a)(1 \div b)$ if $ab \neq 0$.

58. Which of the following statements is false?

(A) The intersection of the sets of irrational and rational real numbers is empty.
(B) The set of positive integers is not a subset of the set of rational numbers.
(C) The set of real numbers is a proper subset of the set of complex numbers.
(D) 0 is an integer.

59. Two cards are simultaneously drawn from an ordinary deck of 52 cards. The probability that they are *not* both of the same suit is

(A) $\dfrac{4}{17}$
(B) $\dfrac{5}{17}$
(C) $\dfrac{12}{17}$
(D) $\dfrac{13}{17}$

60. The prime factors of 96 are

(A) 2 and 3
(B) 6 and 8
(C) 2, 3, and 4
(D) 8 and 12

STOP

If there is still time remaining, you may review your answers.

College Mathematics
ANSWER KEY–SAMPLE EXAMINATION 1

1. 3
2. C
3. 36
4. A
5.

6. 20
7. 8
8. C
9. C
10.

11. A
12. B
13. A
14. D
15. C
16. C
17. A
18. A
19. C
20. C
21. A
22. C
23. B
24. C
25. B
26. C
27. B
28. B
29. D

30.

31. C
32. D
33. A
34. D
35. B
36. C
37. 18
38. A
39. D
40. A
41. B
42. D
43. D

44. C
45. B
46. D
47. 3
48. $\frac{4}{9}$
49. D
50. B
51. C
52. B
53. D
54. D
55. B
56. C
57. A
58. B
59. D
60. A

SCORING CHART

After you have scored your Sample Examination 1, enter the results in the chart below; then transfer your score to the Progress Chart on page 12.

Total Test	Number Right	Number Wrong	Number Omitted
Total: 60			

ANSWER EXPLANATIONS

1. **(3)** $g(-1) = 2 - (-1)^3 = 3$.

2. **(C)** The negation of statement $p \lor q$ is $\sim p \land \sim q$. Verify with truth tables if necessary.

3. **(36)** The answer is the product $2 \times 6 \times 3$.

4. **(A)** $\dfrac{1}{m+n}$ is a fraction for all positive integral m and n. (If, for example, $m = 6$ and $n = 3$, then (B), (C), and (D) are all integers.)

5.

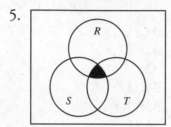

The Venn diagram shows the subset of elements that are in all three sets—in R and in S and in T. (Draw Venn diagrams for (A), (C), and (D).)

6. **(20)** They have $_6C_3$ choices; $_6C_3$ equals $\dfrac{6 \cdot 5 \cdot 4}{3 \cdot 2 \cdot 1}$.

7. **(8)** The equation $\log_4 x = \dfrac{3}{2}$ is equivalent to $x = 4^{3/2} = 8$.

8. **(C)** Let $f(t) = at + b$, where $f(t)$ denotes the temperature at time t. We are given that $f(0) = -4$ and $f(2) = -1$. These yield $f(t) = \dfrac{3}{2}t - 4$, hence $f(3) = \dfrac{1}{2}$.

9. **(C)** The first digit can be 2, 3, or 4. This leaves five possibilities for the second digit and four for the third. The answer is therefore $3 \times 5 \times 4$.

10.

Number(s)	Rational	Irrational	Imaginary
$\sqrt[3]{-125}$	√		
$\dfrac{5}{\sqrt{9}}$	√		
$\sqrt{18}$		√	
$\sqrt{3^2 - 4^2}$			√

Note: $\sqrt[3]{-125} = -5$; $\dfrac{5}{\sqrt{9}} = \dfrac{5}{3}$; $\sqrt{3^2 - 4^2} = \sqrt{-9} = 3i$; but $\sqrt{18} = 3\sqrt{2}$, which is irrational.

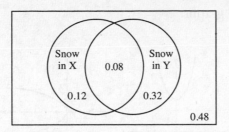

11. **(A)** The relevant probabilities for questions 11 and 12 are shown in the Venn diagram above.

12. **(B)**
    (1) Pr of snow in X   = 0.2
    (2) Pr of snow in Y   = 0.4
    (3) Pr of snow in both cities = (1) × (2)   = 0.08
    (4) Pr of snow in X only = (1) − (3)   = 0.12
    (5) Pr of snow in Y only = (2) − (3)   = 0.32
    (6) Pr of snow in neither city =
        1 − (3) − (4) − (5) =
        1 − 0.08 − 0.12 − 0.32   = 0.48

13. **(A)** The distance along the route is irrelevant here, so choose a convenient distance, say 60 miles. Then it took $60 \div 30 = 2$ hours going, and $60 \div 60 = 1$ hour on the way back. The total journey of 120 miles took 3 hours to complete, hence the average speed was $120 \div 3 = 40$ miles per hour. (Try letting the distance be d miles and note that you get the same average speed.)

14. **(D)** $R \cap S$ contains elements both in R and in S.

15. **(C)** $\{1,2,3, \ldots ,100\}$ has 2^{100} subsets, a large but finite number.

16. **(C)** A restatement is "He does not wear braces and he does not wear glasses."

17. **(A)** $\sim(\forall_x p_x) = \exists_x \sim p_x$. The negation of "$p$ is true for all" is "p is false for some."

18. **(A)** Every fraction whose denominator contains only the factors 2 or 5 can be written as a terminating (nonrepeating) decimal. Divide 2 by 7 and note that the division "never ends."

19. **(C)** Choices (A), (B), and (D) are all false statements.

20. **(C)** If the irrational numbers are $\sqrt{2}$ and $-\sqrt{2}$, for instance, then their sum, product, and quotient are all rational. To show that (C) is false, we suppose that there are numbers p, q, r, where p and r are rational but q is irrational, and such that $p + q = r$. Then it follows that $q = r - p$. Because $r - p$ is rational, it *cannot* equal the irrational number q. Our supposition was false!

21. **(A)** $f(-x) = 2(-x)^2 - 3(-x) + 2 = 2x^2 + 3x + 2.$

22. **(C)** Here are the graphs:

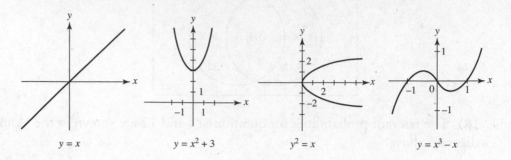

$y = x$ $y = x^2 + 3$ $y^2 = x$ $y = x^3 - x$

23. **(B)** For each x in the domain of a function, there must be a *unique y*. Note, in (B), for example, that there are *two y*-values for $x = 1$.

24. **(C)** The probability that one event *or* another occurs is the sum of the probabilities of the two events minus the probability that they both occur. Since the successive tosses are independent, the probability that they both happen is the product of their probabilities.

    Hence the answer is $\dfrac{1}{6} + \dfrac{1}{6} - \dfrac{1}{36} = \dfrac{11}{36}$.

25. **(B)** Since $x < 0$, $-x > 0$. Each of the numbers in (A), (B), (D) *can*, for appropriate choices of x and y, be negative or zero.

26. **(C)** Choice (A) starts and stops at different points. Each curve in (B) and (D) goes through one point twice.

27. **(B)** Check out some "easy" points: $(0, 1)$, $(1, \dfrac{1}{2})$, $(-1, 2)$. All three lie only on $y = 2^{-x}$.

28. **(B)** $23_{\text{TEN}} = 16 + 4 + 2 + 1 = 2^4 + 2^2 + 2^1 + 2^0 = 10111_{\text{TWO}}$.

29. **(D)** Remember that if f is a function from a set X into a set Y, each element of X must correspond to a *unique* element in Y. In (A), (B), and (C) there are *two* different images of a single element in the domain.

30.

Number	Prime	Composite
4		√
5	√	
25		√
39		√

A prime number has only 1 and itself as factors. Since $4 = 2 \cdot 2$, $25 = 5 \cdot 5$, and $39 = 3 \cdot 13$, then 4, 25, and 39 are composite numbers.

31. **(C)** The point $(1,3)$ lies on the graph of f but not on the graph of g. So p is true, q false. Only $p \wedge q$ is false.

32. **(D)** The slope of $y + 3x = 9$ or $y = -3x + 9$ is -3. Therefore $\frac{k}{3}$ must equal -3.

33. **(A)** $(4 + i)(4 - i) = 16 - i^2 = 16 - (-1) = 16 + 1 = 17$.

34. **(D)** Since $(x + 1)$ is a factor of $f(x)$, $f(-1) = 0$.
    So $(-1)^3 - 2(-1)^2 + 3(-1) + d = 0$ and $d = 6$.

35. **(B)** $4^{2m-n} = (4^m)^2 \div 4^n = 6^2 \div 9 = 4$.

36. **(C)** The denominator of f equals 0 at 1 and -1. Every other real is in f's domain.

37. **(18)** Let the numbers be $6x$ and $11x$. Then $5x = 15$ and $x = 3$. So the smaller number is 18.

38. **(A)** Draw a Venn diagram. Since 30 students $(300 - 80 - 70 - 120)$ did not sign up for either course, the required probability is $\frac{30}{100}$ or $\frac{1}{10}$.

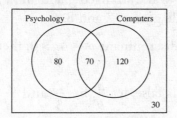

39. **(D)** The subsets are $\emptyset$, $\{a\}$, $\{b\}$, $\{c\}$, $\{a,b\}$, $\{a,c\}$, $\{b,c\}$, and $\{a,b,c\}$. The number of subsets of an n-element set is 2^n.

40. **(A)** The contrapositive of $p \to q$ is $\sim q \to \sim p$.

41. **(B)** The unshaded region is $V \cap W$. The complement is the shaded region.

42. **(D)** The probability equals $\frac{0.15}{0.20} = \frac{3}{4}$.

43. **(D)** The inequalities $x \geq 0$, $y \geq 0$ restrict the graph to the first quadrant.

44. **(C)** Verify that the given statements are illustrated correctly in (A), (B), and (D). Note, however, that (C) is incorrect because in (C), $P \subset R$, contradicting the statement given that $P \cap R = \emptyset$.

45. **(B)** $x^3 - x^2 - 2x = x(x^2 - x - 2) = x(x + 1)(x - 2)$.

46. **(D)** $R \times R$, the Cartesian product, consists only of ordered pairs. Note that (A), (B), (C) are all true.

47. **(3)** $\log_2 2^x = x \log_2 2 = x \cdot 1 = x$.

48. $\left(\dfrac{4}{9}\right)$ You may initially choose any sock from the set of 10, but then, to obtain a matching pair, there are only 4 choices among the remaining 9 socks.

   The probability is therefore $\dfrac{10}{10} \cdot \dfrac{4}{9}$ or $\dfrac{4}{9}$.

49. **(D)** The conditional $p \to q$ is defined as true whenever p is false. The statement is true except when p is true and q is false.

50. **(B)** A counterexample cites values of a and b that satisfy the hypothesis but not the conclusion. Although $(-2)^2 > (-1)^2$, $-2 \not> -1$.

51. **(C)** Since $g(0) = \sqrt{4} = 2$, $f(g(0)) = f(2) = 2 + \dfrac{4}{2} = 4$.

52. **(B)** Most of these data lie between 0 and 150, but there are 2 unusually large values. The mean, based on the sum of the data, will be affected by these large values, whereas the median, representing the middle entry in an ordered list of the data, will not.

53. **(D)** $(x-1)(3-x)^2 > 0$ if and only if $x - 1 > 0$ and $3 - x \neq 0$; i.e., if and only if $x > 1$, $x \neq 3$.

54. **(D)** If the probability of an event is p, the odds in its favor are the ratio of p to $(1 - p)$. Here it is 0.2 to 0.8, or 1 to 4.

55. **(B)** The median score of the arranged grades 6, 7, 7, 7, 8, 9, 10, 10 is halfway between the two middle grades, 7 and 8.

56. **(C)** If $q < 0$, then the discriminant $p^2 - 4q > 0$; therefore the roots are real and unequal.

57. **(A)** To show that (A) is false, let $\dfrac{a}{b}$ be $\dfrac{2}{3}$ and $\dfrac{c}{d}$ be $\dfrac{4}{6}$. Convince yourself that (B), (C), and (D) are true statements.

58. **(B)** Choices (A), (C), and (D) are all true statements.

59. **(D)** One of the cards may be any of 52 (selected from 52 cards); the other (selected from the remaining 51 cards) can be one of 39. The answer is $\dfrac{52}{52} \cdot \dfrac{39}{51} = \dfrac{13}{17}$.

60. **(A)** $96 = 32 \times 3 = 2^5 \cdot 3$; the prime factors are 2 and 3.

College Mathematics
ANSWER SHEET—SAMPLE EXAMINATION 2

1
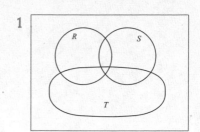

2

3 Ⓐ Ⓑ Ⓒ Ⓓ

4

8 Ⓐ Ⓑ Ⓒ Ⓓ
9 Ⓐ Ⓑ Ⓒ Ⓓ
10 Ⓐ Ⓑ Ⓒ Ⓓ
11 Ⓐ Ⓑ Ⓒ Ⓓ
12 Ⓐ Ⓑ Ⓒ Ⓓ
13 Ⓐ Ⓑ Ⓒ Ⓓ
14 Ⓐ Ⓑ Ⓒ Ⓓ
15 Ⓐ Ⓑ Ⓒ Ⓓ
16

17

18 Ⓐ Ⓑ Ⓒ Ⓓ
19 Ⓐ Ⓑ Ⓒ Ⓓ
20 Ⓐ Ⓑ Ⓒ Ⓓ
21 Ⓐ Ⓑ Ⓒ Ⓓ

22

23 Ⓐ Ⓑ Ⓒ Ⓓ
24 Ⓐ Ⓑ Ⓒ Ⓓ
25 Ⓐ Ⓑ Ⓒ Ⓓ
26 Ⓐ Ⓑ Ⓒ Ⓓ
27 Ⓐ Ⓑ Ⓒ Ⓓ
28

Statement	True	False
$-q < -r$		
$pq < pr$		
$p(q - r) > 0$		
$q + p > r + p$		

29 Ⓐ Ⓑ Ⓒ Ⓓ
30 Ⓐ Ⓑ Ⓒ Ⓓ
31 Ⓐ Ⓑ Ⓒ Ⓓ
32 Ⓐ Ⓑ Ⓒ Ⓓ
33 Ⓐ Ⓑ Ⓒ Ⓓ
34 Ⓐ Ⓑ Ⓒ Ⓓ
35 Ⓐ Ⓑ Ⓒ Ⓓ
36 Ⓐ Ⓑ Ⓒ Ⓓ

37

38 Ⓐ Ⓑ Ⓒ Ⓓ
39 Ⓐ Ⓑ Ⓒ Ⓓ

40

41 Ⓐ Ⓑ Ⓒ Ⓓ
42 Ⓐ Ⓑ Ⓒ Ⓓ
43 Ⓐ Ⓑ Ⓒ Ⓓ
44 Ⓐ Ⓑ Ⓒ Ⓓ
45 Ⓐ Ⓑ Ⓒ Ⓓ
46 Ⓐ Ⓑ Ⓒ Ⓓ

47

Number	Even	Odd
$m + n^2$		
$-m + 2n$		
$2m^2 + n^2$		
$2m + 3n$		

48

49 Ⓐ Ⓑ Ⓒ Ⓓ
50 Ⓐ Ⓑ Ⓒ Ⓓ
51 Ⓐ Ⓑ Ⓒ Ⓓ
52 Ⓐ Ⓑ Ⓒ Ⓓ
53 Ⓐ Ⓑ Ⓒ Ⓓ

54

55 Ⓐ Ⓑ Ⓒ Ⓓ

56 ⟵+++++++++++++⟶
   -6 -5 -4 -3 -2 -1 0 1 2 3 4 5 6

57 Ⓐ Ⓑ Ⓒ Ⓓ
58 Ⓐ Ⓑ Ⓒ Ⓓ
59 Ⓐ Ⓑ Ⓒ Ⓓ
60 Ⓐ Ⓑ Ⓒ Ⓓ

SAMPLE MATHEMATICS EXAMINATION 2

NUMBER OF QUESTIONS: 60

Time: 90 MINUTES

Directions: You will have access to an online scientific calculator during this test.

For multiple-choice questions, select the *best* of the four choices, then type A, B, C, or D. For the other questions, type your numerical answer in the box or click in the appropriate place on the computer screen. (Note: on this practice exam you may circle your choices or write your answers in the boxes provided.)

Notes:

1. *i* represents $\sqrt{-1}$.

2. If the domain of a function *f* is not specified in a question, assume that it is the set of all real numbers for which $f(x)$ is defined.

3. Figures are drawn to scale and lie in a plane, *unless* otherwise specified.

1. Shade the region in the Venn diagram that represents the set $R \cup (S \cap T)$.

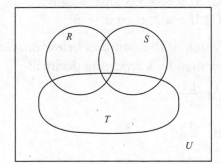

2. Arrange these numbers in increasing order, starting with the smallest number in the top box.

$$|3 - 1|$$

$$|-3| + 1$$

$$-|3|$$

$$1 - |-3|$$

3. The domain of the function $y = \dfrac{4}{(x - 1)^2}$ is

 (A) all real numbers
 (B) all reals except $x = \pm 1$
 (C) all reals except $x = 1$
 (D) all positive numbers except $x = 1$

4. If you can choose to answer 4 essay questions out of 6, how many choices do you have?

5. The contrapositive of "If a triangle is equilateral, then it is isosceles" is

   (A) If a triangle is not equilateral, then it is not isosceles
   (B) If a triangle is isosceles, then it is equilateral
   (C) Some isosceles triangles are not equilateral
   (D) If a triangle is not isosceles, then it is not equilateral

6. Bag I contains 3 nickels and 2 dimes; Bag II contains 1 nickel and 5 dimes. If 1 coin is drawn from each bag, what is the probability that 1 is a nickel and 1 is a dime?

   (A) $\dfrac{17}{30}$

   (B) $\dfrac{1}{2}$

   (C) $\dfrac{1}{28}$

   (D) $\dfrac{1}{30}$

7. If $(2 \times 10^3)^2 \times 5$ is multiplied out, then the number of zeros following the digit 2 is

8. If Z, Q, R denote respectively the sets of integers, of rationals, and of reals, then each point of the Cartesian plane corresponds to an element of

   (A) $R \times R$
   (B) $Q \times Q$
   (C) $Z \times Z$
   (D) R

9. If $P = \{x : x^2 - 2x - 3 = 0\}$ and $Q = \{x : x^2 + x = 0\}$, then $P \cap Q$ equals

   (A) $\emptyset$
   (B) $\{0, -1, 3\}$
   (C) $\{1\}$
   (D) $\{-1\}$

10. The negation of $s \rightarrow t$ is

   (A) $s \wedge {\sim}t$
   (B) ${\sim}s \rightarrow t$
   (C) ${\sim}s \wedge {\sim}t$
   (D) $t \rightarrow {\sim}s$

11. If a, b, and c in the equation $ax^2 + bx + c = 0$ are all positive real numbers, then which statement below is true of every such equation?

   (A) $b^2 - 4ac$ is negative.
   (B) The equation has no real roots.
   (C) The equation has no positive root.
   (D) $b^2 - 4ac$ equals zero.

12. Which statement about real numbers is false?

   (A) If $a \neq 0$, then $a^2 > 0$.
   (B) If $a > 0$, then $\dfrac{1}{a} > 0$.
   (C) If $a > b > 0$, then $a^2 > b^2$.
   (D) If $a < b$, then $a^2 < b^2$.

13. Which of the numbers below *cannot* be represented by a repeating decimal?

   (A) $\dfrac{11}{9}$

   (B) $\dfrac{23}{7}$

   (C) $\sqrt{3}$

   (D) $4\dfrac{1}{3}$

14. Bathroom tiles 1 inch on a side are available in sheets of 10 by 12 tiles. How many sheets are needed to cover a wall 5 ft by 8 ft?

   (A) 30
   (B) 40
   (C) 44
   (D) 48

15. Points in the region enclosed by the parabola and line, shown in the diagram, satisfy the inequalities

   (A) $y < 1 + x$, $y < x^2$
   (B) $y > x^2$, $y < 1 + x$
   (C) $y > 1 + x$, $y < x$
   (D) $y > x^2$, $y > 1 + x$

   (The dotted line segment and dotted curve indicate that the boundaries of the region are excluded.)

   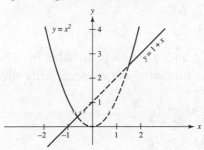

16. A die is tossed. What fraction (in lowest terms) represents the probability that it shows a number greater than or equal to 2?

   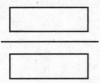

17. For the data 3, 3, 7, 11, 11, 13, 15 the median minus the mean is equal to

18. You have randomly drawn 4 cards from a shuffled deck (of 52 cards—no jokers): an ace, a king, a 7, and a 3. The probability that the next card you draw will give you a pair is

   (A) $\dfrac{1}{16}$

   (B) $\dfrac{3}{13}$

   (C) $\dfrac{1}{4}$

   (D) $\dfrac{1}{3}$

19. If $f(x) = 2x + 1$ and $g(x) = x^2 - 3$, then $g(f(x)) =$

   (A) $4x^2 + 4x - 2$
   (B) $2x^2 - 5$
   (C) $4x^2 + 2x - 2$
   (D) $2x^2 - 2$

20. Which equation has no rational root?

   (A) $x^2 - 1 = 0$
   (B) $x^2 - 2 = 0$
   (C) $x^2 - 4x + 4 = 0$
   (D) $x^2 - x - 2 = 0$

21. The negation of the statement "Some mathematicians are teachers" is

   (A) No mathematicians are teachers.
   (B) Some mathematicians are not teachers.
   (C) Some teachers are not mathematicians.
   (D) All mathematicians are teachers.

22. In how many ways can a group of 12 faculty members choose from among themselves a chairman and an assistant chairman?

23. A die is rolled and a coin is tossed. What is the probability that the die shows a number less than 3 and the coin shows heads?

   (A) $\dfrac{1}{6}$

   (B) $\dfrac{1}{3}$

   (C) $\dfrac{5}{12}$

   (D) $\dfrac{5}{6}$

24. In question 23, what is the probability that the die shows a number less than 3 or the coin shows heads but not both?

  (A) $\dfrac{1}{6}$

  (B) $\dfrac{1}{2}$

  (C) $\dfrac{2}{3}$

  (D) $\dfrac{5}{6}$

25. If $f(x) = \log_2 x$ and $g(x) = 2^x$, then their graphs are symmetric to the

  (A) origin
  (B) x-axis
  (C) y-axis
  (D) line $y = x$

26. If $a > 0$ and $a^x = 0.6$, then $a^{-2x} =$

  (A) -1.2
  (B) -0.36
  (C) $-\dfrac{1}{0.36}$
  (D) $\dfrac{1}{0.36}$

27. If $i = \sqrt{-1}$, then $5\sqrt{-1} + \sqrt{-4} - \sqrt{-9} =$

  (A) 10
  (B) $4i$
  (C) 0
  (D) $-6i$

28. Given that $p < 0$ and $q > r$, indicate whether each of these statements is true or false by checking the approriate box.

Statement	True	False
$-q < -r$		
$pq < pr$		
$p(q - r) > 0$		
$q + p > r + p$		

29. The domain of the function $f(x) = \dfrac{x^2}{x^2 - 4}$ is the set of all reals except

  (A) 0
  (B) 2
  (C) 2 and -2
  (D) 0, 2, and -2

30. Which number is *not* a prime factor of 84?

  (A) 2
  (B) 3
  (C) 6
  (D) 7

31. If p and q are each divisible by 3, which of the following is not necessarily divisible by 3?

  (A) $2q + 3$
  (B) $4p + q$
  (C) $pq + 2$
  (D) $p^2 + q$

32. If $g(x) = \dfrac{\sqrt{x - 3}}{x}$, then $g(4) =$

  (A) $\dfrac{1}{2}$

  (B) $\dfrac{1}{4}$

  (C) $-\dfrac{1}{4}$

  (D) $\pm\dfrac{1}{4}$

33. Which function has a graph symmetric to the y-axis?

  (A) $y = |x|$
  (B) $y = 2x$
  (C) $y = \dfrac{1}{x}$
  (D) $y = x^2 + x$

34. If set $R = \{a, b\}$, set $S = \{1, 2\}$, and set $T = \{2, 3\}$, then the number of elements in $R \times (S \cap T)$ is

  (A) 2
  (B) 4
  (C) 6
  (D) 8

35. $p \rightarrow q$ is *not* logically equivalent to

    (A) if p then q
    (B) p only if q
    (C) p is sufficient for q
    (D) p is necessary for q

36. If $\log_a u = 3$ and $\log_a v = 8$, then $\log_a \frac{u}{v^2} =$

    (A) -13

    (B) $\frac{3}{64}$

    (C) $\frac{3}{16}$

    (D) 5

37. An average of 60 in five tests is considered passing. If a student's average on the first four tests is 55, what grade must he get on the fifth test to pass?

38. In a single throw of a pair of dice, the probability of throwing the sum 8 is

    (A) $\frac{1}{12}$

    (B) $\frac{1}{9}$

    (C) $\frac{5}{36}$

    (D) $\frac{1}{6}$

39. In how many ways can 3 French and 4 German books be arranged on a shelf so that books in the same language are together, if all the books are different?

    (A) 24
    (B) 72
    (C) 144
    (D) 288

40. If g is a linear function such that $g(1) = 3$ and $g(-1) = 9$, then $g(2)$ equals

41. $(2 + \sqrt{3})(3 - \sqrt{3})$ equals

    (A) $3 - \sqrt{3}$
    (B) 3
    (C) $3 + \sqrt{3}$
    (D) $6 + \sqrt{3}$

42. If $R = \{x : x > 2\}$ and $S = \{x : x < 13\}$, then the number of primes in $R \cap S$ is

    (A) 3
    (B) 4
    (C) 5
    (D) infinite

43. Which statement is *not* logically equivalent to "If a kitten meows, then it is hungry"?

    (A) If a kitten is not hungry, then it does not meow.
    (B) If a kitten is hungry, then it meows.
    (C) A kitten meows only if it is hungry.
    (D) For a kitten to meow it is necessary that it be hungry.

44. If you draw 3 cards from a deck of 52, replacing each before drawing the next, what is the probability that they are all black?

    (A) $\frac{2}{17}$

    (B) $\frac{1}{8}$

    (C) $\frac{1}{6}$

    (D) $\frac{3}{2}$

45. Which statement about primes is false?

    (A) Every odd prime is of the form $2^n - 1$, where n is an integer.
    (B) If a product mn of 2 positive integers is divisible by a prime p, then either m or n is divisible by p.
    (C) Every positive integer can be uniquely expressed as a product of primes, except perhaps for the order in which the factors occur.
    (D) There are an infinite number of primes.

46. The range of $y = \log_2 x$ is

    (A) all positive reals
    (B) all positive numbers
    (C) all reals except $x = 0$
    (D) all real numbers

47. If m and n are odd integers, indicate whether each of the following is even or odd by checking the appropriate box.

Number	Even	Odd
$m + n^2$		
$-m + 2n$		
$2m^2 + n^2$		
$2m + 3n$		

48. If a divided by 4 leaves a remainder of 2, and b divided by 4 leaves a remainder of 3, then when $a + b$ is divided by 4 the remainder is

49. The remainder when $3x^3 + 4x^2 - 5x + 1$ is divided by $(x - 2)$ is

    (A) 3
    (B) 7
    (C) 31
    (D) 51

50. A rational number between the rational numbers p and q, for all p and q, is

    (A) $\dfrac{p - q}{2}$

    (B) $\dfrac{p + q}{2}$

    (C) $\dfrac{q - p}{2}$

    (D) $\dfrac{p}{2}$

51. Which equation has no real root?

    (A) $x^3 + x^2 = 0$
    (B) $4x^4 + 1 = 0$
    (C) $2x^4 - 1 = 0$

    (D) $\dfrac{1}{x} + 1 = 0$

52. Which statement about the intersection of a cubic curve and a line is false?

    (A) They need have no intersection.
    (B) They intersect at least once.
    (C) They may intersect twice.
    (D) They cannot intersect more than three times.

53. Suppose 3 of a dozen apples are bruised and 2 are chosen at random from the dozen. The probability that both are bruised is

    (A) $\dfrac{1}{22}$

    (B) $\dfrac{1}{11}$

    (C) $\dfrac{1}{6}$

    (D) $\dfrac{1}{4}$

54. If 60% of a population reads the *Journal*, 45% reads the *Moon*, and 30% reads both papers, what percent of the population reads neither paper?

55.

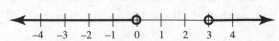

The graph above represents which set?

    (A) $\{x : x < 0 \text{ or } x > 3\}$
    (B) $\{x : 0 < x < 3\}$
    (C) $\{x : x \leq 0 \text{ or } x \geq 3\}$
    (D) $\{x : 0 > x > 3\}$

56. On the given number line, identify the largest value of the function $f(x) = -2(x + 1)^2 + 3$.

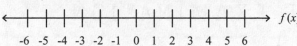

57. If Z is the set of integers, Q the set of rationals, and R the set of reals, then

    (A) $Q \subset Z \subset R$
    (B) $R \subset Q \subset Z$
    (C) $Z \subset Q \subset R$
    (D) $Z \subset R \subset Q$

58. $111_2 + 1_2 =$

    (A) 1110_2
    (B) 1010_2
    (C) 1100_2
    (D) 1000_2

59. A counterexample to the statement "If $ax^2 + bx + c = 0$ has 2 real unequal roots, then $b^2 - 4ac > 3$" is

    (A) $x^2 - 3x + 2 = 0$
    (B) $x^2 - x + 1 = 0$
    (C) $x^2 - 2x + 1 = 0$
    (D) $x^2 - 4x + 3 = 0$

60. Which graph below is not that of a function $y = f(x)$?

    (A)

    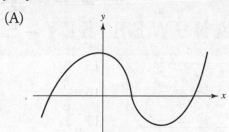

    (B)

    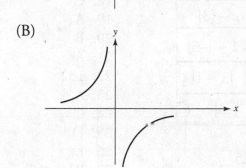

    (C)

    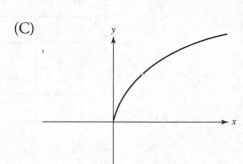

    (D)

    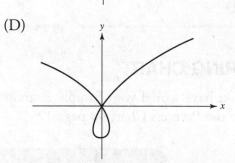

STOP

If there is still time remaining, you may review your answers.

Exam 2

Answer Key—Exam 2

College Mathematics
ANSWER KEY—SAMPLE EXAMINATION 2

1.

2.

$-\lvert 3 \rvert$
$1 - \lvert -3 \rvert$
$\lvert 3 - 1 \rvert$
$\lvert -3 \rvert + 1$

3. C
4. 15
5. D
6. A
7. 7
8. A
9. D
10. A
11. C
12. D
13. C
14. D

15. B
16. $\dfrac{5}{6}$
17. 2
18. C
19. A
20. B
21. A
22. 132
23. A
24. C
25. D
26. D
27. B
28.

√	
√	
	√
√	

29. C
30. C

31. C
32. B
33. A
34. A
35. D
36. A
37. 80
38. C
39. D
40. 0
41. C
42. B
43. B
44. B
45. A
46. D
47.

√	
	√
	√
	√

48. 1
49. C
50. B
51. B
52. A
53. A
54. 25
55. A
56.

57. C
58. D
59. A
60. D

SCORING CHART

After you have scored your Sample Examination 2, enter the results in the chart below; then transfer your score to the Progress Chart on page 12.

	Total Test	Number Right	Number Wrong	Number Omitted
Total:	60			

ANSWER EXPLANATIONS

1. The shaded region consists of elements in R or in the intersection of S and T. Verification is also possible by assigning numbers to the exhaustive disjoint sets, as indicated:

   $R \cup (S \cap T)$
     $= (1,2,4,5) \cup (2,3,5,6 \cap 4,5,6,7)$
     $= (1,2,4,5) \cup (5,6) = 1,2,4,5,6$
   which is the shaded region.

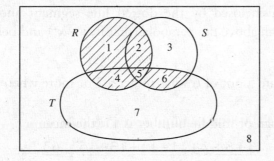

2.

$|3-1|$	$-|3|$
$|-3|+1$	$1-|-3|$
$-|3|$	$|3-1|$
$1-|-3|$	$|-3|+1$

   Note that $|3-1| = |2| = 2$, $|-3|+1 = 3+1 = 4$, $-|3| = -3$, and $1 - |-3| = 1 - 3 = -2$.

3. **(C)** The function $y = \dfrac{4}{(x-1)^2}$ is defined for every real number except 1

   (where the denominator is equal to zero).

4. **(15)** You have $_6C_4$, which equals $_6C_2$ choices; $_6C_2 = \dfrac{6 \cdot 5}{1 \cdot 2} = 15$.

5. **(D)** The contrapositive of $p \rightarrow q$ is $\sim q \rightarrow \sim p$.

6. **(A)** The "favorable" draws are a nickel from bag I and a dime from bag II or a nickel from bag II and a dime from bag I. The probability is, therefore, $\dfrac{3}{5} \cdot \dfrac{5}{6} + \dfrac{1}{6} \cdot \dfrac{2}{5} = \dfrac{17}{30}$.

7. **(7)** Note that $(2 \times 10^3)^2 \times 5 = 4 \times 10^6 \times 5 = 20 \times 10^6$ or 2×10^7.

8. **(A)** If R is the set of reals, then each point in the plane is of the form (x,y) where $(x,y) \in R \times R$.

9. **(D)** $P = \{3,-1\}$; $Q = \{0,-1\}$.

10. **(A)** "$s \rightarrow t$" is symbolic for "if s then t." The negation is "s but not t" or $s \wedge \sim t$.

11. **(C)** If $x > 0$, then $ax^2 + bx + c > 0$. Thus the equation never equals zero for x a positive number. Verify that (A), (B), and (D) can be false.

12. **(D)** Note that if $a = -2$, $b = -1$, then $a < b$ but $a^2 > b^2$.

13. **(C)** $\sqrt{3}$ is not a rational number; a number can be represented by a repeating or terminating decimal if and only if it is rational.

14. **(D)** We divide the area of the wall, in square inches, by the area of a sheet of tiles, in square inches: $\dfrac{5 \times 12 \times 8 \times 12}{10 \times 12} = 48$ sheets.

15. **(B)** The area enclosed by the dotted line segment and dotted arc of the parabola is both above the parabola (that is, $y > x^2$) and below the line (that is, $y < 1 + x$).

16. $\left(\dfrac{5}{6}\right)$ There are 5 out of 6 ways to get a 2 or more when tossing a die.

17. **(2)** The median or middle number is 11; the mean is
$$\frac{3+3+7+11+11+13+15}{7} = \frac{63}{7} = 9.$$

18. **(C)** You have 48 choices. To get a pair, your card must be an ace, king, seven, or three. There are 12 of these left in the deck; therefore the probability is $\dfrac{12}{48}$.

19. **(A)** $g(f(x)) = (2x + 1)^2 - 3 = 4x^2 + 4x + 1 - 3 = 4x^2 + 4x - 2.$

20. **(B)** $x^2 - 2 = 0$ has roots $\pm\sqrt{2}$. Both roots are irrational. Verify that the roots in (A), (C), and (D) are rational.

21. **(A)** The negation of $\exists_x P_x$ (there is a mathematician who is a teacher) is $\forall_x \sim P_x$ (no mathematician is a teacher—literally, "all mathematicians are not teachers").

22. **(132)** The answer is 12×11.

23. **(A)** The die shows a number less than 3 if it shows 1 or 2, with probability $\dfrac{1}{3}$. The coin shows heads with probability $\dfrac{1}{2}$. Multiply probabilities for both events.

24. **(C)** The relevant probabilities are:

P_1 (die shows less than 3) = $\dfrac{1}{3}$,

P_2 (coin shows heads) = $\dfrac{1}{2}$,

P_3 (die shows less than 3 and

coin shows heads) = $P_1 \times P_2 = \dfrac{1}{6}$.

Note that the two events are *independent*.

For the probability that the die shows less than 3 *or* that the coin shows heads but not both, we evaluate

$$P_1 + P_2 - P_3 = \frac{1}{3} + \frac{1}{2} - \frac{1}{6} = \frac{2}{3}.$$

25. **(D)** $a^{-2x} = \dfrac{1}{a^{2x}} = \dfrac{1}{(a^x)^2} = \dfrac{1}{(0.6)^2} = \dfrac{1}{0.36}$.

26. **(D)** The functions are inverses. Graphs of inverses are reflections in the line $y = x$. See question 12, page 340; $\log_2 x$ is shown there in (C), 2^x is shown in (B).

27. **(B)** $5\sqrt{-1} + \sqrt{-4} - \sqrt{-9} = 5i + 2i - 3i = 4i$.

28.

Statement	True	False
$-q < -r$	√	
$pq < pr$	√	
$p(q - r) > 0$		√
$q + p > r + p$	√	

Since $p < 0$ and $q - r > 0$, the product $p(q - r)$ is negative.

29. **(C)** Division by zero is prohibited.

30. **(C)** Since $84 = 4 \cdot 21 = 2^2 \cdot 3 \cdot 7$, the prime factors are 2, 3, and 7; 6 is not a prime number.

31. **(C)** To show this, let $p = q = 3$, for example.

32. **(B)** $g(4) = \dfrac{\sqrt{4-3}}{4} = \dfrac{\sqrt{1}}{4} = \dfrac{1}{4}$. The square root of a positive number is positive, by definition.

33. **(A)** Remember that |x| is positive or zero for all *x*. Its graph is at the right. Can you sketch the graphs in (B), (C), and (D)?

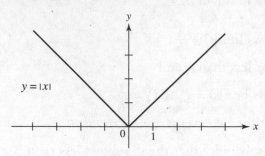

34. **(A)** $S \cap T = \{2\}$. Since there are two elements in *R* and one in $S \cap T$, the Cartesian product $R \times (S \cap T)$ has 2×1 or 2 elements.

35. **(D)** $p \to q$ is equivalent to (A), (B), and (C), and also to "*q* is necessary for *p*," but not to "*p* is necessary for *q*."

36. **(A)** $\log_a\left(\dfrac{u}{v^2}\right) = \log_a u - 2\log_a v = 3 - 2(8) = -13$.

37. **(80)** His total score on the first four tests is 4×55 or 220. If *x* is the score needed on the fifth test in order to average 60 on all 5, then $\dfrac{220 + x}{5}$ must equal 60. So $x = 80$.

38. **(C)** A total of 8 on 1 throw of the pair of dice is obtained in 5 ways (out of 36): 2 and 6, 3 and 5, 4 and 4, 5 and 3, and 6 and 2.

39. **(D)** The 3 French books can be arranged in 3! ways, the 4 German books in 4! ways, and the 2 sets in 2! ways. Multiply $(3! \times 4! \times 2!)$.

40. **(0)** Let $g(x) = ax + b$. Since $g(1) = 3$, we have $a + b = 3$; since $g(-1) = 9$, we have $-a + b = 9$. So $2b = 12$, $b = 6$, and $a = -3$. Then $g(x) = -3x + 6$ and $g(2) = 0$.

41. **(C)** $(2 + \sqrt{3})(3 - \sqrt{3}) = 6 + 3\sqrt{3} - 2\sqrt{3} - 3 = 3 + \sqrt{3}$.

42. **(B)** $R \cap S = \{x : 2 < x < 13\}$. The primes in this set are 3, 5, 7, 11.

43. **(B)** "If *p* then *q*" is logically equivalent to "if not *q*, then not *p*," "*p* only if *q*," and "*q* is necessary for *p*." Choice (B) is the converse of the given statement.

44. **(B)** The answer is the product $\dfrac{1}{2} \cdot \dfrac{1}{2} \cdot \dfrac{1}{2}$.

45. **(A)** 5 is a prime, for example, but there is no positive integer *n* such that $5 = 2^n - 1$.

46. **(D)** Graph (C) on page 336 is for $y = \log_2 x$. Note that its domain is the set of all positive numbers; its range is the set of all reals.

47.

Number	Even	Odd
$m + n^2$	√	
$-m + 2n$		√
$2m^2 + n^2$		√
$2m + 3n$		√

$m + n^2$ is the sum of two odds. Each of the other sums is odd, because each adds an even integer to an odd integer.

48. **(1)** Since there are integers p and q such that $a = 4p + 2$ and $b = 4q + 3$, $a + b$ = $4(p + q) + 5 = 4(p + q + 1) + 1 = 4m + 1$, where m is an integer.

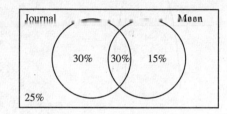

49. **(C)** When $f(x)$ is divided by $(x - a)$, the remainder is $f(a)$.

50. **(B)** Let $p = 1$, $q = 2$ to show that the numbers in (A), (C), (D) are not between p and q.

51. **(B)** $4x^4 + 1 = 0$ is equivalent to $4x^4 = -1$. No real x satisfies this equation, since $4x^4 \geq 0$ for all real x. Find a real root in (A), (C), and (D).

52. **(A)** Every cubic curve and every line intersect at least once and at most three times. Draw several sketches to illustrate this statement.

53. **(A)** The probability is $\dfrac{{}_3C_2}{{}_{12}C_2} = \dfrac{3 \cdot 2}{2 \cdot 1} \div \dfrac{12 \cdot 11}{2 \cdot 1}$ or just $\dfrac{3 \cdot 2}{12 \cdot 11}$.

54. **(25)** Use a Venn diagram to show the percentages of people who read the papers. Subtract from 100 to get the percentage that reads neither paper.

55. **(A)** The hollow circles at 0 and 3 signify *exclusion* of these points.

56.

Note that the largest value of $-2(x + 1)^2$ is $-2(-1 + 1)^2$, or 0. Any value of x other than -1 yields an f, which is less than 3. The graph of $f(x)$ is shown here; its maximum value is 3.

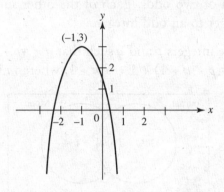

57. **(C)** Every integer is a rational number; every rational number is a real number.

58. **(D)** See question 15 on page 312 and the answer on page 315 for information on adding numbers in base 2.

59. **(A)** $x^2 - 3x + 2 = (x - 1)(x - 2)$, which is zero for $x = 1, 2$. But $b^2 - 4ac = (-3)^2 - 4(2) = 1$, which is not greater than 3.

60. **(D)** For some x-values there is more than one y-value in the graph in (D).

THE SOCIAL SCIENCES—
HISTORY EXAMINATION

Social Sciences—History
ANSWER SHEET—TRIAL TEST

1 Ⓐ Ⓑ Ⓒ Ⓓ Ⓔ   33 Ⓐ Ⓑ Ⓒ Ⓓ Ⓔ   65 Ⓐ Ⓑ Ⓒ Ⓓ Ⓔ   97 Ⓐ Ⓑ Ⓒ Ⓓ Ⓔ
2 Ⓐ Ⓑ Ⓒ Ⓓ Ⓔ   34 Ⓐ Ⓑ Ⓒ Ⓓ Ⓔ   66 Ⓐ Ⓑ Ⓒ Ⓓ Ⓔ   98 Ⓐ Ⓑ Ⓒ Ⓓ Ⓔ
3 Ⓐ Ⓑ Ⓒ Ⓓ Ⓔ   35 Ⓐ Ⓑ Ⓒ Ⓓ Ⓔ   67 Ⓐ Ⓑ Ⓒ Ⓓ Ⓔ   99 Ⓐ Ⓑ Ⓒ Ⓓ Ⓔ
4 Ⓐ Ⓑ Ⓒ Ⓓ Ⓔ   36 Ⓐ Ⓑ Ⓒ Ⓓ Ⓔ   68 Ⓐ Ⓑ Ⓒ Ⓓ Ⓔ   100 Ⓐ Ⓑ Ⓒ Ⓓ Ⓔ
5 Ⓐ Ⓑ Ⓒ Ⓓ Ⓔ   37 Ⓐ Ⓑ Ⓒ Ⓓ Ⓔ   69 Ⓐ Ⓑ Ⓒ Ⓓ Ⓔ   101 Ⓐ Ⓑ Ⓒ Ⓓ Ⓔ
6 Ⓐ Ⓑ Ⓒ Ⓓ Ⓔ   38 Ⓐ Ⓑ Ⓒ Ⓓ Ⓔ   70 Ⓐ Ⓑ Ⓒ Ⓓ Ⓔ   102 Ⓐ Ⓑ Ⓒ Ⓓ Ⓔ
7 Ⓐ Ⓑ Ⓒ Ⓓ Ⓔ   39 Ⓐ Ⓑ Ⓒ Ⓓ Ⓔ   71 Ⓐ Ⓑ Ⓒ Ⓓ Ⓔ   103 Ⓐ Ⓑ Ⓒ Ⓓ Ⓔ
8 Ⓐ Ⓑ Ⓒ Ⓓ Ⓔ   40 Ⓐ Ⓑ Ⓒ Ⓓ Ⓔ   72 Ⓐ Ⓑ Ⓒ Ⓓ Ⓔ   104 Ⓐ Ⓑ Ⓒ Ⓓ Ⓔ
9 Ⓐ Ⓑ Ⓒ Ⓓ Ⓔ   41 Ⓐ Ⓑ Ⓒ Ⓓ Ⓔ   73 Ⓐ Ⓑ Ⓒ Ⓓ Ⓔ   105 Ⓐ Ⓑ Ⓒ Ⓓ Ⓔ
10 Ⓐ Ⓑ Ⓒ Ⓓ Ⓔ   42 Ⓐ Ⓑ Ⓒ Ⓓ Ⓔ   74 Ⓐ Ⓑ Ⓒ Ⓓ Ⓔ   106 Ⓐ Ⓑ Ⓒ Ⓓ Ⓔ
11 Ⓐ Ⓑ Ⓒ Ⓓ Ⓔ   43 Ⓐ Ⓑ Ⓒ Ⓓ Ⓔ   75 Ⓐ Ⓑ Ⓒ Ⓓ Ⓔ   107 Ⓐ Ⓑ Ⓒ Ⓓ Ⓔ
12 Ⓐ Ⓑ Ⓒ Ⓓ Ⓔ   44 Ⓐ Ⓑ Ⓒ Ⓓ Ⓔ   76 Ⓐ Ⓑ Ⓒ Ⓓ Ⓔ   108 Ⓐ Ⓑ Ⓒ Ⓓ Ⓔ
13 Ⓐ Ⓑ Ⓒ Ⓓ Ⓔ   45 Ⓐ Ⓑ Ⓒ Ⓓ Ⓔ   77 Ⓐ Ⓑ Ⓒ Ⓓ Ⓔ   109 Ⓐ Ⓑ Ⓒ Ⓓ Ⓔ
14 Ⓐ Ⓑ Ⓒ Ⓓ Ⓔ   46 Ⓐ Ⓑ Ⓒ Ⓓ Ⓔ   78 Ⓐ Ⓑ Ⓒ Ⓓ Ⓔ   110 Ⓐ Ⓑ Ⓒ Ⓓ Ⓔ
15 Ⓐ Ⓑ Ⓒ Ⓓ Ⓔ   47 Ⓐ Ⓑ Ⓒ Ⓓ Ⓔ   79 Ⓐ Ⓑ Ⓒ Ⓓ Ⓔ   111 Ⓐ Ⓑ Ⓒ Ⓓ Ⓔ
16 Ⓐ Ⓑ Ⓒ Ⓓ Ⓔ   48 Ⓐ Ⓑ Ⓒ Ⓓ Ⓔ   80 Ⓐ Ⓑ Ⓒ Ⓓ Ⓔ   112 Ⓐ Ⓑ Ⓒ Ⓓ Ⓔ
17 Ⓐ Ⓑ Ⓒ Ⓓ Ⓔ   49 Ⓐ Ⓑ Ⓒ Ⓓ Ⓔ   81 Ⓐ Ⓑ Ⓒ Ⓓ Ⓔ   113 Ⓐ Ⓑ Ⓒ Ⓓ Ⓔ
18 Ⓐ Ⓑ Ⓒ Ⓓ Ⓔ   50 Ⓐ Ⓑ Ⓒ Ⓓ Ⓔ   82 Ⓐ Ⓑ Ⓒ Ⓓ Ⓔ   114 Ⓐ Ⓑ Ⓒ Ⓓ Ⓔ
19 Ⓐ Ⓑ Ⓒ Ⓓ Ⓔ   51 Ⓐ Ⓑ Ⓒ Ⓓ Ⓔ   83 Ⓐ Ⓑ Ⓒ Ⓓ Ⓔ   115 Ⓐ Ⓑ Ⓒ Ⓓ Ⓔ
20 Ⓐ Ⓑ Ⓒ Ⓓ Ⓔ   52 Ⓐ Ⓑ Ⓒ Ⓓ Ⓔ   84 Ⓐ Ⓑ Ⓒ Ⓓ Ⓔ   116 Ⓐ Ⓑ Ⓒ Ⓓ Ⓔ
21 Ⓐ Ⓑ Ⓒ Ⓓ Ⓔ   53 Ⓐ Ⓑ Ⓒ Ⓓ Ⓔ   85 Ⓐ Ⓑ Ⓒ Ⓓ Ⓔ   117 Ⓐ Ⓑ Ⓒ Ⓓ Ⓔ
22 Ⓐ Ⓑ Ⓒ Ⓓ Ⓔ   54 Ⓐ Ⓑ Ⓒ Ⓓ Ⓔ   86 Ⓐ Ⓑ Ⓒ Ⓓ Ⓔ   118 Ⓐ Ⓑ Ⓒ Ⓓ Ⓔ
23 Ⓐ Ⓑ Ⓒ Ⓓ Ⓔ   55 Ⓐ Ⓑ Ⓒ Ⓓ Ⓔ   87 Ⓐ Ⓑ Ⓒ Ⓓ Ⓔ   119 Ⓐ Ⓑ Ⓒ Ⓓ Ⓔ
24 Ⓐ Ⓑ Ⓒ Ⓓ Ⓔ   56 Ⓐ Ⓑ Ⓒ Ⓓ Ⓔ   88 Ⓐ Ⓑ Ⓒ Ⓓ Ⓔ   120 Ⓐ Ⓑ Ⓒ Ⓓ Ⓔ
25 Ⓐ Ⓑ Ⓒ Ⓓ Ⓔ   57 Ⓐ Ⓑ Ⓒ Ⓓ Ⓔ   89 Ⓐ Ⓑ Ⓒ Ⓓ Ⓔ   121 Ⓐ Ⓑ Ⓒ Ⓓ Ⓔ
26 Ⓐ Ⓑ Ⓒ Ⓓ Ⓔ   58 Ⓐ Ⓑ Ⓒ Ⓓ Ⓔ   90 Ⓐ Ⓑ Ⓒ Ⓓ Ⓔ   122 Ⓐ Ⓑ Ⓒ Ⓓ Ⓔ
27 Ⓐ Ⓑ Ⓒ Ⓓ Ⓔ   59 Ⓐ Ⓑ Ⓒ Ⓓ Ⓔ   91 Ⓐ Ⓑ Ⓒ Ⓓ Ⓔ   123 Ⓐ Ⓑ Ⓒ Ⓓ Ⓔ
28 Ⓐ Ⓑ Ⓒ Ⓓ Ⓔ   60 Ⓐ Ⓑ Ⓒ Ⓓ Ⓔ   92 Ⓐ Ⓑ Ⓒ Ⓓ Ⓔ   124 Ⓐ Ⓑ Ⓒ Ⓓ Ⓔ
29 Ⓐ Ⓑ Ⓒ Ⓓ Ⓔ   61 Ⓐ Ⓑ Ⓒ Ⓓ Ⓔ   93 Ⓐ Ⓑ Ⓒ Ⓓ Ⓔ   125 Ⓐ Ⓑ Ⓒ Ⓓ Ⓔ
30 Ⓐ Ⓑ Ⓒ Ⓓ Ⓔ   62 Ⓐ Ⓑ Ⓒ Ⓓ Ⓔ   94 Ⓐ Ⓑ Ⓒ Ⓓ Ⓔ
31 Ⓐ Ⓑ Ⓒ Ⓓ Ⓔ   63 Ⓐ Ⓑ Ⓒ Ⓓ Ⓔ   95 Ⓐ Ⓑ Ⓒ Ⓓ Ⓔ
32 Ⓐ Ⓑ Ⓒ Ⓓ Ⓔ   64 Ⓐ Ⓑ Ⓒ Ⓓ Ⓔ   96 Ⓐ Ⓑ Ⓒ Ⓓ Ⓔ

Trial Test

This chapter contains a Trial Test in Social Sciences and History. Take this Trial Test to learn what the actual exam is like, and to determine how you might score on the exam before any practice or review.

The CLEP General Exam in Social Sciences and History measures your knowledge of these areas, including government and political science, geography, economics, psychology, sociology, anthropology, and history (including United States history, Western civilization, and world history).

NUMBER OF QUESTIONS ON THE TRIAL TEST: 125

Time limit: 90 MINUTES

Directions: Each of the questions or incomplete statements below is followed by five suggested answers or completions. Select the one that is best in each case.

1. Membership in the House of Representatives is determined by

   (A) the overall population of the state
   (B) population, but subject to a definite maximum number of members from any one state
   (C) the state as a unit regardless of population
   (D) the number of qualified voters of the state
   (E) all states having the same number of representatives regardless of the size of the state

2. The most important U.S. Supreme Court case affecting membership in the House of Representatives was

   (A) *Brown* v. *Board of Education*
   (B) *Baker* v. *Carr*
   (C) *Jones* v. *Clinton*
   (D) *Schenck* v. *United States*
   (E) *Roe* v. *Wade*

3. In the 19th century, United States Senators were elected by

   (A) popular election
   (B) the state legislatures
   (C) the electoral college
   (D) state conventions
   (E) officials selected from each county in the state

4. The amendment that changed how senators were elected is the

   (A) Thirteenth Amendment
   (B) Fourteenth Amendment
   (C) Fifteenth Amendment
   (D) Seventeenth Amendment
   (E) Nineteenth Amendment

Direct
election of
Senators

5. The period of Japanese history from 1861 to 1945 was marked by

   (A) Japanese isolationism
   (B) the Meiji Restoration and the return to emperor rule
   (C) westernization and modernization
   (D) choices B and C only
   (E) choices A, B, and C

6. Ten men produce 1,000 bushels of tomatoes on ten acres. If ten additional men are hired, the production on the same acreage rises to 1,700 bushels. This phenomenon relates to which one of the following economic concepts?

   (A) Law of diminishing marginal utility
   (B) Supply and demand
   (C) Marginal propensity to consume
   (D) Gross national product
   (E) Law of diminishing returns

7. To the Marxist, profits or surplus value are

   (A) essential to the health of any economy
   (B) payments to the businessman for his labor
   (C) controlled and kept by the capitalists, the bourgeoisie
   (D) the key to a rising standard of living
   (E) constantly increasing in a capitalist society

8. Which of the following can be used to illustrate the cultural impact of China on Japan?

    I. Social and political status of the Samurai class
    II. The Confucian ethical code
    III. Artistic styles in painting, sculpture, and ceramics
    IV. Buddhist religious teaching
    V. Characters used in the written language

    (A) I and II only
    (B) III, IV, and V only
    (C) I, II, III, and IV only
    (D) II, III, IV, and V only
    (E) I, II, III, IV, and V

9. Apes and other higher primates cannot be taught to use highly complex language because

    (A) they are without the biological apparatus of speech
    (B) they are without the ability to learn from communications directed toward them
    (C) they have little mental ability to store or transmit highly abstract ideas
    (D) all of the above
    (E) none of the above

10. The culture concept in social science implies that

    (A) the biological evolution of man is the most important reason for his advances in the past few centuries
    (B) the moral aspects of a thinking, cultured society and people must enlighten its institutions
    (C) the most important lessons for man are to be found in the cultured societies of Europe
    (D) the reason for differences between our own and other societies is that we, as members of our society, learn different things from those that others learn
    (E) art and music are more important than technology in building cultivated tastes

11. The U.S. Supreme Court case *Brown* v. *Board of Education of Topeka, Kansas,* (1954) made a landmark decision over the issue of

    (A) desegregation
    (B) legalized abortion
    (C) religion and the first amendment
    (D) violating the system of checks and balances
    (E) balloting of presidential elections

12. The most advanced primate next to humans are

    (A) baboons
    (B) chimpanzees
    (C) orangutans
    (D) lemurs
    (E) monkeys

13. Which of the following American political figures was unpopular with the democratic followers of Jefferson because of a treaty he had negotiated IN 1794 with England?

    (A) Hamilton Fish
    (B) John Jay
    (C) John Quincy Adams
    (D) James Madison
    (E) Patrick Henry

14. As a result of strong nationalistic movements, which two countries became unified and centralized nations during the 19th century?

    (A) France and Great Britain
    (B) France and Spain
    (C) Czechoslovakia and Finland
    (D) Germany and Portugal
    (E) Italy and Germany

15. Germany violated the neutrality of which of the following nations in both the First and Second World Wars?

    (A) Netherlands
    (B) Norway
    (C) Switzerland
    (D) Belgium
    (E) France

16. The United States Senate has the power to

    Choice 1: approve treaties
    Choice 2: approved appointments of federal judges
    Choice 3: impeach public officials

    (A) Choice 1 only
    (B) Choices 1 and 2 only
    (C) Choices 2 and 3 only
    (D) Choice 3 only
    (E) All three choices

17. A man who lived in a certain country from 1860 to 1960 would have lived through military rule, constitutional monarchy, imperialist expansion, foreign occupation, extraordinary economic development, and a democratic political order that was quickly followed by a long-lasting communist government. The above description best fits which of the countries below?

    (A) Thailand
    (B) China
    (C) Japan
    (D) Egypt
    (E) Brazil

18. The belief that one's culture is the best, better than anyone else's is known as:

    (A) cultural isolation
    (B) cultural universals
    (C) ethnocentrism
    (D) assimilation
    (E) cultural diffusion

19. This totalitarian communist state is currently conducting nuclear tests and has come under the attack of both the United States and the United Nations.

    (A) China
    (B) North Korea
    (C) Iraq
    (D) Hong Kong
    (E) Cuba

20. Anthropologists such as Mary, Louis, and Richard Leakey have provided humankind with a better picture of the evolution of the human race by excavating and reconstructing previous sites of human occupation. This type of anthropology is known as the study of

    (A) cultural anthropology
    (B) physical anthropology
    (C) linguistics
    (D) primatology
    (E) archeology

21. The legal basis for the separation of church and state in the United States is found in the

    (A) First Amendment
    (B) Fifth Amendment
    (C) Tenth Amendment
    (D) The Articles of Confederation
    (E) The Declaration of Independence

22. The American economy is

    (A) pure laissez-faire
    (B) more planned than laissez-faire
    (C) more laissez-faire than planned
    (D) centrally directed as under socialism
    (E) dominated by traditional custom

23. The newest cabinet post made by President Bush since September 11, 2001, is the Department of

    (A) Homeland Security
    (B) Housing
    (C) Terrorism
    (D) Education
    (E) Air Defense

24. "The community is a fictitious body . . . the sum of the several members who compose it." This individualist viewpoint is the basic premise of

    (A) François Quesnay
    (B) Thomas Aquinas
    (C) William Petty
    (D) Jeremy Bentham
    (E) August Comte

25. More characteristic of class than caste is

    (A) vertical mobility
    (B) endogamy
    (C) distinguishing attire
    (D) occupational prohibitions
    (E) prestige differences

26. Both the revolution in Russia in 1917 and the revolution in China in 1949 would have surprised Marx and Engels in that they both were

    (A) highly industrialized capitalistic nations
    (B) followed by democratic elections
    (C) violent proletariat revolutions
    (D) led by the upper landowners that wanted change
    (E) predominantly agrarian-based countries at the time of the revolution

27. The sociological term that reflects such events as the Tiananmen Square incident, the Amritsar Massacre, and the antiwar protests of the 1960s, is

    (A) collective behavior
    (B) primary groups
    (C) civil disobedience
    (D) passive resistance
    (E) rebellion

28. These three concepts—The Common Market, The Eurodollar, and NATO—would indicate that European nations

    (A) are growing further apart, both economically and politically
    (B) are joining together in a common bond of economic and political unity
    (C) have developed a strong military alliance system to reduce the threat from communist Russia
    (D) rely heavily on the United States for economic and political aid
    (E) are becoming economically and politically isolated from the Western world

29. Both Presidents George H. Bush and George W. Bush were involved in the eventual defeat of what dictatorial government?

    (A) Afghanistan
    (B) Cuba
    (C) Iraq
    (D) North Korea
    (E) Libya

30. The only remaining communist Cold War nation still existing in the western hemisphere today is

    (A) Mexico
    (B) Brazil
    (C) South Korea
    (D) Dominican Republic
    (E) Cuba

31. During, the second term of President George W. Bush, his administration was most criticized for its

    (A) support of the right-to-life movement
    (B) invasion of Afghanistan
    (C) failure to prevent the 9–11 disaster
    (D) decision to continue to maintain military forces in Iraq
    (E) friendly relations with communist China

32. Carthage was established as a colony of the

    (A) Greeks
    (B) Phoenicians
    (C) Romans
    (D) Hittites
    (E) Egyptians

33. In the United States at present, the kinship system

    (A) really does not exist
    (B) is formal, highly elaborated, and closely relevant to all the experiences of the family members
    (C) appears only in times of family crises
    (D) puts strong emphasis on the immediate conjugal family
    (E) emphasizes the role of the patriarch

34. Max Weber pointed out that the bureaucratization of society is usually accompanied by

    (A) raising specific educational standards for officeholders
    (B) the decline of the role of "experts"
    (C) greater publicity given to public affairs
    (D) a decline in the role played by intellectuals in public affairs
    (E) a more humane order brought about by efficiency

35. Which of the following developments of the first half of the 20th century seem most clearly to have been forecast in 19th-century Marxian writings?

    (A) The increasing number of people in advanced societies who consider themselves proletarians
    (B) The spread of ownership through the device of corporate stock
    (C) The spread of communism among nonindustrialized peoples
    (D) The rise of wage standards
    (E) Crises of trade and unemployment

36. In the early 1800s, the Industrial Revolution in England and the United States resulted in poor labor conditions for men, women, and children in both factories and mines. By the late 1800s, these conditions had significantly improved. This was because of

    (A) the success of labor unions and pro labor legislation
    (B) the popular growth of communism as an economic system
    (C) capitalists by and large supporting better conditions for the workers
    (D) governments playing a "laissez-faire" policy toward big business
    (E) capitalism being rapidly replaced by socialistic economies

37. The Kentucky and Virginia Resolutions of 1798–1799 were invoked in order to prove the

    (A) right of social revolution
    (B) right of a state to secede when it feels wronged
    (C) right of a state to be the judge of constitutionality
    (D) right to refuse the authority of the Bank of the United States
    (E) right to treat Indians with a strong hand

Questions 38 and 39 refer to a similar time period in history.

38. This location was the site of ancient Mesopotamia and was also called the the cradle of civilization. In order to visit this famous historical site today, one would visit the modern nation of

   (A) Iran
   (B) Turkey
   (C) Pakistan
   (D) Egypt
   (E) Iraq

39. The site referred to in question 38 was located around the rich fertile river valley called the

   (A) Indus River Valley
   (B) Yellow River Valley
   (C) Nile River Valley
   (D) Tigris-Euphrates River Valley
   (E) Congo River Valley

40. Which of the following ideas would Edmund Burke have rejected?

   (A) The specific is to be preferred over the abstract.
   (B) Society can be safely based on reason alone.
   (C) Lawless action is generally destructive.
   (D) It is often an easy jump from democracy to tyranny.
   (E) Society and government are best when the role of human wisdom and human custom are given due respect.

41. Socrates was condemned to death because he

   (A) taught young men to question accepted ideas and practices
   (B) was the teacher of Alexander
   (C) accepted a bribe from the Persians
   (D) denied that there were any fixed standards of good
   (E) taught the Greeks that they were inferior

42. The Edict of Nantes

   (A) outlawed Roman Catholicism in France
   (B) outlawed Protestantism in France
   (C) permitted a limited toleration to Protestants in France
   (D) established freedom of religion in France
   (E) established the doctrine of the trinity in France

43. The patriotic Greek of the 5th century B.C. was primarily loyal to

   (A) the Greek nation
   (B) his emperor
   (C) his religion, which was thought to have no connection with political affairs
   (D) his city-state
   (E) his race

44. The chief object of Spartan education was to develop

    (A) a cultured and artistic citizenry
    (B) good soldiers who were obedient citizens
    (C) an able body of tradesmen
    (D) a select group of priests
    (E) expert technicians

45. "People in the same trade seldom meet together but the conversation ends in a conspiracy against the public, or in some diversion to raise prices." This would most likely be found in the writings of

    (A) John Law
    (B) Adam Smith
    (C) William Petty
    (D) Thomas Mun
    (E) Emile Durkheim

46. The birthplace of democracy was ancient.

    (A) Nero's Rome
    (B) Sparta
    (C) Colonial America
    (D) Pericles' Athens
    (E) Confucius' China

47. "Human history is the chronology of the inevitable conflict between two opposing economic classes." This statement was made by

    (A) John Locke
    (B) Emile Durkheim
    (C) Karl Marx
    (D) Adam Smith
    (E) Francois Quesnay

48. Physicist is to engineer as sociologist is to

    (A) psychologist
    (B) theologian
    (C) social reformer
    (D) historian
    (E) social philosopher

49. The belief that one's patterns of living are superior to those of other groups is termed

    (A) relativism
    (B) ostracism
    (C) ethnocentrism
    (D) assimilation
    (E) totalitarianism

50. As a culture becomes more complex it tends to have within it fewer

    (A) alternatives
    (B) specialties
    (C) universals
    (D) exigencies
    (E) institutions

51. Which one of the following arguments did Malthus try to prove?

    (A) Developments in technology are unlikely to relieve, permanently, the pressure of population on the means of subsistence.
    (B) Poverty is primarily the result of employers' greed.
    (C) Population pressure forces national governments into colonization and imperialistic schemes, which is only proper.
    (D) Intelligent government action, such as subsidies to mothers and taxes on bachelors, can alleviate the effects of the laws of population.
    (E) Poverty is particular to capitalism.

52. United States reaction to the Iraqi invasion of Kuwait in 1990 ultimately resulted in

    (A) the assassination of Saddam Hussein
    (B) United States boycott of oil from Iraq
    (C) United States boycott of oil from Kuwait
    (D) full action of an international military force
    (E) United States position of neutrality in the affair

53. Emile Durkheim described a type of suicide resulting from excessive social integration and called it

    (A) egoistic
    (B) alienative
    (C) altruistic
    (D) anomic
    (E) rational

54. The development of agriculture nearly 12,000–15,000 years ago was a major

    Choice 1: settle permanently in one place
    Choice 2: store surplus food for the winter months
    Choice 3: end malnutrition and famine

    (A) Choice 1 only
    (B) Choice 1 and 2 only
    (C) Choices 2 and 3 only
    (D) Choice 3 only
    (E) All three choices

55. Which of the following usually includes all the others?

    (A) Institutions
    (B) Folkways
    (C) Laws
    (D) Social symbols
    (E) Mores

56. The German Imperial constitution of 1871

    (A) gave Prussia a preferred position in the German union
    (B) was a generally democratic instrument
    (C) declared the equality of all member states
    (D) declared the ruler of Austria to be emperor
    (E) was similar to the British constitution

57. William the Conqueror and the Battle of Hastings of 1066 both played a major role in the development and early history of this nation state.

    (A) Prussia
    (B) Germany
    (C) Spain
    (D) England
    (E) France

58. England and Japan are similar in that they both

    (A) are rich in natural resources
    (B) became imperialistic nations by the late 19th century
    (C) were isolated from the civilized world
    (D) were easily conquered
    (E) saw little benefit in global trade

59. The period of the "Roman peace" (Pax Romana) was

    (A) during the first two hundred years of the Empire
    (B) between the reign of Diocletian and 476 A.D.
    (C) between the last Punic War and the reign of Diocletian
    (D) between the foundation of the Republic and the first Punic War
    (E) during the reign of Charlemagne

60. The Punic Wars were between Rome and

    (A) Macedonia
    (B) Carthage
    (C) Persia
    (D) Athens
    (E) Israel

61. The caliphs were

    (A) the political successors of Mohammed
    (B) prophets of Islam through whom further revelation of God's will was made known
    (C) peoples from Central Asia who adopted the Islamic faith
    (D) a family of Moslem rulers who lived in Spain
    (E) foot soldiers in the armies of Islam

62. The geographical nature of ancient China is such that its mountains, deserts, and plateaus

    (A) have encouraged isolationism and unity among the Chinese people
    (B) made China far more difficult to conquer
    (C) made successful farming highly possible
    (D) allow for a great deal of cultural diffusion
    (E) have welcomed foreigners, making the Chinese culture very diverse

63. The enlightened despots of the 18th century were so styled because they

    (A) saw how important it was to give important concessions to the common people
    (B) were enlightened enough to maintain the monarchic form of government in an age when the people increasingly demanded representation
    (C) were able to expand their domains
    (D) possessed a high degree of learning and a deep belief in religion
    (E) possessed a desire to improve the lot of their subjects and to improve their own education

64. According to Marx and Lenin, the state, in the high stage of communism, will wither away because

    (A) universal coercion will reign over the earth and make national states unnecessary
    (B) the bourgeoisie and proletariat will be able to live in peace without need for the state to mediate between them
    (C) the Communist Party will have consolidated its position to such an extent and rendered the masses so docile that they will no longer need the state
    (D) when there is only one social class, the state, defined as an instrument of class domination, will no longer serve any function and hence will disappear
    (E) the triumphant dialectical process of history will prove statehood to be only a penultimate truth, hence ultimately false in the presence of the final political form, the super-state

65. The Augustinian system of theology held that "Human nature is hopelessly depraved. . . . Only those mortals can be saved whom God for reasons of His own has predestined to inherit eternal life." Which of the following best represents the attitude of the Protestant leaders of the Reformation?

    (A) They knew nothing of Augustine and were ignorant of this idea.
    (B) They strongly opposed this idea since they believed that it would discourage men from doing good works in the hope of winning salvation.
    (C) The idea became very important in the Protestant position.
    (D) They refused to consider the idea, since they thought that Roman Catholic Church fathers such as St. Augustine had no claim to authority.
    (E) They considered it an idea from pagan Rome and without proper Christian charity.

66. The argument most used to support the congressional committee system is that it

    (A) makes sure that minority groups get a fair hearing
    (B) increases congressional control of the executive department
    (C) reduces the cost of lawmaking
    (D) makes possible more careful consideration of bills
    (E) makes sure that presidential wishes will prevail

67. The "heroic age," "time of troubles," "stability," and "decline" are historical concepts found in the historical writings of

    (A) Marx
    (B) Sorokin
    (C) Toynbee
    (D) Becker
    (E) Kant

68. The "id," "ego," and "superego" are all associated with

    (A) Albert Einstein
    (B) Sigmund Freud
    (C) Lewis P. Lipsitt
    (D) Harry Harlow
    (E) Kenneth B. Clark

69. Which country had more of its citizens and soldiers killed in World War II than did the other countries?

    (A) The United States
    (B) Great Britain
    (C) Italy
    (D) France
    (E) USSR

70. Which of the following countries was not in the League of Nations in 1935?

    (A) The United States
    (B) USSR
    (C) The United Kingdom
    (D) France
    (E) Yugoslavia

71. The tearing down of the Berlin Wall in 1989 led to the reunification of which nation?

    (A) Germany
    (B) Scotland
    (C) Berlin
    (D) England
    (E) USSR

72. What Supreme Court decision established the guidelines for the legalization of abortion in the United States?

    (A) *Griswald* v. *Connecticut*
    (B) *Miranda* v. *Arizona*
    (C) *Dred Scott* v. *Sanford*
    (D) *Roe* v. *Wade*
    (E) *Brown* v. *Board of Education*

73. The Soviet Union break-up in 1989 was as result of the

    (A) economic problems coupled with an atmosphere of liberal reform
    (B) horrors of the Stalin era
    (C) successful war effort in Afghanistan
    (D) assassination of Mikhail Gorbachev
    (E) liberal reform that was being initiated in communist China

74. "He (Napoleon) would have liked to establish a colonial empire, but he knew the British fleet ruled the seas, and so, to prevent this vast region from falling to the British, he sold it to the Americans." What was the region called?

    (A) Louisiana
    (B) Florida
    (C) Alaska
    (D) Hawaii
    (E) California

75. The Erie Canal connected

    (A) the Susquehanna and the Potomac
    (B) the Hudson and the Delaware
    (C) Lake Erie and Niagara
    (D) the Hudson and Lake Erie
    (E) Lake Huron and the Ohio

76. Note the following events:

    • Louisiana and Gadsden purchases
    • "54 40 or Fight"
    • Mexican War

    All of the events listed above are associated with

    (A) the Proclamation of Neutrality
    (B) the Monroe Doctrine
    (C) Manifest Destiny
    (D) late-19th-century imperialism
    (E) the American Civil War

Questions 77–78 relate to GRAPH A.

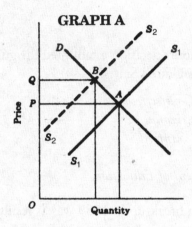

GRAPH A

77. The line $S_2 S_2$ compared to the line $S_1 S_1$ indicates

    (A) an increase in demand
    (B) an increase in supply
    (C) an increase in monopoly
    (D) a decrease in supply
    (E) a decrease in demand

78. The shift from line $S_1 S_1$ to $S_2 S_2$ in Graph A could have occurred because of a

    (A) good year in salt production
    (B) bad year, in that few people desired to purchase "old masters"
    (C) discovery of a new diamond field in Africa
    (D) freeze in the orange groves of Florida
    (E) famine reducing the number of subsistence farmers in a small area of the economy

79. Which of the following statements comes closest to the true Malthusian idea?

    (A) "Population increases rapidly while agriculture lags behind."
    (B) "It is the constant tendency in all animated life to increase beyond the nourishment prepared for it."
    (C) "No progress is possible because of the basic sex drive, which increases population at a geometric rate."
    (D) "Nations which are over-populated must be allowed to expand or send their inhabitants abroad."
    (E) "Things can be produced more cheaply if more is produced."

80. Which practice is most compatible with the supposedly rational nature of "the economic man"?

    (A) Installment buying at high interest
    (B) Borrowing from small loan companies
    (C) Reading a consumer research publication
    (D) Asking a salesman's advice
    (E) Buying more than was on your shopping list

81. During the 1800s, immigrants from this foreign nation initially entered our nation to help meet the demanding need for railroad laborers. Denied entrance into the United States after 1882, it was not until 1943 that they were allowed to become naturalized citizens. These foreign immigrants were

    (A) Italians
    (B) Latinos
    (C) Chinese
    (D) Arabs
    (E) Japanese

82. Little Italy and Chinatown in New York City are both examples of

    (A) ethnocentricity
    (B) cooperatives
    (C) cultural universals
    (D) subcultures
    (E) communal living

83. Under the British Parliamentary Act of 1911, the House of Lords

    (A) lost all power in legislation
    (B) could delay enactment of an ordinary bill for only two years
    (C) was abolished
    (D) was transformed into a house appointed for life terms
    (E) became finally dominant over the House of Commons

84. Besides Israel, which Middle Eastern nation has also been a close ally to the United States?

    (A) Turkey
    (B) Iran
    (C) Libya
    (D) Syria
    (E) Lebanon

85. *Anthropomorphism* is a religious concept meaning

    (A) belief in animal gods
    (B) belief in a god who died and lived again
    (C) rituals in common usage
    (D) attribution of human characteristics to a god or gods
    (E) holding ancestors worthy of worship

86. The behavior expected of any particular group member is his

    (A) role
    (B) status
    (C) performance
    (D) culture
    (E) ideology

87. This political-economic theory is characterized by accumulating wealth (gold and silver) through colonies, an extensive merchant marine, and a favorable balance of trade. This economic concept practiced extensively in Europe during the 16th to 18th centuries was called

    (A) utopian socialism
    (B) marxism
    (C) capitalism
    (D) social darwinism
    (E) mercantilism

88. It was at this time that women participated in the war effort by providing a much needed addition to the industrial labor force. This vital role of the female laborer was to define an entirely new role for women in our society. During which war did women first make their appearance as industrial laborers?

    (A) The Civil War
    (B) The Spanish American War
    (C) World War I
    (D) World War II
    (E) The Viet Nam Conflict

89. From 1845 to 1855 a considerable number of the immigrants to the United States came from

    (A) China
    (B) Ireland
    (C) Greece
    (D) Russia
    (E) Spain

90. As a result of the Congress of Vienna in 1815, Germany

    (A) consisted of thirty-eight states loosely joined in the German Confederation
    (B) was established as a unified state
    (C) existed only as the Holy Roman Empire
    (D) was all included within the bounds of Prussia
    (E) formed a part of the Austrian Empire

91. Under the British system of government, the monarch normally selects a prime minister who commands the support of the

    (A) retiring prime minister
    (B) majority party and with the concurrence of the minority party in the House of Commons
    (C) majority party in the House of Commons
    (D) majority party in the House of Commons and the House of Lords
    (E) commonwealth nations

92. Which country was the moving spirit in organizing the various coalitions against Napoleon?

    (A) Russia
    (B) Austria
    (C) Britain
    (D) Prussia
    (E) Sweden

93. The doctrine of "Manifest Destiny" was most closely associated with which of the following wars involving the United States?

    (A) Civil War
    (B) War of 1812
    (C) World War I
    (D) World War II
    (E) Spanish-American War

94. "Non-slaveholders of the South: farmers, mechanics and working men, we take this occasion to assure you that the slaveholders, the arrogant demagogues whom you have elected to offices of power and profit, have hoodwinked you, trifled with you, and used you as mere tools for the consummation of their wicked designs." These words reflect the viewpoint of this abolitionist newspaper publisher.

    (A) Henry Clay
    (B) Stephen A. Douglas
    (C) William Lloyd Garrison
    (D) George Fitzhugh
    (E) John C. Calhoun

95. "The great object of Jacobinism, both in its political and moral revolution, is to destroy every trace of civilization in the world and force mankind back into a savage state." The Era of the Jacobins, the Committee of Public Safety, and Robespierre are all associated with

    (A) the Declaration of the Rights of Man, 1789
    (B) the National Assembly, 1789–1791
    (C) the Reign of Terror, 1793–1794
    (D) the rise of Napoleon, 1799
    (E) the Stalin purges, 1935–1936

96. "Men, consciously or unconsciously, derive their moral ideas in the last resort from the practical relations on which their class position is based—from the economic relations in which they carry on production and exchange." Which of the following said this?

    (A) Freud
    (B) Goethe
    (C) Kant
    (D) Engels
    (E) Hegel

97. The popular election of U.S. Senators was provided for in the

    (A) Constitution
    (B) Articles of Confederation
    (C) Bill of Rights
    (D) Declaration of Independence
    (E) Seventeenth Amendment

98. The person most responsible for German unification was

    (A) Hitler
    (B) Bismarck
    (C) Von Moltke
    (D) Heine
    (E) Brandt

99. William G. Sumner thought the "social question" (existence of social problems) to be the result of the fact that

    (A) all men are not equally equipped for the onerous struggle against nature
    (B) the virtuous are not ordinarily successful
    (C) political equality is absent
    (D) equality before the law is unattainable
    (E) man knows too little about his society

100. It is difficult for an addict to avoid taking drugs after he has been released from treatment because

    (A) he generally returns to his old circle of drug-using friends
    (B) psycho-physiological dependence on drugs, once established, can never be completely eliminated
    (C) people around him generally expect him to become re-addicted
    (D) Choices A and C only
    (E) Choices A, B, and C

101. The terms *anticlerical* and *worldliness* mean hostility toward the

    (A) business class
    (B) government officials
    (C) white-collar workers
    (D) church
    (E) retail trade

102. Nelson Mandela, F.W. de Klerk, and Bishop Desmond Tutu all are a part of the fight for racial equality in the nation of

    (A) Southern Rhodesia
    (B) Kenya
    (C) India
    (D) Nigeria
    (E) South Africa

103. The Supreme Court has been referred to as a "continuous constitutional convention." The reason for this may be found in the fact that the Supreme Court

    (A) is in session all the time
    (B) changes and enlarges the Constitution by its practice of interpreting the Constitution through its opinions
    (C) is given the right to sit as a constitutional assembly, and to propose, but not ratify or accept, constitutional amendments
    (D) must rule on any proposed amendment regarding its constitutionality
    (E) convokes conventions of high judges which test the Constitution

104. During the 1920s and '30s, Japanese history was marked by the

    (A) growth of democracy
    (B) introduction of industrial development
    (C) return to an isolationist policy
    (D) rise of imperialistic aggression in Asia
    (E) fall of Japan to the Allies

105. Identify the correct chronological order for the origins of the following religions:

    (A) Buddhism, Christianity, Islam
    (B) Confucianism, Islam, Christianity
    (C) Christianity, Zen Buddhism, Confucianism
    (D) Islam, Christianity, Buddhism
    (E) Buddhism, Islam, Confucianism

106. Sadly, the Cold War led to the rise of a number of nations that were split into two, a communist nation and a democratic nation. The only former united nation still existing today with both a communist government and a democratic government is

    (A) Germany
    (B) Viet Nam
    (C) Korea
    (D) the USSR
    (E) Cambodia

107. With the leadership of Nkrumah shortly after the Second World War, this British colony was the first African territory to achieve independence and did so in a somewhat smooth and nonviolent manner. This nation was

    (A) Nigeria
    (B) Ghana
    (C) Ethiopia
    (D) Kenya
    (E) Angola

108. In 2006, the population of the United States reached

    (A) 100 million people
    (B) 200 million people
    (C) 300 million people
    (D) 1 billion people
    (E) 3 billion people

109. In 1298 a.d., he wrote a book that described Cathay and its people. He mentioned strange customs such as the use of paper money, and he told of the wars that Kublai Khan fought with the Japanese. His book inspired later explorers such as Christopher Columbus. Who was the author of this travel book?

    (A) Dante
    (B) Aquinas
    (C) Marco Polo
    (D) Roger Bacon
    (E) Cicero

110. In 1791, the French Constituent Assembly presented France with its first written constitution. This declared France to be

    (A) a limited constitutional monarchy
    (B) an absolute monarchy
    (C) a democracy
    (D) a republic
    (E) a military dictatorship

111. The modern name for what was formerly referred to as Persia is

    (A) Iraq
    (B) Kuwait
    (C) Yemen
    (D) Iran
    (E) Pakistan

112. A general meaning of the term Freudian slip is

    (A) fear of going out in public
    (B) sexual desires toward one's mother
    (C) fear of heights
    (D) an allergic reaction
    (E) the wants and needs of one's subconscious are accidentally expressed

113. This type of sociological study intensely examines many characteristics of one unit (usually a person or people, work group, a community) over a long period of time. This type of investigated behavior study is known as

    (A) the experiment
    (B) the sample survey
    (C) the case study
    (D) the observation
    (E) the control factor

114. If a president were to be impeached, the trial would be in the

    (A) Supreme Court
    (B) Senate
    (C) United States Court of Appeals
    (D) United States District Court
    (E) House of Representatives

115. Religion, rules of conduct, norms, language, and family are all key elements of

    (A) culture
    (B) ethnocentrism
    (C) diversity
    (D) stratification
    (E) domestication

116. Today, the tendency of most American families is toward

    (A) matriarchy
    (B) patriarchy
    (C) elaboration in symbolism supporting the authority of extended kin
    (D) equality of power of husband and wife
    (E) emphasis on the traditional

117. A caste system of social stratification is extremely difficult to maintain in

    (A) an urban society
    (B) a village or rural society
    (C) a highly religious society
    (D) an economically poor society
    (E) a paternalistic society

118. The geographical crossroads of the three monotheistic religions, Judaism, Christianity, and Islam is

    (A) China
    (B) the Western Hemisphere
    (C) Mecca and Medina
    (D) India
    (E) the Middle East

119. The Japanese rulers suppressed Christianity in the 17th century because they

    (A) thought it would divide their people and bring them under the influence of foreign powers
    (B) feared that the peaceful teaching of Christianity would discourage warlike virtues
    (C) believed that Buddhism was the true faith and that all other religions were necessarily false
    (D) said that it was a "white man's" religion
    (E) believed that only God was divine and no man could be

120. Family, religion, and norms are all examples of cultural universals. A cultural universal is

    (A) found only in the Western world
    (B) found predominantly among Asian nations
    (C) when two cultures meet and assimilate into one new culture
    (D) a cultural trait that is common to all societies
    (E) the result of cultural diffusion

121. The writings and viewpoints of Alexis de Tocqueville and Karl Marx would agree that

    (A) the tyranny of the majority was the ominous threat of the future
    (B) organized religion is an important factor in the preserving of liberty
    (C) religion is a good way to calm an oppressed people
    (D) most controversy in modern society would be over property rights and accumulating wealth
    (F) societies with conflicting economic interests can, through compromise and proper institutions, achieve a long life

122. Negative reaction to British rule surfaced in 1857 when rumor had it that rifles were being greased with a mixture of beef and pork fat. This event eventually led to a British colonial rebellion in India called

    (A) Blood Sunday
    (B) the Taiping Rebellion
    (C) the Sepoy Mutiny
    (D) the Gandhi Salt March
    (E) the Tiananmen Square Massacre

123. As the Age of Metternich progressed (1815–1848), which nation came more and more into conflict with Austria and Metternich's political philosophy?

    (A) France
    (B) Russia
    (C) Spain
    (D) England
    (E) Prussia

124. The Twenty-Seventh Amendment to the U.S. Constitution concerns

    (A) equal rights for all citizens, regardless of age, race, background, or sexual orientation
    (B) Congress's authority to raise its own pay
    (C) the voting rights of mentally disabled citizens
    (D) the existence of business monopolies
    (E) Medicare and/or Medicaid being denied to AIDS patients

125. The fall of the Berlin Wall and the collapse of the Soviet Union is best associated with what time period or event below?

    (A) September 11, 2001
    (B) the end of Saddam Hussein in Iraq
    (C) 1989–1991
    (D) the unification of Viet Nam
    (E) the Cuban Missile Crisis of 1962

STOP

If there is still time remaining, you may review your answers.

Social Sciences—History
ANSWER KEY—TRIAL TEST

1. A	26. E	51. A	76. C	101. D
2. B	27. A	52. D	77. D	102. E
3. B	28. B	53. C	78. D	103. B
4. D	29. C	54. B	79. B	104. D
5. D	30. E	55. A	80. C	105. A
6. E	31. D	56. A	81. C	106. C
7. C	32. B	57. D	82. D	107. B
8. D	33. D	58. B	83. B	108. C
9. C	34. A	59. A	84. A	109. C
10. D	35. E	60. B	85. D	110. A
11. A	36. C	61. A	86. A	111. D
12. B	37. C	62. A	87. E	112. E
13. B	38. E	63. E	88. D	113. C
14. E	39. D	64. D	89. B	114. B
15. D	40. B	65. C	90. A	115. A
16. B	41. A	66. D	91. C	116. D
17. B	42. C	67. C	92. C	117. A
18. C	43. D	68. B	93. E	118. E
19. B	44. B	69. E	94. C	119. A
20. E	45. B	70. A	95. C	120. D
21. A	46. D	71. A	96. D	121. D
22. C	47. C	72. D	97. E	122. C
23. E	48. C	73. A	98. B	123. D
24. D	49. C	74. A	99. A	124. B
25. A	50. C	75. D	100. D	125. C

SCORING CHART

After you have scored your Trial Examination, enter the results in the chart below, then transfer your score to the Progress Chart on page 12. As you complete the Sample Examinations later in this part of the book, you should be able to achieve increasingly higher scores.

Total Test	Number Right	Number Wrong	Number Omitted
125			

ANSWER EXPLANATIONS

1. **(A)** The distribution of members in the House of Representatives is determined on the basis of population. The Constitution in Article I, Section 2, Clause 3 provides: "Representatives shall be apportioned among the several states which may be included within this Union according to their respective numbers."

2. **(B)** The case of *Baker* v. *Carr,* decided in 1962, held that federal courts could take jurisdiction of challenges to the apportionment formulas from states for membership in the House of Representatives. The decision was a marked change from past decisions, wherein courts held that such cases were "political" in nature and should be resolved by legislatures instead of by courts.

3. **(B)** In the 19th century, United States Senators were elected by the state legislatures. Article I, Section 3, Clause 1 of the original Constitution reads: "The Senate of the United States shall be composed of two Senators from each state, chosen by the legislature thereof."

4. **(D)** The amendment providing for popular election of United States Senators was 17, ratified in 1913. The ratification reflected the populist spirit, which sought to make the selection of Senators more democratic, thereby removing power of selection from the state legislatures. The power of the state legislatures was described in the original Constitution of 1787.

5. **(D)** With the end of the Tokogawa Shogunate also came the end of its anti-Western and pro-isolationist policies. The restoration of the Meiji rule, a period of Japanese modernization, westernization, and aggressive foreign policy, became the direction of the new government. As a result, Japan entered the late 19th and early 20th century as a world power. Eventually Japan joined with Mussolini and Hitler in a military fascist imperialistic pact.

6. **(E)** The law of diminishing returns states that an input of production (such as labor) and the output it helps to produce tend to diminish as more units of the input factor are applied to the same number of the other factors of production (land and capital).

7. **(C)** Marx says surplus value or profits are controlled and kept by the capitalists. The proletariat or workers sees nothing more than subsistent-level salary.

8. **(D)** Japanese culture and values were strongly influenced both by Chinese Confucianism and Buddhism (Ch'an Buddhism, for example, was transmuted into Zen in Japan). Artistic styles, often transmitted through Korea, frequently reflected Japanese adaptations of Chinese sources. Chinese ideographs were adopted as Japan's first written language. However, the exalted social and political status of the Samurai class as warrior scholars had no equivalent in Ancient China, where soldiers and warlords were held in low esteem by the mandarin scholar gentry.

9. **(C)** Apes and other primates cannot be taught to use highly complex language because they have little mental ability to store or transmit highly

abstract ideas. Some higher primates have been shown to possess potential for learning from communications directed toward them.

10. **(D)** The culture concept in social science implies that the reason for differences between our own and other societies is that we, as members of our society, learn different things from those that others learn. This is the sense in which sociologists use the term *culture*.

11. **(A)** *Brown* v. *Board of Education of Topeka, Kansas*, in 1954 was a landmark decision in that it was the most important pro–civil rights decision in ending segregation in U.S. public schools. As a result of this decision, the process of desegregation of public schools, particularly in the South, was put into play.

12. **(B)** Both the chimpanzee and the gorilla are, next to man, the most advanced form of primate. The size of the chimpanzee brain is one-third that of man's brain today, which was the actual size of man's brain two million years ago when Australopithecus traveled as one of the earliest stages of human evolution.

13. **(B)** John Jay was unpopular with the Democratic followers of Jefferson. In 1794, Jay negotiated a treaty with England. The treaty helped keep America out of the war in Europe between France and England. The Jeffersonians thought that the treaty was favorable to England. They favored France in the European war.

14. **(E)** The unification of Italy, called Risorgimento, was achieved under the leadership of Count Camillo Cavour. Victor Emmanuel II was proclaimed king of a united Italy in 1861. German unification was accomplished mainly through the efforts of Otto von Bismarck. King William I of Prussia was proclaimed emperor of a united Germany in 1871.

15. **(D)** German armies attacked neutral Belgium in 1914 at the beginning of World War I and again in May 1940, early in World War II. Switzerland remained independent in both wars. The neutrality of the Netherlands and of Norway was not violated in World War I. France was aligned against Germany in both wars.

16. **(B)** According to our Constitution, the Senate has the power to approved treaties by a 2/3 vote as well as approve the appointment of federal judges by a majority vote. As for removing a President from office, it is the job of the House to bring charges of impeachment. It is the function of the Senate to sit as the judge and jury thus it is the courtroom for the trial.

17. **(B)** At the beginning of this hundred-year period (1860), China was an absolute monarchy ruled by an emperor. After the Revolution of 1912, China became a republic. In the interim, much of Chinese territory was under foreign occupation. In 1948, Chiang Kai-shek became president under a democratic constitution. One year later, communist forces under Mao Tsetung drove his armies off the mainland and established the Communist People's Republic of China.

18. **(C)** Ethnocentricity is the belief that one culture is superior to another. It is the arrogant attitude that all cultures periodically express. The Yankees are the

best; America is the best nation in the world. The danger of this practice is that we can become prejudiced and subjective toward other cultures. An example of this is Kipling's poem "White Man's Burden" and the attitude that the civilized Western nations (Caucasians) were superior to the Asian and African cultures.

19. **(B)** During the first decade of the 21st century, serious nuclear testing was being conducted by communist North Korea. One of the few communist countries that still remains after the end of the Cold War, North Korea continued to stress the global community as well as the United Nations with their bold attempt to test nuclear weapons.

20. **(E)** While the Leakey family were also physical anthropologists finding numerous remains of human skulls and body parts, the question really deals with the digging up and excavating of human remains. This is known as the study of archeology.

21. **(A)** The First Amendment states: "Congress shall make no law respecting an establishment of religion, or prohibiting the free exercise thereof . . . . " This is the legal basis for the separation of church and state in the U.S.

22. **(C)** The American economy is described as a "free enterprise" system. This would be completely laissez-faire except that there is planning under such agencies as the Federal Reserve System, as well as in committees of Congress and in the various executive departments.

23. **(E)** As a result of September 11th, 2001, and the attack on the World Trade Center, President Bush initiated the creation of a new cabinet post called Homeland Security. This was in response to terrorism and terrorists attacks on the United States.

24. **(D)** Jeremy Bentham (1748–1832), English social philosopher, was the leader of a group called the Utilitarians. He held that each person guides his or her conduct entirely by self-interest.

25. **(A)** In a class system, movement from one class to another (vertical mobility) is possible. In a caste system, endogamy (marriage restrictions), distinguishing attire, occupational prohibitions, and prestige differences tend to prevail.

26. **(E)** Had Karl Marx lived at the time of either the Russian Revolution (1917) or the Chinese Revolution (1949), he would have been dismayed at what would emerge in nonindustrial/agrarian-typed economies. The subsequent revolutions that followed including that of Cuba, Korea, and Viet Nam further support that communism seems to thrive best in agriculture-based societies.

27. **(A)** Collective behavior is a sociological behavior that men and women experience when they are in groups. When collective behavior occurs, individuals that join the group experience intense emotional contagion and are more than willing to follow the direction of the group. Civil rights protests and antiwar protests in the 1960s are both excellent examples of collective behavior.

28. **(B)** With the end of World War II and the rise of communist Eastern Europe, most democratic European nations have become members of both of these organizations and the free nations of Western Europe took steps to develop a closer bond. The goal here was to develop closer ties both politically and economically. Thus, NATO was created along with the development of the European Economic Community or Common Market. Today both organizations have continued to grow, and in particular, the EC (European Community) has become a powerful economic force in world trade.

29. **(C)** Both President George H. Bush and President George W. Bush were involved in the defeat of Iraq in two separate wars. In 1991, Kuwait was invaded by Iraq, but within a short time, a coalition army (Desert Storms) freed Kuwait. Despite a civil war that followed the removal of Iraq's forces from Kuwait, Saddam Hussein remained in power. It was not until the invasion of Iraq by President George W. Bush in 2002 that dictator Saddam Hussein was removed from power.

30. **(E)** The only remaining communist Cold War nation still existing in the Western Hemisphere today is Cuba. The failing health of Cuban leader Fidel Castro who took power in a communist revolution in 1959 leads many Westerners to hope for new and more positive future for the Cuban people.

31. **(D)** The successful invasion of Iraq and the subsequent removal of Saddam Hussein from power has been followed by a far less successful occupation by U.S. military forces. Continued terrorism and guerilla warfare continued throughout the second administration of George Bush. The congressional and gubernatorial elections of November 2006 left a mandate for a definite change in Iraq. The Republican Party and the Bush administration lost control of Congress in the 2006 election and thus represented a mandate to bring our troops home.

32. **(B)** Carthage was established as a colony in North Africa by the Phoenicians about 875 B.C. It was situated opposite Sicily near present-day Tunis.

33. **(D)** In the United States at present, the kinship system puts strong emphasis on the immediate conjugal family, that is, the family consisting of husband, wife, and children.

34. **(A)** Max Weber (1864–1920), German sociologist, described the ideal type of bureaucratic structure in his *Essays in Sociology*. He noted that raising specific standards for officeholders went hand in hand with the bureaucratization of society. To Weber, the bureaucratic society, despite its faults, represented an advance over its predecessors.

35. **(E)** In his writings, particularly in his major work entitled *Das Kapital*, which was published in three volumes between 1867 and 1894, Karl Marx predicted the downfall of capitalism because of its inherent contradictions. This included, in his view, both mass unemployment and wars among the capitalist nations for control of resources and trade.

36. **(C)** The early years of the Industrial Revolution witnessed harsh labor conditions in the mines and factories. Although utopian socialism and scientific

socialism offered some possible solutions, it was, in the end, labor unions and legislation that brought better working conditions for the newly rising working class. England and the United States were the first two industrial nations of the world and were also democratic. Thus, it was the very nature of capitalistic democracy that gave rise to the pro labor legislation and the growth of labor unions; these two factors brought relief to the labor force and continued to provide more and more rights and protection for the working class.

37. **(C)** The Kentucky and Virginia Resolutions of 1798–1799 were drafted by Jefferson and Madison. They were passed by the legislatures of Kentucky and Virginia. They declared the Alien and Sedition Acts, passed by Congress in 1798, to be unconstitutional.

38. **(E)** Ancient Mesopotamia was the site of 'the cradle of civilization." Man's earliest known cities and thus civilizations emerged in this area. This included such cultures as the Hittites, Sumerians, Babylonians, and many others.

39. **(D)** The area bordered by the Tigris and Euphrates rivers was known as Mesopotamia, "the land between the two rivers." The area is in present-day Iraq.

40. **(B)** Edmund Burke (1729–1797), English statesman and political philosopher, would have rejected the idea that society can be safely based on reason alone. Burke emphasized the need for gradual and orderly change and the significance of historical antecedents in sound social and political development.

41. **(A)** Socrates was condemned to death as a threat to Athens because he taught young men to question accepted ideas. The story of his accusation, trial, and conviction is related by Plato in his dialogue *Apology.* The last hours of Socrates' life are described by Plato in the dialogue *Phaedo.*

42. **(C)** The Edict of Nantes was issued by King Henry IV of France in 1598 after a series of bloody wars between Protestants and Catholics. It allowed Protestantism in towns where it was the chief form of worship but barred it from Paris and its surroundings.

43. **(D)** In the 5th century B.C., Greece consisted of a number of city-states, that is, cities and their surroundings. Each citizen was loyal to his city-state such as Athens, Sparta, and Thebes, not to Greece. The cities often fought against each other.

44. **(B)** Sparta was one of the leading city-states in ancient Greece. It was famous for its army. Sons of the ruling class were trained to be soldiers. Only these warriors, called Spartiates, had legal and civil rights.

45. **(B)** Adam Smith (1723–1790) is best known for his classic work *An Inquiry into the Nature and Causes of the Wealth of Nations* (1776). He showed great insight into the operation of economic forces, including the tendency of tradesmen to seek control of the market.

46. **(D)** The birthplace of democracy was first developed and practiced in Athens by Pericles. The foundations to Roman democracy, English democracy and even American democracy can be said to have been inspired by the famous leader of Athens, Pericles.

47. **(C)** Karl Marx (1818–1883) predicted increasing tension between the capitalist class and the working class. The other four ideas are included in his description of capitalism in his three-volume work entitled *Das Kapital.*

48. **(C)** The physicist does research and develops the theoretical basis for the science of physics. The engineer makes practical applications of the physicist's findings. The sociologist does research and develops the theoretical basis for the social science of sociology. The social reformer puts the theories of the sociologist into practice.

49. **(C)** *Ethnocentrism* is the attitude or belief that the way of life of one's own group is superior to that of any other group. *Relativism* is the view that ethical truths depend on the group holding them. *Ostracism* means exclusion from the group.

50. **(C)** Primitive cultures are relatively monolithic. Virtually all behavior is prescribed and universally practiced. More complex cultures accommodate numerous variations in behavior. Hence, they tend to have fewer universals.

51. **(A)** Thomas R. Malthus (1766–1834) wrote the famous *Essay on Population* (1798). He opposed an increase in wages, arguing that it only encouraged larger families. His thesis was that population increased much faster than the food supply. This would not be relieved by developments in technology.

52. **(D)** Led by U.S. forces, Italy, Britain, France, and Saudi Arabia pushed Saddam Hussein's Iraqi invasion forces out of Kuwait in Operation Desert Storm.

53. **(C)** Emile Durkheim (1858–1917), French sociologist, wrote a book entitled *Suicide* in 1897. He analyzed the psychological bases of social behavior. He used the term *altruistic* to describe a type of suicide resulting from excessive social integration.

54. **(B)** The development of agriculture, also known as the Neolithic Revolution, first occurred about 12,000 B.C. It was a major event in human history in that it enabled humankind to settle permanently in one place, end a nomadic lifestyle, and be able to store surplus food for the tough winter months. Even the success of the Industrial Revolution continued to provide a better standard of living and a far better food supply. Yet, this did not end world malnutrition and famine. This economic and social factor has unfortunately continued to the present day.

55. **(A)** In sociology, each of the following is classified as an institution: folkways, laws, social symbols, and mores.

56. **(A)** The German Imperial constitution of 1871 went into effect after the defeat of France in the Franco-Prussian War. Prussia became the dominant state under the constitution. The king of Prussia became Emperor Wilhelm I of Germany.

57. **(D)** William I (the Conqueror) of England is also known in history as Duke William II of Normandy. His army crossed the English Channel and de-

feated the English at the Battle of Hastings in 1066 A.D. He ruled England as William I until his death in 1087.

58. **(B)** During the late 1800s/early 1900s, these two island nations turned to the sea for imperialistic expansion. This need for colonies was spurred on by the continued demands for an industrial society. Britain expanded its empire by becoming heavily involved in Africa. Japan, under the Meiji Restoration, began an aggressive program of modernization so that it too would have its "place in the sun." Japan built a powerful navy and quickly began to expand its empire in southeast Asia.

59. **(A)** The period of the "Roman Peace" (*Pax Romana*) was during the first two hundred years of the Roman Empire. The Empire lasted for five hundred years, from about 31 B.C. to 476 A.D. All the lands around the Mediterranean were part of the Empire. The power and efficiency of the Roman legions kept peace throughout the Empire.

60. **(B)** The Punic Wars (264 B.C.–146 B.C.) were fought between Rome and Carthage. Carthage was founded, as a colony, by the Phoenicians. The Latin word for Phoenicia is *Punicus.*

61. **(A)** In the Islamic religion, the caliph is the religious head of the government as the agent of God. When Mohammed, the Prophet, died, Abu Bakr was chosen as first caliph. Later, Islam split, and different caliphs claimed to be God's agent.

62. **(A)** The geographical nature of China has always encouraged cultural isolation. Until recently, China's mountains to the west and south (Himalayas), its plateaus to the north, its deserts to the northwest, and the Pacific Ocean to the east have provided it with a geographical wall that isolated it from other societies (the Great Wall was added to complete the wall of isolation to the northeast). As a result, despite its size, China developed as one distinct culture.

63. **(E)** The enlightened despots of the 18th century—Joseph II of Austria, Catherine II of Russia, and Frederick II of Prussia—wished to improve both the lot of their impoverished subjects and their own education.

64. **(D)** Marxism sees history in terms of class struggle with the state as an instrument of the dominant class. In the current (final) stage the bourgeoisie is destroyed by the proletariat. With only one class in society, the state will have no function and will disappear.

65. **(C)** Augustine (354–430) taught that divine grace, not human effort, was the source of salvation. This doctrine, called predestination, was a key tenet of the theology of John Calvin (1509–1564) and other leaders of the Protestant Reformation.

66. **(D)** Under the committee system, all bills introduced in the Senate or House of Representatives are referred to the committee in that chamber that is charged with consideration of the particular subject of the bill. Members of each committee specialize in that committee's particular area of legislation so that bills receive special analysis before they are reported to the House or Senate.

67. **(C)** Arnold J. Toynbee, English historian, wrote the scholarly twelve-volume *A Study of History* (1933–1961). He described twenty-one historic civilizations. In his study he found that each undergoes a "heroic age," a "time of trouble," "a period of stability," and a final "decline."

68. **(B)** Sigmund Freud is the founder of psychoanalysis. In 1900, he wrote his book *The Interpretation of Dreams* in which he stressed the role of dreams and the unconscious. One of his most famous concepts was his division of the "self" into the "id, the ego and the superego." His idea and terminology became part of everyday American culture and language.

69. **(E)** The USSR suffered more than 7 million military deaths in World War II. Vast areas of the Soviet Union were overrun by the German armies. Leningrad survived a terrible siege. In addition to the military losses, the USSR lost 13 million civilians in the war for a total of 20 million, by far the heaviest losses of all nations in the conflict.

70. **(A)** Even though President Woodrow Wilson was the architect of the League, the Senate of the United States refused to approve U.S. membership. So the United States did not join the League of Nations.

71. **(A)** East and West Germany were reunited for the first time since World War II after the Berlin Wall was torn down, symbolizing the collapse of Communism in East Germany.

72. **(D)** The *Roe* v. *Wade* decision of 1973 permitted an abortion during the first trimester.

73. **(A)** The Soviet Union break-up in 1989 was larger a result of the economic problems coupled with an atmosphere of liberal reform that was initiated by Mikhail Gorbachev and his programs of glasnost and perestroika. The failure to win in Afghanistan led to further political unrest.

74. **(A)** The region was called Louisiana. This vast territory between the Mississippi River and the Rocky Mountains was sold to the United States in 1803 by Napoleon for $15,000,000. Thirteen states or parts of states were later carved out of this purchase.

75. **(D)** The Erie Canal extended from Albany on the Hudson River westward to Buffalo on Lake Erie. It was formally opened in October 1825.

76. **(C)** Manifest Destiny was a concept developed during the early to mid-1800s in America. It was a belief that America had the natural right to expand its borders west to the Pacific Ocean, north to Canada, and south to Mexico.

77. **(D)** In the graph, the line S_1S_1, moves to S_2S_2 because of an additional cost to the producer. This additional cost causes a decrease in supply represented by movement of the supply curve from S_1S_1 to S_2S_2.

78. **(D)** The shift from S_1S_1 to S_2S_2 which represents a decrease in supply (question #77 above) could have been caused by a freeze in the orange groves in Florida. It could also be caused by a voluntary decrease resulting, for example, from the imposition of a new tax on the producer.

79. **(B)** The concept "It is the constant tendency in all animated life to increase beyond the nourishment prepared for it" is the basic premise of *An Essay on the Principles of Population* (1798). Malthus believed that this tendency would be counteracted by war, famine, disease, or birth control, which he called "moral restraint."

80. **(C)** If "economic man" were to act according to supposedly rational nature, he might well subscribe to a consumer research publication, but he would definitely not act as described in any of the other four choices.

81. **(C)** The Chinese Exclusion Act of 1882 was extended and made permanent in 1902. Chinese immigration to the United States was prohibited, and Chinese could not become naturalized citizens. The law was changed in 1943 to allow Chinese in the United States to become naturalized citizens.

82. **(D)** Subcultures are "cultures within a culture." Within the mother culture, offshoots sometimes develop. The hippies of the 1960s, Chinatown, Little Italy, and the Amish are all subcultures. They have their own unique style of living yet also adhere to some of the traits of mother culture America.

83. **(B)** Prime Minister Herbert Asquith forced the House of Lords to give up its veto power by voting for the Parliament Act of 1911. The House of Lords could still hold up an ordinary bill for two years but no longer.

84. **(A)** Since the end of World War II, Israel and Turkey have been close allies to the United States. Israel has been a symbol of democracy in an otherwise unfriendly Islamic region and Turkey has been a key ally during the era of the Cold War.

85. **(D)** The word *anthropomorphic* comes from the Greek, meaning human form. Anthropomorphism as a religious concept means giving human form or characteristics to a god or goddess. This was a key aspect of the religion of the ancient Greeks.

86. **(A)** The term *role* is used in sociology to mean the way a person is expected to behave in a particular group, i.e., family, work group, school, church, or club. Roles are more formalized in primitive societies than they are, for example, in Europe and America.

87. **(E)** During the first wave of exploration and colonialism (1500s–1700s), mercantilism emerged as both a political and economic theory for the European world. It is characterized by the accumulation of wealth (gold and silver), the building of colonial empires, the creation of extensive merchant marines, and the goal of maintaining a favorable balance of trade.

88. **(D)** It was during World War II that women emerged as an important part of the American labor force. Women participated in the war effort by working in defense industries. This entirely new role for women provided the initiative to break the pattern of the traditional role of the female. Some say it may be considered the beginning of the women's lib movement.

89. **(B)** The decade, 1845–1855, marked a mass migration of Irish immigrants to the United States. This was a direct result of the potato famine taking place in Ireland at that time. Prejudice toward these new Catholic Americans resulted in the origins of the KKK.

90. **(A)** The Congress of Vienna (1814–1815) reorganized Europe after the Napoleonic Wars. The Holy Roman Empire ceased to exist. Thirty-eight states were loosely joined in the German Confederation.

91. **(C)** Under the parliamentary system of government developed by the British, the prime minister is the leader of the majority in the House of Commons. The appointment of the prime minister by the monarch is a mere formality.

92. **(C)** Britain was the moving spirit in organizing the various coalitions against Napoleon. The Quadruple Alliance of 1814, consisting of Russia, Prussia, Austria, and Britain, was organized by Viscount Castlereagh, the British foreign minister. Their combined armies, led by the British duke of Wellington, defeated Napoleon at the Battle of Waterloo in Belgium (1815).

93. **(E)** "Manifest Destiny" was the belief of American expansionists that it was the obvious fate of the United States to spread its system of democracy. The term was used to justify the annexation of Texas, the acquisition of the Oregon territory, the purchase of Alaska, and, finally, the involvement in the Spanish-American War.

94. **(C)** William Lloyd Garrison (1805–1879) was a militant abolitionist. He was publisher of the Boston abolitionist newspaper, *The Liberator*. In the first issue (Jan. 1, 1831), he announced his intention to fight against slavery and said: "I will not retreat a single inch—AND I WILL BE HEARD."

95. **(C)** When the radicals (Jacobins led by Danton and Robespierre) of the French Revolution got control of the National Assembly, in 1793, they launched the Reign of Terror. The Gran Terror, as it was also called, was done to eliminate any opposition to the so-called new democracy. It began with the execution of both the king and queen and continued for nearly a year until the Jacobin radicals were removed from power.

96. **(D)** These were the ideas of Friedrich Engels (1820–895). He was co-author, with Karl Marx, of the *Communist Manifesto* (1848). He collaborated with Marx in the latter's great work, the three-volume *Das Kapital*.

97. **(E)** The Seventeenth Amendment to the U.S. Constitution, adopted in 1913, reads: "The Senate of the United States shall be composed of two Senators from each state, elected by the people thereof." The words "elected by the people thereof" replaced the words "chosen by the legislature thereof" in the original Constitution.

98. **(B)** Bismarck was the chief "architect" of German unification. His use of a "blood and iron" policy led to three wars, the Danish War (1864), the Austro-Prussian War (1866), and the Franco-Prussian War (1870–1871). Consequently, Austria and France no longer remained as obstacles to the German states becoming a united nation in 1871.

99. **(A)** The idea that social problems derive from the fact that all men are not equipped for the onerous struggle against nature was developed by the pioneer American sociologist William Graham Sumner (1840–1910). His classic work, *Folkways,* was published in 1907.

100. **(D)** Addicts usually return to their old circle of friends who expect them to become readdicted, but psycho-physiological dependence on drugs can be completely eliminated as evidenced by the fact that drug treatment centers have on their staffs former drug addicts who have been cured.

101. **(D)** The term *anticlerical* means hostility toward the church. The word *cleric* is derived from the Latin *clericus,* meaning a member of the clergy.

102. **(E)** Bishop Desmond Tutu and Nelson Mandela were black nationalists that played a key role in the liberation of white-controlled South Africa. From the 1980s and into the 1990s, Mandela and F.W. de Klerk, worked together in the transformation of the republic into a politically shared government of both white and black leaders; apartheid officially ended in by the mid 1990s.

103. **(B)** The U.S. Supreme Court interprets the Constitution in difficult cases. Its decisions are given in the form of "opinions," both majority and dissenting. These opinions often have the effect of changing or enlarging the Constitution. Hence, the court may be considered a continuous constitutional convention.

104. **(D)** Immediately after World War I, Japan stepped up its imperialistic policies. Its navy became one of the three largest in the world, and with it, Japan began the conquest of other Asian cultures, including Manchuria and shortly thereafter, mainland China.

105. **(A)** Buddhism developed as a response to Hinduism and spread from India to China in the 3rd century B.C. Several centuries later, Christianity emerged in the Middle East, and was later followed by Islam in the 7th century A.D.

106. **(C)** Sadly, the Cold War led to a number of nations that were split into two, a communist nation and a democratic nation. The only former nation still existing today with both a communist government in the north and a democratic government in the south is that of Korea. Currently, communist North Korea continues to create world tension with their persistence to conduct nuclear tests.

107. **(B)** It was with the end of World War II that Ghana began the African movement toward a national independence. Great Britain spearheaded a peaceful transition of Ghana from a colony to a nation-state in 1957. Shortly thereafter, many other African nations also began to achieve their independence.

108. **(C)** Late in 2006, the population of the United States reached 300 million people. For the past several decades, senior citizens continue to be the largest growing group of Americans.

109. **(C)** Marco Polo, 13th-century merchant and traveler, was born in Venice. He traveled overland to China and reached Peking in 1275. He remained

there twenty years. On his return to Venice he wrote an account of his travels and of Kublai Khan, China's ruler.

110. **(A)** The first written constitution, presented in France in 1791 by the Constituent Assembly, vested sovereign power in the Legislative Assembly. The king was given only a suspensive veto power by which legislation desired by the Assembly could be postponed.

111. **(D)** The modern name for what was formerly referred to as Persia is Iran. After World War I, Turkey, and to a lesser extent its neighbor Persia, experienced revolutions. In 1935, to emphasize its break with the past, Persia took the name of Iran.

112. **(E)** A Freudian slip deals with the innermost subconscious thoughts that surface often when one least expects it.

113. **(C)** A case study is like an ongoing diary that records details of specific individuals or groups over a long period of time. A common tool to the sociologists, it examines closely the behavior of that group or individual. Many case studies are used in education to better understand student behavior.

114. **(B)** If a president were to be impeached, the trial would be in the Senate. Article I, Section 3, Clause 6 provides: "The Senate shall have the sole power to try all impeachments."

115. **(A)** Religion, rules of conduct, norms, language, and family are just some of the key elements of culture. All societies have what is known as cultural universals, which are the basic ingredients common to all cultures throughout the world.

116. **(D)** American culture is in flux and is moving toward equality of power of husband and wife. It is moving away from emphasis on the traditional, away from patriarchy, but not toward matriarchy.

117. **(A)** A caste system of social stratification requires that each individual be easily identified by caste and that he or she remain for life within the caste of birth. In an urban society, individuals tend to become anonymous, intermarry more readily, and thus destroy caste structure.

118. **(E)** The crossroads of the three monotheistic religions is the Middle East. The holy cities of Jerusalem, Bethlehem, Canaan, Mecca, and Medina are all in the Middle East. The birthplace of Christ and Mohammed as well as the Jewish promised land are all, in fact, in close Middle Eastern proximity.

119. **(A)** Christianity had been brought to Japan in 1549 by St. Francis Xavier. For a century, it prospered. Then, in the 17th century, it was violently suppressed. Japan's rulers chose isolation for two centuries. They feared that Christianity, a foreign influence, would be harmful to Japan.

120. **(D)** When introducing the term *culture*, we often refer to cultural universals, which are those traits that are similar to all cultures in the world. Several examples are family, religion, norms (folkways/mores), and government.

121. **(D)** Alexis de Tocqueville (1805–1859), French writer, traveled in America during the 1830s. In his *Democracy in America* (1835) he described, with approval, the political and economic growth he saw. He would agree with the economist Karl Marx that most controversy in modern society would be over property rights, a key tenet of Marxian economics.

122. **(C)** The Sepoy Mutiny in India resulted in changing the power from the hands of trading companies directly to the British government. Some historians feel that it gave the British an excuse to take over India, which became known as the "jewel of the British crown," Britain's richest possession. Sepoy were Indian soldiers fighting in the British army, but when their religious beliefs came into question, they revolted.

123. **(D)** England was one of the four powerful nations at the Congress of Vienna. Although all four nations agreed to prevent future "Napoleons" (thus maintaining a European balance of power), each and every decision made by the Metternich System and the Quadruple Alliance was against the very principles of England's belief in democracy, nationalism, and liberalism. Eventually England withdrew from the Quadruple Alliance.

124. **(B)** The Twenty-Seventh Amendment placed restrictions on Congress's authority to raise its own pay.

125. **(C)** The fall of the Berlin Wall in 1989 and the collapse of the Soviet Union in 1991 marked the end to the Cold War. The Cold War began with the split of Germany into two parts, communist East Germany and democratic West Germany. It ended with the collapse of the Berlin Wall in December of 1989 and the dissolving of the Soviet Union by 1991 into many new republics.

CHAPTER 13

Background and Practice Questions

DESCRIPTION OF THE SOCIAL SCIENCES AND HISTORY EXAMINATION

The CLEP General Examination in Social Sciences and History measures your general knowledge of history, sociology, economics, psychology, anthropology, geography, and political science. It covers material that is generally taught in lower-division college courses for non-social science majors. The exam is given in two parts, each consisting of approximately 60 questions and each requiring 45 minutes to complete. See the following chart for approximate percentages of examination items:

SOCIAL SCIENCES AND HISTORY EXAM	
CONTENT OR ITEM TYPES	**TIME/NUMBER OF QUESTIONS**
40% History	120 questions
17% United States History	90 minutes
15% Western Civilization	
8% World History	
13% Government/Political Science	
10% Sociology	
10% Economics	
10% Psychology	
11% Geography	
6% Anthropology	

The questions on this exam include aspects of the social sciences that may not have been covered in courses you have taken in school. Your ability to answer these questions will depend on the extent to which you have maintained a general interest in these subjects and kept current by reading widely and following current events.

If you want to do well on this test, you should have a very clear sense of chronological relations in history, as well as an understanding of the issues and ideas which have been current in different historical eras. You should have some idea of the relative significance of various ideologies, scientific concepts, and historical events. If you have, on your own or during the course work, read widely in history and sociology (including the history of economic and sociological theories) you will be able to answer a large number of the questions without difficulty. Technical concepts and terms from contemporary economics, social psychology, and political science are tested in a large number of questions. However, if you have an acquaintance with the material emphasized in introductions to these subjects, you are well prepared to answer the questions.

There are a number of accomplishments which the questions endeavor to test. Some questions require mere factual recall. Others ask you to go beyond factual recall to the deduction of a correct answer from the information given in the question and from your own knowledge. Still others are designed to test your ability to apply conceptual principles or theories to particular problems. Many of the questions will demand much of you. You will be asked to judge, to weigh, to rank, to discriminate, and to compare and contrast facts and ideas.

THE KINDS OF QUESTIONS THAT APPEAR ON THE EXAMINATION

Simple Recall

To give you an idea of the various types of questions you will face, we will give some examples here and, where necessary, explain the process by which the right answer is derived. Simple recall questions are straightforward and require no explanation.

EXAMPLES

1. When did the British Navy defeat the Spanish Armada?

   (A) 1066
   (B) 1588
   (C) 1648
   (D) 1688
   (E) 1750
   Answer: (B)

2. What was the name of the treaty ending the Thirty Years' War?

   (A) Treaty of Ghent
   (B) Treaty of Paris
   (C) Treaty of Burgundy
   (D) Treaty of Westphalia
   (E) Treaty of London
   Answer: (D)

EXAMPLES (cont.)

3. Where did General Grant accept the surrender of General Lee in 1865?

(A) Richmond
(B) Vicksburg
(C) Gettysburg
(D) Appomattox
(E) Atlanta
Answer: (D)

4. Who was the prime minister of Great Britain during the negotiations leading to the Treaty of Versailles in 1919?

(A) Winston Churchil
(B) William Pitt
(C) Stanley Baldwin
(D) Lloyd George
(E) Clement Attlee
Answer: (D)

Recall of Multiple Facts

A number of questions will test your ability to recall a number of related facts. An example of this type follows:

EXAMPLE

1. You are in a small country which now is landlocked. In the 19th century, its major city was the capital of an empire with a vast polyglot population. In which of the following countries are you?

(A) Bolivia
(B) Switzerland
(C) Paraguay
(D) Austria
(E) France

Explanation: Austria (D) is the answer, but you must know a number of facts to deduce this answer. France's major city was the capital of a vast polyglot empire in the 19th century. But France is not landlocked. Bolivia, Switzerland, and Paraguay are all landlocked, but their major cities were not centers of large empires in the 19th century. Only Austria fits all the conditions. It is now landlocked after losing vast holdings at Versailles. Its capital city, Vienna, was the center of the vast polyglot Austrian Empire during the 19th century.

Source of Concepts

Another type of question tests your ability to attach major concepts to their original authors.

EXAMPLE

1. Who held that the division of labor was the key to economic progress and that freedom in trade broadened markets, which in turn led to more division of labor and thus economic progress?

    (A) Toynbee
    (B) Marx
    (C) Adam Smith
    (D) Thomas Aquinas
    (E) Aristotle

    Explanation: The interests of all the writers except Adam Smith were centered on issues quite otherwise than the effect of free trade on economic progress. Thus, Adam Smith (C) is the answer.

Application of Principles

Another type of question attempts to examine your facility in applying certain social science principles.

EXAMPLE

1. The marginal propensity to consume in a population is 0.50. Investment expenditures increase by one billion dollars. Everything else being equal, you would expect national income to increase by about how many billion dollars?

    (A) 1
    (B) 2
    (C) 5
    (D) 50
    (E) 500

    Explanation: The student who is acquainted with the "multiplier" concept and the fact that it is tied to the marginal propensity to consume by the formula $M = \dfrac{1}{1-MPC}$ would know that two billion dollars is the answer. He would be applying certain principles from economics to get the answer.

Major Themes of Movements

Yet another type of question deals with the central themes which characterize various schools or traditions of thought.

EXAMPLE

1. History moves in a path which ends only when world-wide stateless communism reigns. The struggle of economic classes is the engine of movement. This viewpoint is characteristic of

   (A) Transcendentalism
   (B) Dialectical Idealism
   (C) Freudianism
   (D) Scholasticism
   (E) Dialectical Materialism

Explanation: (E) The student who knows both that Marxism uses dialectical processes and that Marx thought material conditions the basis of change would see that only the term Dialectical Materialism could fit the ideas in the above viewpoint.

HISTORICAL TIME LINE

The time line that follows will give you an overview of important events in history and the sequence in which they occurred. Keep in mind that no list of this sort is exhaustive; do not use the time line alone as the sole source of review for the history portion of the test. Use it as a brief, introductory review, possibly to help you pinpoint the events and historical periods you need to spend most of your study time on. A day or two before the exam, look at the time line again to stimulate your memory and put your mind into the proper historical gear.

Ancient World

c. 3500B.C.	Sumerian civilization (Mesopotamia)		399 B.C.	Death of Socrates
c. 3100 B.C.	Upper and Lower Egypt united under King Menes (First Dynasty)		334–323 B.C.	Conquests by Alexander (the Great) of Macedonia
c. 3000–1550 B.C.	Indus Valley culture		c. 320 B.C.	Gupta Empire founded India begins a golden age
c. 2700–2200 B.C.	Egyptian Old Kingdom		c. 273–232 B.C.	Reign of Ashoka (India)
c. 2500–1400 B.C.	Minoan civilization (Crete)		264–146 B.C.	Rome's intermittent Punic Wars
c. 1800 B.C.	Hammurabi's code of laws (Babylonia)		221–210 B.C.	Shih Huang–ti (China's "First Emperor"); The Great Wall
c. 1800–1100 B.C.	Shang (Yin) Dynasty (China)		202 B.C.	Han Dynasty established (China)
c. 1375 B.C.	Akhnaton and Egyptian monotheism		105 B.C.	Chinese invent paper
c. 1250 B.C.	Moses and Hebrew law		44 B.C.	Assassination of Julius Caesar
1194–1184 B.C.	Trojan Wars		27 B.C.	Augustus Caesar becomes first Roman emperor
c. 1122–256 B.C.	Chou Dynasty in China		c. 6 B.C.	Birth of Jesus
1025–930 B.C.	Hebrew monarchy		c. 30 A.D.	The Crucifixion
c. 800 B.C.	Homer's epics		70	Roman forces capture Jerusalem
c. 753 B.C.	Founding of Rome		c. 200	Rise of power of the Papacy
745–612 B.C.	Assyrian Empire		331	Founding of Constantinople
c. 630–553 B.C.	Zoroaster (Persia)		c. 400	Peak of Mayan civilization
c. 604 B.C.	Birth of Lao Tzu (Chinese Taoism)		400–1240	Ghana controls Niger trade (Africa)
594–3 B.C.	Solon's laws (Athens)		440	Invasion of Europe by the Huns
563–483 B.C.	Buddha (India)		476	Germanic "barbarians" take Rome
551–479 B.C.	Confucius (China)			
509 B.C.	Roman Republic established			
490–449 B.C.	Greek (Delian League)—Persian Wars			
431–404 B.C.	Peloponnesian Wars			

Medieval World

496	King Clovis of the Franks converted to Christianity	c. 1150	Building of Angkor Wat (Khmers)
527–565	Justinian I rules Byzantine Empire, codifies Roman Law	1192	Yoritomo becomes first shogun to rule Japan
570	Birth of Muhammad	c. 1200–1500	Aztec Empire (Mexico)
c. 600	Buddhism reaches Japan	1211–23	Conquests of Ghengis Khan
622	The Hejira (Muhammad's flight from Mecca [Makkah])	1215	Magna Carta (England)
711	Arab invasion of Spain from Africa	c. 1279	Kublai Khan leads Mongols in completing conquest of China
732	Battle of Tours (Charles Martel leads Franks in victory over invading Arabs)	1337–1453	Hundred Years War (Europe)
		1348–50	Black Death (Europe)
800	Charlemagne crowned Emperor	1450	Gutenberg's movable type perfected
936–973	Otto I Holy Roman Emperor	1450	The Renaissance begins in Europe
c. 1000	Vikings reach North America	1453	Constantinople falls to the Turks
1006	Muslim invasion of India		
1066	Norman conquest of England (Battle of Hastings)	1469	Birth of Nanak, founder of Sikhism (India)
1095	Start of the First Crusade		

United States		World	
1492	Columbus' first voyage to America	1492	"Reconquest" of Spain by Christians
		1492–1517	Columbus' 4 voyages
		1517	Luther's "95 Theses" (beginning of the Reformation)
		1519–22	Magellan circles the globe
		1519	Cortes conquers the Aztecs (Mexico)
		1533	Pizarro invades Peru
		1536	Henry VIII establishes Anglican Church
		1556–1605	Akbar rules Mughal India
		1571	Turkish fleet defeated at Lepanto
		1588	Defeat of Spanish Armada by Royal Navy of England
		1592	Hideyoshi, Japanese unifier, invades Korea
		1500s/1600s	Columbian Exchange takes place between the Old and New Worlds
		1603–1867	Tokugawa Shogunate in Japan
1607	Founding of Jamestown, Virginia	1608	French establish Québec City
		1611	King James version of the Bible
		1618–48	Thirty Years War (Europe)
1619	Virginia establishes House of Burgesses (first legislature)		
1619	First black indentured servants (slaves) arrive in Virginia		
1620	Puritan Separatists (Pilgrims) arrive at Plymouth		
1620	Mayflower Compact		
1636	Harvard founded		
1643	New England Confederation organized	1642–49	English Civil War ("Great Migration" to America)
		1644	Manchu dynasty founded (China)
1647	Public schools founded (Massachusetts)		
1651	First English Navigation Act passed	1651	Dutch settlers in South Africa

	United States		World
1676	Bacon's Rebellion (Virginia)		
1676	King Philip's War (New England)		
		1688	Glorious Revolution (England)
		1688	Bill of Rights (England)
1692	Salem witchcraft trials		
1735	John Peter Zenger trial (free press)		
1754–63	French and Indian War (New France ceded to England)	1751	Diderot's *Encyclopedia* (France)
		1756–63	Seven Years' War (Europe)
		1759	Watt's steam engine
1765	Stamp Act (repealed in 1766)		
1774	"Intolerable Acts" closed Boston Harbor		
1774	First Continental Congress meets		
1775–83	The American Revolution		
1776	Declaration of Independence	1776	Adam Smith's *Wealth of Nations*
		1776	The Enlightenment period begins in Europe
1778	Alliance with France		
1781	Articles of Confederation ratified		
1783	Treaty of Paris officially ends Revolutionary War	1785–86	French economic crisis
1787	Shays' Rebellion (Massachusetts)		
1787	Northwest Ordinance		
1787	Constitutional Convention opens		
1789	Washington becomes first president	1789	French Revolution begins
		1789–91	National Assembly
1790	Slater's first textile mill for spinning cotton		
1791	Bill of Rights ratified	1791–94	National Convention
1793	Cotton gin perfected		
1793	Proclamation of Neutrality		
1794	Whiskey Rebellion	1794	Reign of Terror ends in France
		1794	Mackenzie reaches the Pacific (Canada)
1798–99	Undeclared naval war with France	1795–99	Directory rules France
1798	Alien and Sedition Acts		
1798	Kentucky and Virginia Resolutions		
1803	Louisiana Purchase doubles size of U.S.		

United States		World	
1803	*Marbury v. Madison* (Marshall Supreme Court establishes precedent for judicial review of laws of Congress)		
1804–06	Lewis and Clark expedition	1804–14	Napoleon is Emperor of France
1807	Embargo Act		
1808	Importation of slaves outlawed		
		1809–26	Wars of Latin–American Independence
1812–15	Second war with England (War of 1812)	1812	Napolean fails to defeat Russia
		1815	Battle of Waterloo (Napoleon is defeated)
		1815	Congress of Vienna meets
1816	Protective tariff	1815–48	Age of Metternich
1816	Second Bank of the U.S. chartered		
1820	Missouri Compromise		
1823	Monroe Doctrine		
1825	Erie Canal opens		
1827	Baltimore and Ohio Railroad chartered		
		1830	Revolutions in Europe
1831	Nat Turner slave rebellion		
1832–33	Nullification crisis (tariff)	1832	English (political) Reform Act
1835	Indian removal ("Trail of Tears")		
1836	Republic of Texas established		
1837	Panic of 1837	1837	Rebellion in Canada
		1839–42	Opium Wars (China)
		1845–47	Potato famine in Ireland, heavy Irish Immigration
1846–48	Mexican War	1846	Repeal of English Corn Laws
1847	Mormons reach Utah		
1848	Gold discovered in California	1848	Revolutions in Europe
1848	Women's Rights Convention (New York)	1848	Marx's *Communist Manifesto*
1850	Compromise Bills		
1854	Kansas-Nebraska Act (slavery)	1854–56	Crimean War
1854	Republican Party founded	1854	Perry arrives in Japan
		1857–58	Sepoy "Mutiny" in India John Stuart Mill's *On Liberty*
1859	Drake's oil well (first commercially productive oil well)	1859	Darwin's *The Origin of Species*
1859	John Brown's raid on Harpers Ferry		

United States		World	
1860	Election of Abraham Lincoln		
1861–65	Civil War	1861	Emancipation of Serfs (Russia)
1862	Homestead Act; Landgrant Act	1861–66	Maximillian in Mexico
1863	Emancipation Proclamation		
		1864	Taiping Rebellion in China
1865	Lincoln assassinated		
1865–70	Civil War Amendments (13th–15th)		
1865–76	Southern "Reconstruction"		
1867	U.S. buys Alaska from Russia	1867	Dominion of Canada established (British North America Act)
		1867	Marx's *Das Kapital*
1868	Impeachment of Andrew Jackson	1868	Meiji Restoration (Japan)
1869	First transcontinental railroad	1869	Suez Canal opened
		1870	Italian unification completed
		1871	Franco-Prussian War
		1871	German unification completed
1876	Bell invents telephone		
1876	Hayes-Tilden disputed election		
1877	Edison invents phonograph	1877	Queen Victoria as "Empress of India"
1879	Edison invents electric light		
1879	Standard Oil Trust organized		
1882	Chinese Exclusion Act	1882	British invade and occupy Egypt
1883	Civil Service reform (Pendleton Act)		
		1884	Berlin Conference (on partitioning Africa)
		1885	Indian Congress Party formed
1886	Haymarket riot in Chicago (labor)		
1886	American Federation of Labor founded		
1887	Interstate Commerce Commission		
1887	Dawes Act (Native Americans)		
1889	First Pan American Conference	1889	Japanese Constitution

United States		World	
1890	Sherman Antitrust Act		
1890	Battle of Wounded Knee (last major conflict between Indians and U.S. troops)		
1890	"Closing" of the frontier		
		1894	First Sino-Japanese War
1896	Marconi's wireless telegraph		
1898	Spanish-American War		
1898	Philippine "Insurrection"		
1899	"Open Door" policy in China	1899–1902	Boer War (South Africa)
		1899	Boxer Rebellion (China)
		1900	Freud's *Interpretation of Dreams*
1903	Wright Brothers flight		
		1904–05	Russo-Japanese War (Japan defeats Russia)
		1905	Revolution in Russia
		1905	Einstein's theory of relativity
1908	"Model T" Ford auto		
1909	Perry claims to reach North Pole		
		1910	Revolution in Mexico
		1911	Chinese Republic (Sun Yat-sen)
1914	Panama Canal opened	1914–18	World War I (The Great War)
1914	Federal Trade Commission created		
1917	U.S. enters the war	1917	Russian Revolution
1919	Senate rejects Treaty of Versailles		
1919–20	"Great Red Scare"		
1920	Women's suffrage amendment (19th)	1920	Founding of League of Nations
1921	Washington Disarmament Conference		
1921 & 24	Restrictive immigration laws		
		1922	Fascist dictatorship in Italy Mussolini)
1927	Lindberg's solo flight to Paris	1924	Death of Lenin; Stalin in power
1929	Stock market crash; Great Depression		

United States		World	
		1930	Gandhi's Salt March (India)
		1931	Japan invades Manchuria, second Sino-Japanese War
1933	Roosevelt's "100 Days"; New Deal; "Good Neighbor" policy	1933	Hitler in power (Germany)
		1934–35	Long March (China)
1935–37	Neutrality Acts passed to avoid entrance in World War II (Policy of Isolationism)	1935	Italy attacks Ethiopia
		1936–39	Spanish Civil War
		1937	Japan at war with China
		1938	Munich Conference
		1939–45	World War II
		1939–45	The Holocaust
1941	Japanese attack Pearl Harbor	1941	Germany attacks Russia
1941	The computer perfected	1941	Japanese victories in the Pacific
		1944	"D Day" landings in France
1945	Atomic bombing of Hiroshima and Nagasaki	1945	United Nations organized
		1945	Winston Churchill makes his famous Iron Curtain speech
		1946	Nuremberg war crimes trials
		1946–55	Juan Peron (Argentina)
1947	Truman Doctrine ("Cold War" begins)	1947	Independence for India and Pakistan
1947	Marshall Plan for Europe		
1948	Organization of American States created	1948	Assassination of Gandhi (India)
1948	Television mass-marketing begins	1948	Creation of nation of Israel
		1948–49	Berlin blockade and airlift, First Arab-Israeli War
		1949	NATO established
		1949	Communist victory in China
1950	U.S. enters Korean War		
1953	DNA structure discovered by Watson		
1954	School desegregation decision; integration crises	1954	Battle of Dien Bien Phu (Indo-China)
		1954	Geneva Treaty
		1954	SEATO Alliance formed
1956	Interstate highway system begun	1956	Hungarian Revolution
		1956	Suez crisis, Second Arab-Israeli War
		1957	Russians launch *Sputnik I*, the first space satellite
		1957	Independence for Ghana (Africa)
		1957	European Common Market established

United States		World	
		1959	Castro takes control of Cuba. First communist government in western hemisphere.
1961	Bay of Pigs Invasion of Cuba fails	1961	Berlin Wall constructed
1961	Peace Corps; Alliance for Progress		
1962	Cuban Missile Crisis		
1963	John F. Kennedy assassinated		
1964	U.S. military buildup in Vietnam	1964	Vietnam Conflict escalates
1964	Johnson's "Great Society" and "War on Poverty"		
1966–68	Urban riots	1966–76	Cultural Revolution in China
		1967	Arab-Israeli Six Day War (Third Arab-Israel War)
1968	Assassinations of Martin Luther King, Jr. and Robert Kennedy	1968	"Prague Spring" (Czechoslovakia Uprising)
		1968	Tet Offensive
1969	Men land on the moon		
1969	Anti-Vietnam War demonstrations		
1970	Invasion of Cambodia by Nixon		
1972	Nixon visit to China		
1972	SALT Treaty with USSR		
1972	Watergate break-in		
1973	OPEC oil boycott	1973	Yom Kippur War (Fourth Arab-Israeli War)
1973	U.S. withdrawal in Vietnam	1973	Coup unseats Allende in Chile
1974	Nixon resigns; pardoned by Ford		
		1975	Communist victory in Vietnam
1978	Panama Canal retrocession treaty		
1979	Three Mile Island, Pennsylvania, nuclear accident	1979	Revolution in Iran topples Shah
		1979	USSR invades Afghanistan
1979–81	Hostages seized in Iran	1979	Sandinistas oust Somoza (Nicaragua)
1980s	AIDS epidemic; rising drug problem	1980	Iran-Iraq War begins
1981	"Supply side" economics; tax cuts; debt increase; trade imbalances	1981	Assassination of Egyptian President Anwar Sadat
		1981	Solidarity Movement (Poland)
1983	U.S. aid to Nicaraguan contras	1983	Anti-Apartheid movement (South Africa)
1983	Invasion of Grenada		
1984	Geraldine Ferraro, first woman vice-presidential candidate	1984	Assassination of Indian Prime Minister Indira Gandhi

United States		World	
		1984	Famines in Africa
		1985	Gorbachev made Communist Party Secretary (USSR)
1986	Iran-Contra Scandal	1986	Marcos overthrown (Philippines)
		1986	Chernobyl nuclear accident (USSR)
1987	INF Treaty (armaments)	1987	Glasnost and Perestroika (USSR)
		1987	Meech Lake Agreement on French culture in Quebec
		1988	Riots in Israeli-occupied areas; start of Intifada
1989	Exxon Valdez oil spill (Alaska) environmental concerns	1989	Student demonstrations in China suppressed; Tiananmen Square Massacre
1989	George Bush becomes 41st U.S. president	1989	Nationalist movements in USSR and Eastern Europe
1989	Congress passes Savings and Loan bailout plans	1989	Emperor Hirohito of Japan dead at 87
		1989	Berlin wall dismantled
1990	U.S. forces invade Panama	1990	Lech Walesa wins Poland's runoff presidential election
1990	Drexel Burnham Lambert investment house declares bankruptcy	1990	Nelson Mandela freed
		1990	Iraq invades Kuwait
1990	Clean Air Act of 1977 revised and updated	1990	East and West Germany become unified into one nation
1991	Civil Rights Act passed (job-bias bill)	1991	Access to understanding the Dead Sea Scrolls opened
1991	U.S. Supreme Court Justice Thurgood Marshall resigns	1991	Warsaw Pact disbands
1991	Law professor Anita Hill accuses Judge Clarence Thomas of sexual harassment	1991	Persian Gulf War—Iraq defeated
		1991	South African Parliament repeals apartheid laws
1991	Judge Clarence Thomas becomes 106th Justice of the Supreme Court	1991	Coup d'etat against Gorbachev; Boris Yeltsin elected president of Russia
1991	Major earthquake in San Francisco	1991	Soviet Union breakup after Gorbachev resignation; Commonwealth of Independent States formed
1991	U.S. space shuttle *Atlantis* completes successful mission	1991	Warsaw Pact dissolved
1991	*Rust v. Sullivan* case bars federally funded clinics from providing information about abortions	1991	New Soviet ruling council recognizes independence of Lithuania, Estonia, & Latvia
1991	Coalition forces attack and defeat Iraq		

United States		World	
1992	Gov. Bill Clinton (Democrat) elected 42nd president of the U.S.	1992	"Ethnic cleansing" in former Yugloslavia
1993	NAFTA (North American Free Trade Agreement) approved between U.S., Canada, and Mexico	1993	Bush and Yeltsin sign START 2 Treaty to reduce nuclear weapons
1993	Clinton proposes health care reform bill; Hillary Rodham Clinton leads committee	1993	Civil strife in Bosnia
		1993	Czechoslovakia divides into two separate nations of the Czech Republic and Slovakia
1993	Flooding in Midwest destroys farms and homes, changing landscape	1993	Oslo Agreement between Israel and the Palestinians
		1993	Israeli Prime Minister Yitzhak Rabin and Palestine Liberation Organization Chairman Yasir Arafat win Nobel Peace Prize
1994	Brady Bill (gun control) passed in Congress and signed by President Bill Clinton	1994	First multiracial "free" elections in South Africa—Nelson Mandela becomes president
1994	50th anniversary of D-Day (invasion of Europe on June 6, 1944	1994	The "chunnel" links England and France under the English Channel
1994	Republicans win control of Congress for the first time since 1954	1994	Palestinian autonomy achieved on the Gaza
1994	Whitewater Affair investigation begins	1994	Nelson Mandela inaugurated as president of South Africa.
		1994	Civil War breaks out in Rwanda
1994	Stephen Breyer replaces Harry Blackmun on the Supreme Court	1994	Israel and Jordan sign a peace treaty
1994	Congress approves U.S. involvement in GATT (General Agreement on Tariffs and Trade)		
1995	Federal government shuts down twice because of failure to pass a funding bill	1995	Largest gathering ever of world leaders at fiftieth anniversary of United Nations
1995	Congress approves major overhaul of welfare programs	1995	Ebola virus epidemic in Zaire
1995	Bombing of Oklahoma City federal building	1995	Assassination of Israeli Prime Minister Yitzhak Rabin
1995	United States establishes diplomatic relations with Vietnam	1995	Presidents of Bosnia-Herzogovina, Serbia, and Croatia sign a treaty to end Bosnian civil war
1996	President Clinton signs into law the most sweeping overhaul of welfare programs in sixty years	1996	Boris Yeltsin wins election to become president of Russia
1996	Olympic Games in Atlanta		

United States		World	
		1996	Benjamin Netanyahu wins election to become prime minister of Israel
		1996	Swiss Parliament agrees to search for missing assets of Holocaust survivors
		1996	Kofi Annan of Ghana becomes U.N. Secretary-General
1997	President and Congress agree on a plan to balance the federal budget in six years	1997	Several Asian economies begin to falter (e.g., Indonesia, South Korea, Thailand)
1997	Fund-raising controversy over alleged improprieties in 1996 Democratic campaign	1997	Diana, Princess of Wales, dies in a car accident
1997	Record number of mergers and acquisitions	1997	China regains sovereignty over Hong Kong
1997	Supreme Court overturns Communications Decency Act that attempted to regulate pornography on the Internet	1997	Zairian leader Mobutu Sese Soko steps down after a rebellion and dies in exile
1998	Stock market breaks the 9,000 mark for the first time	1998	Iraq objects to weapons inspections
1998	President Clinton accused in White House scandal; Clinton denies affair with intern, Monica Lewinsky	1998	Tentative agreement is reached to end strife in Northern Ireland
1998	Life sentence to Terry Nichols, convicted in Oklahoma City bombing	1998	Elections in India result in Atal Bihar Vajpayee becoming prime minister
1998	Starr report released outlining case of impeachment proceedings against President Clinton	1998	Serbia clashes with the ethnic Albanians in Kosovo; renewed attacks on Kosovo rebels
1998	House impeaches President Clinton of perjury and obstruction of justice	1998	Good Friday Accord reached in Northern Ireland. Irish Parliament backs peace agreement.
		1998	Europe agrees on the *Euro dollar*
		1998	India, then Pakistan, conducts several atomic bomb tests; world protest and disapproval immediately follow
		1998	Iraq ends cooperation with UN military armed inspectors
		1998	Agreement between Netanyahu and Arafat moves Middle East peace talks forward

United States		World	
1999	United States opens impeachment charges of President Clinton	1999	War erupts in Kosovo as President Milosevic of Yugoslavia massacres and deports thousands of ethnic Albanians
1999	Columbine High School incident results in the death of twelve students and one teacher	1999	Czech Republic, Poland, and Hungary (once part of the Soviet communist bloc) join NATO
1999	John F. Kennedy Jr., wife Carolyn, and sister-in-law Lauren lost at sea in a plane crash	1999	Boris Yeltsin, Russian president, survives impeachment hearings; cabinet reshuffled
1999	The United States turns over the Panama Canal to Panama	1999	Serbs sign agreement to pull troops out of Kosovo after three months of NATO attacks end
		1999	Nelson Mandela, first black president in South African history, steps down; he is succeeded by Thabo Mbeki
		1999	Massive 7.4 earthquake in Turkey leaves over 15,000 people dead
		1999	Barak of Israel and PLO's Arafat announce peace accord
		1999	Russia sends ground troops to Chechnya as conflict with Islamic militants intensifies
		1999	The world awaits the consequences of the Y2K bug
2000	Beginning of stock plunge signaling end of Internet stock boom	2000	Reformists win control of Iranian parliament for the first time since the Islamic Revolution of 1979
2000	U.S. Navy resumes shelling exercise of the military training site located on Puerto Rico's Vieques Islands	2000	British restore parliamentary powers to Northern Ireland after Sinn Fein agrees to disarm
2000	Six-year Whitewater investigation of the Clintons ends without indictments	2000	Presidents of North and South Korea sign peace accord and end a half century of antagonism
2000	U.S. historic presidential election between Bush and Gore is one of the closest in U.S. history. After Florida Supreme Court rules election recount in Florida, U.S. Supreme Court overrides this decision and recount is halted, sealing Bush election victory.	2000	Vicente Fox Quesada elected president of Mexico, ending 71 years of one-party rule by the PRI party
		2000	Nationwide uprising overthrows Yugoslavian president Milosevic

United States		World	
2001	In his final days as president, Clinton issues controversial pardons including Marc Rich, billionaire fugitive financier	2001	Laurent Kabila, Congo president, assassinated; son Joseph takes over amid continuing civil war
2001	George Bush sworn in as 43rd president	2001	Right-wing leader Ariel Sharon elected as Israel's Prime Minister during worst Israeli-Palestinian violence in years
2001	Balance of U.S. Senate shifts as Jim Jeffords changes his party affiliation from Republican to Independent	2001	British livestock epidemic, "foot and mouth disease," reaches crisis levels
2001	Execution of Oklahoma City bomber Timothy McVeigh	2001	NATO ends guerilla warfare in Macedonia
2001	On September 11th, terrorist attacks on the United States hit New York City's World Trade Center and the Pentagon in Washington D.C. Osama Bin Laden and the al-Qaeda terrorists are identified as the parties responsible for the attacks	2001	Former Yugoslavian president Slobodan Milosevic is delivered to the UN tribunal in the Hague to await war-crime trial
		2001	Irish Republican Army announces dismantling of its weapons arsenal, marking a dramatic leap forward in the peace process
2001	Anthrax scare rivets our nation—several deaths recorded	2001	UN-sponsored summit in Bonn, Germany results in Hamid Karzai selected as head of a new transition government in Afghanistan
2001	Enron Corporation, one of the world's largest energy companies, files bankruptcy		
2001	President George W. Bush State of Union labels Iran, Iraq, and North Korea as "axis of evil" and states war on nations that develop weapons of mass destruction	2001	Taliban government collapses after two months of U.S. bombing
		2001	First ever 'same sex marriages' approved in the Netherlands
2001	U.S. troops attack and quickly defeat Taliban forces in Afghanistan. Taliban government collapses on 12/9	2001	Official end of the Soviet Union
		2001	9–11: Terrorists destroy World Trade Center. UN Security Council passes resolution for Iraq attack.
		2001	Pakistan fights Taliban troops on border. Al Qaeda connected (Bin Laden sited in the hills of Pakistan) to both Taliban and Bin Laden
		2001	Ahmed Shah Massoud (pro West supporter) assassinated by Bin Laden and the Taliban two days before 9–11

United States		World	
2002	Enron Scandal impacts Wall Street	2002	Iraq War begins with "coalition forces" (not UN)
2002	Bush states, "Iraq trained Al Qaeda terrorist; weapons of mass destruction exist in Iraq"	2002	Milosevic trials begins on human rights violations
2002	Elections result in Republicans controlling both Houses of Congress	2002	East Timor becomes 191st member of the UN
2002	New cabinet department of Homeland Security created	2002	UN weapon inspections begin in Iraq; Operation "Iraqi Freedom" begins
		2002	Air strikes begin over Baghdad
2003	Secretary of State tells UN "Saddam Hussein is hiding weapons of mass destruction"; Al-samoud missiles found	2003	UN Security Council members— France, Germany, and Russia —say they will veto in the Security Council any act of war on Iraq
2003	Invasion of Iraq highly successful; supported by the American people	2003	Coalition forces invade Iraq—a quick victory: Protest for civil rights occur in Hong Kong
2003	California elected Arnold Schwarzengger as governor		
2003	Bob Hopes dies at 100	2003	China launches first manned mission into space
2003	Space shuttle Columbia explodes—all seven astronauts killed	2003	Chechnya tensions increase and violence occurs in this small Russian province
		2003	Final flight for the Concord
2004	*Exploration Rover* lands on Mars	2004	South Korea becomes most wired internet nation in the world
2004	Controversy begins on Guantanamo detainees; human rights treatment by the U.S. questioned by the UN	2004	Nuclear hardware sent from Pakistan to Iran, North Korea, and Libya
2004	U.S. forces encounter on-going terrorism in Iraq	2004	AL Qaeda terrorists hit subways in Madrid
2004	U.S. occupation of Fallujah begins in Iraq	2004	Israel announces planned withdrawal from 17 settlements in Gaza and West Bank
2004	135,000 troops maintained in Iraq		
2004	Four hurricanes devastate Florida and other parts of the southern United States	2004	Historic Olympic Games end in Athens
		2004	UN calls for all Syrian foreign troops to leave Lebanon; PLO leader Arafat dies in November
		2004	Massive Asian earthquake hits Southeast Asia—death toll reaches 185,000 people!
		2004	10 new nations join the EC— Poland, Malta, Estonia, Lituania, Latavia, Czech Republic, Slovakia, Slovenia, Hungary, and Cyprus

United States		World	
2005	U.S. occupation of Fallujah, Iraq begins	2005	First elections of representatives for 275-member legislature takes place in Iraq
2005	U.S. says Americans forces to be in Iraq at least 18–24 months longer	2005	Pope John Paul II dies
2005	Hurricane Katrina hits the southeastern part of the U.S. (New Orleans, Georgia, and Louisiana hit bad—3000+ dead)	2005	Tensions supporting greater democracy occurs in Kyrgyzstan ("Tulip Revolution"), Georgia, and Ukraine
2005	80% of New Orleans is flooded by Katrina	2005	Mahmoud leader replaces Arafat as Palestinian authority president
		2005	Saddam Hussein trial begins
		2005	Israel informs that all settlers will leave the West Bank and the Gaza Strip
		2005	11 million people approve first parliamentary election in Iraq
2006	U.S. population hits 300 million	2006	Hamas gains majority of legislature in Palestine
2006	President Bush announces that it will take 18 more months before troops can be withdrawn November elections result in the Republicans losing both houses of Congress	2006	World population hits 6.5 billion
		2006	Montenegro becomes 192nd nation in the UN
		2006	Iran confirms the production of uranium
	U.S. Congress approves the Secure Fence Act of 700 miles of fence on the Mexican border	2006	First democratic elections since 1955 in the Democratic Republic of the Congo
		2006	Iraq and Syria renew diplomatic relations

STUDY SOURCES

For review, you might consult the following books. Note that to prepare for this exam, you will need to use several books since no single book covers all the topics on the test.

GENERAL

Frazee, Charles A. *World History the Easy Way.* 2 vols. Hauppauge, NY: Barron's Educational Series, Inc., 1997.

Hunt, Elgin F., and David C. Colander. *Social Science: An Introduction to the Study of Society.* 9th ed. New York: Allyn & Bacon, Inc., 1995.

AMERICAN HISTORY

Brinkley, Alan, Richard Current et al. *American History: A Survey, Vol. 3.* 9th ed. New York: McGraw-Hill, Inc., 1995.

Kellogg, William. *American History the Easy Way.* 2nd ed. Hauppauge, NY: Barron's Educational Series, Inc., 1995.

Norton, Mary Beth et al. *A People and a Nation: A History of the United States.* 4 volumes. 4th ed. Boston: Houghton Mifflin Co., 1994.

WESTERN CIVILIZATION

Kagan, Donald, and Steven Ozment. *Western Heritage.* 6th ed. New York: Macmillan, 1997.

AFRICAN/ASIAN CIVILIZATIONS

Fairbank, John K., Edwin O. Reischauer, and Albert M. Craig. *East Asia: Tradition and Transformation.* 3rd ed. Boston: Houghton Mifflin Co., 1989.

Martin, Phyllis M., and Patrick O'Meara, eds. *Africa.* 3rd ed. Bloomington: Indiana University Press, 1995.

ECONOMICS

Heilbroner, Robert. *The Worldly Philosophers.* 6th ed. New York: Simon & Schuster, 1987.

Heilbroner, Robert, and Lester Thurow. *Economics Explained.* New York: Simon & Schuster, 1994.

SOCIOLOGY

Turner, Jonathan H. *Sociology: The Science of Human Organization.* Chicago: Nelson-Hall, 1986.

POLITICAL SCIENCE

Lawson, Kay. *The Human Polity: An Introduction to Political Science.* 2nd ed. Boston: Houghton Mifflin Co., 1988.

Lose, Richard, ed. *Corwin on the Constitution,* Vol. 1. Ithaca, NY: Cornell University Press, 1981; Vol. 2 1987; Vol. 3 1988.

ANTHROPO-GEOGRAPHY

De Blij, Harm J. *Human Geography: Culture, Society and Space.* 5th ed. New York: John Wiley and Sons, 1995.

SOCIAL SCIENCE GLOSSARY

accommodation An adaptation or adjustment.

amendment A change in the United States Constitution.

Anglican Pertaining to the Church of England or churches following its doctrines and form, such as the Episcopal churches in Ireland or Scotland.

anomie Lacking purpose, identity, or ethical values in a person or society; rootlessness.

Aquinas, Thomas (1225–1274) Italian scholastic philosopher, influenced by the ideas of Aristotle. Wrote *Summa Theologica*, summarizing Christian doctrine and denying any conflict between reason and religious faith.

average revenue Total sales value divided by the number of units sold and equal, therefore, to average price.

Bacon, Roger (1561–1626) English philosopher, essayist, and statesman.

Baker **v.** *Carr* A 1962 Supreme Court decision that ordered state legislatures to apportion representation so that the votes of all citizens would carry equal weight; thus redistricting had to occur where urban areas would have a larger part of representation than rural areas, in proportion to the population of that area.

Baldwin, Stanley (1867–1947) British statesman and prime minister 1923–29; 1935–37.

Bao Dai Chief of state in the Vietnam Republic; leader of the noncommunist Vietnam Nationalists in the late 1940s. He and the French recognized the independence of Vietnam in 1949.

Baptist A member of a Protestant denomination holding that baptism should be given only to adult believers and by immersion in water rather than sprinkling.

Beard, Charles A. Columbia University history professor whose *An Economic Interpretation of the Constitution* (1913) and *Economic Origins of Jeffersonian Democracy* (1915) set forth the thesis that the founding fathers were primarily motivated by their personal economic interests.

Bellamy, Edward Social reformer whose utopian novel, *Looking Backward: 2000–1887*, criticized 19th-century capitalism and advocated a cooperative state.

Bentham, Jeremy English philosopher whose *Introduction to the Principles of Morals and Legislation* explained the philosophy of utilitarianism.

bicameralism A two-house legislature; example—the Senate and the House of Representatives in the Congress (legislative branch) of the United States federal government.

Bossuet, Jacques (1627–1704) An early French Enlightenment historian.

bourgeoisie The middle class in society.

bureaucracy A social structure built on a hierarchy for administering large organizations in a rational, efficient, and often impersonal manner.

Calhoun, John C. Senator from South Carolina who used the concept of states' rights and nullification to voice disagreement with the Tariff of 1828.

caste A social group, characteristic of India, based upon birth and religion, determining the occupation and class of people; usually unchanging.

Cicero, M. Tullius Roman orator who wrote on philosophy, rhetoric, and politics and passed on much of Greek thought to the Middle Ages.

CIO See **Congress of Industrial Organizations (CIO)**.

Clay, Henry Virginia statesman, senator, considered the "Great Compromiser" for his work on the Missouri Compromise of 1820 and the Compromise of 1850. He suggested an American system to stimulate industry, fund internal improvements, and establish a national bank.

Clemenceau, Georges French statesman, one of the Big Four at Versailles in 1919, who, after World War I, negotiated the peace with Germany.

Clemens, Samuel The author Mark Twain, who wrote of Americans in the mid-1800s with stories such as *Huckleberry Finn* and *Tom Sawyer*. He helped coin the expression "Gilded Age" to describe his disenchantment with the materialism of the industrial age.

Cleveland, Grover The 22nd and 24th president of the United States. His honest administration repudiated Tammany Hall. He insisted on sound money, reducing the Wilson Tariff, and authorized an income tax during his administration.

commonwealth The whole body of people in a state; the body politic; a nation or state in which there is self-government; any of the dominions in the British Commonwealth of Nations, especially Australia.

Comte, Auguste French philosopher who founded the philosophy known as positivism.

Condorcet, Marie-Jean (1743–1794) French philosopher who provided a classic exposition of the idea of human progress and the ultimate perfectibility of mankind.

Congress of Industrial Organizations (CIO) A labor union in the United States formed in 1935.

conjugal family A family group made up of a husband and wife; to unite or join together as husband and wife.

Connecticut Plan A compromise proposal providing for a popularly elected House of Representatives, determined by population and three-fifths of its slave population. The Senate would have two senators elected by state legislatures. The proposal was made by Connecticut delegate Roger Sherman at the Consitutional Convention of 1787.

Cooper, James Fenimore One of the first important American novelists. He wrote the *Leather-Stocking Tales*, a group of novels that highlighted the frontiersman, the Indian, and the clash between civilization and the wilderness.

Dante, Alighieri Italian poet, considered the greatest literary figure of the Middle Ages, who wrote in Latin and in Italian. Probably his best-known work is *The Divine Comedy*.

deflation A reduction in available currency and credit that results in a decrease in the general price level.

DeFoe, Daniel English novelist who wrote *Robinson Crusoe* and *Moll Flanders*, and satirical novels.

deGaulle, Charles French soldier who headed the French Committee of National Liberation during World War II and became president of France in 1959.

demographic transition The shift from high birth and death rates through a period of high population growth to a new balance of low birth and death rates.

Dewey, John Educator and philosopher who initiated the theories and practices of progressive education, by advocating "learning by doing."

Diocletian Roman emperor who tried to contain the disintegrating Roman Empire by appointing a loyal general to govern the western provinces while he ruled in the East.

dominion Sovereign or supreme authority; the power of governing and controlling.

Douglas, Stephen A. Illinois senator who endorsed the doctrine of popular sovereignty as an answer to the slavery issue in the territories.

Duke of Sully French statesman who served as Henry IV's finance minister. He established government monopolies and a canal system in England.

Durkheim, Emile The founder of modern sociology who held that secularism, rationalism, and individualism threaten society with disintegration.

Einstein, Albert Scientist best known for his general theory of relativity, ultimately leading to the development of the first atomic bomb.

endogamy Of marrying within one's tribe or social group.

ethnocentrism The tendency to judge other groups and cultures by the norms of one's own and to regard them as inherently inferior.

Faubus, Orville   Governor of Arkansas who ordered the national guard to block Negro students from entering Central High School in Little Rock in 1957.

Fifteenth Amendment   Defines a citizen's right to vote; provided the right to vote for former male slaves after the Civil War. Ratified in 1870.

Fish, Hamilton   Served as a congressman and a senator, and as lieutenant governor and governor of New York. Under President Grant, he served as secretary of state.

Fitzhugh, George   Praised the slave economy and social order of the South as superior to the North in his writings, such as *The Failure of Free Society*.

fixed costs   Costs that do not vary with output, for example, the rent on a factory lease.

Fletcher **v.** *Peck*   The first time the Supreme Court, in 1810, invalidated a state law as contrary to the Constitution. The Court decided that the Georgia legislature had violated a contract when it rescinded the sale of tracts of land.

Fourteenth Amendment   As part of the Reconstruction period after the Civil War, it gave blacks the right to vote and extended the Bill of Rights protections to citizens of the states. Key phrases included "nor shall any state deprive any person life, liberty, or property without due process of law, nor deny to any person within its jurisdiction the equal protection of the laws." Ratified in 1868.

Freedmen's Bureau Act   Passed on March 3, 1865, it coordinated many organizations that had been created to deal with problems faced by freed slaves, particularly labor relations.

Freud, Sigmund   The father of psychoanalysis who held that human behavior is governed by inner forces that are hidden from consciousness.

functionalism   Theory and practice of emphasizing the necessity of adapting the structure and design of anything to its function.

Gadsden Purchase   Approved in 1853, James Gadsden, U.S. minister to Mexico, agreed to buy a strip of land south of the Gila River that would provide a route for a southern railroad to California.

Gaitskell, Hugh   British politician who was leader of the Labour party in 1955.

Gandhi, Mahatma   Spiritual and political leader of India who never held a political office, yet wielded great power with his people. Followed the philosophy of nonviolent civil disobedience in the struggle to end British rule of India.

Gladstone, William   Liberal English leader who promoted land distribution to Irish peasants and won passage of the Reform Bill of 1884.

Goethe, Johann Wolfgang   One of the greatest German literary figures of modern times whose greatest masterpiece was *Faust*.

Good Neighbor Policy   Policy with Latin America established by Franklin D. Roosevelt during the 1930s, advocating cooperation to solve problems and supporting nonaggression and nonintervention.

Great Compromise   Plan discussed at the Constitutional Convention in 1787 regarding a two-house legislature that settled differences between large and small states concerning representation in Congress.

Greeley, Horace   (1811–1872) Newspaper editor, established the *New York Tribune* in 1841, emphasized journalism for an emerging literate middle class; opposed any compromise over the issue of slavery.

Grey, Charles   A Whig in England who secured the passage of the Reform Bill of 1832.

gross national product   Also known as GNP, this figure represents the total of all goods and services produced in a nation in a given year.

habeas corpus   The writ of habeas corpus is the right to know the charge for which an accused person is being held in custody. During times of war, for instance, the Civil War, it was suspended for security reasons.

Hammurabi   King who formed the Babylonian Empire in the Tigris-Euphrates Valley about 1750 B.C. The Code of Hammurabi is the oldest known legal system.

Hannibal   Carthage's great general who led an army from Spain across the Alps and into Italy, yet was unable to seize the city of Rome during the Second Punic War (218–201 B.C.).

Hegel, Georg   German philosopher of the Romantic period who held that ideas develop in an evolutionary fashion that involves conflict.

Herodotus   Considered the "father of history" (484–424 B.C.) who described the Persian invasions of Greece, embellishing facts with fable and hearsay.

Homer   A blind Greek poet, around 750 B.C., known for his epic poems *The Iliad* and *The Odyssey.*

Hughes, Charles Evans (1862–1948)   An American jurist and political figure who was the 10th chief justice of the Supreme Court; he supported U.S. involvement in the League of Nations and worked for limiting naval armaments in the 1920s.

Huxley, Thomas   British scientist who criticized evolutionary ethics in *Evolution and Ethics.* He held that the struggle in nature held no ethical implications except to show how human beings should not behave.

impeach   Part of a process for removal of a public official from office. The House of Representatives first presents and adopts a formal charge against an official, whereupon the Senate acts as a court to consider those charges.

injunction   A court order to prevent a strike by union workers.

installment buying   Paying for a product through timely payments; for example, using a credit card or repaying an auto loan over a specified period of time.

International Monetary Fund (IMF)   Part of the post–World War II economic plan to rebuild European nations.

judicial review   The power of the Supreme Court to decide the constitutionality of laws prepared by the legislative and executive branches of the U.S. government; established by the 1803 case of *Marbury* v. *Madison.*

Kant, Immanuel   A philosopher who acted as a bridge between 18th- and 19th-century thinking; wrote that a careful examination of the structure of the human mind made it possible to arrive at necessary and universal truths.

Kellogg-Briand Pact   Signed by 62 countries in 1928, this agreement renounced the use of war to settle disputes. It was ineffective because there was no way of enforcing decisions.

Keynes, John Maynard   An economic philosopher from England, influencing the ideas of President Franklin D. Roosevelt in the 1930s, where government would increase spending, creating a deficit during a depression to bolster the economy; it was called pump priming during the New Deal period.

Koch, Robert   Along with others, he detected the bacterial origin of several common diseases, thus making possible effective control of epidemics through public sanitation and quarantine.

LaFollette, Robert   United States senator from Wisconsin and a progressive who supported the direct primary, tax reform, and "Wisconsin Idea" for other states to follow when attempting to eliminate corruption in government and provide more service to the people.

laissez-faire   A term that may be defined as noninterference and has been used in government and economics during the late 19th and early 20th centuries to mean a minimum amount of government regulation of business.

Law, John   Scottish mathematician who put his monetary theories into practice in France as controller general with the Banque Royale and the Compagnie des Indes. He favored replacement of specie coin by paper money.

law of diminishing marginal utility   The psychological law that as extra units of a commodity are consumed by an individual, the satisfaction gained from each unit will fall.

Lister, Joseph   Paved the way in Britain for the application of antiseptic surgery in the practice of medicine and in public health policy.

Lochner* v. *New York (1905)   A case that invalidated a state law limiting working hours in bakeries to ten a day or sixty a week on the grounds that it interfered with the rights of individuals and deprived them of freedom of contract.

Locke, John Instrumental in shaping political thinking during the Enlightenment, his *Two Treatises on Government* was seen as justification for revolutions and as government being derived from the consent of the people. Government should also protect the natural rights of people or be overthrown.

Louis X During his brief reign (1314–1316), the real ruler of France was Louis's uncle, Charles of Valois.

Louis XIII His reign (1610–1643) was marked by the dominance of Cardinal de Richelieu as the king's chief adviser and architect of French absolutism.

Louis XV His reign (1715–1774) was characterized by the reinstitution of the parliament's power to allow or disallow laws, some financial pruning and planning, royal scandals, and a lack of political leadership.

Louis XVI His reign began in 1774 and resulted in hampering political and financial reform, which led to the French Revolution and ultimately to the execution of the king in 1793.

Mao Tse-tung (or Zedong) Leader of the Communists in China who led the "Long March" to protect his people from the Kuomintang and later defeated the Nationalists in 1949 to secure control of Mainland China and establish the People's Republic of China or Red China. Died in 1976.

Marcus Aurelius (121–180 A.D.) Roman emperor from 161 to 180 A.D.

marginal propensity to consume The most important variable determining expenditure on consumption is income.

marginal revenue The increase in the total revenue received by a firm from the sale of one extra unit of its output. For a small firm that cannot influence market prices, the extra revenue gained is equal to the price of the sale.

Marshall, John As Supreme Court chief justice, he supported a loose interpretation of the Constitution to help increase the power of the federal government. Established the procedure of judicial review with his decision in *Marbury* v. *Madison* (1803).

Marxism The belief that history can be explained as an economic struggle between classes.

McKinley, William (1843–1901) The 25th president of the United States who backed high protective tariffs and during whose administration the Spanish-American War (1898) gained territory in America's quest for empire. He was assassinated in Buffalo in 1901.

melioristic The belief that the world tends to get better and, especially, that it can be made better by human effort; the betterment of society by improving people's health and living conditions.

Mendel, Gregor Austrian monk whose work on heredity concluded that many traits segregated into dominant and recessive alternatives and that combined traits assorted independently.

Mendès-France, Pierre French premier from 1954 to 1955 who was opposed to complete independence for any of the French territories in North Africa. He was also instrumental in an agreement on the basic provisions for an Indo-Chinese political settlement involving Vietnam.

mercantilism The theory and system of political economy where the economy of the colonies should be controlled by and should benefit the mother country; that government must direct economic activity in order to compete for scarce world resources.

Merton, Robert Sociologist who wrote about "anomie" in *Social Structure and Anomie* regarding alienation when there is a scarcity of socially acceptable institutionalized means to satisfy people's legitimate needs.

Methodist A member of any branch of a Protestant Christian denomination that developed from the evangelistic teachings and work of John and Charles Wesley, George Whitefield, and others in the early 1700s.

Metternich, Klemens von The pivotal figure at the Congress of Vienna, this prince of Austria had organized the coalition that defeated Napoleon. He helped institute monarchy in Europe after 1815.

Mills, C. Wright Sociologist who was the leading advocate of the "power elite" school of thought, arguing that American society is dominated by a power elite that has not seized power, but possesses it by positions of power in formal organizations.

miscegenation The mixing of the races, especially black and white.

Missouri v. Holland A 1920 case that upheld a federal statute to enforce a treaty with Great Britain for the mutual protection of migratory birds flying between the United States and British possessions to the north and south.

Montaigne, Michel French Renaissance writer whose *Essays* expressed skepticism toward accepted beliefs, condemning superstition and intolerance. This collection urged people to live nobly.

Mormon Member of the religious group called the Church of Jesus Christ of Latter-Day Saints, based on the Book of Mormon, which is said to be a lost section of the Bible.

Mun, Thomas An English mercantilist and director of the East India Company.

National Industrial Recovery Act (NIRA) A New Deal act of FDR approved in 1933, setting up a system of industial self-government by drawing up codes of fair trade practices for each industry regarding working conditions and abolishing child labor.

nativism A sociopolitical policy in the United States that favors the interests of native inhabitants over those of immigrants.

Neutrality Acts Several acts passed between 1935 and 1937 that limited America's involvement in the growing tensions of Europe.

Newton, Sir Isaac English mathematician and physicist who formulated the mathematics for the universal law of gravitation and determined the nature of light. His experiments were important to the Scientific Revolution of the late 1600s.

Nietzsche, Friedrich (1844–1900) German philosopher who condemned Christianity as a slave religion and democracy as the rule of mediocrity. He believed that a small group of "supermen" would eventually dominate the world, and may have influenced the thinking of those who accepted Adolf Hitler's rise in Germany.

norms Rules or patterns for behavior.

Northwest Ordinance Approved in 1787 by the Articles of Confederation government, this legislation organized the region north of the Ohio River, including Ohio, Indiana, Illinois, Michigan, and Wisconsin. It provided a plan of government for this territory that would result in three to five states equal to that of the other 13 states. It also banned slavery from the area.

nullification The political belief that a state has the right to not adhere to the guidelines of a federal law. Expressed in 1798 against the Alien and Sedition Acts in the Kentucky and Virginia Resolutions, and against the Tariff of 1828 with the South Carolina Ordinance of Nullification.

Owen, Robert A wealthy British cotton manufacturer who created a model industrial community in Scotland at New Lanark. He paid high wages, reduced working hours, provided sanitary factory conditions, built decent homes for workers, established schools for their children, and permitted the workers to share in management and profits. In 1825, a similar venture in New Harmony, Indiana, failed.

parity Equivalence, maintained by government support of farm-product prices, between farmers' current purchasing power and their purchasing power during a chosen base period.

Pascal, Blaise (1632–1662) French philosopher and mathematician who worked out a number of theorems dealing with probability.

Pendleton Act Passed in 1883, it provided that some government workers would be hired based on competitive examinations. It also set up a Civil Service Commission to administer the tests. It forbade government employees from being forced to give money to political parties.

Petty, William (1623–1687) English political economist.

Pitt, William (1759–1806) British prime minister who supported moderate reform of Parliament during the 1780s, but by the 1790s he secured parliamentary approval to suspend habeas corpus.

planned economy An economy where state authorities, rather than market forces, directly determine prices, output, and production.

Platonism   The philosophy of Plato insofar as it asserts ideal forms as an absolute and eternal reality of which the phenomena of the world are an imperfect and transitory reflection.

Populism   Political movement begun by farmers and labor unions in the 1890s. It sought to limit the power of big business and grant individuals more say in the governmental process.

pragmatism   Theory developed by Charles S. Peirce and William James that the meaning of a proposition or course of action lies in its observable consequences and that the sum of these consequences constitutes meaning.

protectorate   The relation of a strong state to a weaker state under its control and protection; a state or territory so controlled and protected; the authority exercised by the controlling state.

Quaker   A member of a religious sect, the Society of Friends, founded by George Fox, an Englishman, about 1650. Friends believe in plainness of dress,   manners, and religious worship, and are opposed to military service and the taking of oaths.

Quesnay, François (1694–1774)   French physician and political economist.

recession   A moderate and temporary decline in the economy.

remonetization   The restoration of silver for use as legal tender.

Ricardo, David (1772–1823)   English economist who worked out a theory of rent and wages using Malthusian ideas; made poverty seem inevitable and irremediable. Wages tended to remain at the minimum needed to maintain workers, with increased wages encouraging laborers to increase their families.

Riis, Jacob   An immigrant who became a muckraker photographer and journalist exposing the poorer conditions found in slums and tenements. He wrote *How the Other Half Lives,* and was committed to eliminating slums in New York City.

Rodbertus, Johann Karl   German sociologist who was instrumental in introducing French ideas into Germany.

Rostow, Walter   Educated at Yale and Oxford, this English scholar wrote *Essays on the British Economy of the Nineteenth Century* (1948) and other books postulating that societies passed through five stages of economic development from traditional society to a mature society of high mass consumption.

Saint Simon   One of the 12 Apostles.

Salvation Army   An organization founded in England and the United States as part of the Social Gospel movement during the late 19th-century progressive period. Formed to aid urban poor and immigrants during the industrial period.

samurai   The warrior class in feudal Japan.

Say, Jean-Baptiste (1767–1832)   French economist espousing economic liberalism.

secondary groups   Groups in which interaction between members is more superficial than in a primary group and generally based on utilitarian goals.

Senior, Nassau William (1790–1864)   English utilitarian economist who wrote with references to the struggles of the working classes.

Sherman Antitrust Act   Approved in 1890, this act prohibited monopolies by declaring illegal combinations of business that were "in restraint of trade or commerce."

Sismondi, Jean Simonde de (1773–1842)   Swiss historian who attacked the laissez-faire doctrine of the liberal school and was one of the first to call for state action on behalf of the helpless working class.

Smith, Adam   Scottish economist whose *Wealth of Nations* (1776) expressed the idea of laissez-faire; that is, the government should not interfere in business.

socialism   An economic philosophy or political system in which the community, not private individuals, owns and operates the means of production and distribution. All will share in the work and the profits.

Sorokin, Pitirim   Sociologist who argued that societies are oriented toward either "sensate" or "ideational" values.

Spock, Benjamin Dr. Spock's book, *Baby and Child Care,* was widely used as a child-centered guide to child rearing, reflecting the 1950s emphasis on family life and featuring the middle-class woman in her role as a mother at home.

subsidy Monetary assistance by a government to a person, group, or commercial enterprise.

supply and demand Economic terms referring to the amount of goods available for sale and the interest of the consumer in purchasing them.

Supreme Court-packing bill A judiciary reorganization bill submitted to Congress by FDR in 1937, proposing an additional member of the Supreme Court for each one over 70 years of age (five in total) as Roosevelt's reaction to the Court's invalidation of several New Deal pieces of legislation.

Taft, William Howard After easily winning the presidential election in 1908, with the support of progressives and conservatives, he soon found that his only support came from conservatives. He lost a hotly contested three-party election in 1912.

Taft-Hartley Act Legislation passed in 1947 that was considered an anti-union law prohibiting the closed shop, requiring union leaders to take a non-communist oath, and establishing a 60-day cooling-off period before striking.

Taney, Roger B. Supreme Court justice most remembered for his decision in the Dred Scott case of 1857. His opinion asserted that Negroes could not be citizens and Congress could not ban slavery in the territories, thus effectively disallowing the 1820 Missouri Compromise.

tariff A tax or duty imposed by a government on imports or exports.

Thirteenth Amendment Ratified after the Civil War in 1865, this Reconstruction amendment provided that slavery should end.

Thomas, Norman A six-time Socialist party candidate for president between 1928 and 1948, championing such reforms as unemployment compensation and old age pensions.

Thoreau, Henry David Essayist who believed in the right of an individual to disobey an unjust law in a nonviolent manner, that is, through civil disobedience. He believed it was unjust to pay taxes to a nation that permitted slavery. His philosophy was developed during the period of reform movements in the 1840s.

transcendentalism A philosophy developed in the 1840s stressing intuition, belief in individual human dignity, equality, and social reform.

transfer payments Grants or other payments not made in return for a productive service, such as pensions, unemployment benefits, or other forms of income support.

Treaty of Greenville Signed by Little Turtle of the Miami Confederacy, this treaty ended wars with the United States in Ohio and Indiana in the early 1790s.

Turner, Frederick Jackson Historian from the University of Wisconsin who used the 1890 census in an 1893 paper to explain that the American frontier served as a place where democracy grew with each wave of population movement westward. Pioneers had a chance to build the kind of society they wanted in new communities. The frontier also served as a "safety valve" for problems in the East.

variable costs Costs that vary directly with the rate of output, such as labor costs, raw material costs, or fuel and power costs.

Veblen, Thorstein A pessimistic American critic of society and its economic system, whose most important book was *The Theory of the Leisure Class* (1899).

vertical mobility The ability to move up or down the social class ladder, depending on a person's ability to gain economic status.

WASP White Anglo-Saxon Protestants, designated by some nativists in America as the original Americans who epitomized American values, as opposed to immigrants, African-Americans, or various religious groups.

Weaver, James B. Populist candidate for president in 1892 who received 22 electoral votes and over 1 million popular votes.

Weismann, August   German biologist whose theory of the continuity of the germ plasm cast doubt upon the inheritance of acquired characteristics.

welfare state   A social system whereby the state assumes primary responsibility for the economic and social well-being of its citizens.

Wirth, Louis   Sociologist who looked at urbanism and concluded that the many occupations found in cities and the spaces alloted resulted in compartmentalizing the city dweller's life, causing a weakness in social cohesion.

Zeno   Greek philosopher who established the Stoic School, which held that humans must live in harmony within themselves and with nature.

Zorach v. Clauson   A 1952 case that upheld New York City public schools' release-time religious education program, which allowed students to secure religious instruction during school hours on premises other than school property.

Practice Questions on Social Sciences—History

Before attempting a whole sample examination over the vast social sciences area, let's look at some other examples, by specific subject. You should become acquainted with the various kinds of information that you will be asked to provide when you take the entire CLEP Exam. Sometimes it is difficult to decide in which subject area a question belongs, and in some cases we have had to arbitrarily assign a question to a particular discipline.

QUESTIONS ABOUT AMERICAN HISTORY

Directions: Each of the questions or incomplete statements below is followed by five suggested answers or completions. Select the one that is best in each case.

1. The purpose of the Monroe Doctrine was to

   (A) make the world safe for democracy
   (B) let European nations know that the Western Hemisphere was closed to further colonization
   (C) let the world know that America had become isolationist
   (D) free the slaves so that they could fight on the side of the North during the Civil War
   (E) allow Americans to establish control over Latin American nations

2. "He made the American vernacular the medium of a great literary work. The vigor of his prose comes directly from the speech of the great valley of the Far West." This statement refers to which of the following people?

   (A) Frederick Jackson Turner
   (B) James Fenimore Cooper
   (C) Thomas Jefferson
   (D) John Dewey
   (E) Samuel Clemens

3. During a time in which America followed a cautious policy of economic isolationism, tariffs made up more than 85% of the federal government's revenue. This occurred during the time period

   (A) of the early 1800s
   (B) of the Civil War, 1860–1865
   (C) of the early 1900s
   (D) of World War II
   (E) of the 1950s

MAP **A**

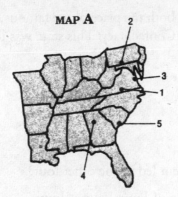

Questions 4–7 pertain to map A.

4. The following events are associated with which president?

   • Opening up the doors and begins trading with communist China
   • The invasion of Cambodia during the Viet Nam War
   • Watergate scandal

   (A) President Dwight Eisenhower
   (B) President John F. Kennedy
   (C) President Lyndon Johnson
   (D) President Richard Nixon
   (E) President Ronald Reagan

5. Which sequence of historical events is chronologically correct?

   (A) Spanish-American War, War of 1812, World War I, Vietnam War
   (B) World War I, World War II, the Spanish-American War, Vietnam War
   (C) War of 1812, Spanish-American War, World War II, Vietnam War
   (D) Spanish-American War, World War I, Vietnam War, World War II
   (E) Vietnam War, World War I, World War II, Spanish-American War

6. Note the following items:

   • March on Washington 1963
   • "I have a dream."
   • Selma demonstration on voting registration

   These events are associated with

   (A) the Black Panthers
   (B) the NAFTA
   (C) the PLO
   (D) Martin Luther King, Jr.
   (E) Governor George Wallace

7. This location was both the place of the famous battle of Gettysburg and also the capitol of the Confederacy. This state was located at

   (A) 1
   (B) 2
   (C) 3
   (D) 4
   (E) 5

8. Which development led to the other four?

   (A) The founding of Jamestown colony
   (B) The Spanish introduce the horse to the Americas
   (C) Thousands of Native Americans dying from new diseases
   (D) Columbus lands in Hispaniola in the Caribbean
   (E) Europeans and American Natives exchange tobacco and potatoes

9. Andrew Jackson, the "people's president," was known for

   (A) creating the spoil system in which he gave jobs to loyal supporters
   (B) the establishment of the Republican Party
   (C) legislation creating land grant colleges
   (D) legislation regulating rail transport
   (E) the regular employment of Negroes in government

10. Which of the following sets represent a major civil rights event in the 20th century?

    (A) Congressional Acts declared unconstitutional—President F.D. Roosevelt
    (B) Salt Talks—President Reagan
    (C) Roosevelt's Corollary—Theodore Roosevelt
    (D) Nullification—President Andrew Jackson
    (E) Little Rock, Arkansas—President Eisenhower

11. Each of the following countries is paired with a decade during which large numbers of its citizens migrated to the United States. Which pair is correct?

    (A) Sweden—1980s
    (B) Germany—1920s
    (C) Russia—1790s
    (D) Ireland—1845–1855
    (E) Italy—1945–1955

12. Note the following headlines:

    - "South Carolina Must Pay Tariff"
    - "National Bank Vetoed"
    - "To the Victors, Go the Spoils"

    These headlines are associated with the presidency of

    (A) Thomas Jefferson
    (B) Andrew Jackson
    (C) Abraham Lincoln
    (D) Theodore Roosevelt
    (E) George Washington

13. "How can an industrialized Northeast, a cotton-growing South, and a small farming West now live side by side in peace in our country?" This question about the United States might have been asked in

    (A) 1780
    (B) 1800
    (C) 1815
    (D) 1850
    (E) 1970

14. The geographical distribution of Negroes to more urban communities in the United States changed most in which period?

    (A) 1840–1860
    (B) 1860–1880
    (C) 1880–1900
    (D) 1920–1940
    (E) 1940–1960

15. Which of the following pairs is correct?

    (A) George Washington—Embargo and Non Intercourse Acts
    (B) Theodore Roosevelt—Stacking the Supreme Court
    (C) Lyndon B. Johnson—Civil Rights Acts of the 1960s
    (D) John F. Kennedy—The Watergate Affair
    (E) Dwight Eisenhower—The Cuban Missile Crisis

16. The United States' membership in which of the following organizations is most consistent with the Monroe Doctrine?

    (A) North Atlantic Treaty Organization
    (B) Southeast Asia Treaty Organization
    (C) International Monetary Fund
    (D) Organization of American States
    (E) United Nations Organization

17. "Every state should agree before an action is taken by the federal government." This states' rights sentiment is similar to the ideas expressed by

    (A) Jackson
    (B) Webster
    (C) Hamilton
    (D) Adams
    (E) Calhoun

18. In which presidential election did traditionally Democratic Georgia, Alabama, and Mississippi vote Republican because of liberal Democratic ticket?

    (A) 1928
    (B) 1932
    (C) 1956
    (D) 1964
    (E) 1968

19. In order to avoid involvement in Europe and Asia in the 1930s, the United States relied chiefly upon

    (A) collective security
    (B) neutrality legislation
    (C) the Kellogg-Briand Pact
    (D) the League of Nations
    (E) the "Good-Neighbor" policy

20. The 2000 election between Bush and Gore was finally solved when the issue of the Florida ballots was solved

    (A) by a vote of Congress
    (B) by the U.S. Supreme Court in a 5–2 decision
    (C) by executive action of President Clinton
    (D) with an amendment to the U.S. Constitution
    (E) by the Florida Supreme Court

21. Some historians say that this American leader should have stood trial for crimes against humanity for his decision to drop the atomic bomb on the cities of Hiroshima and Nagasaki. This president was

    (A) Ulysses Grant
    (B) Franklin D. Roosevelt
    (C) Harry S. Truman
    (D) Richard Nixon
    (E) Lyndon Baines Johnson

22. What do former Presidents Andrew Johnson and Bill Clinton have in common?

    (A) Impeachment charges were brought against them, but they remained in office
    (B) They served only one term
    (C) Both were removed from office as a result of scandals
    (D) They were strong Republican conservatives on foreign policies issues
    (E) They initiated two wars, Johnson the Civil War and Clinton the Persian Gulf War

23. The president connected with the Monica Lewinsky scandal was

    (A) Herbert Hoover
    (B) Bill Clinton
    (C) George Bush
    (D) Jimmy Carter
    (E) Richard Nixon

24. Which time period most accurately reflects the Cold War?

    (A) Churchill's Iron Curtain speech in 1945 to the rise of Boris Yeltsin
    (B) The building of the Berlin Wall in 1961 to 1989, when it was removed
    (C) World War I to World War II
    (D) The entire 20th century
    (E) World War I to Desert Storm

25. With the end of the Cold War, a United States proposal to expand a military alliance in the 1990s caused much controversy. The alliance was

    (A) SEATO
    (B) CENTO
    (C) NATO
    (D) METO
    (E) NAFTA

Answers

1. **B**	6. **D**	11. **D**	16. **D**	21. **C**
2. **E**	7. **A**	12. **B**	17. **E**	22. **A**
3. **A**	8. **D**	13. **D**	18. **D**	23. **E**
4. **D**	9. **A**	14. **E**	19. **B**	24. **A**
5. **C**	10. **E**	15. **C**	20. **B**	25. **C**

QUESTIONS ABOUT WESTERN CIVILIZATION

Directions: Each of the questions or incomplete statements below is followed by five suggested answers or completions. Select the one that is best in each case.

1. Which of the following was known to man before the Neolithic period?

   (A) Use of fire
   (B) Domestication of animals
   (C) Making pottery
   (D) Practice of agriculture
   (E) Permanent dwellings

2. The center of the civilization that we call Minoan was

   (A) in the islands along the Black Sea
   (B) on the island of Crete
   (C) in the central part of Asia Minor
   (D) on the mainland of Greece
   (E) on the Italian peninsula

3. The decline of power among the Greek city-states can be explained by

   (A) the military power of Persia
   (B) soft living
   (C) rivalry and civil war among the city-states
   (D) the pursuit of philosophy and art to the neglect of political action
   (E) inability to deal with sea power

4. Which civilization accepted monotheistic religious beliefs?

   (A) The Roman Republic
   (B) The Greek city-states
   (C) The Hindus of the Indus River Valley
   (D) The Egyptians
   (E) The Hebrews

5. As contrasted with English colonial administration, which of the following is true concerning Spanish colonial administration in the 17th and 18th centuries?

   (A) The authority of the Spanish king declined.
   (B) Spain did not maintain or enforce a mercantilist policy.
   (C) Spain permitted religious dissenters in its colonies.
   (D) Spain allowed less autonomy in its provinces in the New World.
   (E) Spain imposed less of a tax burden upon its colonies.

6. Which of the following would have been a member of the bourgeoisie in France prior to 1789?

   (A) Landed noble
   (B) Peasant
   (C) Merchant
   (D) Lower-class workman in Paris
   (E) Bishop

7. The art center of the Renaissance world was the city of

   (A) Florence
   (B) Paris
   (C) Moscow
   (D) Granada
   (E) Pompeii

8. The "Donation of Constantine" was a document that supposedly established

   (A) Charlemagne's claim to the throne
   (B) the pope's right to political power in the West
   (C) Christianity as the legal religion within the Roman Empire
   (D) the capital of the Roman Empire at the city of Constantinople
   (E) legitimized transfer of power to Byzantium

9. Because of its extensive colonial empire, this nation was among the most populous on earth. As one of the key nations of the "new imperialistic" age, its language was widely used outside its borders. By 1970 it was not among the top ten countries in population, and its influence was much reduced. To what country are we referring?

   (A) Netherlands
   (B) Russia
   (C) U.S.A.
   (D) Japan
   (E) France

10. Summer, cuneiform, ziggurats, and the first written set of laws are all part of the ancient civilization of

    (A) Rome
    (B) Greece
    (C) Harappa
    (D) Mesopotamia
    (E) Huang He Valley

11. "Some say that there are perhaps two nations in this country and great efforts have been made to erase this fact. There is hope these efforts (such as changing the flag design) may succeed." Twice, in 1980 and again in 1995, a separatist movement by a major province to secede from the nation failed. This nation is

    (A) France
    (B) Sweden
    (C) Denmark
    (D) Switzerland
    (E) Canada

12. In the 16th century, England was under the rule of which Protestant family?

    (A) Tudors
    (B) Stuarts
    (C) Hapsburgs
    (D) Medici
    (E) Windsors

13. The Versailles Peace Treaty resulted in a

    (A) more powerful Germany
    (B) Austria gaining additional land for the role it played in the Allied victory
    (C) financial collapse for Germany by 1923
    (D) the immediate rise of Hitler and the Nazi Party
    (E) Germany restoring the monarchy to the throne

14. The Law of the Twelve Tables, the plebian, the tribunes, and the Assembly of Tribes are all associated with what great civilization?

    (A) Athens
    (B) Egypt
    (C) Roman Republic
    (E) Sparta
    (F) Phoenicians

15. The development of early civilizations usually depended on

    (A) the formation of democratic governments
    (B) a plentiful water supply and fertile land
    (C) a location near large deposits of gold and silver
    (D) the existence of large armies
    (E) strong religious centers

16. Which nation below was unified in the 19th century through "blood, sweat and iron"?

    (A) England
    (B) France
    (C) Italy
    (D) Germany
    (E) Russia

17. Note the following headlines:

    • "Auschwitz Commits Genocide"
    • "The Final Solution Results in Millions Dead"
    • "Chamberlain Saves Czechoslovakia by Giving Up the Sudetenland"

    These headlines are each associated with

    (A) events dealing with Nazi Germany during World War II
    (B) imperialism of the 19th century
    (C) the unification of Germany after World War I
    (D) the invasion of Russia by Napoleon
    (E) Vietnam War during the 1960s and '70s

18. In 1904–05, Japan demonstrated its industrial success by modernizing its armed forces and defeating which nation?

    (A) Britain
    (B) France
    (C) Germany
    (D) Spain
    (E) Russia

19. The Huns were

    (A) one of the German tribes
    (B) Asian invaders attacking the Western Roman Empire
    (C) Moslem invaders of Europe
    (D) the people led by Theodoric who conquered Italy
    (E) Vikings who conquered Normandy

20. "If God shows you a way in which you may lawfully get more than in another way (without wrong to your soul or to any other), if you refuse this and choose the less gainful way, you cross one of the ends of your callings, and you refuse to be God's steward." This strong religious sentiment was most representative of

    (A) Scholasticism
    (B) 16th-century Anglicanism
    (C) 17th-century English Puritanism
    (D) Monastic thought
    (E) Christianity in the 1st century A.D.

21. The conservative Austrian foreign minister who played an important role at the Congress of Vienna 1814–15 was

    (A) Talleyrand
    (B) Metternich
    (C) Castlereagh
    (D) Baron Von Stein
    (E) Hindenburg

22. The journals of early travelers such as Ibn Battuta of Morocco, Zheng He of China, and Mansa Musa of Mali are examples of

    (A) works of fiction intended to design the adventure of these travelers
    (B) primary sources describing observations of their travels to other cultures
    (C) secondary sources that record the traveler's interpretations of history
    (D) imperialistic expansion by non-Caucasian cultures
    (E) great Asian and African leaders of their people

23. "As to the speeches which were made either before or during the Peloponnesian War, it is hard for me, and for others who reported them to me, to recollect the exact words. I have therefore put into the mouth of each speaker the sentiments proper to the occasion, expressed as I thought he would be likely to express them." This quote deals with what ancient civilization?

    (A) The Roman Republic
    (B) The Hebrews
    (C) The Roman Empire
    (D) The Greek city-states
    (E) The Phoenicians

Base your answer to questions 24 and 25 on the following poem and on your knowledge of social studies.

> "Here is a new city shall be wrought (built) . . . .
> Shall break a window to the West . . .
> Here flags of foreign nations all
> By waters new to them will call."
> Alexander Pushkin, "The Bronze Horseman"

24. Which Russian ruler's goals are described in the poem?

    (A) Gorbachev
    (B) Peter the Great
    (C) Nicholas II
    (D) Ivan the Terrible
    (E) Catherine the Great

25. Which major Russian policy was developed to implement the plans described in the poem?

    (A) westernization
    (B) isolationism
    (C) appeasement
    (D) status quo
    (E) balance of power

Answers

1. **A**	6. **C**	11. **E**	16. **D**	21. **B**
2. **B**	7. **A**	12. **A**	17. **A**	22. **B**
3. **C**	8. **C**	13. **C**	18. **E**	23. **D**
4. **E**	9. **E**	14. **C**	19. **B**	24. **B**
5. **D**	10. **D**	15. **B**	20. **C**	25. **A**

QUESTIONS ABOUT AFRICAN/ASIAN CIVILIZATIONS

Directions: Each of the questions or incomplete statements below is followed by five suggested answers or completions. Select the one that is best in each case.

1. Chinese culture and influence were most significant in shaping the institutions of which of the following countries?

    (A) India, Japan, and Korea
    (B) Indonesia, Thailand, and the Philippines
    (C) Burma, Pakistan, and Bangladesh
    (D) Japan, Korea, and Vietnam
    (E) Japan, Korea, and the Philippines

2. During the late 19th century through most of the 20th century, the British used passes for identification in several colonies. The Indian nationalist leader Mahatma Gandhi responded with a policy of passive resistance. These events would be associated with

    (A) India only
    (B) South Africa only
    (C) India and South Africa
    (D) China
    (E) Japan

3. Today, mainland China

    (A) is no longer communist
    (B) controls the nationalist island known as Taiwan
    (C) has significantly increased human rights for its people since the Tiananmen Square incident
    (D) continues to build its economic system around collective farms
    (E) took over Hong Kong when the British gave it up in 1997

4. Between 1965 and 1974, which of the following was true concerning Nigeria, Uganda, and Ethiopia?

    (A) Independence was shortly followed by military dictatorship.
    (B) Democratic governments were organized.
    (C) Apartheid became national policy.
    (D) They joined the European Common Market.
    (E) They became independent nations.

5. The samurai were

    (A) Japanese scholars
    (B) a people from Central Asia who invaded Japan
    (C) a Buddhist sect in Japan
    (D) a Japanese warrior class
    (E) Japanese industrialists

6. In which African area did the Leakeys do most of their pioneering archaeological work?

    (A) the Congo Basin
    (B) the Nigerian rain forest
    (C) the Valley of the Kings in middle Egypt
    (D) the Saharan Desert
    (E) Olduvai Gorge

7. The Chinese considered foreigners to be barbarians. This attitude was an example of

    (A) cultural diffusion
    (B) empathy
    (C) interdependence
    (D) chauvinism
    (E) ethnocentrism

8. Kim Il Sung and Kim Jong Il have held power in

    (A) Singapore
    (B) Hong Kong
    (C) North Korea
    (D) South Korea
    (E) Taiwan

9. When the British colony of India became independent in 1947, which new nation was split into two parts nearly 3,000 miles apart because of its Muslim belief?

    (A) India
    (B) Sri Lanka
    (C) Kashmir
    (D) Pakistan
    (E) Nepal

10. The collapse of the "bubble economy" was a trend that occurred during the 1990s in the highly capitalistic nation of

    (A) Indonesia
    (B) Taiwan
    (C) Saudi Arabia
    (D) China
    (E) Japan

11. One of the world's greatest supplies of gold and diamonds comes from this African nation:

    (A) Nigeria
    (B) Egypt
    (C) Ethiopia
    (D) Kenya
    (E) South Africa

12. Mansa Musa, Timbuktu, and Mali are all associated with the African civilizations of

    (A) Western Sudan
    (B) Benin
    (C) Zimbabwe
    (D) Kilwa
    (E) Zanzibar

13. Which pair of religions is best associated with both traditional and modern day sub-Saharan Africa?

    (A) Islam and Hinduism
    (B) Animism and Judaism
    (C) Christianity and Islam
    (D) Animism and Islam
    (E) Christianity and Palestinian

14. One similarity between Japanese Shintoism and African animism is the belief that

    (A) everything in nature has a spirit and should be respected
    (B) only one god exists in the universe
    (C) people's moral conduct determines their afterlife
    (D) religious statues should be erected to honor the gods
    (E) reincarnation is based on how good or how bad you are in your current life

15. "take up the White Man's Burden—
    Send forth the best ye breed—
    Go, bind your son in exile
    To serve your captives' need."

    Rudyard Kipling, *The Five Nations* (1903)

    The words of this poem have been used to support the practice of

    (A) isolationism
    (B) cultural borrowing
    (C) self-determination
    (D) imperialism
    (E) humanitarianism

16. Sun Yat-sen of China and Mahatma Gandhi of India were similar in that both

    (A) rejected violence as a way to aim political power
    (B) supported Marxist philosophy to change existing governments
    (C) led a successful nationalistic movement in their respective countries
    (D) promoted a society ruled by religious leaders
    (E) failed to bring about any permanent change

17. Which statement describes India's foreign policy between 1947 and 1990?

    (A) It imitated its former mother country, Great Britain.
    (B) It supported strong ties with Communist China.
    (C) It joined NATO, developing strong ties with the West.
    (D) It generally followed a policy of nonalignment.
    (E) It maintained a strong and positive relationship with neighboring Pakistan.

18. Examine the following information:

    • President Nkrumah
    • A Western Sudanic Empire
    • The first African colony to become independent after World War II—1957
    • Famous for the trans-Saharan gold salt trade

    These events are associated with

    (A) Ghana
    (B) Songhai
    (C) Zaire
    (D) Rhodesia
    (E) Nigeria

19. During the 1960s, the Biafran Civil War tore this western African nation apart. Despite great oil reserves, this nation still struggles from division caused by strong tribal loyalties. This nation is

    (A) the Republic of South Africa
    (B) Ethiopia
    (C) Rwanda
    (D) Tanzania
    (E) Nigeria

20. The Khmer Rouge, Pol Pot, and the Killing Fields are all associated with the

    (A) Viet Nam War
    (B) Cambodian genocide
    (C) Rape of Nanking
    (D) liberation of the Philippines
    (E) boat people of SE Asia

21. The climate most common to sub-Saharan Africa is

    (A) Savanna Grasslands
    (B) Rain Forest
    (C) Desert
    (D) Mediterranean
    (E) Humid Continental

22. This former British colony is rich in farmland. While the equator passes right through the center of this nation, its elevation (the eastern highlands) provides cool temperature and fertile soil. This nation is

    (A) Nigeria
    (B) Kenya
    (C) Egypt
    (D) Rhodesia
    (E) Congo

23. This Asian nation that has the largest number of Islamic followers is

    (A) Pakistan
    (B) India
    (C) Japan
    (D) Korea
    (E) Philippines

24 Since World War II, this Asian country was the best representative of a capitalistic and democratic government in the entire region. This country is

    (A) China
    (B) Indonesia
    (C) Philippines
    (D) Japan
    (E) Mongolia

25. Which non-Western nation is closet to China in overall population?

    (A) Japan
    (B) Sri Lanka
    (C) Russia
    (D) Bangladesh
    (E) India

Answers

1. **D**	6. **E**	11. **E**	16. **C**	21. **A**
2. **C**	7. **E**	12. **A**	17. **D**	22. **B**
3. **E**	8. **C**	13. **D**	18. **A**	23. **A**
4. **A**	9. **D**	14. **A**	19. **E**	24. **D**
5. **D**	10. **E**	15. **D**	20. **B**	25. **E**

QUESTIONS ABOUT ECONOMICS

Directions: Each of the questions or incomplete statements below is followed by five suggested answers or completions. Select the one that is best in each case.

1. The most important factor in creating the world "population explosion" has been

    (A) higher fertility
    (B) more multiple births
    (C) fewer wars
    (D) more family sentiment
    (E) lower death rates

2. Malthus thought that human population, if unchecked, would tend to grow at

    (A) an arithmetic rate
    (B) a geometric rate
    (C) a constantly slow rate
    (D) an undetermined rate
    (E) a rate determined by the sex ratio

3. Scarcity of resources in relation to desires or needs occurs

    (A) only under capitalism
    (B) only under socialism
    (C) only during wartime
    (D) in all societies
    (E) in money-using societies

4. The percentage of our workforce in agricultural pursuits in 1800 was about

    (A) 20%
    (B) 33%
    (C) 50%
    (D) 75%
    (E) 95%

5. The main reason for organizing the C.I.O. in the 1930s was to

    (A) organize African-Americans and immigrants who seldom belonged to a labor union
    (B) organize mass-production workers
    (C) escape the high fees of the A.F. of L.
    (D) organize craft workers
    (E) organize white-collar workers

6. Currently in what part of the world is the education of women most behind as to percentage and quality?

    (A) North America
    (B) Europe
    (C) Australia
    (D) Islamic Middle East
    (E) Japan

7. "Like Peter the Great westernized Russia, we rapidly transformed our country from a traditional based economic system into a modern industrial economic system and became a leading colonial power by the end of the 19th century." This quote refers to the industrial and economic growth of

    (A) Mongolia under the Tokugawa Shogunate
    (B) China under the Q'ing Dynasty
    (C) South Africa under the Boers
    (D) India led by the Sepoys
    (E) Japan under the Meiji emperor

8. The English economist John Maynard Keynes is associated with the policy of

   (A) trickle-down
   (B) high tariffs
   (C) priming the pump
   (D) balancing the budget
   (E) collective bargaining

9. Historically, the country considered to be the most deficient in natural resources is

   (A) Brazil
   (B) Canada
   (C) Indonesia
   (D) Japan
   (E) Nigeria

10. If anyone can be said to profit from a depression, the group favored would likely be

    (A) people with secure sources of fixed income, such as government bonds
    (B) people who borrowed money before the depression and must repay during it
    (C) industrial owners producing consumer goods
    (D) assembly-line workers in automobile plants
    (E) low-level local government workers

11. Statistical evidence shows that the typical American family behaves in which of the following ways with respect to spending out of income?

    (A) An increasing proportion of income is spent on consumption as income increases.
    (B) The same proportion of income is spent on consumption at all except very low income levels.
    (C) The same proportion of income is spent on consumption at all income levels.
    (D) A decreasing proportion of income is spent on consumption as income decreases.
    (E) The same proportion of income is spent on consumption at all except very high income levels.

GRAPH A

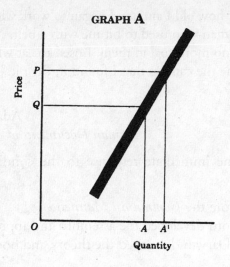

12. The thick black line in Graph A represents

    (A) supply
    (B) cost
    (C) subsidy
    (D) demand
    (E) interest

13. Examine the following economic principles:

    • laissez-faire
    • free competition
    • private ownership
    • profit motive

    These philosophical economic principles were first developed and pro-
    moted by

    (A) Mao Tse Tung
    (B) Karl Marx and Robert Engel
    (C) Adam Smith
    (D) John Stuart Mill
    (E) Vladimir Lenin

14. "I don't know how old I am. . . . I began to work when I was about 9. I first worked for a man who used to hit me with a belt. . . . I used to sleep in the pits that had no more coal in them; I used to eat whatever I could get; I ate for a long time the candles that I found in the pit."

E. Royston Pike
Adapted from *Hard Times,*
Human Documents of the Industrial Revolution

What was one immediate response to the conditions described in this passage?

(A) Marx wrote the *Communist Manifesto*
(B) Henry Ford developed the assembly line approach to production
(C) Charles Darwin developed the theory and book *On the Origin of Species*
(D) Joseph Stalin instituted the collectivization of Russian land
(E) Europe created the EEC, the European Economic Community

15. The various editions of John Stuart Mill's *Principles of Political Economy* indicate that he

(A) became increasingly conservative and antisocialist as he grew older
(B) made remarkably few changes in the views that he first held as a young Benthamite
(C) completely abandoned the socialist views he had held as a young man
(D) increasingly recognized exceptions to a general policy of a laissez-faire society
(E) became more convinced that economic justice and political monarchy were tied together

16. In Western Europe during the medieval time of the 11th and 12th centuries, the right to coin money was

(A) reserved to the Holy Roman Emperor
(B) held only by kings
(C) a monopoly of the Church
(D) held by a number of nobles, kings, towns, and cities
(E) in the care of the state banks

17. Today the capitalistic countries of the United Kingdom, Canada, and the United States are all mainly

(A) market economy
(B) traditional economy
(C) command economy
(D) mixed economy
(E) communist economy

18. In Western Europe, debate and philosophical conflict over the economic and social value of the private property concept would have been of most concern during what two time periods?

    (A) Early Middle Ages and the early Renaissance years
    (B) Early 1600s and mid-1600s
    (C) Beginning of the 1700s to late 1700s
    (D) Mid-1750s and 1800s
    (E) 1850s to the late 20th century

19. The Hanseatic League was

    (A) a trading organization of the Greek city-states
    (B) organized by Marco Polo to help the Italian cities to monopolize and control Middle Eastern and Asian trade
    (C) a group of medieval manors united for protection against the invading tribes
    (D) an association of northern medieval cities and merchants that bonded to protect their commercial interest including sea piracy
    (E) a group of trading nations that crossed Europe into Asia along the secret silk road

20. India's gross national product is about twice that of Sweden. This means

    (A) India is more advanced in technology
    (B) that the average Indian is twice as well-off as the average Swede
    (C) India has sufficient capital
    (D) all of these
    (E) none of these

21. The Federal Reserve Bank has the power to change

    (A) tariffs
    (B) insurance premiums
    (C) the discount rate
    (D) the minimum wage
    (E) stock prices

22. As we enter the 21st century, the transportation of goods in the United States is moving more and more toward

    (A) motor trucks
    (B) canal barges
    (C) pipelines
    (D) railroads
    (E) airlines

23. The theory behind what consumers want and how the society meets consumer demands (market price) was first proposed in the late 18th century when he published his book *The Wealth of Nations*. This economist was

   (A) John Malthus
   (B) Karl Marx
   (C) Adam Smith
   (D) Robert Owen
   (E) Bentham

24. Travel by people between cities in the U.S. is now primarily by

   (A) ship
   (B) railroad
   (C) motor bus
   (D) airplane
   (E) automobile

25. "In these (economic) structures, people looked to past practices plus cultural and religious beliefs to decide what to produce, how to produce it, how products would be distributed, and even when task should be preformed." What type of economy is the author describing?

   (A) Market economy
   (B) Traditional economy
   (C) Command economy
   (D) Mixed economy
   (E) Communist economy

26. The Industrial Revolution had its very first start in

   (A) the United States
   (B) Spain
   (C) Japan
   (D) England
   (E) France

27. In 1933 the purpose of the United States government in devaluing the dollar in terms of gold was to

   (A) raise domestic prices and make American goods cheaper abroad
   (B) lower domestic prices and make American goods more expensive abroad
   (C) establish the gold standard
   (D) stop excessive exports of American goods
   (E) reduce the ability of the gold-producing USSR to exchange gold for industrial and military goods

28. Note the following economic event and concepts:

    - pump priming
    - deficit spending
    - Black Friday

    These are all related to

    (A) the birth of communism in Russia in 1917
    (B) the collapse of the German economy in 1929
    (C) the New Deal and the Great Depression
    (D) the recession of the late 1970s
    (E) the fall of communism throughout eastern Europe

29. From ancient times to the time of Christopher Columbus, the most important body of water for international trade was the

    (A) Mediterranean Sea
    (B) Atlantic Ocean
    (C) Pacific Ocean
    (D) Baltic Sea
    (E) Black Sea

30. The economic system inaugurated by Jean Baptiste Colbert, financial minister and economic advisor to Louis XIV, was

    (A) capitalism
    (B) utopian socialism
    (C) scientific socialism
    (D) laissez faire
    (E) mercantilism

Answers

1. **E**	6. **D**	11. **D**	16. **D**	21. **C**	26. **D**
2. **B**	7. **E**	12. **A**	17. **D**	22. **D**	27. **A**
3. **D**	8. **C**	13. **C**	18. **E**	23. **C**	28. **C**
4. **E**	9. **D**	14. **A**	19. **D**	24. **E**	29. **A**
5. **B**	10. **A**	15. **D**	20. **E**	25. **B**	30. **E**

QUESTIONS ABOUT SOCIOLOGY

Directions: Each of the questions or incomplete statements below is followed by five suggested answers or completions. Select the one that is best in each case.

1. "Caste" and "class" are

   (A) both representative of social strata but to different degrees
   (B) sociological and economical concepts that are identical
   (C) not found in our American society but found in the nation of India
   (D) associated strictly with a capitalistic society
   (E) a result of the Industrial Revolution

2. The marriage of one female to more than one male is called

   (A) monogamy
   (B) celibacy
   (C) polyandry
   (D) polygyny
   (E) endogamy

3. Mormons practiced the act of having multiple wives. What level of social behavior would such an act violate in today's American society?

   (A) A folkway
   (B) The mores
   (C) Law
   (D) Polygamy
   (E) None of the above

4. At the very end of the 20th century and the beginning of the 21st century, which immigrant group came under increasing attack due to their illegal alien status?

   (A) African Americans
   (B) Canadians
   (C) Indians
   (D) Philippinos
   (E) Latin American Hispanics

5. The 2000 Census report indicated that

   (A) people were moving more into rural America
   (B) America's senior citizen population was decreasing
   (C) that there was widespread child abuse in the Roman Catholic Church
   (D) the largest number of people lived in America's suburbs
   (E) the percent of career women had continued to increase since the last census

6. Which type of social system accepts that all classes should be equal and eventually all classes would disappear?

    (A) Capitalistic societies
    (B) Communistic societies
    (C) Fascist societies
    (D) Feudalistic societies
    (E) Caste system societies

7. Stratification is most closely related to social

    (A) identification
    (B) differentiation
    (C) amalgamation
    (D) disorganization
    (E) assimilation

8 Which series represents a trend from little to more social mobility?

    (A) Caste, class, estates
    (B) Estates, caste, class
    (C) Caste, estates, class
    (D) Class, caste, estates
    (E) There is an equal amount of social mobility in each.

9. Which of the following statements is correct?

    (A) Mores are more powerful and more important than folkways.
    (B) Form and content of mores are universally identical.
    (C) There is no sanction (punishment) when you violate mores.
    (D) Violation of mores is not necessary for the overall welfare of the society.
    (E) Violating a folkway will result in taboos and positive injunction.

10. The two most significant influences on childhood socialization (ages 3–11) is the school and the

    (A) computer
    (B) peer group
    (C) television
    (D) religious center
    (E) family

11. Harlow's famous experiments with monkeys in the 1940s showed that

    (A) monkeys and humankind are at a very similar level of development
    (B) social isolation from mothers and peers had irreversible effects on the personality of these monkeys
    (C) monkeys can be taught to communicate with humans at least through sign language
    (D) monkeys need a mother to survive his experiment
    (E) social isolation from mother and peers had no effect on the development of these monkeys

12. A subculture is

    (A) totally opposed to the existing values of the society at large
    (B) better known as a religious cult
    (C) an ethnic group that is an outcast of society that lives mainly in rural areas
    (D) willing to be different yet not willing to totally leave the mother culture
    (E) generally very outspoken about political issues

13. "Childhood moves through cognitive stages of development," according to

    (A) Mead
    (B) Skinner
    (C) Erickson
    (D) Piaget
    (E) Freud

14. Which situation is the best example of the concept of "culture shock"?

    (A) The refusal of the Amish to drive motor vehicles
    (B) The hippies' rejection of "The Establishment" in the 1960s
    (C) The difference in life-styles between Eastern and Western American Indian tribal groups
    (D) The playing of international soccer tournaments on United States soil
    (E) The initial reaction of a Peace Corps volunteer upon entering a developing nation

15. A caste society is characterized by the following:

    Choice 1: Intermarriage is forbidden across caste.
    Choice 2: Most statuses are achieved.
    Choice 3: Occupations are specific to special hereditary groups.

    (A) Choice 1 only
    (B) Choice 3 only
    (C) Choices 1 and 3
    (D) Choices 2 and 3
    (E) All three choices

16. A "sect" religion tends to be

    (A) in accord with the values of the society in which it exists
    (B) lenient toward the indifferent
    (C) a reforming element hoping to make the society more livable
    (D) withdrawn from societal norms and extremely pietistic
    (E) the official religion of the state in which it exists

17. A Russian by the name of Pavlov conducted a series of experiments with animals and discovered conditioned reflex. This finding was the basis of which school of thought?

    (A) psychoanalysis
    (B) behaviorism
    (C) relativism
    (D) the new idealism
    (E) Hegelianism

18. If teaching facts are the sole aim of a teacher, she will probably do better if she is

    (A) nondirective
    (B) permissive and informal
    (C) directive and authoritarian
    (D) disorganized
    (E) group oriented

19. Assigning subjects in an experiment to one treatment or another by flipping a coin is an example of

    (A) randomization
    (B) experimentation
    (C) statistics
    (D) field study
    (E) diary record keeping

20. In *Civilization and its Discontents,* Freud expressed his viewpoint concerning the necessity of controlling the antisocial and aggressive propensities of man. Which of the following authors saw similar ideas in 18th- and 19th-century politics?

    (A) Rousseau
    (B) Locke
    (C) Voltaire
    (D) Hobbes
    (E) Montesquieu

21. Opposition that focuses on the opponent, basically, and only secondarily on the reward is most closely associated with social

    (A) accommodation
    (B) stratification
    (C) competition
    (D) conflict
    (E) differentiation

22. Cases where infants were subjected to prolonged isolation show that

    (A) human beings can acquire culture without human contact
    (B) human beings cannot become socialized unless they are brought up among human beings
    (C) mental-physical development does not depend upon human contact
    (D) people are born with most of the traits they exhibit as adults
    (E) language use comes at a certain age, regardless of the social situation

23. When applying Marxian philosophy to sociology, Karl Marx thought that throughout the history of mankind, the economic and social classes

    (A) were in constant conflict with each other
    (B) accepted the fact that some classes should live better than others
    (C) were all equal in society
    (D) lived in a state of constant harmony
    (E) recognized the right of the powerful class to dominate the society

24. The study of cults shows us that it is often accompanied by isolation from the main society. A classical study of cults is Lofland's study of the "Divine Precepts." According to his findings, the individual most predisposed to cult religious conversion would

    (A) be undergoing political stress, be religiously oriented, but be closed to new religious outlooks
    (B) have a religiously oriented problem-solving perspective, know people in the new religious group, and be personally secure
    (C) be personally secure, be religiously oriented, and be open to new religious outlooks
    (D) be undergoing personal stress, have few if any ties with individuals outside of new religious groups, and be open to new religious outlooks
    (E) be very conservative and believe in the status quo

25. A secondary group is characterized by

    (A) impersonal relationships
    (B) strong emotional ties
    (C) permanence over time
    (D) small size and intimacy
    (E) being with you throughout your life

Answers

1. **A**	6. **B**	11. **A**	16. **D**	21. **D**
2. **C**	7. **B**	12. **D**	17. **B**	22. **B**
3. **C**	8. **C**	13. **D**	18. **C**	23. **A**
4. **E**	9. **A**	14. **E**	19. **A**	24. **C**
5. **E**	10. **E**	15. **C**	20. **D**	25. **A**

QUESTIONS ABOUT POLITICAL SCIENCE

Directions: Each of the questions or incomplete statements below is followed by five suggested answers or completions. Select the one that is best in each case.

1. To which of the following did the U.S. Supreme Court apply the phrase "separate but equal"?

    (A) The formula for racial segregation (1896)
    (B) The nature of federal-state relations (1828)
    (C) The status of Indian tribal governments (1874)
    (D) The Civil War amendments (1865–1870)
    (E) The legal status of men and women (1913)

2. The law that can be considered the most important impetus to trade union organization was the

    (A) Sherman Act of 1890
    (B) Wagner Act of 1935
    (C) Taft-Hartley Act of 1947
    (D) Social Security Act of 1935
    (E) National Recovery Act of 1933

3. The case of McCulloch v. Maryland is considered one of the most important cases decided by the U.S. Supreme Court. In its decision, the court announced a major constitutional concept concerning

    (A) separation of church and state
    (B) judicial review
    (C) segregation
    (D) antitrust regulation
    (E) implied powers

4. Which political concept did we derive from English government when the Constitution was put into existence in the late 18th century?

    (A) limited monarchy
    (B) judicial review
    (C) cabinet system
    (D) bicameralism
    (E) direct democracy

5. The calling of the lords to attend the first parliament and then shortly thereafter the request for commoners or bourgeoisie to also attend parliament all originated with the

   (A) Battle of Hastings
   (B) Doomsday Book
   (C) signing of the Magna Carta
   (D) Act of Supremacy
   (E) creation of the Bills of Rights

6. The position of the Chief Justice of the United States Supreme Court is filled by

   (A) seniority
   (B) promotion
   (C) specific appointment
   (D) election
   (E) rotation among justices

7. The principle of judicial review in the Constitution was established in the case of

   (A) *Marbury* v. *Madison*
   (B) *McCulloch* v. *Maryland*
   (C) *Fletcher* v. *Peck*
   (D) *Missouri* v. *Holland*
   (E) *Zorach* v. *Clauson*

8. The body of legal rules based upon reason as applied in past cases going far back in English history is known as

   (A) constitutional law
   (B) statutory law
   (C) common law
   (D) administrative law
   (E) international law

9. The American Bill of Rights was modeled after the Glorious Revolution and the

   (A) Declaration of Independence
   (B) British Bill of Rights
   (C) Magna Carta
   (D) French Declaration of the Rights of Man
   (E) Napoleonic reforms

10. Ambassadors are appointed by the

    (A) president without the approval of Congress under a special provision of the constitution
    (B) president from a list chosen by the merit system
    (C) president with the consent of the Senate
    (D) retiring ambassadors, with the approval of the president, from a list of technically trained individuals
    (E) president from a list of graduates of the Foreign Service Academy

11. Currently Puerto Rico is an illustration of

    (A) a state
    (B) an incorporated territory
    (C) a protectorate
    (D) a commonwealth
    (E) a dominion

12. The armed forces of the United States are under the control of

    (A) the Departments of War and of the Navy
    (B) President
    (C) Congress
    (D) the General Staff
    (E) the Secretary of Defense

13. The policy of imperialism in the United States from 1890 to 1910 was largely the result of

    (A) the theory of isolation
    (B) an attack by Spain on the United States
    (C) demands for commercial expansion
    (D) a widespread desire to become a world power
    (E) missionary zeal

14. In the Constitution, the states were granted the right to

    (A) exercise only the powers given to them by the Constitution
    (B) settle directly their disputes with Mexico or Canada
    (C) establish their own militia without reference to United States Army standards
    (D) exercise all powers not denied by the Constitution
    (E) veto acts of Congress

15. The Senate must ratify or reject all

    (A) treaties with other nations, by a two-thirds vote of the senators present
    (B) appointments of the president by a majority vote
    (C) treaties or agreements between two states
    (D) decisions of the Supreme Court
    (E) appointments of minor officials by the president

16. The work of the Department of Labor in the president's cabinet is, in the main,

    (A) supporting the American Federation of Labor and other labor organizations in their activities
    (B) collecting statistics on labor conditions and making recommendations to the president
    (C) regulating labor conditions in industry by issuing orders modifying wages or hours, or both
    (D) regulating working conditions of government employees
    (E) providing for binding arbitration in industrial disputes

17. The Prohibition Amendment, ratified in 1919, was

    (A) repealed by the Twenty-First Amendment
    (B) modified but not repealed entirely
    (C) repealed by Congress to meet an economic emergency
    (D) acted upon by popular conventions in each state
    (E) a war measure, not intended to be permanent

18. In some states, voters may originate legislation by

    (A) common consent
    (B) initiative petition
    (C) letters to the legislature
    (D) ordinance
    (E) church rules

19. When the government (state or national) takes possession and ownership of private property for public use, it is exercising the right of

    (A) public ownership
    (B) eminent domain
    (C) state confiscation
    (D) public domain
    (E) *ad hoc* rule

20. An American male in 1983 is white, 50 years old, lives in Topeka, Kansas, makes $100,000 a year as an owner of a small business. You would, on the basis of probability, expect him to vote

    (A) Democratic
    (B) Right to Life
    (C) States Rights or American Independent
    (D) Republican
    (E) Socialist Labor

21. Which of the following do most historians agree is most significant for the continuance of democracy, which is verified in the first ten amendments?

    (A) A written constitution
    (B) Control of finances by legislatures
    (C) Separation of powers
    (D) A large number of political parties
    (E) Protection of civil liberties for all citizens

22. Which state held the balance in the 2000 election between George Bush and Al Gore?

    (A) Washington, D.C.
    (B) New York
    (C) Florida
    (D) California
    (E) Texas

23. "The right of citizens of the United States to vote in any primary or other election for President or Vice-President, for electors for elections for President or Vice-President, or for Senator or Representative in Congress shall not be denied or abridged by the United States or any state by reason of failure to pay any poll tax or other tax." The above statement is taken from which of the following amendments to the United States Constitution?

    (A) Fifth
    (B) Fifteenth
    (C) Twentieth
    (D) Twenty-Third
    (E) Twenty-Fourth

24. Which political philosopher had little impact on the origins of our liberal and democratic government?

    (A) Hobbes
    (B) Voltaire
    (C) Montesquieu
    (D) Locke
    (E) Jefferson

25. What do Ralph Nader and George Wallace have in common?

    (A) They were both Republicans.
    (B) They defected from the union.
    (C) They were all vice presidents in the 20th century.
    (D) They were all assassinated while in office.
    (E) They all ran for President as third-party candidates.

26. Which is an example of the unwritten Constitution?

    (A) The Congress
    (B) The Supreme Court
    (C) The appellate courts
    (D) The presidential cabinet
    (E) The Bill of Rights

27. Which statement is true concerning the Electoral College system? It was

    (A) part of the original Constitution
    (B) passed as a law by Congress
    (C) modified by the Bill of Rights
    (D) part of English Common Law
    (E) added to the Constitution in the 20th century

28. Consider the following events:

    • Lyndon Johnson decided not to seek a second term as president
    • Richard Nixon resigned from the office of president
    • George H. Bush was defeated by Clinton in his attempt to seek a second term

    What statement below reflects why each of these events happen?

    (A) Political scandals hurt the attempts of these men to be re-elected.
    (B) A long drawn out war made them lose public support.
    (C) As incumbent presidents, they lost the popularity and support of the people.
    (D) They were impeached by the Congress of the United States.
    (E) Their economic programs were largely a failure.

29. This president broke the tradition of the two-term president which led to the ratification of the 22nd Amendment (presidency limited to two terms):

    (A) Ulysses S. Grant
    (B) Teddy Roosevelt
    (C) Woodrow Wilson
    (D) Franklin D. Roosevelt
    (E) Harry S. Truman

30. Which statement accurately describes how the Constitution improved the Articles of Confederation?

   (A) The power of the president can be checked by the other two branches.
   (B) Congress is responsible to the state governments.
   (C) States have some power, but most power is given to the national government.
   (D) State courts were equal in power and authority to the national courts.
   (E) The power of Congress was reduced.

Answers

1. **A**	7. **A**	13. **C**	19. **B**	25. **E**
2. **B**	8. **C**	14. **D**	20. **D**	26. **D**
3. **E**	9. **B**	15. **A**	21. **E**	27. **A**
4. **D**	10. **C**	16. **B**	22. **C**	28. **C**
5. **C**	11. **D**	17. **A**	23. **E**	29. **B**
6. **C**	12. **B**	18. **B**	24. **A**	30. **C**

QUESTIONS ABOUT ANTHROPOLOGY

Directions: Each of the questions or incomplete statements below is followed by five suggested answers or completions. Select the one that is best in each case.

1. Which of the following statements about gorillas are true?

   (A) They have a structured, hierarchical social organization.
   (B) They spend nearly all of their time in the trees.
   (C) Their brain size is equal to that of humans.
   (D) They are violent killers.
   (E) Their behavior is unpredictable.

2. Why are present-day hunting and gathering societies of value to the study of anthropology?

   (A) They can learn Western technology so they can raise their standard of living.
   (B) They help us to justify the belief in ethnocentrism.
   (C) Their social organization is similar to that of other primates such as chimps and gorillas.
   (D) These societies may give some indication of how man lived in pre-historic times.
   (E) These societies demonstrate that man can live in a desert climate without technology.

3. The best method to test a two-million-year-old Australopithecus is

(A) carbon 14
(B) seriation
(C) dendrochronology
(D) potassium argon
(E) fluorine

4. The *Origin of Species* is an important anthropological work because it

(A) clearly states that man originated from apes
(B) presents the argument that species have evolved over periods of time
(C) confirmed the authenticity of Piltdown man
(D) states that population will increase at a greater rate than the food supply
(E) states that man was once a chimpanzee

5. The Neolithic period was considered a revolution for humankind because

(A) armies first developed during this time
(B) people descended from trees and became bipedal
(C) it was a change from a hunter-gatherer to a food-producing society
(D) religion first began
(E) a nomadic way of life began

6. A student once demonstrated among other fellow students in a cafeteria the eating of a live goldfish. The reaction of his fellow classmates was that of surprise. This is an example of

(A) cultural assimilation
(B) ethnocentrism
(C) cultural diffusion
(D) cultural universals
(E) culture shock

7. Dian Fossey did her most famous work studying the behavior of African

(A) chimpanzees
(B) orangutans
(C) gorillas
(D) monkeys
(E) lemurs

8. What were the first societies of man characterized by?

(A) They produced a surplus of food.
(B) They were chiefly hunters and gatherers.
(C) They had domesticated plants and animals.
(D) They lived in large, urban-type communities.
(E) They lived in trees.

9. The first civilizations found by archaeologists were in

    (A) Olduvai Gorge
    (B) The Tigris-Euphrates river valley
    (C) Mesoamerica
    (D) The Yellow River valley
    (E) Western Europe

10. Which event in human evolution came first?

    (A) Burial of the dead
    (B) Wall and cave paintings
    (C) Monotheistic religion
    (D) The invention of farming
    (E) The use of fire

11. All primates, including man's ancestors, live primarily in

    (A) desert areas
    (B) extremely cold environments
    (C) plateaus
    (D) mountain areas
    (E) rain forests

12. Which period best reflects the Paleolithic Age?

    (A) Two–three million years ago
    (B) 50,000 years ago
    (C) 12,000 B.C.
    (D) Post-Christ
    (E) The age of farming

13. "I depend primarily on fruits, nuts, roots, berries and the like. . . . I'm armed with small spears, throwing clubs, and sticks . . . and my people are restricted to a very low density of population." This quote was by a

    (A) hunter/gatherer
    (B) seminomadic herder
    (C) horticulturalist
    (D) nonnomadic individual
    (E) farmer

14. Which civilization is associated with the correct location?

    (A) Jarmo, Jericho—Mesoamerica
    (B) Tikal, Chichen-Itza—Nile River valley
    (C) Harrappa, Mohenjo Daro—Tigris-Euphrates River valley
    (D) Rome, Greece—Yellow River valley
    (E) Babylon, Sumer—Mesopotamia

15. Stonehenge, in England, was

    (A) built by the ancient Druids
    (B) an archaeological site of a primitive civilization for its time
    (C) a religious center where the stars were worshipped
    (D) built in a similar fashion to the Egyptian pyramids
    (E) an ancient city

16. The Neolithic Age began independently in Southeast Asia and the New World, yet cultures of these two areas had no contact with each other. This illustrates the concept of

    (A) parallel invention
    (B) culture shock
    (C) ethnocentrism
    (D) cultural diffusion
    (E) cultural assimilation

17. The lowest level or least developed of all the primates are the

    (A) gorillas
    (B) prosimians
    (C) old-world monkeys
    (D) new-world monkeys
    (E) gibbons

18. Which of the following would study and identify skeletal remains?

    (A) Primatologist
    (B) Ethnologist
    (C) Paleontologist
    (D) Archaeologist
    (E) Linguist

19. Mary Leakey and Margaret Mead are cultural anthropologists, which means that they study

    (A) archaeological fossil sites
    (B) human skulls and bones
    (C) contemporary human social life
    (D) monkeys and apes to understand human behavior
    (E) primitive technological societies such as the Eskimos

20. A study of gorillas and their humanlike behavior was made into a famous movie called *Gorillas in the Mist*. This movie portrayed the life of the famous primatologist

    (A) Jane Goodall
    (B) Dian Fossey
    (C) Louis Leakey
    (D) Margaret Mead
    (E) Mary Leakey

Answers

1. **A**	6. **E**	11. **E**	16. **A**
2. **D**	7. **C**	12. **A**	17. **B**
3. **D**	8. **B**	13. **A**	18. **C**
4. **B**	9. **B**	14. **E**	19. **E**
5. **C**	10. **E**	15. **C**	20. **B**

Social Sciences—History

ANSWER SHEET—SAMPLE EXAMINATION 1

1 Ⓐ Ⓑ Ⓒ Ⓓ Ⓔ	33 Ⓐ Ⓑ Ⓒ Ⓓ Ⓔ	65 Ⓐ Ⓑ Ⓒ Ⓓ Ⓔ	97 Ⓐ Ⓑ Ⓒ Ⓓ Ⓔ
2 Ⓐ Ⓑ Ⓒ Ⓓ Ⓔ	34 Ⓐ Ⓑ Ⓒ Ⓓ Ⓔ	66 Ⓐ Ⓑ Ⓒ Ⓓ Ⓔ	98 Ⓐ Ⓑ Ⓒ Ⓓ Ⓔ
3 Ⓐ Ⓑ Ⓒ Ⓓ Ⓔ	35 Ⓐ Ⓑ Ⓒ Ⓓ Ⓔ	67 Ⓐ Ⓑ Ⓒ Ⓓ Ⓔ	99 Ⓐ Ⓑ Ⓒ Ⓓ Ⓔ
4 Ⓐ Ⓑ Ⓒ Ⓓ Ⓔ	36 Ⓐ Ⓑ Ⓒ Ⓓ Ⓔ	68 Ⓐ Ⓑ Ⓒ Ⓓ Ⓔ	100 Ⓐ Ⓑ Ⓒ Ⓓ Ⓔ
5 Ⓐ Ⓑ Ⓒ Ⓓ Ⓔ	37 Ⓐ Ⓑ Ⓒ Ⓓ Ⓔ	69 Ⓐ Ⓑ Ⓒ Ⓓ Ⓔ	101 Ⓐ Ⓑ Ⓒ Ⓓ Ⓔ
6 Ⓐ Ⓑ Ⓒ Ⓓ Ⓔ	38 Ⓐ Ⓑ Ⓒ Ⓓ Ⓔ	70 Ⓐ Ⓑ Ⓒ Ⓓ Ⓔ	102 Ⓐ Ⓑ Ⓒ Ⓓ Ⓔ
7 Ⓐ Ⓑ Ⓒ Ⓓ Ⓔ	39 Ⓐ Ⓑ Ⓒ Ⓓ Ⓔ	71 Ⓐ Ⓑ Ⓒ Ⓓ Ⓔ	103 Ⓐ Ⓑ Ⓒ Ⓓ Ⓔ
8 Ⓐ Ⓑ Ⓒ Ⓓ Ⓔ	40 Ⓐ Ⓑ Ⓒ Ⓓ Ⓔ	72 Ⓐ Ⓑ Ⓒ Ⓓ Ⓔ	104 Ⓐ Ⓑ Ⓒ Ⓓ Ⓔ
9 Ⓐ Ⓑ Ⓒ Ⓓ Ⓔ	41 Ⓐ Ⓑ Ⓒ Ⓓ Ⓔ	73 Ⓐ Ⓑ Ⓒ Ⓓ Ⓔ	105 Ⓐ Ⓑ Ⓒ Ⓓ Ⓔ
10 Ⓐ Ⓑ Ⓒ Ⓓ Ⓔ	42 Ⓐ Ⓑ Ⓒ Ⓓ Ⓔ	74 Ⓐ Ⓑ Ⓒ Ⓓ Ⓔ	106 Ⓐ Ⓑ Ⓒ Ⓓ Ⓔ
11 Ⓐ Ⓑ Ⓒ Ⓓ Ⓔ	43 Ⓐ Ⓑ Ⓒ Ⓓ Ⓔ	75 Ⓐ Ⓑ Ⓒ Ⓓ Ⓔ	107 Ⓐ Ⓑ Ⓒ Ⓓ Ⓔ
12 Ⓐ Ⓑ Ⓒ Ⓓ Ⓔ	44 Ⓐ Ⓑ Ⓒ Ⓓ Ⓔ	76 Ⓐ Ⓑ Ⓒ Ⓓ Ⓔ	108 Ⓐ Ⓑ Ⓒ Ⓓ Ⓔ
13 Ⓐ Ⓑ Ⓒ Ⓓ Ⓔ	45 Ⓐ Ⓑ Ⓒ Ⓓ Ⓔ	77 Ⓐ Ⓑ Ⓒ Ⓓ Ⓔ	109 Ⓐ Ⓑ Ⓒ Ⓓ Ⓔ
14 Ⓐ Ⓑ Ⓒ Ⓓ Ⓔ	46 Ⓐ Ⓑ Ⓒ Ⓓ Ⓔ	78 Ⓐ Ⓑ Ⓒ Ⓓ Ⓔ	110 Ⓐ Ⓑ Ⓒ Ⓓ Ⓔ
15 Ⓐ Ⓑ Ⓒ Ⓓ Ⓔ	47 Ⓐ Ⓑ Ⓒ Ⓓ Ⓔ	79 Ⓐ Ⓑ Ⓒ Ⓓ Ⓔ	111 Ⓐ Ⓑ Ⓒ Ⓓ Ⓔ
16 Ⓐ Ⓑ Ⓒ Ⓓ Ⓔ	48 Ⓐ Ⓑ Ⓒ Ⓓ Ⓔ	80 Ⓐ Ⓑ Ⓒ Ⓓ Ⓔ	112 Ⓐ Ⓑ Ⓒ Ⓓ Ⓔ
17 Ⓐ Ⓑ Ⓒ Ⓓ Ⓔ	49 Ⓐ Ⓑ Ⓒ Ⓓ Ⓔ	81 Ⓐ Ⓑ Ⓒ Ⓓ Ⓔ	113 Ⓐ Ⓑ Ⓒ Ⓓ Ⓔ
18 Ⓐ Ⓑ Ⓒ Ⓓ Ⓔ	50 Ⓐ Ⓑ Ⓒ Ⓓ Ⓔ	82 Ⓐ Ⓑ Ⓒ Ⓓ Ⓔ	114 Ⓐ Ⓑ Ⓒ Ⓓ Ⓔ
19 Ⓐ Ⓑ Ⓒ Ⓓ Ⓔ	51 Ⓐ Ⓑ Ⓒ Ⓓ Ⓔ	83 Ⓐ Ⓑ Ⓒ Ⓓ Ⓔ	115 Ⓐ Ⓑ Ⓒ Ⓓ Ⓔ
20 Ⓐ Ⓑ Ⓒ Ⓓ Ⓔ	52 Ⓐ Ⓑ Ⓒ Ⓓ Ⓔ	84 Ⓐ Ⓑ Ⓒ Ⓓ Ⓔ	116 Ⓐ Ⓑ Ⓒ Ⓓ Ⓔ
21 Ⓐ Ⓑ Ⓒ Ⓓ Ⓔ	53 Ⓐ Ⓑ Ⓒ Ⓓ Ⓔ	85 Ⓐ Ⓑ Ⓒ Ⓓ Ⓔ	117 Ⓐ Ⓑ Ⓒ Ⓓ Ⓔ
22 Ⓐ Ⓑ Ⓒ Ⓓ Ⓔ	54 Ⓐ Ⓑ Ⓒ Ⓓ Ⓔ	86 Ⓐ Ⓑ Ⓒ Ⓓ Ⓔ	118 Ⓐ Ⓑ Ⓒ Ⓓ Ⓔ
23 Ⓐ Ⓑ Ⓒ Ⓓ Ⓔ	55 Ⓐ Ⓑ Ⓒ Ⓓ Ⓔ	87 Ⓐ Ⓑ Ⓒ Ⓓ Ⓔ	119 Ⓐ Ⓑ Ⓒ Ⓓ Ⓔ
24 Ⓐ Ⓑ Ⓒ Ⓓ Ⓔ	56 Ⓐ Ⓑ Ⓒ Ⓓ Ⓔ	88 Ⓐ Ⓑ Ⓒ Ⓓ Ⓔ	120 Ⓐ Ⓑ Ⓒ Ⓓ Ⓔ
25 Ⓐ Ⓑ Ⓒ Ⓓ Ⓔ	57 Ⓐ Ⓑ Ⓒ Ⓓ Ⓔ	89 Ⓐ Ⓑ Ⓒ Ⓓ Ⓔ	121 Ⓐ Ⓑ Ⓒ Ⓓ Ⓔ
26 Ⓐ Ⓑ Ⓒ Ⓓ Ⓔ	58 Ⓐ Ⓑ Ⓒ Ⓓ Ⓔ	90 Ⓐ Ⓑ Ⓒ Ⓓ Ⓔ	122 Ⓐ Ⓑ Ⓒ Ⓓ Ⓔ
27 Ⓐ Ⓑ Ⓒ Ⓓ Ⓔ	59 Ⓐ Ⓑ Ⓒ Ⓓ Ⓔ	91 Ⓐ Ⓑ Ⓒ Ⓓ Ⓔ	123 Ⓐ Ⓑ Ⓒ Ⓓ Ⓔ
28 Ⓐ Ⓑ Ⓒ Ⓓ Ⓔ	60 Ⓐ Ⓑ Ⓒ Ⓓ Ⓔ	92 Ⓐ Ⓑ Ⓒ Ⓓ Ⓔ	124 Ⓐ Ⓑ Ⓒ Ⓓ Ⓔ
29 Ⓐ Ⓑ Ⓒ Ⓓ Ⓔ	61 Ⓐ Ⓑ Ⓒ Ⓓ Ⓔ	93 Ⓐ Ⓑ Ⓒ Ⓓ Ⓔ	125 Ⓐ Ⓑ Ⓒ Ⓓ Ⓔ
30 Ⓐ Ⓑ Ⓒ Ⓓ Ⓔ	62 Ⓐ Ⓑ Ⓒ Ⓓ Ⓔ	94 Ⓐ Ⓑ Ⓒ Ⓓ Ⓔ	
31 Ⓐ Ⓑ Ⓒ Ⓓ Ⓔ	63 Ⓐ Ⓑ Ⓒ Ⓓ Ⓔ	95 Ⓐ Ⓑ Ⓒ Ⓓ Ⓔ	
32 Ⓐ Ⓑ Ⓒ Ⓓ Ⓔ	64 Ⓐ Ⓑ Ⓒ Ⓓ Ⓔ	96 Ⓐ Ⓑ Ⓒ Ⓓ Ⓔ	

Sample Examinations

This chapter has three sample Social Sciences and History examinations, each followed by an answer key, scoring chart, and answer explanations. After you complete each exam, determine your score and mark it on the Progress Chart on page 12. You will see your score climb as you work through each test and become more familiar with the type of questions asked.

SAMPLE SOCIAL SCIENCES–HISTORY EXAMINATION

NUMBER OF QUESTIONS ON THE TRIAL TEST: 125

Time limit: 90 MINUTES

Directions: Each of the questions or incomplete statements below is followed by five suggested answers or completions. Select the one that is best in each case.

1. What do all of the following time periods have in common?

   - 1919–1921
   - 1946–1948
   - 1973–1978

   (A) postwar inflations
   (B) major depressions
   (C) ages of prosperity
   (D) major foreign wars
   (E) conflicts during the Cold War

2. Which of the following migrations involved the greatest number of people?

(A) Norsemen into Britain in the 9th and 10th centuries
(B) English into North America in the 17th century
(C) Blacks from Africa into the Western Hemisphere in the 17th and 18th centuries
(D) Spaniards into Mexico in the 16th century
(E) Asiatics into Hawaii in the 19th century

3. Which of the following societies was a totalitarian-type of government?

(A) Athens
(B) Sparta
(C) The Roman Republic
(D) Asoka's rule
(E) Babylonians under Hammurabi

4. When governments control the major industries such as aircraft, radio and television, this is known as

(A) laissez faire economics
(B) socialism
(C) communism
(D) capitalism
(E) traditional economics

5. Adam Smith contended that

(A) government should run the economy
(B) governments that encourage particular industries with various aids increase real wealth
(C) government should not interfere in the economic affairs of big business
(D) government must do something direct about labor's poverty
(E) government must redirect the activities of most men

6. Who was the African-American woman, born in slavery and later to become the respected editor of a newspaper, who fought hard against the campaign of lynching used in the South during the 1890s?

(A) Harriet Beecher Stowe
(B) Ida B. Wells
(C) Harriet Tubman
(D) Dorothea Dix
(E) Ida Tarbell

7. Based on the United States experience in the Viet Nam War, which conclusion is most accurate?

    (A) War is the only way to contain Communism.
    (B) Communism is not a very strong force.
    (C) Public opinion does not affect national policy.
    (D) Superior military technology does not guarantee victory.
    (E) Unpopular presidents are frequently impeached.

8. Which of the following movements had a lot in common with Calvin's idea of predestination?

    (A) Populism
    (B) Transcendentalism
    (C) Pragmatism
    (D) Puritanism
    (E) Technocratism

9. "It is a symbol of status. It has altered courting patterns. It has contributed to the increase in obesity and heart disease. It has contributed to a host of services and industries. It has helped the growth of suburbs. It has helped to alter state-federal governmental relations." The problematical "it" in the statement is the

    (A) automobile
    (B) elevator
    (C) refrigerator
    (D) subway
    (E) railroad

10. The Supreme Court decision of *Marbury v. Madison* set down the principle of

    (A) states rights
    (B) a two-term president
    (C) checks and balances
    (D) Manifest Destiny
    (E) judicial review

11. The Dred Scott decision, in effect, ruled which of the following unconstitutional?

    (A) Agricultural Adjustment Act
    (B) Sherman Act
    (C) Pure Food and Drug Act
    (D) Missouri Compromise of 1820
    (E) The Second Bank of the United States

12. The following ideas reflect the principles of a 15th- to 17th-century economic system:

    • colonies are needed to supply goods to the mother country
    • a nation's wealth is measured in terms of gold and silver
    • absolute monarchs strongly supported this economic theory

    These principles above reflect the ideas of which economic system?

    (A) Market economy
    (B) Communism
    (C) Socialism
    (D) Mercantilism
    (E) Traditional

13. One of the following countries that had been sending large numbers of immigrants to the United States (in the period from 1890 to the mid-1920s) was given a relatively low quota of immigrants by legislation passed in 1924 in the United States. Which one?

    (A) Great Britain
    (B) China
    (C) Japan
    (D) Germany
    (E) Italy

14. During the 19th century, which two European countries held colonies in Africa?

    (A) France and Switzerland
    (B) Germany and Finland
    (C) Portugal and Spain
    (D) Sweden and Denmark
    (E) Switzerland and Italy

15. Which of the following countries lost territory because of the Munich Conference in 1938?

    (A) Switzerland
    (B) Poland
    (C) France
    (D) Hungary
    (E) Czechoslovakia

16. Which of the following assertions in the 19th century influenced Malthus in his formulation of the theory of natural selection?

    (A) "Population decreases while agriculture forges ahead."
    (B) "It is the constant tendency in all animated life to increase beyond the nourishment prepared for it."
    (C) "No progress is possible because of the basic sex drive which increases population at a geometric rate."
    (D) "Nations which are over-populated must be allowed to expand their inhabitants abroad."
    (E) "Selection of the race which is most military is inevitable."

17. Which best describes the attitude of Mazzini?

    (A) He strongly believed in the racial superiority of the Italians since they had given the world so much.
    (B) He believed that Italian unity could best be attained under the leadership of a patriotic monarch.
    (C) He founded Young Italy, a secret society that called for a unified Italy under a representative government.
    (D) He firmly believed in the cosmopolitan ideal of the 18th century, that all men were citizens of the world rather than of a single nation.
    (E) He thought that true leadership in Italy would have to come from within the Roman Catholic Church.

18. The formation of the Triple Entente and the Triple Alliance were attempts to

    (A) encourage war
    (B) end imperialism
    (C) achieve a balance of power
    (D) divide territory in Africa
    (E) create free trade zones

19. Which of the following belongs in a different category from the others?

    (A) Wagner Act
    (B) Norris-LaGuardia Act
    (C) Taft-Hartley Act
    (D) National Industrial Recovery Act
    (E) Hawley-Smoot Act

20. In order to declare a law unconstitutional, the Supreme Court must have

    (A) at least six yes votes
    (B) a majority vote
    (C) a two-thirds vote
    (D) a yea vote that needs to be also approved by the President
    (E) a unanimous vote

21. The Hundred Years War (1337–1453):

    (A) reflected an intermittent war between two rival nations, England and France
    (B) was fought primarily on the seas and not on land
    (C) demonstrated the ineffectiveness of the longbows in ground warfare
    (D) was a sea battle war between England and Spain
    (E) resulted in a defeat for France as she was finally expelled from English territory

22. Which of the following is the best example of a primary group?

    (A) The graduating senior class in a big school
    (B) A neighborhood
    (C) The Congress of the United States
    (D) A girls' basketball team
    (E) Spectators at a baseball game

23. Both the germ theory of disease and the theory that bacteria can cause milk to sour was advanced by

    (A) Galileo
    (B) Weismann
    (C) Pasteur
    (D) Swann
    (E) Mendel

24. The traditional feudal economy of the Middle Ages is best represented by the

    (A) medieval towns
    (B) manor
    (C) craft guilds
    (D) burgesses
    (E) Italian city-states

25. The production possibility curve indicates

    (A) the maximum output series of any two products
    (B) the minimum output series of any two products
    (C) the gains that can be made by mass production in one product area
    (D) the gains in profit from wider markets
    (E) the gains in profit from controlling prices

26. Cavour is to Italian unification as _____ is to German unification.

    (A) Hitler
    (B) Garibaldi
    (C) Luther
    (D) Bismarck
    (E) Kaiser Wilhelm III

27. Utopian socialism was made famous when a model community was set up in New Lanark, Scotland, by

    (A) Louis Blanc
    (B) Karl Marx
    (C) John Stuart Mill
    (D) Robert Owen
    (E) Leo Tolstoy

28. The utilitarian movement in the early years of the Industrial Revolution stressed a belief in "the greater good and happiness for the greater number." This economic belief was initiated by

    (A) Adam Smith
    (B) David Ricardo
    (C) John Stuart Mill
    (D) William Godwin
    (E) Jeremy Bentham

29. The birth rate in the United States over the last 175 years has

    (A) remained fairly static
    (B) increased greatly
    (C) decreased greatly
    (D) tended to fluctuate wildly around a stable average
    (E) declined in depressed economy periods only

30. "It has a centralized government with one leader, and a common language, and history." This definition applies to a

    (A) clan
    (B) tribe
    (C) family
    (D) nation-state
    (E) city-state

31. Which empire had an empire as great if not greater than that of Rome at its height?

    (A) The Mongolian Empire. 12th–14th century
    (B) William the Conqueror, 11th century
    (C) Russia under the Ivans 15th–16th centuries
    (D) England under Oliver Cromwell, 17th century
    (E) Akbar's Empire, 16th–17th centuries

32. The violation of which of the following norms would result in the least punishment?

    (A) adultery
    (B) incest
    (C) divorce
    (D) polygamy
    (E) theft

33. Besides immigrants of English origin, the next largest group of immigrants that came to America during colonial times was

    (A) South Africans
    (B) Italians
    (C) Russians
    (D) Germans
    (E) Irish

34. The American Declaration of Independence states that "men are endowed by their creator with certain inalienable rights." The same idea is also very clearly expressed in the writings of

    (A) Bossuet
    (B) Duke of Sully
    (C) Machiavelli
    (D) John Locke
    (E) Montaigne

35. Consider the following events:

    - the close of the American frontier
    - the expansion and growth of U.S. naval power
    - Social Darwinism becomes popular in America

    What time period would these events parallel?

    (A) the Washington presidency
    (B) 1845–1855
    (C) 1890–1910
    (D) 1918–1939
    (E) the John F. Kennedy presidency

36. "The value of a commodity is, in itself, of no interest to the capitalist. What alone interests him is the surplus value that dwells in it and is realisable by sale." In which of the following works would this statement occur?

    (A) *Wealth of Nations*
    (B) *Essay on Population*
    (C) *The Protestant Ethic and the Spirit of Capitalism*
    (D) *Theory of the Leisure Class*
    (E) *Das Kapital*

37. The Boers of South Africa were the descendants of settlers who had come to that land from

    (A) England
    (B) the Netherlands
    (C) Germany
    (D) Portugal
    (E) Ireland

38. In 1688, the last Stuart king of England was removed from power, and William and Mary took the throne, accepting Parliament as supreme authority over the monarch. This great event became known as

    (A) the Magna Carta
    (B) the Model Parliament
    (C) the Act of Supremacy
    (D) the Glorious Revolution
    (E) the Triennial Act

39. The belief in the "new imperialism" under which most of Africa and Asia was colonized in the late 19th century was based on the theory expressed by

    (A) "White Man's Burden"
    (B) the Puritan ethic
    (C) Stanley and Livingston
    (D) the Malthusian theory
    (E) John Locke

40. Byzantium had a significant impact on the culture and people of

    (A) the Western Roman Empire
    (B) the Mongolian Empire
    (C) Kievan Russia
    (D) the people of Western Europe
    (E) Islamic societies in the Middle East

41. What factor was a major cause of both World War I and World War II?

    (A) Nationalism and national borders
    (B) The failure of the League of Nations
    (C) The rise of totalitarian fascist states
    (D) The spread of Marxian ideas into Europe
    (E) The dropping of atomic bombs

42. The Boxer Rebellion in China was

    (A) an effort to overthrow the rule of the Manchu emperor
    (B) a revolt against the Japanese rule in Korea
    (C) an attack to remove foreigners from China
    (D) the revolution that established the Chinese Republic
    (E) a fight to establish Confucianism

43. If you wanted to visit the oldest sites of the civilization of the Incas, you would go to

    (A) Mexico
    (B) Guatemala
    (C) Cuba
    (D) Peru
    (E) Venezuela

44. Which best describes the following 18th-century rulers: Catherine II of Russia, Frederick II of Prussia, and Joseph II of Austria? They

    (A) made mock of the "divine right" idea of kingship
    (B) went to considerable lengths to avoid war
    (C) wished to introduce various reforms that were supposed to contribute to the welfare of their subjects
    (D constitutional monarchs
    (E) wished to expand their holdings in South America

45. The "Great Trek" refers to

    (A) the expansion of Canada to the west
    (B) the migration of Europeans to New Zealand
    (C) the movement of Dutch-speaking Boers out of Cape Colony
    (D) the great sheep drives in Australia
    (E) General Custer's march into Montana

Questions 46–49 refer to MAP C. Use this map of Europe and your knowledge of history to answer the questions.

MAP C
EUROPE   1945–1990

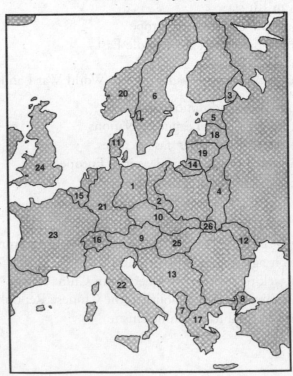

46. Another title or subtitle for this map would be

    (A) Berlin Blockade
    (B) fall of European capitalism
    (C) Arab–Israeli conflict
    (D) Cold War
    (E) rule of Stalin in the USSR

47. This nation was leader of the Warsaw Pact as well as the leader of the communist world. This nation is

    (A) 1
    (B) 2
    (C) 13
    (D) 22
    (E) 27

48. As a result of the "iron curtain" and the post–World War II conflict between Russia and the United States, this nation was split into two. The western part of this nation created a new capital, Bonn. This nation is

    (A) 1
    (B) 2
    (C) 16
    (D) 21
    (E) 23

49. Under the leadership of Tito, this former Communist nation was the only nation to successfully break away from the Soviet Union. Since the early 1990s, it has been split into six smaller nations because of religious and ethnic conflict. This nation is

    (A) 1 and 21
    (B) 10
    (C) 13
    (D) 18 and 19
    (E) 16

50. The best way in economics to define "saving" is to call it

    (A) a time deposit
    (B) an investment
    (C) an act of prudence
    (D) refraining from consumption
    (E) the building of national solvency

51. *Marginal utility* is a term associated with the law of supply and demand. Thus, a high price for a commodity results from

    (A) much labor being required to produce it
    (B) a lower desire to purchase the product
    (C) its great usefulness to people
    (D) its association with an exploitive capitalist system
    (E) its not being mass-produced

52. Which order is correct when ranking primates from lowest to highest?

    (A) Prosimians, new-world monkeys, old-world monkeys, apes
    (B) Lemurs, chimpanzees, baboons, rhesus monkeys
    (C) Baboons, orangutans, man, gorillas
    (D) Old-world monkeys, new-world monkeys, apes, man
    (E) Gibbons, prosimians, gorillas, man

53. Since people interacting take one another into account and modify their behaviors, interaction is

    (A) secondary
    (B) formal
    (C) cohesive
    (D) reciprocal
    (E) marginal

54. Which document on human rights was written shortly after World War II and was a result of the many human rights violations that people had experienced during both world wars.

    (A) The Declaration of the Rights of Man
    (B) The UN Declaration of Human Rights
    (C) The Johnson Civil Rights Legislation of 1964–1965
    (D) The Cambodian Genocide declaration
    (E) Gandhi's pledge of civil disobedience

55. Why did the United States become an active party in the Persian Gulf War?

    (A) To contain the spread of Communism
    (B) To assassinate Saddam Hussein
    (C) To protect the U.S. embassy
    (D) To protect its interests in oil in the Middle East
    (E) To end a civil war taking place there

56. Which of the following is a common trait of a developing nation?

    (A) It is urbanized and industrialized.
    (B) It depends largely on a large farming labor force.
    (C) It has a low infant mortality rate.
    (D) Average life expectancy is about 65–70 years of age.
    (E) Education is a top priority and extensive.

57. The sociologist who analyzed different types of suicide in terms of individuals' attachment or lack of attachment to a group was

    (A) Emile Durkheim
    (B) C. Wright Mills
    (C) Robert Merton
    (D) Louis Wirth
    (E) Pitirim Sorokin

58. The most common way to secure a wife in most simple traditional patrilocal African societies was by

    (A) sororate rules
    (B) purchase
    (C) royal dispensation
    (D) stealing
    (E) capture

59. George Orwell's two books *Animal Farm* and *1984* had one very similar theme or message, which was

    (A) totalitarian states, although dictatorial, do believe in civil liberties
    (B) that communism is the best form of political government
    (C) the general populace supported a powerful secret police that allowed cruel and harsh punishment to be used by the state
    (D) to show readers what a world of horror it would be if communism was allowed to expand at the expense of fundamental human rights
    (E) that the masses support both the government of Big Brother and Napoleon

60. "The young Kaiser William II (1870s–1890s) was jealous of the aged minister who had domineered over Germany so long." Who was the minister?

    (A) Tirpitz
    (B) Dollfuss
    (C) Stein
    (D) Bethman-Hollweg
    (E) Bismarck

61. In European medieval agriculture, the three-field system was a

    (A) means of dividing agricultural land among the three main social classes
    (B) method of rotating crops on the manor
    (C) plan in which both the king and the church received part of the product of the land
    (D) plan to divide manors among various owners
    (E) system of irrigating three or more farms with one canal system

62. When the founding fathers established the electoral college system, they expected that

    (A) mass education would improve the electorate and make direct popular election reasonable
    (B) partisan conflict over the election of a president could be avoided
    (C) a democratic system would evolve whereby the people would select the president according to a weighted formula which equates the popular and electoral votes
    (D) a democratic party system would develop, thus making selection of the president a popular decision
    (E) Washington would serve two terms, after which an amendment would require the election of a president by the House of Representatives

63. Animism is a type of ancient religious belief practiced by traditional

    (A) African tribes and clans
    (B) Middle Eastern civilizations of early Mesopotamia
    (C) Shiite Muslims
    (D) ancient Chinese dynasties
    (E) Aryans that made it a part of Hinduism

64. The philosophical belief that the proletariat communistic revolution would include both city workers and peasants would be opposed only by

    (A) Mao Tse-tung
    (B) Vladimir Lenin
    (C) Joseph Stalin
    (D) Ho Chi Minh
    (E) Karl Marx

65. In the 10th century the ruler of which capital would have called himself "emperor of the Romans"?

    (A) Baghdad
    (B) Cairo
    (C) Kiev
    (D) Constantinople
    (E) London

66. In Cambodia and under the rule of Pol Pot and the Khmer Rouge, the sociological approach to brainwash the masses, feed them little and work them long hours all so that they would be obedient loyal subjects was also a characteristic of America's

    (A) Moonie and Jonestown cults
    (B) Hippie movement
    (C) Yippee movement
    (D) Yuppie subculture
    (E) Black Muslim cult

67. The 19th-century English reform bills of 1832, 1867, and 1884 all had what in common?

    (A) They supported industrial growth for England.
    (B) They increased the power of Parliament while decreasing the king's power.
    (C) They allowed labor unions to exist and have rights.
    (D) They created more and more rights for the masses in the British voting system.
    (E) They ended abusive and unfair child labor in the early factories.

68. "Forced by the prospect of having to fight both the British and American fleet as well as the Latin American rebels, the 'Concert of Europe' broke down and Spanish American colonies were allowed to remain republics." This statement refers to what time period below?

    (A) 1490s–1500s
    (B) 1790s
    (C) 1810s–1820s
    (D) 1940s
    (E) 1850s

69. If greatly diluted amounts of the infection were given in slowly increasing doses, resistance to the disease developed. In 1885, the treatment was tried on a nine-year-old boy bitten by a mad dog. He was cured. Who administered the cure?

    (A) Lister
    (B) Freud
    (C) Pasteur
    (D) Spock
    (E) Koch

70. Using dogs, the animal physiologist whose discovery of the conditioned reflex showed the exclusion of conscious processes from basic behavior patterns was

    (A) Darwin
    (B) Rousseau
    (C) Freud
    (D) Pavlov
    (E) Watson

71. The two-income family is associated with a growing solid middle class in which both the husband and wife began to work. This trend became typical

    (A) during the colonial period in America
    (B) after the Industrial Revolution began in the late 1700s
    (C) after World War I
    (D) after World War II
    (E) during the Kennedy years

72. Which incident below was a major event in the immediate years following World War II ?

    (A) Expansion of U.S. holdings in the Pacific
    (B) Heavy immigration into the United States from southern Europe
    (C) A tendency to feel that the American frontier had finally vanished
    (D) A strong movement to end "Jim Crowism" in the United States
    (E) Growing sentiment against trusts and monopoly

73. Which of the following civil rights originated with the Justinian Code of Rome?

    (A) Freedom of religion
    (B) Freedom of speech
    (C) Freedom of assembly
    (D) The right to vote
    (E) The right to trial by jury

74. The political boundaries of states in Africa came about mainly because of

    (A) geographic and economic ties between tribes
    (B) racial antagonisms
    (C) tribal organization and power
    (D) 19th-century colonial European power politics
    (E) nationalist sentiments in African populations at the end of the 19th century

75. The medieval European intellectual class was drawn almost entirely from

    (A) lawyers
    (B) the clergy
    (C) members of the landed aristocracy
    (D) guildsmen
    (E) royalty

76. The "sun never set" on this nation and it became the greatest naval power when it defeated the Spanish Armada in 1588. This nation is

    (A) France
    (B) Germany
    (C) Japan
    (D) United States
    (E) Great Britain

77. At the turn of the 20th century, the two greatest naval powers were

   (A) Great Britain and the United States
   (B) Japan and France
   (C) Germany and Great Britain
   (D) the United States and China
   (E) Russia and Japan

78. The Tudor ruler, King Henry VIII, declared the "Act of Supremacy" in the early 16th century in England. This act created the first state-controlled religion in all Europe. This religion was

   (A) Anglican
   (B) Methodist
   (C) Presbyterian
   (D) Quaker
   (E) Roman Catholic

79. Which famous 20th century leader made these three famous quotes?

   • "We stand alone"
   • "from Stettin in the Baltic to Trieste in the Adriatic ... an iron curtain has been descended across the continent"
   • "Never in the field of human conflict was so much owed by so many to so few"

   (A) Woodrow Wilson
   (B) Robert De Gaul
   (C) Winston Churchill
   (D) Harry S. Truman
   (E) Theodore Roosevelt

80. The man responsible for gaining independence for Vietnam from French colonial domination was

   (A) Mao Tse-tung
   (B) Mahatma Gandhi
   (C) Ho Chi Minh
   (D) Bao Dai
   (E) Richard Nixon

81. ". . . And yet for the people living in cities, their devalued currency caused by this inflationary period, left this nation crippled with high unemployment and an overall discontented urban population. Most people blamed the Versailles Treaty for their dilemma." This statement would describe

   (A) the United States in 1873
   (B) Germany in 1923
   (C) the United States in 1925
   (D) the United States in 1933
   (E) Great Britain in 1935

82. The growth of the civil rights movement began shortly after World War II and reached its height in the 1960s. The Chief Justice of the Supreme Court during this crucial time period was

    (A) Charles Evans Hughes
    (B) William Howard Taft
    (C) Roger Taney
    (D) Earl Warren
    (E) John Marshall

83. Which of the following books, cited in the 1954 school segregation case, was authored by Gunnar Myrdal?

    (A) *The American Commonwealth*
    (B) *America as a Civilization*
    (C) *An American Dilemma*
    (D) *The Promise of American Life*
    (E) *America's Sixty Families*

84. Review the following key events in colonial America:

    • The Mayflower Compact
    • Virginia House of Burgesses
    • Fundamental Orders of Connecticut

    What do these events have in common?

    (A) They established the right to vote for the American colonist.
    (B) They were early steps in the road to American democracy.
    (C) These were events after the French and Indian War that led to the Revolution.
    (D) These events were all a part of the original colonial settlement in Jamestown.
    (E) The British government used these methods to maintain control over its colonies.

85. American marriage and divorce laws

    (A) are outlined in the Constitution
    (B) vary from state to state
    (C) are uniform for the nation
    (D) have no effect on marriage and divorces
    (E) have not changed over the past 50 years

86. Which group might benefit from inflationary trends?

    (A) Old-age pensioners
    (B) Bondholders
    (C) Land speculators
    (D) Salaried workers
    (E) Educators

87. Land, labor, and capital are all components of

    (A) the Keynes theory of economics
    (B) the factors of production
    (C) Marxian communistic ideology
    (D) prehistoric agrarian societies
    (E) the traditional economy of the manor

88. Consider the following events:

    • The Great Railway Strike 1877
    • The Haymarket Affair 1886
    • The Homestead Strike

    These events resulted in

    (A) an outpouring of support by the public at large for the labor move-
        ment
    (B) the rise of the American communist party
    (C) strong support by big business for labor unions
    (D) the failure of labor to organize against big business
    (E) the federal government supporting big business over labor unions

89. The American family is typically

    (A) matrilocal
    (B) patrilocal
    (C) neolocal
    (D) paleolocal
    (E) rurolocal

90. Urban race riots of the 1960s like the one that occurred in 1965 in Watts,
    Los Angeles, were characterized by

    (A) emotional contagion and absence or weakness of social norms, two
        fundamental components of collective behavior
    (B) strict new protest laws that were soon violated by the radical Black
        Muslim cult
    (C) a time period of American peace in domestic affairs
    (D) Martin Luther King leading the protestors in a violent civil rights
        demonstration
    (E) whites, blacks, and hippies joining together in a cry to end the Viet
        Nam conflict

91. Max Weber said that this man's ideas about Christianity contributed in an
    indirect way to the rise of capitalism. This belief supported a growing mid-
    dle business class. This individual was

    (A) John Calvin
    (B) Durkheim
    (C) Thomas Aquinas
    (D) Henry VIII
    (E) Augustine

92. Which can be defined as any formal ceremony prescribed by the group as having symbolic significance?

    (A) Mores
    (B) Folkways
    (C) Ritual
    (D) Laws
    (E) None of the above

93. "All persons held as slaves within any State or designated part of a State, the people whereof shall then be in rebellion against the United States shall be then, thenceforward, and forever free." The above statement is taken from the

    (A) Abolitionist papers
    (B) Fifteenth Amendment to the Constitution
    (C) Freedmen's Bureau Act
    (D) Thirteenth Amendment to the Constitution
    (E) Emancipation Proclamation

94. A physical anthropologist made the following observation from the remains of an archaeological dig:

    - bipedal
    - 1400–1600 cc brain capacity
    - foramen magnum in the center of the skull
    - no large canine teeth; arc-shaped jaw

    These physical traits would be that of a

    (A) prosimian
    (B) monkey
    (C) chimpanzee
    (D) gorilla
    (E) human being

95. During the French Revolution, new political terms such as *left vs. right* emerged and they remain with us to this day. A *leftist* would be a

    (A) Nazi
    (B) clergyman
    (C) liberal
    (D) status quo individual
    (E) conservative

96. We sometimes hear a peace described as "carthaginian." Judging from what you know of the conclusion of the Third Punic War, this term means

    (A) a soft and lenient peace
    (B) an armistice or temporary cessation of the hostilities
    (C) a peace so severe that it means virtual destruction of the enemy
    (D) a peace that leaves both sides exhausted
    (E) the evolution of a group of allies who stand off a common enemy

97. "I proposed never to accept anything for true which I did not clearly know to be such. I think therefore I am." This quote was said by

    (A) Pascal
    (B) Descartes
    (C) Bayle
    (D) Locke
    (E) Hobbes

98. "The marginal propensity to consume" refers to the

    (A) level of income at which consumer spending just equals income
    (B) inclination on the part of some to "keep up with the Joneses" in their consumer spending
    (C) fraction of extra income that will be spent on consumption
    (D) amount a family (or community) will spend on consumption at different levels of income
    (E) fact that, at low incomes, families spend more on consumption than the amount of their incomes

99. In the effort to counteract a depression or recession, Federal Reserve Banks might

    (A) increase the reserve requirement
    (B) decrease the interest rate charged commercial banks
    (C) sell government securities to individuals
    (D) raise the interest rate charged commercial banks
    (E) raise margin requirements on stock purchases

100. The Mullahs are

    (A) a Muslim
    (B) teachers of Islamic law and dogma
    (C) political leaders of the Muslims
    (D) a ruling dynasty of Baghdad
    (E) followers of Islam who are black

101. A grand jury is

    (A) an organization of outstanding civic leaders
    (B) a group of citizens whose function is to determine the facts in a civil or criminal trial
    (C) the jury used in appellate courts
    (D) a group of citizens responsible for bringing formal charges against a person accused of a serious crime
    (E) a jury that is called in major cases

102. Justices of the Supreme Court who disagree with a decision may prepare a

    (A) concurring opinion
    (B) advisory opinion
    (C) dissenting opinion
    (D) declaratory judgment
    (E) *per curiam* decision

103. The following are examples of one of the several levels of courts in our judiciary system:

    • justices are appointed by the President
    • it has jurisdiction in disputes between states
    • it can overrule an established precedent

    These three examples all apply to

    (A) State Supreme Courts
    (B) The U.S. Supreme Court
    (C) The federal Court of Appeals
    (D) The federal Circuit Courts
    (E) County District Courts

104. The first significant example of colonial unity in America was the

    (A) First Continental Congress
    (B) Albany Congress
    (C) Second Continental Congress
    (D) signing of the Bill of Rights
    (E) Articles of Confederation

105. World War II began

    (A) soon after Hitler became chancellor of Germany
    (B) when Hitler invaded Poland in 1939
    (C) after the bombing attack on Pearl Harbor in 1941
    (D) when the Sudetenland was invaded by the Nazis in 1937
    (E) after a series of German victories had occurred in western and northern Europe

106. Which of the following writers felt that the frontier loosened the bonds of custom, offered new experiences, and had a permanent effect on American institutions?

    (A) Henry George
    (B) Thorstein Veblen
    (C) Charles A. Beard
    (D) Allen Nevins
    (E) Frederick Jackson Turner

107. The Meiji Restoration in Japan (1867–68) was

    (A) an effort to cut all ties with the West and go back to ancient Japanese ways
    (B) the beginning of Japan's modernization
    (C) the capture of Formosa by Japan
    (D) the overthrow of the Japanese emperor
    (E) the reestablishment of the power of the shogunate

108. "Inconvenience, suffering, and death are the penalties attached by nature to ignorance, as well as to incompetence. . . . It is impossible in any degree to suspend this discipline by stepping in between ignorance and its consequences, without, to a corresponding degree, suspending the progress. If to be ignorant were as safe as to be wise, no one would become wise." This quotation came from

    (A) Nikolai Lenin
    (D) Jean Jacques Rousseau
    (C) Cardinal Newman
    (D) Herbert Spencer
    (E) John Locke

109. The Tasadays, the Bushman, the Nuer, the Mbuti, and the Eskimos are all examples of

    (A) nonnomadic cultures
    (B) traditional nomadic societies
    (C) early Neolithic civilizations
    (D) remains of man nearly one million years ago
    (E) isolated cultures that have been able to maintain their unique identity in the 21st century

110. Which statement is true about bills becoming laws in our American Congress?

    (A) Most bills become laws.
    (B) All bills cans start off either in the House or in the Senate.
    (C) Standing and conference committees are a necessary and integral part of the process.
    (D) The Supreme Court can veto a bill passed by both the President and Congress.
    (E) There is no floor debate on a bill; all work is done in committees.

111. In Alvin Toffler's book *The Third Wave* (written in the late 1960s), he says that

    (A) the nuclear family will be replaced by the extended family as a result of our industrialized society
    (B) the American family is in a state of crisis as many alternatives become accepted, such as single parents, remarriages, and gay lifestyles
    (C) mothers and religion will become the primary socializing force in America
    (D) fathers will replace mothers in raising children
    (E) the Norman Rockwell model will become the most common family lifestyle

112. The concept of anomie refers to

    (A) folk society
    (B) a highly normative situation
    (C) a condition marked by normlessness
    (D) a highly dense population
    (E) a warring state armed with atomic weapons

113. Ruth Benedict and Margaret Mead are both famous

    (A) cultural anthropologists
    (B) archaeologists
    (C) paleontologists
    (D) sociologists
    (E) historians

114. The Congo territory was developed and exploited during the last half of the 19th century by a private company that was organized by the king of

    (A) Germany
    (B) Italy
    (C) Portugal
    (D) Belgium
    (E) Sweden

115. Genghis Khan was the leader of

    (A) Mongolian nomads of central Asia
    (B) an ancient Chinese dynasty
    (C) a nation of Asian Muslims
    (D) a sea-going people of southeast Asia
    (E) tribes from northern Japan

116. Surplus value, class conflict, and the inevitability of a proletariat revolution each represent the ideas expressed in the book

    (A) *Leviathan*, by Hobbes
    (B) *Wealth of Nations*, by Smith
    (C) *Essay on Population*, by Malthus
    (D) *Communist Manifesto*, by Marx
    (E) *Expansion and Peace*, by Teddy Roosevelt

117. Which of the following is a major advantage of a corporate form of business organization?

    (A) Lower taxes
    (B) The limited liability of the owners
    (C) Fewer regulations to operate under
    (D) Being inexpensive to start
    (E) It has no say from its shareholders

118. Most public utilities are examples of which type of industry?

    (A) Pure competition
    (B) A cartel
    (C) Monopoly
    (D) Oligarchy
    (E) Partnership

119. Which of the following is a disadvantage of organizing a business as a partnership?

    (A) Taxes are higher than on proprietorships.
    (B) It is easier to raise investment capital when the business is a proprietorship.
    (C) If one partner dies, the remaining partner(s) is (are) responsible for continuing the business.
    (D) Each partner is responsible for business actions taken by the other partner(s).
    (E) One partner can terminate the partnership

120. Which of the following men would least likely agree with the other four concerning man's basic nature?

    (A) Thomas Hobbes
    (B) Machiavelli
    (C) Louis XVI
    (D) Bishop Bossuet
    (E) John Locke

121. Which of the following was the only historical event that took place in the 20th century?

(A) The First Continental Congress meets.
(B) The Panama Canal is completed.
(C) Latin American colonies become free as the Monroe Doctrine takes effect.
(D) Thirteen colonies declare themselves the United States of America.
(E) The United States enters the Spanish-American War.

122. In his famous book *Leviathan*, he reflects the basic principle that "without a supreme being all would be chaos." This quote was by

(A) Locke
(B) Hobbes
(C) Montesquieu
(D) Voltaire
(E) Jefferson

123. If the following historical events below were placed in correct chronological order (with the earliest listed first) that order would be

I. Stamp Act passed by Parliament
II. Articles of Confederation are put in place
III. French and Indian War
IV. Declaration of Independence adopted

(A) III, II, I, and IV
(B) I, IV, II, III
(C) IV, II, III, I
(D) III, I, IV, II
(E) I, II, III, IV

124. Which sociologist is paired with his contribution in the field of sociology?

(A) Harlow—the Zimbardo experiments on human behavior
(B) Max Weber—study of folkways, norms, and mores
(C) Charles H. Cooley—the nature of primary groups
(D) William G. Sumner—defined the term "cultural universals of all societies"
(E) Emile Durkheim—the bureaucracy, the administrative hierarchy of society

125. Studies of feral children give support to the idea that

(A) man inherits most of his behavior patterns from his parents
(B) we must learn to function in society
(C) even if we are isolated from human society for a long period, we can easily learn to live according to its standards
(D) animals share most of the same qualities as man
(E) early childhood socialization has no effect on the early childhood development of said child

STOP

If there is still time remaining, you may review your answers.

Social Sciences–History
ANSWER KEY—SAMPLE EXAMINATION 1

1. A	26. D	51. B	76. E	101. D
2. C	27. D	52. A	77. C	102. C
3. B	28. E	53. D	78. A	103. B
4. B	29. C	54. B	79. C	104. B
5. C	30. D	55. D	80. C	105. B
6. B	31. A	56. B	81. B	106. E
7. D	32. C	57. A	82. D	107. B
8. D	33. D	58. B	83. C	108. D
9. A	34. D	59. D	84. B	109. B
10. E	35. C	60. E	85. B	110. C
11. D	36. E	61. D	86. C	111. B
12. A	37. B	62. B	87. B	112. C
13. E	38. D	63. A	88. E	113. A
14. C	39. A	64. E	89. C	114. D
15. E	40. C	65. D	90. A	115. A
16. D	41. A	66. A	91. A	116. D
17. C	42. C	67. D	92. C	117. B
18. C	43. D	68. C	93. E	118. C
19. E	44. C	69. C	94. E	119. D
20. B	45. C	70. D	95. C	120. E
21. A	46. D	71. D	96. C	121. B
22. D	47. E	72. D	97. B	122. B
23. C	48. D	73. E	98. C	123. D
24. B	49. C	74. D	99. B	124. C
25. A	50. D	75. B	100. B	125. B

SCORING CHART

After you have scored your Sample Examination 1, enter the results in the chart below, then transfer your score to the Progress Chart on page 12.

Total Test	Number Right	Number Wrong	Number Omitted
125			

ANSWER EXPLANATIONS

1. **(A)** Each of the following time periods represent a postwar period (World War I, World War II, and the Viet Nam Conflict) in which inflation surfaced as each of these wars ended. Inflation after a war is rather common in American economics.

2. **(C)** During the 17th and 18th centuries a worldwide slave trade centered in Africa, where blacks were kidnapped by slavers and shipped to the Western Hemisphere, particularly the United States, where they were sold as slaves. Some two million people were involved in this forced migration.

3. **(B)** Ancient Sparta fits the description of a totalitarian state in that it controlled the lives of its people. For example, the state determined whether infants lived or died, how children were to be raised (put in state dormitories from seven on), and that the military was required for all men.

4. **(B)** Socialism is when the state controls the major industries and leaves small businesses to private ownership. Canada is an excellent example of a socialized state in which communications, medicine, and the like are government owned and run.

5. **(C)** Adam Smith (1723–1790), a Scottish economist, wrote *An Inquiry into the Nature and Causes of the Wealth of Nations,* an extremely influential book. In it he developed the theory, usually referred to as "laissez-faire" (let do), that economic forces should be allowed to operate without government interference.

6. **(B)** Ida B. Wells fought for an end to lynching, a terror tactic by whites trying to control black citizens in the south in the 1890s, by using the power of her pen in newspapers published in the United States and in England.

7. **(D)** Guerrilla tactics used by the Vietcong, South Vietnamese supporters of North Vietnam during the 1960s and early 1970s war against the United States, successfully fought the United States with its superior technology and weapons.

8. **(D)** Calvin believed that the fate of the individual was determined by God before birth. This doctrine is called predestination. The Puritans were followers of Calvin. They left England because they did not accept the doctrines of the Church of England.

9. **(A)** The automobile has altered courting patterns, contributed to obesity and heart disease, produced major industries, helped the growth of suburbs and helped to alter state-federal governmental relations. It is also a status symbol. None of the others fit this description.

10. **(E)** It is in the early years of our new nation that the practice of judicial review was established with the *Marbury* v. *Madison* case. Judicial review is the right of the Supreme Court to interpret a law and declare it unconstitutional.

11. **(D)** The Missouri Compromise of 1820 prohibited slavery in the territories north of 36°30' except Missouri. Dred Scott, a slave, was taken into free ter-

ritory and claimed his freedom. The Supreme Court ruled that Dred Scott remained a slave even in free territory. Thus, in effect the Court ruled the Missouri Compromise unconstitutional.

12. **(A)** Mercantilism was an economic system in which the monarchs of Europe supported a policy of exploration and colonization to extract as much wealth as possible from its possessions. During the time of absolutism and strong monarchs (15th–17th centuries), mercantilism was the most popular economic system, under which gold and silver was brought back from the New World.

13. **(E)** The immigration law of 1924 limited immigration to the United States from any country to 2 percent of the people of that nationality residing in the United States in 1890. This drastically reduced the numbers admitted from Eastern Europe and Southern Europe (Italy).

14. **(C)** During the mid to late 19th century, the only combination of European powers controlling colonies in Africa was Portugal and Spain. In fact, these two nations were among the last powers to allow colonial rule in Africa to end. Other Western imperialistic powers in Africa were England, France, Belgium, Italy, and Germany. Thus, choice B is the only correct combination.

15. **(E)** Czechoslovakia was forced to yield to Hitler's claim that the Sudetenland should be ceded to Germany because it contained a majority of ethnic Germans. Neville Chamberlain, Prime Minister of Great Britain, returned from Munich saying "I bring you peace in our time."

16. **(D)** Malthus' essay on population warned of the danger of the world becoming overpopulated. Food supply would not keep pace with the growth of population and therefore the world could become overpopulated. This belief helped justify and spread the idea of colonies being good for the mother country. Many European nations sent representatives to new colonies such as Kenya, South Africa, and so on.

17. **(C)** Mazzini was called "the soul of Italian unification." His belief that each nation had a special mission to perform to contribute to the welfare of humanity in general inspired the Italian people and caused them to fight for Italian unification. To help bring about unification, he organized this secret society in the 1830s.

18. **(C)** The Triple Entente consisted of France, Great Britain, and Russia, while the Triple Alliance consisted of Germany, Austria-Hungary, and Italy. These were formed in the early twentieth century, supposedly for defensive purposes. Yet, they really became two armed camps, dividing Europe in a dangerous manner.

19. **(E)** The Hawley-Smoot Act of 1930 was a tariff act. The others related to labor.

20. **(B)** Decisions of the United States Supreme Court are by a simple majority. Since 1869, the Court has consisted of nine judges. If all nine judges participate in a decision, a vote of five or more for or against the appellant determines the case.

21. **(A)** For over a century, the Hundred Years War (1337–1453) was fought between two rival nations, England and France. It was also the war that Joan of Arc made her heroic appearance as a spark for the French forces. During the battle of Crecy in 1348, the British with their longbow routed the French soldiers. Eventually, the war ended in the French removing England forever from French soil.

22. **(D)** A primary group is closely knit, small in size, and usually has a long duration of contact. This small and closely knit group usually has intimate feelings for one another like a family. The best example noted is thus a girls' basketball team.

23. **(C)** Pasteur developed the germ theory of disease and showed that innoculation could prevent anthrax and tetanus.

24. **(B)** The self-sufficient manor (manorial system) was characterized by a self-contained community that had all the necessities of life. Trade was generally nonexistent, and, in general, a traditional and isolated lifestyle was common.

25. **(A)** The production possibility curve indicates the maximum output series of any two products. The two products often used as illustrations in economics are guns and butter. The curve shows the maximum output of either.

26. **(D)** Bismarck, the "iron chancellor," was the key to German unification. With his policy of "blood and iron" Bismarck brought unity to Germany by both war (blood) and industrialization (iron).

27. **(D)** Robert Owen was the founder of utopian socialism. He set up communities in both England and, later, the United States (New York). Although his model communities eventually failed, they put into motion the fundamental beliefs of socialism that were modified into present-day economic systems.

28. **(E)** Jeremy Bentham was one of several famous economic philosophers of the Industrial Revolution. Similar to the thinking of John Stuart Mill, his theory of utilitarianism was a 19th-century pre-Marxian belief that stated: "The aim of moral social and political action should be the largest possible balance of pleasure over pain; the greatest good and happiness for the greatest number; the useful is good and what is right should be the usefulness of its consequences."

29. **(C)** The factors responsible for the great decrease in the birth rate in the United States during the past 175 years include (1) decrease in the death rate particularly in childhood, (2) decline in the farm population, and (3) widespread adoption of family planning.

30. **(D)** *Nation-state* is a term that developed during the 13th and 14th centuries. As the Middle Ages came to a slow end, powerful lords, then kings, began to unite their smaller kingdoms into larger states or nations. England and France were two of the first nation-states that developed a feeling of oneness: one nation, one nationality, one common history, one tradition, one religion, and so on.

31. **(A)** It was the Mongolian Empire that extended from the China seas into Eastern Europe and reached as far south as the Black Sea. Long after the collapse of the Western Roman Empire, Genghis Khan had created the largest empire in human history.

32. **(C)** The most mild violation of social norms in our society today is divorce. Adultery, incest, polygamy, and theft are all violations of strict mores that we call laws.

33. **(D)** During colonial times, the greatest number of immigrants came from England. If one was to consider slavery, then Africans would also be right up there with the British. Throughout the colonial period, however, the next largest European immigrant was those of German ancestry.

34. **(D)** John Locke (1632–1704), English philosopher, expressed this idea in his *Two Treatises on Government* (1689). Jefferson had read Locke and may have gotten the idea from him but did not copy it directly when he wrote the Declaration of Independence.

35. **(C)** Both the 1890 census and Frederick Turner essay (1893) on the close of the American frontier led to national support that Manifest Destiny was over. If the American nation was going to expand any further, then it would have to go beyond its borders. This "close of the frontier" theory helped fuel further the growth of our naval power, imperial expansion (Spanish American War), and a new emotional arrogance called social Darwinism.

36. **(E)** Karl Marx (1818–1883), the father of socialism and communism, developed his ideas fully in his major work, *Das Kapital* (*Capital*). One of the ideas is that workers receive in wages only part of what they produce. The rest he called "surplus value."

37. **(B)** The first European settlers in South Africa were farmers from the Netherlands. They were called Boers from the Dutch word "boer" which means farmer.

38. **(D)** The Glorious Revolution in 1688 was a peaceful revolution that brought the fall of the Catholic Stuarts from the throne of England. It also established the supremacy of Parliament, making the king accountable to it. William and Mary of Orange accepted the crown only after they accepted the invitation by Parliament to rule, thus signifying Parliament's supremacy. This marked the evolution of England into a limited monarchy.

39. **(A)** Rudyard Kipling wrote this famous poem to symbolize European, or white men's, domination over African and Asian societies. It stresses the superiority of European over non-Western or inferior societies. It specifically refers to the people in the colonies as "half devil and half child." This poem also justifies social Darwinism, or survival of the fittest.

40. **(C)** The Slavs of southern and Eastern Europe were clearly influenced by the culture and religion of Byzantium. With the city Kiev on the Dnieper River, a great deal of cultural and trading contact began to occur with Byzantium. Vladimir I of Kiev converted to Orthodox Christianity; this was a direct result of Russian contact with Byzantium.

41. **(A)** Nationalism was a major cause of both world wars. Ever since the 19th century and the rapid growth of nationalism, this belief had continued to play a leading role, causing border disputes in the pre–World War I years and leading to the creation of alliance systems that were nationalistic in design. With the rise of fascist dictators in the post–World War I era, nationalism was a force for fascist nations to take over other territories.

42. **(C)** In the spring of 1900, a secret society, which Westerners called "The Boxers," started a rebellion in China against foreigners who were occupying their country. More than 300 nationals of England, France, the United States, and other countries were killed.

43. **(D)** The pre-Columbian Inca empire had a population of 6,000,000 and territory extending over 650,000 square miles. It was centered in Cuzco, Peru.

44. **(C)** The 18th-century rulers Catherine II of Russia, Frederick II of Prussia, and Joseph II of Austria were inspired by the ideas of the 18th-century Enlightenment. They wished to introduce various reforms, such as liberal land laws, for the welfare of their subjects.

45. **(C)** After the defeat of the Dutch-speaking Boers in South Africa by the British in 1902, the Dutch Boers (farmers) left Cape Colony and made a "Great Trek" north into the interior of the country, where they established new settlements and farms.

46. **(D)** The Cold War began after World War II with the division of Germany into two parts. It was Winston Churchill in his famous speech who first used the term *iron curtain,* which described the separation of free Europe (Western Europe) from Communist Europe (Eastern Europe). The Cold War ended with the fall of the USSR and Berlin Wall in late 1989.

47. **(E)** The USSR represented the leader of the Communist world in the Cold War and as such organized the Communist response to NATO, which was the Warsaw Pact. This, like NATO, was a military alliance of the Communist-bloc countries committed to protecting the Communist world for democracy.

48. **(D)** West Germany was created in 1949 when the Russian-occupied eastern zone of Germany eventually became East Germany with its capital at Berlin. The remaining three occupied zones—England, France, and the United States—combined and thus created democratic West Germany. The new capital of this nation became Bonn. In the 1990s Germany reunited into one nation after the Cold War ended.

49. **(C)** In 1949, Yugoslavia was the only Communist-bloc nation to break away from the Communist hold of the Soviet Union. Other attempts were made by Hungary, Czechoslovakia, and Poland, but all failed to break away from the Soviet grasp.

50. **(D)** The best way in economics to define "saving" is to call it "refraining from consumption." It is in contrast to consuming all that is produced.

51. **(B)** "Marginal utility" in economics refers to the relation between supply and demand in determining the price of a commodity. High price implies big demand and small supply.

52. **(A)** The ranking of primates from lowest to highest (man) is as follows: prosimians, new-world monkeys (rhesus monkeys), old-world monkeys (baboons), gorillas (gibbons, orangutans, chimpanzees, gorillas) and finally, man.

53. **(D)** When people interact they tend to take one another into account and modify their behavior accordingly. This interaction is said to be reciprocal. Efforts to achieve behavior modification has attained importance in contemporary psychology.

54. **(B)** It was the Armenian genocide that took place during World War I and, in particular, the holocaust that occurred during the early 1940s that brought the human rights issue to the forefront in the postwar discussions. In 1948, soon after the UN was organized, it approved the Universal Declaration of Human Rights. This act set in motion a new modern movement to protect human rights worldwide.

55. **(D)** The Persian Gulf route provides access for oil leaving the Middle East for many industrialized nations.

56. **(B)** A "have not" or "developing" nation is not industrialized or modernized. It depends on traditional agriculture and herding, and thus a large farm labor force is necessary. Most of the population are farmers. Today, more and more of these nations are moving toward an industrialized economy.

57. **(A)** The French sociologist Emile Durkheim (1858–1917) used statistics to support his theories. He analyzed "mechanical" vs. "organic" solidarity. He held that religion and morality originate in the collective mind of society.

58. **(B)** In most patrilocal African societies, the most simple way to secure a wife was by purchase. This was widely accepted. It had no pejorative aspect.

59. **(D)** George Orwell wrote both books in the 1940s, reflecting his fears of a communistic totalitarian world. Thus both are attacks on communism and how a Communist world would result in the lack of any kind of freedom.

60. **(E)** Otto von Bismarck (1815–1898) was premier of Prussia from 1862 to 1890 and Chancellor of Germany from 1871 to 1890. He was called the "Iron Chancellor." The young Kaiser William II was jealous of him and dismissed him in 1890.

61. **(B)** In European Medieval agriculture, the three-field system was a method of rotating crops on the manor. In the absence of artificial fertilizers one of the three fields would lie fallow. The other two would be planted in crops different from the previous year. Exhaustion of the soil was avoided in this way.

62. **(B)** The founding fathers established the electoral college system for choosing a president and vice-president. They provided that the electors be chosen separately in each state and that no Senator or Representative or other United

States officer could be an elector. They expected that partisan conflict over the election of a President would thus be avoided.

63. **(A)** Animism is a belief in nature, and therefore nature rules the society. This term was most often used to describe traditional African societies.

64. **(E)** Only Karl Marx said that industrialization must come before communism. Industrialization must make life difficult for the workers, and then they will rise up and create the proletariat revolution. All these other communist leaders recognized the need for the support of a larger peasant class who clearly outnumbered the proletariat force.

65. **(D)** The "Roman Empire" in the east continued to exist with its capital in Constantinople for more than ten centuries (5th to 15th centuries) after the decline and fall of Rome.

66. **(A)** Cults in the United States emerged in the 1960s as an alternative to the deteriorating American family. Several of the more famous cult movements in North America were the Jonestown cult and that of Reverend Moon. The Jonestown cult ended in massive suicide in Guyana.

67. **(D)** All of these reform bills in 19th-century England were a result of the Industrial Revolution changing the economic structure of the British masses. As the middle class and working class became more and more important, new laws protecting their civil liberties evolved, and new rights such as public education surfaced. Eventually both groups had better representation in the British Parliament.

68. **(C)** From the 1810s to 1820s Latin American nations revolted against the Spanish crown. Leaders such as Bolivar, Martin, and Father Hidalgo supported democratic governments in the Americas. In the end, the revolutions were generally successful and the Monroe Doctrine put the final chapter together, making the Western Hemisphere off-limits to further European colonization.

69. **(C)** The cure was administered by Louis Pasteur (1882–1895), the French bacteriologist. He had developed a vaccine that, in accordance with his theory, could conquer the dread disease hydrophobia (rabies).

70. **(D)** Ivan Petrovich Pavlov (1849–1936), the Russian physiologist, demonstrated the working of the conditioned reflex by an experiment on his dog. He rang a bell just before feeding his dog daily. Soon the dog would salivate when the bell rang and prior to (or regardless of) the feeding.

71. **(D)** The great need for laborers in our industries during World War II caused a great demand for the women laborer/worker. The female contribution to the war effort was rewarded with the beginning of the new "liberated" women. This eventually not only resulted in greater economic and social opportunities for women but also helped the growth of a much larger middle class (the two-income family.

72. **(D)** A strong movement to end "Jim Crowism" in the United States (unequal treatment of blacks) dates from World War II. The other events occurred dur-

ing the last decade of the 19th century or first decade of the 20th century.

73. **(E)** The right to trial by jury is a procedure whereby substantive rights (freedom of speech, press, religion, etc.) may be protected.

74. **(D)** During the 19th century, European powers carved out colonies in Africa by asserting their military power against the Africans and against each other. Most of these colonies gained their independence after World War II.

75. **(B)** The clergy of Medieval Europe had to read and interpret the Bible (often available only in Hebrew, Greek and Aramaic). They also read the commentators (Aquinas) in Latin or in the newly emerging national languages. Thus, as students of religion, philosophy, and literature they were the intellectuals of their time.

76. **(E)** "The sun never sets on the British Empire" was an expression reflecting the vast size of the empire. England had colonies all over the globe, and thus the sun never set on the entire empire at one time. Colonies existed everywhere from the Caribbean to the Middle East to Africa and Asia. As a result, the British maintained one of the largest navies in modern history, and upon defeat of the Spanish Armada it was nicknamed "queen of the seas."

77. **(C)** On the eve of World War I (1913) Great Britain was the greatest naval power in the world. Germany had been building a fleet trying to catch up. The United States was becoming a naval power and had surpassed all but the top two.

78. **(A)** Henry VIII and the Tudor family created the first state-controlled religion in the Western world in 1534. With this "Act of Supremacy", Henry VIII officially broke away from the Church of Rome setting up the new Anglican Church of England.

79. **(C)** Winston Churchill led his country both militarily and psychologically through World War II. At one point, the British stood alone as the only democracy left in Europe after the onslaught of the Nazi war machine. He kept the British people together in both spirit and leadership. After the war, he warned the free world of the dangers of Russian communism and the spread of communistic ideology throughout Eastern Europe.

80. **(C)** Ho Chi Minh led Vietnam in its fight for independence against France. At the Battle of Dien Bien Phu the French army was defeated and driven from Indochina.

81. **(B)** After World War I the German government printed so many marks that by 1923 they were practically worthless. Debtors could easily pay off their debts. People on pensions received money that would buy little or nothing.

82. **(D)** Earl Warren was appointed Chief Justice of the United States Supreme Court in 1953 by President Eisenhower. Under his leadership the Court showed special concern for the civil liberties guaranteed by the Bill of Rights and the Fourteenth Amendment.

83. **(C)** *An American Dilemma*, written by the Swedish sociologist Gunnar Myrdal, was based on a study of the American Negro. It proved that the blacks in America were receiving inferior education and were victims of injustice.

84. **(B)** The Mayflower Compact, the Virginia House of Burgesses, and The Fundamental Orders of Connecticut were all significant steps in the growth of democracy in colonial America. With our democratic British heritage and other key events like the Zenger Trial, the young American nation logically developed into a democratic constitutional government.

85. **(B)** American marriage and divorce laws vary from state to state. Under the Constitution, laws about marriage and divorce are left up to the states, not to the federal government.

86. **(C)** Inflationary trends cause land values to rise rapidly. People on pensions or salaries, or holders of bonds with fixed interest rates, find that their income buys less because of inflation.

87. **(B)** Land, labor, and capital are all components of the factors of production under capitalism. Our capitalistic economy is influence by these components that also have an impact on the four variations of the business cycle.

88. **(E)** The rapid growth of our industrial economy during the second half of the 1800s was followed by an equally and rapidly growing labor movement. When collective behavior failed, workers and unions turned to protests and strikes. Several of the protests turned into violence and riots. The result was support for the business owners over labor by both the government and the public.

89. **(C)** The American family is regarded by sociologists as a new and developing form. Its distinguishing aspect is neither mother, father, ancient nor rural.

90. **(A)** The 1960s was a decade scared with violent protests and riots. Often these events were characterized by urban race riots and antiwar protests. Such was the case in Watts, Los Angeles, when a major race riot occurred in 1965. Sociologists have associated these antiwar protests (like Kent State) and race riots with the fundamental principles of collective behavior. Some of the components of collective behavior are emotional contagion, heightening suggestibility, and absence or weakness of social forms (a liberal society).

91. **(A)** In his *Protestant Ethic and the Spirit of Capitalism* (1920) Max Weber, the German sociologist, developed the idea that John Calvin's teaching about self-denial as a measure of spiritual discipline is closely related to the rise of capitalism.

92. **(C)** Ritual is a formal ceremony prescribed by a group. The form and content of the ceremony are followed exactly on each occasion. The symbolic significance (whether religious or political) is recognized by all members of the participating group.

93. **(E)** These were the words of the Emancipation Proclamation issued by President Abraham Lincoln September 22, 1862, to take effect January 1, 1863.

94. **(E)** All four traits are indicators of the highest level of primate development, that of man. Although apes are partial bipedalist (walk on two feet), their brains are approximately one-third the size of humans' (500–600 cc), their foramen magnum is more to the rear of the skull, and their teeth are more U-shaped. Thus, all four traits fit the description of humans.

95. **(C)** A "leftist" defined by the French Revolution was a liberal, a reformer, and thus someone who wanted change—in fact, quick change. The Jacobins were the true radicals, as they were later called, for they wanted a total end to the monarchy. The "right" were the loyalists or those who were antichange (status quo). Thus they were eventually labeled conservatives.

96. **(C)** At the conclusion of the Third Punic War in 146 B.C., Rome defeated its traditional rival, Carthage, in North Africa. The victor razed Carthage to the ground. This gave rise to the term "a Carthaginian peace."

97. **(B)** René Descartes (1596–1650), French philosopher, mathematician, and scientist, said: "I proposed never to accept anything for true which I do not clearly know to be such." He is best known for his saying: "I think, therefore I am."

98. **(C)** "The marginal propensity to consume" refers, in economics, to the extra amount that people will want to spend on consumption if given an extra dollar of income.

99. **(B)** In an effort to counteract a depression or recession, Federal Reserve Banks might decrease the interest rate charged commercial banks. This would make it easier for banks to lend money to business. This, in turn, would help business to continue to function.

100. **(B)** The Mullahs are Muslim religious teachers trained in traditional Islamic law and doctrine.

101. **(D)** A grand jury is a group of citizens that examines the evidence against a person accused of a serious crime. If the evidence warrants, the grand jury brings formal charges. Then the accused must stand trial.

102. **(C)** Justices of the Supreme Court who disagree with the majority of the Court may prepare a dissenting opinion. In the dissent, the justice states his reason for disagreement.

103. **(B)** The U.S. Supreme Court is the "supreme law of the land." With the addition of judicial review, the highest court makes all final decisions. Possibly the best example was the effect it had on the 2000 presidential election when it ruled in favor of the Bush candidacy in the Florida recount.

104. **(B)** The Albany Congress met in 1754. The Stamp Act Congress met in 1765, the First Continental Congress in 1774, and the Second Continental Congress in 1775. The Articles of Confederation were drawn up in 1778.

105. **(B)** The late 1930s was marked by a policy of appeasement in order to avoid a second world war. The most significant example of appeasement was the Munich Conference in 1938 when the Allies allowed Hitler to occupy the Sudetenland in Czechoslovakia. Shortly thereafter, the Nazis invaded and took over the entire Czech nation. The invasion of Poland in 1939 marked the beginning of World War II and the failure of the Allies' "policy of appeasement."

106. **(E)** The American historian Frederick Jackson Turner (1861–1932) published *The Significance of the Frontier in American History* in 1893. He showed that the frontier exercised the greatest influence on American institutions.

107. **(B)** The Meiji Restoration in Japan (1867–1868) was the beginning of Japan's modernization. The emperor regained power after the Shogunate was overthrown. Then Japan proceeded with modernization along western lines.

108. **(D)** Herbert Spencer (1820–1903), British sociologist, made this statement. He applied the idea of biological evolution to social institutions.

109. **(B)** These primitive technological societies are nearly extinct today but provide us with invaluable insights to how man may have lived thousands of years ago. They were generally hunters and gatherers except for the Nuer, who were herders. These cultures that once existed in the early 20th century were absorbed by the modern shrinking world and are by and large non-existent today.

110. **(C)** Most bills do not become laws. Bills can start off in either house except that money bills must start off in the House of Representatives. Instrumental to the process is the work of standing committees and subcommittees that are used once a bill is introduced. Also, if a bill is on its way to becoming a possible law and the two houses don't agree to the wording, then the bill goes to a conference committee.

111. **(B)** In his book *The Third Wave,* Alvin Toffler discusses the deterioration of the traditional American family (Norman Rockwell type). Such alternative family configurations include single parents, remarriages, group families, and gay families.

112. **(C)** The concept of anomie is used to describe our society where norms of conduct and belief have been weakened or have actually broken down.

113. **(A)** These two famous cultural anthropologists studied the lifestyles of isolated societies that took us back to the early days of the hunter and gatherer. They provide invaluable insights into how humankind may have lived 10,000 years ago.

114. **(D)** The Congo territory was explored and exploited under the leadership of King Leopold II of Belgium. The Congo, in south central Africa, was known as the Belgian Congo until it gained its independence in 1960.

115. **(A)** Genghis Khan was the leader of a nomadic people of Central Asia. Under Genghis Khan's leadership, the Mongols invaded Europe during the 13th century and caused havoc in Poland, Hungary, and much of Russia.

116. **(D)** Marx and Engels developed the idea of scientific socialism that later became known as communism. Basic ideas of this philosophy included surplus value, which is the profit that ends up in the pockets of the capitalist; class conflict, in which the proletariat is in constant battle with the bourgeoisie capitalist; and the inevitability of a proletariat revolution, in which the workers will eventually rise up and overthrow the capitalistic society.

117. **(B)** Limited liability is a major advantage of a corporation in that the corporation can be sued but the individual owners cannot be.

118. **(C)** A public utility is usually a monopoly. The advantage of this is that it is more efficient. Since the breakup of the AT&T phone company, it is easy to comprehend why public utilities should be organized into monopolies.

119. **(D)** One of the major disadvantages of a partnership is that if one partner does something wrong or is corrupt or even inefficient, the other partner(s) is(are) affected. Thus, in a lawsuit, one partner can indeed carry his crime or guilt to his fellow partner or partners.

120. **(E)** John Locke is the true liberal in the group in that he believed in protecting the rights of the individual. Hobbes, Louis XIV, and Bossuet were all supporters of the theory of absolute monarchy and divine right. Machiavelli believed in the power of strong princes that should rule with force. Thus John Locke stands alone as the people's man.

121. **(B)** The only event occurring in the 20th century was the completion of the Panama Canal. The First Continental Congress and the Declaration of Independence by the thirteen colonies occurred in the 18th century. Latin American colonies were freed in the early 19th century, and the Spanish-American War began in 1898.

122. **(B)** In 1651, Thomas Hobbes completed his most famous book, *Leviathan*. This book describes a powerful sea monster in the Bible that is suppose to represent that government (absolute monarchy) must be all-powerful and absolute.

123. **(D)** The French and Indian War—the war between England (and the American colonists) and France (and her Indian allies)—began on the Pennsylvania frontier in 1754. Parliament passed the Stamp Act as a revenue measure in 1765, two years after the war ended. Fifty-five delegates to the First Continental Congress met in Philadelphia beginning September 5, 1774. The Declaration of Independence was adopted by the Second Continental Congress on July 4, 1776. In February 1778, Benjamin Franklin negotiated a treaty of recognition with France and a second treaty creating a formal military alliance.

124. **(C)** Charles H. Cooley was one of the founders of sociology and is particularly known for his work and analysis of primary groups. William G. Sumner is considered the expert on analysis of societies norms. His book *Folkways* discusses the different levels of intensity that society puts in place to regulate its people (norms = folkways, mores, laws). Emile Durkheim's lifelong interest was the study of suicide and he was one of the first sociologists to use sta-

tistical methods of research. Max Weber spent most of his life studying bureaucracy, law, and politics.

125. **(B)** Feral children were kept secluded and isolated by unfit parents. The difficulty to adjust to real life and become socialized shows that socialization is truly a learning process. We are socialized by our environment, which includes our family, friends, and peers. Socialization is critical to the normal development of children. Feral children were denied this right when they grew up in this secluded and isolated environment.

Social Sciences—History

ANSWER SHEET—SAMPLE EXAMINATION 2

1 Ⓐ Ⓑ Ⓒ Ⓓ Ⓔ
2 Ⓐ Ⓑ Ⓒ Ⓓ Ⓔ
3 Ⓐ Ⓑ Ⓒ Ⓓ Ⓔ
4 Ⓐ Ⓑ Ⓒ Ⓓ Ⓔ
5 Ⓐ Ⓑ Ⓒ Ⓓ Ⓔ
6 Ⓐ Ⓑ Ⓒ Ⓓ Ⓔ
7 Ⓐ Ⓑ Ⓒ Ⓓ Ⓔ
8 Ⓐ Ⓑ Ⓒ Ⓓ Ⓔ
9 Ⓐ Ⓑ Ⓒ Ⓓ Ⓔ
10 Ⓐ Ⓑ Ⓒ Ⓓ Ⓔ
11 Ⓐ Ⓑ Ⓒ Ⓓ Ⓔ
12 Ⓐ Ⓑ Ⓒ Ⓓ Ⓔ
13 Ⓐ Ⓑ Ⓒ Ⓓ Ⓔ
14 Ⓐ Ⓑ Ⓒ Ⓓ Ⓔ
15 Ⓐ Ⓑ Ⓒ Ⓓ Ⓔ
16 Ⓐ Ⓑ Ⓒ Ⓓ Ⓔ
17 Ⓐ Ⓑ Ⓒ Ⓓ Ⓔ
18 Ⓐ Ⓑ Ⓒ Ⓓ Ⓔ
19 Ⓐ Ⓑ Ⓒ Ⓓ Ⓔ
20 Ⓐ Ⓑ Ⓒ Ⓓ Ⓔ
21 Ⓐ Ⓑ Ⓒ Ⓓ Ⓔ
22 Ⓐ Ⓑ Ⓒ Ⓓ Ⓔ
23 Ⓐ Ⓑ Ⓒ Ⓓ Ⓔ
24 Ⓐ Ⓑ Ⓒ Ⓓ Ⓔ
25 Ⓐ Ⓑ Ⓒ Ⓓ Ⓔ
26 Ⓐ Ⓑ Ⓒ Ⓓ Ⓔ
27 Ⓐ Ⓑ Ⓒ Ⓓ Ⓔ
28 Ⓐ Ⓑ Ⓒ Ⓓ Ⓔ
29 Ⓐ Ⓑ Ⓒ Ⓓ Ⓔ
30 Ⓐ Ⓑ Ⓒ Ⓓ Ⓔ
31 Ⓐ Ⓑ Ⓒ Ⓓ Ⓔ
32 Ⓐ Ⓑ Ⓒ Ⓓ Ⓔ

33 Ⓐ Ⓑ Ⓒ Ⓓ Ⓔ
34 Ⓐ Ⓑ Ⓒ Ⓓ Ⓔ
35 Ⓐ Ⓑ Ⓒ Ⓓ Ⓔ
36 Ⓐ Ⓑ Ⓒ Ⓓ Ⓔ
37 Ⓐ Ⓑ Ⓒ Ⓓ Ⓔ
38 Ⓐ Ⓑ Ⓒ Ⓓ Ⓔ
39 Ⓐ Ⓑ Ⓒ Ⓓ Ⓔ
40 Ⓐ Ⓑ Ⓒ Ⓓ Ⓔ
41 Ⓐ Ⓑ Ⓒ Ⓓ Ⓔ
42 Ⓐ Ⓑ Ⓒ Ⓓ Ⓔ
43 Ⓐ Ⓑ Ⓒ Ⓓ Ⓔ
44 Ⓐ Ⓑ Ⓒ Ⓓ Ⓔ
45 Ⓐ Ⓑ Ⓒ Ⓓ Ⓔ
46 Ⓐ Ⓑ Ⓒ Ⓓ Ⓔ
47 Ⓐ Ⓑ Ⓒ Ⓓ Ⓔ
48 Ⓐ Ⓑ Ⓒ Ⓓ Ⓔ
49 Ⓐ Ⓑ Ⓒ Ⓓ Ⓔ
50 Ⓐ Ⓑ Ⓒ Ⓓ Ⓔ
51 Ⓐ Ⓑ Ⓒ Ⓓ Ⓔ
52 Ⓐ Ⓑ Ⓒ Ⓓ Ⓔ
53 Ⓐ Ⓑ Ⓒ Ⓓ Ⓔ
54 Ⓐ Ⓑ Ⓒ Ⓓ Ⓔ
55 Ⓐ Ⓑ Ⓒ Ⓓ Ⓔ
56 Ⓐ Ⓑ Ⓒ Ⓓ Ⓔ
57 Ⓐ Ⓑ Ⓒ Ⓓ Ⓔ
58 Ⓐ Ⓑ Ⓒ Ⓓ Ⓔ
59 Ⓐ Ⓑ Ⓒ Ⓓ Ⓔ
60 Ⓐ Ⓑ Ⓒ Ⓓ Ⓔ
61 Ⓐ Ⓑ Ⓒ Ⓓ Ⓔ
62 Ⓐ Ⓑ Ⓒ Ⓓ Ⓔ
63 Ⓐ Ⓑ Ⓒ Ⓓ Ⓔ
64 Ⓐ Ⓑ Ⓒ Ⓓ Ⓔ

65 Ⓐ Ⓑ Ⓒ Ⓓ Ⓔ
66 Ⓐ Ⓑ Ⓒ Ⓓ Ⓔ
67 Ⓐ Ⓑ Ⓒ Ⓓ Ⓔ
68 Ⓐ Ⓑ Ⓒ Ⓓ Ⓔ
69 Ⓐ Ⓑ Ⓒ Ⓓ Ⓔ
70 Ⓐ Ⓑ Ⓒ Ⓓ Ⓔ
71 Ⓐ Ⓑ Ⓒ Ⓓ Ⓔ
72 Ⓐ Ⓑ Ⓒ Ⓓ Ⓔ
73 Ⓐ Ⓑ Ⓒ Ⓓ Ⓔ
74 Ⓐ Ⓑ Ⓒ Ⓓ Ⓔ
75 Ⓐ Ⓑ Ⓒ Ⓓ Ⓔ
76 Ⓐ Ⓑ Ⓒ Ⓓ Ⓔ
77 Ⓐ Ⓑ Ⓒ Ⓓ Ⓔ
78 Ⓐ Ⓑ Ⓒ Ⓓ Ⓔ
79 Ⓐ Ⓑ Ⓒ Ⓓ Ⓔ
80 Ⓐ Ⓑ Ⓒ Ⓓ Ⓔ
81 Ⓐ Ⓑ Ⓒ Ⓓ Ⓔ
82 Ⓐ Ⓑ Ⓒ Ⓓ Ⓔ
83 Ⓐ Ⓑ Ⓒ Ⓓ Ⓔ
84 Ⓐ Ⓑ Ⓒ Ⓓ Ⓔ
85 Ⓐ Ⓑ Ⓒ Ⓓ Ⓔ
86 Ⓐ Ⓑ Ⓒ Ⓓ Ⓔ
87 Ⓐ Ⓑ Ⓒ Ⓓ Ⓔ
88 Ⓐ Ⓑ Ⓒ Ⓓ Ⓔ
89 Ⓐ Ⓑ Ⓒ Ⓓ Ⓔ
90 Ⓐ Ⓑ Ⓒ Ⓓ Ⓔ
91 Ⓐ Ⓑ Ⓒ Ⓓ Ⓔ
92 Ⓐ Ⓑ Ⓒ Ⓓ Ⓔ
93 Ⓐ Ⓑ Ⓒ Ⓓ Ⓔ
94 Ⓐ Ⓑ Ⓒ Ⓓ Ⓔ
95 Ⓐ Ⓑ Ⓒ Ⓓ Ⓔ
96 Ⓐ Ⓑ Ⓒ Ⓓ Ⓔ

97 Ⓐ Ⓑ Ⓒ Ⓓ Ⓔ
98 Ⓐ Ⓑ Ⓒ Ⓓ Ⓔ
99 Ⓐ Ⓑ Ⓒ Ⓓ Ⓔ
100 Ⓐ Ⓑ Ⓒ Ⓓ Ⓔ
101 Ⓐ Ⓑ Ⓒ Ⓓ Ⓔ
102 Ⓐ Ⓑ Ⓒ Ⓓ Ⓔ
103 Ⓐ Ⓑ Ⓒ Ⓓ Ⓔ
104 Ⓐ Ⓑ Ⓒ Ⓓ Ⓔ
105 Ⓐ Ⓑ Ⓒ Ⓓ Ⓔ
106 Ⓐ Ⓑ Ⓒ Ⓓ Ⓔ
107 Ⓐ Ⓑ Ⓒ Ⓓ Ⓔ
108 Ⓐ Ⓑ Ⓒ Ⓓ Ⓔ
109 Ⓐ Ⓑ Ⓒ Ⓓ Ⓔ
110 Ⓐ Ⓑ Ⓒ Ⓓ Ⓔ
111 Ⓐ Ⓑ Ⓒ Ⓓ Ⓔ
112 Ⓐ Ⓑ Ⓒ Ⓓ Ⓔ
113 Ⓐ Ⓑ Ⓒ Ⓓ Ⓔ
114 Ⓐ Ⓑ Ⓒ Ⓓ Ⓔ
115 Ⓐ Ⓑ Ⓒ Ⓓ Ⓔ
116 Ⓐ Ⓑ Ⓒ Ⓓ Ⓔ
117 Ⓐ Ⓑ Ⓒ Ⓓ Ⓔ
118 Ⓐ Ⓑ Ⓒ Ⓓ Ⓔ
119 Ⓐ Ⓑ Ⓒ Ⓓ Ⓔ
120 Ⓐ Ⓑ Ⓒ Ⓓ Ⓔ
121 Ⓐ Ⓑ Ⓒ Ⓓ Ⓔ
122 Ⓐ Ⓑ Ⓒ Ⓓ Ⓔ
123 Ⓐ Ⓑ Ⓒ Ⓓ Ⓔ
124 Ⓐ Ⓑ Ⓒ Ⓓ Ⓔ
125 Ⓐ Ⓑ Ⓒ Ⓓ Ⓔ

SAMPLE HUMANITIES EXAMINATION 2

NUMBER OF QUESTIONS: 125

Time: 90 MINUTES

> **Directions:** Each of the questions or incomplete statements below is followed by five suggested answers or completions. Select the one that is best in each case.

MAP A

EUROPE 1945–1990

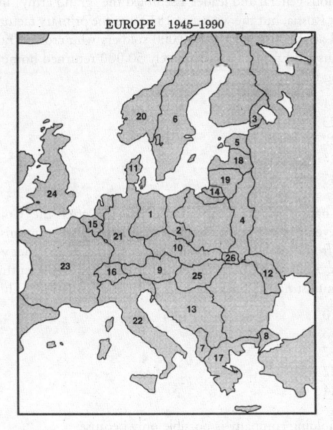

Questions 1–3 refer to Map A.

1. This nation has been the home of the Nazi party since the 1930s. As a fascist nation, it began to invade neighboring nations and actually began World War II when it invaded Poland in 1939.

   (A) 21
   (B) 15
   (C) 24
   (D) 23
   (E) 20

2. It was invaded by Hitler in 1938 when the Nazis took over the Sudetenland region, an area populated with many Germans. Several months later the rest of this nation was successfully taken over by the Nazi army. During the Cold War, this nation attempted to break away from the Soviet-bloc world when its leader, Dubchek, supported a reform movement for civil liberties.

(A) 24
(B) 22
(C) 21
(D) 10
(E) 23

3. A famous general and leader assembled the "grand army" in an attempt to defeat Russia, but the winter of 1812 was the primary factor that led to the grand army's loss. Of the 600,000 soldiers who crossed Europe to attack the Russian Empire, approximately 50,000 returned home in this embarrassing defeat.

(A) 1
(B) 23
(C) 22
(D) 24
(E) 4

4. This nation adapted communism shortly after the Cold War began. However, in 1948, under their leader Tito, this communist nation broke away from "satellites" status and became a trading partner with the United States. After the Cold War ended in the late 20th century, this former communist nation broke into six independent nations. This country is

(A) 10
(B) 13
(C) 17
(D) 22
(E) 24

5. The holding company is possible only because

(A) many stockholders do not permit proxies
(B) some securities do not have voting rights
(C) corporations are permitted to hold stock in other corporations
(D) courts do not enforce the law
(E) stocks can be bought on margin

6. The Securities and Exchange Commission is designed to regulate the securities business for the benefit of

(A) small business
(B) the consumer
(C) the investor
(D) labor
(E) the banking system

7. Adolescent-parent tensions continue to evolve as we enter the 21st century because

   (A) there is an increase in the patriarchal nature of the American family
   (B) the youth subculture or generation gap continues to be a part of teen life
   (C) families are getting larger and larger in our society
   (D) single-parent families have become the most common family structure
   (E) religion has failed to bring families closer together

8. The term *secular power* in medieval European history would be used to describe the powers of a

   (A) king or emperor
   (B) pope
   (C) bishop
   (D) church council
   (E) cardinal

9. A campaign speech was made containing a reference to "two chickens in every pot." What event occurred shortly after the speech which made this reference seem ironic?

   (A) Pullman transportation strike in 1894
   (B) Defeat of the Populists in 1896
   (C) Election of Alfred E. Smith in 1928
   (D) Stock market crash in 1929
   (E) Rationing of gasoline after 1941

10. Levittown is a place and a term that describes

    (A) the shantytowns established during the Depression
    (B) the average American town studied by Robert and Helen Merell Lynd
    (C) the new suburbia that emerged in the 1950s
    (D) a utopian society
    (E) the ideal life depicted on television

11. Which law passed by Congress was part of FDR's New Deal legislation?

    (A) Homestead Act
    (B) Pendleton Act
    (C) Social Security Act
    (D) Morrill Act for education
    (E) Pure Food and Drug Act

12. Which of these ancient empires was geographically the largest?

    (A) Egyptian
    (B) Persian
    (C) Assyrian
    (D) Chaldean
    (E) Hittite

13. Which of the following languages has been the spoken and written word for the Roman Catholic Church?

    (A) Arabic
    (B) Sanskrit
    (C) Greek
    (D) Italian
    (E) Latin

14. Monetary policy in the United States is administered by

    (A) Congress
    (B) the President
    (C) the Federal Reserve Board of Governors
    (D) the Department of Commerce
    (E) the Council of Economic Advisors

15. Malthus' "principle of population" is an instance of the

    (A) law of increasing returns
    (B) law of diminishing returns
    (C) observation that fertility is greater in the tropical than temperate zones
    (D) observation that fertility is greater among the lowest class
    (E) law of diminishing sexual energy

16. The belief in reincarnation is an important part of

    (A) Judaism
    (B) Confucius' teachings
    (C) Hinduism
    (D) Zoroastrianism
    (E) Islam

17. The total value (in dollars) of goods and services produced in the American economy during the year is called the

    (A) net national income
    (B) gross private domestic investment
    (C) gross national product
    (D) net producers domestic gain
    (E) net national product

18. In sociology and psychology, *drives* such as thirst, sex, and hunger are

    (A) behavior that must always be suppressed
    (B) factors which incite behavior in the individual
    (C) glands which secrete endocrines
    (D) mysterious forces which induce people to commit crimes
    (E) called norms

Questions 19–22 pertain to this map.

MAP B
SOUTH AND SOUTHEAST ASIA 1947–1954

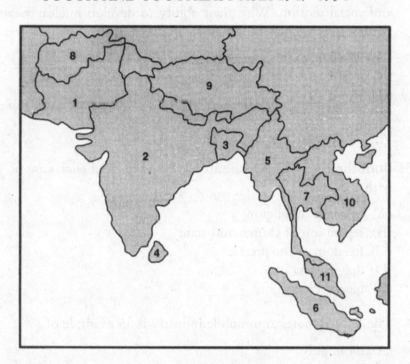

19. This Southeast Asia nation was once a French colony and later, like Korea, was split in two as a result of the Cold War. Today it is once again united under a communist government. This country is

    (A) 5
    (B) 7
    (C) 10
    (D) 11
    (E) 12

20. Which country was ruled until 1959 by a Buddhist religious leader called the Dalai Lama?

    (A) 2
    (B) 4
    (C) 5
    (D) 7
    (E) 9

21. Nicknamed the "jewel of the British crown," this colony eventually received its independence in 1947 but was split into several new states because of its Hindu majority.

    (A) 2
    (B) 5
    (C) 10
    (D) 11
    (E) 12

22. In the short history of these two new, independent nations, constant conflict over border disputes and religion have continued to create political and social tension. With their ability to develop nuclear weapons, these two nations have become a global concern in the 21st century.

    (A) 2 and 1
    (B) 9 and 12
    (C) 7 and 10
    (D) 1 and 8
    (E) 1 and 3

23. Both the Peter Zenger case in 1735 and the Schenck case of 1919 dealt with the issue of

    (A) freedom of religion
    (B) separation of church and state
    (C) freedom of the press
    (D) due process
    (E) blacks' civil rights

24. The United States automobile industry is an example of

    (A) monopoly
    (B) monopolistic competition
    (C) a cartel
    (D) holding company
    (E) oligarchy

25. In a free market economy, price tends to fall whenever

    (A) the quantity supplied increases more rapidly than the quantity demanded
    (B) the quantity demanded increases more rapidly than the quantity supplied
    (C) supply and demand are equal
    (D) both supply and demand increase
    (E) more of a commodity is produced in a mass production technology

26. Nelson Mandela and F.W. de Klerk served notice that "the moral high ground is no longer big enough for both of them." What happened in South Africa to prompt newspapers to discuss these two men?

   (A) The Nobel Peace Prize was being taken away from them by the Nobel Committee.
   (B) A full-scale campaign for the first national election open to all races took place with Nelson Mandela becoming president.
   (C) The National Party and the African National Congress decided to join as a single party under one of these two dynamic leaders.
   (D) Mr. de Klerk decided to step down as president and allow Mr. Mandela, the "true leader who has freed South Africa," to lead the country for the next four years.
   (E) The two leaders agreed that an international peacekeeping agency was needed to end the moral wrongs of apartheid.

27. Nearly half a million years ago, one of the greatest inventions of all time took place. It enabled humankind to survive a rough, challenging environment. This great invention was

   (A) fire
   (B) agriculture
   (C) wheel
   (D) permanent dwellings
   (E) domesticated animals

28. Which event slowed down the growth and spread of communism?

   (A) The rise of labor unions and pro labor legislation in capitalistic nations
   (B) Lenin's call for a proletariat revolution in Czarist Russia
   (C) Mao Tse Tung agrarian revolution in China
   (D) Labor abuses in the early days of the Industrial Revolution
   (E) The suppression of labor movements in England

29. As we enter the 21st century, the latest census report would confirm that:

   (A) men are living longer than women
   (B) the farm population has shown a surprising growth
   (C) the senior citizen population is growing rapidly
   (D) we have hit zero population growth
   (E) there has been a decrease in college attendance

30. Supreme Court justices are

   (A) appointed by the president
   (B) nominated by the Senate and approved by the House
   (C) chosen by electors of the Electoral College
   (D) elected by the populace
   (E) nominated by the president and approved by the Senate

Exam 2

31. In the history of the presidency until 1974, there had never been an instance of

    (A) a vice president becoming president
    (B) a president failing to be elected by the electoral college
    (C) the election of a president by the House of Representatives
    (D) the resignation of a president
    (E) the assassination of a president

32. What do these three amendments have in common?

    • Amendment XIII
    • Amendment XIV
    • Amendment XV

    (A) They all deal with civil rights after the Civil War
    (B) They limit the powers of the presidency
    (C) They are nicknamed the Bill of Rights
    (D) They all deal with the prohibition era
    (E) They increase the power of the federal government

33. "The American expansionists and imperialists of the 1890s appealed to biological evolution and economic and social history (referred to as Social Darwinism) to support their views." Social Darwinism is associated with which of the following American events:

    (A) Entrance into World War I
    (B) Civil War
    (C) Kellogg-Briand Pact
    (D) Spanish American War
    (E) Entrance into World War II

34. The interest which Russia historically manifested in the Dardanelles arose from a desire to have an outlet to the

    (A) Black Sea
    (B) Yellow Sea
    (C) North Sea
    (D) Mediterranean Sea
    (E) Red Sea

35. "L'état, c'est moi." This statement is attributed to

    (A) Louis XVI
    (B) Louis XV
    (C) Louis XIV
    (D) Louis XIII
    (E) Louis X

36. After the Franco-Prussian War completed the unification of Germany, the German Imperial constitution

    (A) made the Prussian king, Kaiser Wilhelm II, the new emperor
    (B) was a generally democratic instrument
    (C) declared the equality of all member states
    (D) declared Metternich the ruler of Austria to be emperor of the Empire
    (E) made Roman Catholicism the state religion

37. In *The Prince*, Machiavelli counsels a ruler that

    (A) it is better to be feared than loved
    (B) it is better to be loved than feared
    (C) he need not worry about arousing the hatred of his subjects
    (D) it is best to be both feared and hated
    (E) it is better to be truthful with one's subjects

38. The father of anthropology who was the first to prove that man's origin was in sub-Saharan Africa and was known for the discoveries of Zinjanthropus and Australopithecus (discovered in Olduvai Gorge) was

    (A) Richard Leakey
    (B) George Mendel
    (C) Charles Dawson
    (D) Louis Leakey
    (E) Jacques DePerthes

39. Which pair of words or phrases best describes a cause-and-effect relationship in connection with "the final solution"?

    (A) putsch—Nordic supremacy theory
    (B) Kristallnacht—rise of the Third Reich
    (C) Babi Yar massacre—passage of the Nuremberg Laws
    (D) master race theory—genocide
    (E) Warsaw Ghetto Uprising—construction of Auschwitz

40. Which Roman emperor ended polytheism by making Christianity the official religion of Rome?

    (A) Julius Caesar
    (B) Constantine
    (C) Octavian
    (D) Nero
    (E) Marcus Aurelius

41. The most significant agent of childhood socialization is

    (A) the peer group
    (B) television
    (C) religious training
    (D) the family
    (E) school

42. The Standard Oil trust was originally organized by

    (A) Carnegie
    (B) Morgan
    (C) Vanderbilt
    (D) Rockefeller
    (E) Gould

43. Which issue in France was significant in the Dreyfus Affair?

    (A) Revolutionist
    (B) Anti-Semitism
    (C) Supremacy of the pope
    (D) Reign of terror
    (E) Absolutism

44. Bismarck, after 1851, believed that Germany could become strong and united only if

    (A) Austria was excluded from German affairs
    (B) she became a republic
    (C) Austria became the leader
    (D) Italy remained divided into small states
    (E) colonies could be gained for Germany

45. The Zulus are

    (A) Bantus who fought the British in South Africa
    (B) the aboriginal peoples of Australia
    (C) the French Protestant settlers in South Africa
    (D) a people who lived in New Zealand before the coming of the British
    (E) a group of Irish revolutionaries

46. A new currency emerged in the mid 1990s in this geographical region that symbolizes both an economic and social bond among their people. This area/region is

    (A) Latin America
    (B) The Caribbean
    (C) Europe
    (D) Southeast Asia
    (E) Russia

47. Which of the following programs of social reform would be, according to the thought of Malthus, based on a correct analysis of the problem of poverty?

    (A) Universal education at public expense
    (B) Guaranteed minimum wage
    (C) Social security
    (D) Consumer subsidies
    (E) Aid to dependent children

48. If people do not consume all their income, but put the unspent amount into a pillow or buy an old security with it, in national income and product terms they are

    (A) saving but not investing
    (B) investing but not saving
    (C) both saving and investing
    (D) neither saving nor investing
    (E) saving, but investing only to the extent that they buy old securities

49. Which of the following is *least* common in our society?

    (A) Group marriage
    (B) Divorce
    (C) Illegitimacy
    (D) Intercourse before marriage
    (E) Homosexuality

50. The student demonstrations for democracy in Tiananmen Square in China were

    (A) violent attacks on government buildings by students
    (B) given relatively little attention from anyone
    (C) allowed to continue peacefully by the government
    (D) attempted to improve academic conditions in school
    (E) suppressed violently by the Chinese government

51. When sociologists talk of "social mobility," they usually have in mind

    (A) horizontal mobility
    (B) interracial marriage
    (C) vertical mobility
    (D) rapid social retrogression
    (E) moral progress

52. The use of canoes and moccasins by the whites are examples of

    (A) parallel inventions
    (B) cultural diffusion
    (C) cultural assimilation
    (D) social mobility
    (E) cultural isolation

53. Which political-economic system practiced the belief that government must be aggressively involved in order to control the success and growth of the economy of a nation?

(A) Mercantilism
(B) Capitalism as defined by Adam Smith
(C) Scientific communism—the fundamental principles of Engel and Marx
(D) Laissez faire economics
(E) Manorialism

54. Which of the following was Veblen's attitude toward marginal utility economics? He considered it

(A) analytically proper
(B) overly inductive and oriented to biology
(C) collectivist in its implications
(D) overly deductive, individualistic, and static
(E) too strongly oriented to the labor movement

55. In the late 19th century, competitive companies in one field entered into agreements to fix prices. When railroad companies in the 1880s engaged in this kind of activity, they were in fact forming

(A) pools
(B) conglomerates
(C) monopolies
(D) trusts
(E) corporations

Questions **56 and 57** refer to the following chart.

U.S. PRESIDENTIAL ELECTIONS 1876–1888				
Year	Candidates	(Party)	Popular vote	Electoral vote
1876	Rutherford B. Hayes	(R)*	4,036,572	185
	Samuel J. Tilden	(D)	4,284,020	184
1880	James A. Garfield	(R)*	4,453,295	214
	Winfield S. Hancock	(D)	4,414,082	155
	James B. Weaver (Greenback-Labor)		308,578	0
1884	Grover Cleveland	(D)*	4,879,507	219
	James G. Blaine	(R)	4,850,293	182
	Benjamin F. Butler (Greenback-Labor)		175,370	0
	John P. St. John (Prohibition)		150,369	0
1888	Benjamin Harrison	(R)*	5,477,129	233
	Grover Cleveland	(D)	5,537,857	168
	Clinton B. Fisk (Prohibition)		249,506	0
	Anson J. Streeter (Union-Labor)		146,935	0

R = Republican; D = Democrat

56. What would be another appropriate title for the above chart?

    (A) The crucial importance of the popular vote in electing the president
    (B) The rapid growth of the American electorate
    (C) The incumbent's advantage in an election
    (D) How the electoral college system operates
    (E) The influence of third parties in election outcomes

57. According to the chart, if one favored the direct election of the president by way of the people's vote replacing the electoral vote, one would turn to the election of

    (A) 1876
    (B) 1880 and 1884
    (C) 1884
    (D) 1888
    (E) 1876 and 1888

58. In 1987, America's Bicentennial observance celebrated the writing of the

    (A) Declaration of Independence
    (B) Monroe Doctrine
    (C) Bill of Rights
    (D) Emancipation Proclamation
    (E) Constitution

59. Which of the following presidents was the only one to serve two full terms?

    (A) President John F. Kennedy
    (B) President Lyndon Baines Johnson
    (C) President Bill Clinton
    (D) President Richard M. Nixon
    (E) President George H. Bush

60. Which is a valid conclusion that can be drawn from the fact that many large cities in the United States still have sections called "Chinatown," "Little Italy," and "Germantown"?

    (A) Racial tension has been fostered by the United States government since the early 1900s.
    (B) Most immigrants are quickly assimilated into the culture of the United States.
    (C) Some sections of large cities are physically isolated from the rest of the city.
    (D) Before becoming citizens, immigrants must live in specified areas of large cities.
    (E) Ethnic goups often try to preserve their cultural heritage.

61. Which would most probably lead to the development of a pluralistic society?

    (A) A policy of open immigration
    (B) A totalitarian form of government
    (C) The requirement that only English be spoken in schools
    (D) The formation of labor unions
    (E) An increased emphasis on social conformity

62. Alexis de Tocqueville's *Democracy in America* had as its basic subject

    (A) American political institutions during the presidency of Andrew Johnson
    (B) modern democracy and an alleged trend toward equality of conditions
    (C) effects of the Industrial Revolution upon America and Europe
    (D) amazing prophecies about the future political development of America and France
    (E) a contrast between English and American democracy

63. What do the following three men all have in common?

    - Earl Warren
    - John Marshall
    - Warren Burger

    (A) Presidents
    (B) State Governors
    (C) U.S. Senators
    (D) Astronauts
    (E) Supreme Court Chief Justices

64. The Huguenots were

    (A) a French family that claimed the throne
    (B) a party that opposed the king's powers in England
    (C) French Protestants
    (D) a fleet that Philip II sent to invade England
    (E) members of the First Estate

65. Why do anthropologists study the behavioral traits of higher primates?

    (A) To see how advanced these higher primates really are.
    (B) It is important to find out why the primates differ so much in their prehensile activities.
    (C) Anthropologists need to find out why humans no longer brachiate.
    (D) The conditions in which the higher primates live resemble the environmental conditions that existed when human cultures began.
    (E) By studying their sexual expression, anthropologists can determine the reasons for human sexual aggression.

66. This great civilization influenced early Russia by diffusing its culture and particularly its religion to Kiev. Once part of the eastern Roman Empire, it was also the home of the great emperor Justinian. The people of this great culture were the

    (A) Huns
    (B) Mongols
    (C) Slavs
    (D) Byzantines
    (E) Chinese

67. The great expansion of business corporations, monopolies, and holding companies took place

    (A) shortly after the Revolutionary War
    (B) prior to 1861 and the Civil War
    (C) near the end of the 19th century
    (D) during the presidency of Franklin D. Roosevelt
    (E) after World War II

68. The formation and social behavior of a baboon troop studied by Jane Goodall reflects that baboons are

    (A) egalitarian
    (B) random and haphazard
    (C) rigidly hierarchical and disciplined
    (D) a system of concentric circles
    (E) low in the order of primate social development

69. He studied the origins and functions of the "self" and laid the foundation of social psychology. This statement refers to

    (A) George Herbert Mead
    (B) Jean Piaget
    (C) Albert Einstein
    (D) John Dewey
    (E) Franklin Frazer

70. In an experiment using a control group,

    (A) change is induced in the control group only
    (B) change is induced in the experimental group only
    (C) more change is induced in the control group than in the experimental group
    (D) less change is induced in the control group than the experimental group
    (E) the control group guarantees the accuracy of the findings

71. In which of the following job categories in the United States has there been an absolute decline over the past thirty years?

    (A) Professional
    (B) Managerial
    (C) Skilled
    (D) Service
    (E) Farm

72. The great expansion of college-bound students began

    (A) at the end of the 19th century
    (B) right after World War I
    (C) during the time of the New Deal
    (D) from the 1960s on
    (E) with the onset of the 21st century

73. Louis XIV is best known for

    (A) making Calvinism the official state religion for the French people
    (B) defeat of the Spanish Armada
    (C) defeat of Britain in the Hundred Years War
    (D) building the Versailles Palace
    (E) being a weak absolute monarch

74. During the Reagan administration, the Iran-Contra Affair reflected U.S. policy toward

    (A) Panama
    (B) Grenada
    (C) Haiti
    (D) Brazil
    (E) Nicaragua

75. "The government bets you can't live on the land for five years and if you can, you win the land." This statement refers to

    (A) the Northwest Ordinance
    (B) veterans' preference after World War II
    (C) the Homestead Act of 1862
    (D) The Morrill Act of 1862
    (E) settlement of the Lone Star Republic im the early 1800s

76. The decade of the greatest growth in the American railroad occurred

    (A) in the 1790s as the nation was first established
    (B) during the Manifest Destiny movement of the 1820s–1850s
    (C) during the Civil War years
    (D) during the post–Civil War era, as industry rapidly expanded
    (E) after America's entrance into World War I in 1917

77. The largest state in area and the smallest in population among the following is

    (A) Nevada
    (B) Texas
    (C) Montana
    (D) Maine
    (E) Alaska

78. Under which president did the stock market make its great advances in the Dow?

    (A) President Nixon
    (B) President Ford
    (C) President Reagan
    (D) President Clinton
    (E) President Bush

79. The immigrants arriving to the United States from the late 1800s to the beginning of World War I in 1914 came from

    (A) western Europe
    (B) southeastern Asia
    (C) Central America
    (D) eastern Europe
    (E) China and Japan

80. In the famous tale of *A Christmas Carol,* Karl Marx would consider the role played by Ebenezer Scrooge to be that of the

    (A) proletariat
    (B) bourgeoisie
    (C) sharecropper
    (D) blue collar worker
    (E) slave owner

81. This was one of the original thirteen states, it was the home of the first colonial legislature—the House of Burgeses—and it was the site of the first settlement, at Jamestown. The state is

    (A) New York
    (B) Delaware
    (C) Virginia
    (D) Pennsylvania
    (E) North Carolina

82. The most populous state in the United States in 1860 was

    (A) Virginia
    (B) Massachusetts
    (C) Illinois
    (D) South Carolina
    (E) New York

83. The largest number of immigrants from 1890 to 1910 came from

    (A) Ireland and Scotland
    (B) China and Japan
    (C) Italy and Eastern Europe
    (D) Latin America
    (E) India and Pakistan

84. This great social philosopher is best known for his work with children: "He concluded that there are two major stages in the development of moral judgment in children. The first stage, ages 3–8 are characterized by respect for authority and the morality of constraint and the second stage, ages 9–12, by the gradual ascent of mutual respect and the morality of cooperation."

    (A) Jean Piaget
    (B) Max Weber
    (C) Margaret Mead
    (D) Sigmund Freud
    (E) Ruth Benedict

85. Ascribed status, unlike achieved status, is based on

    (A) what you do
    (B) who you are
    (C) power and prestige
    (D) intelligence
    (E) your gender

86. During which period was there no margin for saving?

    (A) 1929–1931
    (B) 1941–1944
    (C) 1945–1950
    (D) 1965–1970
    (E) 1989–1991

87. The opposite of Adam Smith's "invisible hand" would be a "visible hand." Which of the following could be considered the "visible hand"?

    (A) God
    (B) Competition
    (C) Price warfare
    (D) Population increase
    (E) Government

88. Immigration in the United States almost came to a standstill in

    (A) 1845–1855
    (B) 1890s
    (C) 1900–1910
    (D) 1919–1939
    (E) 1965–1970s

89. Which is a typical trait of collective behavior that was demonstrated many times in the antiwar protests of the 1960s?

    (A) Protestors do not welcome the media.
    (B) The group and leaders expect to accomplish very little from their actions.
    (C) It is structured and predictable.
    (D) Solidarity is commonly exhibited and intensifies as the protest advances.
    (E) It occurred in isolated and small populated areas.

90. The increased flow of precious metals from the New World to Europe in the 15th and 16th centuries

    (A) caused prices to decrease
    (B) caused trade and contact between the two worlds to expand
    (C) had no effect on price levels
    (D) discouraged speculation
    (E) encouraged small-scale agriculture

91. A sociologist's job is often complicated by the nature of the social condition he is studying. Durkheim, in studying deaths from suicide, had such a problem. The nature of suicide precludes such a particular research treatment. Which of the following research designs would he have had to employ to make significant generalizations and conclusions?

    (A) The case study
    (B) The observation method
    (C) The survey
    (D) The experiment
    (E) A diary

92. Which of the following taught the observance of caste rules as a religious obligation?

    (A) Islam
    (B) Buddhism
    (C) Taoism
    (D) Hinduism
    (E) Judaism

93. "The line of boundary between the territories of the United States and those of Her Britannic Majesty shall be continued westward along the forty-ninth parallel." This provision relates to which of the following?

    (A) Gadsden Purchase
    (B) Louisiana Purchase
    (C) Oregon Territory
    (D) Northwest Ordinance
    (E) Mexican War

94. Henry VII and Henry VIII were members of which royal family?

    (A) Tudors
    (B) Stuarts
    (C) Romanovs
    (D) Hapsburgs
    (E) Bourbons

95. In which of the following cities would there be more Mormons in proportion to the population?

    (A) Atlanta
    (B) Minneapolis
    (C) Salt Lake City
    (D) New York City
    (E) Boston

96. Which of the following smaller states of Europe had only one but nevertheless the largest holding in central Africa before World War I?

    (A) Netherlands
    (B) Belgium
    (C) Denmark
    (D) Norway
    (E) Switzerland

97. The Roman Empire

    (A) was more democratic than the Roman Republic
    (B) in 313 A.D., was split into two (east and west) to make it easier to rule
    (C) fell in both the east and the west in 476 A.D. to the Mongols
    (D) was unable to defeat Hannibal and his army of elephants
    (E) never accepted Christianity into its society

98. "Implied powers" are the powers of the national government that are necessary to

    (A) amend the national Constitution
    (B) prevent the state governments from expanding their powers beyond those given to them by the Constitution
    (C) allow the national government to do the jobs given to it by the Constitution
    (D) allow speedy governmental action in a war
    (E) declare emergency powers and temporarily suspend democracy

99. The Supreme Court decision upholding certain tax-supported benefits for parochial school children was an issue dealing with the

    (A) "general welfare" clause of the U.S. Constitution
    (B) First Amendment
    (C) Fourteenth Amendment
    (D) Fifth Amendment
    (E) Tenth Amendment

100. The Federal Reserve System can control the creation of money by

    (A) setting legal reserve requirements, varying the prime rate, and setting quotas on government printing of currency
    (B) setting legal reserve requirements, varying the discount rate, and varying the prime rate
    (C) setting quotas on bank loans and on the government printing of currency, and by varying the prime rate
    (D) setting legal reserve requirements, varying the discount rate, and by open market operations
    (E) closing banks and the stock market, varying discount rates, and varying the prime rate

101. Those who support the belief in the Bible are often referred to as

    (A) Darwinists
    (B) Primatologists
    (C) Evolutionists
    (D) Creationists
    (E) Von Danikenists

102. The typical American corporation of today is likely to be largely controlled by

    (A) two or three men, who own most of the stock
    (B) a large number of people, each of whom owns a small amount of stock
    (C) managers, who are subject to much pressure from the stockholders
    (D) managers, who are given a very free hand by the stockholders
    (E) a dominant figure who controls the majority of stock

103. Which of these people would have been apt to join one of the craft unions in the American Federation of Labor?

    (A) An automobile assembly line worker in 1937
    (B) A brick mason in 1939
    (C) A department store clerk in 1950
    (D) A nurse in 1965
    (E) A schoolteacher in 1945

104. After he came to power in Turkey, Mustapha Kemal

    (A) attempted to restore traditional Turkish ways
    (B) introduced many modern reforms
    (C) began a war to reconquer the Arab sections of the old Turkish empire
    (D) restored the caliph to power
    (E) tried to reconquer the Balkan peninsula

105. Henry George's "single tax" was to be applied to

    (A) homes
    (B) income
    (C) sales
    (D) land
    (E) imports

106. In the 1980s, the greatest number of American women workers were employed in

    (A) social work
    (B) clerical work
    (C) accounting
    (D) real estate
    (E) libraries

107. David Ricardo used Malthusian ideas to indicate the basic wage. To him, the reason this wage always tends toward bare subsistence is that

    (A) employers are mean
    (B) workers dislike ostentation
    (C) society is unfair
    (D) workers will always reproduce the labor supply to the maximum
    (E) unions are prevented by the state from militant action

108. Consider the following events

    • The dividing of Germany into West and East Germany
    • The dividing of Vietnam into North and South Vietnam
    • The dividing of Korea into North and South Korea

    All three events were a result of

    (A) World War I
    (B) the Vietnam War
    (C) the Cold War
    (D) the Berlin Wall being created
    (E) the Versailles Peace Treaty

109. Which of these peoples were not one of the Germanic tribes?

    (A) Visigoths
    (B) Vandals
    (C) Huns
    (D) Lombards
    (E) Franks

110. The best source of historical data for an archaeologist would be the discovery of _____, but generally, the archaeologist usually finds only _____ when he make a successful dig.

    (A) written remains, written remains
    (B) written remains, material remains
    (C) written remains, verbal remains
    (D) material remains, written remains
    (E) written remains, verbal remains

111. The advance of the Islamic religious jihad in the late 8th century was stopped finally by

    (A) Charlemagne at the Battle of Tours
    (B) the Roman Emperor Octavius and the institution of his policy of Pax Romana
    (C) William the Conqueror at the Battle of Hastings
    (D) the burning of Rome by the Huns
    (E) the joining of two Spanish families of Fernando and Isabel in marriage

112. Which religion was founded in ancient India, spread to China (but didn't take hold), and eventually ended up taking hold in Southeast Asia and Japan?

    (A) Hinduism
    (B) Confucianism
    (C) Shintoism
    (D) Islamic Shiites
    (E) Buddhism

113. A fief was

    (A) a person who swore fealty to a lord
    (B) a grant, usually of land, made in exchange for promised services
    (C) a person bound to the soil
    (D) an oath of loyalty
    (E) a tariff on trade

114. One of the first things the Bolsheviks did in Russia when they came into power in 1917 was to

    (A) have the tsar removed from office
    (B) begin negotiations for peace with the Germans
    (C) make Stalin the head of the state
    (D) drive the Germans completely out of Russian territory
    (E) collectivize the land

115. Stress and strain in adolescence are most characteristic of

    (A) all known societies
    (B) preliterate societies
    (C) peasant societies
    (D) modern industrial societies
    (E) frontier societies

116. Which of the following methods of social science goes deepest into the motivation and problems of people?

    (A) Statistical survey
    (B) Document research
    (C) Interviews
    (D) Case study
    (E) Behavioral model

117. During the constitutional debate in the 1780s, the Federalists

    (A) supported a strong central government to provide order and protection
    (B) emphasized the need for a bill of rights
    (C) were the spokesman for the "common people"
    (D) wanted strong state governments
    (E) feared the abusive power of the new national government

118. Of the following, which is most clearly an example of reducing the domain of ascribed status?

    (A) A young man giving his seat to an older man on a bus that is crowded
    (B) Women who devote their time to their homes and church activities
    (C) Women serving in the armed forces of the United States
    (D) Members of certain racial groups sitting in the back of a bus
    (E) Young people beginning compulsory education at an earlier age

119. Of the following, which stage of human development is closest to modern man, also known as homo sapiens sapiens?

    (A) Neanderthal
    (B) Australopithecus
    (C) Homo Erectus
    (D) Cro-Magnon Man
    (E) Piltdown Man

120. Karl Marx reacted to the capitalist economic system of his time in a famous tract written in 1848. The title of this work was *The Communist Manifesto.* He contended that capitalism was

    (A) an artificial conspiracy imposed on society by greedy people
    (B) a necessary but temporary stage in the evolution of an industrial society
    (C) a retrogressive system that had as its main fault the creation of a proletariat
    (D) going to improve by reforms instituted through state action
    (E) incompatible with Christian morality

121. Consider the following events:

    • A noticeable increase in population occurred with the coming of the Neolithic Age.
    • Man settles down and ideas spread as he begins to make permanent dwellings.
    • Rapid cultural diffusion develops as man begins to establish communities so that he no longer has to be on the move.

    All these events occurred during the:

    (A) Paleolithic Age
    (B) Mesolithic Age
    (C) Neolithic Age
    (D) Industrial Age
    (E) Middle Ages

122. During the Middle Ages, the history of Spain was a mixture of what culture?

    (A) the Holy Roman emperors and the popes
    (B) Western Christians and the Byzantines
    (C) Christians and Muslims
    (D) the Guelphs and the Ghibellines
    (E) Protestants and Catholics

123. A union shop is a shop

    (A) that has voted to allow union representation
    (B) where the majority of the workers are union members
    (C) designated in right to work as having official union status
    (D) where only union members are allowed to work
    (E) that opposes women in the labor field

124. Judicial self-restraint as applied to the Supreme Court can be described as

    (A) a reluctance on the part of the justices to file a dissenting opinion except in rare cases
    (B) an awareness of the need for dignity and propriety in courtroom proceedings
    (C) a careful consideration of the wisdom and social impact of disputed laws
    (D) a careful consideration of the motives of Congress in enacting the disputed laws
    (E) a proper concern for the role and judgment of the legislative branch of government

125. Which statement is accurate on making a federal law?

    (A) The president's veto cannot be overturned.
    (B) The bill must pass both houses and be signed by the president.
    (C) A bill cannot be changed from its original form once introduced.
    (D) The bill can be interpreted by the Supreme Court.
    (E) Most bills eventually become laws as little committee work is needed.

STOP

If there is still time remaining, you may review your answers.

Social Sciences–History
ANSWER KEY–SAMPLE EXAMINATION 2

1. A	26. B	51. C	76. C	101. D
2. D	27. A	52. B	77. E	102. D
3. B	28. A	53. A	78. D	103. B
4. B	29. C	54. D	79. D	104. B
5. C	30. E	55. A	80. B	105. D
6. C	31. D	56. D	81. C	106. B
7. B	32. A	57. E	82. E	107. D
8. A	33. D	58. E	83. C	108. C
9. D	34. D	59. C	84. A	109. C
10. C	35. C	60. E	85. B	110. B
11. C	36. A	61. A	86. A	111. A
12. B	37. A	62. B	87. E	112. E
13. E	38. D	63. E	88. D	113. B
14. C	39. D	64. C	89. C	114. B
15. B	40. B	65. D	90. B	115. D
16. C	41. D	66. D	91. C	116. D
17. C	42. D	67. C	92. D	117. A
18. B	43. B	68. C	93. C	118. C
19. C	44. A	69. A	94. A	119. D
20. E	45. A	70. B	95. C	120. B
21. A	46. C	71. E	96. B	121. C
22. A	47. A	72. D	97. B	122. C
23. C	48. A	73. D	98. C	123. D
24. B	49. A	74. E	99. A	124. E
25. A	50. E	75. C	100. B	125. B

Answer Key–Exam 2

SCORING CHART

After you have scored your Sample Examination 2, enter the results in the chart below, then transfer your score to the Progress Chart on page 12.

Total Test	Number Right	Number Wrong	Number Omitted
125			

ANSWER EXPLANATIONS

1. **(A)** In 1933, the Weimar Republic to the Nazi government and Hitler and his fascist government took over Germany. This new Nazi nation was supposed to last for a thousand years *(Mein Kampf),* but in reality, it lasted only twelve.

2. **(D)** In 1937, Hitler took the German part of Czechoslovakia by force in a quick invasion. Peace efforts were made to avoid a war, and in negotiations with Hitler, Chamberlain of England returned home with the famous "scrap of paper" in which Hitler had agreed to not invade the rest of Czechoslovakia if he was allowed to keep the Sudetenland. Six months later the compromise had failed, for the Nazis had invaded all of Czechoslovakia, taking over the entire country. The stage was set for World War II to begin.

3. **(B)** Napoleon experienced the first failure in his military rule of France when his Grand Army was unable to defeat the Russian army. In 1812, he took the largest army ever assembled across Eastern Europe, but both the cunning Russian military and the winter of 1812 resulted in his first major defeat as ruler of the French people.

4. **(B)** In 1948, under their leader Tito, this communist nation was the only Russian satellite to break away from the Soviet Union. After the death of Tito in the late 1980s, Yugoslavia broke up into six independent nations but not without ethnic and religious tension. During the Cold War, Tito maintained good political and economic relations with the United States.

5. **(C)** A holding company is a corporation that holds stock in another company. This is permitted by law, even though a holding company may not produce any goods or services.

6. **(C)** The Securities and Exchange Commission (SEC) was established by Congress in 1934 under the New Deal to protect investors. The SEC prevents illegal stock market dealing such as prevailed prior to the Great Depression of the 1930s.

7. **(B)** Adolescence is a transition period between childhood and adulthood. This unclear stage leaves the adolescent with some confusion, because the transition is rather sudden and quick. Thus, conflict with parents and society is often common and understandable.

8. **(A)** The term *secular* means worldly or temporal, in contrast to ecclesiastical. In medieval European history, the king or emperor exercised "secular power"; the church exercised ecclesiastical authority.

9. **(D)** In the election of 1928, Republican candidate Herbert Hoover promised two chickens in every pot if he were elected. His election to the presidency was soon followed by the Great Depression of the 1930s, during which there were no chickens in most pots.

10. **(C)** After World War II, William Levitt began mass construction of affordable housing on former potato fields on Long Island. This new suburbia was replicated in Levittown, Pennsylvania.

11. **(C)** The Social Security Act was passed in 1935 under the Democratic administration of Franklin D. Roosevelt. The abolition of slavery came in the Republican administration of Abraham Lincoln; the Pendleton Act in 1883 under Republican President Arthur; the Morrill Act in 1862 under Lincoln; and the Pure Food and Drug Act in 1906 under Republican President Theodore Roosevelt.

12. **(B)** The ancient Persian Empire was the largest. It extended throughout the area we now call the Middle East from Asia Minor in the West to India in the East and from the Caucasus Mountains in the North to the Arabian Sea in the South.

13. **(E)** The official language of the Roman Catholic Church is still Latin. In the past fifty years, however, the vernacular has increasingly been used for actual Mass because it is easier for parishioners to understand and partake in the service.

14 **(C)** Monetary policy in the United States is administered by the Federal Reserve Board of Governors. The seven-member Board of Governors of the Federal Reserve system in Washington exercises control over the nation's money supply and credit conditions. This is referred to as "monetary policy."

15. **(B)** In 1948, under their leader Tito, this communist nation was the only Russian satellite to break away from the Soviet Union. After the death of Tito in the late 1980s, Yugoslavia broke up into six independent nations but not without ethnic and religious tension. During the Cold War, Tito maintained good political and economic relations with the United States.

16. **(C)** Reincarnation, the return of the soul after death in a new living body, is part of the teaching of Hinduism.

17. **(C)** The total value (in dollars) of all goods and services produced in the American economy during a given year is called the gross national product (GNP) for that year. If we subtract depreciation (the using up of capital equipment), we have net national product (NNP).

18. **(B)** In sociology and psychology, *drives* are factors that incite behavior in the individual. The term *drive* indicates an internal force or push that seeks an outlet. In psychoanalysis, *drive* is regarded as an instinct. Examples are thirst, sex, and hunger.

19. **(C)** Viet Nam, once a French colony, was divided at the 17th parallel, which soon put Viet Nam at the forefront of the Cold War. Shortly after the Geneva Agreement of 1954, a communist North Viet Nam and a democratic South Viet Nam had emerged. What eventually followed was the Viet Nam conflict that ended in the communist takeover of South Viet Nam in 1975.

20. **(E)** Tibet was ruled until 1959 by a Buddhist religious leader called the "Dalai Lama." In 1959, the Dalai Lama fled from Tibet. The country is under control of Communist China.

21. **(A)** The "jewel of the British crown," was the colonial possession of India. After the English lost the thirteen American colonies, this became their great-

est possession. When independence came in 1947 through the efforts of Gandhi, the strong religious differences called for the creation of several states, including the division of India and Pakistan into two parts.

22. **(A)** As stated above, these two nations have continued to have strong religious differences into the present. Even Gandhi was unable to bring the two religious groups together, and thus East and West Pakistan (Muslim) and India (Hindu) were created.

23. **(C)** The Peter Zenger case and the Schenck case both dealt with the 1st Amendment, which addresses the freedom of the press.

24. **(B)** Despite foreign competition, the U.S. automobile industry is a monopolistic competition, which means that several key companies control the market. Because we have more than one company, there is competition, but not in the true sense of the word as Adam Smith describes it.

25. **(A)** In a free market economy, price is determined by an equilibrium between supply and demand. When the quantity supplied increases more rapidly than the quantity demanded, the effect is a decline in price.

26. **(B)** All race elections took place for the first time in South Africa, resulting in the election of a black president.

27. **(A)** Approximately 500,000 years ago, humankind invented fire. This great invention provided warmth, enabled human life to cook meat that added protein to the brain, gave humans light at night and thus protection against predators, and finally could be used as a weapon against the human's foes.

28. **(A)** What Marx did not contemplate in his proletariat revolution was that the continual growth of English democracy resulted in both pro labor reform movement and a pro labor legislation (American capitalism followed in a similar reform path).

29. **(C)** For the past decade, the largest growing group of Americans has been senior citizens. With the quality of life in America among the highest in the world, people continue to live longer and longer! Similarly, the senior citizen commands a powerful political vote on the local, state, and national levels.

30. **(E)** The president of the United States nominates the justices of the Supreme Court. After congressional committee discussion, a majority vote of the Senate approves or disapproves of the nominee.

31. **(D)** In the history of the presidency until 1974, there had never been an instance of the resignation of a president. When Richard M. Nixon resigned in 1974, impeachment in the House of Representatives was imminent, and there was every indication that he would be removed by the Senate.

32. **(A)** The American Civil War was followed by a major step toward black equality with the Civil War amendments. Amendments XIII, XIV, and XV abolished slavery, provided citizenship, and instituted voting rights. While civil rights for black Americans was to be a long uphill battle, these amendments were nevertheless a major step in improving their life here in the United States.

33. **(D)** Closely tied to Manifest Destiny, social Darwinism (to Americans) was the idea that the American way of life was superior to other cultures and that therefore the United States was obliged to carry its great society to other peoples. Thus, the belief in American superiority was a form of social Darwinism that first manifested itself in the Spanish American War.

34. **(D)** The Dardanelles are part of the passageway between the Black Sea (dominated by Russia) and the Mediterranean Sea, to which Russia does not have direct access. Hence, Russia has had a historic interest in the Dardanelles.

35. **(C)** Louis XIV of France, who inherited the throne at the age of five in 1643, assumed power in 1661 at the age of 23. He ruled until his death in 1715. He was greatly admired and was called "Le Grand Monarque" or Louis the Great. He is supposed to have said, "L'etat, c'est moi" (I am the state).

36. **(A)** The German Imperial Constitution was adopted after the Franco-Prussian War in 1871. By its terms, King William I of Prussia became Emperor William I of the newly created German Empire.

37. **(A)** Niccolo Machiavelli (1469–1527), Italian political philosopher, is best known for his book, *The Prince*. In it, he counsels a ruler on the best way to acquire and hold political power. In a cynical vein, he advises that it is better to be feared than loved.

38. **(D)** Louis Leakey is not only the father of anthropology but also made it the significant social science that it is today. His revolutionary work in Africa shocked the world when he proved time and time again that man's origin is in the so-called Dark Continent, that of sub-Saharan Africa.

39. **(D)** The "final solution" refers to Hitler's goal of killing all Jews in Europe simply because they were Jewish. The annihilation of a group of people because of its religion is an example of genocide. Hitler's idea of the Germans as a master race required the killing of those whom, like Jews, he considered inferior.

40. **(B)** One of the best known Roman emperors was Constantine the Great. He reorganized provinces within the empire, made strategic economic and political changes, moved the capital to Byzantium, and legalized Christianity. One of his most historical decisions was when he issued the Edict of Milan in 313 A.D. This act ended polytheism by granting freedom of worship to all Christians.

41. **(D)** Despite the changes that the American family has undergone in the last century, it is still the primary socializing agent for children. Even with dual incomes and other changes in the traditional structure, the nuclear family continues to be the primary agent for children.

42. **(D)** The Standard Oil Trust was originally organized in 1882 by John D. Rockefeller. The story is told by Ida Tarbell in *The History of the Standard Oil Company* (1904).

43. **(B)** The Dreyfus Affair began in France in 1894 with the charge that Captain Dreyfus, a Jew, had sold military information to the Germans. He

was sentenced to life imprisonment on Devil's Island. Dreyfus protested his innocence. Anti-Semites, and many leaders of the Church lined up against him. His innocence was finally proven, and he was reinstated as a major in the army.

44. **(A)** Otto von Bismarck (1815–1898), leader of German unification, believed Germany could become strong and unified only if Austria were excluded from German affairs. Bismarck was at heart a Prussian. He feared that Austria, if included, would dispute power with Prussia.

45. **(A)** The Zulus were a warlike tribe that fought against the British in South Africa during the wave of 19th-century imperialism. Several impressive battles were fought that surprised the British army. It was only British military technology that eventually led to the defeat of the Zulu warriors.

46. **(C)** Since the end of World War II, moves to coordinate and unite the European community became an on-going process. In the 1950s, the European Coal and Steel Community and Euratom were created. The greatest and most relevant step occurred in 1958 with the creation of the EEC better known as the Common Market (later the EC = European Community). Probably the boldest step toward greater economic unity was the creation of a common currency the euro (in use since 2000).

47. **(A)** Thomas Malthus (1766–1834), English clergyman and philosopher, was deeply perturbed at the rapid increase in population and the relatively slower increase in the food supply. He foresaw war, plagues, and famine unless population was kept in check. Universal education at public expense offered some hope. The others would only exacerbate the problem.

48. **(A)** If people do not consume all their income, the part not spent is technically saving, no matter what they do with the money. Investing, however, requires that the money be put to work to create new wealth. In national income and product terms, consumption and investment go hand in hand.

49. **(A)** Group marriage, several men and several women living together and cohabiting, is a relatively rare social phenomenon. Each of the other four is far more common in man's various societies.

50. **(E)** The reaction of the Communist Chinese government to these student demonstrations was to quell them.

51. **(C)** When sociologists talk of "social mobility," they usually have in mind vertical mobility, moving from the socioeconomic level into which a person was born into a higher socioeconomic level. In an open society, marked by widespread opportunity, this phenomenon is relatively common.

52. **(B)** America has been called the melting pot of the world. With our diverse ethnic immigrant population, a great deal of cultural diffusion has taken place. Americans love Chinese food, eat many Italian foods, like British music; these are all examples of cultural diffusion. So too is the use of canoes and moccasins by Americans an example of cultural diffusion.

53. **(A)** As the nation-state began to emerge through Europe, so too did these Europeans begin their departure from a traditional economy to a national economy. The new nations of France, England, and Spain employed the use of mercantilism. It meant that the central government would control the economy by setting up colonies to supply the mother country with gold and silver, the mark of economic might for these new nations.

54. **(D)** Thorstein Veblen (1857–1929), American economist and social philosopher, considered marginal utility economics overly deductive, individualistic, and static. Marginal utility economics teaches that the extra utility added by each last unit of a good will be decreasing, although *total* utility will rise with consumption. In his *Theory of the Leisure Class,* Veblen held that, in an affluent society, most goods are useless except for display to establish status.

55. **(A)** With the rise of the giants of industry by the late 1880s, corporations tried to aggressively control production and prices and eliminate the little man. Such was the case of the railroad companies that formed pools in an attempt to fix prices. While these were monopolist steps by big business to end competition, eventually pools were outlawed.

56. **(D)** The chart illustrates how the electoral college system operates. In all four cases, the victor won a majority of the electoral college, but in two of the four elections, the victor did not win a majority of the popular vote. In the electoral college system, a majority of the popular vote is not necessary to win an election (choice A); only a majority of the electoral vote is necessary. Since no incumbents were running in the elections covered, the chart does not illustrate that incumbent's have an advantage (choice C). Nor does the chart present evidence of how third-party candidacies affected the outcome of the elections involved (choice E). Indeed, third-party candidates may have pulled more votes from the winners than from the losers. Only in 1988 is a significant increase in popular vote totals evident (choice B).

57. **(E)** These two elections provide support to those who think we should have the popular vote, not the electoral vote, determine the presidential election.

58. **(E)** The original Constitution was written in 1787 and ratified in 1789. It was eventually to contain twenty-seven changes or amendments. The first ten of these, the Bill of Rights, were added in 1791.

59. **(C)** The only president to serve two full terms was Bill Clinton. President John F. Kennedy was assassinated in his first term, and President Lyndon Baines Johnson chose not to run for a second term with the Viet Nam conflict accelerating. President Richard M. Nixon resigned after Watergate, and President George H. Bush was defeated after one term by Bill Clinton.

60. **(E)** These areas in urban cities contain the most visible signs of ethnicity—restaurants where a group's food is served, churches/religious institutions where the ethnic heritage is evident, stores where ethnic-related products are sold, and streets and homes in which that group's language is heard and spoken.

61. **(A)** Open immigration would enable people from many different areas of the world to migrate to a country. The resulting society would be a pluralistic one because it contained people of various races, languages, and ethnicities or nationalities.

62. **(B)** Alexis de Tocqueville (1805–1859), French writer, traveled throughout the United States in 1831 as an agent of his government. He described his findings in a famous book, *Democracy in America.* In it he wrote: "Nothing struck me more forcibly than the general equality of conditions."

63. **(E)** These three great men all served on the Supreme Court and also rose to the highest position on the Court, that of chief justice. John Marshall was our very first chief justice setting in place the practice of "judicial review." Earl Warren, originally appointed by the conservative President Dwight Eisenhower, became famous throughout the 1960s for his liberal decisions. Warren was followed by Chief Justice Burger who was appointed by President Richard Nixon in the hope to curb the liberal court.

64. **(C)** The Huguenots were French Protestants. They were followers of Calvin and Swiss Protestantism. Persecution in France led many Huguenots to flee to England, Holland, and America.

65. **(D)** The study of the behavior of higher primates is critical in the study of anthropology, for it helps us to better understand how human evolution occurred. Man's ancestors include the ape family, and their behavior has proven to be similar to that of humankind, thanks to the studies of Jane Goodall and Dian Fossey.

66. **(D)** The Byzantine Empire, also known as the Eastern Roman Empire, lasted until 1453 A.D. almost a thousand years longer than the Western Roman Empire. It provided Greta cultural and religious influence all over Eastern Europe and Asia. This cultural contact between the Byzantine civilization and Russia took place through trade by way of Kiev and other city-states in early Russia.

67. **(C)** The great expansion of business corporations, monopolies, and holding companies took place in the later 1880s. The post-Civil War was followed by rapid industrial expansion and the arrival of the giants of industry. Such giants as Rockefeller (oil), Carnegie (steel), Morgan (banking), and Ford (assembly line, automobile) made their presence in American economics.

68. **(C)** Jane Goodall, a colleague of Louis Leakey, did her greatest work in her study of baboon troops. She proved that there are strong similarities between baboons and humans in terms of social organization and leadership.

69. **(A)** George Herbert Mead (1863–1931), American philosopher and social psychologist, in his *Mind, Self, and Society* (1934), held that the self arises as a result of social experience and that the individual experiences himself indirectly from the standpoint of others of the same group. In Freud's psychology, the id is completely unconscious, as is the self prior to conscious development.

70. **(B)** In an experiment, change is induced in the experimental group only. The control group is used to determine the amount or effect of the change on the experimental group.

71. **(E)** There has been an absolute decline in farm employment during the past thirty years. In 1955, there were 8,381,000 people employed in farming. Thirty-five years later (1990), the number was 3,200,000.

72. **(D)** With the election of President John Kennedy, the 1960s marked the surfacing of an affluent middle class. Sometimes referred to as the "Great Society," the 1960s was marked by a growing move toward civil rights legislation and a more liberal society in general. The growth of the rapidly rising middle class and the "two-income family" resulted in the expansion of college-bound students. This growth of the college experience has continued to the present day.

73. **(D)** Louis XIV, the "Sun King" is known for his construction of the Versailles Palace. This grand effort was a display of his wealth and power. It also kept his strong nobility under his suspicious eyes, for they had to spend a significant amount of time at Versailles. Thus, it helped to secure his absolute power.

74. **(E)** During the civil war in Nicaragua in the 1980s, the Reagan administration helped one faction, the Contras. They were provided with funds to purchase weapons from sales of U.S. arms to Iran.

75. **(C)** The Homestead Act of 1862 granted 160 acres of land free to settlers who would live on the land and farm it for a period of five years.

76. **(C)** Railroad mileage in the U.S. increased from 3,000 in 1840 to 190,000 by 1900. The increase by decades was as follows: 1850, 9,000; 1860, 30,000; 1870, 53,000; 1880, 80,000; 1890, 164,000. Thus, the greatest increase in absolute amount was in the 1880s. The greatest increase in railroad mileage was in the post–Civil War era, from the 1880s to the turn of the 20th century.

77. **(E)** Alaska: area, 589,757 square miles; population, 400,481
Texas: area, 267,338 square miles; population, 14,228,383
Montana: area, 147,138 square miles; population, 786,690
Nevada: area, 110,540 square miles; population, 799,184
Maine: area, 33,215 square miles; population, 1,124,660.

78. **(D)** The 1990s saw the greatest economic growth in the history of the American stock market. The greatest rise in the market was under the successful economic period of President Clinton.

79. **(D)** During the years 1885–1914, a torrent of 20 million immigrants arrived in the United States. The rapid expansion of industry from the 1870s on was paralleled with the increased need for blue collar workers. Thus, white unskilled workers from eastern and southern Europe made their way into the United States. The greatest numbers came from Italy and Russia, and Ellis Island welcomed them with open arms.

80. **(B)** The tale *A Christmas Carol* reflects not only the story of the Christmas spirit but also the story of the proletariat worker and the bourgeoisie capitalist. Karl Marx would thus consider Scrooge to be the cold selfish "bourgeoisie" or capitalist who keeps all the profit or "surplus value" for himself.

81. **(C)** Virginia, a middle colony, was the home of the first pilgrim settlement, Jamestown. It was also the birthplace of the first colonial legislature that eventually became the blueprint of American legislative government.

82. **(E)** The most populous state in the United States in 1860 was New York, with 3,880,735. In 1860, the population of Virginia was 1,596,318; Massachusetts 1,231,066; Illinois 1,711,951; and South Carolina 703,708 (slaves in Virginia and South Carolina were counted as 3/5). West Virginia was still part of Virginia in 1860.

83. **(C)** The late 19th century and very early 20th century was the peak of European immigration into the United States. With the growing need for laborers, Eastern Europeans came to the United States looking for opportunity. The largest ethnic migration were Italians and Russian Jews fleeing the pogroms of Russian tsars.

84. **(A)** In preparing for the teaching profession, all future educators get to know the work of Jean Piaget who is best known for his work with children. One of his principal studies concludes that there are two stages of childhood development. The first stage (3–8) is characterized by respect for authority and the second stage (ages 9–12) by the development of mutual respect and cooperation.

85. **(B)** Ascribed status is determined by birth and thus depends on what social scale you are born into. To a degree, you are determined by your family's social class.

86. **(A)** As a result of the Great Depression and the stock market crash, which precipitated the worst depression in our history, both savings and income were at an all-time low.

87. **(E)** Adam Smith (1723–1790) wrote a classic analysis of economic forces entitled *An Inquiry into the Nature and Causes of the Wealth of Nations* (1776). He referred to the unimpeded force operating in the marketplace as "the invisible hand." Government intervention in the free market would be the "visible hand."

88. **(D)** Because of our isolationist policy of the post–World War I period, America entered into an anti-immigration age. Thus immigration was at its lowest in American history between the two wars.

89. **(C)** All collective behavior needs unity or solidarity to be effective. Thus, the very term *collective* means to do together. Collective behavior welcomes the media for publicity and is spontaneous and occurs in largely populated areas.

90. **(B)** The increase in precious metals constituted, in effect, an increase in the money supply. Other things being equal, this steady and substantial increase in coinage was certain to cause an increase in prices.

91. **(C)** A survey of the families and friends of victims would be the best way to do research on suicide. Factors underlying the events leading to the suicide could be helpful for researching the reasons why and the different types of suicide.

92. **(D)** Hinduism, the chief religion of India, developed prior to the 6th century B.C. The caste system became an integral part of Hinduism. Each individual was born into a caste. Four major castes, with many subdivisions, were Brahmans (priests), military, farmers and merchants, and laborers. A lowest group, pariahs (untouchables), were without caste.

93. **(C)** The dispute between Britain and the United States over the Oregon Territory was settled by a treaty in 1846. The forty-ninth parallel of north latitude, constituting the then-existing boundary between the U.S. and Canada to the Rockies, was extended to the Pacific.

94. **(A)** Henry VII, Henry VIII, and Queen Elizabeth I were all members of the Tudor family. The reign of each of these leaders helped expand the power of the English nation. Henry VIII is probably most famous for his departure from the Catholic Church when he established the Anglican Church of England. This state-run church was a direct result of Henry's conflict with the Pope and his desire to have many wives.

95. **(C)** The home of the Mormons has always been Salt Lake City. Recently, the issue of multiple-wives has been explored on *60 Minutes* and other shows as action has been taken against polygamy. Several decades ago the Mormons outlawed polygamy in their religion, but some people still practice it.

96. **(B)** Prior to World War I, Belgium was a major imperial power in Africa because of her control of the Congo, a rich territory extending over 331,850 square miles in Central Africa. The other major imperial powers in Africa prior to 1914 were Britain, France, Germany, Italy, Spain, and Portugal.

97. **(B)** During the 3rd century A.D., the Roman Empire was split into two because it was so large and becoming harder and harder to rule. This was also influenced by the growing number of Germanic and Asian tribes that became more and more of a threat, particularly to the western part of the empire. Eventually, the Huns defeated the western Roman Empire but the east continued to survive for another thousand years.

98. **(C)** The Constitution, in Article I, Section 8, specifically enumerates 17 of the powers of Congress. Then, in clause 18, it gives Congress power "to make all laws which shall be necessary and proper" to do the job given to it by the Constitution. These are called "implied powers."

99. **(A)** The preamble to the Constitution states the reasons for its establishment. One of the reasons is "to promote the general welfare." The Supreme Court looked to this clause in approving public funds for parochial school children.

100. **(B)** In the wake of the rocky stock market of 2001–2002 and the events of September 11, 2001, the Federal Reserve System has stepped in more often to control money by varying discount rates as well as the prime rate.

101. **(D)** Darwin's evolutionary theory was attacked most by the supporters of the Bible. These people are called Creationists. Traditional or conservative religions are often strong advocates of the creationist point of view, i.e., the story of Adam and Eve.

102. **(D)** In the typical American corporation of today, the managers who control the corporation are given a free hand by the stockholders. Rarely, except for the relatively small corporations, is the majority of the stock held by one or a few individuals.

103. **(B)** The American Federation of Labor was established during the 1880s under the leadership of Samuel Gompers. His purpose was to organize skilled workers into craft unions. Brick masons were organized as one of the constituent unions in the AF of L. The rival union organization, the CIO, organized entire industries such as automotive. It came into being in 1935.

104. **(B)** Mustapha Kemal Ataturk (1880–1938), Turkish army officer, came into power after World War I. He carried out a revolution in which both the sultanate and the caliphate were abolished and complete separation of church and state instituted in a new Turkish Republic. Universal suffrage, a parliament, a ministry, and a president were established. Women gained a new freedom.

105. **(D)** Henry George (1839–1897), American economist, wrote *Progress and Poverty* (1879). He believed a "single tax" on land would provide for all the necessary costs of government and even leave a surplus.

106. **(B)** In 1989, the greatest number of American women were employed as clerical workers.

107. **(D)** David Ricardo (1772–1823), British economist, wrote *Principles of Political Economy and Taxation* (1817). He maintained that wages cannot rise above the lowest level necessary for subsistence. Workers reproduce to provide a labor supply that keeps wages at this level. Malthus had previously noted the increase of population in geometric ratio.

108. **(C)** The policy of containment influenced the dividing of nations affected by the Cold War. The dividing of Germany into four zones, then two new countries, began the Cold War in the late 1940s. Subsequent events led to further splits between communism and democracy as the nations of Korea and Vietnam were divided in the 1950s. Today, only Korea is divided, and the fall of the Berlin Wall along with Germany's reunification marked the end of the Cold War.

109. **(C)** The Huns were nomadic horsemen from north central Asia. They occupied China for several centuries. During the 4th century, they invaded the Volga valley of Russia, driving the Visigoths before them. The Visigoths, Vandals, Lombards, and Franks were Germanic peoples.

110. **(B)** The best-case scenario would be to have written records, in fact primary sources, when analyzing and interpreting history. Unfortunately, written records go back only several millennia before Christ, and the period of unwritten human history is far longer. Thus, the next best choice is to rely on

material or physical remains left behind. The teeth are the most durable remains an archeologist can find.

111. **(A)** The Islamic invasions of the 7th and 8th centuries into Europe were finally stopped by Charlemagne at the Battle of Tours. The Moors moved through Northern Africa as far east as India and threatened to take over Europe. It was only because of the great Christian leader Charlemagne that the Islamic invasion did not take over all of Europe. His victory at Tours had a lot to do with his being crowned the Holy Roman Emperor in 800 A.D.

112. **(E)** Buddhism originated as an alternative to Hinduism in which Buddha tried to "liberalize" some of the key prejudiced aspects to the caste system and the effect of religion on it. His ideas were rejected in India and later China but did meet success when his missionary men entered Korea, Japan, and Southeast Asia. Today Buddhism is a major religion in Korea, Japan, Vietnam, and most of eastern Asia.

113. **(B)** A fief in medieval Europe was an estate over which a nobleman exercised control. The grantor would receive a promise of protection or other service in return for the land.

114. **(B)** In November 1917, the Bolsheviks in Russia, led by V. I. Lenin (1870–1914), overthrew the government and came into power. They immediately began negotiations for peace with the Germans. Lenin regarded the war as an imperialist adventure. He thought both sides—the Germans and the Allies—would destroy each other.

115. **(D)** Anthropologists point to excessive stress and strain in adolescence as a characteristic of modern industrial societies. The anthropologist Margaret Mead studied the nonindustrial society of Samoa and reported the relative untroubled adolescence of its members in her *Coming of Age in Samoa* (1928). Her findings have recently been challenged.

116. **(D)** The case study, a method used in the social sciences, delves deeply into the motivation and problems of its subjects.

117. **(A)** During the constitutional debate in the 1780s, the Federalist and Anti-Federalist engaged in a political arena of opposing views on the format of the new centralized government. The Federalists believed in a strong central government and claimed that a bill of rights was unnecessary, while the Anti-Federalists wanted a weak central government so that it would not threaten the rights of the people or the power of the states. The Federalist papers were instrumental in providing support for the eventual approval of the new Constitution.

118. **(C)** The traditional domain ascribed to women in industrial society is that of homemaker. Women serving in the armed forces of the United States constitute a sharp and symbolic break with this ascribed status.

119. **(D)** The closest to modern-day man is Cro-Magnon man, who lived from about 35,000 to 10,000 years ago. He is the evolutionary ancestor to humankind today. Neanderthal and homo erectus are earlier forms of

mankind. Australopithecus, Leakey's great discovery, is one of the very earliest forms of human existence. Piltdown man was a 20th-century hoax.

120. **(B)** In *The Communist Manifesto*, Karl Marx (and his co-author Friedrich Engels) contended that capitalism was a necessary step in the evolution of society to communism. Marx thought that the inevitable struggle between the capitalists and the proletariat would end in the victory of the latter (communism). Hence, capitalism was a necessary stage in the evolution of society.

121. **(C)** The Neolithic or agricultural age has been one of the most important cultural developments in the history of the human race. With farming, man settled down, built permanent homes, and developed a truly modern society. For the first time he no longer had to hunt for food, and survival was a far greater possibility. The human population began to grow rapidly because of this historic stage.

122. **(C)** The Moors of North Africa converted to Islam in the 8th century and became fanatic Muslims. They crossed into Spain in 711 A.D., overran the country, and spread into France. Christians and Muslims vied for control of Spain from the 11th to the 15th centuries, culminating in 1492 when the Muslims were driven from Spain.

123. **(D)** As unions become stronger and stronger, they attempt to set up union shops in which only union members can belong. This guarantees union solidarity and strength for negotiations.

124. **(E)** Judicial self-restraint as applied to the Supreme Court can be described as a proper concern for the role and judgment of the legislative branch of government. The Court prefers not to overrule an act of Congress if it can see any way of finding the act compatible with the Constitution. The Supreme Court decision in the Florida recount for the 2000 election is another example of judicial self-restraint.

125. **(B)** In order for a bill to become a law, the future law must pass through both houses of Congress and be signed by the president. Changes are very common in this process as committees are the work horse of the legislation process. Few bills become laws and a presidential veto can indeed be overridden by a two-thirds vote of both houses. As for the Supreme Court, it has no say on how a bill becomes a law; it can only interpret a law once it is passed.

THE NATURAL SCIENCES EXAMINATION

Natural Sciences

ANSWER SHEET–TRIAL TEST

1 Ⓐ Ⓑ Ⓒ Ⓓ Ⓔ 31 Ⓐ Ⓑ Ⓒ Ⓓ Ⓔ 61 Ⓐ Ⓑ Ⓒ Ⓓ Ⓔ 91 Ⓐ Ⓑ Ⓒ Ⓓ Ⓔ
2 Ⓐ Ⓑ Ⓒ Ⓓ Ⓔ 32 Ⓐ Ⓑ Ⓒ Ⓓ Ⓔ 62 Ⓐ Ⓑ Ⓒ Ⓓ Ⓔ 92 Ⓐ Ⓑ Ⓒ Ⓓ Ⓔ
3 Ⓐ Ⓑ Ⓒ Ⓓ Ⓔ 33 Ⓐ Ⓑ Ⓒ Ⓓ Ⓔ 63 Ⓐ Ⓑ Ⓒ Ⓓ Ⓔ 93 Ⓐ Ⓑ Ⓒ Ⓓ Ⓔ
4 Ⓐ Ⓑ Ⓒ Ⓓ Ⓔ 34 Ⓐ Ⓑ Ⓒ Ⓓ Ⓔ 64 Ⓐ Ⓑ Ⓒ Ⓓ Ⓔ 94 Ⓐ Ⓑ Ⓒ Ⓓ Ⓔ
5 Ⓐ Ⓑ Ⓒ Ⓓ Ⓔ 35 Ⓐ Ⓑ Ⓒ Ⓓ Ⓔ 65 Ⓐ Ⓑ Ⓒ Ⓓ Ⓔ 95 Ⓐ Ⓑ Ⓒ Ⓓ Ⓔ
6 Ⓐ Ⓑ Ⓒ Ⓓ Ⓔ 36 Ⓐ Ⓑ Ⓒ Ⓓ Ⓔ 66 Ⓐ Ⓑ Ⓒ Ⓓ Ⓔ 96 Ⓐ Ⓑ Ⓒ Ⓓ Ⓔ
7 Ⓐ Ⓑ Ⓒ Ⓓ Ⓔ 37 Ⓐ Ⓑ Ⓒ Ⓓ Ⓔ 67 Ⓐ Ⓑ Ⓒ Ⓓ Ⓔ 97 Ⓐ Ⓑ Ⓒ Ⓓ Ⓔ
8 Ⓐ Ⓑ Ⓒ Ⓓ Ⓔ 38 Ⓐ Ⓑ Ⓒ Ⓓ Ⓔ 68 Ⓐ Ⓑ Ⓒ Ⓓ Ⓔ 98 Ⓐ Ⓑ Ⓒ Ⓓ Ⓔ
9 Ⓐ Ⓑ Ⓒ Ⓓ Ⓔ 39 Ⓐ Ⓑ Ⓒ Ⓓ Ⓔ 69 Ⓐ Ⓑ Ⓒ Ⓓ Ⓔ 99 Ⓐ Ⓑ Ⓒ Ⓓ Ⓔ
10 Ⓐ Ⓑ Ⓒ Ⓓ Ⓔ 40 Ⓐ Ⓑ Ⓒ Ⓓ Ⓔ 70 Ⓐ Ⓑ Ⓒ Ⓓ Ⓔ 100 Ⓐ Ⓑ Ⓒ Ⓓ Ⓔ
11 Ⓐ Ⓑ Ⓒ Ⓓ Ⓔ 41 Ⓐ Ⓑ Ⓒ Ⓓ Ⓔ 71 Ⓐ Ⓑ Ⓒ Ⓓ Ⓔ 101 Ⓐ Ⓑ Ⓒ Ⓓ Ⓔ
12 Ⓐ Ⓑ Ⓒ Ⓓ Ⓔ 42 Ⓐ Ⓑ Ⓒ Ⓓ Ⓔ 72 Ⓐ Ⓑ Ⓒ Ⓓ Ⓔ 102 Ⓐ Ⓑ Ⓒ Ⓓ Ⓔ
13 Ⓐ Ⓑ Ⓒ Ⓓ Ⓔ 43 Ⓐ Ⓑ Ⓒ Ⓓ Ⓔ 73 Ⓐ Ⓑ Ⓒ Ⓓ Ⓔ 103 Ⓐ Ⓑ Ⓒ Ⓓ Ⓔ
14 Ⓐ Ⓑ Ⓒ Ⓓ Ⓔ 44 Ⓐ Ⓑ Ⓒ Ⓓ Ⓔ 74 Ⓐ Ⓑ Ⓒ Ⓓ Ⓔ 104 Ⓐ Ⓑ Ⓒ Ⓓ Ⓔ
15 Ⓐ Ⓑ Ⓒ Ⓓ Ⓔ 45 Ⓐ Ⓑ Ⓒ Ⓓ Ⓔ 75 Ⓐ Ⓑ Ⓒ Ⓓ Ⓔ 105 Ⓐ Ⓑ Ⓒ Ⓓ Ⓔ
16 Ⓐ Ⓑ Ⓒ Ⓓ Ⓔ 46 Ⓐ Ⓑ Ⓒ Ⓓ Ⓔ 76 Ⓐ Ⓑ Ⓒ Ⓓ Ⓔ 106 Ⓐ Ⓑ Ⓒ Ⓓ Ⓔ
17 Ⓐ Ⓑ Ⓒ Ⓓ Ⓔ 47 Ⓐ Ⓑ Ⓒ Ⓓ Ⓔ 77 Ⓐ Ⓑ Ⓒ Ⓓ Ⓔ 107 Ⓐ Ⓑ Ⓒ Ⓓ Ⓔ
18 Ⓐ Ⓑ Ⓒ Ⓓ Ⓔ 48 Ⓐ Ⓑ Ⓒ Ⓓ Ⓔ 78 Ⓐ Ⓑ Ⓒ Ⓓ Ⓔ 108 Ⓐ Ⓑ Ⓒ Ⓓ Ⓔ
19 Ⓐ Ⓑ Ⓒ Ⓓ Ⓔ 49 Ⓐ Ⓑ Ⓒ Ⓓ Ⓔ 79 Ⓐ Ⓑ Ⓒ Ⓓ Ⓔ 109 Ⓐ Ⓑ Ⓒ Ⓓ Ⓔ
20 Ⓐ Ⓑ Ⓒ Ⓓ Ⓔ 50 Ⓐ Ⓑ Ⓒ Ⓓ Ⓔ 80 Ⓐ Ⓑ Ⓒ Ⓓ Ⓔ 110 Ⓐ Ⓑ Ⓒ Ⓓ Ⓔ
21 Ⓐ Ⓑ Ⓒ Ⓓ Ⓔ 51 Ⓐ Ⓑ Ⓒ Ⓓ Ⓔ 81 Ⓐ Ⓑ Ⓒ Ⓓ Ⓔ 111 Ⓐ Ⓑ Ⓒ Ⓓ Ⓔ
22 Ⓐ Ⓑ Ⓒ Ⓓ Ⓔ 52 Ⓐ Ⓑ Ⓒ Ⓓ Ⓔ 82 Ⓐ Ⓑ Ⓒ Ⓓ Ⓔ 112 Ⓐ Ⓑ Ⓒ Ⓓ Ⓔ
23 Ⓐ Ⓑ Ⓒ Ⓓ Ⓔ 53 Ⓐ Ⓑ Ⓒ Ⓓ Ⓔ 83 Ⓐ Ⓑ Ⓒ Ⓓ Ⓔ 113 Ⓐ Ⓑ Ⓒ Ⓓ Ⓔ
24 Ⓐ Ⓑ Ⓒ Ⓓ Ⓔ 54 Ⓐ Ⓑ Ⓒ Ⓓ Ⓔ 84 Ⓐ Ⓑ Ⓒ Ⓓ Ⓔ 114 Ⓐ Ⓑ Ⓒ Ⓓ Ⓔ
25 Ⓐ Ⓑ Ⓒ Ⓓ Ⓔ 55 Ⓐ Ⓑ Ⓒ Ⓓ Ⓔ 85 Ⓐ Ⓑ Ⓒ Ⓓ Ⓔ 115 Ⓐ Ⓑ Ⓒ Ⓓ Ⓔ
26 Ⓐ Ⓑ Ⓒ Ⓓ Ⓔ 56 Ⓐ Ⓑ Ⓒ Ⓓ Ⓔ 86 Ⓐ Ⓑ Ⓒ Ⓓ Ⓔ 116 Ⓐ Ⓑ Ⓒ Ⓓ Ⓔ
27 Ⓐ Ⓑ Ⓒ Ⓓ Ⓔ 57 Ⓐ Ⓑ Ⓒ Ⓓ Ⓔ 87 Ⓐ Ⓑ Ⓒ Ⓓ Ⓔ 117 Ⓐ Ⓑ Ⓒ Ⓓ Ⓔ
28 Ⓐ Ⓑ Ⓒ Ⓓ Ⓔ 58 Ⓐ Ⓑ Ⓒ Ⓓ Ⓔ 88 Ⓐ Ⓑ Ⓒ Ⓓ Ⓔ 118 Ⓐ Ⓑ Ⓒ Ⓓ Ⓔ
29 Ⓐ Ⓑ Ⓒ Ⓓ Ⓔ 59 Ⓐ Ⓑ Ⓒ Ⓓ Ⓔ 89 Ⓐ Ⓑ Ⓒ Ⓓ Ⓔ 119 Ⓐ Ⓑ Ⓒ Ⓓ Ⓔ
30 Ⓐ Ⓑ Ⓒ Ⓓ Ⓔ 60 Ⓐ Ⓑ Ⓒ Ⓓ Ⓔ 90 Ⓐ Ⓑ Ⓒ Ⓓ Ⓔ 120 Ⓐ Ⓑ Ⓒ Ⓓ Ⓔ

Trial Test

This chapter contains a Trial Test in Natural Sciences. Take this Trial Test to learn what the actual exam is like and to determine how you might score on the exam before any practice or review.

The CLEP General Exam in Natural Sciences measures your knowledge of biological and physical sciences, including origin and evolution of life, microbiology, biology, ecology, physics, chemistry, astronomy, geology, and other topics.

NUMBER OF QUESTIONS: 120

Time: 90 MINUTES

Directions: Each of the questions or incomplete statements below is followed by five suggested answers or completions. Select the one that is best in each case.

1. What do malaria, amoebic dysentery, and African sleeping sickness have in common?

   (A) All are found in Africa only.
   (B) All are caused by protozoans.
   (C) Each constitutes a serious disease of the central nervous system.
   (D) None is of great significance to humans.
   (E) All are transmitted by direct contact.

2. Cellular structures responsible for oxidizing food and converting energy to adenosine triphosphate are called

   (A) the Golgi apparatus
   (B) ribosomes
   (C) chromoplasts
   (D) mitochondria
   (E) the endoplasmic reticulum

3. According to Weismann's theory of the continuity of the germ plasm,

    (A) embryos recapitulate embryonic forms of their ancestors
    (B) germ plasm remains unaffected by the cytoplasm
    (C) germ plasm can be influenced only by the cytoplasm
    (D) genes exist in pairs on chromosomes
    (E) genes are in linear order along chromosomes

4. The ribosomes associated with the endoplasmic reticulum consist of

    (A) secretory nodes, which control metabolism
    (B) deoxyribose nucleic acid, which synthesizes chromatin
    (C) granular bodies associated with cell division
    (D) ribonucleic acid, which synthesizes protein
    (E) various nucleic acids, each of which is self-perpetuating

5. If a living plant cell is placed in a hypotonic solution,

    (A) turgor pressure decreases
    (B) osmotic pressure increases
    (C) osmotic pressure decreases
    (D) turgor pressure is not affected
    (E) turgor pressure increases

6. In typical ecosystems, the producers are

    (A) heterotrophic
    (B) parasitic
    (C) chemotrophic
    (D) photosynthetic
    (E) saprophytic

7. The light reactions of photosynthesis include those in which

    (A) radiant energy is converted into organic materials
    (B) radiant energy is stored
    (C) carbon dioxide is absorbed
    (D) water is split into hydrogen and oxygen
    (E) sugar is formed and oxygen is released

8. The principal water-absorbing structure of a typical root is the

    (A) hair root
    (B) root cap
    (C) endodermis
    (D) root hair cell
    (E) cortex

9. A photosynthetic organism is one which

    (A) obtains energy by the oxidation of inorganic materials
    (B) utilizes solid materials after eating and digesting them
    (C) obtains its nourishment from decaying organic materials
    (D) lives at the expense of other organisms
    (E) uses radiant energy in food synthesis

10. In plants, a growth response to the stimulus of light is called

    (A) geotropism
    (B) phototropism
    (C) thigmotropism
    (D) photoperiodism
    (E) hydrotropism

11. The growing of plants under soilless conditions is called

    (A) aquatics
    (B) hydrology
    (C) hydrotropism
    (D) hydroponics
    (E) hydrotaxis

12. The graph below indicates plant growth in relation to soil pH. A pH reading below 7.0 is acid; a pH reading above 7.0 is alkaline.

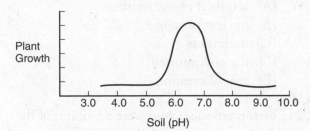

On the basis of the information in the graph, one may conclude that

(A) plant growth causes a shift in soil acidity
(B) most plants grow best in slightly acid soils
(C) no plants can survive in alkaline soils
(D) no plants can survive in acid soils
(E) soil pH has little or no effect on plant growth

13. The enzyme-controlled breakdown of carbohydrates under anaerobic conditions is called

(A) autolysis
(B) decomposition
(C) bacteriophage
(D) fermentation
(E) respiration

14. In plant reproduction, selected cells of the diploid, spore-producing generation undergo

(A) diploidization
(B) oogenesis
(C) spermatogenesis
(D) meiosis
(E) mitosis

15. Structures which are similar because of function are said to be

(A) analogous
(B) homosporous
(C) monoecious
(D) homologous
(E) dioecious

16. In blood transfusions, individuals referred to as universal receivers may receive blood from

(A) group AB only
(B) groups A and AB only
(C) groups B and AB only
(D) group O only
(E) groups O, A, B, AB

17. Many plants produce an orange pigment called carotene which animals convert to

(A) ATP
(B) hemoglobin
(C) vitamin A
(D) phytol
(E) vitamin C

18. Which nerve innervates the semicircular canals?

(A) Auditory
(B) Facial
(C) Trochlear
(D) Spinal accessory
(E) Optic

19. The hormone that controls the rate of food conversion to energy is

(A) insulin
(B) thyroxin
(C) adrenalin
(D) cortisone
(E) secretin

20. Stimulation by the sympathetic nervous system would result in

(A) constricted pupils
(B) dilated arteries
(C) accelerated heartbeat
(D) increased peristalsis
(E) lower blood pressure

21. Progesterone

(A) constricts blood vessels
(B) does not regulate the menstrual cycle
(C) stimulates production of thyroxin
(D) regulates rate of basal metabolism
(E) regulates sodium metabolism

22. The significance of mitosis is that there is

    (A) a quantitative division of the cell
    (B) precise distribution of cell content to the daughter cells
    (C) a qualitative division of cell components
    (D) a reduction of chromosome number
    (E) precise distribution of DNA to each daughter cell

23. Transfer of genetic information from one generation to the next is accomplished by

    (A) RNA only
    (B) DNA only
    (C) codons
    (D) ribosomes
    (E) both RNA and DNA

24. The inherited variations which are so essential to the concept of natural selection have their source in

    (A) acquired characteristics
    (B) nuclear proteins
    (C) mutations
    (D) the environment
    (E) special creation

25. Preformationists who were advocates of the theory of embryo development from structures within the sperm were called

    (A) ovists
    (B) animalculists
    (C) epigenesists
    (D) pangenesists
    (E) phylogenists

---

26. Permanent wilting is a plant condition caused by the loss of water from which there is no recovery, i.e., no restoration of turgidity. The data below show the percentages of soil moisture for selected soil types at the time of permanent wilting for the plants indicated.

Soil Moisture % at Time of Permanent Wilting

	Coarse Sand	Fine Sand	Sandy Loam	Loam	Clay Loam
Corn	1.07	3.1	6.5	9.9	15.5
Sorghum	.94	3.6	5.9	10.0	14.1
Oats	1.07	3.5	5.9	11.1	14.8
Pea	1.02	3.3	6.9	12.4	16.6
Tomato	1.11	3.3	6.9	11.7	15.3

On the basis of this information one may conclude that at the time of permanent wilting

(A) sunlight plays a direct role in wilting
(B) water continues to move from particle to particle in the soil
(C) transpiration continues at a reduced rate
(D) soil moisture varies widely for different plants
(E) soil moisture is fairly constant no matter what plant is involved

27. You would expect to observe caribou and lichens in

    (A) a tropical rain forest
    (B) the arctic tundra
    (C) a grassland
    (D) a deciduous forest
    (E) a coniferous forest

28. Plankton includes aquatic organisms which

    (A) exist below low tide and on the continental shelf
    (B) exist only in darkness
    (C) exist to a depth of 5,000 feet
    (D) float on the surface
    (E) exist in the deepest ocean trenches

29. Marine organisms characteristic of the abyssal zone would be found

    (A) in the inter tidal zone
    (B) on the continental shelf to a depth of 500–600 feet
    (C) in light
    (D) in the deepest ocean trenches
    (E) to a depth of 5,000 feet

30. In studies of predator-prey populations in a hypothetical situation, the data indicated on the graph below illustrate the cyclical population fluctuations of the predators and the prey.

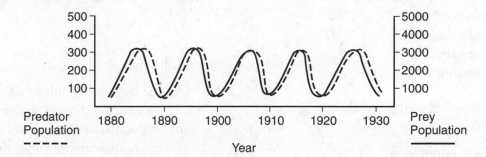

What conclusion may be drawn from these data?

(A) Predators maintain any population above the capacity of a given environment to support it.
(B) Avoidance of predators has no lasting effect on prey population.
(C) Decreases in populations of prey species are followed by decreases in populations of predator species.
(D) Populations of predators are nourished only by surpluses of prey.
(E) Even when exterminating its prey, a predator never exterminates itself.

31. Interrelationships between species are termed *commensalism* when

    (A) both species are benefited
    (B) mates are defended
    (C) one species benefits at the expense of the other
    (D) territories are defended
    (E) one species benefits and the other is not harmed

32. The Cenozoic Era is best described as the age of

    (A) reptiles
    (B) seed ferns
    (C) seed plants and mammals
    (D) primitive fishes
    (E) amphibians

33. In the human circulatory system, blood returns to the heart from the lungs through the

    (A) superior vena cava
    (B) pulmonary veins
    (C) inferior vena cava
    (D) pulmonary artery
    (E) descending aorta

34. Blood is supplied to the muscle wall of the heart by the

    (A) hepatic portal vein
    (B) coronary arteries
    (C) auricular artery
    (D) mesenteric artery
    (E) coronary veins

35. Hookworm larvae gain access to the body

    (A) by penetrating unbroken skin
    (B) by means of insect bites
    (C) through the mouth in contaminated food
    (D) in improperly cooked pork
    (E) in improperly cooked fish

36. Which of the following diseases of humans is transmitted by the bite of ticks?

    (A) Tularemia
    (B) Rocky Mountain spotted fever
    (C) Sleeping sickness
    (D) Psittacosis
    (E) Amebiasis

Questions 37–39

In the diagrams below, water and sugar solutions are separated by cellophane membranes, as indicated. These cellophane membranes are permeable to water molecules and impermeable to sugar molecules. Assume that temperatures are constant and that the cellophane bags are filled equally.

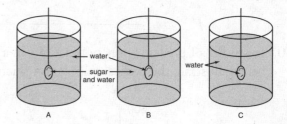

37. In diagram *A*

    (A) the bag will shrink as water molecules move from the bag to the outside
    (B) the addition of sugar to the water in the container will cause the turgidity of the bag to increase
    (C) diffusion does not occur
    (D) water molecules diffuse into the bag because there is a greater concentration of water outside than inside the bag
    (E) there is a net movement of water molecules out of the cellophane bag because of a concentration difference

38. In diagram *B*

    (A) the bag will shrink
    (B) the bag will swell
    (C) there will be a net movement of water molecules into the bag
    (D) there will be a net movement of sugar molecules into the bag
    (E) sugar draws water out of the bag

39. In diagram *C*

    (A) water will diffuse into the bag causing it to swell
    (B) water will diffuse out of the bag causing it to shrink
    (C) there will be no change in the size of the bag
    (D) osmosis occurs in the system
    (E) the addition of glass marbles to the container will cause the bag to shrink

40. An organism which obtains energy from the oxidation of inorganic substances is

    (A) chemosynthetic
    (B) photosynthetic
    (C) parasitic
    (D) saprophytic
    (E) holozoic

41. In a typical lake, the important producers are

    (A) commensals
    (B) zooplankton
    (C) nekton
    (D) phytoplankton
    (E) benthos

42. Photosynthesis

    (A) results in a decrease in dry weight
    (B) requires the energy provided by respiration
    (C) produces carbon dioxide and water
    (D) results in an increase in dry weight
    (E) uses oxygen and glucose as raw materials

43. The failure of one or more pairs of chromosomes to separate during meiosis is called

    (A) polyploidy
    (B) deletion
    (C) translocation
    (D) nondisjunction
    (E) aneuploidy

44. Xylem is the principal constituent of a plant product called

    (A) wood
    (B) bark
    (C) latex
    (D) pith
    (E) resin

45. One side effect that may be produced by the antigen-antibody reaction of the body is

    (A) an allergic reaction
    (B) dehydration
    (C) convulsions
    (D) infection
    (E) pain

46. The body responds to an invasion of viruses by producing

    (A) antibodies
    (B) vaccine
    (C) antibiotics
    (D) antigens
    (E) immune serum

47. The active substance which appears in a virus-infected cell and which prevents infection by a second virus is called

    (A) autolysis
    (B) interferon
    (C) lysozyme
    (D) bacteriophage
    (E) rickettsias

48. It is unfortunate for humans that

    (A) red blood cells are constantly being formed
    (B) blood pressure decreases in the capillaries
    (C) the heartbeat is a regular rhythmic cycle
    (D) the lymphatic system returns fluid to the circulatory system
    (E) hemoglobin bonds more firmly to carbon monoxide than to oxygen

49. The Rh factor is produced due to

    (A) a hormonal reaction
    (B) an antigen-antibody reaction
    (C) a form of anemia
    (D) phagocytosis
    (E) a vitamin deficiency

50. A deficiency of vitamin K may result in

    (A) soft, weak bones
    (B) sterility
    (C) scurvy
    (D) beriberi
    (E) excess bleeding

51. Roughage is important in the human diet because it

    (A) contains vitamins
    (B) speeds up digestion
    (C) stimulates the walls of the large intestine
    (D) slows digestion
    (E) stimulates the production of antibodies

52. "Animal starch," a nutrient stored in various types of animal cells, is more properly known as

    (A) angstrom
    (B) antigen
    (C) myosin
    (D) glycogen
    (E) actin

53. When the thyroid gland produces insufficient amounts of thyroxine,

    (A) tetany occurs
    (B) the basal metabolism rate increases
    (C) irregularities in sodium metabolism develop
    (D) acromegaly develops
    (E) the basal metabolism rate decreases

54. Among the contributions of the ancient Greek scholars

    (A) was the law of independent assortment
    (B) was the concept of biogenesis
    (C) was the concept of recapitulation
    (D) were elements of the theory that living organisms have evolved
    (E) was the preformation theory

55. The physical basis for heredity was established by T. H. Morgan when he demonstrated his

    (A) mutation theory
    (B) principle of eugenics
    (C) gene theory
    (D) theory of recapitulation
    (E) chromosome theory of inheritance

56. Paul Ehrlich is best known for his discoveries in

    (A) immunization
    (B) attenuation
    (C) chemotherapy
    (D) antibiosis
    (E) phytopathology

57. A famous anatomist during the Renaissance was

    (A) Bacon
    (B) Linnaeus
    (C) Phiny
    (D) Vesalius
    (E) Pasteur

58. In general, short food chains are more efficient than long food chains because in short food chains

    (A) there can be no carnivores
    (B) there is more energy produced in each stage
    (C) there are fewer producers
    (D) there is less energy loss
    (E) there are more producers

59. A population displaying a great number of homologous structures is considered to be

    (A) an order
    (B) a class
    (C) a family
    (D) a genus
    (E) a species

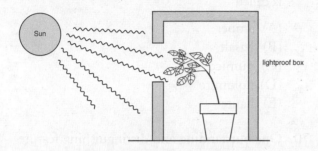

60. Under the conditions of unilateral lighting imposed upon the plant in the diagram above, the plant bends toward the light because

    (A) the plant needs more light in order to carry on photosynthesis
    (B) the plant grows away from darkness
    (C) this is a growth response caused by the unequal distribution of growth-promoting substances in the plant stem
    (D) the plant is attracted to light
    (E) this is a growth response in an attempt to overcome the growth repressing effects of darkness

Directions: Each of the questions or incomplete statements below is followed by five suggested answers or completions. Select the one that is best in each case.

61. After two half-lives of radioactive decay, what percentage of the original number of atoms would remain unchanged?

    (A) 12.5%
    (B) 25%
    (C) 37.5%
    (D) 50%
    (C) 75%

62. The kinetic-molecular theory explains the difference between solids, liquids, and gases. One of the postulates of this theory is that

    (A) molecules are in constant motion and move in straight lines
    (B) molecules of a gas have great attraction for each other
    (C) the kinetic energy of gas molecules is inversely proportional to the temperature
    (D) gas molecules are extremely large in comparison to the distances between them
    (E) when two molecules collide, both always lose energy

63. The basic energy-producing reaction in the sun is the conversion of

    (A) mass to energy due to pressure
    (B) helium to hydrogen
    (C) fuels to heat
    (D) heavy elements into lighter elements
    (E) hydrogen to helium

64. A term to describe the solar system when the earth is presumably in the center is

    (A) rotation
    (B) parallax
    (C) geocentric
    (D) heliocentric
    (E) ecliptic

65. The Milky Way galaxy is best described as

    (A) a spherical grouping of about fifty million stars spread over approximately 2,000 light-years
    (B) the solar system together with its moons and asteroids
    (C) a disk-shaped grouping of billions of stars which spreads over approximately 100,000 light-years
    (D) a galactic system comprising all the constellations
    (E) a spherical grouping of over a billion stars

66. Charged atoms or groups of atoms, which are formed by the gain or loss of electrons, are called

    (A) protons
    (B) neutrons
    (C) moles
    (D) ions
    (E) isotopes

67. When an astronomer detects a shift toward the red end of the spectrum, which of the following may he correctly infer?

    (A) The chemical composition of a star has changed.
    (B) He has discovered a new star.
    (C) A star is stationary.
    (D) The star he is observing is moving closer.
    (E) The star he is observing is moving away.

68. One example of geological crosscutting is

    (A) a fault
    (B) an oxbow
    C) a moraine
    (D) a floodplain
    (E) a stalagmite

69. Fossilized resin from ancient coniferous trees is called

    (A) amber
    (B) basalt
    (C) pumice
    (D) dolomite
    (E) halite

70. One outstanding and distinguishing feature of sedimentary rocks is

    (A) their complete lack of fossils
    (B) that they are formed exclusively of precipitates
    (C) that they are formed exclusively of crystals
    (D) the presence of different layers
    (E) that they are formed by the cooling of magma

71. The form of radiation with the greatest penetrating power is

    (A) alpha particles
    (B) beta particles
    (C) fission
    (D) fusion
    (E) gamma rays

72. As a result of nuclear fission

    (A) there is an increase in mass
    (B) light atomic nuclei fuse
    (C) X-rays are emitted
    (D) much energy is consumed
    (E) longer nuclei split into smaller ones

73. Color aberrations encountered when using lenses are corrected by

    (A) use of convex lenses
    (B) use of concave lenses
    (C) use of achromatic lenses
    (D) reducing the field or the aperture
    (E) proper focusing

74. When an object is immersed in a liquid

    (A) it displaces its own weight
    (B) it displaces a volume equal to its weight
    (C) it displaces a weight equal to its volume
    (D) it is buoyed up by a volume of liquid
    (E) it displaces its own volume of liquid

75. The three ways by which heat may be transferred are

    (A) absorption, adsorption, and radiation
    (B) conduction, convection, and infusion
    (C) vaporization, adsorption, and convection
    (D) diffusion, infusion, and vaporization
    (E) conduction, convection, and radiation

Questions 76 and 77 are based on the following table, which summarizes the parts of the earth's crust as well as some basic information about those parts:

Layer	Thickness (km)	Composition	Temperature (°C)	Density (g/cm³)
Continental crust	30–60	Granitic silicate rock	20–600	2.8
Oceanic crust	5–8	Basaltic silicate rock	20–1,300	3.3
Mantle	2,800	Solid silicate	100–3,000	5.0
Outer core	2,150	Liquid iron-nickel	3,000–6,500	12
Inner core	1,230	Solid iron-nickel	7,000	12

76. About how far is it from the surface of the earth to its center?

    (A) 72 km
    (B) 720 km
    (C) 7,200 km
    (D) 72,000 km
    (E) 720,000 km

77. What is the general relationship between the depth of a layer of the earth and its density?

    (A) the greater the depth, the greater the density
    (B) the greater the depth, the lower the density
    (C) as the depth increases, the density increases and then decreases
    (D) as the depth increases, the density decreases and then increases
    (E) there is no pattern that relates these two factors

78. For every known subatomic particle, there is believed to exist

    (A) an isotope
    (B) an ionized equivalent
    (C) an antiparticle
    (D) coherent radiation
    (E) a thermoelectric effect

79. What name is applied to an atom that carries a negative electric charge?

    (A) catalyst
    (B) electron
    (C) anion
    (D) isotope
    (E) cation

80. The continual change in the plane in which a Foucault pendulum swings is evidence that

    (A) the earth rotates
    (B) the moon revolves around the earth
    (C) the earth revolves around the sun
    (D) the sun is the center of the solar system
    (E) the earth is round

81. When a glass rod is rubbed with a silk cloth

    (A) the glass rod gains protons and becomes negatively charged
    (B) the glass rod gains protons and becomes positively charged
    (C) the glass rod remains neutral
    (D) the glass rod loses electrons and becomes negatively charged
    (E) the glass rod loses electrons and becomes positively charged

82. According to the Second Law of Thermodynamics, ongoing chemical and physical reactions progress from states of high organization to states of low organization unless

    (A) a supply of energy is present
    (B) a catalyst is added
    (C) energy is withdrawn
    (D) the reactants are balanced
    (E) a buffer is added

83. The speed of molecules is dependent upon

    (A) sulfonation
    (B) temperature
    (C) pressure
    (D) concentration
    (E) saturation

84. Work is accomplished when

    (A) direction is imposed upon a moving object
    (B) energy output equals energy input
    (C) a machine operates without expending energy
    (D) force is exerted upon an object, causing it to move
    (E) a weight is held stationary at a certain height

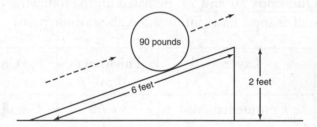

85. In the diagram above, how much effort is required to push the 90-pound barrel up the inclined plane?

    (A) 45 pounds effort
    (B) 30 pounds effort
    (C) 15 pounds effort
    (D) 10 pounds effort
    (E) 5 pounds effort

86. The number of molecules contained in a mole of a substance is called

    (A) the coordination number
    (B) Avogadro's number
    (C) Planck's constant
    (D) the molecular weight of the substance
    (E) the atomic number

87. Compared to the earth, the sun is

    (A) much larger and of greater density
    (B) much larger and of lesser density
    (C) much smaller and of greater density
    (D) much smaller and of lesser density
    (E) about the same size and density

88. According to Newton's third law, there must be a reaction to the force which propels a bullet from the barrel of a rifle. This force is in the

    (A) recoil
    (B) friction of the bullet in the barrel
    (C) pressure used to squeeze the trigger
    (D) shoulder of the person firing the rifle
    (E) inertia of the bullet

89. Fusion reactions for the peaceful production of power have been unsuccessful because

    (A) they are too powerful
    (B) they are too rapid
    (C) there is no practical way to control the temperature
    (D) the cost is prohibitively high
    (E) radioactive electricity is too dangerous

90. Laser-generated light

    (A) is polarized
    (B) is chaotic
    (C) is coherent
    (D) is disordered
    (E) has waves of different frequencies

91. Kinetic theory with respect to gases is based primarily on

    (A) the motion of particles
    (B) the attraction of molecules for each other
    (C) the ionization of gas molecules
    (D) sublimation
    (E) vaporization

92. High-altitude satellites will someday fall to earth because of

    (A) drag caused by cosmic radiation
    (B) drag caused by infrared radiation
    (C) centrifugal force
    (D) centrifugal force and the moon's gravity
    (E) drag caused by air and particles

93. On which of the following is the pH scale based?

    (A) An arithmetic progression of hydrogen ions
    (B) An equal balance between hydrogen and hydroxide ions
    (C) An estimate of the number of hydrogen ions present
    (D) An estimate of the number of hydroxide ions present
    (E) The concentration of hydrogen ions in a liter of solution

94. When an object is transferred from the moon to earth, its mass

    (A) increases
    (B) decreases
    (C) remains constant
    (D) and weight increase on earth
    (E) and weight decrease on earth

95. The thermodynamic measure of disorder is called

    (A) entropy
    (B) spontaneity
    (C) momentum
    (D) redundancy
    (E) valence

96. Through a microscope, minute particles are observed to be in an almost constant state of random movement, a phenomenon called

    (A) surface tension
    (B) capillarity
    (C) osmosis
    (D) diffusion
    (E) Brownian motion

97. Igneous rocks include which of the following?

    (A) Sandstone
    (B) Limestone
    (C) Diamond
    (D) Obsidian
    (E) Shale

98. The atomic number of an element refers to

    (A) the total number of electrons and protons it possesses
    (B) the number of neutrons in the atomic nucleus
    (C) the number of protons in the atomic nucleus
    (D) its sequential number in the atomic scale
    (E) the total number of neutrons, electrons, and protons it possesses

99. A dispersion in which the particles eventually settle out is an example of

    (A) an emulsion
    (B) a solution
    (C) a mixture
    (D) a colloid
    (E) a suspension

100. The alkali metal family of chemical elements includes potassium and

    (A) calcium
    (B) iron
    (C) nickel
    (D) sodium
    (E) aluminum

101. When iron rusts

    (A) iron atoms are reduced and gain electrons
    (B) iron atoms are reduced and lose electrons
    (C) iron atoms are oxidized and gain electrons
    (D) iron atoms are oxidized and lose electrons
    (E) iron atoms react to form iron molecules

102. One primary concern of alchemy was

    (A) sublimation
    (B) vaporization
    (C) solidification
    (D) liquefaction
    (E) transmutation

103. In any given process

    (A) energy may be created
    (B) energy may be destroyed
    (C) energy may neither be created nor destroyed
    (D) the energies of the reactants and products are variable
    (E) energy and work are totally unrelated

104. In accordance with Einstein's theory of relativity, as a body gains speed

    (A) its mass decreases proportionately
    (B) its mass increases proportionately
    (C) only electrons in the outer shells of its atoms are affected
    (D) mass and energy are not related
    (E) only energy is lost

105. Substances which form ions in solution and which can conduct an electric current are called

    (A) reactors
    (B) dispersions
    (C) substrates
    (D) electrolytes
    (E) conductors

106. When different atoms of an element have different masses, they are known as

    (A) ions
    (B) isotopes
    (C) molecules
    (D) electrons
    (E) nuclei

107. Gamma radiation is frequently used successfully to treat tumors and cancer tissue because

    (A) such tissues are immune to radiation
    (B) such tissues are more sensitive to radiation than are healthy tissues
    (C) it acts faster than surgery without the risks of surgery
    (D) the induced rate of radioactive decay is indicative of the extent of cure
    (E) gamma radiation is low-energy radiation

108. Heat is a form of energy caused by

    (A) the exchange of electrons between atoms
    (B) the conversion of matter to energy
    (C) the motion of molecules
    (D) the conversion of energy to matter
    (E) its absorption from the environment

109. By mixing all of the colors of the visible spectrum of light we produce

    (A) infrared light
    (B) black light
    (C) purple light
    (D) green light
    (E) white light

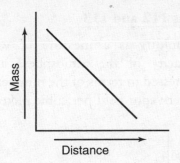

110. The graph above illustrates Newton's Law of Universal Gravitation with respect to the effects of mass and distance.

    From this illustration, one may infer that

    (A) the strength of gravity increases with the mass of the object exerting the pull and diminishes as the distance from the object being pulled increases
    (B) the strength of gravity decreases with the mass of the object exerting the pull and increases as the distance from the object being pulled decreases
    (C) the strength of gravity is not affected by mass
    (D) the strength of gravity is not affected by distance
    (E) the force of gravity is affected by neither mass nor distance

111. The change of certain substances from solid to gaseous states without passing through the liquid state is called

    (A) sublimation
    (B) fusion
    (C) convergence
    (D) thermal coefficient
    (E) reciprocation

Questions 112 and 113

Humidity is a measure of water-holding capacity of the atmosphere and may be expressed in terms of the number of grams of water vapor held per cubic meter of air.

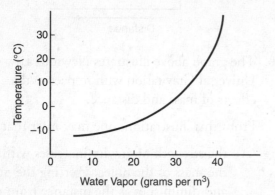

112. According to the illustration above, one may conclude that

    (A) humidity increases at lower temperatures
    (B) humidity decreases at lower temperatures
    (C) temperature does not affect humidity
    (D) higher temperatures decrease humidity
    (E) humidity is directly proportional to temperature

113. From the illustration above, one may also conclude that

    (A) if the humidity increases the temperature will rise
    (B) if the humidity decreases the temperature will rise
    (C) humidity increases uniformly as temperature increases
    (D) saturated air cannot retain its water if the temperature is lowered
    (E) saturated air can hold additional water if the temperature is lowered

114. Although ahead of his time, Roger Bacon contributed to science by stating that intuition or reason is insufficient to justify scientific theory and that, to give certainty to science, there must be

    (A) research
    (B) data
    (C) facts
    (D) observation
    (E) experimentation

115. Electromagnetic waves of extremely high frequency are called

    (A) photons
    (B) matter waves
    (C) gamma rays
    (D) X-rays
    (E) beta rays

Directions: Each group of questions below consists of five lettered choices followed by a list of numbered phrases or sentences. For each numbered phrase or sentence select the one choice that is most closely related to it. Each choice may be used once, more than once, or not at all in each group.

Questions 116–118

    (A) Distillation
    (B) Evaporation
    (C) Radiolysis
    (D) Polymerization
    (E) Transmutation

116. Nuclear reactions that change one element into another

117. The radioactive disintegration of radium to radon

118. The joining of small molecules into larger molecules

Questions 119–120

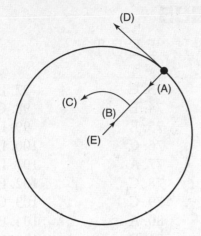

The diagram above represents the circular path of a moving weight tied to the end of a string. The five lettered choices are indicated on the diagram.

119. The velocity of the weight

120. The centripetal force on the moving weight

STOP

If there is still time remaining, you may review your answers.

Natural Sciences
ANSWER KEY—TRIAL TEST

1. B	25. B	49. B	73. C	97. D
2. D	26. E	50. E	74. E	98. C
3. B	27. B	51. C	75. E	99. E
4. D	28. D	52. D	76. C	100. D
5. E	29. D	53. E	77. A	101. D
6. D	30. C	54. D	78. C	102. E
7. D	31. E	55. C	79. C	103. C
8. D	32. C	56. C	80. A	104. B
9. E	33. B	57. D	81. E	105. D
10. B	34. B	58. D	82. A	106. B
11. D	35. A	59. E	83. B	107. B
12. B	36. B	60. C	84. D	108. C
13. D	37. D	61. B	85. B	109. E
14. D	38. A	62. A	86. B	110. A
15. A	39. C	63. E	87. B	111. A
16. E	40. A	64. C	88. A	112. B
17. C	41. D	65. C	89. C	113. D
18. A	42. D	66. D	90. C	114. E
19. B	43. D	67. E	91. A	115. B
20. C	44. A	68. A	92. E	116. E
21. B	45. A	69. A	93. E	117. E
22. E	46. A	70. D	94. C	118. D
23. B	47. B	71. E	95. A	119. D
24. C	48. E	72. E	96. E	120. A

SCORING CHART

After you have scored your Trial Examination, enter the results in the chart below, then transfer your score to the Progress Chart on page 12. As you complete the Sample Examinations later in this part of the book, you should be able to achieve increasingly higher scores.

Total Test	Number Right	Number Wrong	Number Omitted
120			

ANSWER EXPLANATIONS

1. **(B)** Protozoans include some 30,000 single-celled organisms, some of which cause malaria, some types of dysentery, and African sleeping sickness.

2. **(D)** Mitochondria are the sites where energy is transferred from molecules of carbohydrate to those of ATP.

3. **(B)** Reproduction is accomplished, not by cytoplasm, but by germ plasm, which is transmitted essentially unchanged from generation to generation.

4. **(D)** Ribosomes are found scattered in the cytoplasms of living cells and in association with the endoplasmic reticulum. They are composed of ribonucleic acid and protein and function in the synthesis of proteins and enzymes.

5. **(E)** A living plant cell placed in a hypotonic solution, i.e., hypotonic to the cell sap, will increase in turgidity.

6. **(D)** Basic food production for most of the biological world is accomplished by photosynthetic producers.

7. **(D)** Photosynthesis is an energy-storing biochemical reaction in which the radiant energy of sunlight is stored in simple sugars in the form of chemical bonds. During its light reactions, water is split into hydrogen and oxygen.

8. **(D)** Root hair cells are hairlike extensions of the epidermal cells of most kinds of plant roots. These provide greatly increased surfaces for water absorption.

9. **(E)** A photosynthetic organism possesses chlorophyll and, in the presence of radiant energy, synthesizes glucose from carbon dioxide and water and stores energy.

10. **(B)** Growth responses of plants are called tropisms. The growth response of plants to light is called phototropism.

11. **(D)** Hydroponics is the growing of plants in a liquid or moist environment (without soil) to which essential mineral nutrients are added.

12. **(B)** Most plants survive and grow best in soils of slightly acid to neutral soils (pH 5.8–7.0).

13. **(D)** Fermentation is the anaerobic breakdown of carbohydrates by the enzymes produced by living microorganisms such as yeasts.

14. **(D)** In plants, diploid spore-mother cells undergo meiosis to produce haploid spores.

15. **(A)** Analogous structures are similar because of functions; the wing of a bird and the wing of a bee are analogous structures.

16. **(E)** Persons with AB type blood are designated as universal receivers. They may receive blood from any other person, regardless of blood type, since they have both antigen A and antigen B.

17. **(C)** Carotene is a precursor of vitamin A.

18. **(A)** The semicircular canals are innervated by the auditory nerve and are associated with the inner ear and function to keep the body aware of its position with respect to gravity and motion.

19. **(B)** Thyroxin controls the rate of metabolism by controlling the cellular respiration of food.

20. **(C)** The sympathetic nervous system responds to perceived emotional situations such as anger or fear. One body response to anger or fear is accelerated heartbeat.

21. **(B)** The corpus luteum secretes progesterone, which regulates the menstrual cycle and prepares the body for pregnancy.

22. **(E)** Mitosis is both a quantitative and qualitative division of the nucleus of a cell which results in precise and equal distribution of chromatin and, therefore, DNA to each daughter cell.

23. **(B)** Deoxyribonucleic acid (DNA) is the only substance transmitted qualitatively and quantitatively from one generation to the next.

24. **(C)** A mutation is a gene change. Mutations, therefore, are sources of variations and they continue to be handed down to future generations until they mutate again.

25. **(B)** Animalculists were preformationists who believed in a preformation of the individual within the sperm.

26. **(E)** The data indicate that, at the time of permanent wilting, soil moisture is fairly constant, no matter what species of plant is concerned.

27. **(B)** The arctic tundra is treeless and the home of caribou and numerous lichen. It is also the summer breeding ground for numerous migratory birds.

28. **(D)** Plankton consists of free-floating, usually microscopic, plants and animals in a body of water.

29. **(D)** The abyssal zones of the oceans are the deepest ocean trenches.

30. **(C)** The balance between any predator-prey group is delicate; an increase in the population of the prey is typically followed by an increase in the population of the predator, and vice versa.

31. **(E)** Commensalism is a relationship between two species in which one benefits from the other without harming it or giving benefit to it.

32. **(C)** The Cenozoic Era is the last of the great periods of geologic time and is characterized by the advent of mammals and seed plants.

33. **(B)** Pulmonary veins return oxygenated blood from the lungs to the left atrium of the heart.

34. **(B)** Coronary arteries branch from the aorta and carry blood to the heart muscle.

35. **(A)** Hookworm larvae on the ground penetrate unbroken skin, commonly the feet of barefoot children in warm climates.

36. **(B)** Rocky Mountain spotted fever is caused by a rickettsia transmitted to humans through the bite of a tick.

37. **(D)** Sugar molecules inside the bag lower the concentration of water molecules in comparison to the water outside. Therefore, water molecules diffuse into the bag.

38. **(A)** The bag, containing only water, has a higher concentration of water molecules than the surrounding water, which also contains sugar molecules. Water will, therefore, diffuse out of the bag and the bag will shrink.

39. **(C)** A state of equilibrium exists and there will be no net diffusion of water either into or out of the bag.

40. **(A)** Some bacteria, such as iron and sulfur using bacteria, obtain energy through the oxidation of iron and sulfur compounds respectively.

41. **(D)** Phytoplankton are photosynthetic organisms and because they are so numerous, they are important producers.

42. **(D)** Photosynthesis produces the carbohydrate glucose and therefore increases the dry weight of the plant.

43. **(D)** The failure of homologous chromosomes to separate in the anaphase of the first meiotic division, or the failure of the sister chromatids of a chromosome to separate in the anaphase of the second meiotic division, is called nondisjunction.

44. **(A)** Wood is the tree tissue inside the vascular cambium and is a term synonymous with xylem.

45. **(A)** A single injection of a foreign protein into the body may hypersensitize an individual so that future exposure to the same protein results in an allergic reaction.

46. **(A)** A virus invading the body is an antigen. The body's immune system responds by producing antibodies.

47. **(B)** Interferon is produced by body cells into which the foreign nucleic acid of a virus has entered. It renders uninfected cells immune to other viruses.

48. **(E)** Carbon monoxide is a major concern since it has a high affinity for hemoglobin.

49. **(B)** Rh-negative individuals develop antibodies to the Rh antigen, and these destroy Rh-positive cells.

50. **(E)** Vitamin K is essential for prothrombin synthesis, a step in blood clotting.

51. **(C)** Roughage, such as whole-grain cereals, is important to the diet because it stimulates the large intestine.

52. **(D)** In humans and other animals, excess glucose is converted into a starch called glycogen, which is stored in muscles and in the liver, where it is readily available.

53. **(E)** Thyroxine deficiency in humans leads to cretinism in early childhood and to a lowered metabolic rate in adults.

54. **(D)** Anaximander, a Greek philosopher (611–547 B.C.), proposed an explanation of evolution based upon observation and reasoning.

55. **(C)** T.H. Morgan first stated the gene theory of inheritance in 1910.

56. **(C)** Ehrlich studied the effects of chemicals upon body tissues and discovered salvarsan, a chemical used to treat syphilis. He was the first to use a systematic approach to treat chemotherapeutic investigations.

57. **(D)** Vesalius was the greatest anatomist of the 16th century and was noted for performing his own dissections.

58. **(D)** At each level in a food chain there is a loss of energy. For this reason, shorter food chains with fewer energy transfers are more efficient.

59. **(E)** One definition identifies a species on the basis of its number of shared homologous structures.

60. **(C)** Unilateral light is responsible for the unequal distribution of growth-promoting substances in the stem, thus causing uneven stem elongation.

61. **(B)** The half-life of a radioactive substance is the length of time necessary for 50% of its atoms to decay. After two half-lives of radioactive decay, 25% of the original atoms would remain unchanged.

62. **(A)** The kinetic-molecular theory holds that matter is composed of molecules that are in constant motion, move in straight lines, and collide.

63. **(E)** Hydrogen atoms in the sun undergo fusion. Four atoms of hydrogen fuse to form one atom of helium with a minute quantity of mass left over. This mass is converted into energy.

64. **(C)** *Geocentric* describes a concept pertaining to the solar system that supposes that the earth is the center of the system.

65. **(C)** The Milky Way is a large spiral galaxy shaped like a disk and is approximately 5,000 light-years thick and 100,000 light-years in diameter.

66. **(D)** Following the gain or loss of electrons, atoms become either positively or negatively charged and are called ions.

67. **(E)** A shift toward the red end of the spectrum means that the light wavelengths are increasing and indicates that the star being viewed is moving away from the viewer.

68. **(A)** A fault is a fracture of the earth's crust accompanied by a shift of one side with respect to the other.

69. **(A)** Amber is fossilized resin.

70. **(D)** Probably the most distinguishing feature of sedimentary rock is the fact that it has a layered structure.

71. **(E)** Alpha particles have the lowest penetrating power, beta an intermediate amount, and gamma rays the greatest.

72. **(E)** Fission is the "splitting" of larger atoms into smaller ones.

73. **(C)** Color or chromatic aberration is the failure of the different colors contained in white light to meet in a common point, called the focal point, after they pass through a convex lens. It may be reduced by use of an achromatic lens.

74. **(E)** A submerged object displaces its own volume.

75. **(E)** Heat may be transferred by conduction, convection, and radiation.

76. **(C)** Adding up all the depths of the layers gives the distance to the center of the earth, about 7,200 km. Note that the exact distance is not required; only the order of magnitude is necessary.

77. **(A)** A look at the last column shows that as the layers go in toward the center of the earth, the density increases.

78. **(C)** In many situations, such as pair annihiliation, a particle and its antiparticle interact and disappear. An example of an antiparticle is the positron, a particle identical to the electron, except that it has the opposite charge.

79. **(C)** Anions are negatively charged ions. Cations are positively charged.

80. **(A)** A Foucault pendulum is so constructed that it always swings in the same plane. The rotation of the earth makes the pendulum appear to change the plane in which it swings.

81. **(E)** Static electricity can be produced by rubbing a glass rod with a piece of silk, during which the silk takes up electrons to become negatively charged. The glass rod gives up electrons to become positively charged.

82. **(A)** According to the Second Law of Thermodynamics, reactions proceed from low to higher entropy, that is, from order to disorder, unless a supply of energy is present.

83. **(B)** The speed of molecules is directly proportional to their temperature.

84. **(D)** Work is defined as the force exerted upon an object multiplied by the distance the object is moved.

85. **(B)** The ratio of the height of the inclined plane to its hypotenuse determines the effort required to move the barrel up the inclined plane.

86. **(B)** A mole of any substance has Avogadro's number of particles, 6.02×10^{23}.

87. **(B)** The sun is very much larger than the earth and being made primarily of gases (as opposed to the earth, which is solid) is of much lower density.

88. **(A)** According to Newton's third law, to each and every action, there is an equal and opposite reaction.

89. **(C)** Nuclear fusion promises unlimited supplies of energy with much less environmental danger than from fission reactions. However, to date, no useful fusion reactor has been designed.

90. **(C)** Laser-generated light is coherent, ordered, and nonchaotic, and each wave has the same frequency, phase, and direction.

91. **(A)** The current kinetic-molecular theory is a concept based on studies of the motion of molecules.

92. **(E)** All earth satellites will eventually fall back to earth because of drag which is caused by air molecules (even though sparse) and particulate matter in space.

93. **(E)** The pH scale is based on the concentration of hydrogen ions in a liter of solution and is expressed as a logarithmic progression.

94. **(C)** Mass always remains constant. However, on the moon, due to a lower gravity, an object would appear to be lighter.

95. **(A)** Entropy is the thermodynamic measure of disorder and always increases during any spontaneous process.

96. **(E)** Brownian movement is the result of molecular activity. Under the microscope, visible particles appear to be in a state of erratic motion because they are continually being bombarded (bumped) from all sides by molecules in motion.

97. **(D)** Igneous rocks are formed from cooling magma and lava. Obsidian is a glassy rock found where lava has cooled. Shale, limestone, and sandstone are sedimentary rocks, while diamond is a metamorphic rock, being formed from the action of heat and pressure.

98. **(C)** The number of protons in an atomic nucleus is the atomic number.

99. **(E)** Muddy water is a suspension, i.e., it is a dispersion in which the particles eventually settle out.

100. **(D)** The alkali metal family includes sodium, potassium, lithium, cesium, etc.

101. **(D)** Iron atoms are oxidized by oxygen, and in the process they lose electrons.

102. **(E)** In medieval times, alchemy was an endeavor to change base metals into gold, i.e., transmutation.

103. **(C)** The First Law of Thermodynamics states that energy may be neither created nor destroyed.

104. **(B)** Mass and velocity are proportional; as speed approaches the velocity of light, mass approaches infinity.

105. **(D)** Certain molecules ionize (example: HCl ionizes to H^+ Cl^- ions) when placed in liquids and are able to conduct an electric current. These are called electrolytes.

106. **(B)** Isotopes are atoms of the same element that have different mass numbers, that is, varying numbers of neutrons in their nuclei.

107. **(B)** Tumor cells are more sensitive to radiation generally than are healthy cells. Therefore, radiation therapy is often a successful tumor therapy.

108. **(C)** Heat is a form of energy existing in matter resulting from the motion of its molecules. There is no molecular motion at absolute zero.

109. **(E)** Visible light is white and includes wavelengths from red to violet with orange, yellow, green, and blue in between.

110. **(A)** The strength of gravity increases with the mass of the object exerting the gravitational pull and decreases the greater the distance from the object being pulled.

111. **(A)** The direct change from the solid state to the gaseous state is called sublimation. An example is the sublimation of ice or snow when air flows over it at below freezing temperatures.

112. **(B)** ⎫ The ability of the air to hold moisture in vapor form is inversely
113. **(D)** ⎭ proportional to the temperature.

114. **(E)** Roger Bacon is credited with the introduction of the experimental method of science.

115. **(B)** At certain speeds, all matter exhibits wavelengths of extremely high frequency, and these have been observed to affect spaces between atoms in crystals.

116. **(E)** Transmutation, in the historic sense, is the conversion of base metals to gold or silver; in modern physics, it is the transformation of one element into another by one or more nuclear reactions.

117. **(E)** Radioactive decay of certain elements accounts for one form of transmutation, which was unknown before its discovery by Becquerel.

118. **(D)** Polymerization is the joining of small molecules to produce larger molecules using heat, pressure, and selected catalysts.

119. **(D)** ⎫ The weight tied to the end of the string tends to move in a straight line
     ⎬ but is held in circular orbit by the string. Centripetal force acts in the
120. **(A)** ⎭ direction toward the axis or center.

Background and Practice Questions

CHAPTER 16

DESCRIPTION OF THE NATURAL SCIENCES EXAMINATION

The CLEP General Examination in Natural Sciences measures your general knowledge and your ability to use principles and ideas in the biological and physical sciences. It covers material that is generally taught in a college course for non-science majors. The exam is given in two parts, each consisting of approximately 60 questions and each requiring 45 minutes to complete. See the following chart for approximate percentages of examination items:

Natural Sciences Exam	
Content or Item Types	**Time/Number of Questions**
50% Biological Science	120 questions
10% Origin and evolution of life, classification of organisms	90 minutes
10% Cell organization, cell division, chemical nature of the gene, bioenergetics, biosynthesis	
20% Structure, functions, and development in organisms; patterns of heredity	
10% Concepts of population biology with emphasis on ecology	

Natural Sciences Exam

Content or Item Types	Time/Number of Questions
50% Physical Science	
7% Atomic and nuclear structure and properties, elementary particles, nuclear reactions	
10% Chemical elements, compounds and reactions; molecular structure and bonding	
12% Heat, thermodynamics, and states of matter; classical mechanics, relativity	
4% Electricity and magnetism, waves, light, and sound	
7% The universe: galaxies, stars, the solar system	
10% The earth: atmosphere, hydrosphere, structure, properties, surface features, geological processes, history	

The questions on this exam include aspects of natural science that may not have been covered in courses you have taken in school. Your ability to answer these questions will depend on the extent to which you have maintained a general interest in these subjects and kept current by reading science articles and science-based materials in magazines, newspapers, books, and other materials written for the nonscientist.

THE KINDS OF QUESTIONS THAT APPEAR ON THE EXAMINATION

There are two important aspects of the examination questions: (1) the knowledge and abilities they test for, and (2) the formats in which they are presented.

What the Questions Test

Some questions require knowledge of basic scientific concepts, facts, and principles; others require application of knowledge; and a third group requires interpretation and understanding of data presented in various forms (graphs, diagrams, tables, lists). The following questions provide examples of each type of question.

Knowledge of Concepts, Facts, and Principles

Directions: Each of the questions or incomplete statements below is followed by five suggested answers or completions. Select the one that is best in each case.

1. A plant tissue whose cells disintegrate, causing leaves to separate from their stems, is called

    (A) the annulus
    (B) a bud scar
    (C) the collenchyma
    (D) the abscission layer
    (E) the cambium

2. When a glowing wood splint introduced into a tube of gas subsequently bursts into flame, what gas is in the tube?

    (A) Nitrogen
    (B) Chlorine
    (C) Oxygen
    (D) Helium
    (E) Carbon dioxide

Ability to Apply Knowledge

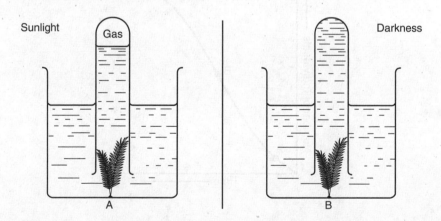

In the diagrams above, aquatic photosynthetic plants are placed under inverted test tubes which are filled with water. Except for light, all environmental and genetic factors are constant and the same for each.

3. After exposing plant A to several hours of sunlight, while plant B is maintained in darkness, it may correctly be concluded that, with respect to gas production,

    (A) plant A carried on photosynthesis
    (B) plant A carried on both photosynthesis and respiration
    (C) darkness inhibits respiration
    (D) sunlight is necessary for gas production
    (E) sunlight inhibits respiration

Ability to Interpret and Understand Data

Directions: The group of questions below consists of five lettered choices followed by a list of numbered phrases or sentences. For each numbered phrase or sentence select the one choice that is most closely related to it. Each choice may be used once, more than once, or not at all.

    (A) Limiting factors of the environment
    (B) High mortality rate
    (C) High reproductive rate
    (D) Short length of time
    (E) Small number of individuals

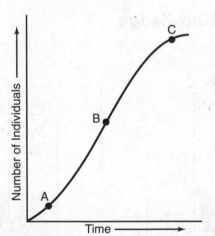

4. A condition limiting the growth rate at position A on the curve

5. A condition limiting the growth rate at position B on the curve

6. A condition limiting the growth rate at position C on the curve

What Formats Are Used

Most questions are in interrogative or sentence-completion form, and require you to select the correct answer from five choices that follow the question. In the preceding group, questions 1–3 are in this format.

A second type lists the answer choices first, and then gives a list of numbered phrases or sentences. You are required to select, for each phrase or sentence, the answer choice that best fits it. Questions 4–6 above, based on a graph, are in this category.

Notice that the directions for the two formats differ.

ANSWERS AND EXPLANATIONS FOR SAMPLE QUESTIONS

1. **(D)** The abscission layer is a layer of plant cells that disintegrates, causing leaves and other structures to separate from the plant.

2. **(C)** A standard laboratory test for oxygen production is that a glowing wood splint bursts into flame in the presence of oxygen.

3. **(D)** Plants A and B are exposed to identical conditions except for sunlight/darkness. There is no evidence that photosynthesis or respiration is occurring. An unidentified gas produced by A is the only observable outcome of this experiment.

4. **(E)** ⎫ The graph represents a standard growth (sigmoid) curve. Over a period
5. **(C)** ⎬ of time a small number of individuals existing under normal conditions
6. **(A)** ⎭ will increase in number while food, space, etc., are ample, but, as the numbers of individuals increase, competition for food, space, etc., increases and the accumulation of metabolic wastes at the same time slows growth.

STUDY SOURCES

For additional review, you might consult the following books, which present a variety of the types of concepts pertinent to a general understanding of the sciences:

HISTORY AND PHILOSOPHY OF SCIENCE

Gardner, Eldon J. *History of Biology.* 2nd ed. Minneapolis: Burgess Publishing Company, 1965.

Hazen, Robert M., and James Trefil. *Science Matters: Achieving Scientific Literacy.* New York: Doubleday, 1991.

Westfall, Richard S. *The Life of Issac Newton.* London: Cambridge Univeristy Press, 1993.

BIOLOGICAL SCIENCE

Crawford, Michael, and David Marsh. *The Driving Force.* New York: Harper and Row, 1989.

Henig, Robin Marantz. *A Dancing Matrix.* New York: Alfred A. Knopf, 1993.

Starr, Cecie, and Ralph Taggart. *Biology: The Unity and Diversity of Life.* 6th ed. Belmont, Calif.: Wadsworth Publishing Company, 1992.

Wallace, Robert A., Jack L. King, and Gerald P. Sanders. *Biosphere.* Scott, Foresman and Company, 1988.

Whitfield, Philip, General Editor. *The Human Body Explained.* New York: Henry Holt and Company, 1995.

Wilson, Edward O. *The Diversity of Life.* New York: W.W. Norton and Company, 1992.

EARTH SCIENCE AND THE ENVIRONMENT

Van Andel, Tjeerd H. *New Views on an Old Planet: Continental Drift and the History of the Earth.* London: Cambridge University Press, 1985.

Levin, Harold L. *The Earth Through Time.* 4th ed. Philadelphia: Saunders College Publishing Company, 1992.

Lutgens, Frederick K. and Edward J. Tarbuck. *The Atmosphere: An Introduction to Meteorology.* 5th ed. Englewood Cliffs, N.J.: Prentice-Hall, 1991.

Tarbuck, Edward J., and Frederick K. Lutgens. *Earth Science.* 5th ed. Columbus, Ohio: Merrill Publishing Company, 1988.

Thompson, Graham R., and Jonathan Turk. *Earth Science and the Environment.* New York: Saunders College Publishing. Harcourt Brace Jovanovich College Publishers, 1993.

PHYSICAL SCIENCE—CHEMISTRY

Allen, Thomas L., and Raymond M. Keefer. *Chemistry, Experiment and Theory.* New York: Harper and Row, 1982.

Ball, Philip. *Designing the Molecular World.* Princeton, N.J.: Princeton University Press, 1994.

Hill, John W. *Chemistry for Changing Times.* New York: Macmillan Publishing Company, 1988.

PHYSICAL SCIENCE—PHYSICS

Chasisson, Eric. *Relatively Speaking.* New York: W.W. Norton and Company, 1988.

Krauskopf, Konrad B., and Arthur Beiser. *The Physical Universe.* 7th ed. New York: McGraw-Hill Book Company, 1993.

Ronan, Colin A., General Editor. *Science Explained: The World of Science in Everyday Life.* New York: Henry Holt and Company, Inc., 1993.

Sherwood, Martin, and Christine Sutton, eds. *The Physical World.* New York: The Oxford University Press, 1991.

ASTRONOMY AND THE UNIVERSE

Hathaway, Nancy. *The Friendly Guide to the Universe.* New York: Viking, 1994.

Jones, Brian. *The Practical Astronomer.* New York: Simon and Schuster, Inc., 1990.

Practice Questions on Natural Sciences

QUESTIONS ABOUT BIOLOGY

Directions: Each of the questions or incomplete statements below is followed by five suggested answers or completions. Select the one that is best in each case.

1. At the tissue level of organization

   (A) cells retain their separate functional identity
   (B) dissimilar cells are associated to conduct a variety of functions
   (C) cells are completely independent
   (D) similar cells are associated in the performance of a particular function
   (E) there is no cellular specialization

2. A cell's metabolic requirements are proportional to its volume. Its ability to meet these requirements and to exchange substances with its environment is

   (A) dependent on its activity
   (B) inversely proportional to its surface area
   (C) dependent on its environment
   (D) a function of both its activity and its environment
   (E) proportional to its surface area

3. All cellular metabolism is controlled by organic catalysts called

   (A) hormones
   (B) vitamins
   (C) auxin
   (D) phlogistons
   (E) enzymes

4. An organism which utilizes radiant energy in food synthesis is

   (A) holozoic
   (B) parasitic
   (C) chemosynthetic
   (D) saprophytic
   (E) photosynthetic

5. The typical consumers in an ecosystem are

   (A) saprophytic
   (B) photosynthetic
   (C) parasitic
   (D) chemosynthetic
   (E) holozoic

Questions 6 and 7

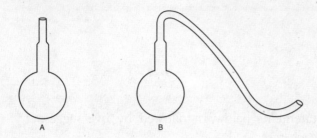

Pasteur placed a nutrient broth in each of two flasks similar to those illustrated above. Both flasks were open to air, but flask B was open only through its curved neck. The broth in each flask was boiled initially to kill the contained organisms, and then the flasks were left standing. Living organisms soon reappeared in flask A but no life appeared in flask B.

6. Since flask B remained free of life indefinitely, it can be concluded that

   (A) life does not arise spontaneously from the nutrient broth
   (B) flask A permits microorganisms to enter readily
   (C) the curved neck of flask B apparently prevents microorganisms from entering the flask
   (D) none of the above
   (E) all of the above, except D

7. The evidence generated by this experiment supports

   (A) Koch's postulates
   (B) The Hardy-Weinberg Law
   (C) the Germ Theory of disease
   (D) Virchow's theory of biogenesis
   (E) the Cell Theory

8. In the "dark reactions" of photosynthesis

   (A) chemical energy is changed to radiant energy
   (B) organic synthesis occurs
   (C) carbon dioxide is absorbed
   (D) radiant energy is released
   (E) radiant energy is changed to chemical energy

9. Photosynthesis

   (A) produces oxygen and inorganic compounds
   (B) produces carbon dioxide and water
   (C) produces carbon dioxide and organic compounds
   (D) produces oxygen and organic compounds
   (E) produces oxygen and water

10. A process which results, in part, in the production of carbon dioxide and water is

    (A) respiration
    (B) photosynthesis
    (C) secretion
    (D) osmosis
    (E) phosphorylation

11. An orientation growth movement by plants in response to an external stimulus is a

    (A) tropism
    (B) synergism
    (C) polymorphism
    (D) cyclosis
    (E) taxis

12. The photoperiodic response for "long-day" plants to short days is

    (A) flowering
    (B) phototropism
    (C) flower inhibition
    (D) parthenocarpy
    (E) photosynthesis

13. Which of the following is an organic compound found in the cell walls of hard wood?

    (A) Lignin
    (B) Suberin
    (C) Pectin
    (D) Cutin
    (E) Resin

14. When you eat a celery "stalk," you are eating

    (A) root tissue
    (B) stem tissue
    (C) leaf tissue
    (D) fruit
    (E) seed

15. Water loss from plants by transpiration would be increased by

    (A) increased air circulation
    (B) darkness
    (C) increased humidity
    (D) lowering the temperature
    (E) decreased air circulation

16. If a species has more than one pair of chromosomes, during meiosis recombination of genes may occur as a result of the reassortment of non-homologous chromosomes and by

    (A) mutation
    (B) fertilization
    (C) polyploidy
    (D) nondisjunction
    (E) crossing-over

17. In plants, selected cells of the haploid, gamete-producing generation

    (A) become or produce spores
    (B) undergo meiosis
    (C) undergo cleavage
    (D) become or produce eggs or sperm
    (E) are polyploid

18. Structures which are similar because of anatomy and development are said to be

    (A) analogous
    (B) dioecious
    (C) monoecious
    (D) homologous
    (E) homosporous

19. The Rh factor assumes serious proportions when

    (A) an Rh-negative mother carries an Rh-positive fetus in a first pregnancy
    (B) an Rh-negative mother carries an Rh-negative fetus in a second pregnancy
    (C) an Rh-positive mother carries an Rh-negative fetus
    (D) an Rh-positive mother carries an Rh-positive fetus
    (E) an Rh-negative mother carries an Rh-positive fetus in a second pregnancy

20. Carotene functions in maintaining

    (A) night vision
    (B) normal blood clotting
    (C) normal nerves
    (D) fertility
    (E) normal tooth and bone development

21. A change in the sequence of nucleotides in DNA is called

    (A) duplication
    (B) transition
    (C) mutation
    (D) transcription
    (E) induction

22. Impairment of the spinal accessory nerves would affect

    (A) muscles of the shoulder
    (B) facial muscles
    (C) the parotid gland
    (D) swallowing
    (E) muscles of the tongue

23. Teeth are innervated by the

    (A) oculomotor nerve
    (B) facial nerve
    (C) vagus nerve
    (D) trochlear nerve
    (E) trigeminal nerve

24. Stimulation by the parasympathetic nervous system would result in

    (A) weaker heartbeat
    (B) erection of hair
    (C) dilated pupils
    (D) higher blood pressure
    (E) increased sweat secretion

25. Pathologic conditions caused by defects in hormonal action are called

    (A) atrophy
    (B) pheromones
    (C) infectious diseases
    (D) deficiency diseases
    (E) functional diseases

26. Oxytocin

    (A) stimulates basal metabolism
    (B) regulates calcium metabolism
    (C) constricts blood vessels
    (D) regulates phosphorus metabolism
    (E) stimulates lactation

27. All of the following may occur during synapsis in meiosis *except:*

    (A) crossing-over
    (B) transduction
    (C) inversion
    (D) translocation
    (E) duplication

28. The appearance of variations in a population may be attributed to either genetic change or

    (A) genetic drift
    (B) changed environmental factors
    (C) nonrandom mating
    (D) parthenogenesis
    (E) adaptive radiation

29. Which one of the following is *not* a type of RNA?

    (A) Template RNA
    (B) Ribosomal RNA
    (C) Messenger RNA
    (D) Gametic RNA
    (E) Transfer RNA

30. The concept that all eggs have existed since the creation of the world is entailed in the beliefs of

    (A) pangenesists
    (B) animaculists
    (C) epigenesists
    (D) ovists
    (E) parthenogenesists

31. The ovary of a flower matures into

    (A) a seed
    (B) an embryo
    (C) a fruit
    (D) the endosperm
    (E) the receptacle

32. You would expect to observe moose and spruce in the

    (A) alpine tundra
    (B) coniferous forest
    (C) tropical rain forest
    (D) grasslands
    (E) deciduous forest

33. Nekton includes marine organisms which

    (A) exist only in darkness
    (B) swim by their own propulsion
    (C) exist to a depth of 5,000 feet
    (D) exist in the deepest ocean trenches
    (E) float on the surface

34. A student of cytogenetics would be concerned with

    (A) convergent evolution
    (B) the cellular basis of inheritance
    (C) prenatal development
    (D) the genetic changes in populations
    (E) parallel evolution

35. A paleontologist is a biologist concerned primarily with studying

    (A) birds
    (B) snakes
    (C) rocks
    (D) insects
    (E) fossils

36. An interrelationship between two organisms in which one receives all of the benefits at the expense of the other is called

    (A) parasitism
    (B) commensalism
    (C) mutualism
    (D) symbiosis
    (E) saprophytism

37. In the human circulatory system, leakage of blood back into the heart is prevented by the

    (A) tricuspid valve
    (B) aortic valve
    (C) ventricular valves
    (D) semilunar valves
    (E) bicuspid valve

38. Blood leaves the human liver through the hepatic vein and returns to the heart through the

    (A) hepatic portal system
    (B) anterior vena cava
    (C) azygous vein
    (D) inferior mesenteric artery
    (E) inferior vena cava

39. The Schick test is used to determine whether or not individuals need immunization, or whether or not immunization procedures have been effective, against

    (A) smallpox
    (B) yellow fever
    (C) polio
    (D) scarlet fever
    (E) diphtheria

40. The greatest significance of sexual reproduction is that it

    (A) ensures invariable genetic lines
    (B) permits new combinations of genes
    (C) ensures that traits are never lost
    (D) eliminates the need for meiosis
    (E) stimulates mating

41. What is the probability that any one child will be a male?

    (A) 1/16
    (B) 1/8
    (C) 1/4
    (D) 1/2
    (E) 3/4

42. In an individual with genotype "AaBb," the probability of producing gametes with dominant genes ("AB") is

    (A) unpredictable
    (B) 1/16
    (C) 1/8
    (D) 1/4
    (E) 1/2

43. Biochemical analysis of normal and sickle-cell hemoglobin reveals that the difference between the two is based on

    (A) sex chromosomes
    (B) transformation
    (C) amino acids
    (D) different antigens
    (E) agglutination

44. An ecological niche

    (A) is a micro-habitat
    (B) is really nondistinguishable
    (C) may be occupied by only one species
    (D) may be occupied by any number of species
    (E) may be occupied by only one individual

45. An organism which exhibits bilateral symmetry

    (A) always has a right and left leg
    (B) always has a right side and a left side
    (C) exhibits universal symmetry internally
    (D) could never possess an anterior or posterior end
    (E) would give birth to living young

46. Enzyme reactions typically have an opposite or contrary reaction. The contrary reaction to the enzyme reaction called hydrolysis is called

    (A) condensation
    (B) reduction
    (C) amination
    (D) phosphorylation
    (E) oxidation

47. Amino acids contain a carboxyl group, —COOH, and an amino group,

    (A) —NO$_2$
    (B) —CH$_3$
    (C) —CH$_2$
    (D) —H$_3$C
    (E) —NH$_2$

48. When a living cell is placed in a fluid and there is net movement of water molecules out of the cell, the fluid is said to be

    (A) isotonic
    (B) hypotonic
    (C) plasmolyzed
    (D) hypertonic
    (E) hydrolyzed

49. An organism capable of synthesizing its own food is described as

    (A) holozoic
    (B) heterotrophic
    (C) autotrophic
    (D) parasitic
    (E) saprophytic

50. Heterotrophic organisms relying upon decomposing organic materials for nutrition are

    (A) parasitic
    (B) autotrophic
    (C) holozoic
    (D) saprophytic
    (E) chemotrophic

51. In 1772, Joseph Priestley demonstrated that green plants

    (A) carry on photosynthesis
    (B) absorb water from the soil
    (C) give off carbon dioxide
    (D) absorb minerals from the soil
    (E) give off oxygen

52. An enzyme-regulated process in living cells resulting in the transfer of energy to ATP is

    (A) reduction
    (B) assimilation
    (C) osmosis
    (D) absorption
    (E) respiration

53. Cellular organelles called ribosomes are the sites of

    (A) enzyme storage
    (B) protein synthesis
    (C) chromosomal replication
    (D) cellular respiration
    (E) photosynthesis in plants

54. What is the principal absorbing structure of typical roots?

    (A) Root cap
    (B) Root hair cell
    (C) Endodermis
    (D) Hair roots
    (E) Xylem

55. The loss of water by transpiration is the result of

    (A) capillarity
    (B) diffusion
    (C) mass movement
    (D) cohesive forces
    (E) adhesive forces

56. The classification of bacteria is determined chiefly by their

    (A) cell membranes and capsules
    (B) movements and environments
    (C) morphological characteristics
    (D) anatomical characteristics
    (E) physiological characteristics

57. The union of a sperm and an egg is called

    (A) germination
    (B) homospory
    (C) fertilization
    (D) reduction
    (E) meiosis

58. The most significant benefit of flowering to humans is

    (A) double fertilization
    (B) the production of fruit and seeds
    (C) pollination
    (D) alternation of generations
    (E) aesthetic

59. Antigens are foreign proteins which stimulate the production of

    (A) fibrin
    (B) globulins
    (C) cytochrome
    (D) antibodies
    (E) lymphocytes

60. A deficiency of vitamin D may cause

    (A) muscular cramps
    (B) stunted growth
    (C) xerophthalmia
    (D) retardation of bone and tooth formation
    (E) paralysis

61. To overcome a thiamine deficiency, you should enrich your diet with

    (A) fresh vegetables
    (B) eggs and dairy products
    (C) citrus fruit
    (D) red meats
    (E) whole-grain cereals

62. Scientific research on the human cerebral cortex reveals that

    (A) the parasympathetic system is centered here
    (B) it controls smooth muscle
    (C) it controls endocrine secretions
    (D) it controls subconscious muscle coordination
    (E) specific areas control specific functions

63. The phases of mitosis occur in the following sequence:

    (A) prophase, anaphase, metaphase, telophase, and interphase
    (B) interphase, telophase, prophase, anaphase, and metaphase
    (C) interphase, prophase, metaphase, telophase, and anaphase
    (D) interphase, telophase, prophase, anaphase, and metaphase
    (E) prophase, metaphase, anaphase, telophase, and interphase

64. The constancy of linkage groups may be altered by

    (A) transduction
    (B) crossing-over
    (C) recombination
    (D) synapsis
    (E) assimilation

65. The "dark" reactions of photosynthesis take place in portions of the chloroplast called

    (A) grana
    (B) stomata
    (C) carotene
    (D) chlorophyll
    (E) stroma

66. Cytoplasmic streaming within living cells is called

    (A) translocation
    (B) transpiration
    (C) helicotropism
    (D) helicotaxis
    (E) cyclosis

67. Cellular respiration in mitochondria may

    (A) result in further energy storage
    (B) form ATP, an energy-yielding molecule
    (C) form ADP, an energy-related substance
    (D) release sugar molecules
    (E) release a variety of cellular hormones

68. Fibrinogen is

    (A) a precursor of certain hormones
    (B) formed from fibrin during clotting
    (C) an antibody to specific antigens
    (D) a source of globulin
    (E) a reservoir of antibodies for immune response

69. Systolic pressure is

    (A) the lowest pressure of the blood, between heartbeats
    (B) the result of a leak in a heart valve
    (C) the blood pressure in veins
    (D) the pressure on the blood as the ventricles contract
    (E) the blood pressure in arteries

70. During the infection process of bacteria by viral particles, it has been demonstrated that

    (A) the virus enters the bacterial cell "head first"
    (B) the virus enters the bacterial cell "tail first"
    (C) only the viral protein enters the cell
    (D) only the DNA of the virus enters the cell
    (E) the complete viral particle enters the cell

71. In the prophase of mitosis,

    (A) homologous chromosomes become paired
    (B) the centriole reappears
    (C) chromosomes are doubled and the duplicate chromatids may be observed
    (D) tetrads of chromatids appear
    (E) synapsis takes place

72. Marine organisms which move by drifting are referred to as

    (A) plankton
    (B) neritic
    (C) littoral
    (D) sessile
    (E) nekton

73. Genes, which control inheritance, are composed of the chemical

    (A) adenosine triphosphate
    (B) ribonucleic acid
    (C) adenosine diphosphate
    (D) deoxyribonucleic acid
    (E) acetylcholine

74. Nephrons

    (A) are functional units of the pancreas
    (B) are functional units of the liver
    (C) are functional units of the spleen
    (D) are functional units of the thyroid gland
    (E) are functional units of the kidney

Questions 75 and 76

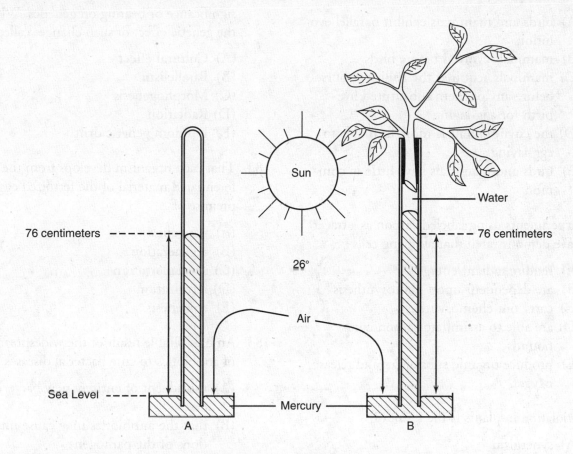

In the diagrams shown above, figure A illustrates a simple mercury barometer, a column of mercury in a sealed glass tube, the open end of which is immersed in a container of mercury which is exposed to atmospheric pressure at sea level. Figure B illustrates a living plant stem, with leaves, sealed in water in the upper end of the glass tubing, which is likewise filled with mercury.

75. What causes the mercury in figure A to rise to a height of 76 centimeters?

    (A) Adhesive forces
    (B) Cohesive forces
    (C) Sunlight heating the mercury, which expands
    (D) Atmospheric pressure on the mercury in the dish
    (E) The vacuum above the mercury in the glass tube

76. The mercury in figure B rises above 76 centimeters because

    (A) the plant stem absorbs mercury, pulling the mercury up the tube
    (B) plants grow better at sea level
    (C) of external and internal forces, including transpirational pull
    (D) the top of the glass tube is not sealed, thus destroying the vacuum
    (E) atmospheric pressure is highest at sea level

77. The existence of monotremes, the egg-laying mammals, suggests that

    (A) birds and mammals exhibit parallel evolution
    (B) mammals evolved before birds
    (C) mammals acquired the ability to nurse before any of them substituted live birth for egg-laying
    (D) the environment is more favorable to egg-laying
    (E) birds and mammals have little in common

78. Experiments using labeled carbon as a tracer have demonstrated that all living cells

    (A) require radiant energy
    (B) are dependent upon photosynthesis
    (C) carry out chemosynthesis
    (D) are able to assimilate carbon compounds
    (E) produce organic substances and release oxygen

79. Etiolation in plants is the result of

    (A) synergism
    (B) insufficient light
    (C) photoperiodism
    (D) parthenocarpy
    (E) taxis

80. Eutrophication of a lake may occur

    (A) when essential nutrients are insufficient
    (B) as a result of too many fish
    (C) during prolonged high temperatures
    (D) when there is insufficient phosphorus
    (E) when there is excess phosphorus

81. Gene frequencies in a population are sometimes modified or changed by factors of little significance or bearing on genetics. What is the genetic effect of such changes called?

    (A) Cultural effect
    (B) Parallelism
    (C) Morphogenesis
    (D) Radiation
    (E) Random genetic drift

82. That each organism develops from the undifferentiated material of the fertilized egg is the premise of

    (A) pangenesis
    (B) regeneration
    (C) special creation
    (D) fertilization
    (E) epigenesis

83. An undesirable result of the widespread use of antibiotics to cure bacterial diseases is

    (A) the advent of entirely new bacterial diseases
    (B) that the antibiotics may cause mutations of the pathogens
    (C) the development of antigenicity
    (D) the development of resistant strains by pathogens
    (E) loss of virulence by some pathogens

84. The adrenocorticotropic hormone is one of seven produced by the anterior lobe of the pituitary gland. Its primary function is to

    (A) stimulate the pancreas to release insulin
    (B) stimulate the thyroid to release thyroxin
    (C) stimulate the adrenal cortex to secrete the hormone cortisone
    (D) stimulate the ovaries to release estrogens
    (E) stimulate skeletal growth

85. When one species cannot survive without the benefits received from another species, the relationship is called

    (A) coordination
    (B) mutualism
    (C) neutralism
    (D) aggregation
    (E) commensalism

86. Sulfur is important in an ecosystem because it is

    (A) important in nerve impulse transmission
    (B) important for salt balance in vertebrate blood
    (C) essential in photosynthesis
    (D) essential for many proteins and certain enzymes
    (E) essential in respiration

87. The movement of ions into a living cell against a concentration gradient with the expenditure of energy is called

    (A) active transport
    (B) osmosis
    (C) plasmolysis
    (D) phagocytosis
    (E) pinocytosis

88. Those viruses which attack and parasitize bacteria are called

    (A) interferon
    (B) bacteriozymes
    (C) rickettsias
    (D) lysozymes
    (E) bacteriophages

89. When no oxygen is available to cells, they may produce ATP by

    (A) glycolysis
    (B) anaerobic respiration
    (C) use of the TCA cycle
    (D) cytochrome interaction
    (E) the citric acid cycle

90. Niacin functions in maintaining

    (A) normal bone formation
    (B) normal nerve functioning
    (C) normal blood clotting
    (D) normal cellular oxidations
    (E) night vision

91. By the conversion of ATP to ADP, cells

    (A) produce amino acids to make proteins
    (B) obtain energy for cellular activities
    (C) synthesize fats
    (D) dissociate to form various ions
    (E) store energy in complex carbohydrates

92. In the farsighted eye,

    (A) light rays converge in front of the retina
    (B) the cornea is defective
    (C) light rays converge in the fovea
    (D) vision is not blurred
    (E) light rays converge behind the retina

93. According to the Watson and Crick model of DNA, the bases are paired as follows:

    (A) adenine-thymine and cytosine-guanine
    (B) adenine-uracil and cytosine-guanine
    (C) adenine-cytosine and guanine-thymine
    (D) adenine-guanine and cytosine-thymine
    (E) adenine-thymine and guanine-uracil

94. Which of the following plants does not produce multicellular embryos?

    (A) Clover
    (B) Elodea
    (C) Tree ferns
    (D) Club mosses
    (E) Spirogyra

95. Which of the genotypes for hemophilia illustrated below would inherit the disease? The gene for hemophilia is recessive.

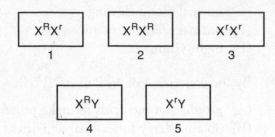

(A) 1, 3, and 5
(B) 2 and 4
(C) 4 and 5
(D) 3 and 5
(E) 1, 2, and 4

96. Fats, like carbohydrates, are composed of carbon, hydrogen, and oxygen, but differ from them by having

(A) proportionally more oxygen
(B) little stored energy
(C) twice as much hydrogen as oxygen
(D) an excess of carbon
(E) proportionally less oxygen

97. Isolation of a population over a long period of time produces

(A) adaptive radiation
(B) hybridization
(C) inbreeding
(D) interspecific competition
(E) parallel evolution

98. As a result of photosynthesis

(A) CO_2 is stored in carbohydrates
(B) light energy is converted into stored chemical energy
(C) entropy is neutralized
(D) energy is released
(E) ATP is energized

99. A deficiency of folic acid could result in

(A) a type of anemia
(B) sterility
(C) beriberi
(D) gray hair
(E) hemorrhage following surgery

100. You would expect to observe buffalo grass and bison in the

(A) desert
(B) tropical rain forest
(C) deciduous forest
(D) arctic tundra
(E) grasslands

101. For the biologist, mutations are

(A) the primary source of variability that permits evolution to occur
(B) seldom inherited complications of inheritance patterns
(C) predictable but impossible to create
(D) nonstable variations of inheritance patterns
(E) are noninherited genetic aberrations

102. Bacterial genes for resistance to antibiotics are readily shared and are carried on bacterial structures called

(A) plasmids
(B) spores
(C) cell membranes
(D) ribosomes
(E) plastids

103. One of the reasons that Mendel was successful when others before him failed was that

(A) he studied the inheritance of single contrasting characters
(B) he understood mutations
(C) he was able to verify his results by making chromosome studies
(D) he concerned himself with genes, not with how they expressed themselves
(E) he was lucky

104. A cellular activity that results in a decrease in dry weight is

    (A) osmosis
    (B) photosynthesis
    (C) diffusion
    (D) respiration
    (E) reduction

105. Pavlov's experiment with dogs involved varying patterns of food presentation and bell-ringing, which, in turn, resulted in a shift of the stimulus causing the dog's salivation. This is a type of reaction called

    (A) imprinting
    (B) proprioception
    (C) conditioned reflex
    (D) visual accommodation
    (E) intelligent behavior

106. Conversion of molecular nitrogen to ammonia or nitrate is carried out only by

    (A) certain bacteria and photosynthesis
    (B) bacteria and fungi
    (C) earthworms and soil bacteria
    (D) lightning, certain bacteria, and blue-green algae
    (E) lightning, decomposition, and fungi

Directions: Each group of questions below consists of five lettered choices followed by a list of numbered phrases or sentences. For each numbered phrase or sentence, select the one choice that is most closely related to it. Each choice may be used once, more than once, or not at all.

Questions 107–108

The following list represents factors that affect the growth, reactions, distribution, and reproduction of living organisms:

    (A) Genetic
    (B) Climatic
    (C) Edaphic
    (D) Biotic
    (E) Fire

107. The factor(s) involved in high soil alkalinity

108. The factor(s) involved in competition between garden beans and weeds

Questions 109–111

    (A) Adenosine triphosphate
    (B) Deoxyribonucleic acid
    (C) Disaccharide
    (D) Nucleotide
    (E) Phospholipid

109. A chemical compound found in chromosomes that stores hereditary information

110. The immediate source of energy for cellular activities

111. Energy-rich molecules formed in the mitochondrion

Answers

1. **(D)** By definition, a tissue is a group of similar cells specialized to perform a particular function or functions.

2. **(E)** Cells exchange substances with their environments through their surface membranes. The ratio of cell surface to cell volume has a direct effect on cellular metabolism and size.

3. **(E)** Enzymes are proteins produced by living cells. Enzymes control cellular metabolism.

4. **(E)** Photosynthesis is the biochemical process which occurs in living cells containing chlorophyll; it occurs only when radiant energy is present and results in the production of the basic food glucose.

5. **(E)** Typical holozoic organisms obtain nourishment by ingesting (eating) their food.

6. **(E)** Flask A permits microorganisms to enter readily and the material broth supports their existence and growth. Flask B severely restricts or prevents the entrance of microorganisms and, due to the lack of microorganisms in its broth, one must conclude that microorganisms do not arise spontaneously.

7. **(D)** Biogenesis is the concept that life arises only from preexisting life, a proposal first suggested by Virchow.

8. **(B)** The dark reactions of photosynthesis include the reduction of CO_2 and its combination into 3- and 6-carbon sugars. This is followed by a series of reactions in which the sugar ribulose is replaced.

9. **(D)** $6CO_2 + 6H_2O + \text{Radiant Energy} \rightarrow C_6H_{12}O_4 + 6O_2$

10. **(A)** $C_6H_{12}O_6 + 6O_2 \rightarrow 6CO_2 + 6H_2O + \text{energy (respiration)}$

11. **(A)** Tropisms are growth responses of plants to environmental stimuli such as light, water, and gravity.

12. **(C)** "Long-day" plants require more than a minimum exposure of 13–14 hours of daylight for flowering. Under conditions of fewer than 13–14 hours of daylight, flowering does not occur.

13. **(A)** Hard woods contain fibers (a type of cell) in addition to tracheids. The cell walls of fibers contain lignin, which resists decay and gives strength.

14. **(C)** Typically, celery has a short, cushiony stem to which the "stalks" are attached. Celery has a compound leaf, i.e., a leaf consists of a petiole, or "stem," and leaflets.

15. **(A)** Transpiration is the evaporation of water from the aerial parts of plants. Any condition which would increase the evaporation of water from an open dish would similarly increase transpiration.

16. **(E)** The two activities responsible for gene recombination in individuals with more than one pair of chromosomes are crossing-over and the reassortment of nonhomologous chromosomes.

17. **(D)** The typical plant life cycle is an "alternation of generations," i.e., the alternation of a diploid, spore-producing generation with a haploid, gamete-producing generation. Following meiosis, haploid spores give rise to the gametophyte generation; haploid gametes, produced by the gametophyte, fuse (fertilization) to produce the zygote, which develops into the diploid sporophyte generation.

18. **(D)** Homologous structures have similarities of structure, embryonic development, and relationships.

19. **(E)** An Rh-negative mother carrying an Rh-positive fetus in a first pregnancy develops antibodies to the Rh antigen, which, in turn, destroy the Rh positive red blood cells of the fetus in a second pregnancy.

20. **(A)** Carotenes are a group of orange to red pigments found in the chromoplastids of certain plant cells. The pigments are converted to vitamin A.

21. **(C)** Any change of the nucleotide sequences in DNA is called a mutation, and the activity that causes it is also called a mutation.

22. **(A)** Spinal nerves typically innervate muscles and organs of the body, while cranial nerves innervate muscles and organs associated with the head.

23. **(E)** Nerve innervations are specific, i.e., the trigeminal nerve innervates the teeth; the optic nerve innervates the eye.

24. **(A)** The sympathetic nervous system typically responds to situations involving anger, fear, etc., with bodily response that provides greater courage, strength, etc. The parasympathetic nervous system tends to counter these by reducing blood pressure, decreasing heart rate, etc.

25. **(E)** Disease may be caused by invading organisms and their products, such as diphtheria or poliomylitis; by deficiencies of minerals and vitamins, such as scurvy or rickets; or by defects in hormonal production and secretion such as goiter. The latter are called functional diseases.

26. **(E)** Endocrine secretions—hormones—are specific in action. Oxytoxin stimulates lactation, or the release of milk.

27. **(B)** Crossing-over, inversion, translocation, and duplication are events which frequently happen to chromatin materials during meiosis.

28. **(B)** The total development of any individual is determined by its genetic makeup as affected by its environment. Changes in genetic makeup through new gene combinations or by mutation, and/or by changed environmental factors are the only causes of variation in a population.

29. **(D)** No type of RNA is designated "gametic RNA." The RNA of gametes is not so designated.

30. **(D)** Ovists contend that miniature organisms were contained in eggs and that all eggs were created together and have existed since the beginning of the world.

31. **(C)** By definition, a fruit is the matured ovary of a flower.

32. **(B)** The coniferous forest biome, the taiga, is dominated by conifers, especially spruces. It is populated by bears, rodents, birds, and moose.

33. **(B)** Nekton includes large fishes, giant squids, and whales which swim in direct relation to their food supply and independent of wave or current actions.

34. **(B)** Cytogenetics is that branch or division of cytology which emphasizes the behavior of the genetic apparatus, or chromosomes of the cell.

35. **(E)** Paleontology is concerned with a study of life of past geological time periods as revealed by fossil remains.

36. **(A)** A parasite derives its food from the living tissue of other organisms.

37. **(D)** Semilunar valves are found at the entrance of both the pulmonary artery and the aorta.

38. **(E)** The hepatic vein empties into the inferior vena cava, which returns blood to the heart.

39. **(E)** The Schick test determines the presence of diphtheria antitoxin in the blood.

40. **(B)** Sexual reproduction is the only reproductive measure which permits new combinations of genes, thus establishing the basis for evolution and adaptation to a constantly changing environment.

41. **(D)** In human sex inheritance, the X and Y chromosome types of sex inheritance are involved. Females are XX. Males are XY and produce sperm carrying either X or Y chromosomes. Eggs carry only an X chromosome. If the fertilized egg contains two X chromosomes, the individual will be female. If it contains an X and a Y chromosome, the individual will be a male.

42. **(D)** The chance of an AB segregation of genes following meiosis in an individual with an "AaBb" genotype is one in four.

43. **(C)** Sickle-cell anemia is due to a mutation and the subsequent substitution of one amino acid for another in the normal hemoglobin protein chain.

44. **(C)** In biotic communities, most populations can be assigned to one of several roles such as a food producer, a first-order consumer, a parasite, a scavenger, etc. Each role is recognized as a niche and only one species occupies a particular and specific niche in a community.

45. **(B)** Animals with bilateral symmetry have right and left sides, a front and back, and are usually active movers.

46. **(A)** Properties of enzymes include inactivation by heat, sensitivity to changes in acidity, limitation (usually) to one substrate, and specificity in regard to the type of reaction carried out. In addition, there is always a contrary reaction. The

contrary reaction to oxidation is reduction, and the contrary reaction to hydrolysis is condensation.

47. **(E)** The amino group is represented as —NH_2.

48. **(D)** A hypertonic solution is one with a higher osmotic pressure than the reference (in this case, the living cell) solution.

49. **(C)** An autotrophic organism is able to manufacture its own food, usually by photosynthesis.

50. **(D)** A saprophytic organism derives its food from nonliving organic matter.

51. **(E)** Priestley discovered the opposing natures of photosynthesis and respiration. Respiration uses oxygen and releases carbon dioxide, while photosynthesis uses carbon dioxide and releases oxygen.

52. **(E)** In respiration the energy of foodstuffs is converted through a series of enzyme-regulated reactions into ATP, adenosine triphosphate, the principal energy storage molecule.

53. **(B)** Ribosomes are RNA-containing organelles that are the sites of the synthesis of proteins.

54. **(B)** Root hair cells increase the absorbing surface area of roots.

55. **(B)** Transpiration is the evaporation of water from the aerial part of plants. Evaporation is the result of the molecular activity called diffusion.

56. **(E)** There are over 2,000 species of bacteria. Bacteria have few morphological/anatomical characteristics. Bacteria are distinguished by their growth in selected nutrient media and by such tests as the production of acid, gas, etc.—all of which are physiological traits.

57. **(C)** By definition, fertilization is the union or fusion of an egg and sperm, which results in the formation of a fertilized egg, or zygote.

58. **(B)** Flowering plants produce the cereal grains in addition to numerous fruits and seeds, all of which are essential to the nutrition of humans and other animals.

59. **(D)** An antigen is any substance which, when introduced into one body, causes the body to produce antibodies against it.

60. **(D)** The physiological function of vitamin D is the regulation of calcium and phosphorus metabolism, hence, bone and tooth formation.

61. **(E)** The chief sources of thiamine are yeast, wheat germ, cornmeal, and enriched (whole-grain) flower products, i.e., the cereals.

62. **(E)** Billions of nerve cell bodies make up the cerebral cortex. By various means (i.e., disease, surgery, electrical stimulation), it has been shown that specific regions of the cerebral cortex control specific functions such as hearing, movement, balance, memory, etc.

63. **(E)** Mitosis is a process consisting of recognized phases which occur in the order prophase, metaphase, anaphase, telophase, and interphase.

64. **(B)** A linkage group consists of a series of inherited traits which are inherited as a "package" because they are in a linear arrangement along a single chromatid. Crossing-over, the exchange of segments between the chromatids of a tetrad, may disrupt this inheritance package.

65. **(E)** The dark reactions of photosynthesis use the energy of ATP, which is formed in the light, for their essential processes, all of which take place in the clear stroma, which surround the grana of the chloroplast.

66. **(E)** A streaming movement of the cytoplasm (cyclosis) within a cell during periods of photosynthesis apparently presents the contained chloroplastids of each cell to maximum light exposure in sequence.

67. **(B)** Enzymes that control respiration are generally found in the mitochondria and, under suitable conditions, the oxidation of pyruvic acid to carbon dioxide and water with the production of ATP molecules can be demonstrated.

68. **(B)** Under the influence of the enzyme thrombin, fibrinogen is converted into fibrin, which gradually forms a mesh in which blood cells become embedded, thus forming a clot.

69. **(D)** Systole is that phase of the heart's action in which blood is forced out of the ventricles.

70. **(D)** Research shows that when a virus is grown in a medium containing radioactive phosphorus-32, the phosphorus is assimilated by the virus and becomes part of the viral DNA. Additional research, using a culture medium containing radioactive sulfur-35, demonstrates that sulfur becomes part of the viral protein but not the DNA. Subsequent studies reveal that only the phosphorus-32 DNA enters bacterial cells while sulfur-35 viral protein does not.

71. **(C)** The prophase is recognized as the phase of mitosis in which the chromatids may be observed in the doubled chromosomes.

72. **(A)** Plankton is the myriad of small, microscopic, free-floating aquatic organisms found at or near the surface and subject to tides and currents.

73. **(D)** The genetic material must be able to contain a code and to copy itself exactly. Deoxyribonucleic acid, often abbreviated DNA, has this capability. In addition, it meets the requirements of being able to mutate and undergo crossing-over.

74. **(E)** Nephrons are the functional units of the kidneys that, while secreting quantities of fluid, reabsorb blood sugar and amino acids as well as urea, various ions, and a large amount of water.

75. **(D)** Atmospheric pressure on the surface of the mercury in the sealed tube pushes the mercury to a height of 760 millimeters. This is the basis of the common mercury barometer.

76. **(C)** Atmospheric pressure on the surface of the mercury and the effects of transpirational pull—the evaporation of water from the stem and leaves of the plant—work together in raising the level of the mercury in figure B above 760 millimeters of mercury.

77. **(C)** Monotremes, the most primitive group of mammals, constitute the lowest evolutionary animal group that nurses its young.

78. **(D)** Carbon is an element basic to all organic compounds and is essential to the synthesis of carbohydrates, fats, and proteins.

79. **(B)** Insufficient light stimulates stem elongation, which, when carried to extremes, is known as etiolation.

80. **(E)** Eutrophication occurs when chemical fertilizers containing phosphorus and nitrogen wash into a lake, causing photoplankton and bottom vegetation to reach high productivity. This tremendous growth blocks out light, causing deeper plants to die while certain decomposers use all the oxygen, thus suffocating the fish.

81. **(E)** Random genetic drift is one of the ways by which changes in gene frequency are explained when mutation and natural selection do not account for evolution.

82. **(E)** According to epigenesis, the individual arises from the undifferentiated material of the egg.

83. **(D)** The widespread use of antibiotics to cure bacterial diseases commonly results in the development of resistance and resistant strains of pathogenic organisms. The use of certain chemicals in controlling insects and other biological pests also results in their development of resistance.

84. **(C)** In response to various sources of stress, the adrenocorticotropic hormone (ACTH) is one of seven hormones produced by the anterior lobe of the pituitary gland. It stimulates the adrenal cortex to release cortisone, which, in turn, causes the stomach to develop ulcerations, shrinks the lymph nodes, increases blood pressure, and lowers the white blood cell count.

85. **(B)** The distinguishing factor of mutualism is that at least one of the species cannot survive without the other.

86. **(D)** While carbon, hydrogen, and oxygen suffice for all carbohydrates and fats, proteins cannot be synthesized without additional elements, including nitrogen and, sometimes, sulfur.

87. **(A)** The transport of ions against a concentration gradient in the direction opposite to that which would occur in osmosis or by diffusion is active transport. The cell expends energy to accomplish this.

88. **(E)** Bacteriophages are viruses that attack and invade bacterial cells converting bacterial DNA to viral DNA.

89. **(B)** Fermentation takes place in yeasts and other cells in the absence of free oxygen, and a similar type of reaction takes place in muscle cells. This process produces lactic acid from which the energy-bearing ATP molecule is formed.

90. **(B)** Niacin is usually thought of as the vitamin that prevents pellagra. Persons consuming insufficient niacin may also develop disorders of the digestive system, skin, and the nervous system.

91. **(B)** In the cellular process that converts ATP to ADP, energy is released for use in cellular activities.

92. **(E)** In the farsighted eye, the misshapen lens focuses the image behind the retina.

93. **(A)** In the complex DNA molecule, the bases adenine and thymine are always paired, as are cytosine and guanine.

94. **(E)** Algae (spirogyra), slime molds, and fungi are the plant groups that do not produce multicellular embryos. All other plants, including mosses and liverworts, and all vascular plants, including club mosses, ferns, gymnosperms, and flowering plants, produce multicellular embryos.

95. **(D)** In human sex-linked inheritance, females, with two X chromosomes, are the "carriers" of the recessive gene for such sex-linked traits as the disease hemophilia. The male Y chromosome lacks a gene for the trait in question. When a male inherits an X chromosome with the recessive gene (X^r), the recessive gene is expressed because no normal gene is present to prevent it.

96. **(E)** In fats, the ratio of hydrogen atoms to oxygen atoms is much higher than 2:1. Tristearin, for example, has the formula $C_{57}H_{110}O_6$.

97. **(A)** Under conditions of isolation, exemplified by Darwin's finches, the production of a number of diverse species from a single ancestral one is referred to as adaptive radiation.

98. **(B)** Photosynthesis results in the conversion of radiant, or light, energy into chemical energy and its storage in the glucose molecule.

99. **(A)** Folic acid is important for normal bone marrow function and a deficiency could result in certain types of anemia.

100. **(E)** Native perennial grasses of the grasslands (prairies) of North America include the so-called buffalo grass, and the predominant animal is the bison.

101. **(A)** Mutations are the primary source of variability that permits evolution to occur. Mutations are recognized today as the source of the accumulated changes described by Darwin in the *Origin of Species*.

102. **(A)** Bacterial genes for resistance to antibiotics are carried on bacterial structures called plasmids. These, in turn, are readily shared or exchanged between different species of bacteria.

103. **(A)** Prior to Mendel, most students of inheritance attempted to study inheritance patterns involving all or groups of supposedly inheritable traits. The usual result was confusion and chaos.

104. **(D)** Respiration is a biochemical process that releases energy and carbon dioxide. Dry weight is lost during respiration because organic compounds are used up.

105. **(C)** In response to a given stimulus, animals, including man, produce a certain response. If a second stimulus is presented simultaneously with the first, the initial response after multiple repetitions will be transferred to the second stimu-

lus and the response will occur even in the absence of the first stimulus. This is called a conditioned reflex.

106. **(D)** Under natural conditions only lightning, certain bacteria, and blue-green algae are able to "fix" nitrogen.

107. **(C)** ⎫ In their environment, all living things are affected by and respond to
108. **(D)** ⎭ various combinations of genetic, climatic, edaphic (soil factors), biotic (living organisms), and fire stimuli.

109. **(B)** Deoxyribonucleic acid, DNA, is found in chromosomes and stores hereditary information in coded form.

110. **(A)** ⎫ In the mitochondria, during cellular respiration, energy is transformed
111. **(A)** ⎭ from carbohydrate molecules to energy-rich adenosine triphosphate (ATP) for use throughout the cell.

QUESTIONS ABOUT ASTRONOMY

Directions: Each of the questions or incomplete statements below is followed by five suggested answers or completions. Select the one that is best in each case.

1. Retrograde motion is the

   (A) apparent backward motion of a planet
   (B) apparent backward motion of the moon
   (C) seasonal movement between the vernal equinox and the autumnal equinox
   (D) reciprocal movement of the earth's axis
   (E) retreat of a meteorite

2. Since the same face of the moon is always visible on earth, we must conclude that

   (A) the earth and moon rotate at the same relative rate
   (B) the earth and moon are rotating in opposite directions
   (C) the moon must make one rotation on its axis while revolving once around the earth
   (D) the earth must make one rotation on its axis while revolving around the moon
   (E) their orbits are equal

3. To say that the solar system is heliocentric means that

   (A) the earth is the center of the solar system
   (B) the sun is the center of the solar system
   (C) the sun is highest in the sky
   (D) the sun is lowest in the sky
   (E) the center reflects the perimeter

4. A star that increases to a maximum brightness and does not return to its original condition is known as a

   (A) nova
   (B) supernova
   (C) giant
   (D) supergiant
   (E) binary star

5. During a solar eclipse

   (A) the earth's shadow is cast on the moon
   (B) the moon's shadow is cast on the earth
   (C) the earth's shadow falls on the sun
   (D) the earth moves between the sun and moon
   (E) the sun moves between the earth and moon

6. An early Egyptian achievement, based on a knowledge of astronomy, was the

   (A) recording of eclipses
   (B) recording of earthquakes
   (C) invention of time
   (D) development of a 365-day calendar
   (E) development of a decimal system

7. Radio waves of broadcasting frequency are reflected by

   (A) ozone in the stratosphere
   (B) an ionized layer of the troposphere
   (C) a nonionized layer of the troposphere
   (D) the exosphere
   (E) the ionosphere

8. An eclipse of the moon

   (A) occurs when the earth passes into the shadow of the moon
   (B) occurs when the moon passes between the sun and the earth
   (C) occurs every eight years
   (D) can occur only during a new moon
   (E) can occur only during a full moon

9. The Hawaiian Islands are just east of the international dateline, and Wake Island is west. When it is July 4 at Pearl Harbor, what is the date at Wake Island?

    (A) July 2
    (B) July 3
    (C) July 4
    (D) July 5
    (E) July 6

10. When a space vehicle is at apogee, it is at

    (A) maximum speed
    (B) minimum speed
    (C) the point farthest away from the sun
    (D) a point in orbit farthest from the earth
    (E) a point in orbit closest to the earth

11. At the time of the summer solstice in the Northern Hemisphere,

    (A) the sun's rays are tangent to the poles
    (B) the sun's rays are perpendicular to the equator
    (C) days and nights are equal over the entire earth
    (D) the sun is directly overhead at the Tropic of Cancer
    (E) the sun is directly overhead at the Tropic of Capricorn

12. Small celestial bodies whose orbits generally lie between Mars and Jupiter are called

    (A) comets
    (B) meteoroids
    (C) asteroids
    (D) planets
    (E) micrometeorites

13. One piece of evidence for the earth's rotation is

    (A) the solar eclipse
    (B) the lunar eclipse
    (C) the changing phases of the moon
    (D) the tilt of the earth's axis
    (E) the circulation of air as reported on weather maps

14. According to Isaac Newton, a combination of the earth's forward motion and "falling" motion, caused by the sun's gravitational force, defines

    (A) the earth's declination
    (B) parallax
    (C) its perturbation
    (D) perihelion
    (E) the earth's orbit

Answers

1. **(A)** Occasionally planets appear to become stationary and then to drift westward for a short time; then the planet resumes its normal eastward motion. This is known as retrograde motion.

2. **(C)** The direction of the moon's rotation is in the same direction as the earth's rotation, and the moon makes only one rotation on its axis during one revolution around the earth. Therefore, the moon keeps the same side directed toward the earth.

3. **(B)** By definition: having the sun as a center.

4. **(B)** A supernova is a star that has collapsed under intense gravitation and then exploded.

5. **(B)** When the moon lies directly between the earth and the sun we witness a solar eclipse.

6. **(D)** The Egyptians were the first to develop a 365-day calendar.

7. **(E)** A layer of the atmosphere characterized by electrical properties and the presence of ionized particles is called the ionosphere. Radio waves from the earth travel upward to these ionized layers and are reflected back to earth.

8. **(E)** In an eclipse, both the sun and the center of the earth lie in the ecliptic plane and so must the moon lie in the ecliptic plane for, if it is too far from the ecliptic plane, it cannot pass into the shadow of the earth to cause a lunar eclipse. When lying in the ecliptic plane, the moon is, by its location, in the "full moon" phase.

9. **(D)** The International Date Line is designated ± 12 hours based on Greenwich time. Points east and west of this line differ in time by 24 hours.

10. **(D)** In an elliptical orbit, a space vehicle at apogee is at the orbit's farthest distance from earth.

11. **(D)** On June 21, the sun is as far north as it will go and is directly over the Tropic of Cancer, 23° 27' north of the equator. This date and this position of the sun mark the summer solstice.

12. **(C)** Asteroids include thousands of small planets between Mars and Jupiter with diameters of a fraction of a mole to almost 500 miles.

13. **(E)** Winds are deflected to the right of their paths in the Northern Hemisphere and to the left of their paths in the Southern Hemisphere, deviations which are the result of the earth's rotation. This deviation is called the Coriolis effect. The circulation of air as indicated on weather maps, is, therefore, a direct effect of the earth's rotation.

14. **(E)** Using his laws of motion, Isaac Newton demonstrated that the earth's orbit depends on its forward motion and its "falling" motion.

QUESTIONS ABOUT EARTH SCIENCE

Directions: Each of the questions or incomplete statements below is followed by five suggested answers or completions. Select the one that is best in each case.

1. A contemporary source of support for the theory of the spheroidal shape of the earth is

   (A) the Foucault pendulum
   (B) photographs taken by astronauts
   (C) computer data
   (D) Coriolis forces
   (E) parallax of stars

2. A crystalline calcite column hanging from a cave ceiling is called a

   (A) stalagmite
   (B) anthracite
   (C) dolomite
   (D) alabaster
   (E) stalactite

3. Lava that solidifies in the air and falls to the earth as solid particles is called

   (A) xenoliths
   (B) laccoliths
   (C) pyroclastics
   (D) batholiths
   (E) pahoehoes

4. About 99% of the earth's atmosphere consists of

   (A) nitrogen and oxygen
   (B) nitrogen
   (C) oxygen
   (D) oxygen and carbon dioxide
   (E) nitrogen and carbon dioxide

5. A weathering of rock by a combination of mechanical and chemical forces is

   (A) hydration
   (B) crosscutting
   (C) lamination
   (D) intrusion
   (E) intumescence

6. A surface separating young rocks from older ones is

   (A) a moraine
   (B) a bench
   (C) a stack
   (D) an unconformity
   (E) a disjunction

7. An earthquake that follows a larger earthquake and originates at or near the same focus is called

   (A) the epicenter
   (B) surface wave
   (C) an aftershock
   (D) seismogram
   (E) reflected wave

8. A dark-brown residue formed by the partial decomposition of plants that grow in marshes and other wet places is called

   (A) coal
   (B) dolomite
   (C) peat
   (D) chert
   (E) coquins

9. Perihelion means

    (A) that the earth is at its summer solstice
    (B) the point in the earth's orbit most distant from the sun
    (C) the point in the earth's orbit nearest to the sun
    (D) that the earth is crossing the Tropic of Cancer
    (E) that the earth is crossing the Tropic of Capricorn

10. Rocks formed by solidification of molten material are called

    (A) sedimentary
    (B) igneous
    (C) fossiliferous
    (D) metamorphic
    (E) monomineralic

11. The gradual domelike buildup of calcite mounds or columns on the floors of caves results in formations called

    (A) stalactites
    (B) diamonds
    (C) gypsum
    (D) dolomite
    (E) stalagmites

12. A fracture line of the earth's crust where one portion has shifted vertically in reference to the other is called

    (A) a fault
    (B) a P wave
    (C) an L wave
    (D) an S wave
    (E) a tremor

13. The condition in which warm air overlying cooler air functions to prevent the upward movement of air is called

    (A) temperature profile
    (B) temperature inversion
    (C) fog
    (D) negative feedback
    (E) heat island

Answers

1. **(B)** Photographs taken from outer space show the earth to be a sphere.

2. **(E)** Crystalline calcite columns called stalactites are formed over long periods of time by dripping water.

3. **(C)** Pyroclastics are particles of solidified lava which have fallen to earth.

4. **(A)** The earth's atmosphere is 78% nitrogen and 21% oxygen. The remaining 1% is primarily argon with small amounts of carbon dioxide, water vapor, and other gases.

5. **(A)** Mechanical weathering is the breaking of rock into smaller pieces, each retaining the characteristics of the original material. Chemical weathering results when chemical actions alter the rock by either the removal or addition of elements.

6. **(D)** Breaks in the rock record are called unconformities. One easily recognized unconformity consists of tilted or folded sedimentary rocks that are overlaid by other, more flat-lying rock strata.

7. **(C)** Aftershocks are earthquakes of less severity that usually follow the primary earthquake.

8. **(C)** As a layer of sphagnum (peat moss) grows over water, older growth is pressed deeper in the water and into darkness where it dies. Initial decay products contain much tannin and this slows down bacterial decay. This becomes the peat of commerce.

9. **(C)** On or about January 3 each year the earth is about 92 million miles from the sun, and is closer than at any other time of the year. This is called perihelion.

10. **(B)** Rock formed by the cooling of magma is known as igneous rock.

11. **(E)** The calcite mounds built up on cave floors are called stalagmites.

12. **(A)** When portions of the earth's crust fracture as a result of earthquakes, these fracture lines are called faults.

13. **(B)** When air is very stable, there is little or no verticle mixing and, therefore, little dilution. Warm air overlying cooler air prevents upward air movement, which results in the atmospheric pollutants being trapped below. This condition is called a temperature inversion.

QUESTIONS ABOUT PHYSICS

Directions: Each of the questions or incomplete statements below is followed by five suggested answers or completions. Select the one that is best in each case.

1. During the process called nuclear fission,

    (A) alpha particles are emitted
    (B) light atomic nuclei fuse
    (C) there is an increase in mass
    (D) radioactive fragments are often formed
    (E) much energy is consumed

2. Chromatic aberration may be eliminated by the use of

    (A) a convex lens
    (B) a concave lens
    (C) monochromatic light
    (D) proper focusing
    (E) a wider lens

3. When a musical note is raised one half step in pitch, it is called

    (A) tremolo
    (B) syncopation
    (C) sharp
    (D) flat
    (E) overtone

4. Pressure in a liquid

    (A) is inversely proportional to depth
    (B) decreases with depth
    (C) is variable at all points at the same level
    (D) is the same at different points at different levels
    (E) is the same at all points at the same level

5. A device in which chemical energy is converted into electrical energy is the

    (A) induction coil
    (B) rectifier
    (C) vacuum tube
    (D) amplifier
    (E) fuel cell

6. The condition created when two wires are connected through such a low resistance that current flow is excessive is called

    (A) a short circuit
    (B) induction
    (C) rectification
    (D) a circuit breaker
    (E) transition

7. Electronics is a field of applied science concerned with

    (A) the flow of electrons along a wire
    (B) the flow of electrons through gases or through a vacuum
    (C) the flow of electrons in liquids
    (D) amplitude modulation
    (E) frequency modulation

8. A prism separates white light because

    (A) parallel rays are reflected
    (B) parallel rays are focused
    (C) the angle of incidence equals the angle of reflection
    (D) the different frequencies are refracted differently
    (E) light rays are absorbed

9. An object traveling at Mach 2 is traveling approximately how many miles per hour?

    (A) 750
    (B) 1,500
    (C) 2,000
    (D) 15,000
    (E) 20,000

10. A shift in the wave length of light or sound, when the source of the light or sound is moving relative to an observer, is known as the

    (A) Bernoullian effect
    (B) Compton effect
    (C) Doppler effect
    (D) Edison effect
    (E) Coriolis effect

11. In scientific terminology, the prefix associated with the exponential expression 10^3 is

    (A) centi
    (B) kilo
    (C) nano
    (D) milli
    (E) pico

12. Magnetic fields produced by an alternating current carried in a wire

    (A) are indefinite and variable
    (B) cannot exist in a vacuum
    (C) cannot be demonstrated
    (D) can be explained by Gilbert's Theory
    (E) cannot penetrate nonmagnetic materials

13. In reference to electrical circuitry, the ohm represents

    (A) the unit of current
    (B) a force between two electric fields
    (C) the difference of potential
    (D) the flow of coulombs
    (E) the unit of resistance

14. Work requires that

    (A) direction be changed
    (B) a force be exerted over a distance
    (C) a definite rate be maintained
    (D) the rate of motion increase
    (E) the rate of motion decrease

15. In using a lever,

    (A) force is gained when the force arm is longer than the weight arm
    (B) force is gained when the force arm is shorter than the weight arm
    (C) force is gained when the force arm and the weight arm are equal
    (D) distance is gained when the force arm is longer than the weight arm
    (E) distance is gained when the fulcrum is central

16. Attics should have provision for ventilation so that hot summer air may be removed by

    (A) conduction
    (B) expansion
    (C) convection
    (D) entropy
    (E) radiation

17. If you swim one kilometer to an island off-shore, how many miles do you swim?

    (A) 0.36 mile
    (B) 0.5 mile
    (C) 0.63 mile
    (D) 0.84 mile
    (E) 1.6 miles

18. Every object remains in its state of rest or in its state of uniform motion unless

    (A) its velocity changes
    (B) its acceleration varies
    (C) internal forces change
    (D) internal forces remain constant
    (E) external forces change that state

19. According to Newton's third law of motion,

    (A) force is proportional to mass times acceleration
    (B) momentum equals mass times velocity
    (C) the weight of a body is equal to the gravitational attraction exerted upon it by the earth
    (D) the weight of a body is equal to the gravitational attraction exerted upon it by the sun
    (E) to every action, there is an equal and opposite reaction

Questions 20–22

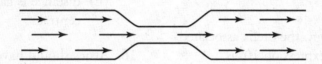

20. A fluid moving through a constriction, as illustrated above, speeds up and at the same time

    (A) its temperature also increases
    (B) its temperature decreases
    (C) its molecules begin to cling together
    (D) the pressure of the fluid within the constriction decreases
    (E) the pressure of the fluid within the constriction increases

21. The phenomenon illustrated is known as

    (A) the Doppler effect
    (B) Borelli's constant
    (C) Bernoulli's principle
    (D) the Mach effect
    (E) Pascal's law

22. One application of the phenomenon illustrated is in the

    (A) calculation of barometric pressure
    (B) verification of translational motion
    (C) design of airplane wings
    (D) determination of wave frequency
    (E) design of internal guidance systems

Questions 23–25

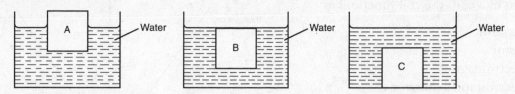

In the figures illustrated above, cubes A, B, and C, which have equal dimensions, are shown in containers of water.

23. With respect to the relative densities of the cubes, it may be concluded that

   (A) cube C has the greatest density
   (B) cube C sinks because its density is equal to the density of water
   (C) cube A has the greatest density
   (D) cube B has the greatest density
   (E) water has less buoyant force than cube A or B

24. Cube C sinks to the bottom because

   (A) cube C has a very low density
   (B) the weight of the displaced water is greater than the weight of cube C
   (C) cube C displaces too much water
   (D) the weight of the displaced water is equal to the weight of cube C
   (E) the weight of the displaced water is less than the weight of cube C

25. The phenomenon illustrated in these figures is best summarized or explained by

   (A) Faraday's postulates
   (B) Boyle's law
   (C) Dalton's theory
   (D) Archimedes' principle
   (E) Kepler's laws

---

26. The energy exerted by a moving bowling ball as it strikes the pins is

   (A) rolling energy
   (B) mass energy
   (C) kinetic energy
   (D) potential energy
   (E) transferred energy

27. If a container of ether is unstoppered in a closed room where there are no air currents or air circulation, we soon smell ether because of the process called

   (A) osmosis
   (B) diffusion
   (C) transpiration
   (D) capillarity
   (E) surface tension

28. When electricity flows through a wire wound in the form of a coil, the coil functions as

    (A) a generator
    (B) a resistor
    (C) an electromagnet
    (D) an electrostatic generator
    (E) an electroscope

29. When the nucleus of a radium atom emits an alpha particle,

    (A) only its atomic number changes
    (B) only its mass changes
    (C) neither its mass nor atomic number changes
    (D) both its mass and atomic number change
    (E) it becomes uranium

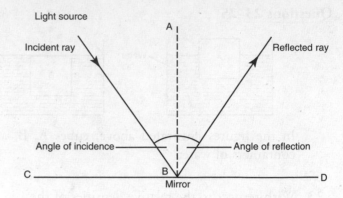

The diagram above illustrates the reflection of a ray of light from a mirror. The imaginary line *AB* is perpendicular to line *CD*.

30. The nature of a reflected ray of light is such that

    (A) the angle of incidence is greater than the angle of reflection
    (B) the angle of reflection always equals the angle of incidence
    (C) the angle of reflection is greater than the angle of incidence
    (D) the angle of reflection varies and changes
    (E) the sum of the angle of incidence and the angle of reflection is a right angle

31. A vibrating string on a musical instrument will produce a low pitch if it is

    (A) short, stretched, and of small diameter
    (B) long, stretched, and of small diameter
    (C) long, loose, and of small diameter
    (D) long, loose, and of large diameter
    (E) short, stretched, and of large diameter

Questions 32 and 33

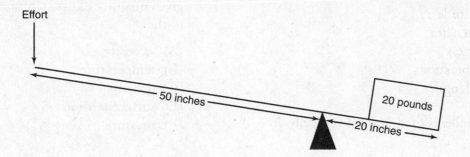

32. The force required to lift the 20-pound load in the illustration above is

    (A) 2 pounds
    (B) 8 pounds
    (C) 10 pounds
    (D) 20 pounds
    (E) 40 pounds

33. What is the mechanical advantage of the lever illustrated above?

    (A) 1
    (B) 2.5
    (C) 5
    (D) 7.5
    (E) 10

---

34. In the transmission of electric power, alternating current is used because

    (A) its voltage is readily transformed
    (B) it is cheaper
    (C) it is readily grounded
    (D) it is ready to use in household appliances
    (E) it has greater resistance

35. Ultraviolet radiation can cause a metal to emit electrons, a process called

    (A) ionization
    (B) facsimile transmission
    (C) electron transformation
    (D) the Compton effect
    (E) the photoelectric effect

36. Materials which transmit no light are referred to as

    (A) luminous
    (B) opaque
    (C) transparent
    (D) lucid
    (E) translucent

37. Concave lenses cause light rays to diverge by

    (A) reflection
    (B) absorption
    (C) diffraction
    (D) dispersion
    (E) diffusion

38. The acoustical engineer is chiefly concerned with

    (A) amplitude
    (B) frequencies
    (C) loudness
    (D) reverberations
    (E) wavelength

39. When a bullet is fired upward vertically, it gains in

    (A) momentum
    (B) speed
    (C) kinetic energy
    (D) potential energy
    (E) inertia

40. Work is the

    (A) direction of movement
    (B) distance of movement
    (C) rate of movement
    (D) product of the rate of movement multiplied by the distance moved
    (E) product of the force on an object multiplied by the distance it moves

41. When a hard rubber ball is rubbed by wool, the ball

    (A) gains electrons and becomes positively charged
    (B) gains electrons and becomes negatively charged
    (C) remains neutral
    (D) loses electrons and becomes positively charged
    (E) loses electrons and becomes negatively charged

42. Transformers

    (A) are coils of wire carrying electric current
    (B) change the voltage of alternating current
    (C) have the capacity to store electric charges
    (D) change the voltage of direct current
    (E) are used to break circuits

43. According to Boyle's Law, when the temperature is constant, the volume of a given quantity of gas is inversely proportional to the

    (A) viscosity
    (B) temperature
    (C) density
    (D) surface tension
    (E) pressure

44. Roger Bacon contributed the

    (A) heliocentric theory
    (B) idea of the rotation of the earth
    (C) experimental approach to science
    (D) concept of buoyancy and density
    (E) idea of the sphericity of the earth

45. The Coriolis force, a significant influence on the movement of ocean waters, is caused by

    (A) the upwelling of cold water
    (B) the gyre
    (C) tidal currents
    (D) the earth's rotation
    (E) tsunamis

46. The inward force that is necessary to keep an object in circular motion is called

    (A) centrifugal force
    (B) inertia
    (C) centripetal force
    (D) net force
    (E) weightlessness

47. When an object exhibits inertia it

    (A) resists changes in its motion
    (B) resists friction and slowing down
    (C) responds directly to friction forces
    (D) exhibits velocity in a specified direction
    (E) possesses direction and magnitude

48. The difference between an induced fusion reaction and a thermonuclear reaction is that, in a thermonuclear reaction, nuclei of

    (A) heavy atoms are split
    (B) heavy atoms are fused
    (C) light atoms are split
    (D) light atoms are fused
    (E) either heavy or light atoms are split

49. The phenomenon called interference is produced when

    (A) light waves are bent
    (B) light waves are parallel
    (C) two or more waves of the same frequency are superimposed
    (D) the velocities of sound in air are identical
    (E) the frequencies of wave vibrations are equal

50. Which of the following molecules contains a double bond?

    (A) H—C≡C—H

    (B)
    ```
        H
        |
    H—C—O—H
        |
        H
    ```

    (C)
    ```
        F
        |
    F—C—F
        |
        F
    ```

    (D)
    ```
      H       H
      |       |
    H—C—O—C—H
      |       |
      H       H
    ```

    (E)
    ```
    H\     /H
      C=
    H/     \H
    ```

51. At the higher altitudes, the existence of a satellite is limited because of drag caused by

    (A) cosmic rays from the sun
    (B) air and other particles in space
    (C) infrared radiation from the sun
    (D) centrifugal force
    (E) both cosmic rays and centrifugal force

52. According to Einstein's theory of relativity, as the speed of a spaceship approaches the speed of light,

    (A) metabolism and mass increase
    (B) metabolism and mass decrease
    (C) metabolism and mass remain constant
    (D) aging, relative to earth, would slow down
    (E) aging, relative to earth, would speed up

53. When a tractor applies a horizontal force of 400 pounds and pushes an object 20 feet across a loading platform, the work accomplished is equal to

    (A) 200 foot-pounds
    (B) 400 foot-pounds
    (C) 2,000 foot-pounds
    (D) 4,000 foot-pounds
    (E) 8,000 foot-pounds

54. When a gas is compressed by pressure and the temperature is held constant,

    (A) its component molecules are compressed
    (B) space between its molecules decreases
    (C) its volume increases
    (D) its molecules speed up
    (E) its molecules slow down

55. The random spreading out of molecules from a higher to a lower concentration is called

    (A) osmosis
    (B) active transport
    (C) diffusion
    (D) passive transport
    (E) capillary action

56. The velocity of an object is a description of

    (A) distance and time
    (B) its acceleration
    (C) its resistance to inertia
    (D) its mass and weight
    (E) its speed and direction

57. What is the mechanical advantage of the block and tackle illustrated?

    (A) 1
    (B) 2
    (C) 3
    (D) 6
    (E) 9

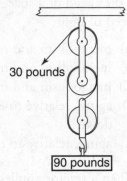

30 pounds

90 pounds

58. The conversion of alternating current to direct current is called

    (A) amplification
    (B) modulation
    (C) transistorization
    (D) induction
    (E) rectification

59. That property of matter which tends to maintain any motionless body at rest is called

    (A) friction
    (B) mass
    (C) inertia
    (D) force
    (E) velocity

60. Electric current in which the direction of flow is reversed at regular intervals is called

    (A) effective current
    (B) alternating current
    (C) direct current
    (D) induced current
    (E) universal current

61. In connection with nuclear reactions, that mass which is just sufficient to make the reaction self-sustaining is called

    (A) a fusion mass
    (B) a fission mass
    (C) a critical mass
    (D) a supercritical mass
    (E) a subcritical mass

62. Echoes are

    (A) decibels
    (B) reflected sound waves
    (C) interference
    (D) reinforcement
    (E) diffracted sound waves

63. Heat energy, in metric or SI units, is expressed in

    (A) calories
    (B) ergs
    (C) joules
    (D) watts
    (E) kilowatts

Questions 64–67

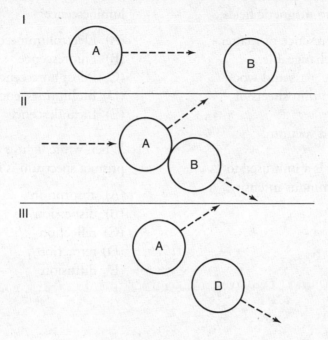

The three diagrams above illustrate a sequence in which ball A is moving toward stationary ball B in diagram I; strikes ball B in diagram II; and both balls are moving after ball A strikes ball B in diagram III.

64. In diagram I, the moving ball (ball A)

    (A) has a momentum equal to that of ball B
    (B) accelerates in direct proportion to its mass
    (C) accelerates in indirect proportion to its mass
    (D) has zero momentum
    (E) has a momentum equal to its mass times its velocity

65. When ball A collides with ball B (diagram II)

    (A) ball A's momentum will increase
    (B) ball A will retain its initial velocity
    (C) ball A's momentum will remain constant
    (D) ball A will slow down
    (E) the force of the collision represents a gain in momentum

66. After the collision of ball A with ball B (diagram III)

    (A) both ball A and ball B will be moving
    (B) ball A will have slowed down and changed direction
    (C) ball A will have lost momentum; ball B will have gained momentum
    (D) the total initial and final velocities of balls A and B will be equal
    (E) all of the above

67. Based upon study and observation of the three diagrams, one may conclude that, in accord with Newton's Second Law,

    (A) momentum decreases mass
    (B) momentum increases mass
    (C) velocity is constant
    (D) a force is necessary for acceleration
    (E) energy is gained following the collision

68. One of the following is not an acceptable statement with respect to magnetic fields:

    (A) They require the presence of matter.
    (B) Lines of force are changeable.
    (C) They can penetrate glass and wood.
    (D) They can penetrate thin sheets of copper.
    (E) They may exist in a vacuum.

69. Which of the following is a unit used to express a measure of luminous intensity?

    (A) volt
    (B) roentgen
    (C) erg
    (D) candela
    (E) luminous flux

70. Which of the following is not an example of luminescence?

    (A) Electroluminescence
    (B) Fluorescence
    (C) Phosphorescence
    (D) Bioluminescence
    (E) Incandescence

71. When white light is directed through a glass prism a spectrum is formed by its

    (A) absorption
    (B) dispersion
    (C) reflection
    (D) refraction
    (E) diffusion

Questions 72 and 73 refer to the following diagram, which illustrates the basic characteristics of waves.

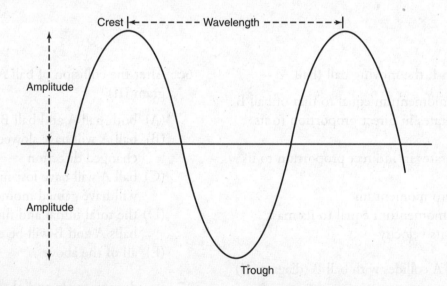

72. Amplitude may be thought of as

    (A) an interaction between two different waves
    (B) the number of crests passing a given point per second
    (C) the distance between two adjacent crests
    (D) a complete cycle, from crest to trough
    (E) one-half of the vertical distance between crests and troughs

73. Interference is

    (A) the simultaneous arrival of two different waves at a single point in space
    (B) the combining of two different waves at some point in space
    (C) the interaction of two or more waves
    (D) "in phase" if two interacting waves are of the same frequency and shape and if they meet crest to crest and trough to trough
    (E) all of the above

74. The total of the number of neutrons and protons in the atomic nucleus is called the

    (A) atomic number
    (B) atomic valence
    (C) mass number
    (D) nucleic number
    (E) ionic number

75. The ratio of the weight of a given mineral to the weight of an equal volume of water is its

    (A) molecular weight
    (B) specific gravity
    (C) specific density
    (D) specific weight
    (E) atomic weight

76. Pressures exerted by the water over a submerged object such as a submarine

    (A) are equal to the area divided by the force
    (B) are dependent upon direction
    (C) are not affected by rate of flow
    (D) are lower nearest the bottom
    (E) are equal to the weight of a column of water above it

77. The Kelvin scale is an absolute scale since its zero point, absolute zero, is

    (A) the freezing point of water
    (B) the temperature at which water reaches its greatest density
    (C) the coldest possible temperature
    (D) the same temperature as outer space
    (E) the temperature of liquid nitrogen

Directions: The group of questions below consists of five lettered choices followed by a list of numbered phrases or sentences. For each numbered phrase or sentence select the one choice that is most closely related to it. Each choice may be used once, more than once, or not at all.

Questions 78–80

    (A) Alpha particle
    (B) Beta particle
    (C) Meson
    (D) Neutron
    (E) Proton

78. A fundamental atomic particle that is electrically neutral

79. The nucleus of a helium atom

80. A particle in the nucleus of an atom having about the same mass as the proton

Answers

1. **(D)** When an atom undergoes fission, it splits into two smaller atoms called fission fragments, and these are usually radioactive.

2. **(C)** Chromatic aberration is the failure of different colors (wavelengths) of light to meet at the focal point after passing through a convex lens. This can be corrected by combining two or more lenses to ensure that the various colors of light meet at the focal point. The use of monochromatic light (light of one or a few nearly similar wavelengths) also eliminates the condition.

3. **(C)** In music, sharps are notes that are raised one half step in pitch.

4. **(E)** Pressure is exerted equally in all directions at a given level.

5. **(E)** In a fuel cell, gaseous hydrocarbons are the oxidizable material, and air supplies oxygen.

6. **(A)** A "short" is an electrical circuit with a very low resistance.

7. **(B)** Electronics is that branch of physics that studies the emission behavior and effects of electrons in vacuums and in gases.

8. **(D)** When white light passes through a prism it is broken up into an array of colors called a spectrum. The shortest rays of light bend the most and are the violet end of the spectrum. The longest rays bend the least and are the red end of the spectrum. All other colors fall in between, i.e., orange, yellow, green, and blue.

9. **(B)** The speed of sound in air at sea level at 0°C is about 741 miles per hour. This rate of speed is rated as Mach 1.

10. **(C)** When the source of a light wave or a sound wave is moving relative to the observer, a change in the observed frequency of light or sound occurs and this change or shift is called the Doppler effect.

11. **(B)** The decimal equivalent to the exponential expression 10^3 is 1,000. The prefix KILO means 1,000.

12. **(A)** When an alternating current is carried in a wire, a changing magnetic field is produced which, in turn, generates a varying electric field.

13. **(E)** The ohm is the unit of electrical resistance in a given circuit.

14. **(B)** Work is performed when an effort or a force causes a body to move.

15. **(A)** A lever is in balance when the effort and load are in balance, i.e., effort x length of force arm = load x length of weight arm. If other factors remain constant, increasing the length of the force arm gives a gain in force.

16. **(C)** Convection currents transfer heat energy in air by a circulatory motion due to variation in density and the forces of gravity.

17. **(C)** A kilometer is 1,000 meters or 0.62 mile.

18. **(E)** Inertia is that property of every object that causes it to remain at rest, or, if in motion, to remain at a constant velocity unless made to change by external forces.

19. **(E)** Whenever something is lifted, pulled, or pushed, it pushes down or resists in return.

20. **(D)** The pressure of a moving fluid (including gases) changes with and is inversely proportional to its speed of motion.

21. **(C)** According to Bernoulli's principle, when a fluid flows through a constriction, it speeds up and its pressure, therefore, decreases.

22. **(C)** An airplane wing is so shaped that air molecules moving over the top surface have farther to travel and, in so doing, they must speed up. This creates a lower air pressure on the top of the wing and the result is lift.

23. **(A)**   ⎫ All matter consists of atoms. The density of a substance depends on the
24. **(D)**   ⎬ masses of its atoms and the closeness in which its atoms are packed. A
given object, when placed in water, displaces a volume of water equal to its weight.

25. **(D)** According to Archimedes' Principle, a floating object displaces an amount of water equal to its own weight.

26. **(C)** Kinetic energy is the energy possessed by a moving object.

27. **(B)** All molecules, except when at absolute zero temperature, tend to remain in constant motion and to spread out throughout all space available to them. This is diffusion.

28. **(C)** The magnetic field around any long straight wire is circular when an electric current passes through the wire. If an electric current is passed through a coil of wire, the strength of the magnetic field is equal to the number of coils of wire and the amount of current in the coil.

29. **(D)** Radium emits charged helium atoms called alpha particles, and these are very heavy. This results in a loss of mass. Radium ($_{88}$Ra) has an atomic number of 88, the 88 representing 88 protons or alpha particles. Since helium is $_2$He and comes from the radium atom, the loss of two from the radium to the helium means that the atom is now $_{86}$R, which is another element—radon.

30. **(B)** When a ray of light strikes an object at a specific angle and is reflected, it bounces off the reflecting surface at the same angle at which it approached.

31. **(D)** Small-diametered musical strings produce a high pitch if stretched tightly and large diametered strings produce a low pitch if strung loosely.

32. **(B)** Effort multiplied by the length of the effort arm equals the load multiplied by the length of the load arm.

33. **(B)** Mechanical advantage is calculated either by dividing the load by the effort or by dividing the length of the effort arm by the length of the load arm.

34. **(A)** Electric power transmission is normally transmitted efficiently at higher voltages. Alternating current is easier to transmit and its voltage is readily transformed.

35. **(E)** The outermost electrons of certain metals are not held strongly by the nucleus. Light of certain frequencies can dislodge surface electrons and this movement of electrons constitutes an electric current, which is called the photoelectric effect.

36. **(B)** Opaque substances do not permit light penetration.

37. **(C)** Parallel rays of light passing through a concave lens bend outward or spread apart and this is called diffraction.

38. **(D)** Reverberations are sound echoes which distort vocal and musical sounds.

39. **(D)** Potential energy is the energy possessed by a body because of its position. A bullet fired into the air has potential energy because it will fall back to earth due to gravity.

40. **(E)** Work is determined by multiplying the force on an object by the distance it is moved.

41. **(B)** The atoms in the wool lose electrons, becoming positively charged; the atoms in the rubber ball gain electrons, becoming negatively charged.

42. **(B)** Transformers are used to increase or decrease the voltage of alternating current.

43. **(E)** At a constant temperature, the volume of a gas is inversely proportional to the pressure.

44. **(C)** Roger Bacon advocated observation and experimentation as sources of scientific information.

45. **(D)** Many factors affect the earth's surface water currents. The most significant factor is the Coriolis force that is caused by the earth's rotation and that deflects currents to the right of their path in the Northern Hemisphere and to the left in the Southern Hemisphere.

46. **(C)** Centripetal force is the inward force that holds an object, such as a satellite, in circular motion in its orbit.

47. **(A)** Inertia is the tendency of a body in motion to remain in motion or the tendency of a body at rest to remain at rest.

48. **(D)** The light atoms of hydrogen isotopes are fused in a thermonuclear reaction.

49. **(C)** When sound waves of the same frequency reach a single point simultaneously they combine in a process called interference.

50. **(E)** The double chemical bond occurs when two electron pairs are shared by bonded atoms.

51. **(B)** Any body anywhere in space is subject to drag caused by the air molecules and other particles found throughout space.

52. **(D)** Speed and time as measured by an observer on a rocket traveling at a speed near the speed of light are different from the speed and time measured by an observer on earth. To the space traveler, light from earth is catching up to the spaceship at one speed; to the observer on earth, light is catching up to the spaceship at a different speed. Both observers are correct.

53. **(E)** Work is defined as weight times distance moved. One foot-pound equals a one-pound weight being moved one foot.

54. **(B)** In a sense, the same number of molecules occupies less space when a gas is compressed and the temperature is held constant.

55. **(C)** Diffusion is the passive transport of molecules or ions from a higher to a lower concentration. Active transport is when the overall change is from a lower to a higher concentration and requires energy.

56. **(E)** Velocity is linear motion in a specific direction.

57. **(C)** Mechanical advantage, in a pulley system, is determined by the number of ropes that support the weight.

58. **(E)** A rectifier is a device used to convert alternating current to direct current.

59. **(C)** The property of any object that keeps it at rest or at a constant velocity unless it is forced to change by external forces is called inertia.

60. **(B)** In alternating current, the direction of current flow is reversed at regular intervals.

61. **(C)** In a nuclear reaction, the minimum mass required to support a self-sustaining chain reaction is called the critical mass.

62. **(B)** Echoes are reflected sound waves.

63. **(C)** The older unit of heat is the calorie; the newer is the joule. One calorie equals 4.184 joules (4.184 J).

64. **(E)** The momentum of any moving body is the product of its mass times its velocity.

65. **(D)** ⎫ When two bodies collide, total momentum after the collision equals
66. **(E)** ⎭ total momentum before the collision. Speed and direction may change because the original momentum is redistributed during the collision.

67. **(D)** The acceleration of a body is directly proportional to the force acting on it and inversely proportional to its mass.

68. **(A)** Magnetic fields exist in vacuums and can also penetrate most kinds of matter.

69. **(D)** The power of a light source is called its luminous intensity. A unit of luminous intensity is the candela.

70. **(E)** Incandescence is the emission of radiation by a hot body which makes the body visible.

71. **(D)** When a ray of light moves from one medium to another, such as air through glass, the ray bends. This is refraction. The different wavelengths of white light are, therefore, separated into the visible spectrum since each has its own refractive index.

72. **(E)** Amplitude is measured from a zero point and is one-half the vertical distance between the crest of a wave and its trough.

73. **(E)** Interference is the combining of two different waves which meet at a point in space. If they meet crest to crest, trough to trough, they are in phase. If they combine out of phase, they cancel out. If waves of different frequencies combine, they reinforce each other part of the time and cancel each other part of the time.

74. **(C)** The total of the number of neutrons and protons in the atomic nucleus equals the mass number.

75. **(B)** The number, which represents the ratio of the weight of a given mineral to the weight of an equal volume of water, is its specific gravity.

76. **(E)** Pressures in fluids increase with depth and are higher as depth increases due to the effects of gravity and the weight of the column of water above an object at any given depth.

77. **(C)** The Kelvin scale is an absolute scale because its zero is the coldest possible temperature, absolute zero.

78. **(D)** Neutrons are fundamental atomic particles that are electrically neutral.

79. **(A)** The nucleus of a helium atom is an alpha particle.

80. **(D)** Neutrons have the same mass as protons.

QUESTIONS ABOUT CHEMISTRY

Directions: Each of the questions or incomplete statements below is followed by five suggested answers or completions. Select the one that is best in each case.

1. When referring to the half-life of a radioactive element, we mean

    (A) an interval of time during which half of its atoms will undergo radioactive decay

    (B) half of the interval of time during which half of its atoms will undergo radioactive decay

    (C) an interval of time in which a specific atom of the element decays by one-half

    (D) an interval of time during which a random atom of the element decays by one-half

    (E) an interval of time during which all atoms of the element undergo one-half radioactive decay

2. In a process called electrolysis,

    (A) there is an interaction between electric currents and magnets

    (B) the motions of electrons in magnetic fields are studied

    (C) chemical compounds are synthesized

    (D) chemical compounds are decomposed by means of electric current

    (E) ionizing radiation may be measured

3. That the volume of a gas is inversely proportional to the pressure at a constant temperature is known as

    (A) kinetic theory of gases

    (B) Boyle's law

    (C) the first law of thermodynamics

    (D) Charles' law

    (E) Boltzmann's law

4. Elements included in the alkali metal family are unique in that they

    (A) are all heavy metals

    (B) have varying combining qualities

    (C) are highly reactive

    (D) all combine in the same ratio with other elements

    (E) have two valence electrons

Questions 5 and 6

$$H \cdot + \cdot H \rightarrow H : H$$

5. The two joined hydrogen atoms shown above illustrate

    (A) surface tension

    (B) ionization

    (C) mass number

    (D) hydrogen bonding

    (E) covalent bonding

6. In the hydrogen molecule, H_2, illustrated

    (A) each atom shares its electron with the other atom

    (B) two hydrogen isotopes are attracted to each other

    (C) positively charged electrons neutralize each other

    (D) the atomic number of each of its hydrogen atoms is four

    (E) hydrogen molecules are held together by surface tension

7. The amino acids in proteins are connected by

   (A) carboxyl groups
   (B) peptide bonds
   (C) double bonds
   (D) alkyl groups
   (E) ester bonds

8. When mercuric oxide is heated, it forms metallic mercury and gaseous oxygen, a type of reaction called

   (A) synthesis
   (B) distillation
   (C) neutralization
   (D) rearrangement
   (E) decomposition

9. The chemical property called acidity is always identified with

   (A) turning phenolphthalein pink
   (B) turning litmus blue
   (C) hydroxide ions
   (D) bitter or soapy taste
   (E) the hydrogen ion

10. Different forms of a chemical element are called

    (A) anions
    (B) allotropes
    (C) ketones
    (D) buffers
    (E) cations

11. Which of the following should give you the least concern?

    (A) Carcinogens in soft drinks
    (B) Strontium 90 in dairy products
    (C) DDT in fresh vegetables
    (D) Riboflavin and niacin in bread
    (E) Herbicidal residues in vegetables

12. Atoms having the same atomic number but having different mass numbers

    (A) have the same number of protons and neutrons
    (B) have the same number of electrons and neutrons
    (C) are called isotopes
    (D) are artificially made by man and do not occur naturally
    (E) cannot be made artificially and occur naturally only

13. A solution can be exemplified by

    (A) a scattering of fine particles in water
    (B) a dispersion of sugar molecules in water
    (C) a dispersion of particles which are larger than molecules but too small to be microscopic
    (D) a dispersion in which the suspended particles eventually settle out
    (E) the immiscibility of the dispersed substances

14. When sodium chloride is dissolved in water, the separation of its ions is called

    (A) dissolution
    (B) dissociation
    (C) neutralization
    (D) adsorption
    (E) electrolysis

15. The energy liberated or consumed in exothermic and endothermic chemical processes is primarily that of

    (A) vaporization
    (B) compression
    (C) chemical bonds
    (D) catalysts
    (E) enzymes

16. In general, the rate of chemical reactions is related to

    (A) the temperature and concentration of the reacting substances
    (B) the exothermic quotient
    (C) the endothermic quotient
    (D) the availability of ions
    (E) the availability of cations

17. A substance consisting of two or more ingredients which are not in chemical combination is called

    (A) an ion
    (B) a mixture
    (C) a molecule
    (D) an oxide
    (E) a compound

18. The atoms of nonmetals tend to gain electrons, resulting in the creation of negatively charged atoms called

    (A) cations
    (B) acid-base pairs
    (C) Bronsted-Lowry ions
    (D) anions
    (E) reduced ions

19. The chemical properties of elements are determined primarily by

    (A) electrons
    (B) ions
    (C) neutrons
    (D) mesons
    (E) protons

20. Mass number represents

    (A) atomic mass expressed in grams
    (B) the number of atoms in one gram atomic mass
    (C) atomic mass
    (D) the sum of the protons and neutrons
    (E) atomic number

21. The chemical reaction:

    $$C_6H_{12}O_6 + 6O_2 \rightarrow 6CO_2 + 6H_2O$$

    represents both the oxidation of glucose when it is burned in a flame and the oxidation of glucose when it is utilized within a living cell. The oxidation reaction in either example involves the

    (A) gain of electrons by atoms being reduced
    (B) loss of electrons by the atoms being oxidized
    (C) gain of electrons by the oxidizing agent
    (D) loss of electrons by the reducing agent
    (E) all of the above

Questions 22 and 23

According to Boyle's law, the pressure and volume of a confined gas are inversely proportional. As a consequence, the product of the pressure and the volume of a gas are constant at a given temperature, i.e., PV = constant.

22. If the pressure of a volume of a gas is halved

    (A) its volume is halved
    (B) its volume is doubled
    (C) its volume remains constant
    (D) its volume decreases according to a geometric progression
    (E) its volume increases according to a geometric progression

23. Which of the following illustrates the pressure-volume relationship for a gas?

   (*P* = pressure and *V* = volume)

(A)

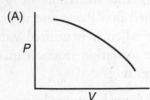

(B)

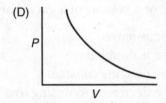

(C)

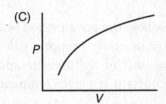

(D)

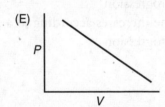

(E)

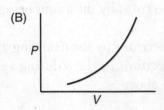

24. The family of chemical elements commonly referred to as the noble gases is characterized chiefly by the fact that its members

   (A) form salts when they combine with metals
   (B) react violently with water
   (C) are inert
   (D) appear on the far left of the periodic table
   (E) exist as diatomic molecules

25. Substances with identical chemical formulas but with different physical and chemical properties are called

   (A) ethers
   (B) ions
   (C) polymers
   (D) esters
   (E) isomers

26. Which chemical element is found in all proteins?

   (A) Sulfur
   (B) Potassium
   (C) Phosphorus
   (D) Manganese
   (E) Nitrogen

27. The atomic number of an element means

   (A) the number of electrons in its nucleus
   (B) the number of neutrons in its nucleus
   (C) the sum of its electrons and neutrons
   (D) the number of protons in its nucleus
   (E) the number of protons in its orbits

28. In the chemical reaction

$$2C_6H_{12}O_6 \rightarrow C_{12}H_{22}O_{11} + H_2O$$

   a disaccharide sugar is formed. This kind of reaction is called

   (A) condensation
   (B) the dark reaction
   (C) oxidation
   (D) the light reaction
   (E) reduction

29. When the disaccharide sugar in the equation above undergoes digestion

   (A) water and CO_2 are the end products
   (B) energy is stored
   (C) water is consumed
   (D) water is the end product
   (E) condensation occurs

30. The family of nonmetallic chemical elements known as the halogens includes

    (A) silicon
    (B) fluorine
    (C) nitrogen
    (D) oxygen
    (E) lithium

31. The chemistry of plastics could well be called the chemistry of

    (A) synergy
    (B) the halogen family
    (C) detergents
    (D) polymers
    (E) biodegradability

32. The smallest existing particle of any chemically pure compound is the

    (A) electron
    (B) proton
    (C) nucleus
    (D) ion
    (E) molecule

33. The changing of one atom into another is called

    (A) ionization
    (B) radiography
    (C) nuclear fusion
    (D) transmutation
    (E) transduction

34. In the process called respiration, which occurs in all living cells, carbon atoms gain oxygen and glucose is

    (A) dissolved
    (B) oxidized
    (C) reduced
    (D) precipitated
    (E) catalyzed

35. $CuO + H_2 \rightarrow Cu + H_2O$

    In the chemical reaction shown above

    (A) H_2 is the oxidizing agent
    (B) CuO is the reducing agent
    (C) H_2 is the catalyst
    (D) CuO acts as a catalyst
    (E) CuO acts as an oxidizing agent

36. An element's atomic mass is

    (A) the total weight of its electrons
    (B) dependent upon uniform temperatures
    (C) its weight relative to that of the carbon-12 atom
    (D) determined by the number of protons in its nucleus
    (E) expressed in grams

Answers

1. **(A)** Half-life is the time in which half of the atoms of a radioactive material will decay.

2. **(D)** In electrolysis, an electric current is passed through a liquid causing a chemical reaction. In industry, sodium may be produced (purified) by the electrolysis of liquid sodium chloride.

3. **(B)** According to Boyle's law, the volume of a gas is inversely proportional to the pressure.

4. **(C)** Alkali metals are very reactive, readily giving up one electron to form ions.

5. **(E)** } A covalent bond occurs when two atoms share a pair of electrons.
6. **(A)** }

7. **(B)** Proteins are composed of amino acids which are united or held together by the C—N—C linkage, commonly called the peptide linkage.

8. **(E)** Heat causes mercuric oxide bonds to break down, thereby permitting the component elements to separate without entering into other compounds— literally, a decomposing of the molecule due to heat.

9. **(E)** Acids are substances whose water solutions contain an excess of hydrogen ions.

10. **(B)** Chemical elements often exist in different forms and these are called allotrophs.

11. **(D)** Riboflavin and niacin are vitamins; all of the other substances listed are hazardous to health.

12. **(C)** Atoms of any element that differ in the number of neutrons in their nucleus are different in mass and are called isotopes.

13. **(B)** Homogenous mixtures have the same composition at the microscopic level throughout. When the dispersed particles are on a molecular scale the mixture is referred to as a solution.

14. **(B)** Dissociation is the separation of the ions of a salt, such as sodium chloride, when it dissolves in water.

15. **(C)** Energy transformations in chemical reactions are concerned with the energy of chemical bonds. Energy loss may be due to the formation of chemical bonds, or energy may be added to break the chemical bonds.

16. **(A)** The rates of chemical reactions are controlled by only a few factors, the most common being the concentrations of the reactants, the temperature, the nature of the reactants, and catalysts.

17. **(B)** A mixture is any portion of matter consisting of two or more substances which can be separated from each other by physical means, i.e., without reacting to form new substances.

18. **(D)** An ion is an atom or a group of atoms functioning as a unit and carrying an electrical charge. Those with positive charges are called cations, those with negative charges anions.

19. **(A)** The chemical properties of elements are an expression of their attraction to or their repulsion from other elements, based primarily on circumstances pertaining to their electrons.

20. **(D)** Mass number is the total number of neutrons and protons in the atom's nucleus.

21. **(E)** In oxidation-reduction reactions a transfer of electrons is involved. Atoms that gain electrons are reduced and atoms that lose electrons are oxidized. The atoms giving up electrons are called reducing agents and the atoms receiving electrons are called oxidizing agents.

22. **(B)** ⎫ According to Boyle's law, the pressure and the volume of a confined gas are
23. **(D)** ⎭ inversely proportional.

24. **(C)** Noble gases are extremely stable and undergo reaction only under rigorous conditions. The first noble gas compound was not prepared until 1962, and, prior to this, it was thought that noble gases were chemically inert.

25. **(E)** Isomers are chemical compounds that have the same number of atoms of the same elements, but differ in structural arrangements and properties.

26. **(E)** Nitrogen is found in all amino acids and, hence, in all proteins.

27. **(D)** The atomic number of an element is the number of protons in its nucleus.

28. **(A)** Disaccharides form by the joining of two monosaccharide units in a condensation reaction in which a molecule of water is split out.

29. **(C)** Disaccharides can react with water in the presence of a catalyst to form monosaccharides. This is digestion and a water-consuming reaction.

30. **(B)** Halogens include fluorine, chlorine, bromine, etc.

31. **(D)** Polymers are molecules composed of two or more small and repeated units that are chemically bonded together. They may be linear, branched, or three-dimensional. Plastic materials are polymers.

32. **(E)** The molecule cannot be further broken down without destroying it and changing its characteristics.

33. **(D)** The concept that atoms (elements) may be changed from one to another is called transmutation.

34. **(B)** When any elements or compounds combine with oxygen they are said to be oxidized. This involves the loss of hydrogen, the loss of electrons.

35. **(E)** In the example given, CuO provides the oxygen that causes H_2 to be oxidized, that is, combined with oxygen. Therefore, CuO is the oxidizing agent and H_2 is the reducing agent.

36. **(C)** An atom's mass is a characteristic of a particular element and the atoms of each element have their own specific atomic mass. Carbon-12 has been assigned an atomic mass of 12; the atoms of all the other elements are assigned atomic masses relative to the atomic mass of the isotope of carbon.

QUESTIONS ABOUT THE HISTORY OF SCIENCE

Directions: Each of the questions or incomplete statements below is followed by five suggested answers or completions. Select the one that is best in each case.

1. The philosopher from Thracé famous for his atomic theory was

   (A) Aristotle
   (B) Democritus
   (C) Thales
   (D) Theophrastus
   (E) Empedocles

2. That living organisms have evolved was first theorized by

   (A) Lamarck
   (B) ancient Greek philosophers
   (C) Darwin and Wallace
   (D) Romans in the first century B.C.
   (E) the geologist Charles Lyell

3. A famous anatomist during the Renaissance was

   (A) Linnaeus
   (B) Michelangelo
   (C) Pliny
   (D) Bacon
   (E) Galen

4. A Roman naturalist, literary man, and government worker who composed an encyclopedia called "Historia Naturalis" ("Natural History") was

   (A) Lucretius
   (B) Galen
   (C) Celsus
   (D) Pliny the Elder
   (E) Dioecorides

5. A pupil of Thales, one of the earliest Greek scholars to be concerned with human evolution, and one who believed in transmutations as a cause of diversity was

   (A) Anaximander
   (B) Galen
   (C) Heraclitus
   (D) Pliny
   (E) Empedocles

6. A stimulus which influenced the thinking of both Darwin and Wallace was

   (A) Lyell's *Principles of Geology*
   (B) Malthus' writing on population
   (C) Lucretius' poem "De Rerum Natura"
   (D) Lamarck's *Philosophie Zoologique*
   (E) the writings of Aristotle

7. The ancient Greek scholar who became the "father of medicine" was

   (A) Aristotle
   (B) Theophrastus
   (C) Alemaeon
   (D) Hippocrates
   (E) Empedocles

8. The 365-day calendar was first proposed by

   (A) Pythagoras
   (B) Archimedes
   (C) the Babylonians
   (D) the Egyptians
   (E) the Greeks

9. The field of immunization had its beginning with the work of

   (A) Lister
   (B) Jenner
   (C) Koch
   (D) Pasteur
   (E) Ehrlich

10. According to Ptolemy,

    (A) the sun is the center of the solar system
    (B) the earth is round, with a circumference of 24,000 miles
    (C) the universe is infinite
    (D) the earth is a flat, floating disc
    (E) the earth is the center of the solar system

11. The concept advocating the particulate or atomic structure of matter was first proposed by

    (A) Theophrastus
    (B) Democritus
    (C) Pliny
    (D) Aristotle
    (E) Plato

12. A highly significant contribution of Isaac Newton was his

    (A) heliocentric theory
    (B) universal law of gravitation
    (C) concept of the atom
    (D) photon theory of light energy
    (E) phlogiston theory

13. Who was the earliest Greek scholar to hold that the entire universe is subject to natural law?

    (A) Aristotle
    (B) Thales
    (C) Anaximander
    (D) Theophrastus
    (E) Empedocles

14. The recording of eclipses was first undertaken by the

    (A) Babylonians
    (B) Egyptians
    (C) Greeks
    (D) Chinese
    (E) Romans

15. Sterile and antiseptic surgical procedures were introduced by

    (A) Fleming
    (B) Semmelweis
    (C) Banting
    (D) Lister
    (E) Gorgas

16. The first to show that a connection exists between electricity and magnetism was

    (A) Henri Becquerel
    (B) Michael Faraday
    (C) Guglielmo Marconi
    (D) Benjamin Franklin
    (E) Han Christian Oersted

17. An early Greek physician whose writings considered medical ethics was

    (A) Galen
    (B) Hippocrates
    (C) Anaximander
    (D) Aristotle
    (E) Theophrastus

18. The Greek scholar who was the first to relate fossils to living plants and animals was

    (A) Anaximander
    (B) Theophrastus
    (C) Empedocles
    (D) Xenophanes
    (E) Aristotle

Answers

1. **(B)** Democritus was one of the first Greeks to advocate the atomic theory.

2. **(B)** The early Greek philosophers Anaximander and Xenophanes formulated ideas concerning the origins of life and evolution.

3. **(B)** Michelangelo made dissections of human internal structures so as to represent the features accurately and in proper relation to each other. His statues give evidence of his knowledge of human anatomy.

4. **(D)** Pliny the Elder (A.D. 23–79) compiled a comprehensive encyclopedia called "Natural History."

5. **(A)** Anaximander proposed that humans evolved.

6. **(B)** Malthus' writing on population presented the theme that humans multiply more rapidly than does food supply, thereby creating conditions for the competition for existence.

7. **(D)** The "Hippocratic Oath" honors Hippocrates as the "father of medicine."

8. **(D)** The Egyptians first proposed the 365-day calendar.

9. **(B)** Jenner was not the first to use vaccinations, but he developed the practicality and usefulness of the procedure.

10. **(E)** Ptolemy developed a model of the universe that accounted for the movements of the planets in circular orbits around a motionless earth.

11. **(B)** Democritus' greatest contribution was his atomic theory, which held that the universe consists of atoms moving in space with all physical change dependent upon the union and separation of atoms.

12. **(B)** Newton was the first person to recognize gravity as a universal force relative to both "the falling apple" and the orbits of the planets.

13. **(B)** Thales supported both the concept of rational inquiry into nature and the school of thought that presumed that the entire universe is controlled by natural law.

14. **(A)** Earliest written records, found in Babylonia and Mesopotamia, describe eclipses and other astronomical events inscribed in the clay and stone tablets of the time.

15. **(D)** Prior to Lister, most surgical procedures were complicated by infection. Lister devised methods of sterilizing the operating room and its equipment by spraying carbolic acid over the hands of the surgeons and the immediate surroundings while the surgery was in progress.

16. **(E)** Oersted was first to demonstate the connection between electricity and magnetism and was the first to propose the principle on which the electric motor is based.

17. **(B)** Hippocrates is called the "father of medicine." His professional writings, entitled "The Law," "The Physician," and "Oath," describe the contemporary attributes and ethics of Greek medicine and of the physicians who practiced it.

18. **(D)** Xenophanes was the first Greek scholar to compare fossils to living organisms.

Natural Sciences

ANSWER SHEET—SAMPLE EXAMINATION 1

1 Ⓐ Ⓑ Ⓒ Ⓓ Ⓔ	31 Ⓐ Ⓑ Ⓒ Ⓓ Ⓔ	61 Ⓐ Ⓑ Ⓒ Ⓓ Ⓔ	91 Ⓐ Ⓑ Ⓒ Ⓓ Ⓔ
2 Ⓐ Ⓑ Ⓒ Ⓓ Ⓔ	32 Ⓐ Ⓑ Ⓒ Ⓓ Ⓔ	62 Ⓐ Ⓑ Ⓒ Ⓓ Ⓔ	92 Ⓐ Ⓑ Ⓒ Ⓓ Ⓔ
3 Ⓐ Ⓑ Ⓒ Ⓓ Ⓔ	33 Ⓐ Ⓑ Ⓒ Ⓓ Ⓔ	63 Ⓐ Ⓑ Ⓒ Ⓓ Ⓔ	93 Ⓐ Ⓑ Ⓒ Ⓓ Ⓔ
4 Ⓐ Ⓑ Ⓒ Ⓓ Ⓔ	34 Ⓐ Ⓑ Ⓒ Ⓓ Ⓔ	64 Ⓐ Ⓑ Ⓒ Ⓓ Ⓔ	94 Ⓐ Ⓑ Ⓒ Ⓓ Ⓔ
5 Ⓐ Ⓑ Ⓒ Ⓓ Ⓔ	35 Ⓐ Ⓑ Ⓒ Ⓓ Ⓔ	65 Ⓐ Ⓑ Ⓒ Ⓓ Ⓔ	95 Ⓐ Ⓑ Ⓒ Ⓓ Ⓔ
6 Ⓐ Ⓑ Ⓒ Ⓓ Ⓔ	36 Ⓐ Ⓑ Ⓒ Ⓓ Ⓔ	66 Ⓐ Ⓑ Ⓒ Ⓓ Ⓔ	96 Ⓐ Ⓑ Ⓒ Ⓓ Ⓔ
7 Ⓐ Ⓑ Ⓒ Ⓓ Ⓔ	37 Ⓐ Ⓑ Ⓒ Ⓓ Ⓔ	67 Ⓐ Ⓑ Ⓒ Ⓓ Ⓔ	97 Ⓐ Ⓑ Ⓒ Ⓓ Ⓔ
8 Ⓐ Ⓑ Ⓒ Ⓓ Ⓔ	38 Ⓐ Ⓑ Ⓒ Ⓓ Ⓔ	68 Ⓐ Ⓑ Ⓒ Ⓓ Ⓔ	98 Ⓐ Ⓑ Ⓒ Ⓓ Ⓔ
9 Ⓐ Ⓑ Ⓒ Ⓓ Ⓔ	39 Ⓐ Ⓑ Ⓒ Ⓓ Ⓔ	69 Ⓐ Ⓑ Ⓒ Ⓓ Ⓔ	99 Ⓐ Ⓑ Ⓒ Ⓓ Ⓔ
10 Ⓐ Ⓑ Ⓒ Ⓓ Ⓔ	40 Ⓐ Ⓑ Ⓒ Ⓓ Ⓔ	70 Ⓐ Ⓑ Ⓒ Ⓓ Ⓔ	100 Ⓐ Ⓑ Ⓒ Ⓓ Ⓔ
11 Ⓐ Ⓑ Ⓒ Ⓓ Ⓔ	41 Ⓐ Ⓑ Ⓒ Ⓓ Ⓔ	71 Ⓐ Ⓑ Ⓒ Ⓓ Ⓔ	101 Ⓐ Ⓑ Ⓒ Ⓓ Ⓔ
12 Ⓐ Ⓑ Ⓒ Ⓓ Ⓔ	42 Ⓐ Ⓑ Ⓒ Ⓓ Ⓔ	72 Ⓐ Ⓑ Ⓒ Ⓓ Ⓔ	102 Ⓐ Ⓑ Ⓒ Ⓓ Ⓔ
13 Ⓐ Ⓑ Ⓒ Ⓓ Ⓔ	43 Ⓐ Ⓑ Ⓒ Ⓓ Ⓔ	73 Ⓐ Ⓑ Ⓒ Ⓓ Ⓔ	103 Ⓐ Ⓑ Ⓒ Ⓓ Ⓔ
14 Ⓐ Ⓑ Ⓒ Ⓓ Ⓔ	44 Ⓐ Ⓑ Ⓒ Ⓓ Ⓔ	74 Ⓐ Ⓑ Ⓒ Ⓓ Ⓔ	104 Ⓐ Ⓑ Ⓒ Ⓓ Ⓔ
15 Ⓐ Ⓑ Ⓒ Ⓓ Ⓔ	45 Ⓐ Ⓑ Ⓒ Ⓓ Ⓔ	75 Ⓐ Ⓑ Ⓒ Ⓓ Ⓔ	105 Ⓐ Ⓑ Ⓒ Ⓓ Ⓔ
16 Ⓐ Ⓑ Ⓒ Ⓓ Ⓔ	46 Ⓐ Ⓑ Ⓒ Ⓓ Ⓔ	76 Ⓐ Ⓑ Ⓒ Ⓓ Ⓔ	106 Ⓐ Ⓑ Ⓒ Ⓓ Ⓔ
17 Ⓐ Ⓑ Ⓒ Ⓓ Ⓔ	47 Ⓐ Ⓑ Ⓒ Ⓓ Ⓔ	77 Ⓐ Ⓑ Ⓒ Ⓓ Ⓔ	107 Ⓐ Ⓑ Ⓒ Ⓓ Ⓔ
18 Ⓐ Ⓑ Ⓒ Ⓓ Ⓔ	48 Ⓐ Ⓑ Ⓒ Ⓓ Ⓔ	78 Ⓐ Ⓑ Ⓒ Ⓓ Ⓔ	108 Ⓐ Ⓑ Ⓒ Ⓓ Ⓔ
19 Ⓐ Ⓑ Ⓒ Ⓓ Ⓔ	49 Ⓐ Ⓑ Ⓒ Ⓓ Ⓔ	79 Ⓐ Ⓑ Ⓒ Ⓓ Ⓔ	109 Ⓐ Ⓑ Ⓒ Ⓓ Ⓔ
20 Ⓐ Ⓑ Ⓒ Ⓓ Ⓔ	50 Ⓐ Ⓑ Ⓒ Ⓓ Ⓔ	80 Ⓐ Ⓑ Ⓒ Ⓓ Ⓔ	110 Ⓐ Ⓑ Ⓒ Ⓓ Ⓔ
21 Ⓐ Ⓑ Ⓒ Ⓓ Ⓔ	51 Ⓐ Ⓑ Ⓒ Ⓓ Ⓔ	81 Ⓐ Ⓑ Ⓒ Ⓓ Ⓔ	111 Ⓐ Ⓑ Ⓒ Ⓓ Ⓔ
22 Ⓐ Ⓑ Ⓒ Ⓓ Ⓔ	52 Ⓐ Ⓑ Ⓒ Ⓓ Ⓔ	82 Ⓐ Ⓑ Ⓒ Ⓓ Ⓔ	112 Ⓐ Ⓑ Ⓒ Ⓓ Ⓔ
23 Ⓐ Ⓑ Ⓒ Ⓓ Ⓔ	53 Ⓐ Ⓑ Ⓒ Ⓓ Ⓔ	83 Ⓐ Ⓑ Ⓒ Ⓓ Ⓔ	113 Ⓐ Ⓑ Ⓒ Ⓓ Ⓔ
24 Ⓐ Ⓑ Ⓒ Ⓓ Ⓔ	54 Ⓐ Ⓑ Ⓒ Ⓓ Ⓔ	84 Ⓐ Ⓑ Ⓒ Ⓓ Ⓔ	114 Ⓐ Ⓑ Ⓒ Ⓓ Ⓔ
25 Ⓐ Ⓑ Ⓒ Ⓓ Ⓔ	55 Ⓐ Ⓑ Ⓒ Ⓓ Ⓔ	85 Ⓐ Ⓑ Ⓒ Ⓓ Ⓔ	115 Ⓐ Ⓑ Ⓒ Ⓓ Ⓔ
26 Ⓐ Ⓑ Ⓒ Ⓓ Ⓔ	56 Ⓐ Ⓑ Ⓒ Ⓓ Ⓔ	86 Ⓐ Ⓑ Ⓒ Ⓓ Ⓔ	116 Ⓐ Ⓑ Ⓒ Ⓓ Ⓔ
27 Ⓐ Ⓑ Ⓒ Ⓓ Ⓔ	57 Ⓐ Ⓑ Ⓒ Ⓓ Ⓔ	87 Ⓐ Ⓑ Ⓒ Ⓓ Ⓔ	117 Ⓐ Ⓑ Ⓒ Ⓓ Ⓔ
28 Ⓐ Ⓑ Ⓒ Ⓓ Ⓔ	58 Ⓐ Ⓑ Ⓒ Ⓓ Ⓔ	88 Ⓐ Ⓑ Ⓒ Ⓓ Ⓔ	118 Ⓐ Ⓑ Ⓒ Ⓓ Ⓔ
29 Ⓐ Ⓑ Ⓒ Ⓓ Ⓔ	59 Ⓐ Ⓑ Ⓒ Ⓓ Ⓔ	89 Ⓐ Ⓑ Ⓒ Ⓓ Ⓔ	119 Ⓐ Ⓑ Ⓒ Ⓓ Ⓔ
30 Ⓐ Ⓑ Ⓒ Ⓓ Ⓔ	60 Ⓐ Ⓑ Ⓒ Ⓓ Ⓔ	90 Ⓐ Ⓑ Ⓒ Ⓓ Ⓔ	120 Ⓐ Ⓑ Ⓒ Ⓓ Ⓔ

This chapter has three sample CLEP natural sciences examinations. Each examination is followed by an answer key, scoring chart, and answer explanations.

SAMPLE NATURAL SCIENCES EXAMINATION 1

NUMBER OF QUESTIONS: 120

Time: 90 MINUTES

Directions: Each of the questions or incomplete statements below is followed by five suggested answers or completions. Select the one that is best in each case.

1. The smallest and least complex unit of living matter is the

    (A) electron
    (B) atom
    (C) organelle
    (D) cell
    (E) molecule

2. Homologous structures, such as the anterior pairs of appendages of vertebrates, are modified for various functions such as flying, swimming, etc. This is called

    (A) mutations
    (B) parallel evolution
    (C) convergent evolution
    (D) adaptive radiation
    (E) metamorphosis

3. If a living cell is placed in an isotonic fluid, there will be

  (A) a net movement of water molecules into the cell
  (B) an increase in turgidity
  (C) no net movement of water molecules into or out of the cell
  (D) a decrease in cell turgidity
  (E) a net movement of water molecules out of the cell

4. Which one of the following factors does *not* influence enzyme activity?

  (A) Temperature
  (B) pH
  (C) Humidity
  (D) Inhibitors
  (E) Concentration

5. Heterotrophs

  (A) utilize radiant energy
  (B) cannot synthesize organic materials from inorganic substances
  (C) are food synthesizers
  (D) oxidize inorganic materials
  (E) synthesize organic materials from inorganic substances

6. The process by which living cell membranes use energy to move ions and molecules into and out of cells, when this cannot be explained by diffusion, is called

  (A) osmosis
  (B) transpiration
  (C) absorption
  (D) imbibition
  (E) active transport

7. A niacin deficiency may best be relieved by enriching the diet with

  (A) eggs and dairy products
  (B) fresh green vegetables
  (C) fresh fruits
  (D) animal products
  (E) citrus fruits

8. Cellular respiration

  (A) stores energy
  (B) uses oxygen and organic compounds as raw materials
  (C) increases dry weight
  (D) occurs only in the presence of radiant energy
  (E) uses carbon dioxide and water as raw materials

9. The movement of genes from one part of a population to another as a result of migration and interbreeding is called

  (A) genetic drift
  (B) gene flow
  (C) natural selection
  (D) directional selection
  (E) nonrandom mating

10. Plants grown in the dark become

  (A) plasmolyzed
  (B) asphyxiated
  (C) synergistic
  (D) etiolated
  (E) parthenocarpic

11. In plants, water is normally conducted upward by a tissue called the

  (A) phloem
  (B) cortex
  (C) cuticle
  (D) pith
  (E) xylem

12. A condition of the human body in which the chemical and physical internal environment is favorable for cellular activities is

  (A) osmotic equilibrium
  (B) chemostasis
  (C) analogous balance
  (D) homeostasis
  (E) neural equilibrium

13. Primitive plants having neither vascular tissues nor multicellular embryos are called

    (A) bryophytes
    (B) thallophytes
    (C) pteridophytes
    (D) spermatophytes
    (E) xerophytes

14. Plants basic in many food chains are

    (A) fungi
    (B) bryophytes
    (C) gymnosperms
    (D) pteridophytes
    (E) algae

15. The first step in the formation of a blood clot is the disintegration of platelets and the release of

    (A) thrombin
    (B) fibrinogen
    (C) fibrin
    (D) thromboplastin
    (E) prothrombin

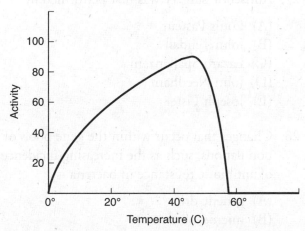

The illustration above represents enzyme activity as a function of temperature.

16. One may conclude, on the basis of the above illustration, that enzymatic activity

    (A) is greatest at 60°C
    (B) is stopped by temperatures above 60°C
    (C) is not affected by temperature
    (D) is independent of temperature
    (E) is greatest at 20°C

17. If you have type A blood, agglutination tests will reveal that

    (A) type A serum will clump part of the time
    (B) type B serum clumps
    (C) both type A and B sera will clump
    (D) type A serum clumps
    (E) neither type A nor type B sera will clump

18. A common enteric bacterium, *Escherichia coli*, is used as a standard to identify water contaminated by sewage, is often identified as the pathogen causing food-borne diseases, and

    (A) is the organism used in a citric acid fermentation
    (B) is the organism used in preparing rabies vaccine
    (C) is the organism of choice for cleaning up toxic wastes
    (D) is one of the organisms suitable for and subjected to genetic engineering techiques
    (E) is the recognized pathogen responsible for vascular wilting diseases of vegetables

19. Nerve impulses from sensory receptors are conducted to the central nervous system

    (A) through the ventral root ganglion
    (B) along a motor neuron
    (C) through the dorsal root ganglion
    (D) through a Doric valve
    (E) across a synapse between connector and motor neurons

20. The transmission of genetic information from one generation to the next requires

    (A) replication of DNA molecules
    (B) replication of RNA molecules
    (C) replication of messenger RNA molecules
    (D) replication of all forms of nucleic acid
    (E) replication of the protein portion of nucleoproteins

21. Transpiration benefits plants by

    (A) assisting in the upward translocation of dissolved minerals
    (B) assisting in the upward translocation of organic substances
    (C) assisting in the downward translocation of organic substances
    (D) helping the plant to retain heat
    (E) maintaining a constant root pressure

22. What is the expected hereditary result of matings involving the interaction of multiple, incompletely dominant genes?

    (A) Inbreeding
    (B) Blending of the involved traits
    (C) Hybridization
    (D) Segregation
    (E) Independent assortment

23. In the prophase of the first meiotic division,

    (A) dyads of chromatids appear following synapsis
    (B) cell plate formation is initiated
    (C) the centriole reappears
    (D) the chromosome number is haploid
    (E) tetrads of chromatids appear following synapsis

24. Floods and fires repeatedly destroyed all life on earth, but acts of special creation repopulated the earth: this doctrine was called

    (A) catastrophism
    (B) adaptation
    (C) uniformitarianism
    (D) natural selection
    (E) Lamarckianism

25. A farmer sprays his crop with a new insecticide that annihilates all but a few of the target population of insects. He continues to use the insecticide and several years later notices the population is back in full force, but the insecticide has little to no effect on the same target population. This is an example of

    (A) natural selection
    (B) genetic selection
    (C) directional selection
    (D) constant selection
    (E) selective breeding

26. The mutation theory was proposed by De Vries to explain abrupt changes in inheritance patterns which

    (A) result from hybridization
    (B) breed true
    (C) do not breed true in subsequent generations
    (D) are environmentally induced
    (E) are based on mitotic errors

27. Antiseptic surgery was first performed by

    (A) Louis Pasteur
    (B) John Tyndall
    (C) Lazaro Spallanzani
    (D) John Needham
    (E) Joseph Lister

28. Changes that occur within the gene pools of populations, such as the increasing incidence of antibiotic resistance in bacteria is

    (A) genetic drift
    (B) microevolution
    (C) macroevolution
    (D) anagenesis
    (E) biogenesis

29. What was Aristotle's greatest contribution to science?

    (A) The theory of the four humors
    (B) The scientific method
    (C) The theory of evolution
    (D) The study of anatomy and medicine
    (E) The atomic theory

30. The basic physiological reaction of vision is

    (A) physical
    (B) chemical
    (C) analgesic
    (D) ketogenic
    (E) electrical

31. Marine organisms found between the limits of high and low tide exist in the

    (A) neritic zone
    (B) abyssal zone
    (C) zone of perpetual darkness
    (D) bathyal zone
    (E) littoral zone

32. Most of the photosynthesis in the oceans is carried out by

    (A) green algae
    (B) blue-green algae
    (C) brown algae
    (D) red algae
    (E) diatoms

33. When corresponding structures of different species are based on similarities in function only, they are said to be

    (A) homologous
    (B) divergent
    (C) parallel
    (D) convergent
    (E) analogous

34. A mutually beneficial interrelationship between living organisms is called

    (A) speciation
    (B) metamorphosis
    (C) symbiosis
    (D) epigenesis
    (E) commensalism

35. The time period described as the age of reptiles is the

    (A) Ordovician period
    (B) Proterozoic Era
    (C) Mesozoic Era
    (D) Cenozoic Era
    (E) Miocene epoch

36. In the digestive system of humans, the stomach-produced enzyme rennin splits the

    (A) ester bond of fats
    (B) phosphate esters of DNA
    (C) peptide bonds of trypsinogen
    (D) phosphate esters of RNA
    (E) peptide bonds in casein

37. Rodent control is necessary to prevent outbreaks of the following bacterial disease:

    (A) psitticosis
    (B) amebiasis
    (C) plague
    (D) typhoid fever
    (E) polio

38. If a couple has three sons, what is the probability that the fourth child will be a daughter?

    (A) 1/16
    (B) 1/8
    (C) 1/4
    (D) 1/2
    (E) 3/4

39. In matings involving individuals that are heterozygous for "A," the genotypes produced would be

    (A) 1/8 *AA*, 3/4 *Aa*, 1/8 *aa*
    (B) 3/8 *AA*, 1/4 *Aa*, 3/8 *aa*
    (C) 1/3 *AA*, 1/3 *Aa*, 1/3 *aa*
    (D) 1/4 *AA*, 1/2 *Aa*, 1/4 *aa*
    (E) 1/2 *Aa*, 1/2 *aa*

40. The frequency of crossing-over between two linked genes is

    (A) controlled by sex chromosomes
    (B) controlled by the law of independent assortment
    (C) controlled by the Hardy-Weinberg Law
    (D) inversely proportional to the distance separating them
    (E) directly proportional to the distance separating them

41. An antigen stimulates the production of

    (A) blood groups
    (B) platelets
    (C) toxins
    (D) an antibody
    (E) Rh

42. Addition of detergents containing phosphates can disturb aquatic ecosystems because the phosphates

    (A) kill bacteria
    (B) poison fish
    (C) stimulate algae growth
    (D) fertilize crop plants
    (E) form deposits in rock

Questions 43–46

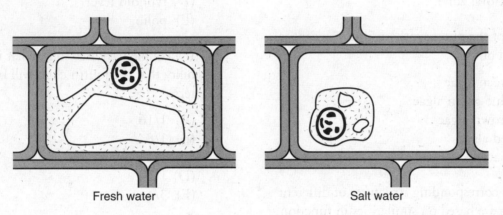

Fresh water   Salt water

The plant cells diagrammed above are located in fresh water and in salt water, respectively, as indicated.

43. Water has moved out of the cell in salt water by a process called

    (A) diffusion
    (B) imbibition
    (C) capillarity
    (D) adhesion
    (E) plasmolysis

44. The cell in fresh water is "plump" with water, a condition referred to as

    (A) rigid
    (B) plasmolyzed
    (C) saturated
    (D) hydrolyzed
    (E) turgid

45. The condition of the cell in the salt water is a result of

    (A) the flow of water out of the cell
    (B) a net movement of water out of the cell
    (C) salt pulling the water out of the cell
    (D) the forces of imbibition
    (E) the force called cohesion

46. In the case of the cell in fresh water

    (A) nothing is able to move into the cell
    (B) adhesive forces hold water in the vacuoles
    (C) the vacuoles continue to lose and to take in water by diffusion
    (D) the cell walls are impermeable to water
    (E) the cell walls are impermeable to salt

47. The figure below shows a food chain. Assume that there are 1,000 units of energy available at the level of the grasses. How much energy will be available by the time the coyote consumes its prey?

   (A) 999 units
   (B) 900 units
   (C) 90 units
   (D) 9 units
   (E) 1 unit

48. Stems increase in diameter mainly because of cell division by the

   (A) cork cambium
   (B) endodermis
   (C) medullary rays
   (D) cortex
   (E) vascular cambium

49. The evaporation of water from the aerial surfaces of plants is called

   (A) translocation
   (B) hydrotropism
   (C) hydroponics
   (D) aquaculture
   (E) transpiration

50. Adrenaline

   (A) regulates potassium metabolism
   (B) constricts blood vessels
   (C) controls bone growth
   (D) regulates thyroxine production
   (E) regulates the pulse rate and muscle tone

51. The primary significance of mitosis is the fact that

    (A) it is quantitative
    (B) the chromosome number is increased
    (C) it results in the production of either eggs or sperm
    (D) the chromosome number is reduced
    (E) it is qualitative

52. The area in the retina of the human eye lacking both rods and cones is called the

    (A) alveolus
    (B) fundibulum
    (C) fovea
    (D) blind spot
    (E) cornea

53. During the initial stages of blood clot formation, blood platelets require

    (A) calcium ions
    (B) the antihemophilic factor
    (C) thrombin
    (D) prothrombin
    (E) cytochrome

54. Simple sugars are stored in the liver as

    (A) glycerol
    (B) maltose
    (C) nucleotides
    (D) glycogen
    (E) casein

Directions: Each group of questions below consists of five lettered choices followed by a list of numbered phrases or sentences. For each numbered phrase or sentence select the one choice that is most closely related to it. Each choice may be used once, more than once, or not at all in each group.

Questions 55–57

    (A) Cuvier
    (B) Darwin
    (C) Lamarck
    (D) Lyell
    (E) Tyson

55. Proposed the doctrine of catastrophism

56. Suggested that the events in the geologic history of the earth were the product of the same natural forces that are active today

57. Proposed the doctrine of uniformitarianism

Questions 58–60

    (A) Cambrian period
    (B) Devonian period
    (C) Jurassic period
    (D) Carboniferous period
    (E) Tertiary period

58. A period of psilopsids, lycopsids, and seed ferns

59. The period of modern mammals and herbacious angiosperms

60. The age of the great coal swamps

Directions: Each of the questions or incomplete statements below is followed by five suggested answers or completions. Select the one that is best in each case.

61. Insofar as the earth's atmosphere is concerned, without supplemental oxygen humans are restricted to the

    (A) ionosphere
    (B) exosphere
    (C) troposphere
    (D) lithosphere
    (E) stratosphere

62. The same side of the moon is always observed from the earth because the

    (A) moon does not rotate
    (B) moon's orbit is an ellipse
    (C) moon's orbit is inclined
    (D) moon's period of rotation equals its period of revolution
    (E) moon's period of rotation is greater than its period of revolution

63. When a space vehicle is at perigee, it is at

    (A) maximum speed
    (B) minimum speed
    (C) the point farthest from the sun
    (D) a point in orbit farthest from the earth
    (E) a point in orbit closest to the earth

64. There are always two calendar days in effect except

    (A) during the summer solstice
    (B) the instant it is noon at Greenwich, England
    (C) the instant it is noon at longitude 180°
    (D) on February 29
    (E) the instant of crossing the International Dateline

65. Low offshore sand ridges that parallel coastlines are called

    (A) baymouth bars
    (B) spits
    (C) barrier islands
    (D) tombolos
    (E) drifts

66. The theory that landmasses move over the surface of the globe is called

    (A) catastrophism
    (B) plate tectonics
    (C) sedimentation
    (D) fossilization
    (E) discontinuity

67. Anhydrous chemicals are completely

    (A) combustible
    (B) without water
    (C) hydrated
    (D) inactive
    (E) without hydrogen

68. Chemical elements that follow uranium in the periodic chart and that have an atomic number higher than uranium (92) are called

    (A) transuranium elements
    (B) isotopes
    (C) transmutation elements
    (D) nucleons
    (E) curies

69. According to the quantum theory, if a quantum of energy is absorbed by an electron moving around an atom,

    (A) the absorbed energy will stimulate the electron and cause it to fluctuate between all of the atom's electron orbits
    (B) the kinetic energy of the electron will fluctuate
    (C) the electron will "descend" to an energy level closer to the atomic nucleus
    (D) the electron will remain at the same orbit energy level
    (E) the electron will move to a "higher" energy level

70. In compounds with ionic bonding

    (A) electrons are created
    (B) the attractive forces between positive and negative charges hold the atoms together
    (C) large energy input is required
    (D) attractions exceed repulsions
    (E) electrons are destroyed

71. Electron microscopes provide a greater magnification than light microscopes because

    (A) there is a laser effect
    (B) electrons travel faster than photons
    (C) their magnifications are greater
    (D) electrons have longer wavelengths than visible light
    (E) electrons have shorter wavelengths than visible light

72. Which of the following is a major advantage of using aluminum for beverage containers?

    (A) It requires very little energy to turn aluminum ore into aluminum metal.
    (B) It takes less energy to manufacture aluminum than it does to manufacture steel.
    (C) Unlike other metals, aluminum can be recycled.
    (D) Obtaining aluminum via recycling is relatively inexpensive.
    (E) There is abundant aluminum in the earth's crust.

73. If one were to observe a variety of samples of quartz, the property that would vary mostly would be

    (A) streak
    (B) density
    (C) specific gravity
    (D) color
    (E) cleavage type

74. How are rocks, ores, and minerals related to each other?

    (A) Ores are highly concentrated forms of valuable rocks.
    (B) Ores are rocks that contain valuable minerals.
    (C) Rocks are made of minerals, which exist as crystals.
    (D) Rocks are combinations of minerals, while ores are a single mineral.
    (E) Ores are combinations of minerals and rocks.

75. Which of the following is an acid?

    (A) NaCl
    (B) NH_3
    (C) $NaNO_3$
    (D) H_3PO_4
    (E) NaOH

76. Which of the following is not an acceptable statement with respect to magnetic fields?

    (A) Lines of force are unchanging.
    (B) They do not require the presence of matter.
    (C) They can penetrate wood.
    (D) They may exist in a vacuum.
    (E) They can penetrate glass.

77. The unit of measurement of electric current is the

    (A) ohm
    (B) volt
    (C) ampere
    (D) coulomb
    (E) watt

78. What are the two major metals obtained from the earth's crust, in terms of quantity?

    (A) Lead and brass
    (B) Gold and silver
    (C) Copper and silver
    (D) Iron and aluminum
    (E) Iron and gold

79. The part of the atom involved in all instances of radioactive change is the

    (A) orbit
    (B) electron
    (C) neutron
    (D) gamma ray
    (E) nucleus

80. The unusable heat energy "lost" to the environment in converting heat to work is known as

    (A) latent heat of fusion
    (B) specific heat
    (C) latent heat of vaporization
    (D) temperature
    (E) entropy

81. The faint outer atmosphere of the sun is known as the

    (A) photosphere
    (B) chromosphere
    (C) corona
    (D) sunspot layer
    (E) spicule

82. Which of the following elements would be least likely to be formed in a star?

    (A) Helium (mass number = 4)
    (B) Carbon (mass number =12)
    (C) Silicon (mass number = 28)
    (D) Iron (mass number = 56)
    (E) Gold (mass number =197)

83. In order to apply a force to one object, one must be able to

    (A) exert a force on the object
    (B) use centrifugal force
    (C) use centripetal force
    (D) overcome gravity
    (E) maintain a constant velocity

84. Energy is defined as the

    (A) rate of doing work
    (B) rate of supply of energy
    (C) capacity to accelerate
    (D) capacity to resist acceleration
    (E) capacity to do work

85. A fundamental particle of negative charge is

    (A) a proton
    (B) an electron
    (C) a neutron
    (D) a meson
    (E) a quark

86. In reference to light or sound waves, the Doppler effect occurs when

    (A) the source and the receiver are in motion relative to one another
    (B) waves are of unequal length
    (C) waves are parallel
    (D) the source and the receiver are stationary
    (E) the source and the receiver are at different temperatures

87. A self-sustaining reaction in which the first atoms to react trigger more reactions is called

    (A) a photochemical reaction
    (B) a chain reaction
    (C) an accelerator reaction
    (D) an electrical reaction
    (E) a biophysical reaction

88. The concept that equal volumes of different gases at the same temperature and pressure contain the same number of molecules is called

    (A) Boyle's law
    (B) Dalton's law
    (C) Gay-Lussac's law
    (D) Avogadro's law
    (E) Charles' law

89. The source of short, consistently timed radio bursts from neutron stars is known as a

    (A) pulsar
    (B) nebula
    (C) quasar
    (D) Red dwarf
    (E) parsec

90. For every force there is a force of reaction which is

    (A) equal and parallel
    (B) unequal and transverse
    (C) equal and transverse
    (D) equal and opposite
    (E) unequal and opposite

91. Electricity produced by a nuclear power plant

    (A) has higher voltage
    (B) has lower voltage
    (C) is radioactive
    (D) is the same as any other electricity
    (E) is direct current only

92. A temperature of 1° Celsius is equal to how many degrees Fahrenheit?

    (A) 5/9°F
    (B) 33.8°F
    (C) 1°F
    (D) −5/9°F
    (E) −33.8°F

93. Which of the following is not consistent with Dalton's atomic theory?

    (A) All matter consists of minute particles called atoms.
    (B) Atoms of a given element are alike.
    (C) Atoms are neither created nor destroyed in chemical reactions.
    (D) Atoms of different elements have the same weight but different electrical charges.
    (E) Typically, atoms combine in small numbers to form chemical compounds.

94. The efficiency of machines is always reduced by

    (A) temperature
    (B) sublimation
    (C) momentum
    (D) friction
    (E) refraction

95. Valence is

    (A) a bundle or quantum of energy
    (B) a measure of acidity
    (C) a measure of alkalinity
    (D) the combining capacity of an ion
    (E) the energy used in doing work

96. Chemical elements classified in the halogen family are commonly referred to as

    (A) noble gases
    (B) inert gases
    (C) alkaline earths
    (D) salt formers
    (E) heavy metals

97. Substances that increase the rate of chemical reactions are called

    (A) ions
    (B) isotopes
    (C) catalysts
    (D) neutralizers
    (E) bases

98. Of the four known forces in the universe, the strong force

    (A) is a force of repulsion
    (B) holds the particles inside the atomic nucleus together
    (C) causes the sun to shine
    (D) holds atoms and molecules together
    (E) produces radioactivity

99. Separation of the components in liquid solution by distillation is dependent upon

    (A) varying solubilities
    (B) heat of solidification
    (C) adsorption
    (D) differences in volatility
    (E) absorption

100. When an acid and a base are brought together in a solution, the hydrogen ions (H^+) of the acid combine with the hydroxide ions (OH^-) of the base to form a salt in a type of chemical reaction called

    (A) condensation
    (B) hydrolysis
    (C) reduction
    (D) oxidation
    (E) neutralization

101. Chemical formulas enable us to determine the kind and number of atoms in a compound, each element's percentage, and

    (A) the number and kinds of isotopes
    (B) its physical properties
    (C) its nuclear reactions
    (D) its half-life
    (E) its molar mass

102. Thermosetting plastics polymerize irreversibly under conditions of

    (A) freezing
    (B) bonding
    (C) volitilization
    (D) heat or pressure
    (E) crystallization

103. By A.D. 1000, when western Europe was beginning to emerge from the Dark Ages, intellectual development was hindered because

    (A) most Arabic and Greek knowledge had been lost
    (B) scientists hesitated to experiment
    (C) alchemy was supreme
    (D) there were formal centers of learning
    (E) the Christian Church advocated Aristotle's logic

104. Naturally radioactive elements can change to other elements with smaller masses subsequent to their emission of

    (A) gamma rays
    (B) X-rays
    (C) alpha particles[1]
    (D) beta rays
    (E) all of the above

105. In nuclear chemistry, $^{16}_{8}O$, $^{17}_{8}O$, $^{18}_{8}O$, represent

    (A) nucleons
    (B) allotropes
    (C) transmutations
    (D) isotopes
    (E) curies

106. Lines that run parallel to the equator of a planet and are identified as being north or south of the equatorial line are known as

    (A) equatorials
    (B) lines of latitude
    (C) lines of longitude
    (D) Greenwich mean time lines
    (E) meridian lines

107. In referring to wave phenomena, the term wavelength means

    (A) the bending of the direction of wave motion
    (B) the interaction of waves arriving simultaneously at the same point
    (C) the distance between crests
    (D) one-half of the distance in height between a crest and a trough
    (E) the number of crests passing a point in a given time

108. The height of transverse sound waves is expressed as

    (A) frequency
    (B) wavelength
    (C) rarefaction
    (D) modulation
    (E) amplitude

109. Einstein showed that, although energy and matter can be converted into each other,

    (A) there is more energy than matter
    (B) there is more matter than energy
    (C) the total amount of energy and matter remains constant in the universe
    (D) the total amount of energy and matter in the universe is unstable
    (E) the conversion of matter to energy requires the input of energy, which is lost

110. In medicine, the X-rays that enable physicians to photograph the skeleton make use of

    (A) radioactive rays
    (B) electron beams
    (C) kinetic energy
    (D) very-high-frequency electromagnetic waves
    (E) Brownian movement

111. Electron emission by certain heated metals is

    (A) the photoelectric effect
    (B) electromagnetic induction
    (C) commutation
    (D) the thermionic effect
    (E) transformation

112. When dissolved in water, inorganic bases produce which of these ions in greatest concentrations

    (A) sulfate ions
    (B) various ions
    (C) hydrogen ions
    (D) nitrate ions
    (E) hydroxide ions

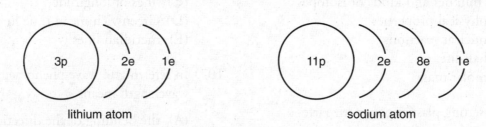

lithium atom   sodium atom

113. The diagrams above show the lithium and sodium atoms. The chemical and physical properties of lithium and sodium are similar because

    (A) both possess an uneven number of protons
    (B) each has a single electron in its outermost energy level
    (C) both possess an uneven number of electrons
    (D) both have the same atomic number
    (E) both are heavy metals

114. Christian theology and Aristotelian philosophy were reconciled in *Summa Theologica*, written by

   (A) Francis Bacon
   (B) Albertus Magnus
   (C) Roger Bacon
   (D) Thomas Aquinas
   (E) Pope Paul III

115. If the corner of a cube of sugar is placed in contact with iodine solution, the entire cube quickly becomes the color of iodine due to

   (A) capillarity
   (B) surface tension
   (C) kinetic energy
   (D) potential energy
   (E) convection

116. If one side of a solid is warmer than the other, the faster moving warm molecules collide with the cooler ones, transferring some of their energy to the slower ones. The transfer of heat energy is called

   (A) convection
   (B) radiation
   (C) adhesion
   (D) conduction
   (E) concussion

117. According to the concept of the conservation of mass, when two or more elements react chemically,

   (A) the sum of their masses equals the mass of the compound formed
   (B) the sum of their masses is less than the mass of the compound formed
   (C) the sum of their masses is greater than the mass of the compound formed
   (D) atoms may be created, modified, or destroyed
   (E) atoms may be changed from one kind to another

118. The process by which substances are separated by utilization of differences in the degree to which they are absorbed to the surface of any inert material is

   (A) fractional distillation
   (B) chromatography
   (C) filtration
   (D) neutralization
   (E) isomerism

119. The maintenance of acid-base balance is accomplished by chemical substances called

   (A) ionizers
   (B) polarizers
   (C) buffers
   (D) neutralizers
   (E) catalysts

120. The equation Cu $(OH)_2$ + H_2SO_4 → $CuSO_4$ + $2H_2O$ is an example of a reaction called

   (A) oxidation
   (B) neutralization
   (C) an exothermic reaction
   (D) a chain reaction
   (E) reduction

If there is still time remaining, you may review your answers.

Natural Sciences
ANSWER KEY—SAMPLE EXAMINATION 1

1. D	25. C	49. E	73. A	97. C
2. D	26. B	50. E	74. D	98. B
3. C	27. E	51. E	75. D	99. D
4. C	28. B	52. D	76. A	100. E
5. B	29. B	53. B	77. C	101. E
6. E	30. B	54. D	78. D	102. D
7. B	31. E	55. A	79. E	103. E
8. B	32. E	56. D	80. E	104. C
9. B	33. E	57. D	81. C	105. D
10. D	34. C	58. B	82. E	106. B
11. E	35. C	59. E	83. A	107. C
12. D	36. E	60. D	84. E	108. E
13. B	37. C	61. C	85. B	109. C
14. E	38. D	62. D	86. A	110. D
15. D	39. D	63. E	87. B	111. D
16. B	40. E	64. B	88. D	112. E
17. B	41. D	65. C	89. A	113. B
18. D	42. C	66. B	90. D	114. D
19. C	43. A	67. B	91. D	115. A
20. A	44. E	68. A	92. B	116. D
21. A	45. B	69. E	93. D	117. A
22. B	46. C	70. B	94. D	118. B
23. E	47. E	71. E	95. D	119. C
24. A	48. E	72. D	96. D	120. B

SCORING CHART

After you have scored your Sample Examination 1, enter the results in the chart below; then transfer your score to the Progress Chart on page 12.

Total Test	Number Right	Number Wrong	Number Omitted
120			

ANSWER EXPLANATIONS

1. **(D)** Of the choices given, the cell is the smallest and least complex unit of living matter. (If one accepts viruses as units of living matter, then these are smaller and less complex.)

2. **(D)** Homologous structures have a basic structural plan that becomes modified or specialized in various directions to meet different modes of life. This is adaptive radiation.

3. **(C)** An isotonic solution is one with an osmotic pressure equal to the reference solution—in this case, the living cell.

4. **(C)** Humidity has no effect on enzyme activity. Most enzymes are highly sensitive to pH and temperature.

5. **(B)** Heterotrophic organisms require organic compounds as food.

6. **(E)** Active transport occurs when cell membranes expend energy to transport ions and molecules in and out of cells at rates or directions that cannot be explained solely by the factors that affect diffusion.

7. **(B)** Among the chief sources of niacin are yeast, green vegetables, and wheat germ.

8. **(B)** Cellular respiration combines oxygen and organic compounds to release energy, carbon dioxide, and water.

9. **(B)** Gene flow is defined as the movement of genes from one population to another by way of interbreeding of individuals in the two populations.

10. **(D)** The absence of light stimulates stem elongation in plants and results in the failure of chlorophyll synthesis. This is etiolation.

11. **(E)** In plants xylem functions chiefly in the upward conduction of water and dissolved minerals and in the support or strengthening of stems.

12. **(D)** Homeostasis is the chemical and physical control over the internal conditions of the body which maintains an environment favorable for carrying out cellular activities.

13. **(B)** Thallophytes, or thallus plants, lack xylem and phloem, the conducting tissues, and they also do not develop multicellular embryos.

14. **(E)** Under normal favorable conditions in the seas and in freshwater lakes and streams, algae are so prolific that they constitute the basic food in many established food chains.

15. **(D)** In blood clotting, in the presence of the antihemophilic factor, blood platelets stick to torn tissue and release thromboplastin and serotonin.

16. **(B)** As indicated on the graph, at temperatures approaching 60°C, enzyme activity stops.

17. **(B)** Type A blood cells contain antigen A and its serum contains antibody B; type B blood cells contain antigen B and its serum contains anitbody A. Type B serum will cause type A blood to clump.

18. **(D)** The common enteric bacterium, *Escherichia coli*, has been found suitable for selected genetic-engineering activities, including genetic alteration for the production of human-type insulin.

19. **(C)** All nerve impulses from sensory receptors are conducted to the central nervous system through a dorsal root ganglion.

20. **(A)** The genetic information of an organism is stored in its DNA molecules, coded according to the sequence of bases along the DNA chain. For the transmission of genetic information to occur, there must be exact duplication of the DNA molecules.

21. **(A)** Transpiration is the evaporation of water from the aerial parts of plants. It has the beneficial effect of transporting dissolved minerals upward from the roots to the stem and leaves.

22. **(B)** The hereditary result of matings involving multiple, incompletely dominant genes is blending of the traits in question. For example, in matings of a wheat homozygous for red grains ($X_1X_1X_2X_2$) with a wheat homozygous for white kernels ($x_1x_1x_2x_2$), the following combinations of genes for color of the grains can be expected: *XXXX, XXXx, XXxx, Xxxx,* and *XXXX* with varying grain colors from dark red to white as the result.

23. **(E)** During the first meiotic division, chromosome reduction has not yet occurred. Hence, the chromatids of any pair of chromosomes are still in groups of four, or tetrads.

24. **(A)** According to *catastrophism* sudden and violent events changed the earth's surface and destroyed all life, and subsequent acts of special creation repopulated the earth.

25. **(C)** Directional selection is defined as selection that changes the frequency of an allele in a constant direction, either toward or away from fixation for that allele.

26. **(B)** Mutations are abrupt and unexpected changes in inheritance patterns that breed true.

27. **(E)** Joseph Lister initiated the era of antiseptic surgery when he began spraying the surgical scene with carbolic acid.

28. **(B)** Microevolution is evolution resulting from small specific genetic changes that can lead to a new subspecies.

29. **(B)** Among Aristotle's most noted contributions was the concept of the scientific method.

30. **(B)** The basic type of reaction in respect to vision or sight is chemical. The chemical reactions occur in the cells of the retina.

31. **(E)** The littoral zone exists from the high tide level to the area 200 meters deep.

32. **(E)** Often called the "grass of the sea," diatoms carry out most of the photosynthesis that takes place in the oceans and are the principal source of food of the animals that inhabit them.

33. **(E)** The key to analogous structures is the word *function*. The wing of a bird and the wing of a bee are similar in only one category: function. Structurally, they are unrelated.

34. **(C)** The term *symbiosis* is a general term meaning "living together," often with mutual benefits.

35. **(C)** The giant reptiles flourished in the geologic time period called the Mesozoic Era.

36. **(E)** Rennin is a digestive enzyme secreted by the stomach which is partially responsible for casein digestion.

37. **(C)** Plague still exists in certain parts of the world and, since it is associated with rodents and their fleas, rodent control is a necessary control measure.

38. **(D)** In each instance of sex determination in humans, the probability that any one individual will be male or female is one-half at the time of conception.

39. **(D)** When both parents are heterozygous, segregation results in gamete types *A* and *a* for both parents. Random fertilization produces three mating types in a ratio of 1:2:1, with one-half being heterozygous for *Aa*.

40. **(E)** Since the probability of crossing-over between two linked genes on a pair of chromosomes is directly proportional to the distance separating them, crossing-over frequencies are greatest in widely separated genes.

41. **(D)** An antigen is any substance that, when introduced into the body, causes the body to produce antibodies.

42. **(C)** Phosphates stimulate the growth of algae, which often form a layer thick enough on the surface of a lake or pond to dramatically reduce oxygen exchange into the water.

43. **(A)** Diffusion in this instance is the movement of water molecules from an area of high concentration of water molecules to or toward an area of low or lower concentration of water molecules.

44. **(E)** Turgid or turgor pressure is a positive pressure developed within living plant cells, and therefore in stems and leaves, as a result of internal water pressure.

45. **(B)** The cell in the salt water has lost water by diffusion, the net movement of water molecules out of the cell.

46. **(C)** Diffusion is the movement of water molecules as a result of their molecular activity. In the case of the cell in fresh water, as in the case of the cell in salt water also, water molecules move freely into and out of the cell.

47. **(E)** At each trophic level, only about 10% of the energy from the previous level is available.

48. **(E)** Cell division by the vascular cambium produces xylem internally and phloem externally, thus adding to the diameter of the stem.

49. **(E)** Water which moistens the cell walls of leaf mesophyll cells evaporates since these cell walls are exposed to the internal gaseous atmosphere of the leaf. This water loss is called transpiration.

50. **(E)** The effects of adrenaline are bodywide, affecting pulse, muscle tone, and the rate of nerve conduction.

51. **(E)** Mitosis is a qualitative distribution of chromatin to each of two different daughter cells. Its primary significance is that each daughter cell receives identical chromatin materials.

52. **(D)** The point where the optic nerve enters the eyeball has neither rods nor cones and, therefore, has no sight capability. It is called the blind spot.

53. **(B)** The antihemophilic factor causes blood platelets to swell into spherical masses and these tend to prevent the loss of other blood components.

54. **(D)** Humans and other animals store simple sugars in the form of glycogen in muscles and in the liver.

55. **(A)** Cuvier suggested that there must have been many floods (catastrophes) that killed most of the organisms living at the time, followed by repeated special creations to repopulate the earth. This idea is called catastrophism.

56. **(D)** ⎤ Lyell opposed catastrophism and special creation. He stated that events
57. **(D)** ⎦ in the geological history of the earth were the products of the same natural forces active today, i.e., erosion, sedimentation, etc. This doctrine is called uniformitarianism.

58. **(B)** The Devonian period was the beginning of true land plants with stomata, vascular tissues, and multicellular embryos.

59. **(E)** During the Tertiary, early modern mammals assumed dominance, together with the flowering (seed) plants.

60. **(D)** During the Carboniferous, giant ferns, clubmosses, and horsetails grew in widespread low and swampy regions of the earth. These later formed layers of dead vegetation which did not decompose. This plant material became coal.

61. **(C)** The trophosphere is the layer of the earth's atmosphere closest to the earth's surface and only the lower half of the troposphere will support life without supplemental oxygen.

62. **(D)** The periods of rotation and revolution of the moon are the same, 27⅓ days. Because of this, the same "face" of the moon is always turned toward the earth.

63. **(E)** Perigee is that point in the orbit of a satellite that is nearest to the earth.

64. **(B)** When it is noon at Greenwich, England, it is 12:00 P.M./00:00 A.M. at the International Date Line. At this instant, only one calendar day is in effect, worldwide.

65. **(C)** Barrier islands are low sand ridges that lie offshore along moderately sloping coastlines.

66. **(B)** Plate tectonics is the concept that continents drift in relation to one another on the earth's surface.

67. **(B)** The term *anhydrous* means free from or without water, especially the water of crystallization.

68. **(A)** Transuranium elements have atomic numbers above 92, are synthetic radioactive elements, and do not exist naturally.

69. **(E)** If a quantum of energy is absorbed by an electron of an atom, the electron moves to a "higher" energy level around the atomic nucleus.

70. **(B)** Molecules with ionic bonds are combinations of atoms bound together in predictable ways, by the attractive forces between positively and negatively charged atoms.

71. **(E)** The wavelength beam of electrons is very short and, therefore, permits a higher degree of resolution than with a light microscope.

72. **(D)** While obtaining pure aluminum metal from its ore (bauxite) is relatively expensive in terms of energy, recycling aluminum is quite inexpensive compared to recycling other metals.

73. **(A)** Samples of quart are all silicon dioxide, SiO_2, and thus have the same density, hardness, and cleavage type. Differences in the streak test results of types of quartz are the result of metal ion impurities in the crystal structure.

74. **(D)** The term *ore* refers to a specific mineral that contains a metal of commercial value (aluminum oxide or bauxite is an ore of aluminum). Rocks are physical combinations of minerals.

75. **(D)** Svante Arrhenius proposed that acids form H^+ ions in water solutions. When H_3PO_4 is added to water, H^+ ions are formed.

76. **(A)** Magnetic fields vary according to their sources, the positions of their sources, and the intensities of their sources.

77. **(C)** Electrical current is measured in amperes, one ampere being equal to one coulomb of charge past a point in one second.

78. **(D)** The two most widely obtained minerals from the earth's crust are iron and aluminum. These are not the two most valuable, but they are the most widely mined.

79. **(E)** In radioactive decomposition as well as in other radioactive changes, the nucleus of the atom is involved.

80. **(E)** Entropy, or change, is a thermodynamic measure of disorder; entropy, or change which increases disorder, in any undisturbed system always increases. Steam in a closed system can be used to push a piston, but its molecules dissipate after escaping into the atmosphere.

81. **(C)** The outer atmosphere of the sun is known as the corona. The photosphere and chromosphere lie beneath the corona but above the surface of the sun.

82. **(E)** Elements formed in the stars are formed by the process of nuclear fusion. Heavier elements require moiré protons to be joined together in the nucleus and are much rarer.

83. **(A)** For every force in one direction, there is an equal force in the opposite direction. To move an object in one direction, a stationary base or anchor is required to overcome the force directed in the opposite direction.

84. **(E)** By definition, energy is the capacity to do work.

85. **(B)** By definition, an electron is a fundamental particle of negative electricity.

86. **(A)** The Doppler effect is the apparent change in the pitch of sounds produced by moving objects when an observer is stationary or moving at a different speed than the producer of the sound.

87. **(B)** In a chain nuclear reaction, neutrons strike other atoms, which, in turn, release neutrons, which strike additional atoms. When a chain reaction can be sustained, the number or amount of fissionable material is described as a critical mass.

88. **(D)** Avogadro explained Gay-Lussac's law of combining volumes and offered the means for determining the molar masses of gases, and this provided a foundation for the kinetic-molecular theory.

89. **(A)** Pulsars are periodic radio wave bursts from neutron stars.

90. **(D)** For every force in one direction, there is an equal force in the opposite direction.

91. **(D)** The nature of electricity is not affected by the source of its production—hydroelectric power plants, nuclear power plants, or plants that burn fossil fuels.

92. **(B)** Celsius temperatures may be converted to Fahrenheit by multiplying the Celsius temperature by 1.8 and adding 32 degrees.

93. **(D)** Dalton's atomic theory holds that atoms are the unit particles of matter and cannot be subdivided, that atoms of a given element are alike and have the same weight, that atoms of different elements have different weights, that in chemical reactions it is atoms that combine, and that the relative weights of the atoms that combine are directly related to the weights of the atoms themselves.

94. **(D)** Friction is a force that opposes motion when two objects in contact with each other attempt to move relative to each other. Friction uses energy and, therefore, reduces mechanical efficiency.

95. **(D)** Valence is the combining capacity of an element—specifically, the number of hydrogen atoms that combine with one atom of that element.

96. **(D)** Elements in the halogen family of chemical elements (e.g., chlorine, iodine) associate readily with other elements and are often referred to as salt formers.

97. **(C)** A catalyst is a substance that initiates or speeds up a chemical reaction without being permanently altered.

98. **(B)** The *strong force* holds the particles inside the atomic nucleus together. The *gravitational force* holds objects to the ground. The *electromagnetic force* holds atoms and molecules together and holds electrons to the atomic nucleus. The *weak force* permits some atomic nuclei to break down, producing radioactivity and causing the sun to shine.

99. **(D)** Distillation is a process of boiling a liquid and condensing its vapor. Two or more liquids will usually have different boiling points so they may be separated by first boiling off the vapor of one liquid and condensing it and then boiling off the vapor of the second liquid and condensing it.

100. **(E)** By definition, the reaction between an acid and a base is called neutralization. For example, if sodium hydroxide (NaOH) reacts with hydrochloric acid (HCl), water and a salt are formed. In this example, the salt is sodium chloride (NaCl). As a chemical equation $HCl + NaOH \rightarrow NaCl + H_2O$.

101. **(E)** A chemical formula is a description, using chemical symbols, of the ratio of atoms in a chemical compound. If the weight ratio and the atomic mass of the elements of a compound are known, the molecular weight of the compound can be calculated.

102. **(D)** The family of plastics referred to as "thermosetting" consists of substances that polymerize irreversibly under heat or pressure, forming a hard mass.

103. **(E)** Albertus Magnus and Saint Thomas Aquinas endeavored to harmonize the teachings of Aristotle with church doctrine. Roger Bacon, in opposition, demonstrated the values of observation and experimentation and argued against the age-old scholastic method of education.

104. **(C)** When an atomic nucleus decomposes by emitting alpha or beta particles, it is said to be radioactive. An example would be the loss of an alpha particle by uranium-238 and its subsequent change to thorium-234.

105. **(D)** Atoms of the same element that have different mass numbers are called isotopes. They have the same number of protons, but different number of neutrons.

106. **(B)** Lines of latitude run parallel to the equator and are identified as being north or south of that imaginary line. Lines of longitude run perpendicular to latitude lines and are identified as being east or west of the prime meridian, located in Greenwich, England.

107. **(C)** Wavelength is the measure of distance between two adjacent crests.

108. **(E)** Amplitude of a sound vibration is one-half of the vertical distance between the crest and the trough.

109. **(C)** Energy and matter can be neither created nor destroyed, but energy and matter can be converted into one another, the total amount in the universe remaining constant.

110. **(D)** X-rays, discovered in 1895 by W.C. Roentgen, are very-high-frequency electromagnetic waves that enable one to photograph the skeleton. X-rays also have numerous other uses in science and industry.

111. **(D)** When certain metals are heated, they emit electrons, a phenomenon called the thermionic effect.

112. **(E)** A base is a substance which produces hydroxyl ions (OH^-) when dissolved in water. Hydroxide ion equals hydroxyl ion.

113. **(B)** In general, the chemical and physical properties of lithium and sodium are similar because the energy level of each atom contains a single electron.

114. **(D)** Thomas Aquinas taught that there is no conflict between faith and reason.

115. **(A)** The force of adhesion between a solid and a liquid based on the relative attraction of the molecules of the liquid in each other and for the solid is called capillarity.

116. **(D)** Conduction is the process whereby heat energy is transmitted directly through materials.

117. **(A)** The law of conservation of mass holds that there is no detectable gain or loss of mass in or as a result of chemical change.

118. **(B)** Various substances may be separated by using the degree to which they are absorbed onto an inert material. If the inert material is paper, the process is called paper chromatography.

119. **(C)** A buffer is any substance capable of neutralizing acids and bases to maintain a given hydrogen ion concentration.

120. **(B)** In a chemical reaction between an acid and a base (in this case, H_2SO_4 and $Cu(OH)_2$, respectively), a salt, $CuSO_4$, and water are formed. This reaction is called neutralization.

Natural Sciences

ANSWER SHEET–SAMPLE EXAMINATION 2

1 (A) (B) (C) (D) (E)   31 (A) (B) (C) (D) (E)   61 (A) (B) (C) (D) (E)   91 (A) (B) (C) (D) (E)
2 (A) (B) (C) (D) (E)   32 (A) (B) (C) (D) (E)   62 (A) (B) (C) (D) (E)   92 (A) (B) (C) (D) (E)
3 (A) (B) (C) (D) (E)   33 (A) (B) (C) (D) (E)   63 (A) (B) (C) (D) (E)   93 (A) (B) (C) (D) (E)
4 (A) (B) (C) (D) (E)   34 (A) (B) (C) (D) (E)   64 (A) (B) (C) (D) (E)   94 (A) (B) (C) (D) (E)
5 (A) (B) (C) (D) (E)   35 (A) (B) (C) (D) (E)   65 (A) (B) (C) (D) (E)   95 (A) (B) (C) (D) (E)
6 (A) (B) (C) (D) (E)   36 (A) (B) (C) (D) (E)   66 (A) (B) (C) (D) (E)   96 (A) (B) (C) (D) (E)
7 (A) (B) (C) (D) (E)   37 (A) (B) (C) (D) (E)   67 (A) (B) (C) (D) (E)   97 (A) (B) (C) (D) (E)
8 (A) (B) (C) (D) (E)   38 (A) (B) (C) (D) (E)   68 (A) (B) (C) (D) (E)   98 (A) (B) (C) (D) (E)
9 (A) (B) (C) (D) (E)   39 (A) (B) (C) (D) (E)   69 (A) (B) (C) (D) (E)   99 (A) (B) (C) (D) (E)
10 (A) (B) (C) (D) (E)   40 (A) (B) (C) (D) (E)   70 (A) (B) (C) (D) (E)   100 (A) (B) (C) (D) (E)
11 (A) (B) (C) (D) (E)   41 (A) (B) (C) (D) (E)   71 (A) (B) (C) (D) (E)   101 (A) (B) (C) (D) (E)
12 (A) (B) (C) (D) (E)   42 (A) (B) (C) (D) (E)   72 (A) (B) (C) (D) (E)   102 (A) (B) (C) (D) (E)
13 (A) (B) (C) (D) (E)   43 (A) (B) (C) (D) (E)   73 (A) (B) (C) (D) (E)   103 (A) (B) (C) (D) (E)
14 (A) (B) (C) (D) (E)   44 (A) (B) (C) (D) (E)   74 (A) (B) (C) (D) (E)   104 (A) (B) (C) (D) (E)
15 (A) (B) (C) (D) (E)   45 (A) (B) (C) (D) (E)   75 (A) (B) (C) (D) (E)   105 (A) (B) (C) (D) (E)
16 (A) (B) (C) (D) (E)   46 (A) (B) (C) (D) (E)   76 (A) (B) (C) (D) (E)   106 (A) (B) (C) (D) (E)
17 (A) (B) (C) (D) (E)   47 (A) (B) (C) (D) (E)   77 (A) (B) (C) (D) (E)   107 (A) (B) (C) (D) (E)
18 (A) (B) (C) (D) (E)   48 (A) (B) (C) (D) (E)   78 (A) (B) (C) (D) (E)   108 (A) (B) (C) (D) (E)
19 (A) (B) (C) (D) (E)   49 (A) (B) (C) (D) (E)   79 (A) (B) (C) (D) (E)   109 (A) (B) (C) (D) (E)
20 (A) (B) (C) (D) (E)   50 (A) (B) (C) (D) (E)   80 (A) (B) (C) (D) (E)   110 (A) (B) (C) (D) (E)
21 (A) (B) (C) (D) (E)   51 (A) (B) (C) (D) (E)   81 (A) (B) (C) (D) (E)   111 (A) (B) (C) (D) (E)
22 (A) (B) (C) (D) (E)   52 (A) (B) (C) (D) (E)   82 (A) (B) (C) (D) (E)   112 (A) (B) (C) (D) (E)
23 (A) (B) (C) (D) (E)   53 (A) (B) (C) (D) (E)   83 (A) (B) (C) (D) (E)   113 (A) (B) (C) (D) (E)
24 (A) (B) (C) (D) (E)   54 (A) (B) (C) (D) (E)   84 (A) (B) (C) (D) (E)   114 (A) (B) (C) (D) (E)
25 (A) (B) (C) (D) (E)   55 (A) (B) (C) (D) (E)   85 (A) (B) (C) (D) (E)   115 (A) (B) (C) (D) (E)
26 (A) (B) (C) (D) (E)   56 (A) (B) (C) (D) (E)   86 (A) (B) (C) (D) (E)   116 (A) (B) (C) (D) (E)
27 (A) (B) (C) (D) (E)   57 (A) (B) (C) (D) (E)   87 (A) (B) (C) (D) (E)   117 (A) (B) (C) (D) (E)
28 (A) (B) (C) (D) (E)   58 (A) (B) (C) (D) (E)   88 (A) (B) (C) (D) (E)   118 (A) (B) (C) (D) (E)
29 (A) (B) (C) (D) (E)   59 (A) (B) (C) (D) (E)   89 (A) (B) (C) (D) (E)   119 (A) (B) (C) (D) (E)
30 (A) (B) (C) (D) (E)   60 (A) (B) (C) (D) (E)   90 (A) (B) (C) (D) (E)   120 (A) (B) (C) (D) (E)

SAMPLE NATURAL SCIENCES EXAMINATION 2

NUMBER OF QUESTIONS: 120

Time: 90 MINUTES

Directions: Each of the questions or incomplete statements below is followed by five suggested answers or completions. Select the one that is best in each case.

1. The term most appropriate to the passage of molecules across cellular membranes is

   (A) selective permeability
   (B) porosity
   (C) mass movement
   (D) capillarity
   (E) imbibition

2. According to the principle of biogenesis,

   (A) organic evolution is a reality
   (B) life comes from preexisting life
   (C) life arose from minerals
   (D) life arose as the result of special creation
   (E) life arises directly from nonliving matter

3. Both inductive and deductive reasoning may be involved in formulating a scientific hypothesis. An example of inductive reasoning is

   (A) the assumption that a particular genetic pattern would result from the mating of two specific parental types
   (B) the consideration of the numbers of different kinds of individuals that resulted from a genetic mating
   (C) the generalization that the inheritance patterns in plants are identical to those in animals
   (D) the prediction of genetic patterns based on reasoning alone
   (E) the presumption of genetic ratios that might result from an experimental mating

4. When a living cell is placed in a hypertonic fluid, there will be

   (A) a net movement of water molecules into the cell
   (B) no net movement of water molecules into or out of the cell
   (C) an increase in cell turgidity
   (D) an increase in Brownian movement
   (E) a net movement of water molecules out of the cell

5. When an organism is incapable of synthesizing its food from inorganic materials, it is described as

   (A) chemosynthetic
   (B) autotrophic
   (C) autophobic
   (D) heterotrophic
   (E) photosynthetic

6. Carotene of plants can be considered a precursor of

   (A) vitamin C
   (B) phytol
   (C) chlorophyll
   (D) hemoglobin
   (E) vitamin A

7. As a result of the process called cellular respiration,

    (A) dry weight increases
    (B) oxygen and organic compounds are produced
    (C) water and carbon dioxide are consumed
    (D) dry weight decreases
    (E) water and organic compounds are produced

8. An energy-releasing process occurring continuously in all living cells is

    (A) respiration
    (B) osmosis
    (C) catalysis
    (D) diffusion
    (E) photosynthesis

9. The chemical compounds called gibberellins

    (A) result in chemosynthesis
    (B) cause unusual cell elongation in plant cells
    (C) cause etiolation in plants
    (D) are inactivated by fungal enzymes
    (E) prevent flowering and seed production

10. The total amount of organic matter in a population is referred to as

    (A) alluvium
    (B) humus
    (C) laterite
    (D) schist
    (E) biomass

11. In plants one of the functions of the xylem is to

    (A) manufacture organic substances from carbon dioxide and water
    (B) reduce transpiration
    (C) increase stem diameter by continued cell division
    (D) conduct water upward
    (E) conduct food substances

12. A grain of wheat is

    (A) a fruit
    (B) a seed
    (C) an epicotyl
    (D) a cotyledon
    (E) a hypocotyl

13. Water loss from plants by transpiration is decreased by

    (A) rainfall
    (B) increased air circulation
    (C) increased temperature
    (D) increased humidity
    (E) decreased humidity

14. Variation in a population may arise due to

    (A) mutation
    (B) independent assortment
    (C) changes in chromosome structure
    (D) changes in the chromosome number
    (E) all of the above

15. In plants, fertilization

    (A) gives rise to the gametophyte
    (B) precedes spore formation
    (C) precedes gamete formation
    (D) restores the diploid condition
    (E) may take place between two spores

16. What is the function of genes?

    (A) To produce mutations
    (B) To produce DNA
    (C) To produce transfer RNA
    (D) To produce all cellular components
    (E) To direct cells to produce specific proteins

17. Within the cytoplasm of living cells, the structures that "read" the genetic code, thereby directing the production of specific enzymes, are the

    (A) ribosomes
    (B) lysosomes
    (C) Golgi complex
    (D) macrosomes
    (E) mitochondria

18. Recombinant DNA research

    (A) permits the creation of entirely new species
    (B) permits the reassortment of genes between different species
    (C) utilizes X-ray techniques
    (D) produces predictable results in every case
    (E) is of no concern to environmental stability

19. Which of the following may be a problem associated with recombinant DNA research and the release of resulting strains of microorganisms into the environment?

    (A) The ultimate cost of development and production
    (B) The extremely limited target areas
    (C) The fact that expectations, at best, are meager
    (D) The fact that all current techniques are uncontrollable
    (E) The difficulty of tracing and recalling such released organisms

20. Nerve impulses along motor nerves leave the central nervous system

    (A) along a dorsal root axon
    (B) along a ventral root axon
    (C) after passing through a dorsal root ganglion
    (D) along a connector dendrite
    (E) along dendrites of sensory neurons

21. The capability of focusing both eyes on the same object is

    (A) stigmatism
    (B) binocular vision
    (C) glaucoma
    (D) hypermetropia
    (E) myopia

22. Parathormone

    (A) dilates blood vessels
    (B) stimulates lactation
    (C) regulates sodium metabolism
    (D) controls blood sugar
    (E) regulates calcium metabolism

23. The mutual exchange of chromosome fragments, which is called crossing-over, occurs during

    (A) interphase
    (B) fertilization
    (C) telophase
    (D) synapsis
    (E) cytoplasmic reorganization

24. The theory proposing the inheritance of acquired characteristics was proposed by

    (A) Alfred R. Wallace
    (B) Charles Darwin
    (C) Jean Baptiste de Lamarck
    (D) Sir Charles Lyell
    (E) Thomas Hunt Morgan

25. The mutation theory was eventually shown to strengthen Darwin's theory of natural selection because it provided

    (A) an explanation for genetic coding
    (B) for cytoplasmic inheritance
    (C) an explanation for pangenesis
    (D) a source of inheritable variations
    (E) the bridge between biometrics and the Mendelean ratios

26. A disease transmitted by an arthropod vector is

    (A) smallpox
    (B) yellow fever
    (C) tuberculosis
    (D) polio
    (E) lockjaw

Exam 2

27. The first to use the word *cell* after studying plant tissue with his microscope was

    (A) Brown
    (B) Leonardo da Vinci
    (C) Hooke
    (D) Grew
    (E) Schleiden and Schwann

28. The primary characteristic of the disease acquired immune deficiency syndrome (AIDS) is that

    (A) it causes a parasitic infection of the digestive tract
    (B) it stimulates the development of several types of cancer
    (C) it causes a defect in a person's natural immunity against disease
    (D) there is no infectious agent
    (E) it causes damage to brain tissues

29. Harvey was the first to verify experimentally

    (A) chemical oxidation
    (B) cell reproduction
    (C) the biogenetic hypothesis
    (D) the nerve impulse
    (E) circulation of the blood

30. You would expect to encounter numerous epiphytes and a variety of arboreal mammals in

    (A) a tropical rain forest
    (B) a deciduous forest
    (C) a coniferous forest
    (D) an alpine tundra
    (E) a taiga

31. Marine organisms found on the continental shelf live in the

    (A) zone of perpetual darkness
    (B) neritic zone
    (C) littoral zone
    (D) abyssal zone
    (E) bathyal zone

32. A diet completely free of cholesterol would include

    (A) a balance of all food types, including lean meat
    (B) fruits and dairy products
    (C) foods of plant origin only
    (D) whole grains and dairy products
    (E) vegetables and lean meat

33. Homologous structures are indicative of

    (A) common ancestry
    (B) convergence
    (C) parallel evolution
    (D) divergence
    (E) similar function

34. An organism which obtains its food from nonliving organic materials is called a

    (A) symbiont
    (B) saprophyte
    (C) commensal
    (D) parasite
    (E) buffer

35. The time period described as the age of glaciers is called the

    (A) Eocene epoch
    (B) Late Mesozoic
    (C) Triassic period
    (D) Early Mesozoic
    (E) Pleistocene epoch

36. Repeated pruning of a row of shrubs commonly results in a dense growth of the shrub branches. The fact that the same shrubs, if not pruned, develop longer main stems with fewer branches is attributed to the action of auxin and is called

    (A) phototropism
    (B) thigmotropism
    (C) disbudding
    (D) apical dominance
    (E) parthonocarpy

37. Inclusion of seafoods in the human diet normally prevents an insufficiency of thyroxin and the development of

    (A) muscular spasms
    (B) anemia
    (C) many enzymes
    (D) goiter
    (E) hemoglobin

38. Pasteurization of milk ensures almost complete protection from the bacterial disease called

    (A) measles
    (B) plague
    (C) smallpox
    (D) polio
    (E) undulant fever

39. In reference to a trait designated as "*A*," the genotypes resulting from a mating between a male parent homozygous for "*A*" and a heterozygous female parent would be

    (A) 1/2 *AA*, 1/2 *Aa*
    (B) 1/4 *AA*, 1/2 *Aa*, 1/4 *aa*
    (C) 3/4 *Aa*, 1/4 *aa*
    (D) 1/4 *Aa*, 3/4 *aa*
    (E) 1/2 *AA*, 1/4 *Aa*, 1-1/4 *aa*

40. Enzymes are specific with reference to

    (A) the units of energy released
    (B) the units of energy absorbed
    (C) the high temperatures required for their activation
    (D) the low temperatures required for their activation
    (E) the substrates they act upon

41. In a single-celled organism such as the amoeba, pinocytic vesicles function by

    (A) bringing some solid particles into the cell
    (B) discharging needlelike barbs containing poison
    (C) propelling the organism
    (D) reacting to environmental stimuli
    (E) excreting waste substances from the cell

42. Amino acid analysis of proteins has been advanced by

    (A) mass spectroscopy
    (B) better understanding of anabolic reactions
    (C) chromatography and electrophoresis
    (D) production and study of autoradiographs
    (E) DNA sequencing methods

43. Saprophytes

    (A) utilize radiant energy
    (B) rely upon the absorption of nutrients from decomposing organic materials
    (C) eat, digest, and assimilate food materials
    (D) oxidize inorganic materials
    (E) exist at the expense of living organisms

44. A diet limited to vegetables will probably lack

    (A) vitamin K
    (B) vitamin B_1
    (C) vitamin B_6
    (D) vitamin B_{12}
    (E) viamin D

Exam 2

Questions 45 and 46

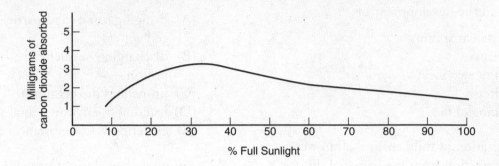

The graph represents the relationship between the rate of photosynthesis (expressed as milligrams of carbon dioxide absorbed per 0.5 square meter of leaf area per hour) and light intensity (expressed as percentages of full sunlight) for woodland ferns.

45. Under the conditions noted above, one may conclude that

(A) ferns use the most sunlight at 100% full sunlight
(B) photosynthesis decreases dry weight
(C) optimum light intensity for ferns is 30–40% full sunlight
(D) photosynthesis increases dry weight
(E) equal increases in light intensity throughout the range of 0–100% of full sunlight bring about equal increases in the rate of photosynthesis for ferns

46. One may also infer that

(A) ferns prefer shade
(B) absorbed carbon dioxide increases to 4 or more milligrams in ferns when exposed to greater than 100% full sunlight
(C) fern leaves are inefficient when it comes to photosynthesis
(D) ferns use more carbon dioxide at 10–50% full sunlight than at 60–100% full sunlight
(E) ferns would grow best in 100% full sunlight

47. Which of the following best describes a nerve impulse?

    (A) The transmission of coded signals along a nerve fiber
    (B) A wave of depolarization passing along a nerve fiber
    (C) A flow of electrons along a nerve fiber
    (D) A chemical reaction
    (E) A wave of contraction passing along the myelin sheath

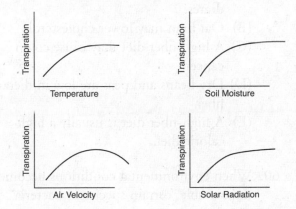

48. The graphs above illustrate the approximate rates of water loss by the aerial parts of plants (transpiration) under varying environmental conditions. On the basis of the information conveyed by the graphs, one may correctly infer that

    (A) air velocity is the principal factor affecting transpiration
    (B) transpiration is affected by multiple factors
    (C) genetic factors exert the primary control over transpiration
    (D) the oxygen concentration in soil moisture has no effect on transpiration
    (E) plants having high concentrations of anthocyanins have high transpiration rates

49. When the dorsal root of a reflex arc is cut,

    (A) stimulation of the distal end causes no reaction
    (B) stimulation of the distal end causes a normal reaction
    (C) the reflex reaction will occur normally
    (D) the sensory stimulus will travel along the ventral root
    (E) new nerve pathways will develop immediately

50. Glucose metabolism is regulated by

    (A) thyrotropin
    (B) epinephrine
    (C) estradiol
    (D) progesterone
    (E) insulin

51. In humans, sex-linked inheritance is concerned with inheritance of

    (A) traits whose genes are located on autosomes
    (B) traits whose genes are located on the X chromosome
    (C) traits whose genes are located on chromosome number 21
    (D) traits whose genes are located on the Y chromosome
    (E) traits whose genes determine sex

52. The inherited variations commonly referred to in treatises on natural selection and evolution, are, in reality,

    (A) merely chance variations
    (B) induced by the environment
    (C) special creations
    (D) mutations
    (E) acquired characteristics

53. Deoxyribonucleic acid consists of simple sugars, phosphate units, and four specific nitrogenous bases:

    (A) cytosine, guanine, thymine, and uracil
    (B) adenine, guanine, thymine, and uracil
    (C) adenine, cytosine, guanine, and thymine
    (D) adenine, cytosine, thymine, and uracil
    (E) adenine, cytosine, guanine, and uracil

54. The best dietary sources of polyunsaturated fats include

    (A) oils of plant origin
    (B) fats of animal origin
    (C) milk, cream, cheese, and butter
    (D) hydrogenated vegetable oils
    (E) trans fats

55. A Renaissance artist renowned for his knowledge of human musculature was

    (A) Albertus Magnus
    (B) Galen
    (C) Michelangelo
    (D) Vesalius
    (E) De Chauliac

56. The ancient Greek scholar who devoted much study to and wrote much about plant reproduction and seed development, and who is referred to as the "father of botany" is

    (A) Aristotle
    (B) Empedocles
    (C) Thales
    (D) Anaximander
    (E) Theophrastus

57. Salts of the heavy metals, such as lead or mercury, when taken into the body, accumulate in the marrow of long bones and interfere with

    (A) coagulation of the blood
    (B) formation of thrombin from prothrombin
    (C) formation of erythrocytes
    (D) maturation of phagocytes
    (E) release of calcium from platelets

58. The primary function of root hair cells is

    (A) anchorage
    (B) storage
    (C) photosynthesis
    (D) absorption
    (E) synergism

59. With respect to dietary fibers, which of the following statements is correct?

    (A) A high-fiber diet is high in carbohydrates.
    (B) Oat bran may lower cholesterol.
    (C) A high-fiber diet may cause colon cancer.
    (D) Dry beans and peas are low in dietary fiber.
    (E) A high-fiber diet is usually a high-calorie diet.

60. When environmental conditions become unfavorable, certain species of bacteria

    (A) develop flagella
    (B) become aerobic
    (C) form spores
    (D) become anaerobic
    (E) develop capsules

61. When certain types of atmospheric particles act as nuclei on which water condensation occurs, these fog-forming nuclei are called

    (A) hydrologic nuclei
    (B) condensation nuclei
    (C) hydroscopic nuclei
    (D) hygroscopic nuclei
    (E) aquifers

62. The earth's orbit around the sun is most like

    (A) a parabola
    (B) a circle
    (C) an ellipse
    (D) a hyperbola
    (E) a spiral

63. One significant scientific contribution of the Babylonians was the

    (A) Pythagorean theorem
    (B) combining of mathematics with experimental theory
    (C) recording of eclipses
    (D) science of alchemy
    (E) principle of Archimedes

64. The laws of conservation of mass were verified experimentally by

    (A) Priestly
    (B) Democritus
    (C) Dalton
    (D) Rutherford
    (E) Lavoisier

65. A star that suddenly increases in brightness and then slowly fades is known as a

    (A) supernova
    (B) nova
    (C) giant star
    (D) visual binary
    (E) white dwarf

66. When a beam of light passes through a colloidal liquid the beam is scattered. This scattering of light is known as

    (A) the Tyndall effect
    (B) a charge-transfer reaction
    (C) close packing
    (D) destructive interference
    (E) the hydrologic effect

67. Deposits of glacial till forming various ridge patterns are called

    (A) bergschrunds
    (B) moraines
    (C) uplifts
    (D) displacements
    (E) sediments

68. An offshore ridge formed by coral is called

    (A) a fjord
    (B) continental shelf
    (C) sediment
    (D) a barrier reef
    (E) an upwelling

69. The smallest particles possessing the properties of elements are

    (A) neutrons
    (B) isotopes
    (C) protons
    (D) atoms
    (E) electrons

70. Throughout the universe, the force that holds atoms and molecules together is called the

    (A) weak force
    (B) nuclear force
    (C) strong force
    (D) electromagnetic force
    (E) fifth force

71. The measure of the disorder of a system is known as

    (A) chaos
    (B) enthalpy
    (C) entropy
    (D) randomness
    (E) nonequilibrium condition

72. Color is primarily the property of those wavelengths of light which are

    (A) absorbed
    (B) reflected
    (C) produced
    (D) attracted
    (E) adsorbed

73. Why is gravity the dominant force throughout the universe?

    (A) The electromagnetic force only holds atoms and molecules together.
    (B) The hypothetical "fifth force" is a repulsive force.
    (C) The weak force allows some atomic nuclei to break down.
    (D) The strong force is vastly stronger than the gravitational force.
    (E) Both the strong force and the weak force have very short ranges.

74. If an object is moving at a constant velocity, which of the following must be true?

    (A) Its speed is constant, but its direction can change.
    (B) Its speed and direction are both constant.
    (C) There are no forces acting on the object.
    (D) Friction must have been reduced to zero.
    (E) It is accelerating, but at a slow rate.

75. An object starts from rest and 5 seconds later it is moving at 100 meters per second (m/s). The acceleration of the object is

    (A) 20 m/s^2
    (B) 95 m/s^2
    (C) 100 m/s^2
    (D) 105 m/s^2
    (E) 500 m/s^2

76. Which term best describes a supersaturated solution?

    (A) concentrated
    (B) immiscible
    (C) asymmetric
    (D) unstable
    (E) dilute

77. Which of the following statements describing cathode rays is *not* correct?

    (A) They are bent by electric fields but not by magnetic fields.
    (B) They cast shadows.
    (C) They travel in straight lines.
    (D) They are bent by both electric and magnetic fields.
    (E) They consist of electrons.

78. Radio waves and light waves differ with respect to

    (A) amplitude
    (B) wavelength
    (C) visibility
    (D) velocities
    (E) diffraction

79. Chemical bonds in which a pair of electrons are shared unevenly between two atoms are called

    (A) hydrogen bonds
    (B) ionic bonds
    (C) nonpolar covalent bonds
    (D) polar covalent bonds
    (E) London dispersion forces

80. In electrical circuits, the unit of resistance is the

    (A) ohm
    (B) watt
    (C) volt
    (D) ampere
    (E) coulomb

81. Which of the following accounts for the high boiling point of water?

    (A) its high molecular weight (molar mass)
    (B) the ability of water molecules to attract to many surfaces
    (C) the ability of water molecules to form hydrogen bonds
    (D) the ability of water molecules to evaporate easily
    (E) the ability of water molecules to dissolve many other substances

82. Simple machines such as levers enable humans to

    (A) gain both force and distance
    (B) gain both mechanical advantage and speed
    (C) decrease the force arm and increase the weight arm without increasing force
    (D) eliminate friction
    (E) trade force for distance, or vice versa

83. Heat transfer is accomplished by conduction, radiation, and

    (A) vaporization
    (B) convection
    (C) expansion
    (D) entropy
    (E) insulation

84. Quantum mechanics is concerned with the

    (A) change in velocity of electrons
    (B) likely location of electrons in atoms
    (C) transmission of heat energy through gases and liquids
    (D) deflection of air flow caused by the earth's rotation
    (E) tendencies of materials to fail as a result of repeated stress

85. A property of matter which tends to make it resist any change in motion is called

    (A) gravity
    (B) force
    (C) mass
    (D) acceleration
    (E) inertia

86. Any physical system is said to possess energy if it

    (A) has the capacity to do work
    (B) has mass
    (C) is at absolute zero
    (D) resists acceleration
    (E) resists gravity

87. A fundamental particle with a positive charge found in the nuclei of all atoms is

    (A) an ion
    (B) a meson
    (C) a proton
    (D) an electron
    (E) a neutron

88. Approximately what percentage of the potential energy of fossil fuels such as coal is actually delivered to homes and businesses as useful energy?

    (A) 95%
    (B) 75%
    (C) 65%
    (D) 35%
    (E) 25%

89. In a chain reaction,

    (A) electricity serves as the trigger
    (B) light energy stimulates atoms
    (C) light energy stimulates molecules
    (D) neutrons combine with photons
    (E) the first atoms to decay trigger additional reactions

90. To say that a football player weighs 220 pounds means that

    (A) his body is attracted by the sun with a force equal to 220 pounds
    (B) his body is attracted by the sun and the moon with a combined force equal to 220 pounds
    (C) his body is attracted by the earth with a force equal to 220 pounds
    (D) he has a negative mass equal to 220 pounds
    (E) he has a positive mass equal to 220 pounds

Exam 2

91. Water held behind a dam represents what kind of energy?

    (A) Kinetic
    (B) Potential
    (C) Mass
    (D) Conserved
    (E) Transformed

92. Which of the following is not currently used as a source of electrical power generation?

    (A) Fission energy
    (B) Fusion energy
    (C) Hydroelectric energy
    (D) Tidal motion
    (E) Geothermal energy

93. In the process called evaporation, the faster molecules of a liquid are able to escape the attractive forces of their slower neighboring molecules. This results in

    (A) an increase in temperature
    (B) a decrease in temperature
    (C) adhesion
    (D) cohesion
    (E) friction

94. Specific gravity is a measure of the relative density of a liquid in relation to

    (A) water
    (B) air
    (C) ice
    (D) mercury
    (E) oxygen

95. Which produces hydrogen gas when interacting with metals?

    (A) Salts
    (B) Acids
    (C) Bases
    (D) Oxides
    (E) Hydroxides

96. The halogen family of chemical elements includes fluorine and

    (A) sulfur
    (B) potassium
    (C) chromium
    (D) bismuth
    (E) iodine

97. When exposed to light, chlorophyll fluoresces. This effect is the

    (A) return of electrons to the chlorophyll molecule
    (B) reflection of light by the chlorophyll molecule
    (C) beginning of glucose synthesis
    (D) absorption of light at one wavelength and the emission of light energy at a different wavelength
    (E) shifting of electrons to the innermost orbits of the chlorophyll atoms

98. One class of organic compounds constitutes the building blocks of proteins and is characterized by possessing

    (A) a carboxyl group only
    (B) an NH_2 group in addition to a carboxyl group
    (C) hydrocarbons
    (D) an alkyl group
    (E) esters

99. In any physical change,

    (A) the reactants disappear
    (B) matter does not lose its chemical identity
    (C) new substances with different properties appear
    (D) energy is released
    (E) energy is absorbed

100. In chemical equations, the total molecular mass of the reactants

(A) equals the total molecular mass of the products
(B) is less than the total molecular mass of the products
(C) is greater than the total molecular mass of the products
(D) is not relative to the total molecular mass of the products
(E) is determined by the atomic number of the reactant

101. The majority of freshwater usage in the world today is for which purpose?

(A) Drinking and washing by people
(B) Agricultural uses
(C) Cooling factories and power plants
(D) Hydroelectric power
(E) Recreational uses

102. Scholasticism represents a philosophical attempt during the Middle Ages to harmonize Roman Catholic beliefs and

(A) the astronomical works of Copernicus
(B) the anatomical and physiological works of Vesalius
(C) Galileo's "behavior of moving objects"
(D) the works and teachings of Aristotle
(E) early Byzantine and Moslem sciences

103. Which of the following is not a major air pollutant today?

(A) Carbon monoxide (CO)
(B) Ozone (O_3)
(C) Unburned hydrocarbons
(D) Nitrogen oxides (NO_x)
(E) Carbon dioxide

104. Chemical processes in which electrons are taken away from atoms or molecules are referred to as

(A) recombinations
(B) tropisms
(C) decompositions
(D) oxidations
(E) reductions

105. During radioactive decay, a given radioactive element may emit

(A) beta and gamma rays only
(B) alpha and gamma rays only
(C) alpha, beta, and gamma rays
(D) alpha, beta, and gamma rays and X-rays
(E) X-rays only

Questions 106 and 107

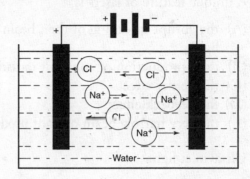

106. After study of the illustration above, one may conclude that

(A) water molecules are attracted by the electrodes
(B) sodium ions are attracted to the positive electrode
(C) sodium chloride dissociates when placed in water
(D) chlorine ions are attracted to the negative electrode
(E) current flow causes an increase in water temperature

107. One may also conclude that

(A) the solution will not conduct current
(B) only sodium ions conduct current
(C) only chlorine ions conduct current
(D) the closed circuit illustrated results in neutrality
(E) when ions are present they are attracted to electrodes having opposite electrical charges

Exam 2

108. Certain metals and alloys, such as nichrome wire, are used in electrical heating devices (toasters, for example) because of their

    (A) low melting point
    (B) high specific resistance
    (C) great current flow
    (D) capacity to discharge electrons
    (E) capacity to modify electrons

109. A unique feature of lasers is

    (A) the abrupt spreading of their beam of light
    (B) their production of coherent radiation
    (C) the Peltier effect
    (D) the Seebeck effect
    (E) the very narrow beam of light produced

110. Ultraviolet light

    (A) is more energetic than visual light
    (B) has a lower frequency than visible light
    (C) has longer wavelengths than visible light
    (D) lies in a low-energy section of the electromagnetic spectrum
    (E) is the light source used in lasers

111. When an electric current is passed through electrodes immersed in an electrolyte, ions of the electrolyte

    (A) precipitate
    (B) dissociate
    (C) crystallize
    (D) combine
    (E) neutralize

112. According to the law of reflection,

    (A) the angle of incidence is equal to the angle of reflection
    (B) the angle of incidence is less than the angle of reflection
    (C) the angle of incidence is greater than the angle of reflection
    (D) the angle of incidence equals the angle of reflection squared
    (E) the angle of reflection equals the angle of incidence squared

113. Which of the following is considered a greenhouse gas that has been increasing in amounts due to human activity?

    (A) carbon dioxide
    (B) water vapor
    (C) ozone
    (D) sulfur dioxide
    (E) carbon monoxide

114. A coil of wire carrying an electric current behaves as

    (A) a stator
    (B) a commutator
    (C) a transistor
    (D) a bar magnet
    (E) a capacitor

Directions: Each group of questions below consists of five lettered choices followed by a list of numbered phrases or sentences. For each numbered phrase or sentence select the one choice that is most closely related to it. Each choice may be used once, more than once, or not at all in each group.

Questions 115–117

    (A) Binary stars
    (B) Black holes
    (C) Dwarfs
    (D) Supernovas
    (E) Variable stars

115. Stars which fluctuate in brightness

116. Stars attracted by their mutual gravitations

117. Stars which increase in brightness multifold

Questions 118–120

    (A) Avogadro's law
    (B) Boyle's law
    (C) Kinetic-molecular theory
    (D) First law of thermodynamics
    (E) Uncertainty principle

118. States that energy may be neither created
     nor destroyed

119. Is based on the concept that we cannot
     know both the position and the momentum
     of an electron at the same time

120. Assumes that gases consist of independently
     moving molecules

STOP

If there is still time remaining, you may review your answers.

Natural Sciences
ANSWER KEY—SAMPLE EXAMINATION 2

1. A	25. D	49. A	73. E	97. D
2. B	26. B	50. E	74. B	98. B
3. B	27. C	51. B	75. A	99. B
4. E	28. C	52. D	76. D	100. A
5. D	29. E	53. C	77. A	101. B
6. E	30. A	54. A	78. B	102. D
7. D	31. B	55. C	79. D	103. E
8. A	32. C	56. E	80. A	104. D
9. B	33. A	57. C	81. C	105. C
10. E	34. B	58. D	82. E	106. C
11. D	35. E	59. B	83. B	107. E
12. A	36. D	60. C	84. B	108. B
13. D	37. D	61. B	85. E	109. E
14. E	38. E	62. C	86. A	110. A
15. D	39. A	63. C	87. C	111. B
16. E	40. E	64. E	88. E	112. A
17. A	41. A	65. B	89. E	113. E
18. B	42. C	66. A	90. C	114. D
19. E	43. B	67. B	91. B	115. E
20. B	44. D	68. D	92. B	116. A
21. B	45. C	69. D	93. B	117. D
22. E	46. D	70. D	94. A	118. D
23. D	47. B	71. C	95. B	119. E
24. C	48. B	72. B	96. E	120. C

SCORING CHART

After you have scored your Sample Examination 2, enter the results in the chart below; then transfer your score to the Progress Chart on page 12.

Total Test	Number Right	Number Wrong	Number Omitted
120			

ANSWER EXPLANATIONS

1. **(A)** Cellular membranes are selectively permeable since they permit different kinds of molecules to pass at varying rates or not at all and this permeability may constantly change.

2. **(B)** According to biogenesis, all life comes from preexisting life.

3. **(B)** Inductive reasoning is reasoning from a part or parts to a whole, or from particulars to general. Deductive reasoning is the derivation of a conclusion by reasoning alone.

4. **(E)** A hypertonic solution has a higher osmotic pressure than the protoplasm of the cell in question and, therefore, water will diffuse out of the cell with a consequent decrease in turgor pressure.

5. **(D)** Autotrophic organisms have the ability to synthesize their food from inorganic materials; heterotrophic organisms lack this ability.

6. **(E)** Carotenoid pigments (carotenes) of yellow and leafy vegetables are precursors in vitamin A synthesis.

7. **(D)** In cellular respiration organic substances are broken down to release their stored energy. This results in a decrease in dry weight.

8. **(A)** All living cells carry on cellular respiration, which is a process that provides energy for the cell's use.

9. **(B)** Like auxins, gibberellins are growth-promoting substances found in plants which cause stem elongation, promote flowering, and play a role in seed germination.

10. **(E)** The total weight of protoplasm in a community is referred to as biomass.

11. **(D)** Xylem is the principal water-conducting tissue in vascular plants.

12. **(A)** A fruit is the matured ovary of a flower. A grain of wheat is a matured ovary of the wheat plant.

13. **(D)** Any factor that affects the evaporation of water from an open container will have a similar effect on transpiration by plants. Transpiration is defined as the evaporation of water from the aerial parts of plants.

14. **(E)** Variation may occur in a population as a result of any chromosomal change affecting its DNA, chromosome number, or structure; the position of genes; or independent assortment during meiosis.

15. **(D)** The fusion of two haploid (N) gametes in plants restores the diploid ($2N$) chromosome number.

16. **(E)** Genes direct cells to produce specific enzymes, all of which are proteins, and these act as the cellular "machines" that control or determine cellular traits.

17. **(A)** All cellullar proteins, including enzymes, are produced by ribosomes, which are composed of RNA and proteins and which follow the instructions received from the DNA code of the nucleus.

18. **(B)** Techniques utilized in the field of recombinant DNA research permit the transfer or reassortment of genes between different species. However, its results are not readily predictable, may affect food chains, and may upset the delicate environment.

19. **(E)** Gene-splicing produces new kinds of individuals within species. The interactions of these new kinds of organisms with the environment are not only unpredictable, but also potentially hazardous if something "goes wrong."

20. **(B)** Motor nerve impulses leave the central nervous system along ventral root axons, while sensory impulses move toward the central nervous system along dorsal roots.

21. **(B)** The human visual system is binocular and stereoscopic, i.e., the images of the two eyes fit together to produce roundness and depth.

22. **(E)** Parathormone is necessary for maintaining the proper calcium ion concentration in the blood. Calcium is involved in nerve impulse transmission, blood clotting, bone and teeth formation, and fertilization.

23. **(D)** Synapsis is the pairing of the chromosomes during the prophase and metaphase of the first meiotic division. Since each chromosome consists of two daughter chromatids during this period, a tetrad of four chromatids exists and crossing-over occurs often.

24. **(C)** Lamarck proposed the theory of the inheritance of acquired characteristics, frequently referred to as the theory of "use and disuse."

25. **(D)** The mutation theory proposed by de Vries strengthened Darwin's theory of natural selection because it provided a good explanation for the source of inheritable variations, something Darwin was not able to do.

26. **(B)** The *Anopheles* mosquito is the vector, or carrier, of the protozoan parasite that causes malaria.

27. **(C)** Robert Hooke was the first to use the term *cell* in describing the microscopic units that comprise the tissues and organs of multicellular plants and animals.

28. **(C)** Although AIDS is a very complex disease distinguished by various symptoms, it is primarily characterized by causing major defects in an individual's immunity to disease.

29. **(E)** William Harvey verified experimentally that the blood circulates. He described arteries and veins and predicted the existence of blood capillaries.

30. **(A)** In the tropical rain forest with its excessive rains, the ground level environment is poor. Therefore, many forms of plants and animals are tree dwellers.

31. **(B)** The neritic environment is identified as a region of shallow water adjoining the seacoast and above the continental shelf.

32. **(C)** Cholesterol is not found in foods of plant origin.

33. **(A)** Homologous structures are similar from the standpoint of structure, embryonic development, and relationship and thus indicate common ancestry.

34. **(B)** A saprophyte is a heterotrophic plant that obtains its nourishment from nonliving organic matter.

35. **(E)** In the Pleistocene epoch climates cooled dramatically and there were two glacial periods during which the ice advanced twice.

36. **(D)** Auxin (plant hormone) is produced primarily by terminal buds, and among its induced responses are stem elongation and lateral bud inhibition. Removal of terminal buds by pruning permits lateral buds to grow into branches.

37. **(D)** Seafood contains small quantities of iodine, and this element is required for normal thyroid function and the production of thyroxin.

38. **(E)** Protection from undulant fever (brucellosis) can be achieved if all milk is pasteurized and if diseased animals are removed from the herd.

39. **(A)** The male parent produces *A*-type gametes only, while the female parent produces both *A*-type and *a*-type gametes in a 1:1 ratio. During random fertilization, zygotes will be 1/2 *AA* and 1/2 *Aa*.

40. **(E)** Enzymes are always specific with respect to the substrate (raw material) worked on.

41. **(A)** Solid food particles such as bacterial cells may be brought into the cell by pinocytosis and released into the cytoplasm as a food vacuole.

42. **(C)** Paper chromatography permits the separation of amino acids and relies upon the different solubilities of amino acids and on their differential absorption on paper.

43. **(B)** Saprophytes are heterotrophic plants which obtain their nourishment from nonliving organic matter.

44. **(D)** While necessary or required proteins may be acquired from an all-vegetable diet, it will probably be deficient in vitamin B12.

45. **(C)** Study of the graph indicates that optimum light intensity for the ferns
46. **(D)** is 30–40%, since this represents the light intensity at which there is greatest absorption of CO_2. Similarly, ferns use more CO_2 at 10–50% of full sunlight than at 60–100%. On the basis of the information given, no other conclusions are valid.

47. **(B)** The resting nerve fiber is polarized, having its outside positively charged and its inside negatively charged. A stimulus causes a wave of depolarization to pass along the fiber, from which it recovers in about 0.001 second.

48. **(B)** Transpiration is the loss of water from the aerial parts of plants; its rate is affected by several environmental factors, including solar radiation, humidity, air movement, soil moisture, and temperature.

49. **(A)** Sensory nerve impulses travel to the spinal cord along the dorsal root of a reflex arc. When the dorsal root has been cut, no sensory nerve impulse may travel to the spinal cord.

50. **(E)** Insulin is produced in the pancreas and is one of the glucose-regulating hormones.

51. **(B)** Sex-linked inheritance in humans is concerned with the inheritance traits whose genes are located on the X chromosome. (The Y chromosome has only a few genes and for different traits.)

52. **(D)** Mutations are the source of the inherited variations and support the theory of evolution by providing the variations needed for natural selection.

53. **(C)** The specific nitrogenous bases of deoxyribonucleic acid are the amino acids adenine, cytosine, guanine, and thymine.

54. **(A)** Polyunsaturated fats are found in largest proportions in plant fats such as sunflower, corn, and soybean oils and in selected fish.

55. **(C)** Michelangelo Buonarroti was a great student of human anatomy who performed many of his own dissections. Evidence of his vast knowledge of anatomy is found in his paintings and sculptures.

56. **(E)** Theophrastus' writings on plants have been preserved and represent the extent of the Greeks' knowledge of science. His greatest work was "Historia Plantarum."

57. **(C)** Erythrocytes are formed in the marrow of long bones. Injury to bone marrow, caused by the deposition of heavy metals, interferes with erythrocyte production.

58. **(D)** Root hair cells increase the absorbing surface of roots and are the principal water-absorbing structures of typical land plant roots.

59. **(B)** Oat bran has a high proportion of soluble fiber, and it is soluble fiber that lowers cholesterol.

60. **(C)** Spore formation is a response of certain bacteria to an environment which becomes unfavorable. Bacterial spores have thick, resistant spore walls and the living bacterial cell within is in a state of suspended animation. When conditions become favorable, the bacterial cell converts back to its active way of life.

61. **(B)** When the atmosphere is saturated with water vapor, minute bits of particulate matter known as condensation nuclei serve as surfaces for the condensation of water vapor.

62. **(C)** Kepler's greatest discovery was the fact that planetary orbits, including that of the earth, are ellipses.

63. **(C)** Ancient civilizations, including the Babylonians, relied on astrology in predicting the future. Astrological events are tied to the behavior of the sun, moon, and planets. It is, therefore, not surprising that early Babylonian writings included references to eclipses.

64. **(E)** Lavoisier showed that mass is conserved.

65. **(B)** Stars that fluctuate in brightness are called variables. In one type, the eruptive variable, a sudden brightening occurs; this is called a nova.

66. **(A)** Colloidal particles scatter light, and this phenomenon is known as the Tyndall effect.

67. **(B)** Glaciers cause the erosion, transportation, and deposition of mineral matter, and this mass of rock debris deposited as residual matter is referred to as a moraine.

68. **(D)** A barrier reef is a long, narrow coral embankment lying offshore.

69. **(D)** Atoms are the smallest units of elements that can exist and that possess all the properties of the specific elements.

70. **(D)** The electromagnetic force is the force that holds atoms and molecules together.

71. **(C)** Entropy is the physical quantity that describes the amount of disorder in a chemical or physical system.

72. **(B)** Those wavelengths of the total visible spectrum which are reflected are blended and perceived by the eye as color.

73. **(E)** The strong force and the weak force have very short ranges and are felt only inside the atomic nucleus. The electromagnetic force acts only to hold atoms and molecules together. Gravity, however, is felt throughout the universe.

74. **(B)** The term *velocity* includes both a speed and a direction so both speed and direction must be unchanging or constant. Friction can certainly reduce speed and change acceleration, but it is not a condition of zero acceleration.

75. **(A)** Acceleration is defined as change in speed divided by the time. The object went from rest, 0 m/s, to 100 m/s. This change of 100 m/s took place over 5 seconds giving (100 m/s)/5 s = 20 m/s^2.

76. **(D)** A supersaturated solution is unstable because of the fact that any disturbance, such as stirring, results in the excess molecules of the solute crystallizing.

77. **(A)** Characteristics of cathode rays include traveling in straight lines, casting shadows, consisting of electrons, and being bent by both electric and magnetic fields.

78. **(B)** Radio waves and light waves are different parts of the electromagnetic spectrum differing primarily in that they have different wavelengths.

79. **(D)** Chemical bonds in which electrons are shared are known as covalent bonds. Uneven sharing results in polar covalent bonds, while even sharing results in nonpolar covalent bonds. Ionic bonds involve the transfer (gain and loss) of electrons between atoms.

80. **(A)** The ohm is the unit of electrical resistance in a material.

81. **(C)** Water's high boiling point (as well as its ability to "bead up" and its high heat capacity) is the result of its formation of hydrogen bonds, or weak attraction between water molecules.

82. **(E)** A lever is a machine which can be used to gain force or distance, since the length of the force arm multiplied by the force used equals the length of the weight arm multiplied by the weight.

83. **(B)** Heat energy is transferred within a medium by conduction, radiation, and convection.

84. **(B)** Quantum theory identifies the smallest units of energy, the quantum, and quantum mechanics explains their behavior inside the atom.

85. **(E)** Inertia is the tendency of a body at rest to remain at rest or the tendency of a body in motion to remain in motion.

86. **(A)** Energy may be defined as the capacity to perform work.

87. **(C)** Protons are one of the fundamental types of particles found in the nuclei of all atoms. Protons have positive charges.

88. **(E)** Only about 1/4 of the energy stored in fossil fuels is actually delivered to its end point. Most useful energy is lost during transmission and generation of the electricity.

89. **(E)** If a nuclear fission reaction is initiated by bombardment of atomic nuclei with neutrons and the subsequent fission results in the release of additional neutrons which, in turn, bombard additional atoms, a chain reaction is created.

90. **(C)** Weight is defined as the force of gravity upon an object.

91. **(B)** Potential energy is that energy possessed by an object because of its position.

92. **(B)** While it has great potential, no functioning fusion plants exist today. This is largely because of our inability to generate and maintain the high temperatures the process requires.

93. **(B)** The heat of vaporization is the heat energy absorbed by the molecules of an evaporating liquid. The result is cooling or a decrease in temperature.

94. **(A)** The specific gravity of a liquid is the ratio of the density of the liquid to the density of water where both densities are obtained in air at the same temperature.

95. **(B)** Acids are well known for their ability to corrode metals. When an acid solution vigorously attacks a metal, hydrogen gas is evolved.

96. **(E)** The halogen family of chemical elements consists of fluorine, chlorine, bromine, iodine, and astatine.

97. **(D)** Fluorescence is the emission of light of one wavelength by a substance subsequent to the absorption of radiant energy of a different wavelength. Subsequent to the absorption of radiant energy by chlorophyll, electrons of

some of its atoms may move to outer electron orbits, resulting in the excited state of these moved electrons. When these moved electrons return to their normal orbits, light of a different wavelength is emitted.

98. **(B)** Proteins are polymers consisting of long chains of amino acids, each unit of which is built from an amino group and a carboxyl group.

99. **(B)** In physical changes, the component building blocks of matter, atoms, do not undergo change. They merely combine and separate in different combinations and arrangements.

100. **(A)** In any chemical reaction, the total molecular mass of the reactants always equals the total molecular mass of the products.

101. **(B)** Over 70% of the freshwater used in the world today is used for agricultural purposes.

102. **(D)** Scholasticism was a philosophical movement during the Middle Ages attempting to combine the teachings of Aristotle and St. Augustine with fixed religious dogma.

103. **(E)** While we hear a great deal about carbon dioxide as a greenhouse gas it is not considered a major air pollutant as the others are.

104. **(D)** By definition, oxidation is the loss of electrons by atoms, ions, or molecules.

105. **(C)** By placing a naturally radioactive substance in a block of lead, a thin radioactive beam may be permitted to come out of the lead through an open hole. When this emitted beam is placed in an electric field, it is split into alpha, beta, and gamma particles.

106. **(C)** Dissociation is the breaking up of a chemical substance into its ionic constituents. In this instance $NaCl$ dissociates to form Na^+ ions and Cl^- ions when placed in water.

107. **(E)** Ionic behavior responds to the concept that like (electrical) charges repel each other and unlike charges attract each other.

108. **(B)** Metals possessing high specific resistance to the conduction of electric current heat up since it takes more energy to push current through wires having high resistance and this energy is converted to heat.

109. **(E)** A laser is a device that can focus a beam of light to concentrate a great amount of electromagnetic energy on a very small area.

110. **(A)** Ultraviolet light is more energetic than visual light and can excite electrons in many kinds of molecules, causing chemical reactions to occur.

111. **(B)** Molecules of an electrolyte dissociate when it conducts an electric current and simultaneously the newly formed ions migrate with anions moving toward the anode and cations moving toward the cathode.

112. **(A)** When electromagnetic waves strike a surface, they are said to be reflected, and careful measurements will reveal that the angle of incidence is equal to the angle of reflection.

113. **(E)** While both water and carbon dioxide are considered greenhouse gases, there is no evidence that human activity has increased the amount of water vapor in the atmosphere.

114. **(D)** The magnetic field generated in a coil of wire when an electric current passes through it behaves in a manner similar to a bar magnet.

115. **(E)** Stars that fluctuate in brightness are known as variable stars.

116. **(A)** Stars which move about each other and which are attracted by their mutual gravitation are called binary stars.

117. **(D)** When a star increases its brightness several million times it is called a supernova.

118. **(D)** According to the first law of thermodynamics, energy may be transformed from one type to another, but may be neither created nor destroyed.

119. **(E)** An electron is displaced by the energy transmitted to it by the photon that strikes it. The electron will then be in a different location. Thus, the energy and the original position of the electron remain unknown, a phenomenon called the uncertainty principle.

120. **(C)** A theory concerning the nature of gases that assumes that gases consist of independently moving molecules is named the kinetic-molecular theory.

NOTES

NOTES

NOTES

NOTES

NOTES

NOTES

NOTES

NOTES

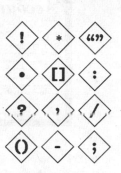

SYSTEM REQUIREMENTS

Windows: This software will run with the following processor:
Intel Pentium II 450 MHz or faster, 128MB RAM on the following Operating Systems:
Windows 2000, XP with a CD ROM Player

Macintosh: This software will run with the following processor:
PowerPC G3 500MHz or faster, 128MB RAM on the following Operating Systems:
MAC OS X 10.2 or higher with a CD ROM Player

Installation Instructions

The product is not installed on the end-user's computer; it is run directly from the CD Rom.

Windows:
Insert the CD ROM. The program will launch automatically. If it doesn't launch automatically:
Click "Run" from the start menu.
Type "D:\CLEP.exe" (where D is the letter of your CD-ROM drive).
Click OK.
Macintosh®:
Insert the CD Rom and open the CD Rom icon.
Double-click on the CLEP X application icon.

BARRON'S LICENSING AGREEMENT/DISCLAIMER OF WARRANTY

Ownership of Rights. The disk in the envelope was created for Barron's Educational Series, Inc., and the editorial contents therein remain the intellectual property of Barron's. Users of the disk may not reproduce it, authorize or permit its reproduction, transmit it, or permit any portion thereof to be transmitted for any purpose whatsoever.

License. Barron's hereby grants to the consumer of this product the limited license to use same solely for personal use. Any other use shall be in violation of Barron's rights to the aforesaid intellectual property and in violation of the Barron's copyright interest in such disks.

Limited Warranty: Disclaimer of Implied Warranties. If this disk fails to function in a satisfactory manner, Barron's sole liability to any purchaser or use shall be limited to refunding the price paid for the same by said purchaser or user. Barron's makes no other warranties, express or implied, with respect to the disk. *Barron's specifically disclaims any warranty of fitness for a particular purpose or of merchantability.*

Consequential Damages. Barron's shall not be liable under any circumstances for indirect, incidental, special, or consequential damages resulting from the purchase or use of the disk.